WID

KT-197-673

Who's Who in Nazi Germany

Robert S. Wistrich is the *Jewish Chronicle* Professor of Jewish Studies at University College, London and holds the Neuberger Chair of modern European history at the Hebrew University of Jerusalem. He is the author of many books including *The Jews of Vienna in the Age of Franz Joseph* (OUP 1989), which won the Austrian State Prize for History; *Antisemitism: The Longest Hatred* (Methuen 1991), which was awarded the Wingate Prize in the UK; *Terms of Survival: The Jewish World Since 1945* (Routledge 1995) and most recently *Weekend in Munich: Art, Propaganda and Terror* (Pavilion Press 1995). He was the historical consultant to the Channel 4 documentary *Good Morning, Mr Hitler!*

WHO'S WHO SERIES

Other Who's Whos (available in USA from Oxford University Press):

Who's Who in the Old Testament
Joan Comay

Who's Who in the New Testament
Ronald Brownrigg

Who's Who in Classical Mythology
Michael Grant and John Hazel

Who's Who in Non-Classical Mythology
Egerton Sykes, new edition revised by Alan Kendall

Who's Who in Shakespeare
Peter Quennell and Hamish Johnson

Who's Who in World War Two
Edited by John Keegan

Who's Who in Jewish History
Joan Comay, new edition revised by Lavinia Cohn–Sherbok

Forthcoming (available from Routledge worldwide):

Who's Who in Military History
John Keegan and Andrew Wheatcroft

Who's Who
in Nazi Germany

Robert S. Wistrich

London and New York

First published 1982
by Weidenfeld & Nicolson

This edition first published 1995
by Routledge
11 New Fetter Lane, London EC4P 4EE

Simultaneously published in the USA and Canada
by Routledge
29 West 35th Street, New York, NY 10001

© 1995 Robert S. Wistrich

Typeset in SABON by
Datix International Ltd, Bungay, Suffolk

Printed and bound in Great Britain by
T J Press (Padstow) Ltd, Padstow, Cornwall

All rights reserved. No part of this book may be reprinted or
reproduced or utilized in any form or by any electronic,
mechanical, or other means, now known or hereafter
invented, including photocopying and recording, or in any
information storage or retrieval system, without permission in
writing from the publishers.

British Library Cataloguing in Publication Data
A catalogue record for this book is available from the British Library

Library of Congress Cataloguing in Publication Data
A catalogue record for this book has been requested

ISBN 0-415-12723-8
0-415-11888-3 (pbk)

Contents

'. . . a careful, scholarly compilation . . . the only volume of its kind that one could read right through − as if it were a straight narrative rather than a work of reference.'

The Jerusalem Post (Israel)

'. . . encompasses a wide selection of personalities connected with Hitler's Germany . . . the information provided is readable and often stimulating and not confined to the bare bones of the usual Who's Who.'

The Observer (London)

'Robert Wistrich deals with the villains and the horrors they perpetrated for the most part briskly, but at times with biting sarcasm . . . the pointed or amusing quotation, the implicit approval or more often damning criticism . . . all contribute to an eminently readable collection. *Who's Who in Nazi Germany* is something of a *tour de force*, with the substance and cutting edge to engross the reader, and bring him back repeatedly for more.'

History (UK)

'. . . Wistrich has probably produced as comprehensive a volume as possible. It provides a wealth of data not otherwise available in any one place.'

American Historical Review

'The author's skilful interweaving of characters and events succeeds in presenting to us a comprehensive record of Hitler's Reich. By cool, dispassionate reporting he exposes a liturgy of evil.'

History Today (UK)

'. . . an instructive reference work, rich in information and containing many surprises, which are generally lacking in other lexica.'

Die Zeit (Hamburg)

'. . . in many respects an outstandingly successful volume.'

Die Welt (Berlin)

Preface

In spite of the ever-growing literature on Nazism and the Third Reich, this is the first comprehensive *Who's Who* on the subject to be written in any language. The objective of the work is to provide a reliable and stimulating source of information and reference for serious students and for the interested lay reader concerning what is a pivotal period in twentieth-century European history. The book is arranged as a collection of compact, succinct biographies listed in alphabetical order and giving basic information about the careers of nearly 350 individuals who were prominent or significant in the Third Reich. Through their lives I have tried to tell the story of Nazism, to link each biography to a facet of the Third Reich so that the interlinking of their careers comes to form an intricate web reflecting the multitude of cross-connections that made up Hitler's Germany. The individuals represented in this volume exercised a very wide range of occupations, social and political roles. In addition to the top rank Nazi Party leaders, SS and Gestapo personalities, Wehrmacht and diplomatic personnel, I have included civil servants, jurists, industrialists, intellectuals, churchmen, academics, artists and entertainers. The actors, writers, film makers, dramatists, painters, sculptors, architects, musicians, philosophers and historians who remained in Nazi Germany and achieved some prominence are an important, if neglected, facet of the reality of the Third Reich.

I have also given attention to the brain-drain from Nazi Germany, including in particular some of the distinguished scientists (physicists, mathematicians, chemists, etc.) and writers who were forced to leave their homeland for racial or political reasons. Entries dealing with Hitler's academic experts in the fields of eugenics, anthropology and racial ideology, with the SS doctors, Commandants of concentration camps and Higher Police and SS leaders implicated in the 'Final Solution' emphasize the criminal, totalitarian character of the régime. On the other hand considerable information is also provided about the German Resistance which embraced a broad span of opinion, including Protestant theologians, Catholic politicians and priests, Social Democrats, conservatives and army leaders.

The most difficult problem in preparing this work was one of selection. Had my focus been narrowed only to Nazi Party leaders, the list of potential candidates would still have run into thousands. On what basis then could I make an adequate selection of entries which would constitute a representative cross-section of German society in the period between 1933 and 1945? To what extent could one disregard the careers of individuals who were primarily active under the Weimar Republic? Many of the subjects in this volume were still alive after 1945 – could one ignore their subsequent fate? Finally, how far should the length of the various biographies reflect the relative importance of their role and according to what criteria was this to be decided? Inevitably, my own attempt to resolve these dilemmas will reveal to a certain degree subjective tastes, preferences and areas of interest and I have not shrunk from exercising value-judgements where this seemed warranted. This is one historical subject where claims to absolute objectivity and detachment sound somewhat artificial and forced, not to say dishonest. In many cases the existing historiographical literature provided a fairly reliable guide as to who should be included but with regard to lesser known figures (though not unimportant in their sphere) the task was more difficult and access to information by no means easy. Indeed, it is doubtful if this work could have been written had I not had the good fortune of working at the Wiener Library as editor of its *Bulletin* from 1974–5 until 1980. The personal files, documentary material, press cuttings and historical works in its great collection on Nazism and the Third Reich provided the indispensable bedrock on which this volume is based. I should like to thank the staff of the Wiener Library in London and its director Professor Walter Laqueur; Mrs Johnson, Mrs Kehr and Janet Langmaid for guiding my first steps; Lord Weidenfeld for suggesting the project and Linda Osband for her editorial assistance; also the staff of Yad Vashem in Jerusalem and of *Der Spiegel* magazine in Hamburg, as well as Joachim Hoelzgen of the London bureau and professor M. R. Marrus (Toronto).

This book is primarily a work of reference but it is also intended to stimulate the interest of the general reader and provide him with a basic tool for further research. To facilitate its readability I have adopted a narrative, chronological approach to each entry and avoided the temptation of providing footnotes for citations. However, a comprehensive bibliography at the back of the book should provide the interested reader not only with some of the background material used in the preparation of this study but also with suggestions for further reading. I have also added a glossary to explain all the major German terms used in the text. A biographical dictionary such as this is not intended to be a substitute but rather a necessary resource material for additional research. The swollen grandeur, the monstrous horror and the tragedy that was Nazi Germany naturally cannot be encompassed in its entirety by a collection of biographies, however representative; but the lives which have been captured in these pages can provide the reader not only with reliable information but also with the human (and all too often inhuman) dimension which is the *sine qua non* for understanding this crucial period in modern history.

ROBERT WISTRICH
London/Jerusalem 1980–1

PREFACE TO THE NEW EDITION

When this book first came out in 1982 it was widely recognised as a unique reference guide to the leading personalities of the Third Reich. In a compact, easily accessible form it focused on top-ranking party leaders, SS and Gestapo personnel, diplomats, administrators, outstanding Wehrmacht generals and army commanders, industrialists, jurists and churchmen. Apart from these pillars of the régime, it also included life portraits of artists, scientists, academics and other intellectuals. There were profiles of entertainers, sportsmen and other celebrities, prominent at the time, if largely forgotten today. I made a special point of including opponents as well as proponents of the régime, both the resistance fighters and the distinguished writers and scientists who fled from Nazi Germany for racial or political reasons. This wide selection enabled the book to provide a more rounded picture of all aspects of life under Hitler and to relieve somewhat the almost unbearable litany of evil that inevitably springs from its pages.

From the outset I was determined to break with the usual format of the *Who's Who*, in order to provide much more than a mere catalogue of names, ranks, dates and numbers. I wanted this to be a book which is not only objective and reliable as a work of reference, but which is also incisive, lively and readable from beginning to end. Hence I have permitted myself the use of pointed quotation, implicit approval or criticism, the note of black humour, the scathing irony or touch of biting sarcasm where necessary. In dealing with such a scale of inhumanity and cruelty, a completely dispassionate and value-free approach would itself surely be suspect. Nevertheless, as reviewers noted at the time in both Britain and Germany, this is not a deliberately judgemental book. It allows the broader story of Hitler's Germany to emerge naturally from the chilling detail of the individual biographies.

This book can and should be read not simply as a kind of dictionary or reference guide but also as a collection of nightmarish short stories which I doubt that any fiction-writer could have made up. It is a world where smooth élite figures, dull apparatchiks, corrupt judges, lawyers and opportunist academics rub shoulders with vicious Gestapo officials and SS murderers; where brilliant generals mix with scholars, writers, playboys and stars of stage and screen; where criminals, dissidents and artists come together as actors in a singular drama whose reverberations are still being felt to this day. Where else, except in a book like this, can one find Martin Heiddeger alongside Heydrich, Karajan with Kaltenbrunner, Richard Strauss next to Julius Streicher?

By interweaving these stories together, I have sought to illuminate the connection between the aesthetic and the barbaric, the normal and the homicidal, the everyday banality and the criminality of the Third Reich. We can surely learn most about the Nazi régime and the wicked ideology which it so ruthlessly implemented by studying the people who made it up, through their individual life-histories. This involves much more than simply dealing with the hard-core of the Nazi Party; hence the effort in this guide to encompass as broad a cross-section of German society as possible, within the limitations of available space.

Wherever possible I have also sought to record the careers of the individuals included in this volume after World War II. Not only was this information generally lacking elsewhere but by pinpointing these details I have been able to show some of the inadequacies and failings in the de-Nazification process. Post-war German courts often handed down derisory sentences and many war criminals were released long before their time was served. This book demonstrates just how easily SS and Gestapo personnel, jurists, bureaucrats, bankers and industrialists involved in the Nazi régime could continue successful careers after 1945, as if nothing had happened.

Today, fifty years after the end of the Third Reich, such a reference volume is more than ever necessary. With the revival of the siren-call of fascism and Nazism in Germany and much of Europe, with the denial of the Holocaust and efforts at relativizing the history of the Third Reich, the need for reliable and accessible information is paramount. I have accordingly updated and extended the earlier edition, adding some new entries and bibliography. May this book serve both as a guide and a warning to those born after 1945, to guard preciously the flame of freedom.

ROBERT S. WISTRICH
Neuberger Chair of modern European history,
Hebrew University of Jerusalem
Jewish Chronicle Professor of Jewish Studies,
University College, London

Jerusalem, November 1994

A

Abetz, Otto (1903–58)   German Ambassador to Vichy France, Otto Abetz was born on 26 May 1903 in Schwetzingen and matriculated in Karlsruhe, where he became an art teacher at a girls' school. He was a supporter of the NSDAP from 1931 and took up relations with French ex-servicemen on its behalf. In January 1935 he entered the Foreign Service under von Ribbentrop (q.v.). His activities as its Paris representative led to his expulsion from France in 1939, but following the German occupation (after the fall of France), Abetz returned in June 1940 and in November received accreditation as German Ambassador – a post he held for four years. The embassy was theoretically responsible for all political questions in occupied and non-occupied France, and for advising the German police and military. Abetz's primary objective was to secure complete collaboration from the French, but as a Party activist – he held the rank of *SS-Standartenführer* – he also sought to seize the initiative as much as possible – suggesting, for example, that all émigré, stateless Jews should be expropriated and expelled to the Free Zone. Abetz regarded anti-semitism as an important lever in undermining the grip of the army and church in Vichy France and replacing it by a pro-German, anti-clerical, populist mass movement. In July 1949 he was sentenced to twenty years' hard labour by a Paris military tribunal, as a war criminal. Released in April 1954 he was burned to death in a motor 'accident' four years later on the Cologne–Ruhr autobahn when something went wrong with the steering wheel of his speeding car. His death may have been a revenge killing for his role in sending French Jews to the gas chambers.

Abs, Hermann (1901–94)   Hermann Abs, once described by David Rockefeller as the 'leading banker in the world', was born in Bonn on 15 October 1901, the son of a lawyer. After studying law and a brief apprenticeship in a Cologne bank, Abs gained experience and connections in international banking abroad in Paris, London, New York and Amsterdam. In 1929 he was already the director of an Amsterdam bank and a year later he became a confidential clerk for the Berlin private banking house of Delbruck, Schickler and Co. By 1935 he was a partner in this firm, whose clients included Hitler and Rosenberg. In 1937 Abs was nominated to the Vorstand (managing board) of Germany's biggest bank, the Deutsche Bank. The bank's profits were greatly augmented by 'Aryanization' and the expropriation of banks in newly annexed territories. Thus, the Deutsche Bank absorbed the Jewish-owned Mendelsohn bank and bought another big Jewish company, Adler and Oppenheimer, at knock-down prices. After the annexation of Austria, Bohemia and Moravia, it took over Austria's giant Creditanstalt Wiener Bankverein as well as Czech banks and industries. Thus, by the end of 1938 Abs, who was in charge of the Deutsche Bank's Foreign Department, was already at one of the nerve centres of German power. Acknowledged as a rising star by Hjalmar Schacht (q.v.), President of the Reichsbank, his good relations with British and American bankers, his commercial and diplomatic skills led to his being entrusted with sensitive missions on behalf of the Third Reich. This also involved resisting efforts by Germany's creditors seeking repayment of the vast loans made to it after World War I. The urbane Abs, solid, discreet and powerful ('a velvet glove around an iron fist') was perfectly suited by his international standing to such diplomacy. A devout Catholic who was never a member of the Nazi Party (though he joined the DAF) his loyalty was never in doubt and his services were indispensable to the Nazi Party and Government in preparing the economic base for German hegemony in Europe. He helped bankroll the German industrial expansion following the Wehrmacht conquests. His clients reaped substantial profits from the economies of a dozen conquered European nations. Between 1939 and 1943 three-quarters of Europe's industrial resources were there for the taking and the Deutsche Bank's own wealth quadrupled as a result of its activities during the Third Reich. By 1942, Abs held 40 directorships, a quarter of which were with firms in lands occupied by German troops. Many of the companies financed by the Deutsche Bank used slave labour and some 6 million Europeans (men, women and children) were used – and often worked to their deaths – in German factories and mines. From 1940 Abs was on the board of directors of IG Farben, which had built a concentration camp adjacent to Auschwitz (called IG Auschwitz by the directors) to produce artificial rubber. Some 50,000 inmates died from starvation and exposure in building it – prisoners at this camp rarely survived more than three months since company policy was to supply a minimal amount of food. The Deutsche Bank was IG Farben's main banker and Abs was its representative on the giant company's supervisory board (*Aufsichtsrat*). Towards the end of the war Abs, along with some other leading German industrialists and bankers, began to plan ahead for after the defeat. He was asked by the British Military Government to help rebuild the German banking system after 1945, on the assumption that it was imperative to get the German economy moving again. Under American pressure Abs was stripped, however, of his 45 directorships and arrested as a suspected war criminal on 16 January 1946, but released after three months thanks to British intervention. A detailed report in 1947 on the Deutsche Bank, which suggested that there was enough evidence to prosecute Abs as a war criminal, was disregarded. By 1948 the banker was in effect managing the German economic recovery programme and had won the trust of the Allies. On 1 March 1948 Abs was appointed Deputy Head of the Reconstruction Loan Corporation and President of the Bank Deutsche Länder, which decided on the allocation of Marshall aid to German industry. Thus not only did Abs escape prosecution at Nuremberg (though the Yugoslavs sentenced him to death in his absence as a war criminal after 1945) but he would successfully rebuild the Deutsche Bank after World War II. Moreover, his pre-war international connections proved invaluable in financial diplomacy on behalf of the Federal Republic. Already in 1951 Abs had negotiated the German foreign debt at the London conference, on behalf of the new German Chancellor, Konrad Adenauer (q.v.). He was seen as indispensable to re-establishing Germany's post-war creditworthiness. Adenauer wanted him as his first Foreign Minister but had to bow to a French veto. Abs would remain Adenauer's close friend and financial adviser. In 1957 Abs became Chairman of the Board of the Deutsche Bank (a post he held until 1967) and then Chairman of its Supervisory Board. At the time, the bank had a controlling interest in nearly one-third of West German industry and was the second largest bank in Europe. He was once again part of that small élite of international bankers, one who had made a brilliant career in the Third Reich and a no less spectacular contribution to the post-war Federal Republic. Praised as a patriot, a financial diplomat and patron of the arts (in 1992 he won the State prize for North Rhine Westphalia for his services to the arts), he died at the age of ninety-two, enjoying wealth, power and honours.

Adam, Wilhelm (1877–1949) Born in Anspach, Bavaria, on 15 September 1877, Wilhelm Adam served as an officer in the Bavarian army during World War I and subsequently acquired a reputation as one of the most able and efficient officers in the Reichswehr. Promoted to Major General in 1930, he was appointed three years later as Commander of the Munich Military Area. In 1935 he was given command of the newly created Armed Forces Academy in Berlin. Adam's earlier association with General von Schleicher (q.v.) and his lukewarm attitude to Hitler's plans – including the building of the West Wall fortifications – made his relations with the Führer somewhat tense, though he survived the crisis of early 1938 which followed the dismissal of two leading generals, von Blomberg (q.v.) and von Fritsch (q.v.). In November 1938, Wilhelm Adam was stripped of his western front command – another sign of Hitler's success in solidifying his control over the army. He died on 8 April 1949 in Garmisch.

Adenauer, Konrad (1876–1967) Born on 5 January 1876 into a Catholic family in Cologne, where he became Deputy Mayor in 1909 and served as Lord Mayor between 1917 and 1933, Adenauer was a member of the republican-democratic wing of the Centre Party during the Weimar period. A resolute opponent of Hitler and National Socialism, Adenauer was dismissed from his position in 1933 and arrested a year later by the Gestapo for continued resistance to the régime. A further arrest followed in 1944 when he was sent to Brauweiler prison. After the fall of the Third Reich, Adenauer co-founded the CDU (Christian Democratic Union) and was elected in 1949 as Chancellor of the German Federal Republic, a position he maintained until his retirement, because of advanced age, in 1963. This was the longest tenure in office of any German statesman since Bismarck, coinciding with a long period of prosperity (the 'economic miracle') and political stability which transformed West Germany into an accepted member of the community of nations. At home and abroad, Adenauer's patriarchal style of leadership, his pro-western orientation and impeccable moral credentials strengthened confidence in the new Germany. His policy favoured close ties with France, European economic co-operation and reconciliation with Israel – in a declaration before the Bundestag on 27 September 1951 Adenauer had acknowledged German crimes against the Jews and the obligation to make 'moral and material amends'. Nevertheless many judges, civil servants, businessmen and police officers with a compromised past continued to serve under his administration. Adenauer's greatest achievement during fourteen years of rule was to provide West Germans with the sense of stability and continuity that could reconcile them to democracy in the post-war period. He died at the age of ninety-one in his villa at Röndorf in April 1967.

Albers, Hans (1892–1960) The blond, daredevil adventurer and irresistible lover of the German screen, Hans Albers was born in Hamburg on 22 September 1892 and began his career as an apprentice in business before turning to acting in the circus and variety. On active service during World War I, Albers was wounded and after the war resumed his acting career in Berlin in operettas, later in plays – first in comic parts, then in character acting. He had outstanding success and started filming, being one of the first actors to appear in talking movies. After 1927 Albers began to establish himself as one of the most prominent film actors and producers in the German cinema. During the Third Reich he was one of the best-loved actors among the public, frequently embodying the spirit of virile heroism, idealism and self-sacrifice in films like Gustav Ucicky's *Flüchtinge* (1933), set in the Far East among a group of Germans trying to escape Bolshevik persecution, or in *Carl Peters* (1941), an idealized Nazi version of the anti-British German colonialist and patriot in East Africa. Albers also starred in Fritz Wendhausen's adaptation of *Peer Gynt* (1934), in *Gold* (1937) and as the alcoholic engineer-hero in *Wasser für Canitoga* (1939) – a film set in the Canadian North, one of the better examples of the Nazi commercial cinema. One of Albers's most seductive performances was in the film spectacular, *Münchhausen* (1943) – for which the screenplay was written by Erich Kastner. After World War II, Albers continued to make films, right up until his death in July 1960. They included *Und über uns der Himmel* (1947), *Der Letzte Mann* (1955), *Das Herz von St Pauli* (1957) and *Kein Engel ist so rein* (1960).

Amann, Max (1891–1957) Born in Munich on 24 November 1891, Amann attended business school and served an office apprenticeship in a Munich law firm before becoming business manager of the Nazi Party in 1921, and after 1922 Director of the Party publishing house, the Eher Verlag. He always enjoyed the full confidence of Hitler, who held him in high regard and unstintedly praised his role in developing the

Völkische Beobachter and the Party's giant newspaper trust after 1933. Their relationship dated back to World War I when Amann had served as Hitler's company sergeant in a Bavarian infantry regiment. During the Beer-Hall *putsch*, Amann along with other Party activists had been arrested and briefly jailed. In 1924 he was elected as an NSDAP candidate to the Munich city council and in 1933 became a Nazi member of the Reichstag for the electoral district of Upper Bavaria/Swabia. The pint-sized Amann was the aggressive, rowdy type of Nazi, brutal, domineering and ruthless towards subordinates. This 'Hercules of the Nazi publishing business' was in the words of Kurt Lüdecke 'a merciless man who sweated lesser Nazi workers for the least possible pay'. Amann was also personally greedy, exploiting his appointment in November 1933 as President of the Reich Association of German Newspaper Publishers and President of the Reich Press Chamber to pillage and plunder the non-Nazi newspaper chains. As chief actor in the *Gleichschaltung* of the press he was a master of the techniques of the legal freeze-out and enforced business deal, by means of which he established Party control of most of the press and gradually eliminated independent publishing.

Hitler's personal wealth owed a great deal to Amann's shrewd business sense. The jovial Bavarian was his personal banker and, apart from overseeing his royalties from *Mein Kampf*, ensured that the Führer received huge fees from his contributions to the Nazi press. But his political services which earned him his appointment as a *Reichsleiter* were no less appreciated. In 1942 Hitler described Amann as 'the greatest newspaper proprietor in the world.... Today the *Zentral Verlag* owns from 70 to 80 per cent of the German press.' Amann enormously enriched himself through his monopoly over the world's largest press and publishing combine. His income increased from 108,000 to 3,800,000 marks between 1934 and 1944; besides his large salary from the Eher Verlag and 5 per cent of the net profits, he owned a substantial interest in the Müller printing company, and was able to pocket millions without paying income tax. As a Party man, Amann's talents were, however, very limited. He was no orator or debater and incapable of writing a single printable line by himself. All articles signed 'Amann', addresses, important letters or announcements were written for him by his right-hand man, Rolf Rienhardt (q.v.).

After the fall of the Third Reich, Amann sought to pose as a businessman who had no ideological commitment to Nazism. His de-Nazification trial showed, however, that of all the Nazi leaders he had made the greatest material gains from his association with the Party. On 8 September 1948 he was sentenced to two-and-a-half years' imprisonment by a Munich court and two months later the Central de-Nazification Court imposed ten years' labour camp on him as a 'Major Offender'. He lost his property, his business holdings and pension rights, dying in poverty in Munich on 30 March 1957.

Axmann, Artur (born 1913) Reich Youth Leader, Artur Axmann was born on 18 February 1913 in Hagen, studied law and by 1928 had founded the first Hitler Youth group in Westphalia. In 1932 he was called into the *Reichsleitung* of the NSDAP to carry out a reorganization of Nazi youth cells and in 1933 became Chief of the Social Office of the Reich Youth Leadership. Axmann gained a place for the Hitler Youth in the direction of State vocational training and succeeded in raising the status of Hitler Youth agricultural work. He was on active service on the western front until May 1940. In August of the same year he succeeded Baldur von Schirach (q.v.) as Reich Youth Leader of the Nazi Party. In 1941 he was severely wounded on the eastern front, losing an arm. During Hitler's last days, Axmann was among those present in the *Führerbunker*, making his escape at the end of April 1945. He was arrested in December 1945 when a Nazi underground was uncovered which he had been organizing. A Nuremberg de-Nazification court sentenced him in May 1949 to a prison sentence of three years and three months as a 'Major Offender'. Axmann subsequently worked as a sales representative in Gelsenkirchen and Berlin. On 19 August 1958 a West Berlin de-Nazification court fined the former Hitler Youth Leader 35,000 marks (approximately £3,000), about half the value of his property in Berlin. The court found him guilty of indoctrinating German youth with National Socialism right until the end of the Third Reich, but concluded that he had been a Nazi from inner conviction rather than base motives. During his trial Axmann told the court that he had heard the shot with which Hitler committed suicide, and had later also seen the body of Martin Bormann (q.v.) lying on a bridge in Berlin. He was found not guilty of having committed any crimes during the Nazi era.

B

Bach-Zelewski, Erich (1899–1972) General of the Higher SS and Police Leader Corps, responsible for anti-partisan warfare on the eastern front during World War II, Erich von dem Bach-Zelewski was born on 1 March 1899 in Lauenburg, Pomerania. A professional soldier from a Junker military family, handsome and typically East Prussian in manner, Bach-Zelewski served in World War I, then in the *Freikorps* and as a Reichswehr officer during the 1920s. In 1930 he joined the NSDAP and a year later he was made an *SS-Untersturmführer*. From 1932 until 1944 he was a member of the Reichstag, representing the Breslau electoral district. After 1934 he commanded SS and Gestapo units in East Prussia and Pomerania. In 1939 Bach-Zelewski was promoted to the position of SS General and two years later became a General of the Waffen-SS assigned to the Central Army Group on the Russian front until the end of 1942. In this period Bach-Zelewski was responsible for many atrocities in which he took a personal part. On 31 October 1941, after 35,000 persons had been executed in Riga, he proudly wrote: 'There is not a Jew left in Estonia.' He also participated actively in massacres of Jews at Minsk and Mogilev in White Russia.

In July 1943 he was appointed by Himmler (q.v.) as anti-partisan chief on the entire eastern front. Subsequently he claimed that in this role he had tried to protect Jews from the *Einsatzgruppen*. Bach-Zelewski was in command of the German units which suppressed the Warsaw rising in the summer of 1944,

being awarded the Knight's Cross in connection with these operations. Highly regarded by Hitler for his brutality and improvisational skills – he was able to conjure armies out of very unpromising material – Bach-Zelewski ended the war as an army Commander. The fact that he testified for the prosecution at Nuremberg, denouncing Himmler and his own fellow police chiefs, spared him extradition to Russia. In March 1951 he was condemned by a Munich de-Nazification court to ten years' 'special labour', which in practice meant being confined to his own home in Franconia. The only one among the mass murderers who publicly denounced himself for his wartime actions, he was never prosecuted for his role in the anti-Jewish massacres. Instead, he was arrested and tried in 1961 for his participation in the Röhm Blood Purge and sentenced to four and a half years; indicted again in 1962 for the murder of six communists in 1933, he was tried before a jury in Nuremberg and received the unusually harsh sentence of life imprisonment. Neither indictment mentioned his wartime role, thereby suggesting that only the murder of ethnic Germans was perceived as an unpardonable crime. He died in a prison hospital in Munich-Harlaching on 8 March 1972.

Backe, Herbert (1896–1947) Reich Minister for Food and Agriculture during the last year of the Nazi régime, Herbert Backe was born on 1 May 1896 in Batum, Russia, the son of German colonists. He attended a Russian secondary school between 1905 and 1914, and was interned during the period of the war, later resuming his studies at Göttingen University in Germany. Assistant lecturer at Hanover Technical High School (1923–4), Backe then turned to tenant farming. He joined the Nazi Party and became head of the farmers' political organization in his district in 1931. From October 1933 he was State Secretary in the Ministry of Food and Agriculture and a year later he launched the so-called Battle of Production (*Erzeugungsschlacht*) aimed at maximizing domestic output and cutting down on food imports. In 1936 he was made Food Commissioner for the Four Year Plan, responsible to Goering (q.v.) for the co-ordination of agrarian and industrial policy. Backe was regarded as an expert not only on agrarian but also on Russian affairs, and from May 1942 he was nominated as Darré's (q.v.) successor, responsible in particular for organizing the foodstuffs sector for the war against Soviet Russia. He was promoted to Reich Minister and *Reichsbauernführer* (Reich Farmers' Leader) at the end of 1943. On 1 April 1944, Backe, whose hard-headed pragmatism and efficiency was increasingly preferred to Darré's ideological 'blood and soil' policies, was appointed Reich Food Minister, serving in Hitler's last cabinet. He died on 6 April 1947, committing suicide by hanging himself at Nuremberg prison.

Baeck, Leo (1873–1956) The central figure of German Jewry during the Nazi period, a great rabbinical scholar, teacher and community leader, Leo Baeck was born in Lissa, Prussia, on 23 May 1873. After obtaining his rabbinical qualification at the Berlin Institute in 1897, he served until 1907 as a rabbi in Oppeln (Upper Silesia) where he wrote his *magnum opus, Das Wesen des Judentums (The Essence of Judaism)* in 1905 – conceived as an answer to the theology of the Protestant Professor Adolf von Harnack. In 1912 when he was called to

serve the most prominent Jewish congregation in Berlin, a position he was to hold for thirty years, Baeck was already well known as a religious philosopher who combined universal scholarship with rabbinical erudition. In 1913 he was appointed lecturer to the *Hochschule für die Wissenschaft des Judentums*, a liberal rabbinical seminary in Berlin, but spent the next few years in the German army as a chaplain during World War I.

In 1922 Rabbi Baeck was elected President of the *Allgemeine Rabbiner-Verband* (Union of German Rabbis), which represented both progressive and orthodox Jews. He was also active from 1926 as Chairman of the *Zentralwohlfahrtsstelle* (Welfare Centre for Jewish Communities) in Germany. Baeck established himself in these years as a non-conformist, independent thinker, a rabbi who represented the respectable, bourgeois community yet remained critical of the prevailing mentality. A non-Zionist, he was nonetheless sympathetic to the re-awakening of Jewish national consciousness – as a young man of twenty-four, he had been one of only two rabbis who abstained from the declaration of protest by German rabbis against Zionism. An optimist, who believed passionately in the Jewish renaissance, Baeck faced his great ordeal as President of the *Reichsvertretung der Juden in Deutschland* – the central representative body of German Jews from the autumn of 1933 until July 1939 – with dignity and nobility of soul. Immediately after the Nazis seized power, Baeck recognized that 'the thousand-year-old history of German Jewry has come to an end', yet he refused all the attractive offers from abroad which would have enabled him to escape from the Third Reich. In Albert Einstein's (q.v.) words: 'What this man meant to his brethren trapped in Germany and facing certain destruction cannot be fully grasped by those whose outer circumstances permit them to live on in apparent security. He felt it an obvious duty to stay and endure in the land of merciless persecution in order to provide spiritual sustenance to his brethren till the end.'

Appointed Chairman of the *Reichsvereinigung der Juden in Deutschland* (1939), Baeck was in constant danger and frequently summoned to the Gestapo, several times arrested, and finally sent to Theresienstadt concentration camp in 1943. Here he was named head of the council of elders in the camp, and continued to teach philosophy and theology. After his miraculous salvation in 1945, he came to Britain where he was elected President of the Council of Jews from Germany and Chairman of the World Union for Progressive Judaism. He was also the first President of the Leo Baeck Institute, a body devoted to transmitting the message of German-speaking Jewry to future generations. Leo Baeck has rightly been described as 'the last representative figure of German Jewry in Germany during the Nazi period'. He died in London on 2 November 1956.

Baeumler, Alfred (1887–1968) An ardent nationalist and old Party member who was one of the leading academic apologists of National Socialism, Alfred Baeumler was born on 19 November 1887 in Neustadt, Austria. He received his doctorate in 1914 after studying at the Universities of Munich, Berlin and Bonn. From 1914 to 1917 he served in the Austrian army, obtaining high distinctions. Professor of Philosophy at Dresden High School from 1928, he was appointed Professor of Political Education at Berlin University in 1933, emerging as the chief liaison man between the universities and Alfred Rosenberg's (q.v.) office charged with the ideological education of the Party. In 1942 he was made head of the Science Division in Rosenberg's Ideology Department. Baeumler's most important contribution

was to transform Nietzsche's thought into a myth at the service of the Nazi world-view by focusing attention on his negation of bourgeois ideology, Christian morality and democratic values. For Baeumler, Nietzsche was 'the philosopher of heroism', of the will to power and the aristocracy of nature, whose activism was synonymous with 'Nordic' and soldierly values. In his *Studien zur Deutschen Geistesgeschichte* (1937) Baeumler wrote: 'If today we see German youth on the march under the banner of the swastika, we are reminded of Nietzsche's "untimely meditations" in which this youth was appealed to for the first time. It is our greatest hope that the state today is wide open for youth. And if today we shout "Heil Hitler" to this youth, at the same time we are also hailing Nietzsche.' Among Baeumler's many books on philosophy and politics were *Nietzsche der Philosoph und Politiker* (1931), *Männerbund und Wissenschaft* (1934), *Politik und Erziehung* and *Alfred Rosenberg und der Mythus des 20 Jahrhunderts* (1943).

Barkhorn, Erich Gerhard (1919–83) Outstanding Luftwaffe fighter pilot, officially credited with 304 kills on the Russian front during World War II, Erich Barkhorn was bonon 20 March 1919 in Königsberg. His first posting was in Ostend in 1941 where he was attached to Fighter Group 52 as a First Lieutenant. Promoted to Captain and then to Major within two years, Barkhorn was sent to the Russian front where he managed not only to survive the war but also to down more enemy planes than any other pilot except his fellow-countryman, Erich Hartmann (q.v.) – according to the claims made by the Luftwaffe statisticians. From 1956 to 1975 he served in the Bundeswehr, reaching the position of Brigadier and Chief of Staff of the 2nd Allied Tactical Airfleet. He died on 12 January 1983.

Bartels, Adolf (1862–1945) German Professor and literary historian who waged a relentless war to eliminate Jews and 'pseudo-Jews' from German literature, Adolf Bartels was born in Wesselburen on 15 November 1862. Himself a well-known *völkisch* author of historical novels, Bartels edited the literary journal *Deutsches Schriftum (German Writings)* until 1933, which specialized in anti-semitic research and articles. Bartels was the founder of a new pseudo-science which flourished under the Third Reich, namely the racial evaluation of literature. In his ferreting out of Jewish and crypto-Jewish authors – according to Bartels, writers like Thomas and Heinrich Mann or Hermann Hesse belonged in the latter category – the veteran literary historian relied on tracing family trees, photographs of ancestors as well as authors, on place of birth and of work, language, style, family and social milieu. A Jewish-sounding name, the use of symbols reminiscent of freemasonry, the mere fact of having written for papers and journals like the *Berliner Tageblatt* or *Simplicissimus* or having advocated liberal views might be adduced as proof of the 'semitic' character of an author's work. In his early books such as *Lessing und die Juden* (1918), *Die Berechtigung des Antisemitismus* (1921), *Der Nationalsozialismus-Deutschlands Rettung* (1924) – a eulogy of the nascent Nazi movement – and *Jüdische Herkunft und Literaturwissenschaft* (1925), Bartels gave expression to his uncompromising racial-biological anti-semitism and determination to 'dejudaize' German literature. He died in Weimar on 7 March 1945.

Barth, Karl (1886–1968) One of the leading Protestant thinkers of the twentieth century and an uncompromising opponent of National Socialism, who was forced to leave Nazi Germany because of his non-conformist attitude, Karl Barth was born in Basel, Switzerland, on 10 May 1886. A little-known Swiss pastor until the publication of his difficult theological work, *Der Römerbrief* (1918), Barth initiated a revolution in Protestant thought by his relentless attack on liberal 'scientific' theology which sought to bridge the gap between reason and revelation. The founder of a new dialectical theology, Barth wished to take Protestantism back to Luther with his insistence that redemption could only come through God's grace, though he rejected the traditional Lutheran subservence to worldly authority. Barth's religious teaching was simultaneously other-worldly and political in the context of National Socialist attempts to exploit vague metaphysical longings and demands. Barth preached an uncompromising return to absolute, unbroken faith – condemning the corruption of the Protestant church establishment, its German nationalism and concessions to worldly interests. From 1923 to 1933 Barth's journal, *Zwischen den Zeiten*, expressed the views of avant-garde Protestant theology. He himself held professorships in Germany, first in Göttingen, then in Münster and finally in Bonn. In July 1933, he founded the journal *Theologische Existenz heute* which strongly opposed the 'German Christians' who supported Hitler. Two years after Hitler's rise to power, Barth was removed from his position at the University of Bonn for refusing to declare an oath of allegiance to the Führer. He returned to the University of Basel, where he continued his academic career and the publication of his multi-volume *Kirchliche Dogmatik*, one of the central works of modern Protestantism, which was to have a world-wide impact. Barth died in Basel on 10 December 1968.

Becher, Kurt (born 1909) An *SS-Standartenführer*, actively involved in negotiations over the fate of Hungarian Jewry, Becher was born in Hamburg on 12 September 1909. In 1934 he joined the

SS equestrian unit and three years later he became a member of the Nazi Party. From September 1939 he was in the SS Death's Head Equestrian Unit I in Poland which participated in executions of Jews in Warsaw and subsequently on the Russian front. As part of the SS Cavalry Brigade in the East, Becher's unit took part in mass shootings of Jews and partisans. For his services, Becher was promoted to the rank of *SS-Obersturmbannführer*. (SS Major). In March 1944, following the German invasion of Hungary, Becher played a key role in establishing SS control of the giant Manfred Weiss armaments firm — the largest in the country and owned by a Jewish family. Assigned by Adolf Eichmann (q.v.) to be chief SS negotiator with the Jewish Relief and Rescue Committee of Budapest, he dealt in particular with the Zionist functionary Rudolf Kasztner. Becher arranged (in return for jewellery and valuables worth millions of Swiss francs) for the ransoming of over 1500 Hungarian Jews from Bergen-Belsen concentration camp to Switzerland. At the same time, on Himmler's instructions, he sought and failed to win Allied acceptance to supply the SS with 10,000 brand new trucks in return for sparing a million Jewish lives. Nevertheless, as part of Himmler's feelers towards a separate peace with the Western Allies, Becher pursued negotiations with the representative of the American Jewish Joint Distribution Committee and with Roswell McCelland of the War Refugee Board, in Switzerland in November 1944.

In April 1945 Himmler (q.v.) appointed Becher as Special Reich Commissioner for all concentration camps. After the German surrender, Becher was arrested and acted as a witness at the Nuremberg trials. However, he managed to avoid prosecution as a war criminal thanks to the intervention of Kasztner (by then, living in Israel) on his behalf — who claimed that Becher had helped in the 'rescue' of Hungarian Jews. Kasztner would pay dearly for this recommendation, being assassinated as a 'collaborator' with the Nazis in Tel Aviv on 4 May 1957. Kasztner would in fact be posthumously cleared of this charge by the Jerusalem High Court, though his trial and the case surrounding it still arouse intense controversy in Israel. Kurt Becher testified in the Eichmann trial in Israel in 1961 (his deposition was made in Germany) although, had he come to the Jewish State, he would himself have had to stand trial as a war criminal. He was able to prosper in his business ventures in the postwar years which included the development of Hungarian agricultural trade with the Federal Republic of Germany.

Beck, Ludwig (1880–1944) German General who served as Chief of Staff of the Armed Forces between 1935 and 1938, Ludwig Beck was born on 29 June 1880 in Biebrich, in the Rhineland. A professional soldier who entered the General Staff in 1911 and after Service during World War I was given various commands in the Reichswehr, Beck was rapidly promoted and on 1 October 1933 appointed Adjutant General in the Reichswehr Ministry. Beck held this position until his elevation to Chief of the Army General Staff in 1935. For the next three years Beck, who was in charge of overall military planning and preparations, came into increasing conflict with Hitler, opposing war on the grounds that Germany was not yet ready and resenting Nazi efforts to increase Party influence at the expense of the army. Beck, a brilliant officer in the Prussian tradition who believed in a limited war based on moral principles rather than a 'revolutionary' war of conquest with uncontrolled conscript armies, was horrified by Hitler's proposal to invade Czechoslovakia in 1938 and by his adventurous policy based on intuition rather than solid planning. The only German general who consistently did everything possible to thwart or delay Hitler's plans, Beck tried to organize resistance to the Führer within the General Staff, but ultimately failed. When he resigned his post on 18 August 1938, the other generals did not follow suit. Beck's resignation removed the last remaining serious challenge to Hitler's war policy and signalled that the breach between the army and the Party had been resolved in favour of the Nazis. Beck continued, however, to adhere to his conviction that Hitler's policy of conquest would bring disaster to Germany and henceforth, until his suicide on 20 July 1944, he was the acknowledged leader of the German Resistance to Nazism. Had the July plot succeeded, Beck would have been designated as Head of State in place of Hitler. Following the failure of the conspiracy, Beck, knowing that he would be executed, chose suicide and at the third attempt succeeded in blowing his brains out, with the help of a German army sergeant.

Benn, Gottfried (1886–1956) Germany's leading expressionist poet and one of the few writers of real stature who supported (if only temporarily) National Socialism, Gottfried Benn was born in Mansfeld on 2 May 1886, the son of a Lutheran pastor. Benn studied theology at Marburg, then embarked on a medical career at the Kaiser Wilhelm Academy in Berlin, serving as a military doctor during World War I and then specializing in venereal and skin diseases. During the 1920s he practised as a physician in Berlin and his medical training doubtless influenced his concern with 'the law of vitality in the age of breeding' and with methods of protecting the German 'race' against decadence caused by interbreeding.

Benn's first volume of poems, aptly entitled *Morgue*, was published in 1912 and reflected his uncompromising pessi-

mism and disillusion with the materialism of Wilhelminian Germany. It was followed by more collections of lyric poetry, short stories, experimental drama and critical, essayistic prose – *Gehirne* (1916), *Das Moderne Ich* (1920), *Gesammelte Prosa* (1927) and *Fazit der Perspektiven* (1930). Taking his inspiration from Goethe, Nietzsche and Spengler (q.v.), Benn rebelled passionately against the demons of a mechanized world, against the rationalism which was paralysing modern civilization and the political doctrines which derived from it, preaching an aesthetic nihilism and the cult of primitive atavism which initially attracted him to Nazism. Benn's irrationalism, expressed in works like *Nach dem Nihilismus* (1932), *Der neue Staat und die Intellektuellen* (1933) or *Kunst und Macht* (1935), led him to see in National Socialism a genuine renaissance of the German nation but he soon became disillusioned with the results, turning into a critic who was himself attacked by Nazi purists.

In 1937 he was expelled from the National Socialist Writers' Association (*Reichsschrifttumskammer*) and prohibited from publishing any more work. He took refuge in the army, the 'aristocratic form of emigration', as he called it, serving as a medical officer between 1939 and 1945. After the war, Benn was looked on askance for his early allegiance to the Nazis, but by 1949 the atmosphere had cleared enough for him to publish the results of his literary ruminations during the Third Reich. It became clear from his wartime writings that he had modified his vitalistic irrationalism and lost all sympathy with Nazi ideology. Benn now adopted a semi-ascetic, completely apolitical stance towards literature and poetry. In 1951 he received the Georg Büchner Prize. Benn died in Berlin on 7 July 1956.

Berger, Gottlob (1895–1975) SS General who was one of Himmler's (q.v.)

foremost experts on racial selection for the SS and on problems concerning its organization and security, Gottlob Berger was born on 16 July 1896 in Gorstetten. A Swabian with many German relatives in South-eastern Europe, Berger was probably the originator of the idea of the Waffen-SS as an international army which would also serve as an instrument for forging together the scattered 'racial' Germans of Axis Europe. A gymnastics instructor and sports champion in his younger days, Berger was appointed *SS-Obergruppenführer* in 1940 and for the next five years was Himmler's Chief of Staff for the military SS and head of the SS main leadership office (*SS-Führungsamtes*). As head of the administrative office of the SS (*SS-Hauptamt*) Berger proved himself a tough and ruthless organizer, and after July 1942 he was Himmler's personal liaison officer with Rosenberg's (q.v.) Reich Ministry for the occupied Eastern Territories, virtually running it at certain periods. In August 1943 Berger was elected a member of the Reichstag for the electoral district of Düsseldorf East. He was also President of the German-Croat Society and of the German-Flemish Study Group, a reflection of his interest in the idea of European union under Nazi auspices. On 31 August 1944 Berger was given command of military operations in Slovakia, in order to 'pacify' the inhabitants – which he did with brutal efficiency – and save the remnants of the puppet State he had helped to create. On 1 October of the same year he was appointed Inspector-General of Prisoners of War while continuing to hold his other positions. After the war, Berger was tried for his role in the murder of European Jewry and condemned on 2 April 1949 by an American tribunal at Nuremberg to twenty-five years' imprisonment. The sentence was commuted to ten years on 31 January 1951, but Berger was released before the end of the year,

having served six and a half years in prison. He died on 5 January 1975.

Best, Werner (1903–89) Senior SS and Nazi Security Police Leader who became Reich Commissioner for occupied Denmark, Werner Best was born on 10 July 1903 in Darmstadt. His parents moved to Dortmund in 1912 and then to Mainz, where Werner Best completed his education. After World War I – his father, a senior postmaster, had fallen in France at the outset of the war in 1914 – Best founded the first local group of the German National Youth League and became active in the Mainz group of the German National People's Party, all before he was twenty. From 1921 to 1925 he studied law at Frankfurt am Main, Freiburg, Giessen and Heidelberg, where he received his doctorate in 1927. During these years he was strongly influenced by the German youth movement with its return to nature, its Germanic myths and *völkisch* world-view. He was twice imprisoned between the end of 1923 and the spring of 1924 by the French authorities during the nationalist struggle in the Ruhr region. In 1929 he was appointed *Gerichtsassessor* (judge) in the Hessian Department of Justice, but was forced to resign from his position two years later when the so-called Boxheim documents were found in his possession. (The name came from the Boxheim estate near Worms, where groups of National Socialists had held meetings to discuss a plan for seizing power after a hypothetical communist revolution.) The documents, which bore Best's signature and contained a blueprint for a Nazi *putsch* and the subsequent execution of political opponents, embarrassed Hitler at a time when he was seeking power by legal means. Nevertheless, Best was made Police Commissioner in Hessen in March 1933 and by July of the same year he was appointed Governor.

Best advanced rapidly in the next six

years, becoming the deputy of Heydrich (q.v.) and Himmler (q.v.), chief legal adviser to the Gestapo (helping it to get rid of 'relics' from the old Weimar legal system and demonstrating how to operate by means of orders for preventive arrests without judicial checks), as well as holding the position of Chief of the Bureau of the Secret State Police at the Reich Ministry of the Interior. The ambitious Best, a cool, amoral technician of power, used his academic and legal skills to justify the totalitarian practice of the Nationalist Socialist Führer State 'which corresponds to the ideological principle of the organically indivisible national community'. The role of the political police was to fight all symptoms of 'disease' in the national organism, 'to discover the enemies of the State, to watch them and render them harmless at the right moment'. As a leading constitutional theoretician and Nazi jurist in the Third Reich, Best did a great deal to give respectability and legitimacy to the political police and the concentration camps. As long as the Gestapo was carrying out the will of the leadership it was, in his view, 'acting legally'.

By 1935 Best was already a *Standartenführer* – during World War II he was promoted to *SS-Obergruppenführer* – and the closest collaborator of Heydrich in building up the Gestapo and the Security Services (SD). Between 27 September 1939 and 12 June 1940 Best was Chief of Section I of the RSHA (Reich Main Security Office) and it was in this capacity that he was charged twenty-five years after the war with complicity in the murder of thousands of Jews and Polish intellectuals in occupied Poland. After leaving the RSHA, Best served for the next two years as Chief of the Civil Administration in occupied France, involved in fighting the French Resistance and in the deportation of Jews. The climax of his career came in Denmark, where he was Reich Plenipotentiary from November 1942 to 1945. In spite

of his record as a 'desk murderer', there is evidence that in Denmark Best sought to sabotage Himmler's orders concerning the implementation of the 'Final Solution'. Only 477 out of more than 7,000 Danish Jews were finally rounded up by German troops who were forbidden by Best to break into Jewish apartments.

Best was originally sentenced to death by a Danish court in 1948 following his extradition, but his sentence was commuted to five years and he was granted a clemency release in August 1951. He returned to West Germany, working for a time in a solicitor's office and then as a lawyer for Stinnes Co., one of the largest German trading concerns. In 1958 he was fined 70,000 marks by a Berlin de-Nazification court for his past activities as a top SS officer. In March 1969 he was held in detention for new investigations concerning responsibility for mass murder, finally charged in February 1972 and released in August of the same year on medical grounds, though the accusations were not withdrawn. One of the most illustrious figures of the Third Reich, the author of a famous book on the police, *Die Deutsche Polizei* (1941), a free-floating intellectual with a blurred sense of morality who devoted his legal talents to the service of a power-mad clique of criminals, Best's role remains ambiguous, at least in relation to his Danish period. A combination of personal ambition, opportunist careerism and ideological inclinations drove him to the apex of the Nazi system where he helped ensure the smooth functioning of a system of terror. Yet at the end of his National Socialist career it would appear that he belatedly began to revert to that respect for law which he had done so much to destroy from within at an earlier period.

Binding, Rudolf Georg (1867–1938) German novelist and poet, born in Basel on 13 August 1867 of wealthy parents (his father, Karl Binding, was an internationally famous jurist), Binding studied at Leipzig and Berlin but did not pursue a professional career, preferring to follow his own inclinations – especially horse-racing and writing. A cavalry Captain in World War I, his autobiographical *Aus dem Kriege* (1925, Engl. trs. *Fatalist at War*, 1929), based on diaries written during the war, is a realistic and prophetic work. Binding cultivated the small genre of legends and short stories, *Novellen* and autobiography, writing much about chivalry, chastity, sacrifice and the manly virtues. A literary self-made man, he was a popular author under the Weimar Republic and the Third Reich. In his *Antwort eines Deutschen an die Welt* (1933) he defended the new Germany against its foreign critics. Binding, who belonged to a small patrician group of neo-classical writers, was a useful apologist for the Nazi régime, but essentially a non-political author. Among his most characteristic works were the highly poetical narrative *Reitvorschrift für eine Geliebte* (1924), the autobiographical *Erlebtes Leben* (1928) and the philosophical dialogues, *Spiegelgespräche* (1933).

Blaskowitz, Johannes (1883–1948) Wehrmacht General who worked out the plan of attack for the invasion of Poland and commanded the Eighth Army there, becoming Commander-in-Chief of the Army of Occupation, Johannes Blaskowitz was born in Peterswalde on 10 July 1883. A professional soldier of the old school, who served in World War I, Blaskowitz rose rapidly under the Third Reich. In 1935 he was promoted to Lieutenant-General and Commander of Defence District II, Stettin. In 1938 he was appointed Field Commander of Army Group 3 (Dresden) and took part in the invasion of Austria and Bohemia, leading the Third Army into the Sudetenland in March 1939. In September 1939 he was Commander-in-Chief of the Eighth Army during the Polish campaign and was subjected to a severe flank attack at Poznan, requiring additional help from von Reichenau's (q.v.) Tenth Army to drive the Poles back. On 27 September Blaskowitz received the surrender of Warsaw and on 22 October 1939 he was made Military Governor of the German occupying forces in Poland.

As Commander-in-Chief, East, Blaskowitz protested at the SS and police bestialities in Poland, complaining that they operated outside the law and that he had no authority over them. He produced two detailed memoranda on their activities and those of the *Einsatzkommandos* against both Jews and the Polish intellectual élite between November 1939 and February 1940, which were addressed to his Commander-in-Chief, Field Marshal von Brauchitsch (q.v.). They documented many instances of raping, horsewhipping, murder and looting of Jewish and Polish shops, warning that the SS 'might later turn against their own people in the same way'. Hitler was reportedly infuriated by Blaskowitz's 'childish attitude' and he was dismissed from several army commands. Nevertheless, he served later on many fronts, never again questioning Hitler's policies. In 1944 he was given command of Army Group G under von Rundstedt (q.v.) which was preparing to defend against the expected Allied invasion in France. Relieved of his command after the defeat in Lorraine, he was transferred to the Netherlands in early 1945, where he surrendered to the British. He committed suicide on 5 February 1948 in Nuremberg prison shortly before his trial as a minor war criminal was due to begin. Fellow prisoners believed that he had been murdered by SS men, but this has never been substantiated.

Blomberg, Werner von (1878–1946) German Field Marshal and Minister of War from 1935 to 1938, Werner von Blomberg was born on 2 September 1878 in Stargard, Pomerania. A tall, impressive-looking, professional soldier from an officers' family, von Blomberg joined the Reichswehr in 1919, after various staff appointments during World War I. From 1927 to 1929 when he served as head of the *Truppenamt* (conscription office) at the War Office, von Blomberg frequently visited Soviet Russia and almost became a Bolshevik, during the honeymoon period of collaboration between the Reichswehr and the Red Army. In 1929 von Blomberg was given command of Defence District I in East Prussia and it was in this capacity that he first met Hitler in 1931, who made a great impression on the intelligent, though easily influenced, officer. Von Blomberg was head of the German delegation at the Disarmament Conference in Geneva and then on 1 January 1933 he was appointed Minister of Defence and promoted to General of Infantry.

Von Blomberg played a crucial role in Hitler's consolidation of power, during the Röhm (q.v.) *putsch* and after the death of President von Hindenburg (q.v.). On 29 June 1934 in an article in the *Völkische Beobachter* he had assured Hitler of the loyalty of the army, and soon after applauded the crushing of the SA, declaring that 'the Wehrmacht, as the sole armed force of the entire nation, while remaining apart from the conflicts of internal politics, will express its gratitude by its devotion and fidelity'. As War Minister, von Blomberg endorsed Hitler's succession to President Hindenburg, swearing the oath of allegiance to the Führer and imposing it on his fellow officers, thereby confirming Hitler's control over the army. In May 1935 he was made Commander-in-Chief of the new Wehrmacht and closely collaborated with Party leaders in planning the military reoccupation of the Rhineland. As a reward for his loyalty, Hitler appointed him the first General Field Marshal of the Wehrmacht in 1936. The steel-helmeted, aristocratic figure of von Blomberg

seemed a guarantee of continuity to the conservative classes, though many of his fellow generals considered him too compliant towards the Nazis.

Von Blomberg's downfall came about through a scandal engineered by Goering (q.v.), who coveted his position, and Himmler (q.v.) who was trying to promote the interests of his armed SS formations. The scandal arose through von Blomberg's marriage – he was a widower at the time with grown-up children – on 12 January 1938 to Eva Gruhn, a pretty, young working-girl who turned out to have been a prostitute with a criminal record who had posed for obscene photographs. Both Hitler and Goering had attended the discreet wedding ceremony as witnesses. Almost immediately, ugly rumours began to circulate as to the lady's past and the dossier compiled by the Berlin Chief of Police, von Helldorf (q.v.), was sent on to Goering, who, together with Himmler, exploited the case to bring down their antagonist. Von Blomberg and his wife were ordered to spend a year in exile, leaving for Capri after the Field Marshal's official resignation on 4 February 1938. The fall of von Blomberg, and that of von Fritsch (q.v.) shortly afterwards, allowed Hitler to end any possibility that the armed forces might act independently or even oppose the Nazi régime. Hitler himself took over the office of Defence Minister and Supreme Commander of the Armed Forces. Von Blomberg died in American detention, a pathetic bedridden old man, on 14 March 1946.

Blunck, Hans Friedrich (1888–1961) President of the Reich Chamber of Literature, novelist and poet Hans Friedrich Blunck was born in Altona, Hamburg, on 3 September 1888. Educated at the Universities of Kiel and Heidelberg, Blunck was appointed a government Councillor in 1920, and in 1925 legal adviser to the University of Hamburg. His literary work reflected his North German peasant background and strong interest in the folklore of the Baltic and North Sea coastal inhabitants. Historical novels, fairy-tales, prehistorical novels combining Nordic Promethean myths, viking saga and poetry predominated in his work which contained a marked dose of *völkisch* and National Socialist ideology. His early writings included a story of the Old Gods, *Streit mit den Göttern* (1925), *Kampf der Gesteine* (dealing with the Stone Age) and *Gewalt über das Feuer* (1928) – a collection of fairy-tales, legends and ghost stories. Apart from fairy-tales in the Low German language, poems and ballads, Blunck also wrote a novel about Brazil, *Die Weibsmühle* (1927), and another about Central America, *Land der Vulkane* (1929). More notorious were his so-called Führer novels, *Hein Hoyer*, the story of a fifteenth-century Hanseatic mercenary leader who becomes a national statesman, *Volkswende* (1930) and *König Geiserich* (1936), described by the Nazi historian of literature, Professor Nadler, as follows: 'a book about the birth of a nation, a book of Führer and Reich, an epic of a new race and a Germanic Christianity.' Other popular works published during the Third Reich included *Die Urvatersage* (1934), *Deutsche Heldensagen* (1938), *Die Jägerin* (1940) and *Sage vom Reich* (1941). Blunck fully collaborated with the Nazis, declaring in 1934 that 'an old world has collapsed and we Germans are showing the way to a new form of life. We carry a new belief in man and mankind in our hearts.' President of the Reich Chamber of Literature (1934–5), a member of the Reich Culture Senate and of the Academy of Literature, Blunck was also a recipient of the Goethe Medal. After World War II, he posed as a lamb of innocence. His two-volume memoirs, *Unwegsame Zeiten* (1952), are notable mainly for their unrepentant, callous whitewash of Hitler's Germany.

Bock, Fedor von (1880–1945) General Field Marshal of monarchist sympathies, the prototype of the Prussian officer, Fedor von Bock was born on 3 December 1880 in Küstrin, Brandenburg. The son of an old aristocratic officers' family – his father was a well-known general – Bock entered the army in 1898 as a Second Lieutenant and from 1912 to 1919 served as a General Staff officer. During World War I he commanded an infantry battalion and was awarded the coveted *Pour le Mérite*. Promoted to Major in 1918, Bock spent four years in the Reichswehr Ministry and by 1931 he was a Lieutenant-General. From 1935 to 1938 Bock, by now General of Infantry, was Commander of Army Group 3 (Dresden). In the spring of 1938, Bock led the Eighth Army into Austria. At the outbreak of World War II, he commanded the Army Group North during the invasion of Poland. Bock was then transferred to Army Group B, which he led during the 1940 invasion which operated on the northern flank in Holland, Belgium and France. Following the fall of France, Bock was promoted to General Field Marshal in July 1940. He then commanded the Army Group Centre during the invasion of the Soviet Union (April–December 1941), but was dismissed by Hitler when the offensive against Moscow was halted. Bock was recalled to take command of Army Group South from January to July 1942, only to be permanently retired after the failure to capture Stalingrad. On 4 May 1945 von Bock was killed in an Allied air raid.

Bonhoeffer, Dietrich (1906–45) Protestant pastor and theologian who was a leading figure in the German Resistance, Dietrich Bonhoeffer was born on 4 February 1906 in Breslau, the son of a well-known psychiatrist and university professor. After studying theology at Tübingen, Berlin and the Union Theological Seminary in New York, Bonhoeffer went to Berlin in 1931 as a lecturer. Following Hitler's rise to power, Bonhoeffer left for London where he preached as a pastor between 1933 and 1935. On his return to Nazi Germany he became a member of the Confessional Church, which asserted that Christianity was incompatible with National Socialism and its racial doctrines. Bonhoeffer not only insisted on the freedom to preach the Gospel, he was ready to risk his life as a Christian in resisting Hitler and in helping Jews to escape. He maintained that 'the church is only a Church, when she exists for those outside herself' and proclaimed its 'unconditional obligation towards the victims of every social system, even if they do not belong to the Christian community'. Bonhoeffer kept in constant touch with churches abroad, visiting England in the spring of 1939 – where he had talks with Bishop Bell and acted as an agent for the conspiracy against Hitler – and then the United States.

During his visit to Sweden in May 1942, Bonhoeffer brought with him concrete proposals from the conspirators, led by General Hans Oster (q.v.), Chief of Staff of the *Abwehr*, and General Ludwig Beck (q.v.), for peace terms, but these were rejected by the British Foreign Office. Bonhoeffer's contacts and his activities made him a prime suspect for the secret police and security services. After his seminary had been closed down a second time in 1940, he had been forbidden by the Gestapo to speak, preach or publish. On 5 April 1943 he was arrested by the Gestapo, charged with subverting the armed forces and imprisoned. After the failure of the July 1944 plot, Bonhoeffer was sent to Buchenwald and then, finally, to Flossenburg concentration camp where he was executed, together with Admiral Canaris (q.v.) and General Oster, on 9 April

1945. As a theologian, Bonhoeffer's ideas and his discussion of a 'religionless Christianity', reinforced by his own martyrdom, exercised a considerable influence on post-war Protestant thought in Britain and America.

Bonhoeffer, Klaus (1901–45) Brother of Dietrich Bonhoeffer (q.v.) and a leader of the Resistance to Hitler, Klaus Bonhoeffer was born in Breslau on 5 January 1901. A lawyer – he was admitted to the bar in 1930 – Bonhoeffer became the legal adviser of Lufthansa, the German civilian air transport company, in 1936. Like his brother, Klaus Bonhoeffer had deep moral objections to National Socialism and worked to overthrow the Third Reich from within, in conjunction with different Resistance groups. Arrested after the failure of the July 1944 plot, he was sentenced to death by the People's Court on 2 February 1945 and shot in Berlin on 23 April as the Russians were storming the city.

Bormann, Martin (1900–45?) Head of the Party Chancellery and private secretary of the Führer, who by the end of World War II had become second only to Hitler himself in terms of real political power, Martin Bormann was born in Halberstadt on 17 June 1900. The son of a former Prussian regimental sergeant-major who later became a post-office employee, Bormann dropped out of school to work on a farming estate in Mecklenburg. After serving briefly as a cannoneer in a field artillery regiment at the end of World War I, Bormann subsequently joined the rightist Rossbach *Freikorps* in Mecklenburg and was connected with the so-called 'Feme' murders. In March 1924 he was sentenced to one year's imprisonment as an accomplice of Rudolf Hoess (q.v.) in the brutal, vengeance murder of Walther Kadow (his former teacher at elementary school), who had supposedly betrayed the proto-Nazi martyr Leo

Schlageter to the French occupation authorities in the Ruhr.

After his release he entered the NSDAP, becoming its regional press officer in Thuringia and then business manager in 1928. From 1928 to 1930 he was attached to the SA Supreme Command and in October 1933 he became a *Reichsleiter* of the NSDAP. A month later he was elected as a Nazi delegate to the Reichstag. From July 1933 until 1941 Bormann was the Chief of Cabinet in the Office of the Deputy Führer, Rudolf Hess (q.v.), acting as his personal secretary and right-hand man.

During this period, the 'model secretary', diligent, adaptable and efficient, began his silent, imperceptible rise to the centre of the power apparatus, slowly acquiring mastery of the bureaucratic mechanism and Hitler's personal trust. He developed and administered the Adolf Hitler Endowment Fund of German industry, a huge fund of 'voluntary' contributions by successful business entrepreneurs to the Führer, which Bormann then reallocated as gifts to almost all the top Party functionaries. In addition to administering Hitler's personal finances, buying the Berghof at Berchtesgaden and running it as well as the whole complex of properties on the Obersalzberg, Bormann acquired the power to control the living standards of *Gauleiters* and *Reichsleiters*, not to speak of members of the Führer's intimate circle. Bormann's brutality, coarseness, lack of culture and his apparent insignificance led the Nazi Old Guard to underestimate his silent persistence and ability to make himself indispensable. Rudolf Hess's flight to Britain opened the way for the 'Brown Eminence' to step into his shoes on 12 May 1941 as head of the *Parteikanzlei* and to gather the reins of the Party into his own hands and steadily undermine all his rivals for power.

Until the end of the war, the short, squat Bormann, working in the anonym-

ity of his seemingly unimportant office, proved himself a master of intrigue, manipulation and political in-fighting. Always the 'narrow Party man' and a fierce guardian of Nazi orthodoxy (he was an arch-fanatic when it came to racial policy, anti-semitism and the *Kirchenkampf* [war between the churches]), Bormann strengthened the position of the Party against the Wehrmacht and the SS, and increased his grip on domestic policy. Increasingly he controlled all questions concerning the security of the régime, acts of legislation, appointments and promotions, especially if they concerned Party personnel. He also established espionage in the army, getting younger officers promoted to spy on the political attitudes of their colleagues. He reopened the fight against the Christian churches, declaring in a confidential memo to *Gauleiters* in 1942 that their power 'must absolutely and finally be broken'. Nazism, based as it was on a 'scientific' world-view, was completely incompatible with Christianity whose influence was regarded by Bormann as a serious obstacle to totalitarian rule. The sharpest anti-cleric in the Nazi leadership (he collected all the files of cases against the clergy that he could lay his hands on), Bormann was the driving force of the *Kirchenkampf*, which Hitler for tactical reasons had wished to postpone until after the war.

Bormann was invariably the advocate of extremely harsh, radical measures when it came to the treatment of Jews, of the conquered eastern peoples or prisoners of war. He signed the decree of 9 October 1942 prescribing that 'the permanent elimination of the Jews from the territories of Greater Germany can no longer be carried out by emigration but by the use of ruthless force in the special camps of the East'. A further decree, signed by Bormann on 1 July 1943, gave Adolf Eichmann (q.v.) absolute powers over Jews, who now came under the exclusive jurisdiction of the

Gestapo. Bormann's memos concerning the Slavs make it clear that he regarded them as a 'Sovietized mass' of sub-humans who had no claim to national independence. In a brutal memo of 19 August 1942 he wrote: 'The Slavs are to work for us. In so far as we do not need them, they may die. Slav fertility is not desirable.' By the end of 1942 Bormann was virtually Hitler's deputy and his closest collaborator, showing an uncanny ability to exploit his weaknesses and personal peculiarities in order to increase his own power. Always in attendance on the Führer, taking care of tiresome administrative detail and skilfully steering Hitler into approval of his own schemes, Bormann acquired the inside track for displacing dangerous rivals like Goering (q.v.), Goebbels (q.v.), Speer (q.v.) and even Himmler (q.v.) whose access to the Führer was controlled by him. Bormann exploited his position of trust to build a Chinese wall against reality, in which Hitler could indulge his fantasies and in which more sensible, conciliatory proposals from other members of the Party were screened from him. Bormann reduced everything to simple, administrative formulae that freed Hitler from the burdens of paper work. He drew up his appointments calendar and decided whom he should see and whom he should not. Hitler rewarded these and other services by the trust he placed in Bormann, whom he once called 'my most loyal Party comrade'. He was made executive head of the *Volkssturm*, the desperate levy *en masse* of the German civilian population organized as the Allies stood poised to invade the Reich. By now virtually the secret ruler of Germany, Bormann did not cease his Machiavellian bureaucratic intrigues against his rivals.

As a result of his machinations Hitler dismissed Goering and Himmler's influence was severely curtailed. It was the indispensable Bormann, the most mys-terious and sinister figure in the Third Reich, who signed Hitler's political testament, who acted as the witness to his marriage to Eva Braun (q.v.) and watched his Führer commit suicide in the Chancellery bunker. Ordered by Hitler 'to put the interests of the nation before his own feelings' and to save himself, Bormann left the *Führerbunker* on 30 April 1945. Accounts of what happened afterwards vary widely. According to Erich Kempka (Hitler's chauffeur), Bormann was killed trying to cross the Russian lines by an anti-tank shell which hit the tank in which they were trying to escape, causing it to burst into flames. Kempka, who was temporarily blinded at the time, claimed nonetheless to have seen Bormann's dead body. Hitler Youth Leader, Artur Axmann (q.v.), on the other hand, believed that Bormann committed suicide and claimed to have seen Bormann's body on 2 May 1945 in the Invalidenstrasse, north of the River Spree in Berlin. Doubts, however, have persisted and numerous sightings of Bormann have been reported, beginning in 1946 when his presence in a North Italian monastery was announced. In the same year, his wife Gerda (a rabid Nazi and daughter of Supreme Party Judge, Walter Buch, q.v.) died of cancer in South Tyrol, though his ten children survived the war. It was then alleged that Bormann had escaped (like other loyal Nazis) via Rome to South America. Rumoured to have settled in Argentina where he was living secretly as a millionaire, allegedly spotted in Brazil and also in Chile, Bormann's traces proved as elusive as the anonymity in which he first rose to power. Having been sentenced to death *in absentia* at Nuremberg on 1 October 1946, he was formally pronounced dead by a West German court in April 1973 but his precise fate remains unknown.

Born, Max (1882–1970) One of the key figures in the development of modern physics and a celebrated refugee from the Third Reich, Max Born was born in Breslau on 12 December 1882. After lecturing at Berlin (1915) and Frankfurt am Main (1919), Born joined the faculty at Göttingen in 1921, where he became Director of the Institute of Theoretical Physics. In April 1933 he was 'placed on leave' by the Prussian Ministry of Education because of his Jewish descent. Though he did not initially wish to leave Germany, he accepted a post at Cambridge University once it was clear that there was no more future for him at Göttingen. Born's outstanding contribution was in the field of quantum theory – he received the Nobel Prize for Physics in 1954 for his work on the statistical foundations of quantum mechanics – and his pupils included such famous German physicists as Werner Heisenberg (q.v.) and Wolfgang Pauli. He was an intimate friend of Albert Einstein (q.v.), whose theory of relativity he defended in the early Weimar years against anti-semitic attacks. From 1936 to 1954 Born was Professor of Natural Philosophy at Edinburgh University. Unlike Einstein, he eventually returned to Germany in his last years. He died on 5 January 1970 at Bad Pyrmont.

Bouhler, Philip (1899–1945) Born in Munich on 2 September 1899, the son of a retired colonel, Bouhler rose to become Chief of the Führer's Chancellery and head of the notorious euthanasia programme. After four years in the Royal Bavarian Cadet Corps and service in World War I (during which he was seriously wounded), Bouhler apprenticed with various publishers. In 1922 he abandoned the University of Munich philosophy school to help edit the *Völkische Beobachter*. From 1925 to 1934 he was *Geschäftsführer* (business manager) of the NSDAP. In 1933 he became a *Reichsleiter* of the Nazi Party and was elected member of the Reichstag for the district of Westphalia. In

1934 he was made Police President of Munich and became Hitler's Chief of Chancery, responsible for the preparation of decrees that were never officially published. At the same time Bouhler was also Chief of the Party's Censorship Committee for the Protection of National Socialist Literature and of the Study Group for German History Books and Educational Material. In 1942 he published *Napoleon, the Comet-Path of a Genius*, which was one of Hitler's favourite bedtime reading books. The soft-faced, bespectacled, mild-spoken Bouhler who 'looked more like an American college-boy than a *Gruppenführer* of the SS' (Gerald Reitlinger) was one of the shadowiest figures in the National Socialist élite. His office was responsible for the euthanasia institutes which used gas chambers filled with carbon monoxide gas to get rid of the mentally sick – and later for the gassing camps for Jews in Poland. On 16 August 1941 Bouhler was ordered by Hitler to halt the euthanasia programme as a result of public protests. At the end of the war, Bouhler increasingly sought Goering's (q.v.) protection and it was at the latter's headquarters at Zell-am-See in May 1945 that Bouhler and his wife committed suicide shortly before the Americans arrived.

Brack, Victor (1904–48) SS Colonel and one of the top officials in the Reich Chancellery who took an active part in the construction of the death camps in Poland during World War II, Victor Brack was born in Haaren on 9 November 1904. After studying economics at Munich, Brack, who was the son of a medical practitioner and friend of Heinrich Himmler (q.v.), became for a time the chauffeur of the future *Reichsführer-SS*. In 1936 he was appointed head liaison officer with the Department of Health by Philip Bouhler (q.v.), though he had no previous medical experience. Subsequently he rose to become Bouhler's deputy and Chief of Section II in the Führer's Chancellery with the rank of *Oberdienstleiter* (approximately equivalent to colonel). Between December 1939 and August 1941 Brack's office, known as T4 in the Reich Chancellery, was responsible, during the 'Euthanasia Action', for disposing of more than 50,000 Germans – including the mentally sick, chronically sick and concentration camp prisoners defined as 'unfit for work', 'politically undesirable elements' and Jews. Brack himself personally interviewed and selected personnel for the euthanasia establishments and in March 1941 offered the services of his network of institutes to Himmler, for the purpose of sterilizing 3–4,000 Jews daily in X-ray clinics. Later in 1941 he prepared to set up mobile gassing vans in Riga and Minsk to exterminate Jews 'unsuitable for work'. Subsequently, he was closely involved in the construction of the death camps and the installation of gas chambers in Poland, operated by some of his personnel from the euthanasia institutes. On 20 August 1947 Brack was sentenced to death at the end of the Doctors' Trial, by an American military tribunal, for his part in the euthanasia programme. He was hanged in Landsberg prison on 2 June 1948.

Brauchitsch, Walter von (1881–1948) Commander-in-Chief of the German Army from 1938 to 1941, Walter von Brauchitsch was born on 4 October 1881 in Berlin, the descendant of an old Prussian military family. An officer in the Imperial army from 1900, he served on the western front as Captain of Artillery during World War I and was awarded the Iron Cross (First Class). After various staff appointments in the Reichswehr between 1919 and 1928, von Brauchitsch was promoted to Lieutenant-General and Artillery Inspector in 1931 and two years later he was made Commander of the First Division

at Königsberg. In 1935 he became Commanding General of the First Army Corps, a year later General of Infantry and in 1937 Commander of the Fourth Army Group, Leipzig. Promoted to General on 4 February 1938, von Brauchitsch was at the same time appointed by Hitler to succeed Werner von Fritsch (q.v.) as Commander-in-Chief of the Wehrmacht, a position he held until December 1941.

Von Brauchitsch was under a personal obligation to the Führer, who not only persuaded his first wife to agree to a divorce but even paid the divorce settlement costs. A few months later von Brauchitsch was able to marry his second wife, née Charlotte Schmidt, who was a rabid Nazi. It was partly due to her influence that the pliable von Brauchitsch proved so weak and compliant towards Hitler and left top army opponents of the régime like General Ludwig Beck (q.v.) in the lurch. Though aware of the conspiracy and himself sceptical of Hitler's aggressive plans, von Brauchitsch felt constrained by his loyalty oath and he backed the Führer even when his own military instincts dictated the reverse. Thus he supported the annexation of Austria in March 1938, the occupation of Czech frontier areas in October 1938 and the military take-over of Czechoslovakia in March 1939. The successes in the early stages of World War II, with the rapid defeats of Poland, France and the Low Countries, all of which took place under his command, added to his prestige and on 17 July 1940 he was made General Field Marshal. On the other hand these successes, which continued during the campaigns in Yugoslavia, Greece and the early stages of the Russian invasion, made von Brauchitsch even more compliant and incapable of standing up to Hitler. After the first setbacks of the Wehrmacht in the Soviet Union, von Brauchitsch began to lose what little influence he still had and plagued by heart disease he was retired on 19 December 1941. Hitler himself now took over as the Supreme Commander of the Wehrmacht. At the end of the war, von Brauchitsch was arrested on his estate in Schleswig-Holstein and taken to England where he was imprisoned for a time. Subsequently interned by the British in a camp in Münster, together with von Rundstedt (q.v.) and von Manstein (q.v.), he was to have been tried by a British military court in 1949. The practically blind, ailing General died, however, of heart failure in the British military hospital in Hamburg-Barmbeck on 18 October 1948.

Braun, Eva (1912–45) Hitler's mistress from 1932 and his wife during the last few hours of his life, Eva Braun was born in Munich, the daughter of a school teacher. Of middle-class Catholic background, she first met Hitler in the studio of his photographer friend, Heinrich Hoffmann (q.v.), in 1929, describing him to her sister, Ilse, as 'a gentleman of a certain age with a funny moustache and carrying a big felt hat'. At that time Eva Braun still worked for Hoffmann as an office assistant, later becoming a photo laboratory worker, helping to process pictures of Hitler. The blonde, fresh-faced, slim, photographer's assistant was an athletic girl, fond of skiing, mountain climbing and gymnastics as well as dancing. After the death of Geli Raubal, Hitler's niece, she became his mistress, living in his Munich flat, in spite of the opposition of her father who disliked the association on political and personal grounds. In 1935, after an abortive suicide attempt, Hitler bought her a villa in a Munich suburb, near to his own home, providing her with a Mercedes and a chauffeur for personal use. In his first will of 2 May 1938 he put her at the top of his personal bequests – in the event of his death she was to receive the equivalent of £600 a year for the rest of her life.

In 1936 she moved to Hitler's Berghof at Berchtesgaden where she acted as his hostess. Reserved, indifferent to politics and keeping her distance from most of the Führer's intimates, Eva Braun led a completely isolated life in the Führer's Alpine retreat and later in Berlin. They rarely appeared in public together and few Germans even knew of her existence. Even the Führer's closest associates were not certain of the exact nature of their relationship, since Hitler preferred to avoid suggestions of intimacy and was never wholly relaxed in her company. Eva Braun spent most of her time exercising, brooding, reading cheap novelettes, watching romantic films or concerning herself with her own appearance. Her loyalty to Hitler never flagged. After he survived the July 1944 plot she wrote Hitler an emotional letter, ending: 'From our first meeting I swore to follow you anywhere – even unto death – I live only for your love.'

In April 1945 she joined Hitler in the *Führerbunker*, as the Russians closed in on Berlin. She declined to leave in spite of his orders, claiming to others that she was the only person still loyal to him to the bitter end. 'Better that ten thousand others die than he be lost to Germany', she would constantly repeat to friends. On 29 April 1945 Hitler and Eva Braun were finally married. The next day she committed suicide by swallowing poison, two minutes before Hitler took his own life. On Hitler's orders, both bodies were cremated with petrol in the Reich Chancellery garden above the bunker. Her charred corpse was later discovered by the Russians. The rest of Eva Braun's family survived the war. Her mother, Franziska, who lived in an old farmhouse in Ruhpolding, Bavaria, died at the age of ninety-six, in January 1976.

Braun, Wernher von (1912–77) German rocket engineer who developed the V-2 (*Vergeltungswaffe* – reprisal weapons) launched against England towards the end of World War II, Wernher von Braun was born in Wirsitz, Prussia, on 23 March 1912. The son of Magnus von Braun, a former Minister of Agriculture under President von Hindenburg (q.v.) and founder of the German Savings Bank, and of a musically talented mother, he developed a strong interest in astronomy and space flight while studying at the Charlottenburg Institute of Technology in Berlin. Engaged in rocket research by the German Army Ordnance Office in October 1932, von Braun was appointed five years later as Technical Director of the immense rocket weapons project at Peenemünde on the Baltic coast. By 1938 he had already developed the prototype of the V-2 – the A-4 rocket, a self-propelled and self-steering apparatus with a range of eleven miles. Von Braun's research in solving problems of guidance, aerodynamics and propulsion was slowed down after 1940 by Hitler's decision to shift men and resources away from rocket research to the Luftwaffe. His pleas for better research facilities were ignored until in 1943 Hitler ordered mass production of the forty-six-foot-long V-2 rocket. Resisting Himmler's (q.v.) attempt to take control of the project, von Braun and two of his chief assistants were arrested by the SS on 14 March 1944 and briefly imprisoned on suspicion of concentrating on space travel rather than making war weapons. They were released thanks to the intervention of General Dornberger and Albert Speer (q.v.) with Hitler, and on 8 September 1944 the first V-2 was launched against England. Some 3,600 rockets were fired in the next seven months against English cities until the launching sites were finally captured by Allied forces.

In March 1945 von Braun evacuated Peenemünde as Russian troops approached and gave himself up to the Americans, together with over a hundred of his scientific colleagues. After interrogation in London, he was released and allowed to continue his research in the United States where he became a naturalized American citizen in 1955 and a leading figure in the American space programme. After 1960 he became Director of the George C. Marshall Space Flight Center in Huntsville, Alabama, playing a crucial part in the development of the American moon flight programme. He designed the US army's Jupiter rocket, which put the United States back into the space race, and his team pioneered the development of the Redstone, which carried America's first astronaut aloft in 1961. The driving force, the inventor and organizing genius behind the American space programme, he designed and developed the huge Saturn 5 rocket, which opened a new era of space exploration in 1969 when it carried the Apollo astronauts to the surface of the moon. In 1970 he was appointed Deputy Assistant Director for planning at NASA (National Aeronautics and Space Administration). Wernher von Braun died of cancer in Alexandria, Virginia, on 16 June 1977 at the age of sixty-five. He was described by the Acting Director of NASA as 'a twentieth-century Columbus who pushed back the new frontiers of outer space with efforts that enabled his adopted country to achieve pre-eminence in space exploration'.

Brecht, Bertolt (1898–1956) Outstanding German playwright and poet who was a militant opponent of Nazism, Bertolt Brecht was born on 10 February 1898 in Augsburg, Bavaria. Drafted as a medical orderly in the last year of World War I, Brecht's disillusion found a voice in his first expressionist dramas, performed in 1922, *Trommeln in der Nacht, Baal* and *Im Dickicht der Städte*. They exhibited a nihilist, anarchist streak underlying Brecht's anti-bourgeois, anti-establishment attitude and his fascination with violence. His greatest theatrical success, *Die Dreigroschenoper* (1928), adapted from John Gay's *The Beggar's Opera* (with music by Kurt Weill, q.v.), was a satire on gangsterism and bourgeois ethics which proved enormously popular with the middle-class public. Other plays such as *Mann ist Mann* (1927) and *Mahagonny* (1929) reinforced Brecht's reputation as a witty parodist of bourgeois respectability. After 1926 he began to study Marxism and to espouse a doctrinaire communism that found expression in his chilling play *Die Massnahme (The Measures Taken)*, which anticipated the totalitarian Stalinist mentality of the late thirties. Though he served the Party till the end of his life, many communists never felt wholly at ease with his work and he was not popular in the Soviet Union.

Brecht's real rise to fame began after 1933 – he went into exile the day after the Reichstag fire – as his work gradually conquered Britain and America. His most famous plays were written in these years of Scandinavian exile in the Danish city of Svendborg and after 1941 in Hollywood and Santa Monica, USA. They included *Der Kaukasische Kreidekreis (The Caucasian Chalk Circle)* and *Leben des Galilei (Life of Galileo)*. Brecht's plays, radio scripts and poems against Nazism were less impressive, if only because they reflected his Stalinist allegiance, unshaken by the Moscow trials, the Spanish Civil War or the Nazi-Soviet pact. In *Die Rundköpfe und die Spitzköpfe* (1938, Engl. trs. *Round Heads, Peak Heads*) and *Furcht und Elend des Dritten Reiches* (1938, Engl. trs. *The Private Life of the Master Race*), Brecht tried to capture the trials and tribulations of the German people under Hitler's yoke and to ridicule racial theories. The wooden prose dialogue disguises, however, a more basic weakness, namely that Brecht's Marxism prevented him from grasping that in the Third Reich it was race not class that counted.

Hitler had liquidated hunger and unemployment, thereby winning the support of the German working classes. It was the Jews, not so much the proletarians, who were being persecuted, a fact barely grasped by Brecht. It is no accident that his satirical play on the 'irresistible' rise of Adolf Hitler, *Arturo Ui,* singularly failed in its intention to explain the rise of fascism on the model of a Chicago protection racket.

After being called before the Committee on Un-American Activities in 1947 for his pro-communist leanings, Brecht left the United States. He initially hoped to settle in Munich, but this proved impossible. At the end of 1949 he went to East Berlin, but held on to his Czech (later Austrian) passport, his Swiss bank account and West German publisher. In East Berlin, Brecht formed, headed, directed and wrote for his own theatre, the Berliner Ensemble, which became an internationally renowned cultural showcase of the communist world. Though he received the Stalin Peace Prize in 1954, Brecht's artistic creativity as a dramatist and poet largely dried up during his last seven years in East Germany. He died on 14 August 1956 in East Berlin.

Breker, Arno (1900–91) Arno Breker, the most famous and successful sculptor in the Third Reich, was born in Elberfeld on 19 July 1900, the son of a stonemason and sculptor. He learned his craft in his father's studio, subsequently studying at the Düsseldorf Academy of Art. Breker then moved to Paris, where he lived from 1927 to 1933 and was strongly influenced by the French sculptor Maillol. Under the Nazi régime, Breker helped to initiate a new style of sculpture with classically monumental figures expressing a strong pathos of gesture, concentrated strength and a rather brutal ideal of hard, heroic masculinity. His perfectly proportioned athletes and warriors were presented as godlike creatures and celebrations of conquest and victory. Breker's sculptures often adorned public buildings or were exhibited at the Great German Art Exhibitions – for example, his bronze figures *The Army* and *The Party* decorated the inner courtyard of the Reich Chancellery in Berlin, built by Albert Speer (q.v.) in 1939. Hitler was enraptured by these muscular, faultless figures and Breker's bust of the composer Richard Wagner stood in Hitler's private retreat in the Berghof. Breker was rewarded by many public honours and commissions for his loyalty to the régime and for his invention of a distinctive Nazi style of sculpture. In 1936 he was awarded the Olympic Silver Medal for Art. In 1937 he became an 'official state sculptor' and received the gift of a giant studio, employing 43 people, among them twelve sculptors. A member of the Prussian Academy of Arts and appointed Professor at the State Technical School for Visual Arts in Berlin in 1938, Breker earned nearly 100,000 marks for his work in that year alone, while paying only a token sum in taxes. In 1940 he received a large private house with a park and another sizeable studio as a personal gift from Hitler. A sculptor of undoubted talent, in spite of his tendency to backward-looking rhetoric and his increasingly bombastic style, Breker was also admired in France. A large exhibition of his work was shown in the Orangerie in occupied Paris in 1942 where the show was opened by the President of the Académie française, who eulogised his artistry. There was an enthusiastic introduction by Jean Cocteau in the exhibition catalogue. The celebration of the male nude body, of a steely masculinity and of sinewy, muscular figures ready for combat, evidently exercised a certain appeal, even outside Nazi Germany, despite the conscious reference to a Nordic racial ideal and the 'Aryan' myth. The hollow, artificial, cold and self-contained brutality in these

figures was ignored by his admirers. After the war, Breker sculpted the heads of many well-known artists like Cocteau, Montherlant, Celine, Ezra Pound and Salvador Dali as well as members of the Wagner family, and Conservative German politicians like Adenauer (q.v.) and Erhard. In 1961 he bought back many of his sculptures in private auction and they stood in his garden in Düsseldorf. His memoirs, *Im Strahlungsfeld der Ereignisse*, were published in 1972. Like Albert Speer (q.v.) Arno Breker enjoyed a certain vogue and a kind of rehabilitation in the two decades before his death, consistently claiming that his art had no political implications.

Brüning, Heinrich (1885–1970) German Reich Chancellor from 1930 to 1932 and leader of the Catholic Centre Party, Heinrich Brüning was born in Münster, Westphalia, on 26 November 1885, the son of an industrialist. After studying philosophy, history and politics – he obtained his doctorate from the University of Bonn in 1915 – he volunteered for military service at the front and rose to command a machine gun company. After World War I, he received his political training as a protégé of Adam Stegerwald and as business manager of the League of German Trade Unions (Christian Unions) from 1920 to 1930. A member of the Catholic Centre Party, representing its conservative, monarchist-oriented right wing, Brüning was elected as a deputy for Breslau in 1924, a position he held until 1933. An aloof, academic type of politician, a sincere Catholic and a leading fiscal expert, Brüning became Chairman of the Centre Party in the Reichstag in 1929. At the end of March 1930 he was appointed Reich Chancellor of a cabinet dominated by the bourgeois centre just when the world economic depression was beginning seriously to hit Germany. Brüning's drastic deflationary policies aimed to sanitize the national finances by cutting expenditure, official salaries and wage rates, reducing unemployment benefits and increasing taxation. Determined to prevent inflation at any cost, his austerity policies were extremely unpopular, paralysing large sectors of the economy as well as reducing the standard of living of the workers. Lacking a solid parliamentary base, Brüning dismissed the Reichstag on 18 July 1930 for failing to support his fiscal programme. Henceforth he governed by decree, using the emergency powers granted by Article 48 of the Weimar Constitution, which made him wholly dependent on the assent of the Reich President Paul von Hindenburg (q.v.). Although he enjoyed the unofficial support of the army and the Social Democrats in the Reichstag, Brüning's position was weakened by the results of the September 1930 elections which greatly increased the strength of the Nazis and communists. They bitterly attacked his policies as the embodiment of all the evils of the post-1918 Weimar 'System'. Brüning was more successful abroad (from 1931 he assumed the additional post of Foreign Minister), bringing an end to reparations at Lausanne in the summer of 1932 and making progress towards revising the Versailles Treaty, thanks to his prestige with the former Allied powers. Under his emergency decrees, the SA and the SS were officially disbanded on 13 April 1932.

Brüning's failure to solve the economic crisis as unemployment mounted over the six million mark encouraged attacks on his policy from both Right and Left in the summer of 1932. The opposition of the big Junker landowners in East Prussia increased as his plans for sanitizing the uneconomical landed estates became known and led to a cooling of his relations with President von Hindenburg, who regarded Brüning's projected policy as 'agrarian Bolshevism'. The backstage intrigues of General von Schleicher (q.v.), who was determined to replace Brüning with a more

amenable figure ready to make concessions to the Nazis, also influenced von Hindenburg to withdraw his support. On 10 May 1932 the almost senile Reich President abruptly called for Brüning's resignation and by the end of the month he had been replaced by Franz von Papen (q.v.). With Brüning's dismissal went the last significant statesman of the Weimar Republic and a decisive blow was struck at the tottering façade of bourgeois democracy in Germany. In July 1933 Brüning gave up the Chairmanship of the Catholic Centre Party and in the summer of 1934 he left for Switzerland, subsequently emigrating to the United States. He accepted a Professorship in Political Science at Harvard, where he became a member of the faculty from 1937 to 1952. In 1951 Brüning returned to Cologne, where he was later appointed Professor Emeritus. He eventually resumed residence in the United States, where he died on 30 March 1970 in Norwich, Vermont. His *Memoiren* were posthumously published in the same year.

Buch, Walter (1883–1949) President of the Nazi Party Supreme Court and one of the highest Party dignitaries, Walter Buch was born in Bruchsal, Baden, on 24 October 1883, the son of an eminent judge. A professional officer who served in World War I, Major Buch left the army after 1918 and worked with the Baden association of ex-servicemen. Entering the NSDAP in 1922, he became leader of the SA commando, Franconia, in Nuremberg in August 1923. In 1927 he was appointed Chairman of the USCHLA (the Investigation and Adjustment Committee), a much feared and secret Party commission in Munich which was sometimes referred to as the 'Cheka in the Brown House'. Essentially a disciplinary body whose functions were to watch unreliable Party members, to crush and expel dissidents as well as to arbitrate in disputes between

NSDAP members, it became to the Party what the Gestapo was for Germans as a whole. The Party tribunal came to exercise an almost unlimited power of life and death over Party members and no appeal against its judgement was possible. The hard-faced Major Buch was able to build up a powerful, independent organization of espionage and secret police within the Party which engaged in surveillance of other Party organizations inside and outside Germany.

In the 1930s it was especially active in Czechoslovakia and other neighbouring countries, controlling foreign groups loosely linked with the Nazi Party. After the Nazi seizure of power, Buch was officially appointed Supreme Party Judge and *SS-Gruppenführer* on 9 November 1934. A few months earlier he had played a leading part in the Blood Purge, accompanying Hitler to Wiessee to arrest Ernst Röhm (q.v.) and directing the SS commando which shot the leading Brownshirts in the courtyard of the Stadelheim prison. Eye-witnesses subsequently described Buch's sadistic enjoyment as he watched his victims expire, some of them old Party comrades whom he killed with his own hand. During the Third Reich, no one was safe from the hatred or vengeance of the supreme executioner of the Party. Buch was also a virulent anti-semite, who did not hesitate to assert that from the Nazi standpoint the Jew was outside the law.

He presided over the Nazi Party Supreme Court which conducted a secret investigation into the Crystal Night pogrom of 8 November 1938 and concluded that the Nazi rank-and-file, who had murdered more than a hundred Jews, were innocent of any crime and had faithfully obeyed 'orders from above'. In an article in *Deutsche Justiz* (21 October 1938) Buch wrote: 'The Jew is not a human being. He is an appearance of putrescence. Just as the fission-fungus cannot permeate wood until it is rotting, so the Jew was able to creep into the German people, to bring on disaster, only after the German nation ... had begun to rot from within.' After the war, Buch was sentenced to five years' forced labour and at his second de-Nazification trial in July 1949 he was classified as a 'Major Offender'. He committed suicide on 12 November 1949, slashing his wrists and drowning himself in Ammer Lake, according to the report of the Bavarian State Police.

Bürckel, Josef (1894–1944) Nazi Governor of Austria, Josef Bürckel was born on 30 March 1894 in Lingfield, in the Palatinate. After serving for four years during World War I, Bürckel became a teacher, abandoning his post in 1926 to become *Gauleiter* of the Nazi Party in the Rheinpfalz. Elected to the Reichstag in 1930 he represented the NSDAP in the Saar region, succeeding von Papen (q.v.) four years later as Plenipotentiary for the Saar Palatinate. In 1935, after the Saar plebiscite, he was appointed Reich Commissioner for the territory. Named *Gauleiter* of Vienna after the union between Germany and Austria, Bürckel was promoted to Reich Commissary on 23 April 1938 and ordered to accomplish 'the political, economic and cultural incorporation of Austria' into the Reich within a year. A talented organizer and shrewd politician, Bürckel sought to bring to a halt the orgy of violence and indiscriminate robbery against Jews, which accompanied the *Anschluss*, by issuing decrees requiring all Nazi commissars who had taken control of Jewish businesses to report their actions. In some cases he even instituted criminal proceedings against those who had stolen assets for themselves. As the top Nazi leader in Austria, Bürckel was nonetheless responsible for applying systematic and ruthless pressure leading to the Jewish deportations from Vienna in 1939–40. Transferred to the Saarland-Lorraine, he was also responsible (together with *Gauleiter* Robert Wagner, q.v.) for the sudden deportation of more than 6,500 Jews without warning from the districts of Baden and Saarpfalz (Saar Palatinate) into unoccupied France on 22–23 October 1940. Bürckel was reported to have committed suicide on 28 September 1944.

Busch, Ernst von (1885–1945) General Field Marshal who was an out-and-out Nazi general, Ernst von Busch was born in Essen-Steele, Ruhr, on 6 July 1885. A professional officer, he had seen active service in World War I and after various staff appointments was made Inspector of Transport Troops in the Reichswehr in 1925. Von Busch was promoted rapidly after the Nazis came to power, reaching the rank of Lieutenant-General in 1937; a year later he was made General of Infantry and Commander-in-Chief of the Eighth Army Corps. After participating in the Polish campaign, von Busch was given command of an army on the western front and awarded the Knight's Cross in 1940. During the invasion of Soviet Russia, von Busch commanded the Sixteenth Army and, in spite of serious difficulties incurred during the winter of 1942, was promoted to General Field Marshal in February 1943. Between 29 October 1943 and 28 June 1944 he commanded the Central Army Group in Russia and was made the scapegoat for its collapse when the Russians opened their summer offensive. Dismissed from his eastern command, von Busch's loyalty was nonetheless rewarded by a transfer to Schleswig and Denmark, where he commanded German forces until the end of the war. A professional soldier of the old school who had never questioned a single Führer order, and even enjoyed sitting in on tribunals of the People's Court, von Busch, though increasingly disillusioned with Hitler's conduct of the war, proved incapable of resisting his spell. He died in British captivity on 17 July 1945.

C

Canaris, Wilhelm (1887–1945) German
Admiral who was Chief of the *Abwehr*,
the military intelligence service of the
High Command of the Armed Forces
(OKW), Wilhelm Canaris was born in
Aplerbeck on 1 January 1887. The son
of a Westphalian industrialist, of Greek
background, Canaris entered the Imperial navy in 1905 and during World War
I commanded U-boats in the Mediterranean as well as carrying out espionage
missions in Spain and Italy. After 1920,
a naval staff officer in the Baltic fleet
who eventually rose to command the
battleship *Schlesien*, Canaris had,
shortly after the war, helped to organize
counter-revolutionary cadres and took
part in the Kapp *putsch*. He appreciated
Hitler's anti-Versailles programme and
his own pathological fear of Russia and
communism found expression in support for open reaction under Weimar.
Nonetheless, the cultivated Canaris disliked the mob violence and brutality of
Nazism and this equivocacy increased
after his appointment as Chief of the
Abwehr on 1 January 1935, a position
he held until February 1944. As head of
the *Abwehr*, Canaris proved himself an
incompetent dilettante whose judgement
was consistently unsound and whose
political and military information about
the enemy was minimal. A pessimistic recluse, whose nerve failed before
each Nazi adventure only to turn into
effusive admiration for Hitler once
it succeeded, Canaris was constantly
beset by Hamlet-like doubts about
his role. His opposition to some of
Hitler's policies and his contacts with
Resistance circles did not prevent him

from fulfilling his duties as head
of counter-intelligence or even proposing such measures during the war as
the identification of Jews by a yellow
star.

He knew all about the crimes of the
Gestapo and, though he had objected
initially to SS methods in Poland (especially the brutal measures against the
Polish intelligentsia, nobility and clergy),
he obliged his subordinates to co-operate with the Security Services. His relationship to his former pupil Reinhard
Heydrich (q.v.), whom he had trained
as a naval officer, was one of bitter
rivalry while at the same time they were
socially intimate neighbours. He protected himself and his men from the
prying SD by obtaining documents concerning Heydrich's alleged non-Aryan
antecedents, yet at his funeral Canaris
delivered a eulogy in which he described
the Gestapo Chief as a 'great man and a
true friend'.

Canaris's double role in the *Abwehr*
and his desire to bring Hitler down,
mixed with a patriotic dread of Germany's defeat, prevented him from
taking a clear-cut stand in the Resistance. Nevertheless, he did play an important part (along with his former *Abwehr*
deputy, Hans Oster, q.v.) in the Hitler
bomb plot, particularly after his dismissal in February 1944 as head of the
Abwehr and his appointment as Chief
of the Office for Commercial and Economic Warfare. Following his arrest and
imprisonment for several months, Canaris was executed for treason on 9
April 1945 in Flossenburg concentration
camp, along with Dietrich Bonhoeffer

(q.v.) and Hans Oster, with the sound of Allied gunfire already approaching in the background.

Carossa, Hans (1878–1956) German poet and novelist, regarded as one of the most popular and best-selling authors in the Weimar years, Hans Carossa was born in Tölz, Bavaria, on 15 December 1878, the son of a physician. After studying medicine at the Universities of Munich, Würzburg and Leipzig, he served in World War I as an army doctor and was wounded on the western front. He continued to practise as a family physician in Munich until 1929, using his professional experience as source material for his literary work. An autobiographer and confessional novelist *par excellence*, Carossa's early works included *Eine Kindheit* (1922), *Rumänisches Tagebuch* (1924), *Verwandlungen einer Jugend* (1928), and the best-selling *Der Arzt Gion* (1931) about the disruptive effects of the war – all of which were translated into English. After 1933 Carossa continued writing novels which reached a wide public, managing to remain apolitical and avoiding any dealings with Nazi officialdom as far as possible. Among his best-known books in this period were *Führung und Geleit, Lebensgedenkbuch* (1933), *Geheimnisse des reifen Lebens* (1936) and *Das Jahr der schönen Täuschungen* (1941). In 1938 he received the Goethe Prize and in 1942 he was appointed President of the European Writers' Union – a brainchild of Goebbels (q.v.) – which made him unwittingly appear as an apologist of the Nazi régime. Carossa's warm, simple, graceful style, his urbanity and Olympian serenity, his preoccupation with themes like love, friendship and the art of living, largely accounted for his popularity and the fact that he was readily tolerated by a régime eager to preserve the façade of normality and an abstract, humanitarian idealism. He died in Rittsteig bei Passau on 12 September 1956.

Choltitz, Dietrich von (1894–1966) German commanding officer in charge of Nazi-occupied Paris who ordered the capitulation of his forces on 25 August 1944, allegedly in disregard of Hitler's orders to burn the city. Dietrich von Choltitz was born in Schloss Wiese-Graflich on 9 November 1894, entering the army in 1914 and pursuing a military career which led to his appointment in 1942 as Major General, his promotion in February 1944 to Lieutenant-General and in August 1944 to Wehrmacht Commander of Greater Paris. Imprisoned by the French, he was soon released and in 1951 published his memoirs *Soldat unter Soldaten*, in which he bitterly denounced Hitler's 'contempt of the fundamental laws of morality and dignity both in his attitude to the enemy and his own people'. While describing the destruction of Poles and Jews as 'an offence against God's laws of life', von Choltitz was no less inclined to put Allied bombing measures against the Germans on the same plane.

Clauberg, Karl (1898–1957) SS doctor who conducted notorious experiments in sterilizing Jewesses at Auschwitz death camp during World War II, Karl Clauberg was born in Wupperhof on 28 September 1898. After serving in the infantry during World War I, Clauberg studied medicine in Kiel, Hamburg and Graz, receiving his doctorate in 1925. Chief physician at a university women's hospital in Kiel, Clauberg joined the NSDAP in 1933 and fully subscribed to Nazi ideology, eventually rising to the rank of *SS-Brigadeführer*. Appointed Professor of Gynaecology and Obstetrics at the University of Königsberg on 30 August 1937, Clauberg published a large number of scientific works in his field. By 1940 he had written over fifty research papers and several books, including *Die weiblichen Sexualhormone* (1933) and *Innere Sekretion der Ovarien* *und der Placenta* (1937) which was translated into Spanish and English.

Appointed Director in 1940 of a gynaecological clinic in Upper Silesia, Clauberg had himself approached Heinrich Himmler (q.v.), knowing of his interest in 'negative demography' (i.e. sterilization without operation), and asked to be allowed to sterilize women by the injection of irritating chemicals into the uterus. He was put to work by Himmler in Ravensbrück concentration camp in July 1942 and then offered the facilities of Experimental Block 10 of Auschwitz to continue his diabolical experiments. At his disposal was placed a large retinue of internee doctors, including the Polish camp doctor, Wladyslas Dering (subject of a famous libel case in England in 1964 concerned with medical experiments at Auschwitz). From 1942 to 1944 Clauberg conducted his quickfire mass sterilization injections without anaesthetic on Jewesses and sometimes gypsies, causing untold suffering and death to his victims. On 7 June 1943 he proudly reported to Himmler: 'The time is not far distant when I shall be able to say that one doctor, with, perhaps, ten assistants can probably effect several hundred, if not one thousand sterilizations on a single day.'

At the end of the war Clauberg was deported by the Russians and tried in 1948 for the part he had played in the 'mass extermination of Soviet citizens'. Sentenced to twenty-five years' imprisonment, he was amnestied after ten years as a prisoner of the Russians. He returned to the North German town of Kiel under the Adenauer-Bulganin agreement for the repatriation of German prisoners. On his return to Germany, Clauberg showed no contrition for his crimes, even boasting of his 'scientific achievements'. In October 1955 the Central Council of Jews in Germany filed an action with the West German authorities for the prosecution of Dr Clauberg. He was accused of 'repeatedly inflicting grave bodily injury' on the Jewish women inmates he used in his sterilization experiments in Auschwitz. On 22 November 1955 he was placed under arrest by the Kiel police. On 9 August 1957 he died in a Kiel hospital, shortly before his trial was due to begin.

Conti, Leonardo (1900–45) Reich Health Leader and head of the Department of Health in the Ministry of the Interior, Leonardo Conti was born in Lugano, Switzerland, on 24 August 1900. The son of a Swiss-Italian father and a mother who subsequently became 'Reich Leader of Midwives', Conti studied medicine in Germany and in November 1918 was a co-founder of the antisemitic *Kampfbund für Deutsche Kultur* and an active leader of the *völkisch* student movement. A member of the *Freikorps*, he participated in the Kapp *putsch* and belonged to the Old Guard of the Nazi Party, joining the SA in 1923 and becoming its first physician in Berlin. Conti built up and organized the medical services of the SA and also founded the Nazi Doctors' Association in the Berlin district. A general practitioner of medicine in Berlin from 1927 – he was the doctor of the Nazi 'martyr' Horst Wessel (q.v.) – Conti joined the SS in 1930. Two years later he became a delegate in the Prussian legislature and in April 1933 he was appointed a Prussian State Councillor by Goering (q.v.). Head of the Public Health Department in the Reich Leadership from 1934, he was made Chief of the Berlin Health Service and put in charge of medical arrangements for the Berlin Olympic Games in 1936. A specialist on 'race questions', Conti in an interview following the Nazi decree of 1938, which forbade Jewish physicians to practise their profession except among Jews, remarked: 'It is only the elimination of the Jewish element which provides for the German doctor the living space due to him.' On 20 April 1939 Conti was appointed *Reichsgesundheits führer* (Reich Health Leader) and State Secretary for Health in the Reich and Prussian Ministry of the Interior. Originally put in charge of the euthanasia programme, he was quickly succeeded by Philip Bouhler (q.v.); but as a protégé of Martin Bormann (q.v.), he maintained his position as Reich Health Leader until August 1944. Elected a member of the Reichstag in August 1941, Conti was promoted in August 1944 to the rank of *SS-Obergruppenführer*. He hanged himself in his Nuremberg cell on 6 October 1945.

Courant, Richard (1888–1972) Professor of Mathematics and for thirteen years Director of the world-famous Mathematical Institute at Göttingen, whose activities he greatly expanded through his organizational and fund-raising talents, Richard Courant was one of the most distinguished casualties of the Nazi education policy introduced in 1933. Born in Lublinitz, Silesia, on 8 January 1888, he studied at the Universities of Breslau, Zürich and Göttingen where he received his doctorate in 1910. Appointed Professor of Mathematics at Münster (1919) and then at Göttingen (1920–1) he collaborated with his great teacher David Hilbert to develop methods of applying theories of quantum mechanics to the problems of physics. An outstanding scholar and teacher, Courant made original contributions to functional analysis and differential equations and authored the classic *Methoden der mathematischen Physik* (1924). Though legally entitled to an exemption – he had been severely wounded in World War I during service as a frontline infantry officer – Courant was stripped of his *venia legendi* in April 1933 under the notorious *Arierparagraph*, which prescribed the retirement of all civil servants of 'non-Aryan' descent. The anti-semitic purge which led to the dismissals of Courant, the re-

nowned physicist Max Born (q.v.) and Emmy Noether (q.v.) effectively destroyed the foremost mathematical centre in Germany. Asked at a banquet by the Nazi Minister of Education about the state of mathematics since it had 'been freed of Jewish influence', David Hilbert (for forty years the doyen of German mathematics) replied: 'But, Herr Minister, there is no mathematics left at Göttingen.' Courant himself departed to Cambridge as a visiting lecturer (1933–4) and then emigrated to the USA where he was Professor and head of the Mathematics Department at New York University until 1958. During World War II he organized a team of scientific scholars working on military projects and subsequently received the US Navy's Distinguished Public Service Award. In 1958 the Courant Institute of Mathematical Sciences which he had founded at NYU was named after him. He died on 27 January 1972.

Cramm, Baron Gottfried von (1909–76) The best German tennis player of his era and considered before World War II as the finest player never to have won the Wimbledon men's singles' title, Gottfried von Cramm was born in Hanover on 7 July 1909. A lithe, superlatively fit and hard-working strokemaker with a menacing serve whose classic style was developed on German courts, the tall, blond sportsman was one of his country's best ambassadors abroad, his dress, demeanour and good looks earning him the epithet 'Beau Brummell of Tennis'. One of the aristocrats of the sport, always perfectly flannelled – von Cramm never wore shorts – and with impeccable court manners, he first emerged in 1932 as a player of world calibre when representing Germany in the Davis Cup. Together with his country's top player, Daniel Prenn (q.v.), von Cramm helped Germany to a surprise fourth round victory over Britain and a week later defeated the top

Italian players in a 5–0 German victory in the European zone final. In the Davis Cup final of 1932 Germany lost 2–3 to America but von Cramm defeated the great server Frank Shields, displaying an impressive variety of shots and remarkable mobile defence. After Prenn was forbidden by the Nazis to play Davis Cup tennis for Germany, von Cramm emerged as the nation's leading representative and in 1934 was the first German to win the French men's singles' championships in Paris, with a glorious display of tennis. Seeded third at Wimbledon he lost in the fourth round and, in spite of winning both his singles against France in the Davis Cup, was on the losing side.

In 1935 von Cramm's dynamic game was only bettered by that of Britain's Fred Perry, who defeated him in four sets in the French final and again in the Wimbledon final where von Cramm had been seeded second. Almost single-handedly the Baron took Germany to the inter-zone final of the Davis Cup in the same year. In 1936 von Cramm gained his revenge on Perry in the French final which he won in five sets, but at Wimbledon he pulled a thigh muscle in the second game of the men's singles' final and lost to Perry in straight sets. In 1937 the splendid but unlucky German star reached his third successive Wimbledon final, but lost to his close friend, the brilliant Californian, Donald Budge. In the inter-zone final of the Davis Cup, von Cramm rose to superlative heights and was unlucky to be defeated by Budge in the fifth set of the deciding rubber by 8–6. He also lost the American final to Budge in five sets.

These narrow defeats sealed von Cramm's fate (he had never pretended to be a Nazi sympathizer), for had he brought the Davis Cup to Germany not even Hitler would have dared to imprison so popular a sports hero. As it was, von Cramm was imprisoned by the Gestapo on his return from Australia in 1938, after the court had been instructed to convict him. Occasional news of the Baron's fate trickled through and it was rumoured that he had tried to commit suicide and that his aged mother had personally appealed to Hitler. Released in 1939 his entry was refused at Wimbledon. During World War II von Cramm survived three Nazi interrogations. After 1945 he returned to first-class tennis and won the German singles' title in 1949 at the age of forty. In 1951 he reappeared at Wimbledon and, in spite of the absence of twelve years from grass, played brilliantly though losing to Jaroslav Drobny in the first round.

Von Cramm was the top German tennis player for twenty years, winning the German International Championships at Hamburg on six occasions and representing his country thirty-seven times in the Davis Cup. Following his retirement from the game, von Cramm became a successful businessman and continued to be active in the administration of tennis in Germany, being appointed President of the Rot-Weiss LTC and an honorary member of the committee of the German Lawn Tennis Association. Von Cramm died in an automobile accident on 9 November 1976 on the road between Alexandria and Cairo.

D

Dagover, Lil (1897–1980) A prominent German film actress born on 30 September 1897 at Madiven, Java, the daughter of a forest ranger in the service of the Dutch authorities. Sent at the age of ten to Baden-Baden to study, she later entered the cinema thanks to her marriage in 1917 to the actor Fritz Dagover who was twenty-five years her senior. Discovered by the director Robert Wiene (a colleague of her husband's), she appeared in his classic expressionist film *The Cabinet of Dr Caligari* and in a number of other prestigious German productions during the early 1920s, including Carl Froelich's *Kabale und Liebe* (1920), Fritz Lang's *Der Müde Tod* (1921) and Murnau's *Tartuffe* (1925). Apart from three trips – one to Sweden in 1927, another to France in 1928–9 and one to Hollywood in 1931 – most of Lil Dagover's career and fate was linked to that of the German cinema, where her role was usually that of the frail heroine with the 'haunted' look. She continued to star in a great number of films during the Nazi era, to which she brought a talent and presence they did not always deserve. Among her best performances were her roles in *Der Kongress Tanzt* (1931), in Gerhard Lamprecht's *Der Höhere Befehl* (1935) and in Veit Harlan's (q.v.) *Die Kreutzersonate* (1936). She also acted in the Deutsches Theatre Berlin, the Salzburg Festival, at forces shows and at war theatres. At one time she was reported to have been a close friend of Hitler. In 1944 she received the War Merits Cross. Lil Dagover continued her career in post-war Germany, appearing in *Königliche Hoheit, Die Barrings* (1955), *Buddenbrooks* (1959) and playing supporting parts until the late 1970s in such films as *Der Fussgänger* (1974), *Der Richter und sein Henker* (1975) and *Die Standarte* (1977). She died in January 1980 in München-Geiselgasteig at the age of eighty-two.

D'Alquen, Gunter (born 1910) Chief Editor of the SS weekly, *Das Schwarze Korps (The Black Corps)*, Gunter d'Alquen was born in Essen on 24 October 1910, the son of a Protestant merchant and reserve officer. After attending secondary school in Essen and joining the Hitler Youth in 1925, d'Alquen entered the NSDAP at the age of seventeen and was an SA man and Youth Leader in the Party between 1927 and 1931. He played an active part in the National Socialist Students' Association and later joined the SS on 10 April 1931, becoming an SS Captain within three years. D'Alquen never completed his university studies, concentrating instead on a journalistic career. In 1932 he joined the staff of the *Völkische Beobachter* as a political correspondent, catching the eye of Heinrich Himmler (q.v.) who in March 1935 appointed him editor of the official SS paper, *Das Schwarze Korps*. As the mouthpiece of revolutionary Nazism and chief spokesman of the SS in the German press, d'Alquen's paper frequently attacked intellectuals, students, distinguished scientists, recalcitrant business firms, black marketeers, churchmen and other groups or trends in German society which had aroused Himmler's wrath.

Apart from its notorious anti-semitism and censorious role in national affairs, the paper saw itself as a bastion of German morale during World War II, concentrating its attention on German victories at the front. D'Alquen himself became a prominent SS war reporter after September 1939 and towards the end of the war was appointed by Himmler as head of the Wehrmacht propaganda department. Among his publications were an official history of the SS, *Die SS. Geschichte, Aufgabe und Organization der Schutzstaffeln der NSDAP* (1939). He also edited *Das ist der Sieg* (1940) and *Waffen-SS im Westen* (1941). In July 1955 d'Alquen was fined 60,000 marks (£5,000) by a Berlin de-Nazification court, deprived of all civic rights for three years and debarred from drawing an allowance or pension from public funds. He was found guilty of having played an important role in the Third Reich, of war propaganda, incitement against the churches, the Jews and foreign countries, and incitement to murder. He had glorified the SS State and Hitler's infallibility, brought democracy into contempt and encouraged anti-semitism. After a further investigation into his earnings from Nazi propaganda, d'Alquen was fined another 28,000 marks by the Berlin de-Nazification court on 7 January 1958.

Daluege, Kurt (1897–1946) Commander-in-Chief of the Police of the German Reich and subsequently Deputy Protector of Bohemia and Moravia (in succession to Heydrich, q.v.), Kurt Daluege was born in Kreuzburg, Upper Silesia, on 15 September 1897. During World War I he served as a volunteer in an assault division. After receiving an engineer's training at Berlin Technical High School, Daluege briefly worked as a foreman in an engineering firm before becoming the leader of a unit in the notorious Rossbach *Freikorps*.

A swashbuckler and rowdy in his early years, Daluege joined the NSDAP in 1922 and on 22 March 1926 founded and led the first SA group in Berlin and North Germany. Leader of the Berlin SA until 1928, he then transferred to the SS, organizing special shock-battalions for surprise attacks on opponents, and for the next five years was Commander of SS units in East Germany. In the spring of 1933, the young SS officer was closely linked to Goering (q.v.) and given the special task of purging the police apparatus and political opponents of the régime. In May 1933 he was put in charge of the police division in the Prussian Ministry of the Interior and made Commander of all Prussian Police Forces. As the chief mediator between the SS and the Prussian State hierarchy, Daluege transformed the Prussian police machine into an instrument of the Nazis and a significant political factor in consolidating the new régime.

A coldly calculating figure, reputed to be an excellent organizer, Daluege used the links he had forged with the *Schutzpolizei* and political police to attract discharged, dissatisfied, restless police officers to the SS and to infiltrate the regular police with SS men. In 1933 Daluege was appointed Ministerial Director and a Prussian State Councillor and became a member of the Reichstag, representing the electoral district of East Berlin. A year later he was made *SS-Obergruppenführer* and in 1936 Commander of the German *Ordnungspolizei* (which comprised the urban and administrative police, the coastal police, fire service, passive defence, etc.) and Chief of its High Command. Already Chief of Security Police in the central office of the SD, Daluege also established the *Kameradschaftsbund Deutscher Polizeibeamten* – a National Socialist umbrella organization of police officials. Responsible for the suppression of internal revolt, for protecting the lives of Hitler and other Nazi leaders, Daluege was the most powerful policeman in the SS, second in rank only to his rival, Heinrich Himmler (q.v.), who controlled the political police. It was under Daluege's supervision that the *Ordnungspolizei* was comprehensively Nazified and militarized. After Heydrich's death, Daluege became Deputy Protector of Bohemia and Moravia in 1942, later being held responsible for the destruction of Lidice and other terrorist measures taken against the Czech population. He was executed by the Czechs on 24 October 1946.

Dannecker, Theodor (1913–45) SS Captain in charge of the deportation of Jews from France (1942), Bulgaria (1943) and Italy (1944) to Auschwitz, Dannecker was a young Bavarian lawyer from Munich who became one of Adolf Eichmann's (q.v.) indispensable agents in the implementation of the 'Final Solution'. Sent to Paris in September 1940 by Eichmann's Bureau IV B4, the branch of the RSHA in Berlin devoted to 'Jewish' matters, Dannecker headed its French bureau and *Judenreferat* (Jewish section), receiving his orders directly from Eichmann. As the 'Jewish expert' of the Gestapo and Eichmann's deputy with the Paris Sipo-SD, *SS-Hauptsturmführer* Dannecker claimed the credit for being the first to propose continuous Jewish deportations from France to the East and was constantly prodding the Vichy authorities to take more active anti-semitic measures. Xavier Vallat, the first French Commissioner for Jewish Questions, who clashed with him over the long-range German policy on the Jews in France, described Dannecker as 'a fanatical Nazi who went into a trance every time the word Jew was mentioned'. Dannecker was recalled to Berlin in October 1942 for abusing his independence and in January 1943 was transferred to Eichmann's office in Sofia, Bulgaria, where he continued to supervise deportations of Jews. Posted

to Verona in October 1943 and to Hungary in the summer of 1944, Dannecker became Jewish Commissary for Italy in October 1944, remaining with the Eichmann commando to the end of the war. Dannecker committed suicide in an American prison camp in Bad Tölz on 10 December 1945.

Darré, Richard-Walther (1895–1953) Reich Farmers' Leader and Reich Food Minister in Hitler's Germany, Walther Darré was born on 14 July 1895 in Belgrano, Buenos Aires, Argentina. After attending school in Heidelberg and Bad Godesberg, Darré continued his education at King's College, Wimbledon, and fought as an artillery officer on the western front in World War I. After demobilization, Darré briefly joined the Berlin *Freikorps*, then resumed his agricultural studies, qualifying in 1922 as an agronomist (*Diplomlandwirt*). An early friend of Heinrich Himmler (q.v.), whom he first met in the right-wing, back-to-the-land movement, the *Artamanen*, Darré began to organize farmers in the NSDAP in the late 1920s. Though not one of the 'Old Fighters', Darre rose rapidly in the Party hierarchy after 1930, impressing Hitler with the 'blood and soil' ideology he expressed in early works such as *Das Bauerntum als Lebensquell der Nordischen Rasse* (1928), *Um Blut und Boden* (1929) and *Neuadel aus Blut und Boden* (1930). In these and other works, Darré claimed that the Nordic race had been the true creators of European culture (in contrast to the 'nomadic' Jews), that the German peasant was the driving-force of history, the substance of Germanism and the ultimate custodian of national uniqueness.

Darré proposed the creation of a 'Germanic aristocracy of the soil', a new ruling class – rooted in the agrarian community which would dominate the *Ständestaat* (corporatist State) that he hoped to recreate. A lower-middle-class pigbreeder, who consistently viewed economic life from the racial-biological standpoint and believed in the peasantry as the eternal 'life-source' of the Germanic race, he was the driving-force behind the activization of Nazi agrarian policy between 1930 and 1933, exploiting the dissatisfaction and unrest in rural areas to win the farmers over to National Socialism. With the shift in Nazi Party strategy towards cultivating the rural peasant population and urban *Mittelstand*, Darré's romantic, anti-industrial 'blood and soil' ideology came into vogue, influencing both Himmler and Hitler. On 4 April 1933 Darré was made head of the organization of German farmers and for the next twelve years he was *Reichsbauernführer* (National Farmers' Leader). He was appointed Reich Minister for Food and Agriculture on 29 June 1933. A member of the Reichstag from November 1933, *Reichsleiter* and *SS-Gruppenführer*, member of the Academy of German Law and Honorary President of the German Agricultural Society, Darré received the Golden Party Badge in 1936 and many other honours. He was also Chief of the SS Central Office for Race and Resettlement and author of numerous books on racial topics, on the pig in ancient folklore, the peasantry, etc., including *Das Schwein als Kriterium für Nordische Völker und Semiten* (1933), *Der Schweinemord* (1937), *Im Kampf um die Seele des deutschen Bauern* (1943) – works which demonstrated his primitive racism, his anti-semitism and the *völkisch* cult of the peasant.

As Minister of Agriculture, Darré proclaimed the entail farm legislation (*Erbhofgesetz*), which aimed to preserve the peasantry as a privileged class and bulwark against the world of capitalism. Darré was convinced that only a large number of peasant family holdings, economically secured from the 'chaos of the market', could ensure the racial health of the German nation. His de-

fence of the rural *Mittelstand* brought Darré into conflict with Hjalmar Schacht's (q.v.) free market economics and the financial policy of the Reichsbank. Moreover Darré's ideological policies failed to increase the birth rate, to stop the transformation of the peasant into a capitalist farmer, or to prevent the flight from the land. His incompetence and impracticality gradually led to a loss of influence and, by 1939, the Food Estate Leader ceased to have Hitler's confidence. During World War II pragmatic and military considerations assumed greater importance and it was Himmler who was given the power of decision over agricultural settlements in occupied territories. Darré's opposition to the concept of 'defence farms', his increasingly marginal status as a 'theoretician' and above all his failure to organize the German food supply efficiently led to his dismissal in May 1942. Captured in 1945, he was eventually sentenced to five years in prison by an American military tribunal at Nuremberg for the confiscation of property from Polish and Jewish farmers and for having ordered German Jews to be deprived of basic foodstuffs, thereby deliberately provoking the starvation of civilians. Darré was released in 1950 and lived in Bad Harzburg for the last years of his life. He died in a private clinic in Munich on 8 September 1953.

Delp, Alfred (1907–45) Jesuit priest and member of the Kreisau Circle which sought to overthrow the Hitler régime and re-Christianize Germany as a prelude to a new order, Alfred Delp was born in Mannheim on 15 September 1907. Entering the Jesuit order at the age of eighteen, Delp was ordained as a priest in 1937. Between 1937 and 1941 he collaborated on the journal *Stimmen der Zeit*. A year later he joined the German Resistance and was arrested at the end of July 1944, following the failure of the assassination attempt against

Hitler. Tried by the People's Court and subjected to the withering scorn of its President, Roland Freisler (q.v.), Delp was sentenced to death and hanged in Berlin on 2 February 1945.

Dibelius, Friedrich Karl Otto (1880–1967) Protestant bishop and a leading figure in the church Resistance to the Nazis, Otto Dibelius was born in Berlin on 15 May 1880. From 1907 to 1925 he was a pastor (after 1915 in Berlin) and the following year he was appointed General Superintendent of the Evangelical (Lutheran) Church in Prussia. When the Nazis came to power, Dibelius was dismissed from his post, but for the next twelve years he was a prominent figure in the Confessional Church, founded by his close associate, Pastor Niemöller (q.v.). Dibelius, like Niemöller, opposed the concept of the totalitarian State and its efforts to supplant Christian doctrine by neo-paganism or the Nazi 'co-ordinated' German Christian movement. In an open letter to the Nazi Minister of Ecclesiastical Affairs, Hans Kerrl (q.v.), in 1937, Dibelius pointed out that when 'the State seeks to become the Church and assume power over men's souls', then the Evangelical Church would be 'bound by Luther's words to resist in God's name'. In his conclusion, Dibelius did, however, display the parochial tendency of the church to ignore the monstrous crimes of the régime against non-Christians, as long as its own institutional edifice was left untouched. 'The church struggle', he observed, 'might be terminated in three months if only the State would cease to interfere with the freedom and independence of the church.'

Dibelius was acquitted of treason by a special court and survived the war in spite of his known opposition to Nazism. Though he knew from Kurt Gerstein (q.v.) the horrific details of the extermination of Jews at Belzec and other death camps in Poland, he did not publicly protest. After the war he became Protestant Bishop of Berlin-Brandenburg (in the eastern zone), and from 1949 until 1961 he was Chairman of the Council of the Evangelical Church in Germany. He was the first German to become, in 1954, a President of the World Council of Churches. In 1960 he became *persona non grata* in the German Democratic Republic for disputing the right of the communist government to be considered an 'Authority' (in the theological sense) for Christians. 'In a totalitarian order', Dibelius declared, 'there is no justice whatsoever as Christians understand it ... no justice at all.' He died in Berlin on 31 January 1967.

Diels, Rudolf (1900–57) The founder and first head of the Gestapo, Rudolf Diels was born in Berghaus, in the Taunus, on 16 December 1900, the son of a Protestant farmer. He volunteered and was accepted for military service at the end of World War I. A student of law at the University of Marburg after 1919, Diels in his youth acquired a reputation as a boisterous drinker and great womanizer. An ambitious and perspicacious official, Diels entered the Prussian Ministry of the Interior in 1930 and two years later was appointed a senior government adviser in the police section, charged with taking measures against both communists and Nazis, under the direction of the Social Democratic Minister, Karl Severing. The conservative Diels proved to be a turncoat 'democrat', a bureaucratic opportunist who defected in 1933 to the Nazis and Hermann Goering (q.v.), placing his profound knowledge of political police techniques at the latter's disposal and emerging as his assistant minister. Diels persuaded Goering to establish a secret police force in June 1933, becoming Chief of Department IA in the Prussian State Police. This was the origin of the Gestapo and, as its first head, Diels carried out a purge of Republican police officials, thereby helping to dig the grave of constitutional government in Germany.

He provided Goering with secret files that consolidated his patron's position in the Party and were capable of ruining his political adversaries. Though he assured Himmler (q.v.) in 1933 that he intended to 'put into practice the principles evolved by the SS in my professional field as far as the Prussian political police is concerned', Diels soon found himself caught in a power struggle between Goering and the SS leader. At the end of September 1933 Goering had to sacrifice his confidant and favourite assistant to the intrigues of his rivals, though later appointing him Deputy Police President of Berlin. Diels judged it safer to flee to Karlsbad, Bohemia, for five weeks until he was recalled by Goering to resume his duties as head of the Gestapo. Diels was finally dismissed on 1 April 1934 (being replaced by Himmler), but was protected from Heydrich's (q.v.) intrigues by his patron. In May 1934 Diels was appointed *Regierungspräsident* (a local government post) of Cologne and for the next six years he was also in private employment as inland shipping administrator of the Hermann Goering Works.

In 1940 he became *Regierungspräsident* of Hanover, but was dismissed after refusing to carry out a district leader's orders to arrest Jews in the city. He was saved from arrest by Goering (whose cousin he had married) on a number of occasions and rescued by him from a Gestapo prison after the July 1944 plot against Hitler. After the fall of the Third Reich, Diels worked as an administrator in Lower Saxony and as an Under-Secretary in the Bonn Ministry of the Interior until 1953. His self-justificatory memoirs, *Lucifer ante portas: Von Severing bis Heydrich*, appeared in 1950, glossing over his own role in paving the way for the totalitarian police system perfected by Himmler and Hey-

drich. In his book *Der Fall Otto John* (1954) Diels attacked the Nuremberg trials (where he had appeared as a prosecution witness) for trying to 'exterminate' the Prussian spirit in Germany as well as abusing the anti-Nazi Resistance and the policies of the Allied governments. He died on 18 November 1957 while on a hunting expedition, accidentally shooting himself as he took a gun out of his car.

Dietrich, Otto (1897–1952) Reich Press Chief of the NSDAP from 1933 to 1945 and Hitler's chief publicity agent, Otto Dietrich was born in Essen on 31 August 1897. A war volunteer on the western front during World War I, he was awarded the Iron Cross (First Class). After the war he studied at the Universities of Munich, Frankfurt am Main and Freiburg, receiving his doctorate in political science in 1921. A research assistant in the Essen Chamber of Commerce, later deputy editor of the Essen *Nationalzeitung*, Dietrich had also been business manager, after 1928, of the *Augsburger Zeitung*, a German-national evening paper. Through his marriage – he was the son-in-law of Dr Reismann, the influential owner of the *Rheinisch-Westfälische Zeitung* – he established links with the representatives of Rhineland heavy industry such as Emil Kirdorf (q.v.) and himself became the legal adviser of a big steel trust. On 1 August 1931 Dietrich, who was a convinced Nazi, was appointed Press Chief of the NSDAP and a year later he joined the SS, rising to the rank of *SS-Obergruppenführer* in 1941.

In his role as publicist and press chief, Dietrich organized the great Nazi propaganda campaigns during the elections of 1932, becoming Hitler's constant companion as he endlessly criss-crossed Germany by car and plane. Hitler's envoy in the heavy industrial region of the Ruhr where he helped undermine Gregor Strasser's (q.v.) radical Nazi power-base, Dietrich also used his family connections to mediate between the NSDAP and captains of industry like Fritz Thyssen (q.v.). Dietrich was an active publicist on behalf of the Nazi Party after the seizure of power and his documentary work *Mit Hitler an die Macht* (1933), which represented the Führer's 'peaceful struggle for the soul of the German people', sold over 250,000 copies. Other publications included *Die Philosophischen Grundlagen des Nationalsozialismus* (1935), *Das Wirtschaftsdenken im Dritten Reich* (1936), *Weltpresse ohne Maske* (1937) and *Auf den Strassen des Sieges; mit dem Führer in Polen* (1939). From 1937 to 1945 Dietrich was State Secretary in Goebbels's (q.v.) Ministry of Propaganda as well as Press Chief of the Reich Government, playing a decisive role in reorganizing the press and in disciplinary matters. The driving force behind the Editors' Law, which castrated the independence of newspaper editors as well as publishers, Dietrich cooked the German news to Hitler's prescriptions, especially after the outbreak of World War II. To ensure the complete regimentation of editors and journalists, Dietrich issued daily directives on how to present the news from the front, which were prepared with Hitler's approval. On 22 February 1942 Hitler expressed his admiration for Dietrich's resourcefulness in one of his rambling table talks: 'Dr Dietrich may be physically small, but he is exceptionally gifted at his job.... I am proud of the fact that with his handful of men I can at once throw the rudder of the press through 180 degrees – as happened on 22 June 1941 [the day Germany invaded Russia]. There is no other country which can copy us in that.'

Dietrich's unquestioning subservience to Hitler did, however, lead him to make mistakes and wildly mistaken prophecies, such as his rash statement on 9 October 1941 before German and for-

eign journalists. 'The campaign in the East has been decided,' he declared, '... the further development will take place as we wish it. With these last tremendous blows we have inflicted on the Soviet Union she is militarily finished. The English dream of a war on two fronts has definitely come to an end' *(ist endgültig ausgeträumt)*. In fact Moscow was not taken and the furious Goebbels had to try and repair the damage. Dietrich nonetheless retained his position and the Führer's confidence until the end of the Third Reich. Imprisoned in 1945, he was eventually tried and sentenced in April 1949 to seven years' imprisonment for crimes against humanity. He was released from Landsberg prison on 16 August 1950 for good behaviour. He died in Düsseldorf in 1952 at the age of fifty-five. His political settling of accounts with Hitler, the biography of an eye-witness, entitled *Zwölf Jahre mit Hitler (*Twelve Years with Hitler*)*, which had been composed in a British internment camp immediately after the war, was posthumously published in 1955.

Dietrich, Sepp (1892–1966) One of Hitler's earliest supporters, head of the *Leibstandarte-SS* Adolf Hitler Regiment and later Commander of the Sixth SS Panzer Army during World War II, Sepp Dietrich was born in Hawangen on 28 May 1892, the son of a poor Bavarian peasant family. Employed in hotels and public houses, then a butcher's apprentice in Munich, Dietrich joined the Imperial army in 1911 and served as a paymaster sergeant during World War I. After the war he drifted from one job to the next, joined the Oberland *Freikorps* and was an early member of the NSDAP. A participant in the Munich Beer-Hall *putsch*, his strong-arm prowess at Party political meetings brought him to Hitler's attention and in 1928 he was made Commander of the Nazi leader's bodyguard. Elected a member of the Reichstag for Lower Bavaria in 1930, he was promoted to SS Lieutenant-General a year later. The tough Bavarian often acted as Hitler's chauffeur on his automobile tours of Germany and, after the Nazis seized power, he was promoted rapidly. Head of the *Leibstandarte-SS* Adolf Hitler Regiment, he was made a General of the Waffen-SS, appointed to the Prussian State Council, and on 4 July 1934 he was given the rank of SS General for his prominent role in the Röhm purge.

As Chief of the *Stabswache* (staff guard), it was Dietrich who led the assassination squad which murdered Ernst Röhm (q.v.) and other SA leaders, some of whom were formerly personal comrades. During World War II, Sepp Dietrich was one of the few 'old Nazis' to make a name for himself as a soldier, holding commands in Poland, France, Greece, Russia, Hungary and Austria. Though lacking military experience and no great strategist, Dietrich displayed considerable powers of leadership, personal magnetism and a marked streak of ruthlessness. Awarded many decorations, including the Oak Leaves with Swords on 31 December 1941 and the Brillianten to Oak Leaves in August 1944, Dietrich's courage and hardness were never in doubt. Hitler paid him this tribute in February 1942: 'The role of Sepp Dietrich is unique. I have always given him the opportunity to intervene at sore spots. He is a man who is simultaneously cunning, energetic and brutal. Under his swashbuckling appearance, Dietrich is a serious, conscientious, and scrupulous character.... He is a Bavarian Wrangel, someone irreplaceable. For the German people Sepp Dietrich is a national institution. For me personally there is also the fact that he is one of my oldest companions in the struggle.'

The legend of his military valour was consciously built up by Nazi propaganda during the war, ignoring the atrocities for which he was responsible as a divisional commander in the Kharkov-Kherson district between 1941 and 1943. As Commander of the First SS Panzer Corps in Normandy he was given the task of containing the Anglo-American beachhead, but proved unable to throw back the Allied forces. In December 1944 he was given command of the Sixth Panzer Army during the Ardennes counter-offensive, Hitler's last great gamble to turn the tide of the war by cutting the Allies off from their supply bases. Dietrich did his best but was aware that the task assigned to him was impossible, and by this time he was thoroughly disillusioned with Hitler's conduct of the war. At Malmédy (Belgium), during the Battle of the Bulge on 17 December 1944, he was responsible for the shooting down in cold blood by German tanks of nearly a hundred American prisoners of war, a crime for which he was later sentenced by an American military tribunal.

At the end of the war Dietrich's SS troops fought in Hungary and he was also entrusted by Hitler with the last-ditch defence of Vienna before the advancing Russian forces. His Sixth SS Army had to be withdrawn and he was finally captured by the American Seventh Army in May 1945. A year later he was tried and given a life sentence (commuted to twenty-five years) for his role in the massacre of the captured American soldiers at Malmédy. Dietrich was secretly released on 22 October 1955 from the American war crimes prison at Landsberg on the recommendation of a joint Allied-German clemency board (a decision that aroused some angry reactions at the time); he was rearrested and charged in August 1956 with aiding and abetting in the murder of Röhm and six other leading Brownshirts over twenty years earlier. Found guilty by a Munich court of being an accessory to premeditated murder, he was sentenced to nineteen months' imprisonment. He was released for reasons of health in

February 1959. He died of a heart attack in Ludwigsburg on 21 April 1966.

Dimitrov, Georgi (1882–1949) Bulgarian communist leader who was the star defendant at the Reichstag fire trial of 1933 and later became Prime Minister of Bulgaria, Georgi Dimitrov was born on 18 June 1882 in Radomir. At the age of twelve he was apprenticed to a printer in Sofia and while still in his teens helped found a printers' union. Dimitrov was a member of the pre-war Bulgarian Social Democratic Party, a leader of its left wing and a deputy for ten years in the National Assembly. After World War I – during which he had been imprisoned without trial for opposing Bulgarian participation – Dimitrov became a prominent leader of the Bulgarian Communist Party and his activities obliged him to live the life of an exile, in Moscow, Berlin and Vienna. At the time of his arrest following the mysterious fire of 27 February 1933 in the Berlin Parliament, Dimitrov, at that time the head of a clandestine communist network in western Europe, was in the company of two other Bulgarians. They were arrested as part of a Nazi attempt to prove that the burning of the Reichstag was communist-inspired and to obtain a verdict which would justify massive repression and terror against their political adversaries in Germany. The trial before the Supreme Court in Leipzig was an international sensation – 120 journalists from all over the world attended the sessions – in which Dimitrov emerged as the central figure, turning the tables on his accusers and driving them on to the defensive. He succeeded in reducing the Prussian Minister President and Minister of the Interior, Hermann Goering (q.v.), to quivering, impotent rage. Goering lost control of himself, shouting: 'I didn't come here to be accused by you. As far as I am concerned you are a rogue who should have been hanged long ago,' and had to be cau-

tioned by the judges. The Nazis were bitterly disappointed by the results of the trial, which proved a propaganda débâcle abroad. Dimitrov and the other communist defendants were acquitted – the young Dutchman Marinus van der Lubbe (q.v.) was, however, found guilty of starting the fire and subsequently executed – and it was widely believed abroad that the real culprits were Goering and the Nazi Party.

Although the Reichstag fire failed in its propaganda objectives abroad, it produced the desired results at home, strengthening the hands of the Nazis in the March 1933 elections, enabling Hitler to disqualify the eighty-one legally elected communist deputies and to obtain extraordinary powers through the so-called 'Enabling Law'. Dimitrov's defiant conduct throughout the trial won him the admiration of the whole world and made him a hero among communists. Even in Germany a saying went the rounds, which paid tribute to his courage: 'There is one man left in Germany and he is a Bulgarian.' Acquitted on 23 November 1933, Dimitrov was finally released at the end of February 1934 (in an exchange of prisoners), thanks to the pressure of international public opinion, thus denying Goering the revenge he had sworn to inflict for his public humiliation. Appointed General Secretary of the Comintern (Communist International) in 1935, Dimitrov presided over a major shift in communist tactics against fascism and backed the policy of forming Popular Fronts to strengthen the western bourgeois democracies. It was Dimitrov who in 1935 provided the classic communist definition of fascism as 'the openly terroristic dictatorship of the most reactionary, most chauvinistic and most imperialistic elements of Finance-Capital'. After the occupation of Bulgaria by Soviet forces at the end of World War II, Dimitrov emerged as the leader of the Bulgarian communists and was appointed Prime

Minister on 6 November 1946. He died in Moscow on 2 July 1949.

Dirksen, Herbert von (1882–1955) German career diplomat who served as Ambassador to Moscow, Tokyo and London between 1928 and 1939, Herbert von Dirksen was born on 2 April 1882 in Berlin. On his father's side he was descended from generations of Prussian civil servants, while his mother came from a family of Cologne bankers. A typical product of the Wilhelminian era, von Dirksen boasted in his memoirs (printed for private circulation in 1935) that he was 'proud of my purely Germanic blood' just as his father had been proud of his ennoblement in 1887 'before a whole batch of more or less Jew-tainted families was ennobled by the liberalistic Emperor Frederick III'. The young von Dirksen, a pupil of the König Wilhelm Gymnasium in Berlin, had originally studied law, passing his examination as a junior barrister in 1905. After a round-the-world tour he served as an assistant judge in 1910. During World War I he was on active service at the front, receiving the Iron Cross (Second Class), and immediately afterwards entered the diplomatic service. Attached to various missions in Eastern Europe – he was at Kiev (1918–19), chargé d'affaires in Warsaw (1920–1) and Consul-General at Danzig (1923–5) – von Dirksen was made head of the East European division of the Foreign Office from 1925 to 1928. In the same year he succeeded Count von Brockdorff-Rantzau as Ambassador to Moscow and continued the policy of Russo-German co-operation, designed to obliterate the humiliation of the Versailles Treaty.

During von Dirksen's five years in Moscow, there was open economic and secret military co-operation. German technicians and experts helped in modernizing Soviet industry, but the hoped-for economic and political understanding fell through. With the rise of the Nazis to power, von Dirksen was transferred to Tokyo in 1933, where he remained until 6 February 1938, assuring Hitler that Japan was 'a reliable partner for the anti-Comintern', although the Foreign Office had favoured an alliance with China. On his way to Japan he wrote his *Zwischenbilanz (Intermediate Balance-sheet)*, private memoirs which reveal him as an egocentric, ambitious and bitter man, full of resentment at the insufficient appreciation of his services shown by Hitler and von Ribbentrop (q.v.), whom he despised. These memoirs were also outspokenly anti-semitic, a trait which disappeared in the published version, where he claimed to have felt nothing but shame at the anti-Jewish pogrom of November 1938.

On 7 April 1938 von Dirksen succeeded von Ribbentrop as Ambassador to London, a post he held until the outbreak of World War II, when he retired from active service in the Foreign Office. During the war he lived mainly at his country estate in Gröditzberg, Silesia. In June 1947 he was cleared by a de-Nazification court which regarded his membership of the Nazi Party as a mere formality and declined to see him as a supporter of the régime. In 1954, shortly before his death, von Dirksen publicly criticized Konrad Adenauer's (q.v.) foreign policy as too pro-western, advocating more contacts and dealings with the East German régime to bring about an eventual reunification. Von Dirksen, who was a foreign policy adviser to Silesian Germans expelled from their former homeland, also demanded a more activist diplomacy to recover Silesia from the Poles. His published memoirs were translated into English under the title, *Moscow, Tokyo, London* (1951).

Dirlewanger, Oskar (1895–1945) A high SS officer who founded a special SS battalion made up of criminals and desperadoes in 1940, Dirlewanger was born in Würzberg on 26 September 1895. During World War I, he reached the rank of lieutenant and won the Iron Cross. Between 1919 and 1921 he was involved in the suppression of communist risings in the Ruhr and Saxony, serving also in the *Freikorps* in Upper Silesia. In 1922 he obtained a degree in political science and a year later joined the Nazi Party. He ran a knit-wear factory in Erfurt for a few years before becoming an SA leader in Esslingen in 1932. After serving a two-year sentence in 1934 for seducing a dependent, Dirlewanger joined the Condor Legion in 1937, fighting for Franco in the Spanish Civil War. By 1939 he was *Obersturmführer* in the Waffen-SS and a year later, in September 1940, he initiated the creation of a special detachment of convicted criminals, murderers and incendiaries, within the SS Death's-Head Units. This SS-Sonderbataillon 'Dirlewanger' provoked revulsion, even in some SS circles, by its cruelty and the murderous havoc it created in combating partisans in Poland and White Russia. An investigation into its activities was launched in August 1942 and its findings submitted to an SS court, but on Himmler's orders no action was taken against Dirlewanger. In 1943 Dirlewanger was decorated with the German Cross in gold and a year later promoted to *SS-Standartenführer* in the Waffen-SS. His unit was active in the suppression of the Polish uprising in Warsaw (August 1944) and of the Slovak national uprising in October 1944, where it behaved with typical brutality. In May 1945 Dirlewanger's men were taken into Soviet captivity but he fled westwards and was arrested in Altshausen. He died in a French prison on 7 June 1945, probably as a result of torture and ill-treatment.

Dix, Otto (1891–1969) German expressionist painter whose work depicted the horrors of war and the hunger and poverty of the post-war years with extraordinary realism, Otto Dix was born on 2 December 1891 at Untermaus near Gera, Thuringia, the son of an industrial worker. A leading member of the *Neue Sachlichkeit* (New Objectivity) movement, along with George Grosz and Max Beckmann, Dix's work was full of bitter social criticism, exposing the unembellished stark truth of the trenches: himself a soldier in the ranks during World War I, his series of etchings of the mass slaughter, *Der Krieg* (1924), convincingly vented his disgust at the butchery and inhumanity of the war. Dix's paintings reflected not so much the golden twenties of Weimar culture as a nightmarish world of cripples, prostitutes, outsiders and humiliated victims of society. His satiric attacks on the bourgeoisie, on the acceptance of corruption and the nihilistic social apathy of his contemporaries earned him comparison with the famous nineteenth-century French artist, Daumier.

Originally apprenticed as a decoration painter after graduating from elementary school, Dix had studied at the art academy in Dresden on a scholarship. In 1927 he was appointed Professor at the Dresden State Academy, a position he held until his dismissal when the Nazis came to power in 1933. Henceforth the painter was under continuous surveillance by the Gestapo and his works were eventually banned as 'decadent art' from German art galleries and museums. Two hundred and sixty of his paintings and etchings were removed from public display in 1937 and, on Goebbels's (q.v.) order, many of them were burnt. The previous year Dix and his family had moved to a remote farm retreat on the shores of Lake Constance, where they lived in obscurity until the end of the war. In 1945 Dix was drafted into a 'People's Defence Unit' by the Nazis and shortly afterwards was made a prisoner of war by the French at a camp in Colmar, Alsace. He returned to

Germany after the war, accepting a Professorship at Düsseldorf Art Academy in 1950. In his later work, Dix moved far away from the 'New Objectivity', painting tranquil landscapes and portraying Christian religious themes. He died in July 1969 at Singen, Lake Constance.

Doenitz, Karl (1891–1980) Grand Admiral who was Commander-in-Chief of the German Navy after 1943 and subsequently Hitler's designated successor, Karl Doenitz was born on 16 September 1891 in Grünau, near Berlin. The son of a successful engineer, he joined the Imperial navy in 1910, becoming an officer three years later. At the beginning of World War I Doenitz was transferred to the Naval Air Arm, becoming a flight-observer and later a seaplane squadron leader. From 1916 to 1918 he served with the U-boat fleet and was captured after the sinking of his submarine near Malta at the end of the war. In 1919 Doenitz joined the small German navy, becoming an inspector of torpedo boats, serving in cruisers (he commanded the *Emden*) and then on 27 September 1935 he was appointed to raise and command the new U-boat arm, once Hitler had decided to abandon the restrictions imposed by the Versailles Treaty. A convinced National Socialist and admirer of Hitler, Doenitz was promoted to Vice-Admiral in 1940 (in the same year he received the Knight's Cross), to Admiral in 1942, to Grand Admiral on 30 January 1943 and successor to Admiral Erich Raeder (q.v.) as Supreme Commander of the German Navy, on the same date. In April 1943 Doenitz was decorated with the Oak Leaves of the Knight's Cross and on 30 January 1944 his loyalty to National Socialism was recognized by the award of the coveted Golden Party Badge.

As head of the U-boat arm, Doenitz played an important role in World War II, proving himself an able tactician in directing the Battle of the Atlantic against Allied supply shipping. The submarine fleet probably came closer than any other weapon to winning the war for Germany, sinking some fifteen million tons of Allied shipping and threatening completely to disrupt Britain's supply routes. It was Doenitz who pioneered the concept of the 'wolf pack', with his U-boats waiting for Allied convoys in groups – by early 1943 there were 212 U-boats at his disposal operating in packs and another 181 in training. He constantly urged Hitler and Raeder to spare no efforts in building up the German submarine fleet, but the invention of microwave radar enabled the Allies to inflict heavy losses on the U-boat packs which German production lines were unable to replace in sufficient numbers. In Hitler's last will, Doenitz was appointed his successor as Reich President and Supreme Commander of the Armed Forces.

The Grand Admiral set up an 'Acting Reich Government' in Flensburg-Mürwik, in the far north of Schleswig-Holstein on the Danish border, attempting to negotiate an orderly end to the war against the Allies in the West. On 1 May 1945 he went on the radio to state that it was his first task 'to save Germany from destruction by the advancing Bolshevik enemy. For this aim alone the military struggle continues. As far and as long as this aim is impeded by the British and Americans, we shall be forced to carry on our defensive fight against them as well.' In fact, Doenitz knew that effective German resistance was at an end and his proposals to end the war in the West while continuing to fight the Russians were rejected. The rump Doenitz government came to an end on 23 May 1945 when the new Head of State was captured by the British. Much to his own surprise, Doenitz was sentenced to ten years' imprisonment by the Nuremberg Tribunal on 1 October 1946 for war crimes and crimes against peace. Exactly ten years after sentence, he was released from Berlin's Spandau prison. Admiral Doenitz died on 24 December 1980.

Dohnanyi, Hans von (1902–45) Austrian lawyer who became a member of the *Abwehr* and an important figure in the July 1944 plot against Hitler, Hans von Dohnanyi was born in Vienna on 1 January 1902, the son of a Hungarian pianist. From 1929 to 1938 he worked in the Reich Ministry of Justice, occupying himself with legal reform. Partly of Jewish descent, he was 'Aryanized' according to a special order of Hitler and was able to serve in important positions in various ministries though not to join the Nazi Party. Appointed a judge of the Supreme Court, von Dohnanyi transferred a year later to the *Abwehr* and was employed as a special leader on the staff of the High Command of the Armed Forces under Major-General Hans Oster (q.v.). The brother-in-law of Pastor Dietrich Bonhoeffer (q.v.), von Dohnanyi's connections with the Resistance dated back to before the war and on 5 April 1943 he was picked up by the Gestapo on suspicion of being involved in a conspiracy against Hitler. Released for lack of evidence, he was arrested again shortly before the July 1944 plot and this time removed to Sachsenhausen concentration camp where he was subjected to particularly brutal treatment. Shortly before the end of the war, on 8 April 1945, von Dohnanyi was murdered at the camp in circumstances that have never been clarified.

Dörpmuller, Julius (1869–1945) Riech Minister of Transport from 1937 to 1945, Julius Dörpmuller was born in Elberfeld on 24 July 1869. After studying engineering at Aachen Technical College, he entered the Prussian railway service and also spent some time working for the Chinese Imperial Railways before 1914. At the end of World War I he found himself in Russia after fleeing

from China, and managed to return safely to Germany where he continued his work with the railroad system. In 1926 he was appointed Director General of German State Railways. After the Nazis came to power, he was frequently honoured and decorated, and his engineering expertise was highly regarded by Hitler who appointed him Chairman of the *Autobahn* Management Committee. In 1937 he was nominated *Reichsverkehrminister* (Reich Minister of Transport), a post which he held until the fall of the Third Reich. He died in Malente, Schleswig-Holstein, on 5 June 1945.

Drexler, Anton (1884–1942) Co-founder of the *Deutsche Arbeiterpartei* in Munich, where he was born on 13 June 1884, Anton Drexler was one of the forerunners, and briefly also the Honorary Chairman, of the NSDAP. A machine-fitter who had lost his job in Berlin for refusing to accept the Social Democrats as the voice of the German working class, he became a locksmith in a locomotive works in Berlin after 1902. Physically unfit for the army, the idealistic Drexler found an outlet for his patriotism by joining the *Vaterlandspartei* (Fatherland Party) during World War I. Drexler urged the workers to fight for a German victory and demanded action against profiteers and speculators, while at the same time denouncing the Marxism of the Social Democrats. In March 1918 he set up a Committee of Independent Workmen, which combined German national racism – directed at excluding Jews and foreigners from State and society – and the liberation of the working man on the basis of a supra-class platform.

On 5 January 1919 Drexler joined forces with the journalist, Karl Harrer, head of the *Politischer Arbeiterzirkel* (Political Workers' Circle) in Munich, to form the first cell of the future NSDAP, the German Workers' Party. A mixture of secret Society and drinking club with about forty regular members when Adolf Hitler (q.v.) joined the group in 1919, it advocated the union of all 'producers' against loan capital and interest slavery, called for profit sharing and bridging the gap between intellectual and physical labour. Superimposed on this quasi-socialist programme was an intense nationalism and anti-semitic racism fed by the trauma of the lost war. The German labouring classes were seen as the victims of a diabolical conspiracy of international 'Jewish' capital, ideas which found a fertile soil in postrevolutionary Munich and impressed the young Hitler. The latter had read Drexler's pamphlet *Mein Politisches Erwachen (My Political Awakening)* and derived the core of his Nazism from these first attempts to create a classless, popular Party, which was anti-capitalist, anti-liberal, anti-Marxist and anti-semitic, while espousing the cause of German national resurgence. The ingenuous, unworldly Drexler, who co-authored the twenty-five theses which constituted the National Socialist programme announced on 24 February 1920, proved however to be no match for Adolf Hitler who had wrested the leadership from him by the summer of 1921. Two years later, Drexler had left the Party and in 1924 he was elected to the Bavarian legislature on another list. He never again participated in the Nazi movement and died, a forgotten figure, in Munich on 24 February 1942.

Duesterberg, Theodor (1875–1950) Vice-President of the *Stahlhelm*, the association of German nationalist ex-soldiers and a candidate of the German Nationalist Party in the presidential elections of 1932, Theodor Duesterberg was born in Darmstadt on 19 October 1875. After serving as a Lieutenant-Colonel in World War I, Duesterberg founded the *Stahlhelm* on 23 December 1918, together with the manufacturer Franz

Seldte (q.v.), calling on ex-servicemen 'without distinction of class' to fight against 'the slavery of the Versailles Diktat'. The *Stahlhelm* sought to mobilize the spirit of the frontline soldier against 'the heresy of Internationalism, Pacifism and Marxism', demanding 'adequate *lebensraum*' for Germany. By 1931 it consisted of twenty-three federal units with as many as 14,000 local groups and a million uniformed men with military training at its disposal. The largest of the para-military organizations, its leaders included men belonging to the old aristocracy with important connections in the army, the industrial and political élites. In 1931 the *Stahlhelm* was among the rightist nationalist groups which sought to combine in the Harzburg Front with the Nazis to overthrow Chancellor Brüning (q.v.) and establish a 'truly national government'. The Front failed in its objective and when Duesterberg ran in the presidential elections of March 1932, the Nazis destroyed his chances by revealing that he was of partly Jewish descent. His candidature was withdrawn for the run-off elections in April 1932. When Hitler came to power on 30 January 1933 he nonetheless offered Duesterberg a post in his cabinet, which the latter refused, in contrast to his colleague Seldte, who became Reich Minister of Labour. Following the bloodbath of June 1934, Duesterberg was temporarily sent to a concentration camp for criticizing the Nazis. He survived the Third Reich and, after the war, published a booklet *Der Stahlhelm und Hitler* (1949) in which he denounced the 'insane Jew hatred preached by Hitler' and criticized the 'hard-hearted indifference ... even among the so-called educated classes' to the reign of terror unleashed during the Röhm (q.v.) *putsch* which led Germany down the road to disaster. The *Stahlhelm's* own role in consistently undermining the Weimar Republic and thereby abetting the National Socialists was ignored. Duesterberg died on 4 May 1950 in Hameln.

Dwinger, Edwin Erich (1898–1981) Leading German novelist whose works were very popular among *bündisch* youth groups in the Weimar Republic and whose powerful evocation of World War I experience in the East was much admired by the Nazis, Edwin Dwinger was born on 23 April 1898 in Kiel. The son of a technical officer in the German navy and of a mother of Russian origin, Dwinger volunteered as a cavalry officer and went to the eastern front in 1915, where he was severely wounded and fell into the hands of the Russians. Sent to Irkutsk and later to eastern Siberia, Dwinger served in Admiral Kolchak's White Army against the Bolsheviks and took part in their catastrophic retreat through Siberia. Eventually he escaped via Mongolia, returning to Germany in 1920. Dwinger's best-selling trilogy based on his Siberian notebooks, beginning with *Die Armee hinter Stacheldraht* (1929, Engl. trs. *Prisoners of War*, 1930), *Zwischen Weiss und Rot* (1930, Engl. trs. *Between White and Red*, 1932) and culminating with *Wir Rufen Deutschland* (1932), contains unforgettable scenes depicting the suffering of POWs in Siberia, the fighting between Reds and Whites during the Russian Civil War, the sense of comradeship and community in the face of danger, and the courage and idealism brought out by war. The third part of the trilogy suffers, however, from Dwinger's didacticism, his belief that he had a vital message for the German people and the world – the necessity to combine ethnic solidarity with a sense of duty, and a socialism of the heart that could rise above class distinctions and transcend both capitalism and Bolshevism.

Dwinger's anti-communism made him acceptable to the Nazis, who considered him an expert on 'Soviet mass murder'. In 1935 he received the Dietrich-Eckart

Prize and in the same year he was made an *Obersturmführer* in an *SS-Reiterstandarte* (cavalry regiment). Dwinger continued to write best-selling books under the Third Reich, including *Die Letzten Reiter* (1935) about the fate of *Freikorps* men from the Baltic, *Spanische Silhouetten* (1937), impressions of the Spanish Civil War as seen from Franco's side, *Auf halbem Wege* (1939) and *Der Tod in Polen. Die Volksdeutsche Passion* (1940). During World War II, Dwinger was a war correspondent with a Panzer division in the USSR, receiving authorization from the personal staff of the *Reichsführer-SS* to study the operations of the SS in the occupied territories. In a letter to Himmler (q.v.) on his return, Dwinger thanked him for his generous assistance and declared his readiness to participate in the new order for Soviet Russia. Dwinger set down his impressions in *Wiedersehen mit Sowjetrussland. Tagebuch vom Ostfeldzug* (1942). However, his public opposition to National Socialist *Ostpolitik* in the Soviet Union – Dwinger did not accept the official view that the Russians were 'sub-humans' – and his contacts with the Russian General Wlassow in the autumn of 1943 led to his house arrest. Dwinger's anti-Bolshevism did not lead him to embrace Nazi racial theories about the inferior Slavs.

After World War II Dwinger continued to write prolifically and to find a readership in Germany. His works included *Wenn die Dämme brechen – Untergang Ostpreussens* (1950), *General Wlassow – Eine Tragödie unserer Zeit* (1951) and a novel about the Cossacks, *Sie suchten die Freiheit. Schicksalweg eines Reitervolkes* (1953). Dwinger's utopian war novel, *Es geschah im Jahre 1965* (1957), about a nuclear world war provoked something of a furore, with the author being accused of taking sadistic pleasure in the prospects of a global conflagration. Dwinger died on 17 December 1981 at the age of eighty-three in Gmund am Tegernsee.

E

Eckart, Dietrich (1868–1923) Bavarian Catholic poet who was Hitler's first mentor and the 'spiritual' godfather of National Socialism, Dietrich Eckart was born on 23 March 1868 in Neumarkt, Upper Palatinate. A journalist by training, a mediocre poet and dramatist, Eckart's lack of success in pre-war Wilhelminian Germany fuelled his hatred of Jews and Marxists whom he blamed for his own failures and later for Germany's defeat in World War I. After a long period of bohemian vagrancy in Berlin, Eckart returned to Munich in 1915 and entered politics after the abortive November revolution of 1918. He invented the Nazi battle-cry *'Deutschland Erwache!'* (Germany Awake!), the title of one of his poems, and, as the first poet of the movement, became the forerunner of National Socialist lyric art. In 1919 he began publication of the nationalist weekly *Auf Gut Deutsch*, which attacked the Versailles Treaty, Jewish war profiteers, Bolshevism and Social Democracy. Among its earliest contributors were Gottfried Feder (q.v.) and the young Baltic émigré, Alfred Rosenberg (q.v.). Eckart helped obtain the funds which enabled Hitler to buy up the *Völkische Beobachter*, which became the official organ of the NSDAP on 17 December 1920. Eckart was its first editor and publisher until he was eventually succeeded by Rosenberg.

In the role of visionary poet and seer, Eckart exercised a remarkable personal ascendency over the young Hitler, who looked up to him as a teacher and father-figure whose services to National Socialism were 'inestimable'. It was Eckart who introduced Hitler to Munich Society, who improved his social graces and his German, grooming him for the role of messianic saviour and reinforcing his ultra-nationalist, anti-semitic ideas. Not surprisingly, *Mein Kampf* was dedicated to Dietrich Eckart, whose name appears at the end of Volume 2 in bold type. A dialogue between Hitler and Eckart, published in Munich in 1923 under the title *Der Bolshewismus von Moses bis Lenin (Bolshevism from Moses to Lenin)*, reflects their common belief that the Jews represented the occult power of revolutionary subversion throughout history and were responsible for deflecting man from his natural path. In this pamphlet the primitive, brutal nature of Eckart's anti-semitism and its influence on the young Hitler find their concrete manifestation. By the time of the Munich Beer-Hall *putsch*, Eckart was already seriously ill, his health undermined by drunkenness and morphine addiction. Briefly imprisoned in Stadelheim, he died of heart failure not long after his release, on 23 December 1923. He was buried in Berchtesgaden.

Eichmann, Adolf (1906–62) SS Lieutenant-Colonel who was Chief of the Jewish Office of the Gestapo during World War II and implemented the 'Final Solution' which aimed at the total extermination of European Jewry, Adolf Eichmann was born in Solingen on 19 March 1906. The déclassé son of a solid middle-class Protestant family which had moved to Linz, Austria, where Eichmann spent his youth, he failed to complete his engineering studies. After working briefly as an ordinary labourer in his father's small mining enterprise and then in the sales department of an Upper Austrian electrical construction company, Eichmann became a travelling salesman for the Vacuum Oil Company between 1927 and 1933. On 1 April 1932 he joined the Austrian Nazi Party at the suggestion of his compatriot Ernst Kaltenbrunner (q.v.). Having lost his job he sought employment across the border in Bavaria in July 1933, joining the exiled Austrian legion and undergoing fourteen months' military training. In September 1934 he found an opening in Himmler's (q.v.) Security Service (SD) which provided him with an outlet for his bureaucratic talents. By the beginning of 1935 he was the official responsible for 'Jewish questions' at the Berlin head office of the SD, specializing in the Zionist movement. He acquired a smattering of Hebrew and Yiddish, and briefly visited Palestine in 1937 to explore the possibilities of Jewish emigration from Nazi Germany to Palestine. Appointed assistant to the SD leader of the SS main region, Danube, Eichmann's first big opportunity came after he was sent to Vienna by the Gestapo to prepare the ground for the *Anschluss*.

From August 1938 he was in charge of the 'Office for Jewish Emigration' in Vienna set up by the SS as the sole Nazi agency authorized to issue exit permits for Jews from Austria, then Czechoslovakia and later the old German Reich. Eichmann's acquired expertise in 'forced emigration' – in less than eighteen months approximately 150,000 Jews left Austria – and extortion was to prove an ideal training-ground for his later efficiency in 'forced evacuation', i.e. the registering, assembly and deportation of Jews to extermination centres in the East. By March 1939 he was already handling forced deportations to Poland and, in October of the same year, he was appointed special adviser on the 'evacuation' of Jews and Poles. In December 1939 Eichmann was transferred to *Amt* IV (Gestapo) of the Reich Main Security Office (RSHA) where he took over *Referat* IV B4 dealing with Jewish affairs and evacuation.

For the next six years Eichmann's office was the headquarters for the implementation of the 'Final Solution'; though it was not until the summer of 1941 that his 'resettlement' department began the task of creating death camps, developing gassing techniques and organizing the system of convoys that were to take European Jewry to their deaths. It was in 1941 that Eichmann first visited Auschwitz and in November of the same year he was promoted to SS Lieutenant-Colonel. He had already begun to organize the mass deportation of Jews from Germany and Bohemia, in accordance with Hitler's order to make the Reich free of Jews as rapidly as possible. The Wannsee Conference of 20 January 1942 consolidated Eichmann's position as the 'Jewish specialist' of the RSHA and Heydrich (q.v.) now formally entrusted him with implementing the 'Final Solution'. In this task Eichmann proved to be a model of bureaucratic industriousness and icy determination even though he had never been a fanatical anti-semite and always claimed that 'personally' he had nothing against Jews. His zeal expressed itself in his constant complaints about obstacles in the fulfilment of death-camp quotas, his impatience with the existence of loopholes such as the free zone in Vichy France or the uncooperativeness of the Italians and other German allies in expediting their Jews. When even Himmler became more 'moderate' towards the end of the war, Eichmann ignored his 'no gassing' order, as long as he was covered by immediate superiors like Heinrich Müller (q.v.) and his old friend, Kaltenbrunner.

Only in Budapest after March 1944 did the desk-murderer become a public personality, working in the open and playing a leading role in the massacre of Hungarian Jewry. In August 1944 the 'Grand Inquisitor' of European Jewry could report to Himmler that approximately four million Jews had died in the death camps and that another two million had been killed by mobile extermination units. Though arrested at the end of the war, Eichmann's name was not yet widely known and he was able to escape from an American internment camp in 1946 and flee to Argentina. He was eventually tracked down by Israeli secret agents on 2 May 1960, living under an assumed name in a suburb of Buenos Aires. Nine days later he was secretly abducted to Israel, to be publicly tried in Jerusalem. The trial, which aroused enormous international interest and some controversy, took place between 2 April and 14 August 1961. On 2 December 1961 Eichmann was sentenced to death for crimes against the Jewish people and crimes against humanity. On 31 May 1962 he was executed in Ramleh prison.

Eicke, Theodor (1892–1943) Inspector of Concentration Camps and SS Guard Formations (SS Death's Head Formations) during the Third Reich, Theodor Eicke was born on 17 October 1892 at Kampont, Alsace-Lorraine, the son of a station-master. He was discharged from the Imperial army after reaching the rank of sub-paymaster and being decorated with the Iron Cross (Second Class). He joined the police administration in Thuringia after qualifying as an inspector in 1920. Eicke was briefly employed by the security police and the criminal police and by the police administration in Ludwigshafen on the Rhine. He lost various jobs because of his anti-republican political activities, but in 1923 he was hired as a commercial executive by I. G. Farben (Ludwigshafen), also looking after their anti-espionage service. Eicke joined the NSDAP and the SA on 1 December 1928 and was transferred to

the SS on 20 August 1930 where he was quickly promoted. Appointed *SS-Standartenführer* on 15 November 1931, he was put in charge of the SS regiment in the Rhine-Palatinate.

Sentenced to two years' penal servitude in March 1932 for political bomb attacks, he fled to Italy on Himmler's (q.v.) instructions, returning to Germany in mid-February 1933. The aggressive, restless Eicke soon clashed, however, with the *Gauleiter* of the Rhine-Palatinate, Josef Bürckel (q.v.), who declared him a 'dangerous lunatic', ordering his detention at the Psychiatric Clinic in Würzburg on 21 March 1933. Eicke was struck off the SS rolls, but reconfirmed in his old rank on 26 June 1933 and promptly appointed by Himmler as the new Commandant of Dachau. In May 1934 he was entrusted by the SS leader with the take-over of the concentration camps by the SS and with their reorganization. On 4 July 1934 Eicke was given the post of *Inspekteur der Konzentrationslager und SS-Wachverbände (SS-Totenkopfverbände)* and a week later he was promoted to *SS-Gruppenführer*. The brutal, energetic Eicke had earned his promotion by his important role in suppressing the so-called Röhm (q.v.) *putsch* and executing the SA chief in his cell at Stadelheim prison, Munich, on 1 July. In his new role, Eicke proved to be a dedicated servant of Himmler and Heydrich (q.v.), replacing the guard police at Dachau by SS Death's Head Formations, the toughest and most ruthless Nazi elements.

Under Eicke's régime, no pity was to be shown for 'enemies of the State' and prisoners were treated with maximum, impersonal severity. He laid down exact instructions on corporal punishment, beatings, solitary confinement and shooting of offenders who were considered as 'agitators', mutineers or refractory elements who refused to obey instructions or work while on detail. Dachau, with its SS motto that 'tolerance is a sign of weakness', became a model for the German concentration camp system as a whole. Rudolf Hoess (q.v.), later Commandant of Auschwitz, recalling his Dachau training, observed: 'The purpose of Eicke's everlasting lectures and orders to the same effect was ... to turn his SS men completely against the prisoners, to stir up their feelings against the prisoners....' Eicke's writing paper bore the maxim: 'Only one thing matters: the command given', and he warned his SS guards of severe penalties for any trace of softness. Eicke saw his task in terms of establishing a military discipline in accordance with SS ideals of 'loyalty, bravery and devotion to duty', telling his concentration camp commanders in 1939 that they must be ready to 'carry out even the hardest and most difficult of orders without hesitation'. On 14 November 1939 he was appointed Commander of the first SS-Totenkopf Division which he raised in Dachau and took over the organization and employment of the SS Death's Head Formations used in action in Poland. Promoted in 1943 to SS General and General of the Waffen-SS, Eicke was killed on 16 February of the same year during an air reconnaissance on the eastern front.

Einstein, Albert (1879–1955) One of the greatest physicists of all time, Nobel Prize winner and discoverer of the special and general theory of relativity, Albert Einstein was born on 14 March 1879 in Ulm, Württemberg, of Jewish parents. He spent his early years in Munich where his father set up a small electrochemical business. As a boy he was fascinated by algebra and geometry, though he detested the barracks discipline of German schools. In 1896 he entered the Swiss Federal Polytechnic School in Zürich, graduating in 1900 and receiving his doctorate from Zürich in 1905. Unable to get an academic position, he took a post with the patent office in Bern while continuing to pursue

his concern with the fundamental problems of physics. In 1905 he published four brilliant papers in the *Annalen der Physik* which were to transform twentieth-century scientific thought. He established the special theory of relativity, predicted the equivalence of mass (m) and energy (e) according to the equation $e = mc^2$, where (c) represents the velocity of light; he created the theory of Brownian motion and founded the photon theory of light (photoelectric effect) for which he received the Nobel Prize in 1921. Einstein joined the German University of Prague in 1910 and then in 1913 through Max Planck (q.v.) received a Professorship at the Prussian Academy of Science in Berlin.

In 1916 Einstein published his *Die Grundlagen der allgemeinen Relativitätstheorie (Relativity, the Special and the General Theory: A Popular Exposition, 1920)*, which profoundly modified the simple concepts of space and time on which Newtonian mechanics had been based. His prediction of the deflection of light by the gravitational field of the sun was borne out by a British team of scientists at the time of the solar eclipse in 1919, making Einstein a household name. Throughout the Weimar years he was lionized, especially abroad, though in Germany not only his work but also his pacifist politics aroused violent animosity in extreme right-wing circles. Anti-semites sought to brand his theory of relativity as 'un-German' and during the Third Reich they partially achieved their objective, when Einstein's name could no longer be mentioned in lectures or scholarly papers, though his relativity theory was still taught.

During the 1920s Einstein travelled widely in Europe, America and Asia and identified himself with various public causes such as pacifism, Zionism, the League of Nations and European unity. When Hitler came to power in January 1933 Einstein was in California and he never returned to Germany, being almost immediately deprived of his posts in Berlin and his membership of the Prussian Academy of Sciences. His property was seized and a price put on his head by Nazi fanatics. His books were among those burned publicly on 10 May 1933 as manifestations of the 'un-German spirit'. As an outspoken opponent of National Socialism his name became synonymous with treason in the Third Reich. Einstein emigrated to the United States where he became a Professor at the Institute of Advanced Studies (Princeton) and an American citizen in 1940. Alarmed at the prospect that Hitler's Germany might acquire an atomic bomb after two German physicists had discovered the fusion of uranium, Einstein signed a letter to President Roosevelt in August 1939 which sparked off the Manhattan project. It was one of the great ironies of his career that the pacifist Einstein, through this action, should have helped initiate the era of nuclear weapons to whose use he was completely opposed. A lifelong opponent of nationalism, Einstein regarded the Third Reich as a catastrophe for civilization.

Active in Jewish causes he was offered the Presidency of the State of Israel, but declined, 'being deeply touched by the offer but not suited for the position'. His simplicity, benevolence and good humour as well as his scientific genius gave Einstein a unique fame and prestige among physicists, even though after the mid-1920s he diverged from the main trends in the field, especially disliking the probabilistic interpretation of the universe associated with quantum theory. The best-known refugee from Nazism and one of its most adamant critics, Einstein died in Princeton on 18 April 1955.

Elser, Johann Georg (1903–45) A Swabian carpenter and cabinet-maker who narrowly failed to assassinate Hitler in November 1939, Johann Georg Elser

was born in the village of Hermaringen, Württemberg, on 4 January 1903. The son of a timber merchant, he attended elementary school in Königsbronn and at the age of fourteen was apprenticed as a turner in a local iron factory. In 1922 he passed his journeyman's exam as a cabinet-maker and became a specialist in carpentry and metal work. For the next decade Elser lived as a wandering craftsman, sometimes working in clock factories or repairing furniture. In 1928–9 he joined the militant communist group, the *Rotfrontkämpferbund* (Red Front Fighters' Association), but although he had regularly voted communist before 1933, Elser was not politically minded, nor did he have any contacts with underground or Resistance organizations. A reserved, slow-spoken individual who carried out his assassination plan single-handed, Elser had been perturbed by the Munich agreements and the danger of war. He took his decision in the autumn of 1938 and planned the assassination attempt meticulously, accumulating a stock of explosives, designing a special clock mechanism and hiding his machine in a wooden column behind the speakers' rostrum in the Munich Bürgerbräukeller where Adolf Hitler was due to speak on 8 November 1939, before the 'Old Fighters'.

Elser's explosive device went off at twenty minutes past nine, destroying half the hall, killing seven people and wounding sixty-three. Hitler had unfortunately left the building ten minutes earlier, immediately after concluding his anniversary speech. Elser was arrested the same evening at the Swiss frontier and brought to Berlin, where he was interrogated at the Prinz Albrechtstrasse. Eventually he confessed to the Gestapo, but the Nazis preferred to blame the British Secret Service and Otto Strasser's (q.v.) Black Front for the assassination attempt. Elser was sent to Sachsenhausen concentration camp as 'Hitler's special prisoner', where he was kept along with other 'prominent prisoners' such as Léon Blum, Paster Niemöller (q.v.) and the former Austrian Chancellor, Kurt von Schuschnigg. He was given a carpenter's bench and allowed to make what he pleased. In 1944 he was moved to Dachau and kept alive, possibly in the hope of being used in a show trial after the war. On 9 April 1945 he was murdered by the Gestapo on a secret order from Himmler (q.v.) and his death attributed to an Allied bombing raid. There appears to be no evidence for the assertion that Elser was himself a Nazi agent. His motives were those of a lone resister who became convinced that Hitler's elimination would prevent more bloodshed and ameliorate the condition of the working man.

Epp, Franz Xaver Ritter von (1868–1947) Conservative General who was one of the most influential protectors of the Nazi Party in its early days, Franz Ritter von Epp was born in Munich on 16 October 1868, the son of a painter. A professional soldier, he entered the service of the Royal Bavarian Ninth Infantry Regiment in 1887 and in October 1896 was appointed First Lieutenant. During 1901–2, von Epp was in China with a German colonial detachment and between 1904 and 1907 he took part as a volunteer in the cruel and inglorious colonial war against the Hereros in German South-West Africa. During World War I, von Epp had a distinguished record – he was awarded the *Pour le Mérite* and the Iron Cross (First and Second Classes). On 8 February 1919 the Epp *Freikorps* was established and utilized in the liberation of Munich, being noted for its brutality. It was responsible for the murder of Gustav Landauer, the anarchist revolutionary, and for the massacre of socialists at Greising, a Munich suburb. For a brief period, von Epp was military dictator of Bavaria, which became a centre of opposi-

tional and Nazi activity against the government in Berlin and the communists.

Among von Epp's paid informers was Lance Corporal Adolf Hitler (q.v.), who had attracted the attention of his aide-de-camp, Ernst Röhm (q.v.). It was through Röhm that von Epp raised 60,000 marks for converting the *Völkische Beobachter* into a Nazi Party mouthpiece, obtaining the money from the Reichswehr treasury and Bavarian capitalists. Von Epp's troops were used by the republican government to crush the communists in the Ruhr, and he also exerted his influence on behalf of the SA in Bavaria, becoming its area commander in Munich in 1926. Three years earlier, during the abortive November *putsch*, von Epp had sat on the fence, distancing himself from the coup once it had failed. In 1928 he joined the NSDAP and immediately became a Reichstag deputy for the electoral district of Upper Bavaria-Swabia. He was also put in charge of the *Wehrpolitisches Amt* (the defence political office) of the Nazi Party. On 9 March 1933 von Epp dismissed the government of Bavaria and was appointed Governor, a position he held until the fall of the Third Reich. The conservative monarchist was also made head of the Colonial Policy Office of the Reich Leadership on 5 May 1934 and three months later Hitler appointed him Master of the Hunt in Bavaria. In July 1935 he was promoted to General of Infantry, but by this time his real power had been much deflated. From the beginning of 1934 he had clashed with Himmler (q.v.) and Heydrich (q.v.) over the 'improper use of protective custody' in Bavaria, expressing anxiety that 'confidence in the law' might be undermined. His outmoded authoritarian concepts condemned him to little more than a figurehead role in the Third Reich. At the end of the war, von Epp fell into the hands of the Americans and died in an American internment camp on 31 January 1947.

Esser, Hermann (1900–81) One of Hitler's earliest comrades in arms, a co-founder of the Nazi Party, Hermann Esser was born on 29 July 1900 in Röhrmoss, near Munich, the son of a civil servant. While still a teenager, he volunteered for military service, serving for one year during World War I. A radical socialist, who briefly worked on a left-wing provincial paper, he co-founded the German Workers' Party (forerunner of the NSDAP) with Anton Drexler (q.v.) in October 1919. Early in 1920 he met Hitler in the press department of the regional army headquarters and in the same year he was appointed the first editor of the *Völkische Beobachter* and Chief of Party Propaganda. From the outset Esser specialized in lurid descriptions of 'Jewish' scandals, appealing to the basest human instincts. Unsavoury, crude, of low moral character, Esser was nonetheless one of the most effective rabble-rousers in the early days of Nazism, his fiery speeches contributing to the Party's initial successes in Bavaria. Esser did not take part in the unsuccessful Hitler *putsch* of November 1923, remaining in bed – Hitler subsequently accused him of personal cowardice – and afterwards fleeing to Austria. On his return to Germany in January 1924 he was sentenced to three months' imprisonment by a Munich court.

The scandals in Esser's private life led other Nazis, especially the Strasser brothers and Goebbels (q.v.), to call for his exclusion from the Party. Gregor Strasser (q.v.) called his behaviour egoistic and *unvölkisch*, while Otto Strasser (q.v.) compared him to Julius Streicher (q.v.) as two 'sexual perverts' and 'demagogues of the worst kind'. Even Alfred Rosenberg (q.v.), who did not share the Strassers' 'revolutionary' ideas, held Esser in contempt and threatened to sue him for libel, dropping the suit at the last moment so as not to harm the Party. In 1926 Esser also quarrelled with Streicher, and this time Hitler (who had put up with Esser because he was useful) broke off personal relations with him, siding with the *Gauleiter* of Franconia. Nevertheless Hitler continued to use Esser as a speaker for certain kinds of public meetings and made him editor of the new, illustrated Party newspaper, *Illustrierter Beobachter*, a position he held from 1926 until 1932.

In 1929 Esser became a member of the County Council of Upper Bavaria and of the Munich City Council, and in 1932 of the Bavarian diet. In 1933 he was elected a member of the Reichstag, representing the electoral district of Upper Bavaria-Swabia. He persuaded General Ritter von Epp (q .v.) to make him Bavarian Minister of Economics, a position he held until 1935 when his intrigue against the Bavarian Minister of the Interior, Adolf Wagner (q.v.), failed and he was deposed. While in the post Esser had forced Bavarian industrialists to pay large sums to the State treasury, but it was above all his scandalous personal life – it was alleged that he had immorally assaulted the under-age daughter of a prominent Munich businessman – which prompted Hitler to act. Nonetheless the Führer did not dare to break completely with Esser, who knew too many compromising secrets and unsavoury details of Party life.

In 1935 he was put in charge of the Tourist Division in the Reich Propaganda Ministry and made President of the Reich Group Tourist Traffic (*Fremdenverkehr*). On 12 December 1939 he was appointed Vice-President of the Reichstag, but this was a mere sinecure which did not carry any influence. During World War II Esser faded completely into the background, aside from publishing in 1939 a viciously anti-semitic book, *Die Jüdische Weltpest (The Jewish World Pest)*, in the style of Julius Streicher. Apart from being the main speaker at the twenty-third anniversary of the founding of the NSDAP, celebrated by the 'Old Fighters' in the

Munich beer cellar on 24 February 1943, Esser remained out of the limelight. At the end of the war, this led to his being regarded as of minor importance and he was released by the Americans in 1947, after having been held in detention for two years. Esser then went into hiding until he was taken into custody on 9 September 1949, this time by German police. A Munich de-Nazification court reclassified him as a 'Major Offender' for having been the oldest propagator of Nazi ideas and for his past Jew-baiting activities. On 13 March 1950 an appeal court confirmed the verdict of five years' forced labour against him, but with time deducted for several years spent in detention he was released in 1952. He would probably never have been re-arrested had he not furnished titillating details for a syndicated story on 'Hitler, the Great Lover' which appeared in 1949 in an illustrated Munich magazine. Henceforth, Esser maintained a low profile until his death at the age of eighty on 7 February 1981.

Euringer, Richard (1891–1953) German novelist and lyric poet born on 4 April 1891 in Augsburg, Richard Euringer served as an aeroplane pilot in World War I and subsequently headed a Bavarian pilot-training school. During the Weimar years he tried to make a living as a worker in a sawmill and as an office boy in a bank. His early works like the war novel *Fliegerschule 4* (1929) showed the adventurous side of war, while *Die Arbeitslosen* (1930) dealt with the problem of unemployment. From 1931 a contributor to the leading Nazi newspaper, the *Völkische Beobachter*,

Euringer was considered, along with Johst (q.v.), Grimm (q.v.) and Kolbenheyer (q.v.), as one of the most active National Socialist authors and a herald of the coming Third Reich. His outstanding success was *Deutsche Passion* (1933), a radio play which revived some traits of medieval mysteries and received the first National State Prize in Nazi Germany. In the same year, Euringer was appointed chief librarian of the Essen public library, though he had no previous training for such a position, and in 1934 he became a member of the advisory board of the Reich Radio Chamber and the Reich Chamber of Literature. A freelance author from 1936, Euringer was the leading practitioner and theorist of the *Thingspiel* – open-air epic theatre which combined Nazi agit-prop, battle scenes, circus performance, choral declamations and fanfares. The elements of *Thingspiel* were fire, water, earth and air, stones, stars and solar orbits, mermaids, fairies, nymphs and fauns – according to Euringer, it was 'the theatre of nature' through which the people honoured their martyrs and enacted the cult of the dead, replete with blood-oaths and exorcism. Euringer's works included *Die Jobsiade* (1933), *Totentanz* (1934) and *Chronik einer Deutschen Wandlung* (1936) and a number of successful political *Zeitromane* (period novels). In his *Deutsche Dichter unsere Zeit* (1939) he wrote: 'My books are the continuation of my vocation as a soldier through other means.' This was a characteristic statement of the official ideology underlying Nazi drama and literature. Euringer died in Essen on 29 August 1953.

F

Falkenhausen, Alexander Freiherr von (1878–1966) German General who served from 1940 to 1944 as the Military Governor of occupied Belgium and northern France, Alexander von Falkenhausen was born on 29 October 1878 in Blumenthal, Silesia. A professional soldier of the old Prussian school, descended from a Junker family, he was military attaché to the German embassy in Tokyo in 1912, and during World War I was attached to the Turkish army, serving in Palestine. He received the *Pour le Mérite* decoration for courage in combat. From 1927 to 1930 von Falkenhausen was Commandant of the Infantry School in Dresden. In 1934 he succeeded General von Seeckt (q.v.) as head of the German Military Mission in China, where he remained for over four years, training the army of Chiang Kai-Shek and helping to develop a modern Chinese arms industry.

In 1939 he was recalled by Hitler to active service in Germany and on 1 September 1940 appointed General of Infantry. During his four years as Military Governor of Belgium and northern France, von Falkenhausen sought to protect the native population from the worst excesses of occupation. A correct, chivalrous officer who disliked Nazi extremism and the methods of the SS, von Falkenhausen nonetheless approved the deportation orders for all foreign Jews in Belgium and ordered Belgian hostages to be executed. Though he initially opposed the imposition of the Jewish badge in Belgium, he was obliged to yield to pressure from the Reich Main Security Office. Under his administra-

tion, Belgian Jews were deprived of employment, their firms 'Aryanized' without compensation and they were obliged to do compulsory labour service. Von Falkenhausen, however, was suspected of complicity with the German Resistance movement and relieved of his command shortly before the attempt on Hitler's life. After the failure of the July 1944 plot he was sent to Dachau concentration camp, where he was saved by American troops in May 1945, just as he was about to be executed. Later re-arrested by the Americans and handed over to the Belgian authorities, he was tried and convicted by a Brussels military tribunal on 7 March 1951 for executing hostages and ordering the deportation of 25,000 Belgian Jews. Sentenced to twelve years' imprisonment, he was released after three weeks as an act of clemency and in recognition of the fact that he had also protected Belgians from the SS. Von Falkenhausen died in Nassau on 31 July 1966.

Falkenhorst, Nikolaus von (1885–1968) Commander-in-Chief of German troops in Norway between 1940 and 1944, Nikolaus von Falkenhorst was born in Breslau on 17 January 1885. Descended from an old military family, he joined the army in 1907 and during World War I was given various regimental and staff appointments. A member of the *Freikorps* in 1919, he was taken over by the Reichswehr and between 1925 and 1927 served in the Operations Division of the War Ministry. Appointed Brigadier on 1 October 1932, von Falkenhorst was military attaché in

Prague, Belgrade and Bucharest between 1933 and 1935. On 1 July 1935 he was promoted to Major General and Chief of Staff of the Third Army (Dresden) and in 1937 to Lieutenant-General. In 1939 he commanded the Twenty-first Army Corps during the Polish campaign and was promoted to General of Infantry. He was Commander-in-Chief of German forces in Norway from 1940 until his dismissal on 18 December 1944 for opposing the policies of Josef Terboven (q.v.), the Reich Commissioner for Norway. Von Falkenhorst pursued a harsh policy towards prisoners of war: he handed over captured British commandos to be executed, for which he was sentenced to death by a British military tribunal in 1946. The sentence was later reduced to twenty years' imprisonment. Von Falkenhorst was released on 23 July 1953 for reasons of health. He died in Holzminden on 18 June 1968.

Fallada, Hans (1893–1947) Prominent novelist whose work faithfully reflected the *Zeitgeist* of the Great Depression as it affected the peasants of North Germany, the lower middle classes and petty functionaries, Hans Fallada was born as Rudolf Ditzen in Greifswald on 21 July 1893. After secondary school and agricultural studies, Fallada worked as a farm supervisor on various North German country estates and was imprisoned for having swindled the owners. A disastrous adolescence was reflected in Fallada's unstable private life and recurring morphine addiction. As a freelance writer Fallada became famous for his ability to portray the effects on individual Germans of the years immediately preceding, during and after the great slump of 1929. His *Bauern, Bonzen und Bomben (Farmers, Functionaries and Fireworks)*, published in 1931, recounted the story of the farmers' revolt in Holstein, which he had witnessed as a local news reporter, showing up right-wing violence as well as mocking the

Social Democrats. His brilliant ear for dialogue and gift for simple, accurate social observation were also displayed in the best-selling *Kleiner Mann – was nun? (Little Man – What Now?)* published the following year, and one of the most successful, symptomatic novels of the Depression. This novel, with its cover drawn by George Grosz, described the cares of a young shop assistant and his working-class wife in the Germany of the slump. It made Fallada's name and displayed the realism which had earlier prompted Kurt Tucholsky to describe him as 'the best imaginable political guide to the *fauna Germanica*'. During the Third Reich, Fallada continued to write prolifically, being tolerated by the Nazis, though somewhat suspect because of a tendency towards decadence. Among his later works were *Wer einmal aus dem Belchnapf frisst* (1934), *Wir hatten mal ein Kind* (1934), *Wolf unter Wölfen* (1937), *Der eiserne Gustav* (1939) and *Damals bei uns daheim* (1942). His half-hearted collaboration with the Nazis, and later with the East German authorities, reflected an adaptation to circumstances rather than any profound convictions. He died in Berlin of drink and drugs on 5 February 1947.

Faulhaber, Cardinal Michael von (1869–1952) Archbishop of Munich and a leading figure in the Roman Catholic ecclesiastical hierarchy during the Third Reich, Michael von Faulhaber was born in Klosterheidenfeld, Lower Franconia, on 5 March 1869. Professor of Old Testament exegesis at Strasbourg from 1903, he was appointed Bishop of Speyer in 1911 and Archbishop of Munich-Freising in 1917. In 1921 he was made a Cardinal. A Bavarian monarchist, von Faulhaber's attitude to the Weimar Republic was highly ambiguous. At times he impugned its legality, describing its origin in November 1918 as characterized by perjury and high treason. Under the Third Reich he tried to steer a middle course, maintaining good working relations with the Nazi authorities while seeking to preserve the vital interests of the Catholic church.

The Concordat of 1933 between the régime and the church inhibited open opposition, though von Faulhaber did protest when it became apparent that the Nazis were consistently violating the agreement. Shortly before Christmas 1933, the Cardinal preached a series of sermons in St Michael's Church, Munich, which stood up for the values of the Old Testament against Nazi neo-paganism. Published shortly afterwards under the title *Judentum, Christentum, Germanentum* (1934), the sermons defended the principles of racial tolerance and humanity against unbridled national-ism, trying indirectly to protect the Jewish origins of Christianity from Nazi attack. The Cardinal's call to respect the Jewish religion was undoubtedly an act of considerable courage, but his pointed distinction between Israel *before* the coming of Christ and modern post-Christian Jews reflected traditional Catholic ambiguity. 'Antagonism to the Jews of today', the Cardinal insisted, 'must not be extended to the books of pre-Christian Judaism', suggesting that his prime motive was to defend the tradi-tion and authority of the Catholic church, rather than the Jews themselves. Nevertheless, Cardinal Faulhaber did on several occasions condemn racial hatred as a poisonous weed in German life and warned 'that God always punished the tormentors of His Chosen People, the Jews'. During the anti-semitic pogrom of 9 November 1938 he provided a truck for the Chief Rabbi of Munich to sal-vage religious articles from his syna-gogue, though there was no open protest by Faulhaber or any other Catholic bish-ops against the atrocities.

The Cardinal had earlier visited Hitler at Berchtesgaden on 4 November 1936 and come away impressed by his diplo-matic finesse, believing that he would continue to respect the rights of the Catholic church. This proved to be an illusion, as was made apparent in the papal encyclical *Mit Brennender Sorge (With Deep Anxiety)* of 1937, partly drafted by von Faulhaber, which pro-tested against Nazi violations of the Con-cordat with the Holy See. Nonetheless, the Cardinal was supportive of Nazi foreign policy at the time of the *An-schluss* with Austria and the Czech crisis of 1938. In November 1939 he celebrated Hitler's 'miraculous' escape from Johann Georg Elser's (q.v.) assassination attempt with a solemn mass in Munich. In spite of various approaches from the Resistance, von Faulhaber remained non-committal about the plot against Hitler, eventually denouncing it after interrogation by the Gestapo in 1944. Thus, in spite of his courageous defence of Catholic principles, attempts to present von Faulhaber as a champion in the struggle against Nazi tyranny would appear to be exaggerated. He died in Munich on 12 June 1952.

Feder, Gottfried (1883–1941) Leading ideologist of National Socialism in its early days and a representative figure in the Old Guard, Gottfried Feder was born in Würzburg on 27 January 1883. An engineer by profession, he became increasingly interested in economics and, in the aftermath of World War I, became well known in Bavaria as the leading propagandist for the abolition of inter-est. It was Feder who made the idea of 'breaking the interest slavery of inter-national capitalism' a major economic plank in the original Nazi platform of 1920, which he drew up together with Anton Drexler (q.v.), Hitler and Dietrich Eckart (q.v.). Feder held high finance responsible for the inflation and econ-omic chaos in post-war Germany which had become a 'slave of the international stock market'. His speeches were pep-pered with attacks on industrialists and financiers mixed with anti-semitic rhetoric, denunciations of the Versailles Treaty, Weimar and the Reichstag. One of the leading members of the small German Workers' Party of 1919 (forerunner of the NSDAP), Feder's eclectic socialism initially made a deep impression on Hitler, who regarded him as a guide in economic matters.

Editor of the *National Socialist Library* and a number of other Nazi publications in Nuremberg and Darmstadt, Feder was one of the most prominent Party ideologues in the 1920s and a leader of its populist, racist and anti-industrial wing. Elected a Nazi deputy to the Reichstag in 1924 for the district of East Prussia, Feder advocated the expropriation of Jewish property and unprofitable large, landed estates, as well as a freeze on interest rates. He put forward his quasi-socialist ideas in a number of publications and books, including *Das Programm der NSDAP und seine weltanschaulichen Grundlagen* (1931), *Was Will Adolf Hitler?* (1931), *Kampf gegen die Hochfinanz* (1933) and the anti-semitic tract *Die Juden* (1933). Feder's economic policies and his influence as Chairman of the Economic Council of the NSDAP led, however, to a falling off of financial support for the NSDAP. Both Hjalmar Schacht (q.v.) and Walther Funk (q.v.) – future Ministers of Economic Affairs in the Third Reich – warned Hitler against Feder's social credit schemes which would ruin the German economy. Hitler realized that only by abandoning Feder's aggressive anti-capitalism could he win the support of the big industrialists which was vital to his electoral campaign.

Under the Third Reich, Feder's influence declined drastically and in July 1933 he was given the insignificant post of Under-Secretary in the Ministry of Economic Affairs. Put in charge of settlements policy, he tried to reverse the population imbalance between town and country by settling labourers in semi-peasant villages around decentralized fac-

tories, but the plan was thwarted by a powerful lobby of Junkers, generals and the official farm organization. Dismissed from the Ministry of Economic Affairs in December 1934, Feder ceased to play any role in the politics of the Third Reich and returned to private life. He died in Murnau, Upper Bavaria, on 24 January 1941.

Fischer, Eugen (1874–1967) Professor of Anthropology and the first Nazi Rector of the University of Berlin, Eugen Fischer was born in Karlsruhe on 5 June 1874. In 1921 he co-authored (together with Erwin Baur and Fritz Lenz) one of the standard works of German racialism, *Menschliche Erblehre und Rassenhygiene (Human Hereditary Teaching and Racial Hygiene)*. The pseudo-science of 'racial hygiene', an offshoot of genetics and eugenics, of which Fischer was a leading exponent, exercised a special fascination for the Nazis, providing a kind of zoobiological legitimacy for their crimes. From 1927 until his retirement in 1942 Fischer was Director of the Kaiser Wilhelm Institute for Anthropology, Human Hereditary Teaching and Eugenics in Berlin, one of the centres for the dissemination of the racial hygiene idea. From 1937 a member of the Prussian Academy of Sciences, he was also a regular contributor to the *Archiv für Rassen- und Gesellschaftsbiologie*, the central organ of the German Association for Racial Hygiene. In 1959 he produced a slender volume of gossipy memoirs, *Begegnungen mit Toten (Encounters with the Dead)*, which carefully avoided mention of the millions of innocent people who suffered through the application of the Nazi racial theories he had espoused. In spite of his past activities, Professor Fischer was made an 'honorary member' of the reconstituted post-war German Anthropological Association. He died in Freiburg on 9 July 1967.

Flick, Friedrich (1883–1972) Wealthy industrialist, supporter of the Nazi movement and one of the most prominent employers of slave labour in the Third Reich, Friedrich Flick was born on 10 July 1883 in Ernsdorf, Westphalia. Shortly before World War I he began to work in the iron industry and rose rapidly in the ranks of the Ruhr industrialists until by the early 1930s he had achieved a dominant position in the largest steel-producing firm in Germany, United Steel Works (*Vereinigte Stahlwerke*). In 1932 Flick gave 50,000 Reichsmarks to the Nazi movement as a political insurance premium against the eventuality of their coming to power; but he gave nearly twenty times this sum to the campaign to re-elect President Paul von Hindenburg (q.v.), as well as backing the liberal and Catholic parties. A typical example of the politically amoral capitalist, Flick increased his financial support for the Nazis in 1933, providing seven million marks for Hitler and the NSDAP during the next decade; as a member of the Circle of Friends of Heinrich Himmler (q.v.), he also contributed 100,000 marks annually to the activities of the SS. In 1937 Flick formally joined the NSDAP and a year later was made a *Wehrwirtschaftsführer*. Flick, who was especially skilled in stock-exchange affairs and forming syndicates, was Director or Chairman of the Board of innumerable iron, steel and coal works in the Third Reich. During World War II Flick's enterprises bought and used 48,000 slave labourers, 80 per cent of whom died. Jewish concentration camp inmates were often sent to work in his various munitions plants.

At his trial in Nuremberg in 1947 for complicity in helping Hitler achieve power and extend his conquests, Flick assumed a pose of injured innocence with regard to this and other crimes, asserting that 'nothing will convince us that we are war criminals'. By January 1951 all the German industrialists impris-

oned for war crimes, including Flick who had been sentenced to seven years, had been released as an act of clemency by the American High Commissioner for Germany, John J. McCloy. Though the Flick group lost many of its assets, it was rapidly rebuilt, controlling by 1955 over a hundred companies with a registered capital of more than twenty-two million dollars and an annual business turnover exceeding two billion dollars, including Daimler-Benz, the makers of Mercedes cars. Flick was reported to be the richest man in post-war Germany and the fifth wealthiest individual in the world. Yet he consistently refused to pay any compensation to the slave labourers on whose backs part of his earlier fortune had been built. In 1968 his company *Dynamit Nobel* stated that it had 'neither a legal nor a moral obligation to make payment' for the use of slave labour during World War II and in 1970 his lawyers, replying to an appeal from McCloy, repeated that the Flick group 'categorically refused to fulfil the demands of the Claims Conference' (Conference of Jewish Material Claims against Germany). Flick died in Konstanz on 20 July 1972 at the age of ninety, leaving a fortune of over one billion dollars to his playboy son, with not even a cent for the concentration camp inmates who helped make him rich.

Forster, Albert (1902–54) Reich Governor of the Free State of Danzig, Albert Forster was born on 26 July 1902 in Fürth, where he became a local Nazi Party and SA leader during the late twenties. A bank employee by profession, Forster was made *Gauleiter* of Danzig in October 1930, reorganizing the disrupted Nazi Party in the free city. In the same year he was elected a member of the Reichstag for the electoral district of Franconia, where he had earlier been politically active under *Gauleiter* Julius Streicher (q.v.). He also became head of the shop assistants' group which had been integrated into the German Labour Front. Forster gradually took control of government policy in Danzig Free State, being made Reich Regent there just before World War II, after having directed clandestine and open preparations for its seizure by the Germans. An SS Lieutenant-General, Forster had a black record of atrocities against the Poles, who sentenced him to death in May 1948 after he had been extradited there the previous year to stand trial. The sentence of the Danzig court was subsequently commuted to life imprisonment.

Franck, James (1882–1964) Nobel Prize winner in Physics, James Franck was born in Hamburg on 26 August 1882 and studied chemistry at Heidelberg and Berlin, where he received his doctorate in 1906. Associate Professor of Physics at Berlin (1916–18), he was appointed head of the physics division at the Kaiser Wilhelm Institute, Berlin-Dahlem (1918–20), and from 1920 to 1933 he was Professor and Director of the Physics Institute at Göttingen. In 1926 Franck was awarded the Nobel Prize jointly with Gustave Herz for discovering the laws governing the impact of an electron on the atom. The advent of the Nazis in 1933 forced the Jewish-born Franck to emigrate to the USA, where he became a faculty member at Johns Hopkins and then at the University of Chicago after 1938. He continued to make important investigations in the field of photochemistry and the structure of matter (especially the kinetics of electrons), and designed new methods of experimentally confirming the assumptions on which modern atomic theory rests. During World War II Franck participated in the technical utilization of nuclear energy in the first atomic reactor in the world at Chicago. In the 'Franck report' of June 1945, signed by seven leading scientists, he issued a passionate

warning about the consequences of the atomic bomb being dropped on Japan. He died at the age of eighty-two on 22 May 1964 while visiting Göttingen, which forty years earlier he had helped transform into a 'Mecca of atomic physics'.

Frank, Hans (1900–46) The Nazi Party's leading jurist and Governor-General of Poland during World War II, Hans Frank was born in Karlsruhe on 23 May 1900, the son of a barrister who had been struck off the list for corruption. After a brief spell in the *Freikorps*, Frank joined the *Deutsche Arbeiterpartei* and then in September 1923 became a storm trooper. In November of the same year he participated in the march on the Felderrnhalle. In 1926 he passed the State bar examinations and began to practise as a lawyer in Munich. In the years before 1933 he defended Hitler in several hundred actions, emerging as the star defence counsel of the NSDAP and head of its legal office in 1929. Already Hitler's personal lawyer, Frank was rewarded with a series of high offices following the Nazi seizure of power in 1933. Bavarian Minister of Justice, Reich Leader of the NSDAP (head of the Party law division), Reich Minister of Justice, President of the Academy of German Law as well as the International Chamber of Law, Hans Frank became Reich Minister without Portfolio in 1934.

In spite of these imposing titles, Frank never belonged to Hitler's innermost circle of power, perhaps because of his profession – Hitler detested and despised lawyers – and his middle-class origins. Moreover, the fact that he had raised formal objections at the time of Röhm's (q.v.) murder in 1934 led to a gradual decline in his political influence. Frank's dreams of resurrecting German popular law, his misunderstanding of the relations between Nazi praxis and the Party programme, and his vacillating, insecure personality compounded of romantic idealism and a nihilistic admiration for self-confident brutality prevented him from playing a front-rank role.

Nevertheless, following the conquest of Poland, Frank was appointed Governor-General and made responsible for civil administration in the 'vandal *Gau*' as he called it. Frank treated the Poles as slaves of the Greater German Reich, to be mercilessly subordinated, exploited and wiped out as a national entity. The cream of Poland's intelligentsia were exterminated, the country's art treasures were ransacked for private gain and, while the Poles starved, Frank set up tables in extravagant luxury, ruling his vassal kingdom from the old royal palace in Cracow. 'If I put up a poster for every seven Poles shot,' he boasted to a Nazi newspaper correspondent, 'the forests of Poland would not be sufficient to manufacture the paper for such posters.'

Frank's policy towards Jews was even more brutal. In a notorious speech on 16 December 1941, Frank declared: 'I ask nothing of the Jews except that they should disappear. They will have to go.... We must destroy the Jews wherever we meet them and whenever opportunity offers so that we can maintain the whole structure of the Reich here.... We can't shoot these 3.5 million Jews, and we can't poison them, but we can take steps which, one way or another, will lead to extermination, in conjunction with the large-scale measures under discussion in the Reich.' Subsequently, Frank complained that the extermination policy which he approved in principle divested him of valuable labour-power and he found himself at loggerheads with the SS and police authorities in Poland – especially *SS-Obergruppenführer* Krüger – who were eroding his jurisdiction on all sides. In spite of his own brutal inhumanity, Frank never really grasped the anti-utilitarian aspects

of the Nazi genocide policy nor the nature of the system he loyally served.

In July 1942 following the execution of his friend Dr Carl Lasch (First President of the German Law Academy) on embezzlement charges, Frank in a lecture tour of German universities called for a return to constitutional rule. Within a month he was stripped of all his Party honours and legal offices, being replaced as *Reichskommissar* of Justice by Otto Thierack (q.v.) though he remained as Governor-General of Poland, a post that Hitler regarded as the most unpleasant he could give anyone. After the fall of the Third Reich, the 'slayer of Poles' and exterminator of Jews was brought to trial at Nuremberg, abjectly confessing his guilt, pleading contrition and declaring that '... a thousand years will pass and the guilt of Germany will not be erased'. By this time Frank had become reconciled to the Catholic church and even attacked Hitler as a betrayer of millions of Germans. He was executed as a war criminal in Nuremberg prison on 16 October 1946.

Frank, Karl-Hermann (1898–1946) Fanatical Sudeten German *Freikorps* leader who became Minister of State and virtual ruler of the Czech 'Protectorate', Karl-Hermann Frank was born on 24 January 1898 in Karlsbad. After serving the last years of World War I in the Austrian army and having failed in his bookselling business in Karlsbad, Frank joined the Sudeten German Nazi Party, becoming a member of the Czech Parliament in 1937. Second-in-command to Konrad Henlein (q.v.) in the Sudeten German Party, Frank was appointed deputy *Gauleiter* of the NSDAP in the Sudetenland on 30 October 1938. Following the Nazi occupation of Prague in March 1939, Frank became chief of police, with the title of Secretary of State to the Protectorate, and was given the rank of *SS-Gruppenführer*. The right-hand man of Neurath (q.v.), Daluege (q.v.) and Heydrich (q.v.) (whom he eventually succeeded as *Reichsprotektor*), he was described by none other than Adolf Eichmann (q.v.) as a Jew-hater of the 'Streicher kind' and distinguished himself by exceptional ferocity in the execution of his duties. From 20 August 1943 until the end of the war he was Minister of State with the rank of Reich Minister for Bohemia and Moravia. After extradition by the Americans, he was sentenced to death by a Czech court and publicly executed in Prague before 5,000 spectators on 22 May 1946.

Frank, Walter (1905–45) The self-appointed custodian of German historiography during the Third Reich, Walter Frank was born in Fürth, Bavaria, on 12 February 1905. The son of an army official, he grew up in a Protestant, nationalist atmosphere at home and in his youth became an ardent adherent of Nazi ideology and a convinced anti-semite. Frank studied at the University of Munich under Professor Alexander von Müller, the pro-Nazi President of the Bavarian Academy of Sciences, and graduated in 1927 with a dissertation on the nineteenth-century German anti-semitic agitator, Adolf Stoecker. In 1928 his monograph was published under the title *Hofprediger Adolf Stoecker und die Christlich-Soziale Bewegung*. A revised second edition appeared seven years later, better adapted to Nazi requirements. In 1933 Frank published his study *Nationalismus und Demokratie im Frankreich der Dritten Republik*, which was notable for its efforts to unmask the nefarious role of the 'international Jew' in the French Republic. An old Party member, Frank became increasingly prominent under the Third Reich in organizing and integrating anti-Jewish scholarship in Germany.

A dynamic, ambitious personality and a powerful speaker, on 1 April 1936 he was appointed President of the newly founded *Reichsinstitut für Geschichte des Neuen Deutschland* (Reich Institute for the History of the New Germany), which gave him the pivotal position from which to influence German historiography in the Nazi spirit. In the spring of 1936 the *Forschungsabteilung Judenfrage* (Research Department for the Jewish Question) was created within the *Reichsinstitut*, and Frank, who was its Director, thus defined its purpose: 'In German politics, Israel's kingdom terminated in the spring of 1933. In German scholarship, however, Israel through its governors reigned longer.... We don't want dictatorship but we want the leadership in the scientific life of our nation.... In this process of an army-formation the *Reichsinstitut* ... is the first army corps....' Frank himself edited the nine-volume *Forschungen zur Judenfrage* (1937–44), which was perhaps the most notorious product of his Institute. However, by the spring of 1941 his influence began to decline with the flight of his protector Rudolf Hess (q.v.) to England and the establishment of a rival anti-Jewish institute sponsored by Alfred Rosenberg (q.v.) who rapidly outdistanced him. Frank committed suicide on 9 May 1945 at Gross Brunsrode, near Braunschweig.

Freisler, Roland (1893–1945) President of the Berlin People's Court (*Volksgericht*) and known as the 'hanging judge' for his ruthless and fanatical application of Nazi law, Roland Freisler was born on 30 October 1893 in Celle, the son of an old Hessian peasant family. During his military service in World War I, Freisler was captured by the Russians and imprisoned in Siberia for several years. He learned to speak Russian fluently, became a Bolshevik Commissar and for a time a convinced communist – Hitler could never overcome his aversion to this aspect of Freisler's past – until he escaped in 1920 and returned to Germany. After studying law at Jena, Freisler began to practise as a lawyer in Kassel in 1923, joining the Nazi Party a year later. In 1932 he was elected as a Nazi delegate to the Prussian legislature and a year later to the Reichstag as a member for the district of Hessen-Nassau. In 1933 Freisler was also made head of the personnel department in the Prussian Ministry of Justice. From 1934 to 1942 he was a State Secretary in the Ministry in charge of combating sabotage. A leading Nazi writer on the question of reforming the criminal law, Freisler was also a member of the German Law Academy, a Prussian State Councillor and held the rank of *SA-Brigadeführer*. As State Secretary in the Reich Ministry of Justice he participated in the Wannsee Conference of 20 January 1942, which discussed the 'Final Solution' of the Jewish problem in Europe.

In August 1942 he succeeded Thierack (q.v.) as President of the *Volksgericht*, a tribunal designed to provide speedy justice in cases of treason, defined broadly as any form of opposition to the ideology of the Third Reich. As the 'People's Judge', Freisler proved himself a true sadist in legal robes, heaping vulgar abuse on prisoners before sending them to execution and fully justifying his reputation as the German Vyshinsky. The exceptional brutality and sarcasm, the vile taunts which he inflicted on the German generals, officers and other leaders implicated in the July plot of 1944 were actually recorded on soundtrack as part of a film made of the first of the bomb-plot trials: they showed Freisler to be an able pupil of the Soviet techniques used in the late 1930s against the Old Bolsheviks. Freisler was killed by an Allied bomb in the cellar of the People's Court on 3 February 1945 while presiding over another treason trial.

Frick, Wilhelm (1877–1946) Reich Minister of the Interior from 1933 to 1943 and one of Hitler's closest advisers

during the *Kampfzeit*, Wilhelm Frick was born on 12 March 1877 in Alsenz, in the Palatinate, the son of a Protestant schoolmaster. From 1896 to 1901 Frick studied law at Göttingen, Munich, Berlin and Heidelberg, where he received his doctorate. From 1904 to 1924 Frick worked in the Munich police as a government official, heading the political police section after 1919. Frick did not serve at the front during World War I, but was an early sympathizer of the NSDAP and Hitler's liaison man at Munich police headquarters in the early 1920s. Among his 'services' to right-wing circles in this period was help to the 'Feme' murderers (*Freikorps* members) to escape capture. After his participation in the Munich Beer-Hall *putsch*, Frick was arrested and sentenced to fifteen months' imprisonment (suspended in 1924), but was nonetheless allowed to continue as head of the criminal section of the Munich police. In 1924 Frick was elected as one of the first National Socialist deputies to the Reichstag and one year later was appointed head of its parliamentary faction.

On 23 January 1930 Frick became the first National Socialist Minister in a provincial government, responsible for education and the Ministry of the Interior in Thuringia. His actions in this post, which he held until 1 April 1931, gave an early foretaste of what the Nazi seizure of power would mean for the rest of Germany. The police force was purged of officers with republican sympathies, Nazi candidates for office were illegally favoured, a special chair was created for the doyen of Nazi racists, Hans Günther (q.v.), at the University of Jena, the anti-war film *All Quiet on the Western Front* was banned, along with jazz music, and rabid militaristic, anti-semitic propaganda was allowed to flourish unchecked. Special German freedom prayers were instituted at Thuringian schools on Frick's instructions, which glorified the German *Volk*, its national honour and military power, while denouncing 'traitors' and 'destroyers'. When the Nazis came to power in January 1933 Frick was appointed Minister of the Interior, a key position which he held until August 1943, and he was directly responsible for measures taken against Jews, communists, Social Democrats, dissident churchmen and other opponents of the régime. His training as a jurist enabled him to cover Nazi crimes with a veil of pseudo-legalistic verbiage as he drafted and signed laws abolishing political parties, independent trade union organizations and all provincial legislatures, as well as sending some 100,000 opponents of the régime to concentration camps by 1935.

He was responsible for drafting and administering the laws that gradually eliminated the Jews from the German economy and public life, culminating in the Nuremberg race laws that reduced them to second-class citizenship in the Reich. It was Frick who framed the extraordinary law that declared all Hitler's actions during the Blood Purge of the SA in June 1934 to be legal and statesmanlike. It was quickly passed by the puppet Reichstag in the spirit of Frick's dictum that 'Right is what benefits the German people, wrong is whatever harms them'. Although nominally Himmler's (q.v.) superior, Frick singularly failed to impose any legal limitations on the power of the Gestapo and the SS, never seriously interfering with their encroachments on his area of jurisdiction. As Minister of the Interior he failed to lift a finger to protect German Jewry from the atrocities inflicted during the Crystal Night pogrom of 9 November 1938. By this time Frick's importance had declined, since he had already fulfilled his main function of helping Hitler to consolidate his power legally, thus paving the way for the establishment of a totalitarian police state.

As Germany became fully militarized during World War II, Frick's power was further reduced. On 24 August 1943 he was appointed *Reichsprotektor* of Bohemia and Moravia, a position he held until the end of the war, though real authority was concentrated in the hands of his nominal subordinate, Karl-Hermann Frank (q.v.). At the Nuremberg trial, Frick (who refused to testify) was charged and found guilty of crimes against peace, war crimes and crimes against humanity committed in concentration camps in the Protectorate. The dedicated Nazi bureaucrat and loyal implementer of Hitler's ruthless aims was hanged at Nuremberg on 16 October 1946.

Friedeburg, Hans George von (1895–1945) The last Supreme Commander of the German Navy who negotiated its unconditional surrender at Rheims in May 1945, Hans George von Friedeburg was born in Strasbourg on 15 July 1895. He joined the Imperial navy during World War I serving as a cadet, and after promotion to Naval Lieutenant in 1916 he was transferred to U-boat service a year later. In 1933 Friedeburg was promoted to Lieutenant-Commander and Adjutant to the Reich War Ministry. In the same year he introduced Heinrich Himmler (q.v.) to the High Command circle and the head of the Army Administration section, Walter von Reichenau (q.v.). The following year, the young Naval Captain was himself promoted to the High Command through Himmler's influence. At the end of World War II, Friedeburg, who had meanwhile risen to the rank of Admiral, was given supreme command of the German navy. He exercised this function for eight days – from 1 to 9 May 1945 – before co-signing the official German capitulation to Soviet forces in Berlin. On 23 May 1945 he committed suicide in Mürwik.

Fritsch, Werner Freiherr von (1880–1939) Chief of the High Command of the German Army from 1934 to 1938 and an opponent of Hitler's war programme, Werner von Fritsch was born in Benrath, near Düsseldorf, on 4 August 1880. The son of a First Lieutenant in the XI Prussian Hussars' Regiment in Düsseldorf, the aristocratic von Fritsch was a professional soldier of the old Prussian school, gifted, unbending and ascetic in his life-style. He entered the War Academy in 1901 and ten years later was appointed to the General Staff. After service in World War I, he was promoted to Lieutenant-Colonel in 1922 and in 1926 headed a department in the Reichswehr Ministry. Promoted to Major General and given command of a cavalry division in 1930, von Fritsch's single-minded dedication to his army career made him a popular figure in the General Staff. Made Commander of Military District III (Berlin) in 1932, he was promoted to Lieutenant-General. A friend of President von Hindenburg (q.v.), the traditionalist General was the latter's nomination as Chief of the High Command of the German Army in February 1934. On 2 May 1935 von Fritsch was promoted to Commander-in-Chief of the Wehrmacht and participated actively in its reconstruction and rearmament.

Though he never disguised his hostility and contempt for the Nazi Party and the SS, von Fritsch kept his distaste to himself, remarking in May 1937: 'I have made it a guiding principle to confine myself to the military domain and to keep aloof from all political activity. I lack all talent for it.' The prototype of the 'unpolitical soldier', von Fritsch was nonetheless alarmed when Hitler revealed his plans to use armed force against Austria and Czechoslovakia at the Hossbach Conference of 5 November 1937. Von Fritsch realized that this aggressive programme would mean a European war and tried to dissuade Hitler on the grounds that Germany was not militarily prepared for such an enterprise. At the beginning of 1938 von

Fritsch became the victim of a complicated intrigue engineered by Himmler (q.v.), who saw in him an obstacle to his plans for expanding the role of the SS, and Goering (q.v.), who coveted his position as Commander-in-Chief of the army. With the help of Heydrich's (q.v.) Security Services, fake charges of homosexuality were concocted against von Fritsch who was a bachelor, seemingly uninterested in women. It was alleged that he had been paying blackmail to an ex-convict since 1935 to cover up homosexual offences, a charge he categorically denied when confronted with it by Hitler in an interview in the Chancellery library on 24 January 1938. At this interview (where Goering and Himmler were also present) a notorious male prostitute and blackmailer named Hans Schmidt was produced, whose false testimony convinced Hitler that the charges were true. On 4 February 1938 Hitler announced that von Fritsch – and his colleague Werner von Blomberg (q.v.) – had resigned 'for reasons of health', though by this time the Führer knew that the army chief was the victim of a Gestapo frame-up. The Blomberg-Fritsch crisis was too golden an opportunity for Hitler to miss, to rid himself of the last remaining representatives of conservatism in high positions and to gain complete control over the armed forces.

On 18 March 1938 von Fritsch was eventually acquitted by a military court of honour of the charges made against him. Significantly, the dismissed Commander-in-Chief made no real gesture of defiance, beyond challenging Himmler to a duel, and refused to support any attempt by army officers to overthrow Hitler with the fatalistic comment: 'This man is Germany's destiny, and this destiny will run its course to the end.' A letter of 2 December 1938 written by von Fritsch to his friend, Baroness Margot von Schutzbar, suggests an underlying ambivalence in his attitude to Hitler. In the letter, von

Fritsch stated that after World War I he came to the conclusion that for Germany to regain its power it would have to be the victor in three battles: against the working class (already accomplished), against the Catholics and against the Jews – the latter, added von Fritsch, 'is the most difficult'. Recalled to the army in an honorary position, as Colonel-in-Chief of his old regiment (the Twelfth Artillery Regiment), von Fritsch died in strange circumstances during the Polish campaign. On 22 September 1939 near Praga, before Warsaw, he walked into the field of fire of a Polish machine gunner, as if seeking his own death.

Fritzsche, Hans (1900–53) Head of Radio Broadcasting in the Reich Ministry of Propaganda under Joseph Goebbels (q.v.), Hans Fritzsche was born on 21 April 1900 in Bochum, Westphalia, the son of a civil servant. Following war service as a private, Fritzsche studied modern languages, history and philosophy at Greifswald and Berlin, without passing his examinations. In 1923 he joined the German National People's Party and a year later he became editor of the Telegraphen Union news agency controlled by Alfred Hugenberg (q.v.) and of the International News Service, a division of the latter's huge press combine. In 1932 Fritzsche was appointed head of the German radio news service. A conservative nationalist rather than a Nazi, Fritzsche changed his spots when Goebbels chose him to head the news service in the Press Section of the Reich Ministry of Propaganda on 1 May 1933. On the same day Fritzsche joined the NSDAP. As head of the German Press Section, Fritzsche was responsible for the 'co-ordination' of all news outlets in Nazi Germany, regularly instructing German editors on what could be printed, controlling information released to the outside world and ensuring that the official Nazi version of the news was faithfully presented. From 1940 he was Ministerial Director and head of the Home Press Division in Goebbels's Ministry and of the parallel office under Government Press Chief Otto Dietrich (q.v.).

In November 1942 Fritzsche left the Press Section and became head of the Radio Division in the Ministry of Propaganda. Already known as one of the leading political commentators on the German wireless since 1937, Fritzsche had built up a mass audience for his broadcasts by relying on reasoned argument rather than the familiar Nazi-style bombast and demagogy. At the same time he faithfully reflected the basic themes of National Socialist propaganda and helped create the image of Hitler as an irresistible political and military genius who had raised the German nation to the pinnacle of its power and prestige. As *Bevollmächtiger für die Politische Gestaltung des Grossdeutschen Rundfunks* (Plenipotentiary for the Political Supervision of Broadcasting in Greater Germany) after 1942, Fritzsche, like his master, Joseph Goebbels, concentrated on maintaining German morale in the face of growing military setbacks.

At his trial in Nuremberg, Fritzsche was one of the very few Nazis – apart from Albert Speer (q.v.) – who appeared to regret his wartime role and revised his earlier estimate of Hitler and National Socialism. On 1 October 1946 he was acquitted by the Nuremberg court of participation in war crimes. In 1947 a German de-Nazification court re-examined his role in inciting anti-semitism and deceiving the German people about their real situation in the later part of the war. On 29 September 1950 he was released from detention. In his memoirs, *Hier spricht Hans Fritzsche (Hans Fritzsche Speaking)*, first published in Zürich in 1948, the former Nazi radio commentator strenuously protested his innocence of all charges against him. He died in Cologne on 27 September 1953.

Fromm, Friedrich (1888–1945) Chief

of Army Equipment and Commander of the Reserve Army during World War II, Friedrich Fromm was born in Berlin on 8 October 1888. A professional soldier who served in World War I, with the rank of First Lieutenant in 1918, Fromm subsequently joined the Reichswehr. After holding a series of staff posts, he was promoted to Colonel on 1 February 1933 and head of the Army Department in the Reich War Ministry. In September 1939 he was made Chief of Armaments and Commander-in-Chief of the Reserve Army, positions he held until the July plot of 1944. Fromm played an ambiguous role in the conspiracy against Hitler, blowing hot and cold, his vacillation arising out of a weak-minded opportunism and desire to be certain that success was assured, before he committed himself to the Resistance. At the time of the bombing attempt on Hitler's life at the Rastenburg field headquarters, Fromm was at the Ministry of War in Berlin. He was lost to the conspiracy from the moment that he accidentally learned from General Keitel (q.v.) on the telephone that Hitler was still alive. He promptly ordered the arrest of his own Chief of Staff, Colonel Graf von Stauffenberg (q.v.), who had just arrived from Rastenburg, suggesting to his partner that he shoot himself.

Though Fromm was arrested by the conspirators, they were soon delivered into his hands by loyal officers and after a summary court-martial he had his former associates, including von Stauffenberg and Friedrich Olbricht (q.v.), despatched by a firing squad in the War Ministry yard. This act of savagery, designed to cover up the traces of his own participation in the conspiracy, was then followed by another piece of treachery. Under his eyes General Ludwig Beck (q.v.), military leader of the conspiracy, was persuaded to commit suicide, twice attempting unsuccessfully to blow his brains out, until he was finished off by a sergeant with a

shot in the neck. Fromm's cowardly betrayal was of no avail. The next day he was arrested on the orders of Heinrich Himmler (q.v.), who had already replaced him as head of the Reserve Army and was determined to implicate him in the plot against Hitler. Sentenced to death by the People's Court, Fromm was himself executed by a firing squad on 19 March 1945.

Funk, Walther (1890–1960) Minister of Economic Affairs from 1937 to 1945, Walther Funk was born in Trakehnen, East Prussia, on 18 August 1890. After studying law, economics and philosophy at the Universities of Berlin and Leipzig, Funk became a financial journalist and joined the staff of the conservative Berlin *Börsenzeitung* in 1916. Chief editor of its business section from 1920, he was appointed Editor-in-Chief of the paper in 1922, a lucrative position which he held for the next ten years. An ardent nationalist and anti-Marxist, Funk joined the Nazi Party in the summer of 1931, becoming Hitler's personal economic adviser. Enjoying the confidence of big business, he was a leading contact man between the NSDAP and the big Rhineland industrialists, including Emil Kirdorf (q.v.), Fritz Thyssen (q.v.), Albert Voegler (q.v.) and Friedrich Flick (q.v.), who regarded him as a 'liberal Nazi' and a potential moderating influence. Not only the coal and steel interests, but also the big banks, insurance companies and directors of the giant chemical concern, I. G. Farben, channelled money to the Nazis through Funk. In return, Funk stressed the importance of private initiative and free enterprise to the Führer and, as Chief of the Office for Economic Policy in the Reich Leadership of the Party, guaranteed that the voice of heavy industry would be heard. In January 1933 Funk was appointed Press Chief of the Reich Government and, from 2 March, Secretary of State in Goebbels's (q.v.) Ministry of Propaganda as well as Chairman of the Board of Directors of the Reich Broadcasting Company. Subsequently, Funk was made Vice-President of the Reich Chamber of Culture which he had helped Goebbels to create. In November 1937 he succeeded Hjalmar Schacht (q.v.) as Reich Minister of Economics; a year later he also replaced him as Plenipotentiary for the War Economy and in January 1939 as President of the Reichsbank.

A notorious homosexual and habitual drunkard, the greasy-looking, dwarfish Minister of Economics, though a man of many parts and an important figure in the earlier financial structuring of the Third Reich, proved after 1938 to carry little weight in the upper echelons of the Party. Though a member of the Ministerial Council for Reich Defence and after September 1943 of the Central Planning Commission, Funk had no real economic programme of his own and in 1944 most of the important wartime responsibilities of his Ministry were handed over to the more efficient Albert Speer (q.v.).

Indicted at Nuremberg in 1945 along with other Nazi leaders, Funk strongly protested his innocence, claiming that he had only been an official implementing the plans of the top Party leadership, especially those of Goering (q.v.). However, it was established that as President of the Reichsbank, Funk had come to a secret agreement with Himmler (q.v.) that gold, jewels and other valuables taken from murdered Jews were to be deposited in the so-called 'Max Heiliger' account of his bank and credited to the SS. Funk knew that these enormous deposits of currency and valuables originated from the extermination camps. Found guilty of war crimes, crimes against peace and crimes against humanity, Funk was sentenced to life imprisonment by the Nuremberg Tribunal on 1 October 1946. Released from Spandau prison in 1957 for health reasons, Funk died in Düsseldorf on 31 May 1960.

Furtwängler, Wilhelm (1866–1954) One of the finest conductors of the twentieth century, Wilhelm Furtwängler was born in Berlin on 26 January 1886. After studying in Munich, Furtwängler became Director of Opera at Mannheim in 1915, subsequently succeeding Richard Strauss (q.v.) as conductor of the Berlin opera concerts. In 1922 he was appointed Director of the Berlin Philharmonic, a position he held until the end of World War II. He also led the Vienna Philharmonic from 1927 to 1930. A traditional conservative who disliked the modernism of Schoenberg and was one of the great exponents of romantic music, Furtwängler chose to remain in Nazi Germany, along with most of the outstanding figures of the German music world.

The leading conductor at the Berlin State Opera from the autumn of 1933 to December 1934, Furtwängler was for a time out of favour with Hitler because of his spirited defence of the composer Paul Hindemith (q.v.), denounced by official Nazi propaganda as a musical 'degenerate'. Nevertheless, he arrived at a mutually beneficial accommodation with the Nazis, who used the conductor's international reputation as an advertisement for their cultural policy. The magnificent symphony music and opera performances of the Berlin Philharmonic Orchestra and the Berlin State Opera under his direction helped to obscure the degradation of the other arts under the Third Reich. Appointed a Prussian State Councillor and in 1936 Director of the Bayreuth Festival, Furtwängler's activity during the remaining years of the Third Reich was the subject of much criticism abroad. Cleared by a German de-Nazification court in 1946, Furtwängler was reappointed four years later as Director of the Berlin Philharmonic, a position he held until his death in Baden-Baden on 30 November 1954.

G

Galen, Clemens August Graf von (1878–1946) Cardinal Archbishop of Münster and one of Hitler's most determined opponents, Clemens von Galen was born in Dinklage on 16 March 1878. He began his career as a bishop's chaplain in Münster in 1904. After a period as a priest in Berlin, von Galen became Pastor of St Lambert Church in Münster in 1929 and in 1933 he was appointed Archbishop. When the Nazis came to power, Cardinal von Galen took the oath of allegiance to the régime and opposed church interference in politics. Resentful of the Versailles Treaty, he thanked and blessed the Führer when German troops re-entered the demilitarized Rhineland in 1936. At the beginning of World War II, the Cardinal also adopted a patriotic stance, exhorting his congregation to defend the Fatherland, while at the same time warning against feelings of vindictiveness, the killing of hostages and unarmed prisoners of war.

Von Galen's opposition to the régime had nonetheless been growing steadily since 1933 and he did not disguise his contempt for Nazi propaganda against the Catholic church. He was firmly opposed to National Socialist race doctrines and openly criticized government practices which he regarded as contrary to Christian teaching. In 1934 he issued a closely reasoned refutation of Alfred Rosenberg's (q.v.) calumny of Christianity in his notorious *Myth of the Twentieth Century*. Von Galen's answer appeared as a pamphlet and as a supplement to his diocesan gazette in Cologne and Münster, thereby reaching hundreds of thousands of Catholics. In 1941 in a series of sermons he preached against the police State and the unlawful 'destruction of worthless life', earning the nickname of the 'Lion of Münster' for his courageous defiance. In a blistering sermon on 3 August 1941 in Münster Cathedral, Cardinal von Galen called the euthanasia programme 'plain murder', telling his congregation that he was suing those responsible for this criminal act under Paragraph 211 of the Penal Code.

Von Galen's sermons were the most effective, single episcopal protest against the régime and they shook the Nazi leadership sufficiently to persuade Hitler to suspend and give up the euthanasia measures. Though Himmler (q.v.) demanded his arrest and Martin Bormann (q.v.) called for his execution, Goebbels (q.v.) urged moderation, warning that the Archbishop's arrest would mean 'writing off Münster and the whole of Westphalia for the duration of the war'. Hitler himself, who wanted to avoid a confrontation with the Catholic church, swore to exact retribution from von Galen but only after the end of the war. The result was that the Cardinal continued to exercise his functions, though he was confined to Münster and the Gestapo kept track of his activities. Finally arrested after the assassination attempt of 20 July 1944, the Cardinal survived the end of the war in Sachsenhausen concentration camp. He died in Münster on 22 March 1946.

Galland, Adolf (1912–94) Famous German fighter ace and Commander-in-Chief of the Luftwaffe Fighter Arm from

1941 to 1945, Adolf Galland was born in Westerholt, Recklinghausen, in 1912, the son of a well-to-do estate bailiff of French descent. An adept glider pilot before he was twenty, Galland joined the Lufthansa civilian airline in 1932. Between 1937 and 1938 he took an active part in the Spanish Civil War, flying three hundred missions with the Condor Legion and developing novel techniques of close support. During the German invasion of Poland, Galland had a staff post but returned to a Fighter Group in April 1940, serving in France and then leading German formations during the Battle of Britain. Over the skies of England they had to face RAF fighter squadrons directed by radar, which came as a surprise 'and a very bitter one'. Galland, who never made the mistake of underestimating his opponents, nonetheless survived and was credited during World War II with more than a hundred aircraft destroyed. He was the second Luftwaffe pilot to be awarded the Knight's Cross with Oak Leaves, Swords and Diamonds.

After the death of Werner Moelders in November 1941 Galland succeeded him as Commander of the Fighter Arm of the Luftwaffe. A year later he was promoted to Major General, becoming at the age of only thirty the youngest general in the German armed forces. During the next two years, though handicapped by shortages of every kind, Galland took all available opportunities to improve technical and tactical knowhow and managed to inspire his pilots with his own devotion to duty and to their concerns. Nevertheless, he was blamed for the gradual collapse of the Fighter Arm under the Allied aerial onslaught, falling out with both Hitler and Goering (q.v.) who blindly refused to accept the realities of Germany's situation. Galland was relieved of his command in January 1945, but allowed by Hitler to return to combat duty. He was made head of the new *Jagdverband* 44,

flying the highly sophisticated jet-powered Me 262 fighters with other dismissed officers. The new jets, however, had come off the production lines too late and in too few numbers to alter the course of the war. After the war, Galland spent six years in Argentina as technical adviser to the air force. In his memoirs *Die Ersten und die Letzten, Jagdflieger im zweiten Weltkrieg* (1953) Galland claimed that future group commanders of the German air force had been needlessly sacrificed during the Battle of Britain, due to the mistaken strategy of the Luftwaffe. Following his return in 1954 from Peron's Argentina, Galland worked as an industrial consultant in Düsseldorf and for a time was even considered a likely candidate as chief of the new West German air force.

George, Heinrich (1893–1946) One of the great film stars of the Weimar period who became a strong supporter of the Nazis, Heinrich George was born on 9 October 1893 in Stettin, the son of a civil servant. He started his career as an actor at Kolberg before World War I and made his film début in Robert Wiene's *Der Andere* (1913), but only took off as a star of stage and screen after 1925. In 1926 he appeared in Fritz Lang's *Metropolis*, in 1929 in Richard Oswald's *Dreyfus* and in 1931 he was the male star of *Berlin Alexanderplatz*. An actor-manager of real talent, George was known to have had communist leanings, which probably explains why after his 'conversion' of 1933 he threw himself with such fervour and enthusiasm into official Nazi art. Beginning with his role in *Hitlerjunge Quex* (1933) and in productions like Ucicky's *Das Mädchen Johanna* (1935), Carl Froelich's *Heimat* (1938) and Herbert Maisch's *Friedrich Schiller* (1940), George appeared in and produced many films, achieving an outstanding international success. Even more important was his theatrical career under the Third

Reich. Named Director of the Schiller Theatre in Berlin, he excelled in productions of the classics such as Goethe's *Goetz von Berlichingen*, or the plays of Schiller, Kleist, Shakespeare and Calderon. He also starred in Hans Steinhoff's (q.v.) adaptation of Ibsen's drama, *An Enemy of the People* (*Ein Volksfeind*), brought to the screen in 1937. George was not only willing to accept honours and titles from the régime but also to propagandize on its behalf, even appearing in such a virulently anti-semitic film as Veit Harlan's (q.v.) *Jud Süss* (1940) in the role of the Duke of Württemberg. George's last film, *Kolberg* (1944), also with Harlan, glorified the city where he had once made his acting début, and it was here that he was arrested by Russian troops. He died in Soviet custody in the camp of Sachsenhausen near Berlin on 26 September 1946.

Gerstein, Kurt (1905–45) SS Lieutenant who was head of the Waffen-SS Institute of Hygiene in Berlin and did his best secretly to spread the facts of the 'Final Solution' to a world that did not want to listen, Kurt Gerstein was born in Münster on 11 August 1905. By profession an engineer and mining assessor and from 1925 a member of a Protestant youth movement, Gerstein joined the NSDAP in May 1933 but continued to be an active member of Pastor Niemöller's (q.v.) Confessional church with close links to the Christian anti-Nazi Resistance. In 1936 he was arrested by the Gestapo for distributing religious tracts and expelled from the Nazi Party. After a second spell in a concentration camp in 1938, Gerstein managed in 1941 to join the Health Department of the SS, where few questions were asked about his past. His initial motive was to find out the truth about the murder of mental patients in the euthanasia institutes such as Grafeneck and Hadamar. In January 1942 Gerstein was put in charge of the Technical Disinfection Department within the section for 'Health Technique' and was responsible for handling 'poisonous disinfectant gases'. In the late summer of 1942 he was sent on a mission by the SS Health Department to persuade Globocnik (q.v.) and Christian Wirth (q.v.) to introduce 'Zyklon B' gassing into Polish death camps, in place of gas engines.

In August 1942 he visited Belzec death camp (in the Lublin district) and witnessed the breakdown of the diesel motor that delivered the gas used in the mass extermination of Jews and other 'undesirables'. Gerstein's eye-witness report, left behind in a prison confession made in 1945, contains a uniquely detailed description of the death camps as seen through the eyes of a German official. According to his own account, Gerstein's activity as a 'Zyklon B' demonstrator 'was from the first an agent's activity on behalf of the Confessional Church'. He had 'but one desire', namely 'to gain an insight into this whole machinery and then to shout it to the whole world'. Returning from his inspection tour of Belzec in late August 1942, Gerstein recounted what he had witnessed to a chance companion travelling on the same Warsaw–Berlin express, the Swedish diplomat, Baron von Otter. Gerstein requested that the diplomat 'report at once to his government and the Allies, as every day was bound to cost the lives of thousands and tens of thousands of people'. (The Swedish government though made fully aware of the technical procedures of killing and other details never passed on the information.) Gerstein also urged friends in the Dutch underground to broadcast his information by radio to Great Britain but, though the British Foreign Office knew it to be correct, the news was rejected by British officials as atrocity propaganda. Gerstein also tried to report to the Papal envoy in Berlin, but the latter, most reluctant to offend the Nazis, showed him the door. All his efforts to inform his church friends and opinion abroad proved futile as did his premise that, if the facts became known, the liquidations would be stopped. Even the Protestant Bishop of Berlin, Otto Dibelius (q.v.), a member of the church Resistance to whom Gerstein recounted in detail the extermination of Jews at Belzec, proved unable to act. Overwhelmed by a sense of personal responsibility and guilt, the despairing Gerstein committed suicide in a French prison on 17 July 1945.

Gisevius, Hans Bernd (1904–74) German Vice-Consul in Zürich during World War II and a liaison man between the US Office of Strategic Services (OSS) and the peace camp within the *Abwehr*, Hans Bernd Gisevius was born in Arnsberg on 14 July 1904. At the outset of the Nazi régime, he joined the Gestapo though he had previously been a staunch conservative, a follower of von Hindenburg (q.v.) and a member of the *Stahlhelm*. During the four months he spent as a Gestapo official, Gisevius contributed to bringing down its first chief, Rudolf Diels (q.v.). Subsequently transferred to the Police Department in the Prussian Ministry of the Interior, Gisevius was involved in a number of conspiracies against Hitler which came to nothing. During the war he entered the *Abwehr*, working for it from his base in Switzerland as German Vice-Consul. He was a frequent visitor to Allen Dulles, Chief of the US Office of Strategic Services, passing on messages from General Beck (q.v.) and Goerdeler (q.v) and keeping him posted on the activities of the German Resistance. Gisevius survived an investigation by the Gestapo and escaped back to Switzerland, after the abortive July plot of 1944. He returned to Germany in 1945 as a privileged prosecution witness at the Nuremberg trials, testifying against Goering (q.v.) and on behalf of Schacht (q.v.) and Wilhelm Frick (q.v.). His two-

volume memoirs, *Bis zum Bitteren Ende*, were published in 1946 (Engl. trs. *To the Bitter End*, 1947) and described in exciting detail the activities of the German Resistance as well as giving a close-up view of leading Nazi personalities. While strongly condemning the ruthless terror and immorality of the Hitler régime, Gisevius also pointed to the silent acquiescence of millions of Germans who 'played at hide-and-seek with themselves', feigning ignorance of the police State and never taking the trouble to seek further information about the fate of its victims. After the war, Gisevius spent some years in the United States and West Berlin, before eventually settling in Switzerland. He died in West Germany on 23 February 1974.

Globke, Hans (1898–1973) Civil servant in the Reich Ministry of the Interior who co-authored an official commentary on the Nuremberg racial laws of 1935 and provided the legal basis for further anti-Jewish legislation, Hans Globke was born in Düsseldorf on 10 September 1898. A loyal servant of the Weimar Republic, Globke became administrative councillor to the Prussian Ministry of the Interior in 1929. Though never a member of the NSDAP, Globke applied his legal skills to consolidating the Nazi hold on power by helping to formulate the emergency legislation that gave Hitler unlimited dictatorial powers. He was also the author of the law concerning the dissolution of the Prussian State Council in 10 July 1933 and of further legislation which 'co-ordinated' all Prussian parliamentary bodies. Together with Wilhelm Stuckart (q.v.), Globke co-authored the *Kommentare zur Deutschen Rassengesetzgebung* (1936), a commentary on the new Reich Citizenship Law based on the community consciousness of 'the racially homogeneous German people, bound by common blood'. The exercise of civil rights in Nazi Germany was henceforth to be founded on *völkisch* concepts of the natural inequality and the 'dissimilarity of races, peoples and human beings'. Since all political rights depended on membership of the *Volk*, the commentary made it clear that 'all persons of alien blood – hence especially Jews – are automatically excluded from attaining Reich citizenship' and therefore from holding any public office. Globke was also the initiator of the idea of compelling all German Jews to adopt the middle names of Israel and Sarah. During the war, Globke was further involved in the elaboration of laws that provided a juridical basis for the persecution of Jews and guidelines for the 'Germanization' of conquered peoples in the occupied territories. His past record did not prevent Globke from prospering in the post-war Federal Republic, where he was appointed State Secretary of the Chancellery and Chief of its Personnel Division in 1953, a position he held for the next ten years. His earlier involvement in the Third Reich made him a prime target of East German propaganda – the communist régime had tried him *in absentia* and given him a life sentence – and on several occasions he offered to resign. He was, however, vigorously defended by the Federal Chancellor of West Germany, Konrad Adenauer (q.v.), who, though himself an impeccable anti-Nazi, chose to believe Globke's claim that he tried to mitigate the legal measures demanded by Hitler. After his retirement from public life in 1963, Globke moved to Switzerland. He died in Bad Godesberg on 13 February 1973 at the age of seventy-five.

Globocnik, Odilo (1904–45) *SS-Obergruppenführer* who was in charge of Operation Reinhard, the plan for the extermination of Polish Jewry during World War II, Odilo Globocnik was born in Trieste on 21 April 1904. The son of an Austrian Croat family of petty officials and a builder by profession, he joined the Nazi Party in Carinthia (Austria) in 1930 and became a 'radical' leader of its factory cells in the province. In 1933 Globocnik entered the SS and was appointed deputy district leader of the NSDAP in Austria. Imprisoned for over a year on account of political offences, Globocnik re-emerged as a key liaison man between Hitler and the Austrian National Socialists. Appointed provincial Nazi chief of Carinthia in 1936, he was promoted to *Gauleiter* of Vienna on 24 May 1938. Dismissed from his position for illegal speculation in foreign exchange on 30 January 1939 and replaced by Josef Bürckel (q.v.), Globocnik was pardoned by Himmler (q.v.) and appointed on 9 November 1939 as SS and Police Leader for the Lublin district in Poland. He was chosen by Himmler as the central figure in Operation Reinhard (named after Reinhard Heydrich, q.v.), no doubt because of his scandalous past record and well-known virulent anti-semitism.

Put in charge of a special company of SS men not subordinate to any higher authority and responsible only to Himmler, Globocnik founded four death camps in Poland – Belzec, Sobibor, Majdanek and Treblinka – and drew rich rewards from the slaughter of nearly three million Jews whose property, down to their spectacles and the gold from their teeth, was seized by the SS. As his situation reports show, Globocnik carried out Himmler's orders with brutal efficiency and by November 1943 Operation Reinhard had been completed and the death camps under his control liquidated. It had consisted of four separate tasks: the extermination of Polish Jewry, the exploitation of manpower, the realization of the immovable property of liquidated Jews and the seizure of hidden valuables and movable property. According to Globocnik's final accounting to Himmler, the overall value of the cash and valuables accruing to the Reich between 1 April and 15 December 1943 from Operation Reinhard came to 180 million Reichsmarks. For helping himself too liberally to some of this plunder, Globocnik was discharged to Trieste together with his SS commando, where he was made Higher SS and Police Leader for the Adriatic region.

At the end of the war, Globocnik succeeded in evading arrest by returning to his native country in the mountains south of Klagenfurt. He was eventually tracked down and, according to some accounts, arrested on 31 May 1945 by a British patrol at Weissensee, Carinthia, committing suicide by swallowing a cyanide capsule a few minutes after being apprehended. According to other versions, Globocnik was hunted down and killed either by partisans or by a Jewish vengeance squad in June 1945.

Gluecks, Richard (1889–1945) SS General and Inspector of Concentration Camps during World War II, Richard Gluecks was born on 22 April 1889. After serving in World War I as an artillery officer, Gluecks became a businessman in Düsseldorf. An early recruit to the NSDAP, he worked after 1936 under Theodor Eicke (q.v.), the first Inspector of Concentration Camps. Rising to the rank of *SS-Brigadeführer* and in charge of Eicke's staff at Oranienburg – headquarters of the concentration camp inspectorate – Gluecks succeeded his former boss shortly after the outbreak of World War II. His official title until March 1942 was *Der Reichsführer SS – Inspekteur der Konzentrationslager*. It was Gluecks who in February 1940 chose the site of Auschwitz as a concentration camp for Poles to be confined in 'political detention'; later it was transformed into the foremost extermination centre for European Jewry. One of the shadowiest figures in the 'Final Solution', Gluecks was head of *Amtsgruppe* D in the *SS Wirtschafts-und Verwaltungshauptamt* (SS Economic and Administrative Head Office) under Lieutenant-

General Pohl (q.v.). As head of the concentration camp inspectorate, a subdivision of Pohl's empire, he was the direct superior of Rudolf Hoess (q.v.) and other death camp commandants in occupied Poland. All written and oral extermination orders were transmitted by Heinrich Himmler (q.v.) through Pohl and Gluecks to be passed on to the various concentration camp commanders. Gluecks not only exercised full control over the medical services at Auschwitz and other camps, being responsible for the SS doctors who made the selections for extermination, but he also decided together with Himmler and Pohl how many Jewish deportees should be liquidated and how many spared for hard labour. In November 1943 he was promoted to *SS-Obergruppenführer* and made a Lieutenant-General of the Waffen-SS. At the end of the war Gluecks appeared to have vanished, but it was later claimed that he had committed suicide at Flensburg Naval Hospital on 10 May 1945, where he was undergoing treatment for shock following an Allied bombing raid. It is also possible that he was the victim of a small band of Jewish avengers roaming through Germany at the end of the war who sought to track down and execute mass murderers.

Goebbels, Joseph (1897–1945) Master propagandist of the Nazi régime and dictator of its cultural life for twelve years, Joseph Goebbels was born into a strict Catholic, working-class family from Rheydt, in the Rhineland, on 29 October 1897. He was educated at a Roman Catholic school and went on to study history and literature at the University of Heidelberg under Professor Friedrich Gundolf, a Jewish literary historian renowned as a Goethe scholar and a close disciple of the poet Stefan George. Goebbels had been rejected for military service during World War I because of a crippled foot – the result of contracting polio as a child – and a sense of physical inadequacy tormented him for the rest of his life, reinforced by resentment of the reactions aroused by his diminutive frame, black hair and intellectual background. Bitterly conscious of his deformity and fearful of being regarded as a 'bourgeois intellectual', Goebbels overcompensated for his lack of the physical virtues of the strong, healthy, blond, Nordic type by his ideological rectitude and radicalism once he joined the NSDAP in 1922. The hostility to the intellect of the 'little doctor', his contempt for the human race in general and the Jews in particular, and his complete cynicism were an expression of his own intellectual self-hatred and inferiority complexes, his overwhelming need to destroy everything sacred and ignite the same feelings of rage, despair and hatred in his listeners.

At first Goebbels's hyperactive imagination found an outlet in poetry, drama and a bohemian life-style, but apart from his expressionist novel, *Michael: ein Deutsches Schicksal in Tagebuchblättern* (1926), nothing came of these first literary efforts. It was in the Nazi Party that Goebbels's sharp, clear-sighted intelligence, his oratorical gifts and flair for theatrical effects, his uninhibited opportunism and ideological radicalism blossomed in the service of an insatiable will-to-power. In 1925 he was made business manager of the NSDAP in the Ruhr district and at the end of the year was already the principal collaborator of Gregor Strasser (q.v.), leader of the social-revolutionary North German wing of the Party. Goebbels founded and edited the *Nationalsozialistischen Briefe* (*NS Letters*) and other publications of the Strasser brothers, sharing their proletarian anti-capitalist outlook and call for a radical revaluation of all values. His National Bolshevik tendencies found expression in his evaluation of Soviet Russia (which he regarded as both nationalist and social-ist) as 'Germany's natural ally against the devilish temptations and corruption of the West'.

It was at this time that Goebbels, who had co-authored the draft programme submitted by the Nazi Left at the Hanover Conference of 1926, called for the expulsion of 'petty-bourgeois Adolf Hitler from the National Socialist Party'. Goebbels's shrewd political instinct and his opportunism were demonstrated by his switch to Hitler's side in 1926, which was rewarded by his appointment in November of the same year as Nazi district leader for Berlin-Brandenburg. Placed at the head of a small, conflict-ridden organization, Goebbels rapidly succeeded in taking control and undermining the supremacy of the Strasser brothers in northern Germany and their monopoly of the Party press, founding in 1927 and editing his own weekly newspaper, *Der Angriff* (*The Attack*). He designed posters, published his own propaganda, staged impressive parades, organized his bodyguards to participate in street battles, beer-hall brawls and shooting affrays as a means to further his political agitation. By 1927 the 'Marat of Red Berlin, a nightmare and goblin of history' had already become the most feared demagogue of the capital city, exploiting to the full his deep, powerful voice, rhetorical fervour and unscrupulous appeal to primitive instincts. A tireless, tenacious agitator with the gift of paralysing opponents by a guileful combination of venom, slander and insinuation, Goebbels knew how to mobilize the fears of the unemployed masses as the Great Depression hit Germany, playing on the national psyche with 'ice-cold calculation'. With the skill of a master propagandist he transformed the Berlin student and pimp, Horst Wessel (q.v.), into a Nazi martyr, and provided the slogans, the myths and images, the telling aphorisms which rapidly spread the message of National Socialism.

Hitler was deeply impressed by Goebbels's success in turning the small Berlin section of the Party into a powerful organization in North Germany and in 1929 appointed him Reich Propaganda Leader of the NSDAP. Looking back many years later (24 June 1942), Hitler observed: 'Dr Goebbels was gifted with the two things without which the situation in Berlin could not have been mastered: verbal facility and intellect.... For Dr Goebbels, who had not found much in the way of a political organization when he started, had won Berlin in the truest sense of the word.' Hitler had indeed cause to be grateful to his Propaganda Leader, who was the true creator and organizer of the Führer myth, of the image of the Messiah-redeemer, feeding the theatrical element in the Nazi leader while at the same time inducing the self-surrender of the German masses through skilful stage management and manipulation. A cynic, devoid of genuine inner convictions, Goebbels found his mission in selling Hitler to the German public, in projecting himself as his most faithful shield-bearer and orchestrating a pseudo-religious cult of the Führer as the saviour of Germany from Jews, profiteers and Marxists. As a Reichstag deputy from 1928, he no less cynically gave open voice to his contempt for the Republic, declaring: 'We are entering the Reichstag, in order that we may arm ourselves with the weapons of democracy from its arsenal. We shall become Reichstag deputies in order that the Weimar ideology should itself help us to destroy it.'

Goebbels's deeply rooted contempt for humanity, his urge to sow confusion, hatred and intoxication, his lust for power and his mastery of the techniques of mass persuasion were given full vent in the election campaigns of 1932, when he played a crucial role in bringing Hitler to the centre of the political stage. He was rewarded on 13 March 1933 with the position of Reich Minister for Public Enlightenment and Propaganda, which gave him total control of the communications media – i.e. radio, press, publishing, cinema and the other arts. He achieved the Nazi 'co-ordination' of cultural life very quickly, astutely combining propaganda, bribery and terrorism, 'cleansing' the arts in the name of the *völkisch* ideal, subjecting editors and journalists to State control, eliminating all Jews and political opponents from positions of influence. On 10 May 1933 he staged the great ritual 'burning of the books' in Berlin, where the works of Jewish, Marxist and other 'subversive' authors were publicly burned in huge bonfires.

He became a relentless Jew-baiter, demonizing the stereotyped figure of the 'International Jewish Financier' in London and Washington allied with the 'Jew-Bolsheviks' in Moscow, as the chief enemy of the Third Reich. At the Party Day of Victory in 1933, Goebbels attacked the 'Jewish penetration of the professions' (law, medicine, property, theatre, etc.), claiming that the foreign Jewish boycott of Germany had provoked Nazi 'counter-measures'. Goebbels's hatred of the Jews, like his hatred of the privileged and clever, stemmed from a deep-rooted sense of inferiority and internalization of mob values; at the same time it was also opportunist and tactical, based on the need to create a common enemy, to feed popular resentment and to mobilize the masses.

For five years Goebbels chafed at the leash as the Nazi régime sought to consolidate itself and win international recognition. His opportunity came with the Crystal Night pogrom of 9–10 November 1938, which he orchestrated after kindling the flame with a rabble-rousing speech to Party leaders assembled in the Munich *Altes Rathaus* (Old Town Hall) for the annual celebration of the Beer-Hall *putsch*. Later, Goebbels was one of the chief secret abettors of the 'Final Solution', personally supervising the deportation of Jews from Berlin in 1942 and proposing that Jews along with gypsies should be regarded as 'unconditionally exterminable'. He combined verbal warnings that, as a result of the war, 'the Jews will pay with extermination of their race in Europe and perhaps beyond' with careful avoidance in his propaganda material of discussing the actual treatment of the Jews, i.e. any mention of the extermination camps. Goebbels's anti-semitism was one factor which brought him closer to Hitler, who respected his political judgement as well as his administrative and propagandist skills. His wife Magda and their six children were welcome guests at the Führer's Alpine retreat of Berchtesgaden. In 1938 when Magda tried to divorce him because of his endless love affairs with beautiful actresses, it was Hitler who intervened to straighten out the situation.

During World War II relations between Hitler and Goebbels became more intimate, especially as the war situation deteriorated and the Minister of Propaganda encouraged the German people to ever greater efforts. After the Allies insisted on unconditional surrender, Goebbels turned this to advantage, convincing his audience that there was no choice except victory or destruction. In a famous speech on 18 February 1943 in the Berlin Sportpalast, Goebbels created an atmosphere of wild emotion, winning the agreement of his listeners to mobilization for total war. Playing adroitly on German fears of the 'Asiatic hordes', using his all-pervasive control of press, film and radio to maintain morale, inventing mythical 'secret weapons' and impregnable fortresses in the mountains where the last stand would be made, Goebbels never lost his nerve or his fighting spirit. It was his quick thinking and decisive action on the afternoon of 20 July 1944, when he isolated the conspirators in the War Ministry with the help of detachments of loyal troops,

which saved the Nazi regime. Shortly afterwards he achieved his ambition to be warlord on the domestic front, following his appointment in July 1944 as General Plenipotentiary for Total War.

Given the widest powers to move and direct the civilian population and even to redistribute manpower within the armed forces, Goebbels imposed an austerity programme and pressed for ever greater civilian sacrifice. But with Germany already close to collapse, it was too late to accomplish anything beyond further dislocations and confusion. As the war neared its end, Goebbels, the supreme opportunist, emerged as the Führer's most loyal follower, spending his last days together with his family, in the *Führerbunker* under the Chancellery. Convinced that the Nazis had finally burnt all their bridges and increasingly fascinated by the prospect of a final apocalypse, Goebbels's last words on dismissing his associates were: 'When we depart, let the earth tremble!' Following the Führer's suicide, Goebbels disregarded Hitler's political testament, which had appointed him as Reich Chancellor, and decided to follow suit. He had his six children poisoned with a lethal injection by an SS doctor and then himself and his wife Magda shot by an SS orderly on 1 May 1945. With characteristic pathos and egomania he declared not long before his death: 'We shall go down in history as the greatest statesmen of all time, or as the greatest criminals.'

Goerdeler, Carl (1884–1945) Lord Mayor of Leipzig from 1930 to 1937 and the civilian leader of the German Resistance to Hitler, Carl Goerdeler was born in Schneidemühl on 31 July 1884. After studying law, he became a civil servant, and from 1920 to 1930 he served as second Mayor of Königsberg. A devout Protestant and a monarchist at heart, Goerdeler was appointed Lord Mayor of Leipzig in 1930 and price commissioner under the Brüning cabinet. He continued as an economic adviser to the government in the early years of the Nazi régime, accepting the post of Reich Commissioner of Prices in November 1934, responsible for overseeing prices in areas where supervision had formerly been carried out by various ministries. In 1935 he resigned from this watchdog post in protest against government policies, which rejected his economic liberalism and proposals for local administrative reform. Goerdeler rejected the frenzied rearmament programme of the Nazis as well as their anti-semitism, resigning in 1937 as Mayor of Leipzig when a bust of the Jewish composer Felix Mendelssohn was removed from its place in front of City Hall. In the same year Goerdeler emerged as the leader of the conservative, nationalist Resistance to Hitler, using his position as principal contact man abroad of the Stuttgart firm of Bosch to warn influential people in Britain, France and America against the threat of Nazi Germany.

The headstrong, energetic Goerdeler became the driving-force of civilian Resistance circles by the outbreak of World War II, travelling widely abroad and exploiting his excellent domestic contacts with German officials, diplomats and business leaders. An admirer of the military, he tried hard to arouse the generals against the régime, composing a memorandum in July 1940 intended for the German officer corps, in which he described the desolation of a conquered Europe under Nazi domination. In spite of his great knowledge of home and international affairs, Goerdeler's peace plan of 1943 was surprisingly lacking in realism, envisaging a Greater Germany without Hitler, that still included Austria, the Sudetenland, East and West Prussia, Poznan, Silesia and Alto Adige. Not prepared to give up the bulk of Hitler's territorial gains, Goerdeler thought in terms of a strong, post-war

German national State which would serve as a bulwark against the communist East. He was convinced that the British and Americans could be induced into separate peace negotiations by the offer of German military help against Soviet Russia, and was bitterly disappointed by the Allied policy of unconditional surrender.

Goerdeler's political and social attitudes on the domestic front were also somewhat anachronistic. He wished to preserve a strong executive power, stable authority and a healthy élite within a democratic framework of law, confident that he could win instant allegiance from the German people simply by confronting them with the evidence of Nazi crimes. With regard to the 'Jewish Question', Goerdeler appeared to accept some of the premises of the Nuremberg Laws while seeking to abolish the strictly 'racial' measures. In a letter to Field Marshal von Kluge (q.v.), whom he still hoped to win over to the Resistance in the summer of 1943, Goerdeler argued that 'to continue the war with no chance of victory was an obvious crime'. He regarded both Goebbels (q.v.) and Himmler (q.v.), the latter with somewhat more justification, as potential allies 'since these two men have realized that they are lost with Hitler'.

Goerdeler's mania for drawing up memoranda and lists for a post-Hitler Germany proved his undoing, after the failure of the 20 July 1944 plot. A variety of documents incriminating the man who would have been Chancellor of Germany had the conspiracy succeeded were found by the Gestapo, including the list of members of his future cabinet. Goerdeler's various indiscretions contributed to incriminating other members of the Resistance who figured on his lists. Arrested and sentenced to death by the People's Court on 8 September 1944, Goerdeler was not executed for another five months while Himmler pursued secret peace feelers of his own. He was finally hanged on 2 February 1945 in the Prinz Albrechtstrasse prison.

Goering, Emmy (1893–1973) Second wife of Hitler's heir apparent, Hermann Goering (q.v.) and Nazi Germany's first lady (though she never quite lived up to the role), Emmy Sonnemann was born in Hamburg on 24 March 1893. A statuesque actress of Wagnerian proportions, Emmy Sonnemann performed at the National Theatre in Weimar and in 1934 became a *Staatsschauspielerin* (State actress) in the Berlin State Theatre. Her marriage to Goering on 20 April 1935 was a quasi-royal affair and the birth of her only daughter, Edda, two years later, was also a national event. Since the Führer was unmarried, Frau Goering, as the wife of the second ranking personality of the Third Reich, played a leading role in the social life of the Nazi élite. Both she and her husband were the butt of many popular sex jokes which circulated unofficially among the public. In one of these jokes Emmy Goering wakes up to see her naked husband with his back to her indulging in a bizarre ceremony with his marshal's baton. Challenged by his wife, Goering explains, 'I am promoting my underpants to overpants.' In 1948 Emmy Goering was convicted of being a Nazi and banned from the stage for five years. She died in Munich on 8 June 1973.

Goering, Hermann (1893–1946) Commander-in-Chief of the Luftwaffe, President of the Reichstag, Prime Minister of Prussia and, as Hitler's designated successor, the second man in the Third Reich, Hermann Goering was born in Rosenheim on 12 January 1893. The son of a judge who had been sent by Bismarck to South-West Africa as the first Resident Minister Plenipotentiary, Goering entered the army in 1914 as an Infantry Lieutenant, before being transferred to the air force as a combat pilot. The last Commander in 1918 of the Richthofen Fighter Squadron, Goering distinguished himself as an air ace, credited with shooting down twenty-two Allied aircraft. Awarded the *Pour le Mérite* and the Iron Cross (First Class), he ended the war with the romantic aura of a much decorated pilot and war hero. After World War I he was employed as a showflier and pilot in Denmark and Sweden, where he met his first wife, Baroness Karin von Fock-Kantzow, whom he married in Munich in February 1922. Goering's aristocratic background and his prestige as a war hero made him a prize recruit to the infant Nazi Party and Hitler appointed him to command the SA Brownshirts in December 1922. Nazism offered the swashbuckling Goering the promise of action, adventure, comradeship and an outlet for his unreflective, elemental hunger for power.

In 1923 he took part in the Munich Beer-Hall *putsch*, in which he was seriously wounded and forced to flee from Germany for four years until a general amnesty was declared. He escaped to Austria, Italy and then Sweden, was admitted to a mental hospital and, in September 1925, to an asylum for dangerous inmates, becoming a morphine addict in the course of his extended recovery. Returning to Germany in 1927, he rejoined the NSDAP and was elected as one of its first deputies to the Reichstag a year later. During the next five years Goering played a major part in smoothing Hitler's road to power, using his contacts with conservative circles, big business and army officers to reconcile them to the Nazi Party and orchestrating the electoral triumph of 31 July 1932 which brought him the Presidency of the Reichstag. Following Hitler's appointment as Chancellor on 30 January 1933, Goering was made Prussian Minister of the Interior, Commander-in-Chief of the Prussian Police and Gestapo and Commissioner for Aviation.

As the creator of the secret police,

Goering, together with Himmler (q.v.) and Heydrich (q.v.), set up the early concentration camps for political opponents, showing formidable energy in terrorizing and crushing all resistance. Under the pretext of a threatened communist coup, Prussia was 'cleansed' and hundreds of officers and thousands of ordinary policemen were purged, being replaced from the great reservoir of SA and SS men who took over the policing of Berlin. Goering exploited the Reichstag fire – which many suspected that he had engineered – to implement a series of emergency decrees that destroyed the last remnants of civil rights in Germany, to imprison communists and Social Democrats and ban the left-wing press. He directed operations during the Blood Purge, which eliminated his rival Ernst Röhm (q.v.) and other SA leaders on 30 June 1934. On 1 March 1935 he was appointed Commander-in-Chief of the Air Force and, with Udet (q.v.) and Milch (q.v.), was responsible for organizing the rapid build-up of the aircraft industry and training of pilots. In 1936 his powers were further extended by his appointment as Plenipotentiary for the implementation of the Four Year Plan, which gave him virtually dictatorial controls to direct the German economy. The creation of the state-owned Hermann Goering Works in 1937, a gigantic industrial nexus which employed 700,000 workers and amassed a capital of 400 million marks, enabled him to accumulate a huge fortune.

Goering used his position to indulge in ostentatious luxury, living in a palace in Berlin and building a hunting mansion named after his first wife Karin (she had died of tuberculosis in 1931) where he organized feasts, state hunts, showed off his stolen art treasures and uninhibitedly pursued his extravagant tastes. Changing uniforms and suits five times a day, affecting an archaic Germanic style of hunting dress (replete with green leather jackets, medieval peasant hats and boar spears), flouting his medals and jewellery, Goering's transparent enjoyment of the trappings of power, his debauches and bribe-taking, gradually corrupted his judgement. The 'Iron Knight', a curious mixture of *condottiere* and sybarite, 'the last Renaissance man' as he liked to style himself with characteristic egomania, increasingly confused theatrical effect with real power. Nevertheless, he remained genuinely popular with the German masses who regarded him as manly, honest and more accessible than the Führer, mistaking his extrovert bluster and vitality for human warmth. Goering's cunning, brutality and ambition were displayed in the cabal he engineered against the two leading army Generals, von Fritsch (q.v.) and von Blomberg (q.v.), whom he helped to bring down in February 1938, in the misplaced hope that he would step into their shoes.

Following the Crystal Night pogrom of 9 November 1938, it was Goering who fined the German Jewish community a billion marks and ordered the elimination of Jews from the German economy, the 'Aryanization' of their property and businesses, and their exclusion from schools, resorts, parks, forests, etc. On 12 November 1938 he warned of a 'final reckoning with the Jews' should Germany come into conflict with a foreign power. It was also Goering who instructed Heydrich on 31 July 1941 to 'carry out all preparations with regard to ... a general solution [*Gesamtlösung*] of the Jewish question in those territories of Europe which are under German influence....' Goering identified with Hitler's territorial aspirations, playing a key role in bringing about the *Anschluss* in 1938 and the bludgeoning of the Czechs into submission, though he preferred to dictate a new order in Europe by 'diplomatic' means rather than through a general European war. Appointed Reich Council

Chairman for National Defence on 30 August 1939 and officially designated as Hitler's successor on 1 September, Goering directed the Luftwaffe campaigns against Poland and France, and on 19 June 1940 was promoted to Reich Marshal.

In August 1940 he confidently threw himself into the great offensive against Great Britain, Operation Eagle, convinced that he would drive the RAF from the skies and secure the surrender of the British by means of the Luftwaffe alone. Goering, however, lost control of the Battle of Britain and made a fatal, tactical error when he switched to massive night bombings of London on 7 September 1940 just when British fighter defences were reeling from losses in the air and on the ground. This move saved the RAF sector control stations from destruction and gave the British fighter defences precious time to recover. The failure of the Luftwaffe (which Hitler never forgave) caused the abandonment of Operation Sea Lion, the planned invasion of England, and began the political eclipse of Goering. Further failures of the Luftwaffe on the Russian front and its inability to defend Germany itself from Allied bombing attacks underlined Goering's incompetence as its supreme commander. Technical research was run down completely, not surprisingly with a Commander-in-Chief who prized personal heroism above scientific know-how and whose idea of dignified combat was ramming enemy aircraft.

Goering rapidly sank into lethargy and a world of illusions, expressly forbidding General Galland (q.v.) to report that enemy fighters were accompanying bomber squadrons deeper and deeper into German territory in 1943. By this time Goering had become a bloated shadow of his former self, discredited, isolated and increasingly despised by Hitler who blamed him for Germany's defeats. Undermined by Bormann's (q.v.) intrigues, overtaken in influence by Himmler (q.v.), Goebbels (q.v.) and Speer (q.v.), mentally humiliated by his servile dependence on the Führer, Goering's personality began to disintegrate. When Hitler declared that he would remain in the Berlin bunker to the end, Goering, who had already left for Bavaria, misinterpreted this as an abdication and requested that he be allowed to take over at once; he was ignominiously dismissed from all his posts, expelled from the Party and arrested. Shortly afterwards, on 9 May 1945, Goering was captured by forces of the American Seventh Army and, to his great surprise, put on trial at Nuremberg in 1946.

During his trial Goering, who had slimmed in captivity and had been taken off drugs, defended himself with aggressive vigour and skill, frequently outwitting the prosecuting counsel. With Hitler dead, he stood out among the defendants as the dominating personality, dictating attitudes to other prisoners in the dock and adopting a pose of self-conscious heroism motivated by the belief that he would be immortalized as a German martyr. Nevertheless, Goering failed to convince the judges, who found him guilty on all four counts: of conspiracy to wage war, crimes against peace, war crimes and crimes against humanity. No mitigating circumstances were found and Goering was sentenced to death by hanging. On 15 October 1946, two hours before his execution was due to take place, Goering committed suicide in his Nuremberg cell, taking a capsule of poison that he had succeeded in hiding from his guards during his captivity.

Gottschalk, Joachim (1904–41) One of Germany's most popular young actors, Joachim Gottschalk was born on 10 April 1904, the son of a doctor. Having gradually established a reputation at Leipzig and Frankfurt am Main, Gottschalk was called to Berlin in 1938, appearing in a number of films which earned him wide success. These included Gustav Ucicky's *Aufruhr in Damascus* (1939) and *Ein Leben Lang* (1940) and Liebeneiner's *Du und Ich* (1939). After the outbreak of war, Gottschalk found himself increasingly ostracized because of his Jewish wife, whom he refused to divorce in spite of constant pressure from Nazi officials. In 1941 the Gestapo accused his wife of *Rassenschande* (racial defilement), giving her and her eight-year-old son one day to pack and leave the country. The strain had become intolerable and, after killing their child, the Gottschalk couple committed suicide on 6 November 1941, before Gestapo agents could raid their home. News of the tragic death of the handsome young actor and his family spread quickly through Berlin's artistic quarter, nearly causing a revolt in the film studios.

Greim, Robert Ritter von (1892–1945) Air force General with an excellent record as one of the top Luftwaffe pilots, Robert Ritter von Greim was born in Bayreuth on 22 June 1892, the son of an officer in the Bavarian army. After serving in World War I as a fighter pilot (he was credited with downing twenty-eight Allied planes), von Greim studied law for three years at the University of Munich. From 1924 to 1927 he organized the Canton Military Air Force, and then became the manager of commercial air training centres at Würzburg, Nuremberg and Munich. In 1934 he re-entered the Wehrmacht as a Major and became Commodore of the Richthofen Fighter Group. In 1935 Goering appointed him First Squadron Leader of the newly created Luftwaffe and four years later he was made its Chief of Personnel. In 1940 von Greim helped direct air attacks against Great Britain and between 1941 and 1944 distinguished himself on the eastern front as one of the outstanding Luftwaffe pilots. He received the *Ritterkreuz* (Knight's

Cross) in June 1940, the Oak Leaves to Knight's Cross in April 1943, and Swords in 1944. From 1942 Commanding General of the V *Fliegerkorps* and from February 1943 to 1945 Commander of the air force (*Luftflotte*) on the eastern front, von Greim found himself promoted by Hitler on 23 April 1945 to succeed Goering as the new Commander-in-Chief of the Luftwaffe. Together with Hanna Reitsch (q.v.), the famous woman test-pilot, von Greim was summoned from Munich by Hitler to report to his underground headquarters in the *Führerbunker* in Berlin, especially in order to receive his new assignment and also to be promoted to Field Marshal. During the flight into the burning city on 25 April 1945, von Greim's plane was hit by Russian anti-aircraft shell and he was wounded, but his partner Hanna Reitsch managed to land the plane near the Chancellery. In spite of their entreaties to remain in the bunker, von Greim and Hanna Reitsch were ordered to leave Berlin once the promotion had been made and somehow succeeded in escaping from the exploding nightmare of flames that had enveloped the crumbling capital of the Third Reich. They flew to the headquarters of Admiral Karl Doenitz (q.v.), who had been named by Hitler as his political successor. General von Greim committed suicide in prison at Salzburg on 24 May 1945.

Greiser, Arthur (1897–1946) President of the Danzig Senate and Nazi *Gauleiter* of the Warthegau during World War II, Arthur Greiser was born in Schroda, Posen, on 22 January 1897, the son of a civil servant. During World War I he served as a naval officer, and, after a period in the *Freikorps* and later as an unsuccessful businessman, co-founded the *Stahlhelm*, a veterans' organization in Danzig in 1924. Greiser joined the NSDAP and the SA in 1929 and the following year he entered the SS as one of Himmler's (q.v.) earliest adherents.

From November 1930 Greiser was deputy district leader of the NSDAP in Danzig and leader of the Party faction in the diet. On 20 June 1933 he became Deputy President of the Danzig Senate and on 28 November 1934 he succeeded Hermann Rauschning (q.v.) as President, a post he retained until 1 September 1939. Greiser was then made head of the Civil Administration in Posen and on 21 October 1939 he became *Gauleiter* and Reich Governor of the Warthegau – the Polish western regions annexed to the German Reich, which also included the district of Lodz (Litzmannstadt). From July 1940 Greiser was a member of the Reichstag for the Warthegau electoral district and in 1943 he was promoted to the rank of SS General. As *Gauleiter* for the Warthegau and Lodz, he was in charge of the mass deportation and extermination of Jews and Poles to secure room for Germans from the Baltic States, Volhynia, the Balkans and the Reich proper. As a result of his measures the German population in his region swelled from 325,000 in 1939 to almost 950,000 by the end of 1943. Greiser had a black record of cruelty towards the Polish population, advocating in a letter to Himmler of 1 May 1942 that tubercular Poles be sent for 'special treatment' to Chelmno death camp. Greiser also supervised the anti-Jewish terror which led to the burning of synagogues, the sending of thousands of Jews to forced labour, deportations to Germany, to the *Generalgouvernment* (occupied Poland) and to the extermination camps. Towards the end of the war he fled to the Bavarian Alps, where he eventually surrendered to the Americans. Extradited to Poland and tried by a Polish court, he was sentenced to death and hanged on 20 June 1946 in front of his former palace in Poznan after being paraded around the town in a cage.

Grimm, Hans (1875–1959) German author who gave to the Nazis one of their most potent slogans, *Volk ohne Raum (People without Space)*, the title of his monumental two-volume novel published in 1926 which attracted immediate attention and sold nearly 700,000 copies. Hans Grimm was born in Wiesbaden on 22 March 1875, the son of a former university professor who was also a founding member of the Colonial League (*Kolonialverein*). At the age of twenty he decided to try his own hand at world trade and went to England to learn the export business. Leaving London in 1896 for the Cape Colony, he spent the next fourteen years in South Africa and German South-West Africa, mostly as an independent merchant. This experience decisively moulded his political outlook, his emotional attitudes and his preoccupation with Germany's colonial aspirations. For Grimm, the theme of *lebensraum* was inextricably linked with overseas colonies and was the only panacea for Germany's social problems and political ills. In *Volk ohne Raum*, the political novel which later became obligatory reading in all Nazi schools, Grimm declared: 'The cleanest, most decent, most honest, most efficient and most industrious ... white nation on earth lives within too narrow frontiers.' Grimm, who saw himself as the German Rudyard Kipling (while lacking his universal appeal), had struck a literary goldmine in this largely autobiographical and virulently anti-British account of a German settler's life in British South Africa at the turn of the century. In this classic of 'blood and soil' literature, which was chosen by Hitler's Germany to represent the entire German world of letters at the Chicago World Exhibition of 1936 (no other German work was displayed there), Grimm gave full expression to his obsession with colonial imperialism, with the 'white man's burden' and his love-hate resentment towards England.

Though he never joined the Nazi Party, Grimm's world-view once crystallized showed the same patterns of thought as official Nazi ideology. He agreed with Hitler's élitism and his call for German racial purity, and described National Socialism as 'the second German Reformation', a 'grandiose' attempt at completing Luther's work through a return to true Nordic being. Grimm sought to propagandize this Nazi message abroad in his two speeches, *Amerikanische Rede* (1936) and *Englische Rede* (1938), depicting Germany, England and the USA as the future world triumvirate and apex of the Nordic race, destined to throw back the challenge of *Vermassung* (mass-mindedness) and Bolshevism. Grimm distrusted the revolutionary radicalism in the Nazi movement and was at one time threatened by Goebbels (q.v.) with arrest and committal to a concentration camp (a threat that never materialized), but this did not prevent him after the war from comprehensively whitewashing Adolf Hitler and Nazism.

In answer to a message broadcast to the German people on 29 November 1945 by the Archbishop of Canterbury, Grimm wrote his ultra-nationalist apologia *Die Erzbischofschrift – Antwort eines Deutschen* (Engl. trs. *Answer of a German*) attacking the 'soul-murder' perpetrated against the Germans by the victorious Allies, denouncing the Nuremberg trials, de-Nazification and the concept of collective guilt. He claimed that Nazism in its early years had brought great benefits to Europe; that it had 'saved the awakening German people and along with them the tightly packed Central European masses from the great desertion to communism, and that means from total mass-mindedness'. Moreover Grimm found nothing to reproach Nazism for in the pre-1939 period 'except for the Röhm affair and the night of the Jew-baiting', and he even blamed warmongering Britain for the outbreak of World War II. According to Grimm, British 'anti-Teutonism' was the moral equivalent of German anti-semitism and, since 1895, British policy had been based solely on the slogan *Germania est delenda* (Germany must be destroyed). The British failure to understand National Socialism had been a 'tremendous disaster for Europe'. It was superstitious fear of Germany which had led Britain to wage preventive wars and oppose the 'good European' Adolf Hitler, who only wished to protect the continent against the menace from the East. In his book *Warum – woher, aber wohin?* (1954), Grimm elaborated his earlier assertions, presenting Hitler as a visionary figure, a 'German martyr', a somnambulant seer and as 'the greatest statesman Europe had ever known', whose legacy would determine the fate of future European generations. In a series of speeches in different cities of Schleswig-Holstein, Grimm continued in the early 1950s to display his enthusiasm for National Socialist ideals, until the Federal authorities eventually banned him from addressing public meetings. He died unrepentant at his ancient homestead in Lippoldsberg an der Weser on 27 September 1959.

Groener, Wilhelm (1867–1939) Second-in-command of the German army at the end of World War I and subsequently Minister of Defence in the last years of the Weimar Republic, Wilhelm Groener was born in Ludwigsburg on 22 November 1867. A professional soldier, attached to the General Staff of the Imperial army from 1899, Groener was promoted to Lieutenant-Colonel and placed in charge of war production in 1916. In October 1918 he succeeded General Ludendorff (q.v.) as First Quartermaster-General and on 9 November informed the Emperor Wilhelm II that he no longer commanded the loyalty of his troops and should abdicate, for which he was never forgiven by the German military caste.

Groener also took responsibility for urging the new republican government to accept the Versailles Treaty in the name of the Supreme Command, despite the opposition of many top officers. Already during the war Groener had worked closely with the socialist leader Friedrich Ebert, subsequently making a pact with him in November 1918 pledging the support of the army in consolidating the new government if Bolshevism and anarchy were put down. To this end, Groener authorized the formation of volunteer units of loyal, anti-revolutionary soldiers. Between 1920 and 1923 Groener served as Reich Minister of Communications and in January 1928 he was appointed Minister of Defence, a post he held until May 1932. During 1931–2 he also served as Minister of the Interior and was the strong man of the Brüning cabinet. Groener's loyalty to the Weimar Republic was exceptional among the top Reichswehr generals as was his determined opposition to Nazi infiltration of the armed services.

On 22 January 1930 Groener issued an order of the day in which he warned against Nazi attempts to use the Wehrmacht for the political aims of the Party, urging regular soldiers to stand above politics and to 'serve the State'. His fateful mistake was to make General von Schleicher (q.v.) his right-hand man and entrust him with the army's relations with other ministries and with the political leadership. When Groener took measures to ban the SA in April 1932, von Schleicher began to intrigue against him with the Nazis and to instigate a smear campaign against his chief, accusing him of being under the influence of Marxists and pacifists. Already ill with diabetes, exhausted and sickened by his protégé's betrayal, Groener nonetheless defended his banning of the SA on 10 May 1932, to be met by a torrent of abuse from Nazi deputies, led by Hermann Goering (q.v.). Bitterly disillusioned, Groener resigned three days

later, a serious blow to the disintegrating Republic. He died in Bornstedt on 3 May 1939.

Gross, Nikolaus (1898–1945) Trade union secretary and member of the anti-Nazi Resistance, Nikolaus Gross was born on 30 September 1898 in Niederwenigern (Ruhr). A miner who rose to become a trade union official and editor in 1930 of the *Westdeutschen Arbeiterzeitung* (*West German Workers' Paper*), Gross opposed Nazism from the outset and later sought to organize resistance among Catholic workers in preparation for the July plot of 1944. Arrested on 12 August 1944, he was sentenced to death by the People's Court and eventually executed on 23 January 1945.

Gross, Walter (1904–45) Head of the Nazi Party Office for Racial Policy (*Rassenpolitisches Amt der NSDAP*), Walter Gross was born in Kassel on 21 October 1904. A physician by training, he entered the NSDAP in 1925 and seven years later became a member of the Reich leadership of the National Socialist German Doctors' Alliance in Munich. In 1933 Dr Gross founded and headed the Reich Bureau for Enlightenment on Population Policy and Racial Welfare, which in April 1934 was integrated into the Racial Policy Department of the NSDAP. In September 1942 Gross became head of this department and also head of the Science Division in the Ideology Department (*Amt Rosenberg*). A member of the Reichstag for the electoral district of Oppela from 1936, Gross was one of the most fanatical and influential advocates in the Party of the doctrines of racial purity, which he considered essential for the preservation of German national culture against the 'imperialistic designs of the Jewish people on German soil'. In a lecture at the Institute for the Study of the Jewish Question, Gross observed: 'As far as the historical appearance of the Jew in

Europe is concerned, we believe that the hour of his death has irrevocably arrived.' His zoological anti-semitism found typical expression in his pseudo-scientific work, *Die rassenpolitischen Voraussetzungen zur Lösung der Judenfrage* (1943), written as the Nazi 'Final Solution' was being implemented in Europe.

Grüber, Heinrich (1891–1975) Protestant Dean of Berlin who risked his life to save Jews from Nazi persecution, Heinrich Grüber was born in Stolberg, Rhineland, on 24 June 1891. Of Huguenot stock, he studied theology in Bonn, Berlin and Utrecht before becoming an active social worker and the director of a home for retarded boys. Staunchly opposed to Hitler, he came into contact with Pastor Niemöller (q.v.) and the Confessional Church who entrusted him with setting up an organization, the 'Büro Grüber', at his vicarage in Kaulsdorf, near Berlin, to help save Christians of Jewish descent. The Büro dealt with emigration and employment abroad, care for the aged, welfare and the education of Jewish children. Grüber constantly negotiated with the Nazi authorities, including Eichmann's (q.v.) Gestapo office, on behalf of Jewish organizations and sometimes found secret helpers in the Wehrmacht and different Reich ministries. After the outbreak of war he was frequently harassed by Gestapo threats and in December 1940 he was arrested and sent to Sachsenhausen concentration camp, then transferred to Dachau. He suffered from a heart complaint, had his teeth knocked out and most of his helpers were murdered by the Nazis. Released in 1943 he resumed contact with Evangelical Church clergymen in exile. In 1945 he became Dean of St Mary's Church in Berlin and founded the *Evangelische Hilfsstelle für Ehemals Rassisch Verfolgte* (Evangelical Aid Society for Former Victims of Racial Persecution). From 1949

to 1958 Grüber was the chief representative of the Evangelical Church in East Berlin, resigning his position in protest against anti-Christian smears in the DDR. He was also unpopular in West Germany for his advocacy of nuclear disarmament and his attacks on West German militarism, not to mention his insistence on the collective guilt of the German nation for Nazi crimes. Grüber argued that every German 'who glosses over his past failings is a potential criminal of tomorrow' and denounced the official whitewashing of the German people in the post-war period. He was the only German witness to come to Jerusalem in 1961 to testify in the Eichmann trial to the existence of 'another Germany'. Dean Grüber continued to emphasize the moral obligation of the Germans to the Jewish people and to warn the authorities against minimizing periodic outbursts of neo-Nazi activity in the Federal Republic. His memoirs, *Erinnerungen aus Sieben Jahrzehnten*, were published in 1968. He died of a heart attack seven years later at the age of eighty-four.

Gründgens, Gustaf (1899–1963) One of the most popular actors in Nazi Germany, who achieved success on both stage and screen, Gustaf Gründgens was born in Düsseldorf on 22 December 1899. He began his theatrical career as an actor in Hamburg in the mid-1920s and by the end of the decade had achieved a considerable impact in the Berlin State Theatre. His performance as Mephistopheles in Goethe's *Faust* was the sensation of the 1931–2 season. Subsequently, Gründgens was appointed as Director General of the Prussian State Theatre in October 1934. Gründgens had established himself as a movie actor with his role as the chief gangster in *M*, the first sound film of Fritz Lang. Other early films included *Luise, Königin von Preussen* (1931), *York* (1931) and his appearance as King Charles VII in a monumental film about Joan of Arc, *Das Mädchen Johanna* (1935). Gründgens also gave memorable performances as Professor Higgins in Erich Engel's *Pygmalion* (1935) and as a decadent, dandyish Joseph Chamberlain, replete with monocle and flower in his buttonhole, in the anti-British film, *Ohm Krüger*. Gründgens's earlier communist sympathies did not affect his career in Nazi Germany and he even enjoyed the support of Hermann Goering (q.v.), through whom he was made a Prussian State Councillor in 1936. He continued as *Generalintendant* of the Prussian State Theatre until 1945. Gründgens was married to the famous actress, Marianne Hoppe – his earlier marriage to the daughter of Thomas Mann had been dissolved – and managed to maintain his popularity as a glamorous screen idol throughout and even beyond the Third Reich. He eventually committed suicide in Manila on 7 October 1963. His life inspired the film *Mephisto* (1981), based on a controversial novel by Klaus Mann, son of Thomas Mann (q.v.).

Grynszpan, Hirschel (born 1921) The seventeen-year-old Polish Jew, whose assassination of the legation secretary at the German embassy in Paris on 7 November 1938 was exploited by the Nazis to launch the notorious Crystal Night pogrom, was born in Hanover in 1921. His father Zindel Grynszpan had come to Germany from the East in 1911, ironically enough to escape anti-semitism. His son Hirschel, one of eight children, had left home in 1936 before finishing school and led a rootless existence in Brussels and Paris. Already emotionally disturbed, it appears that he intended to kill the German Ambassador in revenge for the expulsion of some 15,000 Polish Jews, including his own family, who at the end of October 1938 were unceremoniously dumped across the Silesian border at Zbaszyn. This brutal German

action carried out without any warning had reduced the Grynszpan family to complete destitution. On 7 November 1938 Grynszpan bought a revolver, went to the German embassy and shot the first diplomat who admitted him to his office – Ernst von Rath – the embassy Councillor who happened to be a known anti-Nazi, already under surveillance by the Gestapo. Two days later Nazi Germany erupted in the *Reichskristallnacht* (Crystal Night), an orgy of mob violence against German Jewry, skilfully orchestrated by Hitler and incited by the rabble-rousing speeches of Joseph Goebbels (q.v.). German cities were strewn with the broken glass of Jewish shops, engulfed in the smoke of synagogues set on fire, and Jewish houses were destroyed. The assault had been well prepared, for Jews were systematically expropriated and expelled, no less than twenty thousand were transported to concentration camps and a collective payment of a billion marks was imposed on the Jewish community, which was held responsible for the damage which Nazi hooligans inflicted on it! Grynszpan himself was charged with the murder of von Rath, but never tried before World War II. After the outbreak of the war and the collapse of France in June 1940, he was handed over to the Nazis by the Vichy authorities. Goebbels evidently planned a gigantic show trial to be held in May 1942, which would blame Grynszpan and world Jewry for the outbreak of the war between France and Germany. The plans were dropped when rumours and an anonymous letter surfaced which claimed that von Rath had engaged in protracted, homosexual relations with Grynszpan. The mere suggestion of scandal and the change for the worse in Franco-German relations evidently persuaded the Nazis to postpone the trial indefinitely. The fact that he faced criminal proceedings probably saved Grynszpan's life, for instead of being sent to Auschwitz he was kept first in Sachsenhausen and then in Moabit prison in Berlin. In 1957 it was revealed that he was alive and living under a false name in Paris. His father also survived and gave evidence at the Eichmann trial in Jerusalem in 1961.

Guderian, Heinz (1885–1954) German tank General and architect of the successful blitz operations in Poland, France and the Soviet Union during World War II, Heinz Guderian was born in Kulm (Chelmno) on 17 June 1888. After training in the military academy and service in World War I, he joined the Reichswehr in 1919, alternating between regimental and staff duties. Attached to the Third Telegraph Battalion at Koblenz and involved in work with radio, Guderian early on acquired a knowledge of communications techniques which enabled him during World War II to become the first corps Commander to direct battles from a mobile radio communications vehicle at the front. Promoted to Lieutenant-Colonel in 1931 and Chief of Staff of the Inspection of Mechanized Troops, Guderian specialized in developing the armoured corps of the armed forces. The mechanized warfare expert of the Wehrmacht, Guderian was promoted to Brigadier and Chief of Staff to the GOC, Panzer troops in 1934. His advocacy of the type of armoured warfare which subsequently revolutionized modern battle, his recognition that tanks would play a decisive role in the future as the core of a powerful, combined attack force and that other weapons would have to be subordinated to its requirements, was supported by Hitler against the conventional military orthodoxy. Promoted to Major General in 1936 and two years later to Lieutenant-General and acting Commander of the Sixteenth Army Corps, Guderian became Commander-in-Chief of all Panzer troops in 1939.

On the outbreak of war and during the invasion of Poland, Guderian's ideas

on tank warfare – expressed in his book, *Achtung: Panzer!*, published three years earlier – were vindicated when his armoured corps acted as a spearhead in smashing the Polish infantry divisions defending the Danzig corridor. Awarded the Knight's Cross in October 1939 for the success of his blitz operations, Guderian repeated the performance in France as part of Kleist's (q.v.) *Panzergruppe*, smashing through the Ardennes on 10 May 1940 and reaching Sedan three days later with the tank divisions of his Nineteenth Armoured Corps. By 20 May 1940 his tanks had broken through to Abbeville on the coast and three days later they were in Boulogne and Calais. Ordered to halt by Hitler, they were prevented from stopping the escape of the British Expeditionary Force from Dunkirk. Guderian then advanced rapidly to the south-east as far as the Swiss border, again surprising the High Command by the speed of his progress. Awarded the Oak Leaves to Knight's Cross in July 1941, Guderian showed the same drive and mastery of *Blitzkrieg* during the invasion of Russia as he had displayed on the western front, his *Panzergruppe* pushing forward to within two hundred miles of Moscow. Ordered to turn south and link up with Kleist's Panzers in Army Group South, Guderian's forces helped encircle and capture four Soviet armies in September 1941.

Hesitancy at the top and the diversion south stretched the military campaign, however, into the autumn and winter, enabling the Russians to use the respite afforded by the breakdown of the German mechanized assault to raise new armies and replace those which had been captured. Guderian fell out with Field Marshal von Kluge (q.v.) and then with Hitler, who refused to accept his view that German advance positions could not be maintained in winter conditions. He was dismissed in December 1941 and remained inactive until he was recalled as Inspector-General of the armoured forces in February 1943. Following the forced retreats of the autumn/winter 1943, Guderian began to see the military situation as hopeless and canvassed the possibility of removing Hitler from command of the army, without committing himself to the Resistance. Following the failure of the 20 July plot against Hitler, Guderian was promoted to Chief of the General Staff of the OKW (Army High Command) on 21 July 1944. He was then appointed a member of the court of honour which investigated officers implicated in the conspiracy. Together with Keitel (q.v.) and von Rundstedt (q.v.), he was responsible for turning over hundreds of his comrades to the People's Court for execution, after expelling them from the army. He also issued orders warning his General Staff to behave in the future as good Nazis.

Guderian's disagreements with Hitler nonetheless continued as he sought in vain to switch troops to the eastern front to avoid total collapse in the face of the great Soviet offensive which he predicted would come. By early 1945 he was arguing strongly for an immediate armistice with the West. This led to his dismissal on 21 March. He was subsequently captured by the Americans on 10 May 1945. Six years later he published his memoirs, *Erinnerungen eines Soldaten*, which ruthlessly exposed the dilettantism that had led to the defeats of the German armies in Soviet Russia. The most successful German tank commander of World War II, gifted with sure intuition, speed of thought and execution, the ability to create surprise, strategic and tactical understanding, as well as the capacity to inspire his troops, Guderian played a decisive role in the early successes of the Wehrmacht. It was the theories and operational skills of this Panzer pioneer which made the *Blitzkrieg* possible. Though loyal to Hitler and backed by him against the more traditionalist generals, Guderian too finally became a victim of the Führer's increasingly erratic military decisions. He died in Schwangau bei Füssen on 15 May 1954.

Günther, Hans (1891–1968) The leading ideologist of Nazi racialism, Hans Günther was born in Freiburg on 16 February 1891. A social anthropologist, his books beginning with *Kleine Rassenkunde des Deutschen Volkes* (*Short Ethnology of the German People*) were widely distributed in many editions during the Third Reich, continuing the work of earlier racial theorists like Arthur de Gobineau and Houston S. Chamberlain. The *Short Ethnology*, for example, sold more than 270,000 copies between 1929 and 1943 and established new criteria for defining the racial 'ideal type' of the Nordic Aryan based on outward appearance, anthropological measurement of skulls and historical creativity. In 1930 Günther was appointed to the chair of social anthropology at the University of Jena as one of the first acts of the Nazi Minister in Thuringia, Wilhelm Frick (q.v.). Later, Günther became Professor of Racial Science at the University of Freiburg. On his fiftieth birthday in 1941 he was awarded the Goethe Medal and his work was praised by Alfred Rosenberg (q.v.) as of 'the utmost importance for the safeguarding and development of the National Socialist *Weltanschauung*'. Günther recognized that there were no pure races and that not all 'Aryans' were Nordic; equally, he did not regard the Jews as a race but as a *Rassengemisch* (racial mixture) in which the 'physical and spiritual hereditary endowments of non-European peoples are predominant'. In Günther's anthropology, 'the proportion in which the races are mixed' was the decisive factor and his theories were used to justify Nazi legislation aimed at strengthening the German race. Günther depicted the Nordic race as the great creative force in history whose threatened mongrelization would endanger the future of civilization unless its ranks were eugenically purged of all disintegrating influences. Foremost among these 'ferments of disintegration' were the 'non-European' Jews, a mixture of Asiatic and Oriental stock, responsible for such decomposing ideas as liberalism, democracy and socialism. Günther's pseudo-scientific race theories served as a convenient justification for Hitler's central idea, that the Aryan-Germanic races must unite in an apocalyptic struggle for civilization that necessitated the elimination of the Jews from Europe.

After World War II, Günther carried on where he left off as a political publicist and ethnologist, as if the Third Reich and the 'Final Solution' had never occurred. His earlier works were gradually reissued, including his biological studies of the ancient Greeks and Romans, and in 1963 *Frömmigkeit Nordischer Artung* (first published in 1934). Günther now updated his old organic philosophy based on the Nordic myth, to attack the Americanized mass society and the Soviet totalitarian State. The unrepentant doyen of Nazi racialists argued that mankind would do well to return to National Socialism as a cure for its ills. He died in Freiburg on 25 September 1968.

Gürtner, Franz (1881–1941) Reich Minister of Justice from 1932 until his death in 1941, Franz Gürtner was born in Regensburg on 26 August 1881, the son of a locomotive engineer. After high school in Regensburg, he attended the University of Munich where he studied law. During World War I he served on the western front and in Palestine, receiving the Iron Cross (First and Second Classes). After the war Gürtner pursued a successful legal career, being appointed Bavarian Minister of Justice on 8 November 1922, a position he held until his nomination by Franz von Papen (q.v.) as Reich Minister of Justice on 2 June

1932. As a *Deutschnationale* (German National) Party member, Gürtner was sympathetic to right-wing extremists like Hitler, seeing to it during his trial in 1924 following the Beer-Hall *putsch* that the judiciary was lenient and that a light sentence was given to the Nazi Party leader. During the trial Hitler was allowed to interrupt the proceedings as often as he wished, to cross-examine witnesses at will and to speak on his own behalf at almost any length. Gürtner obtained his early release from Landsberg prison and later persuaded the Bavarian government to legalize the banned NSDAP and allow Hitler to speak again in public. After serving as Minister of Justice in the cabinets of von Papen and von Schleicher (q.v.), Gürtner was retained by Hitler in this post and made responsible for 'co-ordinating' jurisprudence in the Third Reich. Though a bureaucrat of the old school and a non-Nazi conservative, Gürtner nonetheless merged the association of German judges with the new National Socialist Lawyers' Association and provided a veil of constitutional legality for the Nazi State.

At first Gürtner also tried to protect the independence of the judiciary and a remnant of legal norms, especially against the high-handed, arbitrary and brutal methods of the SA, who in the summer of 1933 came into conflict with the police and the administrative organs of the State. The ill-treatment of prisoners at concentration camps in Wuppertal, Bredow and Hohnstein (Saxony), under the jurisdiction of local SA leaders, provoked a sharp protest from the Ministry of Justice. Gürtner observed that prisoners were being beaten to the point of unconsciousness by whips and blunt instruments, commenting that such treatment 'reveals a brutality and cruelty in the perpetrators which are totally alien to German sentiment and feeling. Such cruelty, reminiscent of oriental sadism, cannot be explained or excused by militant bitterness however great.' The protest proved to be in vain, for Hitler pardoned all those SA leaders and camp guards who were sentenced in the Hohnstein trial. Gürtner also complained about confessions obtained by the Gestapo under torture, but this practice, too, was upheld by Hitler. By the end of 1935 it was already apparent that neither Gürtner nor the Reich Minister of the Interior, Frick (q.v.), would be able to impose limitations on the power of the Gestapo or control the SS camps where thousands of detainees, who had been charged with no crimes, were being held without trial. During World War II the feeble resistance of the Ministry of Justice was weakened still further as alleged criminals were increasingly dealt with by the Gestapo and SD, without recourse to any court of law. Gürtner, who was genuinely appalled by the summary justice of shooting prisoners in concentration camps on the instructions of the security police, found his objections once again brushed aside by Hitler. Instead of resigning he stayed on in the vain hope of 'preventing the worst', thereby merely lending his prestige as a conservative bureaucrat to the systematic perversion of justice in the Nazi State. He found himself providing official sanction and legal grounds for a series of criminal actions, beginning with the institution of *Ständegerichte* (drumhead court-martials) that tried Poles and Jews in the occupied eastern territories, and later for decrees that opened the way for implementing the 'Final Solution'. Gürtner died on 29 January 1941 in Berlin before the full implications of Nazi criminality had become apparent, but cannot be exonerated from having facilitated their path.

Gütt, Arthur (1891–1949) Nazi population expert and head of the National Hygiene Department in the Reich Ministry of the Interior, Arthur Gütt was born on 17 August 1891 in Michelau. After completing his medical studies, Gütt became a circuit leader of the NSDAP (Kreis Labiau) in 1923. A leading advocate of the new science of eugenics, Gütt emphasized the need to encourage large-size families and preserve German racial health and purity against the threat of biological degeneration. When the Nazis came to power in 1933, Dr Gütt was appointed Ministerial Adviser for Racial Culture and Heredity, attached to the Public Health Department. The following year he became Ministerial Director and co-authored an official commentary on the sterilization laws with Ernst Rudin (q.v.), entitled *Gesetz zur Verhütung Erbkranken Nachwuchses vom 14. Juli 1933 ... (Law for the Prevention of Hereditary Disease in Posterity)*. In June 1935 Gütt became head of the Office for Population Policy and National Hygiene on the staff of the *Reichsführer-SS* and President of the State Academy of the Public Health Service. Gütt was the architect of the sterilization law of 24 November 1936 dealing with habitual offenders and immoral offences. He was also the author of a number of works in the field of racial hygiene, including *Die Bedeutung von Blut und Boden für das Deutsche Volk* (1933), *Dienst an der Rasse als Aufgabe der Staatspolitik* (1934), *Blutschutz und Ehegesundheitsgesetz* (1936), *Handbuch der Erbkrankheiten* (1940) and *Die Rassenpflege im Dritten Reich* (1940). In September 1939 Gütt retired from his position in the Ministry of the Interior at his own request. A year later he was nonetheless promoted to SS Major General. By the time of his death in 1949 his role in developing the legal foundations of Public Health Organization in the Third Reich had been largely forgotten.

H

Haber, Fritz (1868–1934) Nobel Prize winner in chemistry, Fritz Haber was born in Breslau on 9 December 1868, the son of a prosperous chemical and dye merchant, who was an alderman of the city. After a period in business, Haber, who was essentially self-taught in his chosen field of physical chemistry, began research in Karlsruhe in 1894. He was especially interested in the influence of electricity on organic substances and was the first to demonstrate the significance of electrode potential in oxidation and reduction. In 1904 he developed a successful synthesis of ammonia from hydrogen and nitrogen, for which he was awarded the Nobel Prize in 1918. Another outstanding achievement was his optical analysis of gases which led to the gas interferometer that bears his name. From 1906 Professor of Physical and Electrochemistry in Berlin, Haber was appointed five years later as Director of the new Kaiser Wilhelm Research Institute in Berlin-Dahlem. In 1916 he became chief of the chemical warfare service at the Institute, which had been turned over entirely to war work. During the 1920s, under Haber's direction, the Institute became the leading centre in the world for physical chemistry. Although Haber was a completely assimilated Jew and personally immune because of his war service and long-standing academic status from the immediate effects of the Nazi civil service purge at German universities in 1933, it effectively brought his career to an end. Ordered to dismiss all Jews on his staff, Haber objected to the new measures and to any privileged status for himself,

resigning on 30 April 1933 in a letter of protest to the Prussian Ministry of Education. Following a visit to Cambridge in the summer of 1933, Haber, whose health had deteriorated, decided to head south for a sanatorium in Italy, but died en route of a heart attack, in Basel (Switzerland) on 29 January 1934. A year later a memorial meeting was held in his honour, arranged by Max Planck (q.v.) under the auspices of the Kaiser Wilhelm Institute in defiance of orders from the Ministry of Education. The meeting, which stressed Haber's patriotic services to Germany and his scientific achievements, was the only public demonstration of protest made by German scientists during the Third Reich. Haber's most important books included his *Grundriss der technischen Elektrochemie auf theoretischer Grundlage* (1898), *Die elektrolytischen Prozesse der organischer Chemie* (1910) and *Über die Synthese des Ammoniaks* (1922).

Hadamovsky, Eugen (1904–44) Chief of Staff of the Nazi Party's Reich Propaganda Office until his removal in April 1942, Hadamovsky was born in Berlin on 14 December 1904. Already as a schoolboy he enrolled in the illegal Black *Reichswehr* and then became a member of the *Freikorps*. Later he travelled for a time in Austria, Italy, Spain and North Africa, working as a car mechanic and locksmith, before returning to Berlin in 1928. After some hesitation, he joined the NSDAP in December 1930 and by 1932 he was working in the Reich Propaganda office in Munich. His success in organizing the radio transmission of Hitler's rallies in 1933 obliged Goebbels (q.v.) to appoint him as head of German radio broadcasting later that year. Co-founder of the Reich Radio Chamber, he became its Vice-President in November 1933. As Head of the Reich Radio he ensured the removal of all 'racially undesirable collaborators' and despite Goebbels's intrigues he held Hitler's confidence for a time, until his position became undermined during the war years. Hadamovsky was a typical career-ist who could never quite disguise his parvenu traits or inability to fulfil all the expectations of him. He aped Goeb-bels's behaviour with women, while behind his back the latter mocked his vanity and inefficiency. In 1942 he was removed from his office as Head of Broadcasting for the Reich for incompe-tence. In 1943 he joined the Wehrmacht and fell as a tank officer on the eastern front in 1944. Among his writings on propaganda and his journalism he con-tributed *Der Rundfunk im Dienst der Volksführung* (1934), *Hitler erobert die Wirtschaft* (1935) and *Hitler kämpft um die Frieden Europas* (1936).

Halder, Franz (1884–1972) German General who was Chief of the Army General Staff between 1938 and 1942, Franz Halder was born on 30 June 1884 in Würzburg into a Roman Catholic officers' family. During World War I he served as a General Staff officer and joined the Reichswehr Ministry in 1919, remaining in the army and receiving thirty regimental and staff appointments between 1921 and 1930. In 1930-1 he joined the Organization Department of the General Staff and in 1935 he was promoted to Major General, followed by his appointment as Lieutenant-Gen-eral in 1937 and as Chief of Staff of the German Army in 1938, replacing Gen-eral Ludwig Beck (q.v.) who had been forced to resign. Halder was aware of the resentment of army officers towards

Hitler, and in 1938 even went so far as to promise the latter's opponents that he would support a *putsch* so as to avoid a European war. Halder and the Commander-in-Chief of the Wehrmacht, Walter von Brauchitsch (q.v.), both of them torn between their dislike of Nazism and their oath of loyalty to the Führer, nonetheless considered using the army to arrest Hitler should he declare war on France and Britain. After the Munich agreement the plot came to noth-ing and Halder gradually found himself drawn into Hitler's orbit, being inti-mately involved in the planning of the early battles in World War II, even though he had initially opposed the war and Hitler's strategy. Although the High Command of the Army was increasingly subordinate to Hitler's own interference – after the war Halder claimed that this intervention had been disastrous and had paralysed the armed forces – the Chief of Staff supported the policy as long as it brought success and he contrib-uted substantially to the early victories on the eastern front. His dismissal on 24 September 1942 arose out of a disagree-ment with Hitler's decision to divert forces to take Stalingrad. After the July plot of 1944, Halder was arrested and only narrowly avoided execution, being confined in a concentration camp until the end of the war, when he was liber-ated by the Americans. The quiet, la-conic Halder, a professional soldier of exceptional ability and an able writer, claimed in his best-selling pamphlet, *Hitler als Feldherr* (1949), that the Führer was a fanatic whose principles of strategy were catastrophic; that he had no human contact with his troops and was completely indifferent to their wel-fare; that he wasted lives and material to win superfluous victories; that he believed will power to be more impor-tant than military science and brought about Germany's defeat by removing control of the army from the profes-sional generals. What Halder did not explain was how he could serve Hitler for so long and whether he had not betrayed the essential principles of the Army General Staff in doing so. He died on 2 April 1972 in Aschau, Upper Bavaria.

Hammerstein-Equord, Kurt Freiherr von (1878–1943) Chief of the Army Command between 1930 and 1934, Kurt von Hammerstein was born on 26 September 1878 in Hinrichshagen. Attached to the General Staff during World War I, von Hammerstein was a patriotic officer of the old school who had little in common with Hitler or the Nazi movement, which he regarded with aristocratic contempt. Appointed in 1930 as Chief of the General Staff of the Reichswehr, von Hammerstein did not hesitate to express to Reich President von Hindenburg (q.v.) the doubts of the army command concerning Hitler's suitability as Chancellor in 1933. His antipathy to Nazi political control led to his dismissal on 1 February 1934. Five years later von Hammerstein was recalled to take command of an army group in the West, then transferred to another command in Silesia before being finally dismissed from the army for his anti-Nazi feelings. He became involved in the Resistance, but died in Berlin on 25 April 1943 before the conspiracy against Hitler was implemented.

Hanfstaengel, Ernst (1887–1975) Chief of the Foreign Press Department of the Nazi Party and a well-heeled personal friend of Hitler from the early days of the movement, Ernst Hanfstaengel was born in Munich on 2 February 1887, the son of cultivated, wealthy parents who owned an art-publishing business in Munich. Hanfstaengel's mother was American and descended from a family that had produced two distinguished Civil War generals. Originally it was intended that Hanfstaengel should take over the New York branch of the family

business and he was sent to study at Harvard University, where he graduated in 1909. After spending more than ten years in the United States he returned to Munich after World War I. He first heard of Hitler through Captain Smith, the assistant military attaché at the American embassy in Berlin, who had been impressed by the oratory of the little-known agitator. Hanfstaengel went to a political meeting of Hitler's and became an instant convert to Nazism. His friendship was important in the early days of the movement in opening the doors of respectable Munich society to Hitler, and he also loaned the Party a thousand dollars (a huge sum during the inflation) against a mortgage, to enable it to buy up and secure the *Völkische Beobachter*. Hanfstaengel participated in the abortive Munich Beer-Hall *putsch* of 1923, and it was to his country home at Uffing that Hitler fled after its failure. Two days later Hitler was arrested and, during his imprisonment, Hanfstaengel continued to help him and the Party in various ways. The eccentric, gangling Bavarian with his sardonic wit and love of practical jokes was a great favourite in Hitler's inner circle. His virtuoso piano-playing and clowning provided much needed light relief and soothed Hitler's nerves both before and after he became Reich Chancellor of Germany. In 1931 he was appointed Foreign Press Chief of the Nazi Party and used his influence and contacts abroad to improve the image of the movement and later of the régime. By the mid-1930s, however, he had come under a cloud for his moderate political views and frank comments about some of the top Nazi leaders. Goebbels (q.v.) in particular resented his close personal ties with Hitler and constantly cast aspersions on his character. Hitler, too, came to look on him as more of a businessman than a politician, later claiming that he was 'insufferable in his avarice' and judged success in purely monetary terms. In

March 1937, fearing liquidation, Hanfstaengel fled to England and then went on to the United States where he spent part of World War II as an 'adviser' on the Third Reich to President Roosevelt and the American government. Briefly interned after the war, he soon returned to Germany where he published a memoir translated into English as *Hitler: The Missing Years* (1957). He died in Munich on 6 November 1975.

Harlan, Veit (1899–1963) German actor, director and producer who stood closer to National Socialist ideology than any other important film maker in the Third Reich, Veit Harlan was born on 22 September 1899 in Berlin, the son of the novelist and dramatist, Walter Harland. He made his début in the theatre at the age of sixteen and for eleven years played at the Berlin State Theatre, until in 1927 he began a new career as a film actor. In 1934 he made his début as a movie director with a popular comedy, *Krach im Hinterhaus*, followed by *Kater Lampe* (1935) and the highly successful *Die Kreutzersonate* (1937). Harlan's movie about German youth, *Jugend* (1938), with its condemnation of puritanism and defence of adolescent love, witnessed the début in German films of the young Swedish actress, Christina Söderbaum, who was to become the director's third wife, starring in nearly all his subsequent films. The Harlan-Söderbaum duo were profoundly committed to Nazi ideology as exhibited in such movies as *Verwehte Spuren* (1938), *Das Unsterbliche Herz* (1939) and above all in *Jud Süss* (1940), the anti-semitic film which was shown in the East every time a liquidation or deportation of Jews was planned. (After World War II Harlan claimed that he was not anti-semitic, that he had been an 'involuntary' accomplice of the Nazis and that Goebbels (q.v.) was responsible for the anti-Jewish scenes in *Jud Süss*!) Harlan's films were technically well made but suffered from pomposity, blatant propagandist intent and a lack of imaginative inspiration. Movies like *Der Grosse König* (1941) about Frederick the Great and *Kolberg* (1944) about the resistance of a small Baltic port near Danzig to Napoleon's troops were primarily exaltations of Prussian militarism, glorifying courage, patriotism, sacrifice and duty. *Kolberg*, the most expensive film in the history of the German cinema – it cost $8\frac{1}{2}$ million marks and Harlan had at his disposal all the resources of the army, State and Party – was also the last one produced in the Third Reich and contained a desperate appeal for resistance to the bitter end. After 1945 Harlan was imprisoned several times and finally tried before the court of assizes at Hamburg, which found him not guilty of 'crimes against humanity' on 29 April 1949. He disappeared from public life until 1951 when he made his film comeback with *Unsterbliche Geliebte*, starring Christina Söderbaum. Despite an attempted boycott of the work of this Hitlerian film maker, Harlan directed a dozen films after 1951, mostly featuring his Swedish wife. These included *Hanna Amon* (1951), *Die Blaue Stunde* (1952), *Sterne über Colombo* (1953), *Verrat an Deutschland* (1954), *Das Dritte Geschlecht* (1957), *Liebe Kann wie Gift sein* (1958) and *Die blonde Frau des Maharadscha* (1962).

Harnack, Wolf Alexander Oskar Ernst von (1888–1945) A Social Democrat and member of the Resistance movement against Hitler, von Harnack was born on 15 July 1888 in Marburg, the son of a prominent theologian and church historian, Adolf von Harnack. After World War I, he entered the SPD and held various positions in the Prussian civil service, including that of *Regierungspräsident* in Merseburg. In 1933 he was dismissed from his post following the Nazi purge of the civil administration. After joining the Resistance, he was arrested and imprisoned on 20 July 1944 following the failure of the conspiracy. On 1 February 1945 von Harnack was sentenced to death by the People's Court and hanged on 3 March.

Hartmann, Erich (1922–93)   Ace German pilot in World War II credited by the Luftwaffe with 352 kills, a record that was disputed by British and American airmen who believed it to be grossly exaggerated. Hartmann, who was born in Weissach on 19 April 1922, flew on the eastern front where opposition to German fighter pilots was much less severe, and in 1944 he was appointed Squadron Commander of Fighter Group Fifty-three. The same year he was captured by the Russians and held in a POW camp, from which he was only released in 1955. Hartmann received many decorations, winning the Knight's Cross with Oak Leaves, Swords and Diamonds – the sixth and last Luftwaffe pilot to do so.

Hassell, Ulrich von (1881–1944) Veteran career diplomat and foreign affairs expert of the Resistance, Ulrich von Hassell was born in Anklam, Pomerania, to an old aristocratic North German family. After studying law, he entered the Foreign Office in 1908 and after 1911 held many important posts abroad, beginning as Vice-Consul in Genoa. After World War I he was embassy Councillor in Rome (1919), Consul-General in Barcelona (1921–6), Ambassador in Copenhagen (1926–30) and Belgrade (1930–2) and finally in Rome between 1932 and his deposition in 1938. A gentleman of the old school, married to the daughter of the founder of the German Imperial navy, Grand Admiral von Tirpitz, von Hassell was a representative figure of the German nobility whose deep-rooted Prussian patriotism and militarism was modified by a Christian outlook and feeling for European solidarity. Initially mildly tolerant and even sympa-

thetic to Nazism, von Hassell became increasingly worried by Hitler's adventurist policies abroad and the moral disintegration of Germany at home. As Ambassador to Italy he became convinced that the Italo-German rapprochement and war against Britain and France would be disastrous for Germany. His cultivated contempt for the vulgarity of the Nazis led to his removal from the diplomatic service during the shake-up of 4 February 1938 when von Ribbentrop (q.v.) became Foreign Minister.

Disillusioned by his experiences, von Hassell joined forces with General Beck (q.v.) and Goerdeler (q.v.) as the diplomatic head of the anti-Hitler Resistance. After his retirement he travelled widely in Europe seeking contacts and engaging in endless negotiations on behalf of the Resistance. After World War II began, he strove manfully to win over the top generals, including Halder (q.v.), von Brauchitsch (q.v.), Rommel (q.v.) and Fromm (q.v.), to the principle of a negotiated peace. Failing to persuade them to carry out a military *coup d'état* in which Hitler would be arrested and brought to trial, he became increasingly disgusted by their lack of moral fibre and firm resolve. Von Hassell was also disappointed by the absence of British response to his plans for a post-Hitler Germany, which would still have retained almost all of the Führer's conquests, including Austria, the Sudetenland and the 1914 border with Poland. (In 1914 Poland did not exist, which meant that in effect his group envisaged the old border with Tsarist Russia.) No less anachronistic was his idea of a restored Hohenzollern monarchy and his belief that the western Allies would militarily support a Hitlerless Germany against the supreme danger – the Bolshevization of Europe. On 27 April 1942 von Hassell was informed by his old colleague, Ernst von Weiszäcker (q.v.), that he was being closely watched by Himmler's (q.v.) secret police. By early

1943 several other members of his circle were also under observation. Henceforth the focal point of the Resistance shifted to the eastern front and the efforts of General Henning von Tresckow (q.v.) and then Claus von Stauffenberg (q.v.) to assassinate Hitler. With the failure of the plot of 20 July 1944 von Hassell knew that the Gestapo would shortly arrest him and received them calmly, while working at his desk, on 28 July. He was tried and sentenced to death by the People's Court and hanged at Plötzensee prison on 8 September 1944. After the war his diaries *Vom Andern Deutschland. Aus den Nachgelassenen Tagebüchern 1938–1944 (The Other Germany: Diaries 1938–1944)*, which had been buried in the garden of his Bavarian home, were published and provided a uniquely detailed source of information about the daily activities of the German Resistance.

Hauptmann, Gerhart (1862–1946) Germany's greatest playwright in the Wilhelminian and Weimar eras and one of the very few outstanding literary figures who remained in Nazi Germany, Gerhart Hauptmann was born in Obsersalzbrunn, Silesia, on 15 November 1862, the son of a farmer. After studying sculpture at an art school in Breslau and then science and philosophy at the University of Jena (1882–3), Hauptmann spent the next two years in Rome working as a sculptor. He returned to Berlin to complete his studies, later settling in Silesia and devoting himself to writing. His literary work was closely connected with the landscape, people, dialect and culture of his native region and influenced in the 1890s by social themes and the conditions of the working class. The only German naturalist writer of real stature, Hauptmann's early social dramas beginning with *Vor Sonnenaufgang (Before Dawn, 1889)* and his most famous work *Die Weber (The Weavers, 1892)*, which depicted the unsuccessful weavers' revolt of 1844, shocked the theatrical public. Regarded as a socialist and champion of the common man, Hauptmann was in fact a prolific writer of great versatility and wide artistic sympathies for whom the fate of the individual was ultimately more important than any political ideology.

In works like the poetic comedy *Der Biberpelz* (1893), *Hanneles Himmelfahrt* (1896), *Die Versunkene Glocke (The Sunken Bell, 1897)* and *Rose Bernd* (1903) he was already moving towards the neo-romanticism of his later plays, in which fairy-tales and saga elements mingle with poetic mysticism and mythical symbolism. In his novel *Der Narr in Christo, Emanuel Quint (The Fool in Christ, Emmanuel Quint, 1910)*, the story of a Silesian carpenter's son possessed by pietist ecstasy, Hauptmann found a modern parallel to the life of Christ. The quality of the stream of plays, novels and some verse which flowed from his pen was recognized by the award of the Nobel Prize for Literature in 1912. Hauptmann's sunny disposition, his Olympian serenity and golden touch gave him the status of a latter-day Goethe under the Weimar Republic. He became the charismatic poetic personality of the age, at home in almost all the literary genres, from elaborate fairy-tales, comedies and tragedies to psychological novels, poetic and philosophical epics. *Till Eulenspiegel* (1928), an epic in hexameters fusing reality and fantasy, politics, mythology and history, was one of the great poetic phantasmagorias of modern consciousness. Hauptmann managed to preserve his legendary serenity under the Third Reich, though he once confessed to a friend that 'my period ended with the burning of the Reichstag'. The fact that the most popular playwright, the representative figure and national symbol of Weimar culture, remained in Nazi Germany and continued to have his plays produced, was eagerly exploited by the régime. Goebbels (q.v.)

in particular constantly reminded the world of the fact that the once-ardent socialist had made his peace with the Nazis, whatever Hauptmann's private feelings on the matter.

The final phase of Hauptmann's dramatic work was *Die Atriden-Tetralogie* (1941–8), a cycle of plays which expressed his horror at the cruelty of his own time through the use of tragic Greek material. Other works written under the Third Reich included the autobiographical *Das Abenteuer meiner Jugend* (1937), the epic *Der Grosse Traum* (1942) and the novel fragment *Der Neue Christophorus* (1943) which contained his final religious and philosophical thinking in poetic symbolism. Though he was essentially indifferent to politics, the American authorities initially banned his plays from theatres in their sector in West Berlin after the war on the grounds of his earlier submissiveness to the Nazi régime. Hauptmann died in Agnetendorf on 6 June 1946.

Haushofer, Albrecht (1903–45) Professor of Political Geography at the Berlin School of Politics, author of classical tragedies in blank verse and a member of the German Resistance, Albrecht Haushofer was born in Munich on 7 January 1903. Son of the former general and founder of *Geopolitik*, Professor Karl Haushofer (q.v.), he studied history and geography in Munich. From 1928 to 1938 he was general secretary and a regular contributor to the *Gesellschaft für Erdkunde* (Geographical Society) and in 1939 he was appointed Professor of Political Geography at the University of Berlin. Albrecht Haushofer was probably the architect of Rudolf Hess's (q.v.) flight to Britain in May 1941 to seek British collaboration against the Russians. Hess had been a disciple of Albrecht's father, and his son had acted as his adviser before 1933 until accusations of non-Aryan ancestry had obliged the deputy Führer to get rid of him. Never-

theless, their close relationship had been maintained and, after Haushofer had been forced to abandon a brief appointment in the Foreign Office in March 1938, Hess had obtained his reinstatement as the head of an Information Section. Haushofer's extensive knowledge of Britain continued to influence Hess, who also protected the family from the Party fanatics who objected to Professor Karl Haushofer's half-Jewish wife. It was Haushofer who, in the interests of the Resistance, encouraged Hess's fixed idea of promoting a peace between Great Britain and Nazi Germany, instigating the plan which led to the abortive flight of Hitler's deputy to Scotland. After Hess's flight, Albrecht Haushofer came under observation but was not arrested until December 1944. Opposed to Nazism and in favour of restoring an authoritarian monarchy, Haushofer had established contacts with the Hassell-Goerdeler-Popitz group, with the Kreisau Circle and even with some members of the so-called 'Red Orchestra'. Following his arrest as an accomplice of Adam von Trott zu Solz (q.v.), Haushofer was imprisoned in Berlin's Moabit prison, where he wrote his *Moabiter Sonnette*, unexpectedly retrieved and published after his death. Haushofer was illegally shot by an SS section on the night of 23 April 1945, during the battle for Berlin, with the Russians already in the burning city. Among his dramatic works which had once been performed in Berlin theatres were the trilogy *Scipio, Sulla* and *Augustus* (written between 1934 and 1939), *Die Makedonen* (1941) and *Chinesische Legende* (1943).

Haushofer, Karl (1869–1946) The founder of the theory of 'Geopolitics' which provided an important ideological bridge between traditional German imperialism and National Socialism, Karl Haushofer was born in Munich on 27 August 1869. Educated at cadet school, university and the War Academy, he served in the Bavarian army, was briefly attached to the Japanese army and commanded a reserve division during World War I, reaching the rank of Brigadier. In his youth Haushofer travelled widely in India, China, Russia, Korea and Europe on various diplomatic missions and put this wide experience to use when he became Professor of Geography at the University of Munich in 1921 (a position he held until 1939). In the same year he first met Hitler and began to exert a considerable influence on Nazi Party thinking, especially through the intermediary of his pupil, Rudolf Hess (q.v.). As President of the Society for Geopolitics, as well as in his lectures and writings, Haushofer synthesized in a systematic form some of the ideas previously developed by the American Admiral Mahan and famous historians from Herodotus to Ranke, to demonstrate the interconnection between politics and geography. Ideologists of Nazism, such as Hess, Rosenberg (q.v.) and Darré (q.v.), as well as the young Hitler, absorbed from Haushofer the concept of *lebensraum* in a vulgarized, pseudo-scientific form. To the biological doctrine of race was added an expansionist category of space and the conviction that German destiny would be decided in the East. In his periodical *Die Geopolitik* and in such writings as *Der Nationalsozialistische Gedanke in der Welt* (1934), *Wehrwille als Volksziel* (1934) and *Deutsche Kulturpolitik* (1940), Haushofer continued to provide a respectable rationalization for Nazi expansionism, though by 1938 he was already disillusioned with many aspects of National Socialism. He had never been a fully-fledged Nazi, partly because of his half-Jewish wife, and he continued to believe that peace with the British was crucial to German policy – the same idea that inspired Rudolf Hess's abortive mission to the Duke of Hamilton. Haushofer was arrested after the implication of his son Albrecht in the July 1944 plot and committed suicide on

13 March 1946 in reaction to the latter's death.

Heidegger, Martin (1889–1976) Existentialist philosopher considered by many to be one of the foremost thinkers of the twentieth century, Martin Heidegger was born in Messkirch, Baden, on 26 September 1889, the son of an old Swabian peasant family. Heidegger's early schooling at high schools in Konstanz and Freiburg was followed by theological and philosophical studies at the University of Freiburg (1909–13). In 1916 he obtained his *Habilitation* (qualification for teaching at university level) and in 1922 was appointed to teach philosophy at the University of Marburg. In 1928 Heidegger succeeded his former teacher Edmund Husserl in the chair of philosophy at Freiburg. In April 1933 he was named *Rektor* (Chancellor) of the university, drawing analogies in his inaugural address between the 'knowledge service' of scholars and the army or labour service of soldiers and workers. Heidegger was the most eminent German philosopher to embrace National Socialism, though the period of his official implication in the movement lasted barely a year. The fundamental ontology of his major philosophical work *Sein und Zeit* (1927), with its search for 'authentic' values, for a new self-assertion of the German spirit against the modern cosmopolitan world, its preoccupation with *Angst* and dehumanization, already anticipated aspects of his later involvement with Nazism. Heidegger's emphasis on rootedness, on intimacies of blood and the freedom of death, his denial of freedom of choice and dislike of urban intellectualism, fitted easily enough into National Socialist ideology.

In a series of speeches as Rector of Freiburg University in 1933–4, Heidegger even went beyond his official obligations, praising the genius of Adolf Hitler for leading the German people out of the corruption of 'rootless and impotent thinking' and declaring that it was the 'supreme privilege' of the academic community to be reunited with the German *Volk* and to serve its will. Heidegger saw in Nazism the promise of a totally new beginning in German destiny and in Hitler 'the only present embodiment and future embodiment of German action and its law' (3 November 1933). In a series of lectures in 1935 (reproduced in 1953 in his *Introduction to Metaphysics*) Heidegger actually spoke of the 'inner truth and greatness of this [i.e. Nazi] movement', by which he meant 'the encounter between global technology and modern man' allegedly expressed in its philosophy. On the other hand, Heidegger was not noticeably anti-semitic and as Rector prohibited the planned burning of 'decadent' works by Jewish or communist authors in front of the university. He also refused to ratify the dismissal of two anti-Nazi colleagues at the University, finally resigning his rectorship in February 1934. Subsequently, Heidegger withdrew from politics into philosophical quietism, continuing to lecture and publish under the Third Reich such works as *Hölderlin und das Wesen der Dichtung* (1936), *Platons Lehre von der Wahrheit* (1942) and *Vom Wesen der Wahrheit* (1943). In 1944 he was enrolled in a compulsory work-brigade involved in the construction of earthworks on the banks of the Rhine. From 1945 to 1951 Heidegger was prohibited from teaching in any public capacity by the Allied powers. In 1951 he was appointed Honorary Professor and resumed his teaching at Freiburg, giving occasional seminars until 1967.

After World War II Heidegger's influence, especially on French existentialism (Sartre's philosophy is incomprehensible without reference to his German predecessor), was enormous, and his theories on the nature of language and poetry were also widely discussed. On the ques-

tion of Hitlerism and the Holocaust, the policies of the Third Reich and his own involvement, he maintained, however, a complete public silence until his death in Messkirch on 26 May 1976. A month later, a long interview appeared in the German magazine *Der Spiegel* – it had been recorded a decade earlier on condition that it only be used posthumously – where Heidegger claimed that at the time he had seen no alternative to Nazism if Germany were to survive. Nowhere in this last statement concerning his own past did Heidegger explicitly repudiate National Socialism or have anything to say about the philosophical implications of the bestialities committed during the Third Reich.

Heinkel, Ernest Heinrich (1888–1958) German aircraft engineer, born in Grunbach (Wurttemberg) on 24 January 1888, Heinkel studied mechanical engineering at the Technical Academy in Stuttgart and was deeply affected by the Zeppelin disaster of 1908, after which he was convinced that the airplane was the means of transport of the future. During his engineering studies he built his own plane which he crashed in 1911, suffering severe wounds. During World War I Heinkel was director of an Austrian and a Hungarian airplane factory whose products were successfully flown and used by the Austro-Hungarian army and the German navy. In 1922 he founded the Heinkel-Flugzeugswerke at Warnemunde, making at first seaplanes, and later bombers and fighters which achieved fame in World War II. The fast Heinkel He-70, the prototype of the streamlined airplane, was an international success. The middle-range bomber, He-111, was until well into World War II the standard machine of the German bomber squadrons. Heinkel also built the first jet plane, the He-178, which was successfully tested on 27 August 1939 and the first rocket aircraft, the He-176, which on its test flight surpassed all previous speeds for this type of machine. Like his great rival, Wilhelm Messerschmitt (q.v.), Heinkel was appointed a *Wehrwirtschaftsführer* and made a great contribution to strengthening the Luftwaffe. By the end of 1944 he employed in his factories 55,123 persons, of whom 30,455 were foreign workers. After the war, Heinkel was classified as a 'fellow-traveller' by a de-Nazification court on 18 January 1949. In the 1950s he returned to airplane construction but in order to survive he had to enter into close ties and eventually be absorbed by the aircraft company Messerschmitt-Bolkow-Blohm (MBB). Heinkel published his memoirs, *Sturmisches Leben,* in 1953 and died on 30 January 1958.

Heisenberg, Werner (1901–76) Awarded the Nobel Prize for Physics in 1932, Werner Heisenberg was the most brilliant of the younger generation of theoretical physicists who decided to remain in Germany rather than emigrate after the Nazis came to power. Born in Würzburg on 5 December 1901, Heisenberg studied physics at Munich under Arnold Sommerfeld. Between 1924 and 1927 he worked with Niels Bohr at Copenhagen, both men profoundly influencing the subsequent development of atomic physics. From 1927 to 1941 he was Professor of Physics at the University of Leipzig and, from 1941 to 1945, Director of the Kaiser Wilhelm Institute for Physics, Berlin-Dahlem, and Professor of Theoretical Physics at Berlin University. In the late 1920s Heisenberg's uncertainty principle and his work in quantum mechanics, along with that of Schrödinger, de Broglie, Bohr, Einstein (q.v.) and Max Born (q.v.), helped revolutionize the conceptual world of modern physics. His principle of indeterminacy suggested that chance, not determinism, statistical laws, not causal mechanisms, governed the physical universe. The

'Aryan' physicists in Nazi Germany led by Johannes Stark (q.v.) totally rejected Heisenberg's quantum mechanics, attacking him as a 'theoretical formalist' and the 'spirit of Einstein's spirit', who shared the fundamental perspectives of 'Jewish physics'. An ominous article in the SS organ *Das Schwarze Korps* (15 July 1937) entitled 'White Jews in Scholarship' even suggested that Heisenberg and other so-called 'Jews in character' rather than ancestry should disappear.

For the next year Heisenberg's fate was in the hands of the SS bureaucracy until Himmler (q.v.) exonerated him, partly as a result of a family intervention – the physicist's mother had appealed to the mother of the *Reichsführer-SS* whom she knew slightly – and partly because of the support he received from the scientific community, from some German diplomats and even from high-ranking circles in the SS itself. Nevertheless, Heisenberg was not called to succeed Arnold Sommerfeld, whose chair of theoretical physics at the University of Munich was vacant. Subsequently, he wrote that 'the years before the Second World War have always appeared to me, in so far as I spent them in Germany, as a time of endless loneliness'.

Heisenberg, who had not signed the 1934 declaration of physicists supporting Hitler and was never a Nazi, suffered from the loss of international contacts and the administrative measures that were damaging the structure of academic physics in Germany. He tried to defend the integrity of scientific values against the inroads of the politicians and the Nazi ideologues and to preserve what could be salvaged from the traditions and institutions of German science. During the war, as the decline in German atomic physics became evident and military considerations were paramount, Werner Heisenberg and his group received more encouragement from the authorities. But the German atomic research programme still lacked the necessary funds, material and manpower and no nuclear weapons project was ever initiated. Heisenberg's close involvement in the programme reflected his naivety about politics and the way in which science had become intertwined with the economic and military situation. There is no evidence that he ever saw the need to insist on the application of scientific values to the world outside the laboratory. After 1946 Heisenberg became Director of the Max Planck Institute for Physics at Göttingen. He wrote many books and papers on quantum mechanics, atomic physics and cosmic rays. Among his most important works were *Die Physikalischen Prinzipien der Quantentheorie* (1944, 3rd edn), *Die Physik der Atomkerne* (1949, 3rd edn), *Die Naturbild der Heutigen Physik* (1955) and *Schritte über Grenzen* (1971).

Helldorf, Wolf Heinrich Graf von (1896–1944) Berlin's Chief of Police and later a member of the Resistance to Hitler, Graf von Helldorf was born in Merseburg on 14 October 1896 and served during World War I as an officer, being awarded the Iron Cross (First and Second Classes). After the war he joined the notorious Rossbach *Freikorps* and was involved in the Kapp *putsch* (1920), which led to his exile in Italy where he remained for four years. He joined the NSDAP in 1926 and became an SA leader in Berlin in 1931. A member of the Prussian *Landtag* in 1932, he was elected as a Nazi deputy to the Reichstag on 12 November 1933. In the same year he was appointed SS leader with the rank of General in the Brandenburg district and *SA-Gruppenführer*. From July 1935 von Helldorf served as Berlin's Police President – for two years he had been Chief of Police in Potsdam – and indulged in various rackets, including the confiscation of passports belonging to wealthy Jews for resale at prices averaging 250,000 marks. Graf von Helldorf,

who had never been a convinced National Socialist, was one of the major figures involved in the conspiracy against Hitler's life in 1944, which led to his arrest and torture. He was eventually hanged on 15 August 1944.

Henlein, Konrad (1898–1945) Reich Governor and *Gauleiter* of occupied Sudetenland during World War II, Konrad Henlein was born on 6 May 1898 in Maffersdorf, near Reichenberg (Bohemia), of a German father and Czech mother. Educated at a commercial college and employed as a bank clerk after military service during World War I (he was a prisoner of war in Italy until 1919), Henlein became the gym instructor of a Sudeten German club in Asch in 1925. In 1931 he was appointed leader of the German Gymnastic Union in Czechoslovakia and in October 1933 he founded the Sudeten German *Heimatfront* (Patriotic Front) to replace the prohibited NSDAP. Two years later it changed its name to the *Sudetendeutsche Partei* (SDP), demanding autonomy for the Sudeten German minority within the framework of the Czech State. In the elections of 1935 the SDP obtained forty-four seats and in effect represented over half of the German-speaking population of Czechoslovakia. Only the communists and Social Democrats refused to identify with its demands for full cultural autonomy and the transformation of Czechoslovakia into a federal State on the Swiss model. From 1935 onwards, the SDP was secretly in receipt of subsidies from the Third Reich via the *Volksdeutsche Mittelstelle* (controlled by Werner Lorenz, q.v.) and the German embassy in Prague, as well as being granted 15,000 marks a month from the *Ausland* Organization. As a fifth column the SDP played a key role in subverting the Czech State, enabling Hitler to manipulate the dispute between the Sudeten Germans and the Czech government from within. Gradually all regional and local organizations, sporting societies, cultural associations, choral and musical societies, etc., in the Sudetenland were infiltrated and transformed into Nazi cells.

Though Henlein continued to bamboozle the British with his denials that he had any connection with National Socialism or the Third Reich, by 1937 his Party was openly pro-Nazi and anti-semitic. At a secret meeting with Hitler after the annexation of Austria on 28 March 1938, Henlein and the Führer agreed on a common strategy based on the principle: 'We must always demand so much that we can never be satisfied.' Henlein did not return to Czechoslovakia until it was already occupied by German troops as a result of the Munich agreements. Already an SS Lieutenant-General and member of the Reichstag, on 1 May 1939 he was appointed head of the Civil Administration in the Sudetenland and *Gauleiter* of the region, positions he held until the end of World War II. In June 1943 the Reich Governor of the Sudetenland was promoted to *SS-Obergruppenführer*. Following capture by the Americans, Henlein committed suicide in an Allied POW camp in May 1945.

Hess, Rudolf (1894–1987) Deputy Leader of the Nazi Party and after Goering (q.v.) the No. 3 man in Nazi Germany, Rudolf Hess was born in Alexandria, Egypt, on 26 April 1894. He volunteered for the army in 1914 to escape from his father's domination and the hateful prospect of a commercial career, serving first as a shock troop leader and then as a flier. In 1919 he joined the *Freikorps* under General Ritter von Epp (q.v.) and entered the Nazi Party in January 1920, after hearing Hitler speak. A student of political science at the University of Munich, Hess was profoundly influenced by the geopolitical theories of Professor Karl Haushofer (q.v.), which he transformed into a vague,

pseudo-scientific philosophy of expansionism. Hess's sole original contribution to National Socialist ideology was the introduction of the concept of *lebensraum*. After his arrest and imprisonment for his part in the attempted Beer-Hall *putsch* of 1923 (he spent seven months in Landsberg fortress), Hess helped Hitler to write *Mein Kampf* as well as taking down most of the dictation for the book. The sections on *lebensraum*, the role of the British Empire in history and the organization of the NSDAP were influenced by his ideas.

From 1925 to 1932 Hess had no official rank in the Nazi Party but acted as Hitler's private secretary, his confidant and blindly loyal follower. Introverted, shy, deeply insecure and dependent on an idealized father-figure, Hess made up for his lack of intelligence, oratorical ability or capacity for political intrigue by a dogged subservience and devotion to Hitler which was as naive as it was sincere. In December 1932 Hitler made him Chairman of the Central Political Commission of the NSDAP and shortly afterwards he was promoted to the rank of SS General. On 21 April 1933 the almost unknown Hess became Deputy Leader. In this position he largely exercised subordinate representative functions and supervised charitable duties, acting as the Führer's shadow but proving incapable and unwilling to take any initiatives of his own. His most important privilege was to announce Hitler from the tribunal at mass meetings, with the wide-eyed, ecstatic enthusiasm of the true believer. Hess masked his lack of independence, his clumsiness in thought and deed, by an unrestrained cult of the Führer that exceeded even the most sycophantic eulogies of the Nazi élite. In June 1934, shortly before the Röhm (q.v.) purge, Hess exhibited the total extinction of all personality implied in his own Leader worship, when he declared: 'The National Socialism of all of us is anchored in uncritical loyalty, in

the surrender to the Führer that does
not ask for the why in individual cases,
in the silent execution of his orders.'
For Hess, Hitler was 'pure reason in
human form', a venerated God-like
figure without whom his own neurotic
personality could not function. Even at
Nuremberg in 1946 he clung to this idealized image: 'It was granted me for many
years to live and work under the greatest
son whom my nation has brought forth
in the thousand years of its history.'
During the Third Reich, Hess's dog-like
fidelity was rewarded by many high positions. Reich Minister without Portfolio
from 2 December 1933, a member of the
Secret Cabinet Council from 4 February
1938 and in August 1939 appointed a
member of the Ministerial Council for
Reich Defence, Hess reached the apex
of his career in 1939 when he was made
successor   designate   to   Hitler   and
Goering.

One sensational, absurd act, his self-
appointed, wholly unofficial peace mission to Britain, not only brought his
Party career to an end but transformed
the Nazi leader into one of the most
famous psychiatric cases of the century.
On 10 May 1941 Hess secretly left Germany in a Messerschmitt 110 fighter on
a solo flight to Scotland, where he bailed
out within twelve miles of the Duke of
Hamilton's home. He hoped through
the intermediary of the Duke, whom he
had briefly met at the Berlin Olympics
of 1936, to convince the British government that Hitler had no wish to destroy
a fellow-Nordic nation, that he only
wanted a free hand to pursue his *lebensraum* politics in eastern Europe. Hess
evidently believed that this would be in
Britain's best interests since its empire
would be left in peace. However, if Britain did not rid itself of the Churchill
government and come to an understanding, then it would be utterly destroyed.
Much to his surprise, Hess was simply
imprisoned and treated as a prisoner of
war. In Germany, Hitler declared him

insane and the Nazi press portrayed him
as 'a deluded, deranged and muddled
idealist, ridden with hallucinations trace-
able to World War [I] injuries'.

During captivity, Hess did indeed
appear to crack up completely, taking
flight in neurosis and a paranoid fear
that his food was being poisoned. When
brought to trial at Nuremberg in 1946
he appeared to be suffering from total
amnesia (which he afterwards claimed
was feigned), staring vacantly into space
and behaving like a broken man. Although there were some doubts about
his sanity, Hess was nonetheless sentenced to life imprisonment, having been
found guilty of crimes against peace and
conspiracy to commit other crimes listed
in the indictment. Rudolf Hess was imprisoned in the Allied military prison in
Berlin-Spandau and kept there at the
insistence of the Russians until his death
in 1987 at the age of ninety-two. His
long imprisonment was punctuated by
periodic calls for his release on humanitarian grounds as well as speculations
about his mental health and even his
true identity. He became a martyr for
neo-Nazis all over the world who have
turned his name into a rallying cry and
his burial place in northern Bavaria into
a shrine for their movement.

Heusinger, Adolf (1897–1982)   Chief of
the Operations Section of the General
Staff during World War II, Adolf Heusinger was born on 4 August 1897 in
Holzminden, the son of a school teacher.
After entering the Imperial army as a
cadet in 1915, Heusinger fought on the
western front during World War I. After
joining the Reichswehr, he served on the
General Staff from 1931 and was promoted in 1937 to Major in the Operations Section of the Army High Command (OKW). On 1 October 1940 Heusinger was appointed Brigadier and made
Chief of Operations in the High Command. In 1941 he was promoted to
Major   General   and   in   1943   to

Lieutenant-General. Following the dismissal of Kurt Zeitzler (q.v.) and before his replacement by General Guderian (q.v.) as Army Chief of Staff, Heusinger was in effect running the operational side of the German military machine. He was present at Hitler's headquarters in Rastenburg, East Prussia, on 20 July 1944 reporting on the situation following the Russian breakthrough on the eastern front, when a tremendous explosion blasted the room, shattering the central table and destroying the ceiling. Heusinger, who was only slightly wounded, was arrested two days later and tried in August by the People's Court, accused of having known about the conspiracy. He was released in October 1944 but relieved of active duty. A witness in the Nuremberg trials, Heusinger, who had never been a genuine Nazi, was kept in Allied detention until 1948. A year later he was appointed military adviser to Konrad Adenauer (q.v.) and in 1951 he was involved as a specialist in discussions concerning the European defence community. After 1952 General Heusinger took a leading part in planning the new Bundeswehr (the West German armed forces), serving as its Inspector-General from June 1957 until 1961. He had earlier succeeded General Speidel (q.v.) as Chief of the Armed Forces in the Federal Ministry of Defence. From 1961 until his retirement three years later, Heusinger was Chairman of the NATO armed forces based in Washington.

Heyde, Werner (1902–64) Professor of Neurology and Psychiatry at the University of Würzburg at the age of thirty-seven and from 1939–42 also head of the euthanasia project or so-called 'mercy killing' of physically and mentally handicapped persons in Germany and Austria, Werner Heyde was born in Forst/Lausitz on 25 April 1902, the son of a manufacturer. An SS medical doctor (he eventually held the rank of

SS Colonel), Heyde had joined the NSDAP in 1933 and rapidly emerged as the top expert in 'mercy killing' in the Third Reich. In 1939 he was selected to head Organization T4, based at Tiergartenstrasse 4, in a suburb of Berlin (the nub of the entire administration of the euthanasia programme), which strove to implement Hitler's orders concerning the 'destruction of worthless life'. Some 100,000 German men, women and children were killed under his directions as head of the Reich Association for Hospitals and Sanatoria by special doctors using lethal injections, starvation, carbon monoxide and 'Zyklon B' gas. Heyde also headed a travelling circus of psychiatrists who investigated the emotional life of concentration camp inmates at Dachau, Buchenwald and other camps, selecting both Jews and 'Aryans' for execution in his institutes. Sentenced to death *in absentia* by a German court in 1946, he escaped into the British zone by slipping off the back of an American army truck taking him for interrogation to Nuremberg and settled down to practise under the alias of Dr Fritz Sawade in Flensburg, Schleswig-Holstein. Employed as a labour court medical expert and official consultant by the Chief Medical Officer of Schleswig-Holstein, he was knowingly shielded by top State officials who knew his real identity and preserved a conspiracy of silence about his past. On 12 November 1959 the eminent psychiatrist gave himself up to a court at Frankfurt. He was to have been the main defendant in the biggest postwar euthanasia trial held at Limburg County Court, but on 13 February 1964, five days before his trial was due to start, Dr Heyde committed suicide in his cell at Butzbach prison, hanging himself with his trouser belt from a radiator pipe.

Heydrich, Reinhard (1904–42) Head of the Reich Main Security Office and the leading organizational architect of the

Nazi 'Final Solution', Reinhard Heydrich was born in Halle, a provincial town in Prussian Saxony, on 7 March 1904. The son of a Dresden music teacher who had founded the First Halle Conservatory for Music, Theatre and Teaching, Heydrich joined the *Freikorps* in 1919 and was strongly influenced in his early years by the racial fanaticism of *völkisch* circles. On 30 March 1922 he entered the Reichsmarine in Kiel, serving for a time under Wilhelm Canaris (q.v.) who nurtured his taste for naval intelligence work. In 1931 Heydrich was forced to resign from the navy by Admiral Raeder (q.v.) for 'conduct unbecoming to an officer and a gentleman', after compromising the virtue of a shipyard director's daughter. In July of the same year he joined the NSDAP and then the SS, attracting the attention of Himmler (q.v.) and rising rapidly through the ranks. Appointed SS Major on 25 December 1931, then SS Colonel and Chief of the SD (Security Service) in July 1932, Heydrich was promoted to *SS-Brigadeführer* on 21 March 1933 and, in reward for his murderous services during the Röhm (q.v.) *putsch*, became SS Lieutenant-General on 1 July 1934.

Tall, slim, blond-haired, with slanting, deep-set blue eyes, Heydrich with his military bearing and ice-cool hardness seemed to epitomize the 'Nordic-Aryan type' of Nazi mythology. His athleticism – he was a first-class fencer, an excellent horseman and a skilled pilot – allied to his talent as a violinist and his orderly, disciplined exterior impressed Himmler, who selected him as his right-hand man. As Himmler's assistant in securing control of the Munich and then the Bavarian police after the Nazi seizure of power, Heydrich assured the successful 'co-ordination' of the political police in the other German *Länder* during 1933–4. Heydrich soon intrigued his way to becoming Chief of the Berlin Gestapo and by 1936 was given command of the security police throughout the Reich.

An able technician of power, ruthless, cold and calculating, without any compunction in carrying out the most inhuman measures, Heydrich made himself indispensable to the masters of the Third Reich. Yet the arrogant facade disguised a deeply split personality, a neurotic temperament and pathological self-hatred which found its outlet in a boundless greed for power, morbid suspiciousness and exhibitionism. A sense of 'racial' inadequacy, the gnawing uncertainty caused by his suspected half-Jewish origins – utilized for blackmail purposes by his rivals for power though never established as a fact – added to his built-in sense of inferiority, aggravating his tendency to see treachery, intrigue and potential hostility everywhere. As head of the SIPO, the unified, centralized, militarized and Nazified security police (including political and criminal police), Heydrich reacted with pitiless harshness in dealing with 'enemies of the State'. His cynicism and contempt for human beings led him to exploit the basest instincts – sadism, envy, intolerance – in weaving his gigantic spider's web of police surveillance in the Third Reich. He filed extensive dossiers not only on enemies of the Party but also on his rivals and colleagues, using the police apparatus to set his opponents at each other's throats. 'Scientific' studies of the *modus operandi* of potential enemies of the State like Marxists, Jews, Freemasons, Liberal Republicans, religious and cultural groups went hand in hand with arrests, torture and murder of those who stood in the way of the totalitarian police apparatus.

The 'Blond Beast', who controlled the sole intelligence service of the Party after 1935, specialized in devious methods of blackmail alongside the weapons of open terror and persecution. His hand was most probably in the Tukhachevsky Affair – which led to the purge of the top Red Army generals in the Soviet Union – and he fabricated the scandalous intrigue which brought down the leading German generals, von Blomberg (q.v.) and von Fritsch (q.v.), in 1938. His proclivity for dirty tricks was again in evidence when he masterminded the mock attack on the Gleiwitz radio transmitter which provided Hitler's excuse for invading Poland. In 1939 Heydrich was appointed head of the Reich Main Security Office (RSHA) which incorporated the Gestapo, the criminal police and the SD. A gigantic political machine for centralizing and transmitting information to all corners of the Nazi world, it gave Heydrich the opportunity to perfect the techniques of secret police power. The most satanic consequence of this accumulation of power was revealed in Heydrich's implementation of the order for the wholesale extermination of European Jewry. Already before the war, Heydrich had concentrated the management of Jewish affairs in his hands, though in 1938 the emphasis was still on a policy of forced emigration. One of the instigators of the Crystal Night pogrom of November 1938, Heydrich had sent Eichmann (q.v.) to Vienna to organize a 'Centre for Jewish Emigration' and, impressed by his success, had created a similar centre in Berlin.

After the conquest of Poland, Heydrich ordered the concentration of Polish Jews in ghettoes and the appointment of Jewish councils, a characteristically perfidious way of forcing the Jewish communities to 'collaborate' in their own destruction. With Eichmann's help, he organized the mass deportations of Jews from annexed parts of Poland, from Germany and Austria to the territory of the Generalgouvernement. In his directive of 21 September 1939 Heydrich distinguished, however, between the 'final aim, requiring longer periods of time' (and necessarily top secret), and the stages required for achieving it. Ghet-

toes were only a temporary solution, much like the expropriation of Jewish wealth by the Gestapo and the forced evacuation of Jews from Germany had been before 1939–40. On 31 July 1941, following the invasion of the Soviet Union (in the first six weeks of the campaign Heydrich had, with typical exhibitionist bravado, flown with the Luftwaffe), Goering (q.v.) commissioned him to carry out 'a total solution of the Jewish question in those territories of Europe which are under German influence'. Both the terms *Gesamtlösung* (total solution) and *Endlösung* (final solution) were used in the document and Heydrich was delegated to take responsibility for all the necessary organizational, administrative and financial measures. His *Einsatzgruppen*, which had already killed tens of thousands of Poles and Jews with the co-operation of the German military, were to murder in all a million Russian and Polish Jews as well as many Soviet officials.

To co-ordinate the action of various government and Party agencies, Heydrich convened the Wannsee Conference on 20 January 1942 to discuss the ways and means of implementing the 'Final Solution of the European Jewish Question'. In the circumlocutory language used to disguise the policy of mass murder which he had a considerable part in devising, Heydrich described how Jews capable of work 'are brought to these areas [in the eastern occupied territories] and employed in road building, in which task undoubtedly a large part will fall out through natural diminution'. In other words they would be sent to their death through hunger, exhaustion or disease and, where required, by murder squads. The surviving remnant would be given appropriate 'treatment' as they represented a 'natural selection', constituting the 'germ-cell of a new Jewish development should they be allowed to go free'. Having laid the groundwork for the 'Final Solution' (appropriately enough Operation Reinhard, the code-word for the extermination of Polish Jewry, was named after him), Heydrich left his Berlin headquarters to assume the post of Deputy Reich Protector of Bohemia and Moravia on 23 September 1941. Taking up residence in Prague, Heydrich adopted 'the policy of the whip and the sugar', speeding up repression and ordering mass executions while attempting to win over the workers and peasants by improving social conditions.

Overestimating his success in 'pacifying' the Czechs, Heydrich abandoned normal security precautions and drove about in an open car without armed escort. On 27 May 1942 he was gravely wounded by two Free Czech agents, trained in England and parachuted into Czechoslovakia, who opened fire on his car and rolled a bomb under it. The assassins were discovered, along with more than a hundred other Resistance men, sheltering in a church, and massacred by the SS. Heydrich died of his wounds on the morning of 4 June 1942 and was eulogized at his funeral by Hitler, Himmler and his old rival Admiral Canaris. The reprisals were terrifying in their savagery. The Germans razed to the ground the entire village of Lidice, executing all its male inhabitants. Nearly a thousand Czechs were condemned to death by a German court-martial in Prague and a smaller number in Brno. A 'special action' in Berlin killed 152 Jews and more than 3,000 were deported from the Theresienstadt ghetto and exterminated. In death as in life, Heydrich's name seemed inextricably linked with terror and intimidation for its own sake.

Hilferding, Rudolf (1877–1941) Leading Social Democrat and twice Minister of Finance during the Weimar Republic, Rudolf Hilferding was born on 10 August 1877 in Vienna, the son of wealthy Jewish parents. Trained as a pediatrician, Hilferding turned to socialism while still a medical student and contributed his first study of Marx's economic theories to the German socialist publication, *Die Neue Zeit*, in 1902. One of the leading representatives of the Austro-Marxist school, Hilferding became a teacher at the Social Democratic Party (SPD) training centre in Berlin in 1906. From 1907 to 1915 he was political editor of *Vorwärts*, the central organ of the German SPD. The author of several important theoretical works on political economy, Hilferding published his Marxist classic *Das Finanzkapital* in 1910, a book which considerably influenced Lenin's writings on imperialism. At the outbreak of World War I, Hilferding, like the majority of the SPD, approved the granting of war credits, but at the end of 1918 he went over to the Independent Social Democrats (USPD), becoming chief editor of their newspaper, *Die Freiheit*. In 1922 he rejoined the Majority Socialists and from 1924 to 1933 served as an SPD deputy in the Reichstag. Appointed Minister of Finance in the Stresemann cabinet from August to October 1923, Hilferding contributed to stabilizing the mark, but could not stop the inflation altogether. He was again Finance Minister under the socialist cabinet of Hermann Müller in 1928–9 on the eve of the world economic depression. Editor of the outstanding socialist periodical, *Die Gesellschaft*, Hilferding was not only the leading financial expert of the SPD but also its chief theoretician in the Weimar years. A resolute anti-Nazi, Hilferding as a prominent socialist and Jew was obliged to flee Germany in March 1933, escaping to Denmark, then moving on to Switzerland and finally settling in France in 1938. In 1934 he had drafted the Prague programme for the exiled German Social Democrats and throughout the decade he continued to warn the rest of the world of the dangers emanating from Hitler's Germany. Hilferding was arrested in unoccupied southern France in February 1941 by the Vichy police, taken to the border of occupied France and handed over to the Germans. He died on 2 February 1941 in a Parisian prison, from injuries brutally inflicted by the Gestapo.

Himmler, Heinrich (1900–45) *Reichsführer-SS*, head of the Gestapo and the Waffen-SS, Minister of the Interior from 1943 to 1945 and organizer of the mass murder of Jews in the Third Reich, Heinrich Himmler was born in Munich on 7 October 1900. The son of a pious, authoritarian Roman Catholic schoolmaster who had once been tutor to the Bavarian Crown Prince, Himmler was educated at a secondary school in Landshut. He served as an officer cadet in the Eleventh Bavarian Regiment at the end of World War I, later obtaining a diploma in agriculture from Munich Technical High School where he studied from 1918 to 1922. After working briefly as a salesman for a firm of fertilizer manufacturers, the young Himmler joined a para-military, nationalist organization and participated in the Munich Beer-Hall *putsch* of November 1923 as standard-bearer at the side of Ernst Röhm (q.v.). Secretary to Gregor Strasser (q.v.) and his deputy district leader in Bavaria, Swabia and the Palatinate, he was also acting propaganda leader of the NSDAP from 1925 to 1930. After marrying in 1927, Himmler returned to poultry farming for a time but was singularly unsuccessful in the business of raising chickens. In January 1929 he was appointed head of Hitler's personal bodyguard, the black-shirted *Schutzstaffel* (SS), at that time a small body of 200 men which was subsequently to become under his leadership an all-embracing empire within the Nazi State.

Elected in 1930 to the Reichstag as Nazi deputy for Weser-Ems, Himmler concentrated on extending SS member-ship – which reached 52,000 by 1933 – and securing its independence from control by Röhm's SA, to which it was initially subordinated. He organized the Security Service (SD) under Reinhard Heydrich (q.v.), originally an ideological intelligence service of the Party, and together the two men ensured that the Nazis consolidated their power over Bavaria in 1933. In March 1933 Himmler was appointed Munich Police President and shortly afterwards he became Commander of the political police throughout Bavaria. In September 1933 he was made Commander of all political police units outside Prussia and, though formally under Goering (q.v.), became head of the Prussian Police and Gestapo on 20 April 1934. The turning-point in Himmler's career was his masterminding of the purge of 30 June 1934 which smashed the power of the SA and paved the way for the emergence of the SS as an independent organization charged with 'safeguarding the ... embodiment of the National Socialist idea' and translating the racism of the régime into a dynamic principle of action.

By 17 June 1936 Himmler had successfully completed his bid to win control of the political and criminal police throughout the Third Reich, becoming head of the Gestapo in addition to his position as *Reichsführer* of the SS. A very able organizer and administrator, meticulous, calculating and efficient, Himmler's astonishing capacity for work and irrepressible power-lust showed itself in his accumulation of official posts and his perfecting of the methods of organized State terrorism against political and other opponents of the régime. In 1933 he had set up the first concentration camp in Dachau and in the next few years, with Hitler's encouragement, greatly extended the range of persons who qualified for internment in the camps. Himmler's philosophical mysticism, his cranky obsessions with mesmerism, the occult, herbal remedies and homeopathy went hand in hand with a narrow-minded fanatical racialism and commitment to the 'Aryan' myth. In a speech in January 1937 Himmler declared that 'there is no more living proof of hereditary and racial laws than in a concentration camp. You find there hydrocephalics, squinters, deformed individuals, semi-Jews: a considerable number of inferior people.' The mission of the German people was 'the struggle for the extermination of any sub-humans, all over the world who are in league against Germany, which is the nucleus of the Nordic race; against Germany, nucleus of the German nation, against Germany the custodian of human culture: they mean the existence or non-existence of the white man; and we guide his destiny'. Himmler's decisive innovation was to transform the race question from 'a negative concept based on matter-of-course anti-semitism' into 'an organizational task for building up the SS'. Racism was to be safeguarded by the reality of a race society, by the concentration camps presided over by Himmler's Deaths Head Formations in Germany, just as during World War II the theories of 'Aryan' supremacy would be established by the systematic extermination of Jews and Slavs in Poland and Russia. Himmler's romantic dream of a race of blue-eyed, blond heroes was to be achieved by cultivating an élite according to 'laws of selection' based on criteria of physiognomy, mental and physical tests, character and spirit. His aristocratic concept of leadership aimed at consciously breeding a racially organized order which would combine charismatic authority with bureaucratic discipline. The SS man would represent a new human type – warrior, administrator, 'scholar' and leader, all in one – whose messianic mission was to undertake a vast colonization of the East. This synthetic aristocracy, trained in a semi-closed society and superimposed on the Nazi system

as a whole, would demonstrate the value of its blood through 'creative action' and achievement.

From the outset of his career as *Reichsführer* of the SS, Himmler had introduced the principle of racial selection and special marriage laws which would ensure the systematic coupling of people of 'high value'. His promotion of illegitimacy by establishing the State-registered human stud farm known as *Lebensborn*, where young girls selected for their perfect Nordic traits could procreate with SS men and their offspring were better cared for than in maternity homes for married mothers, reflected Himmler's obsession with creating a race of 'supermen' by means of breeding. Himmler's notorious procreation order of 28 October 1939 to the entire SS that 'it will be the sublime task of German women and girls of good blood acting not frivolously but from a profound moral seriousness to become mothers to children of soldiers setting off to battle' and his demand that war heroes should be allowed a second marriage expressed the same preoccupation.

The small, diffident man who looked more like a humble bank clerk than Germany's police dictator, whose pedantic demeanour and 'exquisite courtesy' fooled one English observer into stating that 'nobody I met in Germany is more normal', was a curious mixture of bizarre, romantic fantasy and cold, conscienceless efficiency. Described as 'a man of quiet unemotional gestures, a man without nerves', he suffered from psycho-somatic illness, severe headaches and intestinal spasms and almost fainted at the sight of a hundred eastern Jews (including women) being executed for his benefit on the Russian front. Subsequent to this experience, he ordered as a 'more humane means' of execution the use of poison gas in specially constructed chambers disguised as shower rooms.

The petty-bourgeois eccentric whose

natural snobbery led him to welcome old aristocratic blood into the SS, revived a web of obsolete religious and cosmological dogmas linking new recruits to their distant Germanic ancestors. He cultivated the 'return to the soil' and the dream of German peasant-soldier farms in the East while at the same time proving himself a diabolically skilful organizer of rationalized modern extermination methods. The supreme technician of totalitarian police power who saw himself as a reincarnation of the pre-Christian Saxon, Henry the Fowler, advancing eastwards against the Slavs – he organized the thousandth anniversary of Henry's death in 1936 – Himmler perfectly expressed in his own personality the contradictions of National Socialism. For him, the SS was at one and the same time the resurrection of the ancient Order of the Teutonic Knights with himself as grand master, the breeding of a new *Herrenvolk* aristocracy based on traditional values of honour, obedience, courage and loyalty, and the instrument of a vast experiment in modern racial engineering. Through this privileged caste which was to be the hard core of German imperial dominion in Europe, the nucleus of a new State apparatus would emerge with its tentacles impinging on all spheres of life in the expanded Third Reich. By recruiting 'Aryans' of different nationalities into his Waffen-SS Himmler envisaged the creation of 'a German Reich of the German Nation' based on the feudal allegiance of its communities to the lordship and protection of the Führer, embodying a Germany that would become the centre of a higher political entity.

By the end of the 1930s the possibility of forging this Greater Germanic Reich of the future came closer to realization as Himmler reached the peak of his power. In October 1939 Hitler appointed him *Reichskommissar für die Festigung des Deutschen Volkstums* (Reich Commissar for the Strengthening

of Germandom) and he was given absolute control over the newly annexed slice of Poland. Responsible for bringing people of German descent back from outside the Reich into its borders, he set out to replace Poles and Jews by *Volksdeutsche* from the Baltic lands and various outlying parts of Poland. Within a year over a million Poles and 300,000 Jews had been uprooted and driven eastwards. With the characteristic self-pitying and ascetic ethos of self-abnegation that he inculcated into the SS, Himmler informed the *SS-Leibstandarte* Adolf Hitler Regiment: 'Gentlemen, it is much easier in many cases to go into combat with a company than to suppress an obstructive population of low cultural level, or to carry out executions or to haul away people or to evict crying and hysterical women.' It was Himmler's master stroke that he succeeded in indoctrinating the SS with an apocalyptic 'idealism' beyond all guilt and responsibility, which rationalized mass murder as a form of martyrdom and harshness towards oneself. Nowhere was this more apparent than in Himmler's notorious speech on 4 October 1943 to the SS Group Leaders in Poznan.

One principle must be absolute for the SS man: we must be honest, decent, loyal, and comradely to members of our own blood and to no one else. What happens to the Russians, what happens to the Czechs, is a matter of utter indifference to me. Such good blood of our own kind as there may be among the nations we shall acquire for ourselves, if necessary by taking away the children and bringing them up among us. Whether the other peoples live in comfort or perish of hunger interests me only in so far as we need them as slaves for our *Kultur*. Whether or not 10,000 Russian women collapse from exhaustion while digging a tank ditch interests me only in so far as the tank ditch is completed for Germany. We shall never be rough or heartless where it is not necessary; that is clear. We Germans, who are the only people in the world who have a decent attitude to animals, will also adopt a decent attitude to these human animals, but it is a crime against our own blood to worry about them and to bring them ideals. I shall speak to you here with all frankness of a very grave matter. Among ourselves it should be mentioned quite frankly, and yet we will never speak of it publicly. I mean the evacuation of the Jews, the extermination of the Jewish people.... Most of you know what it means to see a hundred corpses lying together, five hundred, or a thousand. To have stuck it out and at the same time – apart from exceptions caused by human weakness – to have remained decent fellows, that is what has made us hard. This is a page of glory in our history which has never been written and shall never be written.

In carrying out his task as supreme overseer of the 'Final Solution', Himmler proved himself a fanatical disciple of race theory with an unswerving dedication to its translation into stark reality. By the time of the invasion of the Soviet Union all the necessary levers of power were in his hands. He controlled the Reich Main Security Office through Heydrich (q.v.) and then Kaltenbrunner (q.v.), the criminal police under Nebe (q.v.), the Foreign Political Intelligence Service under Schellenberg (q.v.) and the Gestapo under Heinrich Müller (q.v.). Through the SS he ruled supreme over the concentration camps and the death camps set up in Poland, while in the Waffen-SS he had a powerful private army whose strength he had expanded from three to thirty-five divisions, making it a rival military force to the Wehrmacht. In addition to these vast powers, Himmler controlled the political administration in the occupied territories and in August 1943 he was made Minister of the Interior, giving him jurisdiction over the courts and the civil service. Himmler utilized these powers mercilessly to exploit the 'inferior' eastern peoples for slave labour, to gas millions of Jews on Hitler's orders, to plan mass abortions and the sterilization of entire ethnic groups. Under his authoriza-

tion a special SS pseudo-science developed which caused untold suffering to innocent civilians. He eagerly supplied 'asocial individuals', criminals, gypsies, Jews, etc., for so-called 'freezing experiments' (to see how much cold a human being could endure) or high altitude tests on human guinea pigs in decompression chambers. Himmler treated the results of these murderous, pseudo-medical experiments as if they had been performed on bacterial cultures. The same police dictator who was disgusted at cruelty to animals and never abused his power for personal profit was totally indifferent to the millions of human beings crushed by the mass murder machine which he controlled.

Following the July plot of 1944 Himmler's position was strengthened still further and the Wehrmacht was forced to accept him as Commander-in-Chief of the Reserve Army in addition to all his other offices. He was even given supreme command of the Army Group Vistula in spite of his lack of military experience. Towards the end of the war Himmler, however, had become convinced that Germany was on the verge of collapse and tried to approach the Allies for peace negotiations through the head of the Swedish Red Cross, Count Folke Bernadotte. He ordered the mass slaughter of Jews to be stopped on his own initiative and proposed the surrender of the German armies in the West, including Denmark and Norway, to General Eisenhower while continuing the struggle in the East. Himmler, who by this time had lost all sense of reality, evidently believed that the Allies would consider him an acceptable leader for a reconstituted Germany and even dreamed of setting up a National Socialist government in Schleswig-Holstein in May 1945 which would negotiate with the West on equal terms. Hitler, learning of the betrayal of his most loyal follower, was enraged, repudiating him in his political testament and stripping him of all his offices. Even Admiral Doenitz (q.v.), who had succeeded Hitler in the last days of the war, rejected Himmler's services. Following the German surrender, Himmler took on a false identity and tried to escape, but was captured and arrested by British troops. Brought to Lüneberg, Himmler killed himself on 23 May 1945 by swallowing a poison vial concealed in his mouth, before he could be brought to trial.

Hindemith, Paul (1895–1963) One of the foremost composers of the early twentieth century and a prominent refugee from the Third Reich, Paul Hindemith was born on 16 November 1895 in Hanau. After studying at the Frankfurt Conservatory, Hindemith began his career as a viola player, establishing himself through his string quartets as the most important of the younger generation of German composers, combining experimental and traditional techniques in a distinctive, modern style. A composer of many parts he tried his hand in various musical genres, including traditional *lieder*, ragtime music, jazz, operas and setting the song-cycles of Rilke and Trakl to music. His early atonal compositions showed affinities with Schoenberg and Stravinsky, though later he opposed the twelve-note system pioneered by Schoenberg and his followers. His most successful early operas were *Cardillac* (1926) and *Mathias der Maler* (1934), based on the life of the painter, Matthias Grünewald. He also composed children's operas such as *Wir Bauen eine Stadt* (*We are Building a City*, 1931), numerous sonatas and chamber works as well as the viola concerto, *Der Schwanendreher* (1935), based on medieval German folk songs. The songs he composed for the Berlin cabaret *Neues vom Tage* (*News of the Day*, 1929) particularly aroused Nazi anger, prompting Goebbels (q.v.) to rant against the 'atonal musicians who out of sheer sensationalism stage scenes involving nude

women in their bathtub in the most disgusting and obscene situations, and further befoul these scenes with the most atrocious dissonance of musical impotence'.

From 1927 to 1937 Hindemith was Professor at the Berlin *Hochschule für Musik* (College for Music) where he taught composition. Defended by such influential figures as Furtwängler (q.v.), Hindemith's works were performed as late as 1934, until the Nazis imposed a total ban on his work for its alleged dissonance and alien rhythms. His compositions were subsequently held up to public ridicule and featured in a 'degenerate music' exhibition along with those of Schoenberg, Mahler, Stravinsky, Weill (q.v.) and other '*Geistesjuden*'. After leaving Nazi Germany in 1938, Hindemith eventually settled in the United States where he taught at Yale University from 1940 to 1953. He became an American citizen in 1946. Hindemith succeeded in establishing a new musical form, so-called *Gebrauchsmusik* (utility music), written for specific performances by amateur school groups or chamber music organizations, which strengthened the contact between the composer and his public. In 1953 he returned to Europe to teach at the University of Zürich. He died in Frankfurt am Main on 28 December 1963.

Hindenburg, Paul von (1847–1934) General Field Marshal who became a German national hero during World War I and was Reich President from 1925 to 1934, Paul von Hindenburg was born in Poznan (Posen) on 2 October 1847. After serving in the Austro-Prussian war (1866) and the Franco-Prussian war (1870–1), von Hindenburg was appointed to the General Staff eight years later and before his retirement in 1911 had risen to the rank of Commanding General of the Fourth Army. Early during World War I, von Hindenburg was recalled to the army and made

Commander in East Prussia. Credited with victory at the Battle of Tannenberg in August 1914 over a much larger Russian force, von Hindenburg was appointed Commander-in-Chief of the German armies in the East in November and promoted to General Field Marshal. On 29 August 1916 he succeeded General von Falkenhayn as Supreme Commander of all the German armies. Together with General Erich Ludendorff (q.v.), his Chief of Staff, von Hindenburg became virtual dictator of Germany towards the end of the war, intervening in civilian affairs, regulating labour and mobilizing the rest of the economy for total warfare. Together they succeeded in stemming the Allied advance in the West. The costly offensive launched by von Hindenburg in France (March–July 1918) led to an Allied counter-offensive and, with the help of fresh American troops, the German armies were defeated and forced to surrender. Following the abdication of the Emperor Wilhelm II, von Hindenburg eventually retired to his East Prussian estate in Neudeck.

After the death of the first President of the Weimar Republic, Friedrich Ebert, in 1925, von Hindenburg was persuaded to run for office by a coalition of nationalists, Junkers and other conservative groups. His successful campaign led to his nomination in May 1925 as Reich President. During the next five years he strictly upheld the republican constitution, although increasingly under the influence of the army and his fellow Junkers. In 1930 he appointed the Catholic Centre Party leader, Heinrich Brüning (q.v.), as Chancellor, allowing him to rule by decree as the world depression began severely to affect the German economy. With Brüning's help, von Hindenburg was re-elected President in April 1932, receiving over nineteen million votes and defeating Hitler's challenge as well as that of the communist candidate, Ernst Thaelmann (q.v.).

As von Hindenburg came more deeply under the influence of the Right, and in particular of General von Schleicher (q.v.), his relations with Brüning cooled and he began to look more sympathetically on the growing Nazi Party. On 30 May 1932 he demanded Brüning's resignation, appointing von Papen (q.v.) in his place, and then on 3 December 1932 replacing him with von Schleicher. Neither appointment succeeded in containing the Nazis, since Hitler refused anything less than 'unequivocal leadership of the government' as he told von Hindenburg in an interview in August 1932. The increasingly senile Reich President gradually modified his low opinion of 'the Bohemian corporal' (Hitler), under the influence of his son Oskar and his Reich Chancellery chief, Otto Meissner (q.v.). Together with von Papen they persuaded the ageing Field Marshal to remove von Schleicher and appoint Hitler as Chancellor on 30 January 1933. While he was still consolidating his power, the Nazi leader continued to pay lip service to the authority of the virtually impotent von Hindenburg, exploiting his name and status as a folk hero for his own ends. By the time of von Hindenburg's death in Neudeck on 2 August 1934, the Third Reich was already firmly established and by the end of the month his presidential functions had been transferred by plebiscitary decision to the Führer and Chancellor, Adolf Hitler.

Hitler, Adolf (1889–1945) Founder and leader of the Nazi Party, Reich Chancellor and guiding spirit of the Third Reich from 1933 to 1945, Head of State and Supreme Commander of the Armed Forces, Adolf Hitler was born in Braunau am Inn, Austria, on 20 April 1889. The son of a fifty-two-year-old Austrian customs official, Alois Schickelgruber Hitler, and his third wife, a young peasant girl, Klara Poelzl, both from the backwoods of lower Austria, the young

Hitler was a resentful, discontented child. Moody, lazy, of unstable temperament, he was deeply hostile towards his strict, authoritarian father and strongly attached to his indulgent, hard-working mother, whose death from cancer in December 1908 was a shattering blow to the adolescent Hitler. After spending four years in the *Realschule* in Linz, he left school at the age of sixteen with dreams of becoming a painter. In October 1907 the provincial, middle-class boy left home for Vienna, where he was to remain until 1913 leading a bohemian, vagabond existence. Embittered at his rejection by the Viennese Academy of Fine Arts, he was to spend 'five years of misery and woe' in Vienna as he later recalled, adopting a view of life which changed very little in the ensuing years, shaped as it was by a pathological hatred of Jews and Marxists, liberalism and the cosmopolitan Habsburg monarchy. Existing from hand to mouth on occasional odd jobs and the hawking of sketches in low taverns, the young Hitler compensated for the frustrations of a lonely bachelor's life in miserable male hostels by political harangues in cheap cafés to anyone who would listen and indulging in grandiose dreams of a Greater Germany.

In Vienna he acquired his first education in politics by studying the demagogic techniques of the popular Christian-social Mayor, Karl Lueger, and picked up the stereotyped, obsessive anti-semitism with its brutal, violent sexual connotations and concern with the 'purity of blood' that remained with him to the end of his career. From crackpot racial theorists like the defrocked monk, Lanz von Liebenfels, and the Austrian Pan-German leader, Georg von Schoenerer, the young Hitler learned to discern in the 'Eternal Jew' the symbol and cause of all chaos, corruption and destruction in culture, politics and the economy. The press, prostitution, syphilis, capitalism, Marxism, democracy and

pacifism – all were so many means which 'the Jew' exploited in his conspiracy to undermine the German nation and the purity of the creative Aryan race. In May 1913 Hitler left Vienna for Munich and, when war broke out in August 1914, he joined the Sixteenth Bavarian Infantry Regiment, serving as a despatch runner. Hitler proved an able, courageous soldier, receiving the Iron Cross (First Class) for bravery, but did not rise above the rank of Lance Corporal. Twice wounded, he was badly gassed four weeks before the end of the war and spent three months recuperating in a hospital in Pomerania. Temporarily blinded and driven to impotent rage by the abortive November 1918 revolution in Germany as well as the military defeat, Hitler, once restored, was convinced that fate had chosen him to rescue a humiliated nation from the shackles of the Versailles Treaty, from Bolsheviks and Jews.

Assigned by the Reichswehr in the summer of 1919 to 'educational' duties which consisted largely of spying on political parties in the overheated atmosphere of post-revolutionary Munich, Hitler was sent to investigate a small nationalistic group of idealists, the German Workers' Party. On 16 September 1919 he entered the Party (which had approximately forty members), soon changed its name to the National Socialist German Workers' Party (NSDAP) and had imposed himself as its Chairman by July 1921. Hitler discovered a powerful talent for oratory as well as giving the new Party its symbol – the swastika – and its greeting 'Heil!'. His hoarse, grating voice, for all the bombastic, humourless, histrionic content of his speeches, dominated audiences by dint of his tone of impassioned conviction and gift for self-dramatization. By November 1921 Hitler was recognized as Führer of a movement which had 3,000 members, and boosted his personal power by organizing strong-arm squads to keep order at his meetings and break up those of his opponents. Out of these squads grew the storm troopers (SA) organized by Captain Ernst Röhm (q.v.) and Hitler's black-shirted personal bodyguard, the *Schutzstaffel* (SS). Hitler focused his propaganda against the Versailles Treaty, the 'November criminals', the Marxists and the visible, internal enemy No. 1, the 'Jew', who was responsible for all Germany's domestic problems.

In the twenty-five-point programme of the NSDAP announced on 24 February 1920, the exclusion of the Jews from the *Volk* community, the myth of Aryan race supremacy and extreme nationalism were combined with 'socialistic' ideas of profit-sharing and nationalization inspired by ideologues like Gottfried Feder (q.v.). Hitler's first written utterance on political questions dating from this period emphasized that what he called 'the anti-semitism of reason' must lead 'to the systematic combating and elimination of Jewish privileges. Its ultimate goal must implacably be the total removal of the Jews.' By November 1923 Hitler was convinced that the Weimar Republic was on the verge of collapse and, together with General Ludendorff (q.v.) and local nationalist groups, sought to overthrow the Bavarian government in Munich. Bursting into a beer-hall in Munich and firing his pistol into the ceiling, he shouted out that he was heading a new provisional government which would carry through a revolution against 'Red Berlin'. Hitler and Ludendorff then marched through Munich at the head of 3,000 men, only to be met by police fire which left sixteen dead and brought the attempted *putsch* to an ignominious end. Hitler was arrested and tried on 26 February 1924, succeeding in turning the tables on his accusers with a confident, propagandist speech which ended with the prophecy: 'Pronounce us guilty a thou-

sand times over: the goddess of the eternal court of history will smile and tear to pieces the State Prosecutor's submission and the court's verdict for she acquits us.' Sentenced to five years' imprisonment in Landsberg fortress, Hitler was released after only nine months during which he dictated *Mein Kampf* (*My Struggle*) to his loyal follower, Rudolf Hess (q.v.). Subsequently the 'bible' of the Nazi Party, this crude, half-baked hotchpotch of primitive Social Darwinism, racial myth, anti-semitism and *lebensraum* fantasy had sold over five million copies by 1939 and been translated into eleven languages.

The failure of the Beer-Hall *putsch* and his period of imprisonment transformed Hitler from an incompetent adventurer into a shrewd political tactician, who henceforth decided that he would never again confront the gun barrels of army and police until they were under his command. He concluded that the road to power lay not through force alone but through legal subversion of the Weimar Constitution, the building of a mass movement and the combination of parliamentary strength with extra-parliamentary street terror and intimidation. Helped by Goering (q.v.) and Goebbels (q.v.) he began to reassemble his followers and rebuild the movement which had disintegrated in his absence. In January 1925 the ban on the Nazi Party was removed and Hitler regained permission to speak in public. Outmanoeuvring the 'socialist' North German wing of the Party under Gregor Strasser (q.v.), Hitler re-established himself in 1926 as the ultimate arbiter to whom all factions appealed in an ideologically and socially heterogeneous movement. Avoiding rigid, programmatic definitions of National Socialism which would have undermined the charismatic nature of his legitimacy and his claim to absolute leadership, Hitler succeeded in extending his appeal beyond

Bavaria and attracting both Right and Left to his movement.

Though the Nazi Party won only twelve seats in the 1928 elections, the onset of the Great Depression with its devastating effects on the middle classes helped Hitler to win over all those strata in German society who felt their economic existence was threatened. In addition to peasants, artisans, craftsmen, traders, small businessmen, ex-officers, students and déclassé intellectuals, the Nazis in 1929 began to win over the big industrialists, nationalist conservatives and army circles. With the backing of the press tycoon, Alfred Hugenberg (q.v.), Hitler received a tremendous nationwide exposure just as the effects of the world economic crisis hit Germany, producing mass unemployment, social dissolution, fear and indignation. With demagogic virtuosity, Hitler played on national resentments, feelings of revolt and the desire for strong leadership using all the most modern techniques of mass persuasion to present himself as Germany's redeemer and messianic saviour. In the 1930 elections the Nazi vote jumped dramatically from 810,000 to 6,409,000 (18.3 per cent of the total vote) and they received 107 seats in the Reichstag.

Prompted by Hjalmar Schacht (q.v.) and Fritz Thyssen (q.v.), the great industrial magnates began to contribute liberally to the coffers of the NSDAP, reassured by Hitler's performance before the Industrial Club in Düsseldorf on 27 January 1932 that they had nothing to fear from the radicals in the Party. The following month Hitler officially acquired German citizenship and decided to run for the Presidency, receiving 13,418,011 votes in the run-off elections of 10 April 1931 as against 19,359,650 votes for the victorious von Hindenburg (q.v.), but four times the vote for the communist candidate, Ernst Thaelmann (q.v.). In the Reichstag elections of July 1932 the Nazis emerged as the largest political party in Germany, obtaining nearly fourteen million votes (37.3 per cent) and 230 seats. Although the NSDAP fell back in November 1932 to eleven million votes (196 seats), Hitler was helped to power by a camarilla of conservative politicians led by Franz von Papen (q.v.), who persuaded the reluctant von Hindenburg to nominate 'the Bohemian corporal' as Reich Chancellor on 30 January 1933. Once in the saddle, Hitler moved with great speed to outmanoeuvre his rivals, virtually ousting the conservatives from any real participation in government by July 1933, abolishing the free trade unions, eliminating the communists, Social Democrats and Jews from any role in political life and sweeping opponents into concentration camps.

The Reichstag fire of 27 February 1933 had provided him with the perfect pretext to begin consolidating the foundations of a totalitarian one-party State, and special 'enabling laws' were ramrodded through the Reichstag to legalize the régime's intimidatory tactics. With support from the nationalists, Hitler gained a majority at the last 'democratic' elections held in Germany on 5 March 1933 and with cynical skill he used the whole gamut of persuasion, propaganda, terror and intimidation to secure his hold on power. The seductive notions of 'National Awakening' and a 'Legal Revolution' helped paralyse potential opposition and disguise the reality of autocratic power behind a façade of traditional institutions. The destruction of the radical SA leadership under Ernst Röhm in the Blood Purge of June 1934 confirmed Hitler as undisputed dictator of the Third Reich and by the beginning of August, when he united the positions of Führer and Chancellor on the death of von Hindenburg, he had all the powers of State in his hands. Avoiding any institutionalization of authority and status which could challenge his own undisputed position as supreme arbiter, Hitler allowed subordinates like Himmler (q.v.), Goering (q.v.) and Goebbels (q.v.) to mark out their own domains of arbitrary power while multiplying and duplicating offices to a bewildering degree.

During the next four years Hitler enjoyed a dazzling string of domestic and international successes, outwitting rival political leaders abroad just as he had defeated his opposition at home. In 1935 he abandoned the Versailles Treaty and began to build up the army by conscripting five times its permitted number. He persuaded Great Britain to allow an increase in the naval building programme and in March 1936 he occupied the demilitarized Rhineland without meeting opposition. He began building up the Luftwaffe and supplied military aid to Francoist forces in Spain, which brought about the Spanish fascist victory in 1939. The German rearmament programme led to full employment and an unrestrained expansion of production, which reinforced by his foreign policy successes – the Rome–Berlin pact of 1936, the *Anschluss* with Austria and the 'liberation' of the Sudeten Germans in 1938 – brought Hitler to the zenith of his popularity. In February 1938 he dismissed sixteen senior generals and took personal command of the armed forces, thus ensuring that he would be able to implement his aggressive designs.

Hitler's sabre-rattling tactics bludgeoned the British and French into the humiliating Munich agreement of 1938 and the eventual dismantlement of the Czechoslovakian State in March 1939. The concentration camps, the Nuremberg racial laws against the Jews, the persecution of the churches and political dissidents were forgotten by many Germans in the euphoria of Hitler's territorial expansion and bloodless victories. The next designated target for Hitler's ambitions was Poland (her independence guaranteed by Britain and France) and, to avoid a two-front war, the Nazi dictator signed a pact of friendship and non-

aggression with Soviet Russia. On 1 September 1939 German armies invaded Poland and henceforth his main energies were devoted to the conduct of a war he had unleashed to dominate Europe and secure Germany's 'living space'.

The first phase of World War II was dominated by German *Blitzkrieg* tactics: sudden shock attacks against airfields, communications, military installations, using fast mobile armour and infantry to follow up on the first wave of bomber and fighter aircraft. Poland was overrun in nineteen days, Denmark and Norway in two months, Holland, Belgium, Luxemburg and France in six weeks. After the fall of France in June 1940 only Great Britain stood firm. The Battle of Britain, in which the Royal Air Force prevented the Luftwaffe from securing aerial control over the English Channel, was Hitler's first setback, causing the planned invasion of the British Isles to be postponed. Hitler turned to the Balkans and North Africa where his Italian allies had suffered defeats, his armies rapidly overrunning Greece, Yugoslavia, the island of Crete and driving the British from Cyrenaica.

The crucial decision of his career, the invasion of Soviet Russia on 22 June 1941, was rationalized by the idea that its destruction would prevent Great Britain from continuing the war with any prospect of success. He was convinced that once he kicked the door in, as he told Jodl (q.v.), 'the whole rotten edifice [of communist rule] will come tumbling down' and the campaign would be over in six weeks. The war against Russia was to be an anti-Bolshivek crusade, a war of annihilation in which the fate of European Jewry would finally be sealed. At the end of January 1939 Hitler had prophesied that 'if the international financial Jewry within and outside Europe should succeed once more in dragging the nations into a war, the result will be, not the Bolshevization of the world and thereby the victory of Jewry, but the annihilation of the Jewish race in Europe'. As the war widened – the United States by the end of 1941 had entered the struggle against the Axis powers – Hitler identified the totality of Germany's enemies with 'international Jewry', who supposedly stood behind the British-American-Soviet alliance. The policy of forced emigration had manifestly failed to remove the Jews from Germany's expanded *lebensraum*, increasing their numbers under German rule as the Wehrmacht moved East.

The widening of the conflict into a world war by the end of 1941, the refusal of the British to accept Germany's right to continental European hegemony (which Hitler attributed to 'Jewish' influence) and to agree to his 'peace' terms, the racial-ideological nature of the assault on Soviet Russia, finally drove Hitler to implement the 'Final Solution of the Jewish Question' which had been under consideration since 1939. The measures already taken in those regions of Poland annexed to the Reich against Jews (and Poles) indicated the genocidal implications of Nazi-style 'Germanization' policies. The invasion of Soviet Russia was to set the seal on Hitler's notion of territorial conquest in the East, which was inextricably linked with annihilating the 'biological roots of Bolshevism' and hence with the liquidation of all Jews under German rule.

At first the German armies carried all before them, overrunning vast territories, overwhelming the Red Army, encircling Leningrad and reaching within striking distance of Moscow. Within a few months of the invasion Hitler's armies had extended the Third Reich from the Atlantic to the Caucasus, from the Baltic to the Black Sea. But the Soviet Union did not collapse as expected and Hitler, instead of concentrating his attack on Moscow, ordered a pincer movement around Kiev to seize the Ukraine, increasingly procrastinating and changing his mind about objectives. Underestimating the depth of military reserves on which the Russians could call, the calibre of their generals and the resilient, fighting spirit of the Russian people (whom he dismissed as inferior peasants), Hitler prematurely proclaimed in October 1941 that the Soviet Union had been 'struck down and would never rise again'. In reality he had overlooked the pitiless Russian winter to which his own troops were now condemned and which forced the Wehrmacht to abandon the highly mobile warfare which had previously brought such spectacular successes. The disaster before Moscow in December 1941 led him to dismiss his Commander-in-Chief von Brauchitsch (q.v.), and many other key commanders who sought permission for tactical withdrawals, including Guderian (q.v.), Bock (q.v.), Hoepner (q.v.), von Rundstedt (q.v.) and Leeb (q.v.), found themselves cashiered.

Hitler now assumed personal control of all military operations, refusing to listen to advice, disregarding unpalatable facts and rejecting everything that did not fit into his preconceived picture of reality. His neglect of the Mediterranean theatre and the Middle East, the failure of the Italians, the entry of the United States into the war, and above all the stubborn determination of the Russians, pushed Hitler on to the defensive. From the winter of 1941 the writing was on the wall but Hitler refused to countenance military defeat, believing that implacable will and the rigid refusal to abandon positions could make up for inferior resources and the lack of a sound overall strategy. Convinced that his own General Staff was weak and indecisive, if not openly treacherous, Hitler became more prone to outbursts of blind, hysterical fury towards his generals, when he did not retreat into bouts of misanthropic brooding. His health, too, deteriorated under the impact of the drugs prescribed by his quack physician, Dr Theodor Morell. Hitler's personal decline, symbolized by his increasingly rare public appearances and his self-enforced isolation in the 'Wolf's Lair', his headquarters buried deep in the East Prussian forests, coincided with the visible signs of the coming German defeat which became apparent in mid-1942.

Rommel's (q.v.) defeat at El Alamein and the subsequent loss of North Africa to the Anglo-American forces were overshadowed by the disaster at Stalingrad where General von Paulus's (q.v.) Sixth Army was cut off and surrendered to the Russians in January 1943. In July 1943 the Allies captured Sicily and Mussolini's régime collapsed in Italy. In September the Italians signed an armistice and the Allies landed at Salerno, reaching Naples on 1 October and taking Rome on 4 June 1944. The Allied invasion of Normandy followed on 6 June 1944 and soon a million Allied troops were driving the German armies eastwards, while from the opposite direction the Soviet forces advanced relentlessly on the Reich. The total mobilization of the German war economy under Albert Speer (q.v.) and the energetic propaganda efforts of Joseph Goebbels (q.v.) to rouse the fighting spirit of the German people were impotent to change the fact that the Third Reich lacked the resources equal to a struggle against the world alliance which Hitler himself had provoked.

Allied bombing began to have a telling effect on German industrial production and to undermine the morale of the population. The generals, frustrated by Hitler's total refusal to trust them in the field and recognizing the inevitability of defeat, planned, together with the small anti-Nazi Resistance inside the Reich, to assassinate the Führer on 20 July 1944, hoping to pave the way for a negotiated peace with the Allies that would save Germany from destruction. The plot failed and Hitler took implacable vengeance on the conspirators, watching with satisfaction a film of the grisly executions carried out on his orders. As disaster came closer, Hitler buried himself in the unreal world of the *Führerbunker* in Berlin, clutching at fantastic hopes that his 'secret weapons', the V-1 and V-2 rockets, would yet turn the tide of war. He gestured wildly over maps, planned and directed attacks with non-existent armies and indulged in endless, night-long monologues which reflected his growing senility, misanthropy and contempt for the 'cowardly failure' of the German people.

As the Red Army approached Berlin and the Anglo-Americans reached the Elbe, on 19 March 1945 Hitler ordered the destruction of what remained of German industry, communications and transport systems. He was resolved that, if he did not survive, Germany too should be destroyed. The same ruthless nihilism and passion for destruction which had led to the extermination of six million Jews in death camps, to the biological 'cleansing' of the sub-human Slavs and other subject peoples in the New Order, was finally turned on his own people. On 29 April 1945 he married his mistress Eva Braun (q.v.) and dictated his final political testament, concluding with the same monotonous, obsessive fixation that had guided his career from the beginning: 'Above all I charge the leaders of the nation and those under them to scrupulous observance of the laws of race and to merciless opposition to the universal poisoner of all peoples, international Jewry.' The following day Hitler committed suicide, shooting himself through the mouth with a pistol. His body was carried into the garden of the Reich Chancellery by aides, covered with petrol and burned along with that of Eva Braun. This final, macabre act of self-destruction appropriately symbolized the career of a political leader whose main legacy to Europe was the ruin of its civilization and the senseless sacrifice of human life for the sake of power and his own commitment to the bestial nonsense of National Socialist race mythology. With his death nothing was left of the 'Greater Germanic Reich', of the tyrannical power structure and ideological system which had devastated Europe during the twelve years of his totalitarian rule.

Hoepner, Erich (1886–1944) Wehrmacht General and leading member of the Resistance against Hitler, Erich Hoepner was born in Frankfurt an der Oder on 14 September 1886. A politically minded General, he had taken part in the Kapp *putsch* in his younger days and, in September 1938, as Commander of the Sixteenth Panzer Corps in Thuringia, he was assigned to the task of disarming the SS should it attempt to interfere in the army's plans for removing Hitler. The plot came to nothing and Hoepner took an active part in the military campaigns against Poland, France and the Soviet Union. Along with Guderian (q.v.) he was considered the leading exponent of armoured warfare in the Wehrmacht, being given command in 1941 of the Fourth Armoured Corps on the eastern front, but was unjustly dismissed in December of the same year for retreating in the face of a Russian counter-offensive when Moscow was in his sights. Hoepner was publicly humiliated in an order of the day and even denied the right to wear uniform, a treatment which turned him once more into an active conspirator. Hoepner was designated to take over command of the home forces should General Fromm (q.v.) prove unreliable and was also considered for the post of Minister of War in a new provisional government. After the failure of the July plot of 1944 he was arrested and tried by the People's Court, being subjected to the brutal jibes of its president, Roland Freisler (q.v.). Hoepner, who preferred to go on trial rather than accept the offer of a cere-monial suicide, appeared unconvincing in his evidence, having been brutally mistreated by his Gestapo interrogators while under arrest. On 8 August 1944 he was hanged by wire suspended from meathooks at Plötzensee prison in Berlin.

Hoess, Rudolf (1900–47) Commandant of the concentration and extermination camp at Auschwitz between 1940 and 1943, Rudolf Hoess was born in Baden-Baden on 25 November 1900, the son of pious Catholic parents. His father, a shopkeeper who wanted his son to become a Roman Catholic priest, was a dogmatic, overpowering influence in his early life. After his father's death, the fifteen-year-old Rudolf Hoess secretly joined the army, serving on the Turkish front and becoming at seventeen the youngest NCO in the German forces, as well as receiving the Iron Cross (First and Second Classes) for bravery. In 1919 he joined the East Prussian Volunteer Corps for Protection of the Frontier and became a member of the Rossbach *Freikorps*, taking part in battles in the Baltic region, the Ruhr and Upper Silesia. In 1923 he was involved in a brutal political murder – one of his accomplices was Martin Bormann (q.v.) who subsequently protected him at a later stage in his career – for which he was sentenced to ten years' imprisonment. He was released under the Amnesty Law of 14 July 1928, having served less than half his sentence, and for the next six years worked on the land in Brandenburg and Pomerania in various service groups. In 1934 Himmler (q.v.) invited him to join the active SS and, in June of the same year, he was posted to the protective custody camp at Dachau as a block overseer. Transferred to Sachsenhausen in 1938 and promoted to SS Captain two years later, Hoess was appointed Commandant at Auschwitz on 1 May 1940, a position he held until 1 December 1943.

During his three and a half years at Auschwitz, Hoess proved himself the ideal type of the passionless, disinterested mass murderer, the quiet bureaucrat who never personally attended selections for the gas chambers or mass executions. To all appearances a kindly, unselfish, introverted family man and animal-lover, Hoess took a perfectionist pride in his 'work', noting in his memoirs that 'by the will of the *Reichsführer-SS*, Auschwitz became the greatest human extermination centre of all time'. It was Hoess, the perfect example of the conscientious, self-disciplined, petty-bourgeois automaton whose golden rule was 'Only one thing is valid: orders!', who ensured the smooth functioning of the extermination system at Auschwitz, treating mass murder as a purely administrative procedure. What concerned Hoess was not the indescribable suffering of his victims but rather the practical difficulties of carrying out his assignment with maximum efficiency – questions involving the precise adherence to timetables, the size of transports, the types of oven and methods of gassing. He took pride in being the first to utilize successfully 'Zyklon B' – the squeamish Hoess, who could not bear shootings and bloodshed, found gas to be infinitely more rational, bloodless and hygienic. Hoess's sense of duty, his absolute submission to authority, his conscientious adherence to the SS motto 'Believe! Obey! Fight!' immunized him to any emotion except that of self-pity.

In his autobiography, *Kommandant in Auschwitz* (which first appeared in Germany in 1958), Hoess recalled that from his earliest youth he was brought up 'with a strong awareness of duty'. In his parents' home 'it was insisted that every task be exactly and conscientiously carried out. Every member of the family had his own special duties to perform.' He regarded this compulsion to obey orders and to surrender all personal independence as a hallmark of his own mo-

rality and bourgeois decency. 'I am completely normal', he observed in his book. 'Even while I was carrying out the task of extermination I lived a normal life and so on.'

So efficiently did Hoess carry out his 'duties' at Auschwitz that approximately two-and-a-half million inmates were liquidated and in 1944 he was commended by his superiors as 'a true pioneer in this field, thanks to new ideas and new methods of education'. Hoess found it difficult to uproot himself from his 'work' at Auschwitz, but in November 1943 he was made head of No. 1 branch of *Amtsgruppe* D of the WVHA (SS Economic and Administrative Main Office), later becoming the deputy of SS General Richard Gluecks (q.v.), Inspector-General of Concentration Camps. Hoess was arrested by military police near Flensburg, Schleswig-Holstein, on 2 March 1946 and handed over to the Polish authorities just over two months later. At the end of March 1947, Hoess was sentenced to death by a Polish military tribunal. The execution was carried out on 7 April 1947, next to the house inside the Auschwitz camp where he had lived with his wife and five children and where he had sent millions of innocent men, women and children to their deaths.

Hofacker, Caesar von (1896–1944) Lieutenant-Colonel on the staff of General Heinrich von Stuelpnagel (q.v.), the Military Governor of France, and closely involved in the officers' plot against Hitler, Caesar von Hofacker was born on 2 March 1896. The liaison man between von Stuelpnagel and his cousin, Lieutenant-Colonel Claus von Stauffenberg (q.v.), in Berlin, von Hofacker was also implicated in efforts to bring Field Marshal Erwin Rommel (q.v.) into the conspiracy when the final defeat of the German army appeared to be imminent. Following his arrest after the failure of the July 1944 plot, von Hofacker was tortured by the Gestapo, blurting out Rommel's name to his interrogators and thereby sealing the latter's fate. Von Hofacker was tried and found guilty of treason by the People's Court, dying in agony on a meathook on 20 December 1944.

Hoffmann, Heinrich (1885–1957) Hitler's official photographer, his close confidant and friend, Heinrich Hoffmann was born in Fürth on 12 September 1885. As a youngster, Hoffmann learnt his profession after school while working in his father's photography shop. During World War I he served as a photographer in the Bavarian army, publishing his first book of photographs in 1919. In the same year he first met Hitler, the beginning of an intimate personal relationship. Hitler would often visit the Hoffmanns' home in Munich for relaxation. It was through the photographer that the future leader of the Third Reich first met Eva Braun (q.v.) who worked in his shop, and Hoffmann also frequently drove him to the Wagner home in Bayreuth to see Frau Winifred Wagner (q.v.). In 1920 Hoffmann joined the NSDAP and soon belonged to the inner circle of Hitler's intimate companions. The only man allowed to photograph the Führer, he accompanied him everywhere on his road to power and later, during World War II, travelled with him to all the various fronts. Hoffmann's two-and-a-half million photographs provide a unique record of twenty-five years of German history and helped to make him an enormously wealthy man, as well as enriching Hitler himself and enhancing his popularity. In the 1930s he published the pictorial booklets on each of the major Party rallies. Perhaps his greatest success was *Hitler, wie ihn Keiner Kennt* (*The Hitler Nobody Knows*), published in 1933, which showed a relaxed, genial, friendly and accessible Führer. For the new edition four years later, the pictures of the

murdered Ernst Röhm (q.v.) had disappeared down the memory-hole.

Other books of Hoffmann's, consisting of plates and portraits with captions, which enjoyed heavy sales, included *Jugend um Hitler* (1934), *Hitler in seiner Heimat* (1938), *Hitler in Italien* (1938), *Hitler Befreit Sudetenland* (1938, with an introduction by Konrad Henlein) and *Das Antlitz des Führers* (1939). In 1938 Hoffmann was appointed Professor by Hitler and in January 1940 the court photographer became a member of the Reichstag for the electoral district of Düsseldorf East. His status in the Party, which had gone up when his daughter Henny married Baldur von Schirach (q.v.), the Reich Youth Leader, was not however based on politics as much as on his artistic and business connections with the Führer. Hitler shared Hoffmann's taste in paintings and gave him the responsibility of sifting through paintings submitted for the annual Grand Art Show. It was Hoffmann's idea that Hitler should receive a royalty for every photograph of himself which appeared on a postage stamp, which led to the accumulation of enormous sums of money to the Führer's account. Hoffmann was tried as a Nazi profiteer in 1947, sentenced to ten years' imprisonment (later reduced to three, then raised to five years in 1950) and nearly all of his personal fortune was confiscated. He died in Munich on 16 December 1957.

Höhn, Reinhard (born 1904) German jurist born in Graefenthal, Thuringia, on 29 July 1904, Höhn was one of a younger breed of technocrats and middle-class academics who made spectacular careers in the Third Reich. After studying law at various German universities, Höhn became a prominent official in the Young German Order, which was close to the German National People's Party and the Stahlhelm. He entered the Nazi Party on 1 May 1933 and the SS a year later. By 1935 he was an adjunct

Professor at Heidelberg, a year later he was a member of the Academy of German Law and from 1939 until 1945 he was Director of the Institute of Research on the State at the University of Berlin. Since 1935 Höhn had been Heydrich's legal adviser as head of the main section in the SD Central Office in Berlin. His philosophy of law supported the leadership principle (*Führerprinzip*) and the complete subjection of the individual to the National Socialist *Volksgemeinschaft*, defined as a 'species community' based on blood and soil. In his lectures during the war, Höhn gave legal justification to draconian penalties (including the death sentence), even for minor crimes, especially against Poles and other occupied peoples. The will of the German racial community as embodied in the Führer had supplanted, in Höhn's teaching, any residues of individual rights and democratic safeguards provided by a liberal–rational legal system. After the war, Höhn disappeared from view for a number of years. In 1956 he became the head of one of Europe's leading managerial schools.

Hossbach, Friedrich (1894–1980) General of Infantry and Hitler's Wehrmacht Adjutant between 1934 and 1938, Friedrich Hossbach was born in Unna on 21 November 1894. He began his military career as a cadet in October 1913 and was promoted to Lieutenant in October 1914, spending the war on the eastern front. In 1920 he joined the Reichswehr and seven years later he was appointed a Captain in the War Office. Promoted to Major in 1934, Hossbach became Adjutant to the Führer and Chief of the Central Section of the General Staff and Wehrmacht, a position he held until 28 January 1938. Made a Colonel on 1 March 1937, Hossbach gave his name eight months later to a famous memorandum – the Hossbach Protocol – when he recorded the minutes of the conference given by Hitler to the Commanders-

in-Chief of the land, air and sea forces and to the Foreign Minister at a secret meeting held in the Reich Chancellery. At this conference Hitler outlined a long-term plan of continental expansion, asserting the right to greater *lebensraum* of the German 'racial community' and his determination to overthrow Austria and Czechoslovakia in the near future. The full account, based on Colonel Hossbach's careful notes, was revealed at the Nuremberg trials and is one of the most complete and important statements of Hitler's foreign policy intentions. Hossbach was dismissed from his post as Adjutant at the time of the Blomberg–Fritsch (q.v.) crisis, but restored to the General Staff in 1939. Promoted to Major General on 1 March 1942, made Lieutenant-General exactly five months later and then General of Infantry on 1 November 1943, Hossbach was given command of the Sixteenth Panzer Corps. He spent the next two years on the Russian front, taking over as Commander of the Fourth Army on 28 January 1945, only to be dismissed two days later for withdrawing his troops in East Prussia in disregard of the Führer's orders. General Hossbach died on 10 September 1980.

Huch, Ricarda (1864–1947) Poetess and a prominent writer of the neo-romantic school, who specialized in historical novels, Ricarda Huch was born on 18 July 1864 in Braunschweig. After receiving her doctorate in history at Zürich in 1892, she worked in the town library for a while as a secretary before taking up a teaching position in Bremen. She subsequently lived in Vienna, Munich and Heidelberg. Among the works which she was best known for were *Die Geschichte von Garibaldi* (1906), *Der Sinn der Heiligen Schrift* (1918) and *Michael Unger, Frühling in der Schweiz* (1938). In 1931 she was awarded the Goethe Prize, but resigned after 1933 from membership of the Prussian Academy of Fine Arts in protest at the Nazi dismissals policy directed against Jews. After the fall of the Third Reich, whose brutal methods she thoroughly detested, the octogenarian writer urged the German public to honour the men and women of the Resistance as heroes who had fought against a ruthless system of terror that had dishonoured and brought about Germany's ruin. The eighty-three-year-old authoress died a year after this appeal, in Schonberg im Taunus on 17 November 1947.

Hugenberg, Alfred (1865–1951) German press and film tycoon who by joining forces with Hitler helped him to gain power according to the letter of the Weimar Constitution, Alfred Hugenberg was born in Hanover on 19 June 1865. A co-founder in 1890 of the Pan-German League, whose aggressively nationalist war-cry was 'Deutschland wach auf', Hugenberg began his spectacularly successful business career as a Director of the Krupp concern – he was Chairman of the Board between 1909 and 1918 – before setting up on his own. During the inflation of the early 1920s, Hugenberg made huge profits and bought up scores of provincial newspapers. Gradually he built up a great chain of newspaper and news agencies, obtained a controlling interest in UFA (Universum Film AG) – Germany's largest producer of feature films and newsreels – and used his near monopolistic position in the communications industry to mobilize German middle-class opinion against the Weimar Republic. Hugenberg controlled the Scherl publishing house, one of the largest newspaper, periodical and book publishing firms in Berlin; he took over Vera Verlag, which owned or managed fourteen provincial newspapers; he bought up Ala-Anzeiger AG, which gave him a dominant position in the advertising field; and he gained control of the Telegraphen

Union, another publishing firm. This was the greatest concentration of power operating on German public opinion, and it was mobilized to support an ultra-nationalist programme and at the same time to declare war on pacifism, internationalism, democracy and socialism.

Hugenberg was an industrialist who made a fortune by preaching conservative reaction and helped to put the Nazis in power in order to expand further his economic interests. A Reichstag deputy of the *Deutsch-Nationale Volkspartei* (German National People's Party) from 1920, he was made its sole Chairman on 21 October 1928, a position he held until its disbandment (under intense Nazi pressure) on 28 June 1933. In 1929 Hugenberg joined forces with the Nazi movement in a massive campaign against the reparations envisaged by the Young Plan and placed his huge propaganda machine for the first time at Hitler's disposal. Thus, at the outset of the world economic crisis, Hitler's name became widely known to the German people, thanks to the short-sightedness of an old-fashioned, diehard conservative leader convinced that he could manipulate the Nazis for his own ends. The German Nationalists, who essentially represented the agrarian lobby in the Reichstag – the industrial backers of Hugenberg's party were increasingly alienated by his high-handed, inflexible policies – proved, however, to be no match for the National Socialists in their tactical alliance between 1929 and 1933.

In January 1933 Hitler still needed Hugenberg's Nationalists to bring the Nazi share of the popular vote over the 50 per cent margin and to provide an aura of social respectability and Prussian tradition to his destruction of democratic institutions. Hugenberg was therefore made Minister of Economics and Agriculture in Hitler's first cabinet on 30 January 1933. In the elections of 5 March 1933, the Nationalists, however, gained only 8 per cent of the votes cast and Hugenberg's hopes of being able to control Hitler began to fade away. The SA was used to harass Hugenberg's supporters, his own economic ideas were attacked in the Nazi press as reactionary and his Nationalist Party was subverted from within. On 27 June 1933 he was virtually forced to resign and the next day his own party was dissolved. Henceforth he was kept out of politics until his death at the age of eighty-six, managing to outlive both Hitler and the Third Reich. Although obliged to sell off some of his huge combine to the Nazi Party as a result of economic and political pressures, Hugenberg was allowed to retain control of his newspaper and publishing business until 1943. Even then, when the Nazi-controlled Eher Verlag entered negotiations to take over his Scherl Verlag, Hugenberg drove a hard bargain, coming out with a substantial block of shares of Rhenish-Westphalian industry in his briefcase. Hugenberg was able to retain this property after the war and emerge scot-free, since the Detmold de-Nazification court classified him in 1949 as a 'fellow-traveller' and chose not to penalize him for his role as a gravedigger of Weimar democracy and an accomplice of Hitler. Hugenberg's fellow-travelling was in many ways the embodiment of the complicity of the German middle classes as a whole, whose outlook he had done much to shape and condition. He died on 12 March 1951, in Kukenbruch bei Rinteln.

J

Jannings, Emil (1884–1950) Prominent stage and screen actor who was already a great star in the Weimar period and continued to be a highly successful and popular film idol under the Third Reich, Emil Jannings was born in Rohrschach, Switzerland, on 23 July 1884. The son of an American-born father and a German mother, Jannings was raised in middle-class comfort, but ran away from home to become a sailor at the age of sixteen. Two years later he decided to become a professional actor and began his stage career in 1906, appearing in Königsberg, Nuremberg and Leipzig. Discovered by the famous theatrical director Max Reinhardt, he was subsequently given parts at the Deutsches Theatre, emerging as one of the leading stage actors in Weimar. Powerfully built, with an enormous stage presence, Jannings's film debut began in 1919 and his work extended to the end of the Third Reich, establishing him along with Heinrich George (q.v.), Gustaf Gründgens (q.v.) and Werner Krauss (q.v.) as one of a quartet of outstanding movie actors whose careers survived the collapse of republican democracy in Germany. In the 1920s Jannings starred in a number of important and influential films, including his *tour de force* role in Murnau's *Der Letzte Mann* (1924), where he played the part of an old doorman of a great hotel, too old for his job, who loses status and self-respect along with his uniform when he becomes a lavatory attendant. Jannings also played the circus acrobat in Dupont's *Variété* (Variety, 1925) which so impressed Hollywood that he was offered (along with the producer and chief cameraman) an irresistible contract with Paramount and left for America. He won an Oscar in 1927/8 as best actor for his performances in his first two American films, *Way of all Flesh* (1927) and Josef von Sternberg's *The Last Command* (1928), but his thick German accent put an end to his Hollywood career with the advent of talking movies. He returned to Germany, starring in *Der Blaue Engel* (The Blue Angel, 1930), where he superbly portrayed Professor Rath, the pompous solid citizen enslaved by his passion for Marlene Dietrich.

Though never a Party member, Jannings became an enthusiastic supporter of Nazi ideology after 1933 and one of the leading actors and producers in the Third Reich, gladly accepting roles in anti-British and other propaganda films. Made a *Reichskultursenator*, he was one of Hitler's favourite film actors and was never short of work. In 1938 he was awarded a medal by Goebbels (q.v.) and appointed as head of Tobis, the company that produced his films. In 1941 he was honoured as 'Artist of the State'. The following year he played the part of Bismarck in Wolfgang Liebeneiner's *Die Entlassung*. Among his best-known performances were the title roles in Hans Steinhoff's *Robert Koch* (1939) and in *Ohm Krüger* (1941), a lavish anti-British Boer War epic and an explicitly political film. Jannings died in Stroblhof, Austria, on 2 January 1950, a lonely and embittered man, having been blacklisted by the Allied authorities and prevented from exercising his profession after 1945.

Jaspers, Karl (1883–1969)   German philosopher and psychopathologist who opposed National Socialism, Karl Jaspers
was born in Oldenburg on 23 February
1883. After receiving his medical degree
in 1909, Jaspers took up a lecturing
position in psychology at the University
of Heidelberg. In 1922 he was appointed
Professor of Philosophy and soon established himself as a leading existentialist
thinker. Concerned with concrete individual existence as the basis of all phi-
losophizing, believing in freedom of
choice and action, Jaspers opposed
abstract sociological and psychological
theories which made the individual lose
sight of his freedom and responsibility.
In *Die Geistige Situation der Zeit*, published in 1931 (Engl. trs. *Man in the
Modern Age*, 1933), Jaspers pointed to
the dangers of a mass society ruled by
'anonymous powers' and the imminent
collapse of human values, without actually mentioning the menace of National
Socialism. Nevertheless, his general philosophy with its quasi-religious sense of
an all-encompassing transcendent reality, its concern with communicable
truth and its appeal to reason brought
him into conflict with Nazism, whose
mysticism and racial doctrines he completely rejected. From 1937 to 1945 Jaspers was forbidden to teach in Germany,
but made no attempt to compromise
with or please the régime. After the war
he taught philosophy at the University
of Basel. His criticism of the German
tendency to cover up unpleasant memories of the past and blot out Nazi
crimes, expressed in his book *Die Schuld-
frage, Ein Beitrag zur Deutschen Frage*,
published in 1946 (*The Question of
Guilt*, 1947), was indifferently received,
but his works continued to be widely
read. These included *Psychologie der
Weltanschauungen* (1919), *Reason and
Existence* (1935, trs. 1956), *Existenz-
philosophie* (1938), *The Great Philosophers* (2 vols., 1962, 1966), *The Atom
Bomb and the Future of Man* (1958, trs.

1961) and *The Future of Germany*
(1967), the last two dealing with current
political questions. Describing his position in the Third Reich, his pupil, the
political scientist and historian Hannah
Arendt, wrote: 'What Jaspers represented then, when he was entirely alone,
was not Germany but what was left of
humanitas in Germany.' He died in
Basel on 26 February 1969.

Jeschonnek, Hans (1899–1943)   Air
Force Chief of Staff during World War
II, Hans Jeschonnek was born in Hohen-
salza on 9 April 1899. During World
War I he served as an officer in the
Prussian infantry before being transferred to the air force. In November
1938 he was promoted to Colonel and
in August 1939 to Major General. From
1 February until his suicide in East Prussia in August 1943, Jeschonnek was General Staff Chief of the Luftwaffe, closely
involved in its general planning and in
all its major campaigns. Jeschonnek was
promoted to General of Fliers in July
1940 after the fall of France, and on 1
April 1942 he was made General and
appointed Chief of the Luftwaffe Leadership Staff. By 1943 it was apparent that
the air force was unable to support effectively a holding campaign in the West
or to perform adequately on the Russian
front. Increasingly, the Luftwaffe was
obliged to go on the defensive and to
concentrate on protecting Germany
itself. Disillusioned by this turn of events
and by Goering's (q.v.) incompetent leadership, Jeschonnek took his own life on
19 August 1943. Against his express
wishes, Goering attended the funeral
and deposited a wreath from Hitler.

Jodl, Alfred (1890–1946)   Chief of the
Operations Staff of the High Command
of the Armed Forces (OKW) from 1939
to 1945 and Hitler's closest military adviser, Alfred Jodl was born in Würzburg
on 10 May 1890, the son of a distinguished military family. A professional

soldier who saw front-line service during World War I as an officer and joined the General Staff as a Captain in 1919, Jodl had known Hitler since 1923 and was one of the 'Party soldiers' who hero-worshipped him. From 1935 he served in the war plans division of the General Staff and with the creation of the OKW he was made head of its Land Operations Department. Promoted to Major General in April 1939, he was appointed Chief of the Wehrmacht Operations Staff and throughout the war directed, under Hitler and Keitel (q.v.), all the German campaigns except that against the Soviet Union. Advising Hitler on strategy and operations as his personal Chief of Staff, Jodl rarely contradicted him openly – he was second only to Keitel in his fanatical belief in the Führer's genius – though he sometimes persuaded him to yield by diplomatic means. As Hitler more and more took over Jodl's real job as head of Operations in the OKW, he and his staff had to assume independent leadership in certain theatres of war, acting as a second General Staff. In the last stages of World War II, Jodl even issued instructions to front commanders without Hitler's approval, but managed to retain the Führer's confidence and his own position for the duration of the war where others had failed. Intellectually superior and less subservient than Keitel, Jodl was more concerned with the military conduct of the war than any other general and less involved in political affairs.

On 30 January 1943 he was awarded the coveted Golden Party Badge and a year later he was promoted to General. Jodl's advice, particularly in the last years of the war, was not always strategically sound, for all his intellectual ability and prudence. His opposition to the Kursk offensive in 1943 contributed to the massive German defeat at Stalingrad. He also misjudged the situation on the western front in the autumn of 1944, where the German army found

itself overstretched in men and supplies following the Ardennes offensive. A week after Hitler's suicide, it was Jodl, representing Admiral Karl Doenitz (q.v.), who signed the surrender of the Wehrmacht to the Allies at Rheims on 7 May 1945. Tried by the International Military Court at Nuremberg as a major war criminal, Jodl defended himself in precise and sober fashion, claiming that it was 'not the task of a soldier to act as judge over his supreme commander'. Because he had condoned many illegal acts such as the shooting of hostages and been deeply involved even in Hitler's more criminal schemes, Jodl was found guilty on all four counts for which he was charged, including war crimes and crimes against humanity. He was hanged at Nuremberg on 16 October 1946. A German de-Nazification court subsequently found that Jodl had restricted himself to operational questions which did not transgress international law and posthumously exonerated him on 28 February 1953 of the crimes for which he had been executed.

Johst, Hanns (1890–1978) Expressionist playwright and writer who became the Nazi poet laureate and head of the Reich Theatre Chamber, Hanns Johst was born in Seehausen bei Riesa, Saxony, on 8 July 1890. He originally hoped to become a missionary, then studied medicine at the Universities of Leipzig, Munich and Vienna and trained as a male nurse. After military service during World War I, Johst turned to writing expressionist dramas including *Der König* (*The King*) in 1920 and *Thomas Paine* in 1927. In 1929 Johst was made President of the Nazi poets' organization in the *Kampfbund für Deutsche Kultur*. Three years later he wrote his famous jingoist drama, *Schlageter*, glorifying the proto-Nazi martyr, Albert Leo Schlageter, who had been executed by the French in 1923 during their occupation of the Rhineland. Johst's sycophantic dedication – 'Written for Adolf Hitler, in affectionate veneration and unchanging loyalty' – and the contents of the drama impressed Hitler. It was constantly performed as a Nazi classic during the Third Reich and one of the play's lines, 'When I hear the word culture, I slip back the safety catch of my revolver', came to epitomize the ethos of National Socialist art. Appointed dramatic adviser to the Berlin State Theatre in February 1933 and then President of the Academy of German Poetry, Johst was named a Prussian State Councillor in January 1934 and the following year he became President of the Reich Chamber of Literature. Together with Goebbels (q.v.), Johst was now in a unique position to mould the arts, and especially the theatre, in the direction of National Socialist ideology in order 'to save the German people from the complete materialism of a purely realistic world'. A prolific, if mediocre, novelist and poet as well as a playwright, Johst's works included *Der Kreuzweg* (1921), *Lieder der Sehnsucht* (1924), *So gehen sie hin* (1930), *Mutter ohne Tod* (1933), *Maske und Gesicht* (1935) and *Ruf des Reiches* (1940). On account of his activities during the Third Reich, Johst was categorized as a 'fellow-traveller' by a Munich de-Nazification court on 7 July 1949 and fined 500 marks. A few weeks later Johst's appeal led to a stiffer sentence – defined as a 'Major Offender' he was condemned to three-and-a-half years' labour camp, half his property was confiscated and he was forbidden to exercise his profession for ten years. He died in Ruhpolding, Bavaria, on 23 November 1978.

Jordan, Pascual (1902–80) Born in Hanover on 18 October 1902, Pascual Jordan studied physics, mathematics and zoology at Göttingen where he became a *Privatdozent* (university lecturer) in 1926. Along with Werner Heisenberg (q.v.) and Max Born (q.v.),

Jordan was one of the founders and foremost proponents of quantum physics as well as the author of numerous books and essays on theoretical physics, biophysics and astrophysics, in which he sought to popularize the new theories. These works included *Elementare Quantenmechanik* (1929) and *Anschauliche Quantentheorie* (1936). His book *Die Physik des 20 Jahrhunderts* (*The Physics of the 20th Century*), published in 1936, was notable for giving full credit to the achievements of Einstein (q.v.), Bohr, Hertz, James Franck (q.v.) and other Jewish scientists. Jordan was one of a group of younger conservative physicists who mistakenly believed that they could temper the radicalism of the Nazis through co-operation. From 1929 to 1944 Professor of Theoretical Physics at the University of Rostock, Jordan transferred to Berlin in 1944–5 and then to Hamburg where he lectured from 1947 to 1970. In 1942 Jordan received the Max Planck Medal and his services as a war propagandist and ideologist were recognized by the Nazi régime. Between 1957 and 1961, Jordan was a Christian-Democratic MP in the Bundestag, frequently calling for a return to the 'true front spirit'. In 1965 he protested against the recognition of the Oder-Neisse Line as Poland's western border. In 1973 he wrote that 'what the German people most urgently needs today is the overcoming of its national inferiority complex' – complaining that every attempt to assert German self-confidence was immediately denounced as 'fascistoid'. Jordan himself was a frequent target of such attacks from the Left in the postwar period. Following his death in Hamburg in August 1980, the neo-Nazi *Deutsche National-Zeitung* described him as one of Germany's 'greatest minds' and an authentic nationalist.

Jünger, Ernst (born 1895) Outstanding novelist and essayist who probably undermined the Weimar Republic more effectively than any other single author and helped foster a mental climate in which Nazism could flourish, Ernst Jünger was born in Heidelberg on 29 March 1895. At the age of seventeen he ran away from home to join the Foreign Legion, spent a few weeks in Africa – his adventures were subsequently retold in his *Afrikanische Spiele* (1936, Engl. trs. *African Diversions*, 1954) – before being brought back by his father, a wealthy chemist who later owned a pharmaceutical factory. Jünger joined the German army as a volunteer in 1914 and was decorated for his distinguished and heroic service with the coveted *Pour le Mérite*, the highest military award in Imperial Germany. His book *In Stahlgewittern* (1920, Engl. trs. *The Storm of Steel*, 1929) with its glorification of war, of vitalism and death-dealing, and its archetypal hero figures, was the first of Jünger's novels and it established him as the foremost literary representative of the 'front generation' and its 'inner experience' of the trenches. After studying zoology between 1923 and 1925 and interesting himself in geology and botany, Jünger turned back to writing, developing a skilfully impersonal style 'without heart, without love, without compassion', that seemed to turn men into things and establish a rigid order beyond the nihilism and chaos of human existence.

Works like *Das Abenteurliche Herz* (1929) and *Blätter und Steine* (1934) with their de-anthropomorphizing techniques revealed Jünger as an existentialist with a three-dimensional approach to the essence of things, the abstract realm of ideas and the symbols of destiny. Jünger was too much of a non-conformist to fit easily into a totalitarian mass movement, though his half-romantic, half-technocratic nationalism in the 1920s made him appear as a proto-Nazi and intellectual promoter of National Socialism from the sidelines. For a time close to Goebbels (q.v.), he nonetheless re-

jected the latter's entreaties to join the NSDAP and refused to be placed on the Party's Reichstag list in 1928. At the end of the 1920s he played with National Bolshevism and drew close to the circle around Ernst Niekisch (q.v.), seeing in Soviet Russia a seductive expression of will-to-power combined with total mobilization.

Jünger's attempted synthesis of fascism and communism envisaged a movement in which idealized 'worker-soldiers' would constitute a disciplined élite, which would subordinate instinct by force and technocratic power. *Der Arbeiter* (1932) was the high point of his National Bolshevism, hailed by Niekisch for its adaptation of the Russian revolutionary spirit to the German mentality. After the Nazis came to power, Jünger was offered and personally refused a seat in the Reichstag as well as in the Prussian Academy of Poetry. Nevertheless he continued to earn large financial dividends from officially sponsored reprints of his works and, together with Gottfried Benn (q.v.) and Gerhart Hauptmann (q.v.), was the most distinguished writer to remain active in Nazi Germany. Jünger shared with the Nazis their emphasis on the collective *Fronterlebnis* (front-line experience), their totalitarian spirit and their underlying nihilism, even if he was too aristocratic and individualist to join the Party. In *Der Arbeiter* he had looked forward to the 'annihilation of the values of the free-floating spirit' and the destruction of bourgeois standards, claiming that 'the best answer to the high treason of the spirit against life is high treason of the spirit against the spirit; and to be part of this blasting operation is one of the great and cruel pleasures of our time'. But if Jünger played his part in paving the way for later Nazi atrocities by his openly nihilistic attitudes, his later books also contained an implicit rejection of their methods, if not their ideology. His novel *Auf den Marmorklippen* (1939, Engl. trs. *On the Marble Cliffs*, 1947) expressed a veiled antipathy to the tyranny of the régime and in 1940 its printing was stopped after 35,000 copies had been sold.

Jünger rejoined the army (the favoured form of aristocratic 'inner emigration'), serving on the staff of the German military command in Paris between 1940 and 1942, then in Soviet Russia for three months, before returning to Paris once more. In October 1944 he was discharged from the army for 'unsatisfactory military conduct' and in the following month his son was killed.

At this time Jünger completed his secretly circulated indictment of the Hitlerian system, *Der Friede* (1944, Engl. trs. *The Peace*, 1948), a courageous denunciation of totalitarian tyranny, which revealed that the author had shed his earlier nationalism. Jünger's war diaries, first published under the title *Strahlungen* (1949), are no less disdainful of the Nazi spirit to which he had once made no trifling contribution. After World War II, Jünger continued to write prolifically and was widely recognized as the most significant and interesting of the authors who had been active under the Third Reich.

K

Kaltenbrunner, Ernst (1903–46) A fanatical Austrian Nazi and leading police official, who rose to become Chief of the Reich Main Security Office, Ernst Kaltenbrunner was born on 4 October 1903 in the valley of the Inn, near Braunau, the birthplace of Adolf Hitler. Descended from a family of country artisans (his father and grandfather were, however, lawyers), Kaltenbrunner was educated in Linz, where Adolf Eichmann (q.v.) was one of his boyhood friends, and subsequently studied law at Graz University. He took his doctorate in law in 1926, setting up his practice as a lawyer in Linz. Active in one of the first groups of Austrian National Socialist students and for a time a militant in the Independent Movement for a Free Austria, Kaltenbrunner eventually joined the Nazi Party in 1932. A year later he became a member of one of the more or less camouflaged SS organizations in Austria and a spokesman for the Party in Upper Austria, providing legal advice to members and sympathizers.

In 1934 Kaltenbrunner was arrested by the Dollfuss government, and again in May 1935 he spent six months in prison on a conspiracy charge, being struck from the bar for his political activities. Shortly before his second arrest he had been appointed Commander of the Austrian SS. After his release he worked assiduously with Seyss-Inquart (q.v.) for the *Anschluss* with Germany and, as a reward for his services, was appointed by the latter on 2 March 1938 as Minister for State Security in Austria and promoted to *SS-Gruppenführer*. At the same time he became a member of the Reichstag. During the next three years Kaltenbrunner was successively appointed as Commander-in-Chief of the SS and the police for the regions of Vienna, the Upper and Lower Danube, and then in April 1941 Lieutenant-General of Police. He created an impressive intelligence network radiating from Austria south-eastwards, which caught the attention of Himmler (q.v.), who to general surprise recommended him in January 1943 as head of the *Reichssicherheitshauptamt* (RSHA) in Berlin in succession to Reinhard Heydrich (q.v.). In this key position as head of the security police and the Security Service (SD), Kaltenbrunner not only controlled the Gestapo but also the concentration camp system and the administrative apparatus for carrying out the 'Final Solution of the Jewish Question'.

A giant of a man, nearly seven feet tall, with massive broad shoulders, huge arms, a thick square chin and deep scars from his student duelling days, Kaltenbrunner excelled in brutal repression and providing human fodder for the concentration camps. Excitable, deceitful, self-indulgent – he was an alcoholic and a chain-smoker – Kaltenbrunner took a personal interest in various methods of execution used in the camps under his aegis and especially in the gas chambers. Under his ruthless prodding, the RSHA organized the hunting down and extermination of several million Jews. During the war he was also responsible for the murder of Allied parachutists and prisoners of war. Kaltenbrunner had a passion for military intelligence and counter-espionage and in February

1944 he succeeded in swallowing up the foreign and counter-intelligence department of the *Abwehr* under Admiral Canaris (q.v.) which was reduced to a branch of his RSHA office. Towards the end of 1944 Kaltenbrunner tried to step into Himmler's place as the recognized mediator with the International Red Cross and to establish contact with the Allies through Allen Dulles, head of the United States Office of Strategic Services in Europe. These efforts came to nothing and, at the end of the war, Kaltenbrunner fled to the Tyrol, removing his headquarters to Alt-Aussee. He was picked up by an American patrol and brought before the International Military Tribunal at Nuremberg, charged with war crimes and crimes against humanity. He was hanged in Nuremberg prison on 16 October 1946.

Karajan, Herbert von (1908–89) Outstanding Austrian conductor born in Salzburg on 5 April 1908, Herbert von Karajan studied at the Mozarteum and originally intended to become a pianist. He first attracted public notice in 1927 when substituting at short notice to conduct a performance of Mozart's *The Marriage of Figaro* in Ulm. He conducted there for the next seven years, becoming Music Director of the Ulm Opera. From 1935 to 1941 von Karajan was General Music Director and conductor in Aachen. From 1938 he also conducted at the Berlin State Opera and the Berlin Philharmonic Orchestra. A highly imposing figure both on and off the podium, the autocratic, imaginative and eloquent von Karajan (a member of the NSDAP from 1933) ranked with the leading virtuoso conductors of his time. After the war, he became Director of the *Gesellschaft der Musikfreunde* in Vienna (1949), toured with the Vienna Philharmonic and also with the new London Philharmonia Orchestra. His main energies, however, were devoted to the Berlin Philharmonia after he suc-

ceeded Furtwängler (q.v.) as its conductor in 1954, and to the Salzburg Festivals. In 1956 he was appointed Director of the Vienna State Opera, and in subsequent years consolidated his reputation as the finest conductor of his age.

Kaufmann, Karl (1900–69) *Gauleiter* of Hamburg and a prominent Nazi functionary, Karl Kaufmann was born in Krefeld on 10 October 1900, of Roman Catholic parents. After serving in World War I, in 1920 he joined the Erhardt *Freikorps* Brigade in Upper Silesia and the Ruhr. One of the co-founders of the NSDAP in the Ruhr in 1921, he was appointed *Gauleiter* of the Rhineland district three years later, a position he held until 1928. From 1928 until 1930 he was a member of the NSDAP faction in the Prussian legislature and in 1930 he was elected as a delegate to the Reichstag. In the same year he was dismissed from all his Party appointments as a result of accusations dating back several years that he had embezzled Party funds, blackmailed political opponents and worn an Iron Cross that had never been awarded to him. In 1933 he was reinstated as district leader and appointed *Reichsstatthalter* of Hamburg, a position he held until the end of the war. He took an active part in the atrocities in Fuhlsbüttel concentration camp. In 1941 Kaufmann was promoted to *SS-Obergruppenführer* and a year later he was appointed Reich Commissioner for Overseas Shipping. After the war, Kaufmann lived as a businessman in Hamburg until an investigation in 1948 led to a sentence of one year and two months. On 22 April 1949 he was released on health grounds from British internment. Arrested by the Hamburg authorities on 3 August 1950, he was set free soon afterwards. Arrested once again on 5 January 1953 on account of his associations with other Nazi chiefs, he was released on 29 March 1953.

Keitel, Wilhelm (1882–1946) General Field Marshal and Chief of Staff of the High Command of the Armed Forces (OKW) from 1938 to 1945, Wilhelm Keitel was born in Helmscherode, Braunschweig, on 22 September 1882. A professional soldier who served as an artillery officer on the General Staff during World War I and suffered severe wounds, Keitel was a member of a *Freikorps* in 1919 and received various regimental appointments during the next six years. In 1929 he was made head of the Army Organization Department, a position he held until 1934, when he was promoted to Major General. From 1935 to 1938 Keitel was head of the Armed Forces Office at the War Ministry and during this period he was again promoted to Lieutenant-General (1936) and General of Artillery (1937). Following the fall of his close friend and collaborator, von Blomberg (q.v.), and Hitler's assumption of supreme command himself, Keitel was appointed on 4 February 1938 *Chef des Oberkommando der Wehrmacht* (Chief of Staff of the High Command of the Armed Forces) and in November of the same year he was promoted to Colonel General. Awarded the Golden Party Badge of the NSDAP in April 1939, Keitel was made General Field Marshal in July 1940 after the fall of France, personally conducting the French armistice negotiations at Compiègne.

Keitel initially opposed the invasion of the Soviet Union, but subsequently praised Hitler's relentless conduct of the Russian campaign. The Führer's closest military adviser in the High Command, Keitel was involved in all important strategic decisions but was held in contempt by other generals for his undignified compliancy and inability to disagree with Hitler. His submissive docility and servile flattery – after the victory in the West he called Hitler 'the greatest commander of all times' – earned him the nickname *Lakeitel* (lackey) in army circles. Second only to Hitler in the hierarchy of command, Keitel's total loyalty was highly valued by the Führer but had disastrous consequences in bringing about the acquiescence of other generals who might otherwise have questioned certain orders. From the outbreak of the war in Poland Keitel condoned measures leading to mass murder, beginning with the wiping out of the Polish intelligentsia, nobility and clergy. In an instruction to the High Command in March 1941 Keitel noted that 'the *Reichsführer-SS* acts independently upon his own responsibility', and on 27 July he signed an order that gave Himmler (q.v.) absolute powers in implementing terror in Russian-occupied territory. Keitel revealed to army commanders that they would have to carry out the execution of political commissars themselves or hand them over to the Gestapo, sanctioning such measures on the grounds that 'we are dealing here with the destruction of a world philosophy'.

On 16 December 1942 he justified the massacres carried out by *Einsatzgruppen* operating on Russian soil. 'It is not only justified therefore, but the duty of the troops to use every method without restriction, even against women and children provided it ensures success. Any act of mercy is a crime against the German people.' Keitel was also responsible for issuing the Night and Fog decree allowing the seizure of 'persons endangering German security', who vanished without trace into oblivion. These and other orders led Keitel to be brought before the Nuremberg Tribunal, after he had signed the unconditional capitulation of the German forces in Berlin on 8 May 1945. He was found guilty of war crimes and crimes against humanity and was executed in Nuremberg prison on 16 October 1946.

Keppler, Wilhelm (1882–1960) Hitler's personal adviser on economic affairs and chief liaison between the Nazi Party and the business world, Wilhelm Keppler was born in Heidelberg on 14 December 1882. An industrialist, engineer and early member of the NSDAP, Keppler was introduced to Hitler by Heinrich Himmler (q.v.) and was used by the Nazi leader to secure financial support from business circles during his rise to power. He was the intermediary in contacts with the wealthy banker, Baron Kurt von Schröder (q.v.), and conservative circles designed to bring down General von Schleicher (q.v.). On 5 March 1933 Keppler was elected to the Reichstag for the electoral district of Baden and in July of the same year he was appointed Reich Commissioner for Economic Affairs. In 1936 Keppler became personal adviser to Goering (q.v.) in the implementation of the Four Year Plan, with special responsibility for securing raw materials for industry. During the preparations for the *Anschluss* with Austria, Keppler was secretary at the Vienna embassy, and from March to June 1938 acted as Reich Commissioner in Austria. He was sent on similar missions to Slovakia and Danzig to pave the way for their incorporation into the Reich. Keppler, who had entered the SS on 21 March 1935, was the founder of the *Freundeskreis Heinrich Himmler* (Circle of Friends of Heinrich Himmler), the source of enormous contributions from the business world to the SS, especially during World War II. In return, Keppler, who was chairman of numerous industrial firms controlled by the Third Reich, was employed by Himmler to administer confiscated industries for the SS in occupied Poland and Russia. During World War II, Keppler was Secretary of State with special duties in the Foreign Office and on 30 January 1942 he was promoted to *SS-Obergruppenführer*. At the end of the war, Keppler was interned and sentenced to ten years' imprisonment at the Wilhelmstrasse trial on 14 April 1949. He was released on 1 February 1951 as a result of the clemency

action by the American High Commissioner. Keppler died on 13 June 1960.

Kerrl, Hans (1887–1941) Reich Minister for Ecclesiastical Affairs from 1935 until his death in 1941, Hans Kerrl was born in Fallserleben, the son of a Lutheran school teacher, on 2 December 1887. During World War I he served as a Lieutenant and received the Iron Cross (First and Second Classes). Kerrl was Reich Commissioner in the Prussian Ministry of Justice from 23 March until 20 April 1933, during which period he placed a ban on any Jewish notary engaging in official business and forbade Jewish lawyers to practise in Prussia. Elected to the Reichstag on 12 November 1933 for the electoral district of South Hanover-Braunschweig, Kerrl was made Reich Minister without Portfolio on 17 June 1934. A sympathizer with the 'German Christians', Kerrl was appointed Minister for Church Affairs on 16 July 1935 and was responsible for the Nazi co-ordination of the Christian churches. Kerrl's policies sought to bring the exercise of spiritual and pastoral functions in the Evangelical Church completely under government control, arousing the opposition of a number of Protestant churchmen and theologians. He died in Berlin on 15 December 1941.

Kesselring, Albert (1885–1960) General Field Marshal of the air force and later Commander-in-Chief of the German troops in Italy, Albert Kesselring was born in Marktsheft, Bavaria, on 20 November 1885, the son of a town education officer. He joined the army as a cadet in 1904, becoming an officer in the Bavarian artillery. During World War I he served as Adjutant and General Staff officer, and after the war joined the Reichswehr on regimental service with the artillery until 1932, when he was promoted to Brigadier. Transferred to the air force in 1935 as Chief of the Luftwaffe Administrative

Office, he was promoted a year later to Lieutenant-General and Chief of the General Staff of the Luftwaffe. In 1937 Kesselring was appointed General of Fliers and a year later he became Commander-in-Chief of Air Fleet I (Berlin). At the outbreak of war in 1939 Kesselring successfully commanded two air fleets employed in the Polish campaign and then in the invasion of Belgium in 1940. Commander-in-Chief of Air Fleet II during the Dutch campaign, Kesselring was promoted to General Field Marshal on 19 July 1940, after the fall of France. In addition to the bombing attacks on Rotterdam, he ordered the Luftwaffe's heavy bombing of the British Expeditionary Force evacuating Dunkirk. Later in 1940 Kesselring directed the damaging bomb attacks on air bases in South-East England during the Battle of Britain. Only Goering's (q.v.) tactical blunder in redirecting the Luftwaffe on to targets in London allowed British fighter defences to recover.

From December 1941 to March 1945 Kesselring was Commander-in-Chief in the South, responsible for Italy and the Mediterranean basin. He shared the direction of Rommel's (q.v.) campaign in North Africa, taking control during the latter's absences and supervising the German withdrawal from Tunisia. From 1943 to 1945 the extremely able Kesselring commanded German forces in Italy, a country he knew well and where he was instrumental in holding up the Allies against heavy odds. His skilful, defensive campaign in the face of Allied air superiority and brilliantly executed retreat delayed the Allied advance northwards for more than a year. His record was blotted, however, by the countermeasures he took in reprisal for an attack by Italian partisans on German soldiers, which led to the sickening Ardeantine cave massacre of March 1944 where 335 Italian civilians were shot. In March 1945 Hitler sent Kesselring to

North-West Europe to try and halt the Allied advance, but the situation was already beyond repair in spite of his military skills. Kesselring remained loyal to the Führer to the end despite efforts by Hitler's opponents in the Wehrmacht to win him over to their side. In May 1947 Kesselring was sentenced to death by a British military court in Venice for having ordered the execution of Italian hostages. His sentence was later commuted to life imprisonment, and in October 1952 he was released because of ill-health. Highly regarded on the Allied side as one of the most able German generals during World War II, Kesselring died in Bad Nauheim on 16 July 1960.

Kirdorf, Emil (1847–1938) Ruhr coal-king and the first major figure from the business world to join the Nazi Party, Emil Kirdorf was born in Mettmann on 8 April 1847. He began his career as an industrialist in the 1870s when he co-founded the Gelsenkircher Mine Works. Later he also participated in the creation of the Rhine-Westphalian Coal Syndicate – a bituminous coal cartel in which he played an active role right up to April 1925 – and another powerful cartel, the United Steel Works. An extreme authoritarian and right-wing nationalist, Kirdorf was much feared as a ruthless industrial employer and hater of the trade unions. He organized and controlled the Ruhr treasury fund established by the big Rhineland industrialists to protect their mining interests. In 1927 the octogenarian survivor of the early phase of German monopoly capitalism joined the NSDAP. He resigned a year later (a fact long concealed by the Nazis), distrustful of the socio-economic radicalism of the Nazi left wing, but maintained cordial personal relations with Hitler. It was Kirdorf who persuaded Hitler to write a secretly printed pamphlet designed to reassure big business circles that the 'socialism' of the

NSDAP need not be taken seriously and would not endanger their interests. Kirdorf was attracted by the extreme nationalism and anti-Marxism of Hitler, but in the years between 1929 and 1933 he supported the German National People's Party more than the NSDAP. Having retired from active business by this time and having no access to corporate or associational funds, there is no hard evidence that he was a heavy financial contributor to the Nazi Party, as has frequently been asserted. It is nonetheless true that he was a fellow-traveller, sympathetic to nationalist aims and impressed by Hitler's charismatic power over the masses. In 1934 he rejoined the Nazi Party and was eagerly appropriated by the régime as a respectable patron and supporter from the business world. Kirdorf died in Mühlheim an der Ruhr on 13 July 1938.

Kleist, Ewald von (1881–1954) General Field Marshal and highly successful Commander of Panzer forces in the early years of World War II, Ewald von Kleist was born in Braunfels, Hessen, on 8 August 1881, the descendant of a famous aristocratic family. After field service during World War I, von Kleist joined the Reichswehr, serving in various staff appointments between 1919 and 1929, when he was promoted to Brigadier. From 1932 to 1935 the Commander of a cavalry division and promoted again to Lieutenant-General, he was appointed in 1936 as Commandant of Breslau and made General of Cavalry. Retired in the spring of 1939, he was recalled at the outbreak of war to command the Twenty-Second Army Corps during the Polish campaign. During the battle for France in 1940 Colonel General von Kleist commanded the armoured corps which broke through the Ardennes, beginning the rout of the French army, and raced to the Channel coast with a speed that astonished both the Allied generals and the German High Com-

mand. In April 1941 von Kleist was given command of the forces that captured Belgrade during the Serbian campaign. Following the invasion of Soviet Russia, von Kleist's *Panzergruppe* I (First Panzer Army) captured Kiev on 19 September 1941 and took part in the drive to the Caucasus during the summer offensive of 1942 with von Kleist as Commander-in-Chief of Army Group A. At first his forces made rapid progress in their efforts to reach the rich Grozny oil fields, but then the tide of battle turned as they ran short of petrol and units were diverted to support the attack on Stalingrad in the autumn of 1942. Though forced to begin a long retreat from the Rostov area, von Kleist was rewarded for his services by promotion to General Field Marshal on 31 January 1943 and then in March 1944 by the award of the Swords to Oak Leaves of the Knight's Cross. Dismissed from his command by Hitler shortly afterwards, von Kleist was captured by Allied forces in 1945 and tried for war crimes in Yugoslavia, being sentenced to fifteen years' imprisonment. Released in 1949, he was handed over to the Russians and died in Soviet captivity in October 1954. A commander of the old school, who had for a time worked in Resistance circles, von Kleist proved himself a competent and skilful general during the war, capable of adapting to the new techniques of armoured warfare, pioneered by gifted subordinates like General Guderian (q.v.).

Kluge, Günther Hans von (1882–1944) General Field Marshal and Army Group Commander in Russia and France, Günther von Kluge was born in Poznan on 30 October 1882. A Prussian field artillery officer from 1901, von Kluge served as a General Staff officer during World War I and was rapidly promoted, especially after the Nazi rise to power. A Major General in September 1933, promoted to Lieutenant-General in April 1934, von Kluge was given command of Military District VI (Münster) in September of the same year. During the Polish and French campaigns at the beginning of World War II, von Kluge commanded the Fourth Army and was promoted on 19 July 1940 to the rank of General Field Marshal, following the fall of France. After the invasion of the Soviet Union he was again given command of the Fourth Army, which reached the outskirts of Moscow before being battered by the Russian counteroffensive and forced to retreat in December 1941. In spite of this failure he was promoted to replace von Bock (q.v.) as Commander-in-Chief of Army Group Centre on 16 December 1941. Von Kluge's troops achieved little success on the Russian front during 1942–3 but the pliant, subservient Field Marshal retained the confidence of Hitler. On his sixtieth birthday (30 October 1942) he received a cheque from Hitler to the value of 250,000 marks, half of it to be spent on improving his estate.

It was shortly after this massive bribe that von Kluge first came into contact with members of the German Resistance who beseeched him, for the time being without success, to join in the plot against Hitler. On 3 July 1944 von Kluge was appointed by the Führer to succeed von Rundstedt (q.v.) as Commander-in-Chief of the western front, but failed to hold the Allied armies. His vacillating character and weak-minded opportunism was revealed by his attitude during the abortive plot of July 1944. Von Kluge had promised his aid to the conspirators 'in the event of the attempt being a success', but backed out of the rebellion as soon as he learned that Hitler had only been wounded in the assassination attempt. His cowardice, however, did not save him. Relieved of his command on 17 August 1944 for not discovering the plot in time and for his military failures (he was replaced by Walther Model, q.v.), von Kluge was ordered back to Berlin. Fearing he would be judged and hanged in Germany, von Kluge committed suicide by taking a cyanide pill on 19 August 1944 while travelling between Paris and Metz. In his letter of farewell he once more proclaimed his admiration for Hitler's 'greatness' and 'genius' and his loyalty until death, while calling on the Führer to end the 'hopeless struggle'.

Knochen, Helmut (born 1910) Commander of the security police in occupied France from 1940 to 1944, Helmut Knochen was born on 14 March 1910 in Magdeburg, the son of a school teacher. He studied at the Universities of Leipzig, Halle and Göttingen, obtaining his doctorate in 1935 with a thesis on an English playwright. Knochen had joined the SA on 1 May 1933 and worked for a time as an editor in the official press agency of the Nazi Party before entering the Security Service (SD) in 1937. For the next three years he worked in *Amt VI* (SD *Ausland*), studying the refugee press in France, Belgium and Holland. After his highly successful role in the kidnapping of two British intelligence agents at Venlo (for which he was awarded the Iron Cross, First and Second Class), the young SS Colonel was chosen to lead a special commando of about twenty men into France in June 1940. The task of this small unit, which was responsible to Himmler (q.v.) and Heydrich (q.v.) in Berlin, was to keep an eye on all enemies of the Nazi régime in France, chiefly Jews, communists, Freemasons, anti-fascists and German refugees. As Himmler's representative in France, Knochen found himself hampered by the German military administration under General Otto von Stuelpnagel (q.v.) which fiercely opposed any encroachment on its domain. Not until May 1942 did Knochen's security police achieve its administrative autonomy. By this time in sole charge of the Gestapo-SD in France, the cultured, polished Knochen succeeded in reorganizing and extending his apparatus despite interference from Berlin, where Heinrich Müller (q.v.), who had succeeded Heydrich, resented his subtle methods and independent temperament. Knochen remained at his post until 18 August 1944, when he was recalled to Berlin by Ernst Kaltenbrunner (q.v.) who stripped him of his rank, a decision later reversed by Himmler. Knochen hid after the war, but was eventually caught and sentenced to life imprisonment by a British court in June 1946 for the execution of captured airmen. On 10 October 1946 he was handed over to the French authorities and, after a long internment, eventually appeared before a Parisian military tribunal which sentenced him to death on 9 October 1954. A presidential decree commuted the sentence to forced labour for life on 10 April 1958. Knochen's sentence was once more reduced by a decree of 31 December 1959 to twenty years' penal servitude from the date of sentence. He was pardoned and repatriated by General de Gaulle early in 1963, retiring in comfort to Baden-Baden where he has been living on a West German government pension.

Koch, Erich (1896–1986) Honorary Lieutenant-General (SS), *Gauleiter* of East Prussia and Reich Commissar of the Ukraine from 1941 to 1944, Erich Koch was born in Elberfeld on 19 June 1896. After undistinguished military service during World War I, Koch became a railway clerk until he was dismissed in 1926 for anti-republican political activity. Having joined the NSDAP in 1922, he was involved in the revolt against the occupation in the Ruhr and was imprisoned several times by the French authorities. Between 1922 and 1926 he was one of the Party district leaders in the Ruhr and a supporter of the radical wing of the NSDAP led by Gregor Strasser (q.v.). From 1928 Koch was *Gauleiter* of the Party in East Prussia and leader of

its faction in the provincial diet. From 1930 a member of the Reichstag for East Prussia and appointed a member of the Prussian State Council in July 1933, Koch was made *Oberpräsident* of East Prussia in September of the same year. His autocratic rule never permitted the SA or the SS to come to the fore, as in other *Gaue*, but Koch's advocacy of collectivization in agriculture made him unpopular with the peasants and he was ruthless in arresting his critics, or expelling them from the Party. During World War II Koch proved himself one of Hitler's cruellest satraps in the conquered eastern territories, his criminal orders causing the deaths of hundreds of thousands of innocent men, women and children, their deportation to concentration camps and the razing of their villages to the ground.

In addition to East Prussia, he was appointed head of the civil administration in Bialystok (1941) and from October 1941 to 1944 he was *Reichskommissar* in the Ukraine with control of the Gestapo and the police. His first official act in the Ukraine was to close local schools, declaring that 'Ukraine children need no schools. What they'll have to learn later will be taught them by their German masters.' In a speech in Kiev on 5 March 1943 Koch was explicit about the methods he intended to use to build a slave State in the Ukraine and his complete contempt for Slav *Untermenschen* ('sub-humans'): 'We are a master race', Koch insisted, 'which must remember that the lowliest German worker is racially and biologically a thousand times more valuable than the population here.' Thanks to his twisted policy of brutal 'Germanization' and the repression, murder and exploitation of Poles, Ukrainians and Jews, Koch's empire was soon infested with partisans.

After the loss of the Ukraine, Koch returned to Königsberg and then, after the fall of East Prussia, he disappeared in West Germany until his arrest by

British security officers in Hamburg at the end of May 1949. His extradition was demanded by the Polish and Soviet governments who regarded him as one of the worst war criminals, directly involved in the extermination of the Polish intelligentsia, Soviet partisans and hundreds of thousands of Jews in Bialystok and the Ukraine. On 14 January 1950 Koch was delivered by the British to a prison in Warsaw, but his trial did not begin until 19 October 1958 when he was charged with the responsibility for the death of 400,000 Poles (his crimes in the Ukraine were not dealt with). Koch was sentenced to death on 9 March 1959 by the Polish district court in Warsaw, for having planned, prepared and organized mass murder of civilians, but his sentence was commuted to life imprisonment on account of his ill health. In a state of partial collapse through most of his trial (rousing himself only to protest that he was a 'Christian', a good 'socialist' and a friend of the workers), Koch was fortunate to benefit from an article in the Polish penal code which prevented the execution of bedridden persons. Erich Koch died in prison at Barczewo on 12 November 1986.

Koch, Ilse (1906–67) Known as the 'Bitch of Buchenwald' for her sadistic cruelty and power-mad behaviour towards prisoners under her supervision, Ilse Koch was the wife of Karl Koch, Commandant of Buchenwald, whom she had married in 1936. A powerfully built, formidable nymphomaniac who had accompanied her husband to Buchenwald in 1939, she was especially fond of horse-riding exercises – a riding hall costing a quarter of a million marks and not a few human lives was specially constructed for her at the camp – to the accompaniment of the Buchenwald SS band. She also liked to ride through the camp, whipping any prisoner who attracted her attention. Her taste for col-

lecting lampshades made from the tattooed skins of specially murdered concentration camp inmates was described as follows by a witness at Nuremberg: 'The finished products [i.e. tattooed skin detached from corpses] were turned over to Koch's wife, who had them fashioned into lampshades and other ornamental household articles.' Her husband, who had become a millionaire from his unscrupulous racketeering and exploitation of concentration camp labour and production for private use, was, however, brought before an SS court in 1944 in a famous case of corruption. Sentenced to death, he was reprieved and then executed by his accuser, von Waldeck-Pyrmont (q.v.), Higher SS and Police Leader of Thuringia, shortly before the end of the war. Ilse Koch was more fortunate. Though sentenced to life imprisonment in the Buchenwald trial of 1947, her sentence was reduced to four years and she was soon released. Re-arrested in 1949, she was tried before a West German court for the killing of German nationals and the intense publicity in the national press made her name a byword for horror. On 15 January 1951 she was sentenced to life imprisonment for murder. She committed suicide in a Bavarian prison on 1 September 1967.

Kolbe, Georg (1877–1947) Outstanding German sculptor who adapted to the Nazi régime, Georg Kolbe was born in Waldheim on 13 April 1877 and studied art in Dresden, Munich and Paris at the Académie Julian in 1898. Originally trained as a painter, Kolbe decided to turn instead to sculpture after a meeting with Rodin in Rome. In 1903 he settled in Berlin, remaining there for the rest of his life apart from travels to Greece, Italy and Egypt. Kolbe worked mainly in bronze, modelling classically proportioned nudes and also executing on occasion a few portrait heads. Rodin and later Maillol were the decisive influences on his work. Kolbe's early figures were highly expressive and imaginative – especially the *Dancing Girl* of 1912. During the later period, in particular after 1933, his style became repetitively aggressive and nationalistic. During the Third Reich he indulged in the kind of monumental figures whose cheap pathos was largely geared to the Nazi mythology of the Nordic-Germanic 'master race'. In the spirit of bringing art to the people, his studio became a favoured venue for guided tours by members of the 'Strength through Joy' organization. He died in Berlin on 15 November 1947.

Kolbenheyer, Erwin Guido (1878–1962) Best-selling author in the Third Reich and a leading apologist of the Nazi régime, Erwin Guido Kolbenheyer was a Hungarian *Volksdeutsche*, born on 30 December 1878 in Budapest, where he attended elementary school. After a spell in Karlsbad he moved to Vienna, where he studied philosophy and the natural sciences (1900–4). Kolbenheyer became a freelance writer, specializing in historical novels, the earliest of which was *Amor Dei, ein Spinozaroman* (1908) and the best known being his notorious *Paracelsus* trilogy which, for all its Germanomania, its pretentiousness and metaphysical preaching, won him much acclaim in the 1920s. The trilogy, beginning with *Die Kindheit des Paracelsus* (1917), followed by *Das Gestirn des Paracelsus* (1921) and *Das Dritte Reich des Paracelsus* (1926), was written in a semi-archaic language in order to reproduce the spirit of the times. The emphasis on 'Teutonism' in Kolbenheyer's works, the fact that the heroes of his novels and dramas were invariably 'typical Germans' fighting against a hostile world or mystics revolting against medieval scholasticism and the international church, reflected the extreme nationalism of the Sudeten German minority among whom he had lived. Not only in his historical novels

but also in more theoretical studies such as *Die Bauhütte* (1925), Kolbenheyer anticipated many features of National Socialism and he prophesied that the fate of the German nation would be to turn away from the alien creed of Judeo-Christianity. He defended the Nazi burning of the books as a necessary act of 'purification' and wrote a poem in honour of Hitler, praising 'the man who won a way towards the light for his people'. Kolbenheyer received the Goethe Prize of the City of Frankfurt in 1937 and continued to publish widely read books like *Karlsbader Novellen 1786* (1935) and the novel *Das Gottgelobte Herz* (1938). His work was a prime example of the genre of Nazi literature which enabled naked violence and political cynicism to be dissolved into a fog of idealistic mysticism. He died in Munich on 12 April 1962.

Kollwitz, Kathe (1867–1945) The great socialist painter of proletarian Germany and, arguably, the most powerful graphic artist of the late Wilhelminian period, Kathe Kollwitz (née Schmidt) was born in Königsberg on 8 July 1867. Her charcoal drawings, lithographs and etchings were devoted to the battle against working-class poverty and the barbarity of war. The driving power of her literal, sentimental and intensely emotional work was human sympathy and a deep feeling for the oppressed. From 1919 to 1933 she was Professor at the Academy of Art in Berlin, where she continued to live until 1943. Although permitted to exhibit for a while under the Third Reich, her work was silenced by the Nazis. She died unsung, shortly before the liberation, in Moritzburg near war-torn Dresden, on 22 April 1945.

Kramer, Josef (1907–45) Commander of the Birkenau and Bergen-Belsen concentration camps, Josef Kramer became notorious as the 'Beast of Belsen' – a term coined by the international press in 1945 after the discovery of piles of corpses and mass graves by British troops entering the camp. Kramer had been Rudolf Hoess's (q.v.) Adjutant at Auschwitz in 1940 and Commandant of Birkenau during the mass slaughter season of 1944. He had also previously served at Dachau, Esterwegen, Sachsenhausen, Mauthausen and Natzweiler, where he was Commandant in 1943. Kramer played a personal part in the killing of some eighty prisoners there, including women, in order to complete the famous anatomical collections of Professor Hirt of Strasbourg University. At the so-called Doctors' Trial he described in detail how he had introduced poison to kill his victims in the gas chamber and how he had felt no qualms 'because I had been ordered to kill these eighty internees in this way, as I have told you. Anyway, this is how I was brought up.' Kramer was transferred to Belsen from Birkenau on 1 December 1944 and managed within a short time to make another Auschwitz out of this 'privileged' camp, even though there were no gas chambers there. Under his dull, brutal administration, chaos developed in the overcrowded camp with prisoners being left to rot in every stage of emaciation and disease and corpses piling up in the barracks. Kramer was arrested by the British troops and tried by a British military court at Lüneberg, which condemned him to death on 17 November 1945.

Krauss, Werner (1884–1959) Already a star of stage and screen in the Weimar period and, together with Emil Jannings (q.v.) and Heinrich George (q.v.), one of the three great actors of the Third Reich, Werner Krauss was born at Gestungshausen, Coburg, on 23 July 1884. From his film début in 1916 until the advent of talkies Krauss made no fewer than 104 movies and emerged as one of the outstanding interpreters of the expressionist cinema. He was the malig-

nant Dr Caligari in Robert Wiene's famous film, starred in Murnau's *Tartüff* (1925), in Froelich's *Kabale und Liebe* (1921), in Pick's *Scherben* (1920), in *Danton* (1921), *Wachsfigurencabinett* (1924), appeared in Jean Renoir's *Nana* (1927), in Ucicky's *Mensch ohne Name* (1932), and in theatrical and historical films based on Dostoievsky's *The Brothers Karamazov* (1921), on Shakespeare's *Othello* (1922) and the life of Napoleon (1929). In the theatre he excelled in the role of Agamemnon, as the old man Hilse in Hauptmann's *Die Weber* and as the Captain of Kopenick in Zuckmayer's famous play. Under the Third Reich, Krauss was made Vice-President of the *Reichstheaterkammer* (1933–6) and in April 1934 named as an 'Actor of the State' (*Staatsschauspieler*). His Stakhanovite exertions in Goebbels's (q.v.) dream factory consolidated his position as a celluloid idol – one who was vain, ambitious and infinitely adaptable. Among his best-known performances in these years were as Napoleon I in Franz Wenzler's *Hundert Tage* (1934), as the anthropologist Virchow in *Robert Koch, der Bekämpfer des Todes* (1939) and in the principal role in Pabst's film about the famous doctor and alchemist *Paracelsus* (1942). Most notorious of all was his virtuoso contribution to the anti-semitic movie *Jud Süss* (1940), a cinematic curtain-raiser for the Nazi Holocaust and the most diabolically racist film made in the Third Reich. Krauss played half-a-dozen Jewish parts in the film, evidently steeping himself in the ghetto atmosphere, just as the Jews of the East were about to be exterminated from the face of the earth. Krauss's sheer dedication to his craft – his pedantic mastery of the grotesque 'semitic' accents of the characters he played in this film – was a macabre testimony to his professionalism. As a result of this film he did not act again for several years after the war. He became an Austrian national in 1948 and died in Vienna on 20 October 1959.

Krupp von Bohlen und Halbach, Alfried
(1907–67) Son of Gustav Krupp von
Bohlen und Halbach (q.v.), he acquired
sole control of the historical firm in
1943 and was a central figure in the
Nazi war economy. Alfried Krupp von
Bohlen was born in Essen on 13 August
1907. From 1936 to 1943 he was one of
the Managing Directors of the firm in
Essen, whose armament factories contributed immensely to German military
strength. From the outbreak of war in
1939 Alfried Krupp von Bohlen, who
was in charge of the crucial department
of Mining and Armaments, ensured that
a continuous supply of his firm's tanks,
munitions and armaments reached the
German forces. He was responsible for
moving entire factories from the
German-occupied territories, which
were transported to Germany and rebuilt by Krupps. In 1942, for example,
he supervised the take-over of the iron
and steel industry of the Ukraine. For
the reconstruction of the Mariupol
electro-steel works at the Berthewerke
in Breslau, Krupp von Bohlen did not
shrink from using concentration camp
inmates from a nearby camp which he
had visited on one of his inspection
tours. In July 1943 Krupps were even
allowed to collect Jews from Auschwitz
to work in Essen, where conditions were
little better than in the Polish death
camps. Following an agreement with
Albert Speer (q.v.), Minister for Armaments and War Production, Krupp von
Bohlen employed 45,000 Russian civilians as forced labour in his steel factories
as well as 120,000 prisoners of war and
6,000 other civilians in the coalmines in
conditions below the minimum health
standard. Krupp von Bohlen also set up
a shell factory at Auschwitz and his
officials frequently visited the occupied
countries to recruit slave labour.

In 1943 Alfried Krupp von Bohlen
became sole director and proprietor of
the Krupp industrial empire, which had
been exempted from inheritance tax by
the Lex Krupp – a special law which
incorporated the family's 175 German
companies and their sixty foreign subsidi-
aries into a single tax entity – and he
was made *Wehrwirtschaftsführer* with
the task of mobilizing the entire resources of the German armament industry. The Essen works and other parts of
the Krupp empire, however, were either
destroyed or severely damaged by Allied
bombing attacks after March 1943.
Hitherto undeviatingly loyal to the
Nazis, Krupp von Bohlen now began to
press for compensation for war damage
and recovery of debts as the inevitability
of Germany's defeat became apparent.

Captured by the Canadians shortly
before the end of the war, Krupp von
Bohlen was tried by the Nuremberg Military Tribunal along with nine directors
of the firm and sentenced on 31 July
1948 to twelve years' imprisonment as a
major war criminal, having all his property confiscated. The barbaric treatment
handed out to prisoners of war and
other inmates of the Krupp labour
camps, as well as his pivotal role in the
German military effort and plundering
of occupied territories, ensured a verdict
of guilty. Alfried Krupp von Bohlen
served only three years of his sentence
before he was released from Landsberg
prison on 4 February 1951, following a
general amnesty for convicted industrialists and marshals issued by the American
High Commissioner, John J. McCloy,
himself a banker in private life. His
immense personal fortune – estimated
at between 45 and 50 million pounds ster-
ling – and his confiscated corporate property were returned to him. In 1953 he
was permitted to return to his former
position as head of the family firm and,
in spite of the Allied High Commission's
order that it sell its coal and steel holdings, the Krupp Works rapidly regained
its former standing as the leading steel
producer in Europe. On 30 July 1967,
when Alfried Krupp von Bohlen died of
heart failure after an incurable illness,

his unwieldy, sprawling giant of a firm – 110,000 workers, £500 million turnover, £75 million exports – was, however, on the verge of collapse. As a final act of policy he had been obliged to abandon control of his huge family enterprise to the big German banks, whose financial intervention alone saved the firm. After his death Krupps once again rose like a phoenix from the ashes following a successful reorganization, but as a family dynasty its history was over.

Krupp von Bohlen und Halbach, Gustav (1870–1950) German armaments tycoon who was appointed by Hitler as 'Führer of the Reich Estate of German Industry', Gustav Krupp von Bohlen und Halbach was born in The Hague, Holland, on 7 August 1870 into a prominent banking family. After studying law at Heidelberg, he served as a diplomat in a number of German embassies abroad before marrying Bertha Krupp in 1906 and gradually taking over the Friedrich Krupp Works in Essen, Kiel, Magdeburg and Berlin. Head of the leading armaments firm in Germany and Europe (which had played a key role in World War I) and from 1931 Chairman of the Association of German Industry, the 'King of the munition makers' was initially a 'violent opponent' of Hitler, according to his fellow industralist, Fritz Thyssen (q.v.). Krupp von Bohlen even warned President von Hindenburg (q.v.) on 29 January 1933 – the day before Adolf Hitler was appointed Chancellor – against the folly of such a step. Yet within a short time he became in Thyssen's words 'a super Nazi' following a meeting at Goering's (q.v.) Reichstag President's Palace on 20 February 1933 which was hosted by Hjalmar Schacht (q.v.). At this meeting, where three million marks were collected from leading industrialists on behalf of the Nazi Party, Hitler promised to eliminate the Marxists and restore the Wehrmacht – a point of special interest to Krupp von

Bohlen as the largest producer of guns, tanks and ammunition in Germany. Goering drove home the point by emphasizing that the Third Reich would end disarmament and irksome democratic controls – the forthcoming elections would be the last in Germany for at least ten years and 'probably even for the next hundred years'. Hitler kept his promise by restoring Krupp von Bohlen and other industrialists to leadership positions in the employers' associations and dismissing Nazi 'radicals' who had tried to seize control of the economy. In May 1933 he appointed Krupp von Bohlen as Chairman of the Adolf Hitler Spende in Berlin, an industrialists' fund administered by Martin Bormann (q.v.) which contributed liberally to the Nazi Party in return for special favours in the economic sphere. After 1933, the Krupp family contributed more than ten million marks annually to Hitler and the Nazi Party as well as additional sums to the 'Circle of Friends of Heinrich Himmler' who financed 'special tasks of the SS'.

During World War II the giant Krupp Works benefited extensively from the German conquest of territories in the East, employing approximately 100,000 slave labourers, including Russian prisoners of war, in fifty-seven labour camps in the Essen area, which were guarded by barbed wire and SS guards. Atrocious sanitary conditions (lack of medical supplies, water, toilets, overcrowding that bred disease, etc.), inadequate clothing and extremely meagre food characterized these Krupp labour camps which were scarcely surpassed by the Polish death camps. An estimated 70–80,000 slave labourers died as a result of the cruel methods of coercion employed in the Krupp Works. Krupps also built a large fuse factory at Auschwitz where Jews were worked to exhaustion and later gassed to death.

After the war Krupp von Bohlen was regarded by the Allies as a major war criminal and was indicted at Nuremberg for complicity in Hitler's war of aggression. The older Krupp von Bohlen, however, did not stand trial because of his 'physical and mental condition', after having been examined by a medical panel selected by the American military tribunal. It concluded that he was suffering from senility after a stroke and would not be able to follow the proceedings. Gustav Krupp von Bohlen died in Blühnbach bei Salzburg on 16 January 1950.

Kube, Wilhelm (1887–1943) *Gauleiter* and governor of White Russia during the war years, Kube was born in Glogau (Silesia) in 1887, the son of a professional soldier. Between 1908 and 1912 Kube studied history and political science at the University of Berlin, where he was Chairman of the German *Völkisch* Academic Union. Between 1920 and 1923 he was General Secretary of the German National People's Party, as well as its representative on the Berlin city council. In 1924 he became a Reichstag deputy for the German National Freedom Party and chairman of its Berlin section. At the beginning of 1928 Kube joined the NSDAP, sitting as a deputy in the Reichstag and as chairman of the Nazi caucus in the Prussian Landtag. In 1933 he was appointed by Goering (q.v.) as *Oberpräsident* (governor) of the Brandenburg district (including Berlin) and from November he represented the Frankfurt/Oder electoral constituency in the Reichstag. He was removed from all his positions in September 1936 by Major Walter Buch (q.v.), chief judge of the Party court, on charges of blackmail, seduction of colleagues' wives and embezzlement. Kube's career recovered thanks to Himmler (q.v.) who had been impressed by his willingness to volunteer for the Waffen-SS at the age of fifty-three. In July 1941 he was appointed *General*

Kommissar of White Russia, in charge of civil administration, and at first he co-operated closely with the SS in exterminating the Jews of Minsk and Belorussia. His report to Hinrich Lohse (q.v.) on 31 July 1942 pointed out with satisfaction that in the previous ten weeks 55,000 Jews had been liquidated. Before 1939 Kube had been a fanatical anti-semite but soon even he would be shocked by the brutal actions of the SS and police commanders against the Jews and the local population in White Russia. In particular, he was frustrated by the transport of Jews from the Reich to the Minsk ghetto, who were being earmarked for extermination. He complained to Heydrich (q.v.), who categorically dismissed his arguments for the exemption of German-speaking Jews from the 'Final Solution'. In a letter to Lohse on 16 December 1941, Kube repeated that 'people who come from our *Kulturkreis* are quite different from the bestial native hordes'. Kube's change of attitude and his policy of employing Jewish workers led to constant conflicts with Senior SS and Police Leaders.

Kube angrily complained that the *Aktionen* which had been resumed in Minsk, in April 1943, had led to unheard-of outrages. He regarded the removal of gold fillings from hundreds of Jews intended for execution as 'conduct unworthy of the Germany of Kant and Goethe'. As late as July 1943 Kube was still ignoring official instructions to cease all private employment of Jews, which led to a serious warning from Rosenberg's (q.v.) office which was responsible for the Eastern Occupied territories. On 22 September 1943 Kube was shot in his headquarters by a Russian chambermaid (a member of the partisans) before SS charges against him could be considered. Hitler ordered a State funeral for his veteran party comrade.

L

Lammers, Hans Heinrich (1879–1962) Chief of the Reich Chancellery from 1933 to 1945 and Hitler's closest legal adviser, Hans Heinrich Lammers was born in Lublinitz, Upper Silesia, on 27 May 1879, the son of a veterinary surgeon. After studying law at Breslau and Heidelberg, he was appointed a county court judge in Beuthen in 1912. After military service during World War I, Lammers joined the Reich Ministry of the Interior as a senior government adviser and in 1933 he was promoted to head of the Reich Chancery when the Nazis came to power. An unimaginative bureaucrat who combined a sense of protocol with natural brutality, Lammers's legal expertise was much appreciated by Hitler who had known him for many years and looked to him as his most important subordinate in State matters. For months at a time Lammers and his staff would carry on Chancery business at Hitler's private retreat on the Obersalzberg and he was frequently consulted by the Führer on legal matters. A member of the German Law Academy and a Prussian State Councillor, Lammers was made Reich Minister without Portfolio in 1937 and two years later on 30 November 1939 he became Ministerial Councillor for Reich Defence. In 1940 Lammers was promoted to Honorary SS General. From January 1943 onwards, Lammers presided over cabinet meetings in Hitler's absence and, together with Martin Bormann (q.v.), usurped a great deal of power by controlling access to the Führer. From 1943 all orders to be signed by Hitler had to be cleared first by a triumvirate consisting of Lammers, Bormann and Field Marshal Keitel (q.v.). Bormann's intrigues against him and Lammers's involvement in Goering's (q.v.) telegram of 23 April 1945, informing Hitler that he was assuming control of the country, led to an order for his arrest. Imprisoned and interned by the Allied authorities after the war, Lammers was accused at the Wilhelmstrasse trial of 1949 of formulating and giving legal authority to Nazi anti-Jewish measures leading to the 'Final Solution'.

While admitting knowledge of the Führer's order to Heydrich (q.v.) to implement the 'Final Solution of the Jewish Question', Lammers denied all involvement in its execution. The International Military Tribunal at Nuremberg sentenced him to twenty years' imprisonment, but the United States High Commissioner halved the sentence and, after another reduction, Lammers was released from Landsberg prison on 16 December 1951. He died in Düsseldorf on 4 January 1962.

Landau, Edmund (1877–1938) A leading German mathematician who did important work in the theory of functions and was one of the founders of modern number theory, Edmund Landau was born on 14 February 1877 in Berlin, the son of the famous Professor of Gynaecology, Leopold Landau. Born in Warsaw, his father had been active in Jewish affairs, an interest shared by his Zionist-oriented son. In 1909 Edmund Landau succeeded Herman Minkowski as Professor of Mathematics at Göttingen and in the same year published the first systematic account of modern number theory, *Handbuch der Lehre von der Verteilung der Primzahlen* (2 vols.). He was subsequently elected a full member of the Academies of Berlin, Göttingen, Halle, Leningrad and Rome. For several years a member of the Hebrew University's Board of Governors, Landau briefly took over the chair of mathematics at Jerusalem in 1927, returning to Göttingen the following year. His status as a long-standing civil servant initially spared him from the dismissals effected at Göttingen in April 1933, but anti-semitic demonstrations and boycotts organized by Nazi students made his position untenable. Following his compulsory retirement as a result of the Nuremberg Laws in 1935, Landau returned to Berlin, where he died on 19 February 1938.

Laue, Max von (1879–1960) A leading German physicist and former pupil of Max Planck (q.v.), Max von Laue was born in Pfaffendorf, near Coblenz, on 9 October 1879. Professor of Theoretical Physics at Zürich (1912–14), Frankfurt (1914–19) and Director of the Institute of Theoretical Physics at the University of Berlin (1919–43), von Laue's pioneering work in X-ray crystallography won him fame and the Nobel Prize for Physics in 1914. His research into the diffraction of X-rays in crystals was the starting point of much subsequent work in the field. Deputy Director of the Max Planck Institute of Physics (1921–51) he used his influence where possible to counter the Nazi policy of dismissals after 1933, regretting as he did the loss to Germany of so many outstanding Jewish scientists. In January 1934 he courageously paid tribute to the Nobel Prize winner Fritz Haber (q.v.), a victim of the racial purge, in two widely read scientific journals – an action which earned him an official reprimand from the Ministry of Education. Von Laue was one of the most active opponents of

Johannes Stark (q.v.), the leader of the 'Aryan Physics' school who sought to realign modern physics with National Socialist ideology. Convinced that political interference would destroy the standards and effectiveness of German science, von Laue successfully opposed Stark's election to the Prussian Academy of Sciences. Von Laue's eminence, his age and his patriotism protected him during the Third Reich in spite of his uncompromising independence and refusal to co-operate with the Nazis. In a letter to Max Born (q.v.) in 1944, Albert Einstein (q.v.) observed that what distinguished von Laue from other scientists who remained in the Third Reich was his human stature. 'It was particularly interesting in his case to observe how he tore himself loose step by step from the traditions of the herd under the effect of a strong feeling of justice.' After the collapse of Nazi Germany, von Laue was a witness in several de-Nazification trials. He was responsible for re-establishing the laboratories of the Imperial Institute of Physics and Technology and participated actively in the reconstruction of German cultural life. He died in Berlin on 23 April 1960.

Leander, Zarah (1907–81) Red-headed Swedish actress and singer who became 'the Nazi cinema's flesh-and-blood monument to feminine allure ... She projected a screen-filling *décolletage* beneath which, with chaste and steady rhythm, beat a woman's heart' (Richard Grünberger). Born on 15 March 1907 in Karlstad, Sweden, the daughter of a pastor, Zarah Heidberg married at the age of sixteen the actor Nils Leander, an inveterate alcoholic whom she soon left. Following her success in a Viennese musical comedy and as the star of Geza von Bovary's *Première* (1937), the Scandinavian actress was offered a long-term contract by the German UFA studios. Over the next eight years the most beautiful woman of the Nazi cinema became a semi-official personage in the Third Reich, the 'chastity-belted *Ewige Weib* of the Nazi screen'. Her films were projected throughout the territories conquered by the Wehrmacht. For the most part they were musicals and romantic love stories set in past centuries or exotic climes. She starred in *Zu Neuen Ufern* (1937), in Carl Froelich's *Heimat* (1938), in *Der Blaufuchs* (1938), *Es war eine Rauschende Ballnacht* (1939), *Das Lied der Wüste* (1939) and *Das Herz der Königin* (1940), and in Rolf Hansen's films *Der Weg ins Freie* (1941), *Die Grosse Liebe* (1942) – a smash hit – and *Damals* (1943), achieving a fame unrivalled by any German woman artist.

Never an adherent of Nazism, Zarah Leander, who remained a Swedish citizen, avoided politics and propaganda activity, preferring the artistic and bohemian milieu in Berlin, throwing lavish and noisy receptions in her home and engaging in eccentric conduct which infuriated Goebbels (q.v.) and other Nazi potentates. During a bombing raid on Berlin in 1943 her villa caught fire and Zarah threw all her wardrobe through the windows to avid passers-by. A few hours later she flew back to Stockholm. After several years in retreat in the Swedish countryside, she returned to Vienna, the scene of her first triumph, to resume her film career, appearing in *Cuba Cubana* (1952), *Ave Maria* (1953), *Bei Dir war es Immer so Schön* (1954) and *Der Blaue Nachffalter* (1959). As late as 1965 Zarah Leander appeared in musical comedy in West Berlin and two years later in the Italo-German production *Come Imparai ad Amare la Donne*. She spent her last years in quiet retirement in Sweden, where she died in August 1981.

Leber, Julius (1891–1945) Former Social Democratic Party deputy and a leading figure in the German Resistance, Julius Leber was born in Biesheim, Alsace, on 16 November 1891. From a poverty-stricken background, Leber worked for a time in a rug factory and then joined the Social Democratic Party. During World War I he served as an officer in the Imperial army and was decorated for his bravery in combat. In 1920 he completed his doctorate in political science at Freiburg and took an active part in the overthrow of the right-wing Kapp *putsch* in Berlin. In 1921 he was appointed editor of the *Volksbote* in Lübeck and three years later became a member of the SPD parliamentary faction in the Reichstag. A strong opponent of Hitler and National Socialism, Leber was a marked man after 30 January 1933 and narrowly escaped an attempt on his life the day after the Nazis came to power. From 1933 to 1937 he was imprisoned and sent to concentration camps at Esterwegen and Oranienburg as a 'danger to the State'. After his release Leber became closely involved in the resistance to Hitler, establishing contacts with the Kreisau Circle, a small group of officers and professional people who regarded Nazism as a disaster for Germany. One of the leading Social Democrats around Goerdeler (q.v.), Leber's left-wing views drew him politically close to Claus von Stauffenberg (q.v.), the dynamic General Staff officer who became the driving-force of the Resistance after 1943. Leber was to have been von Stauffenberg's candidate for Reich Chancellor had the conspiracy against Hitler succeeded. Leber, together with his fellow Social Democrat Adolf Reichwein (q.v.), was, however, arrested before the July plot was put into operation, as a result of contacts with communist agents, one of whom proved to be working for the Gestapo. On 20 October 1944 Leber was condemned to death by the People's Court for high treason and hanged at Plötzensee prison on 5 January 1945.

Leeb, Wilhelm Ritter von (1876–1956) General Field Marshal who commanded the Army Group North in the early phase of the Russian campaign, Wilhelm Ritter von Leeb was born in Landsberg, Bavaria, on 5 September 1939, to an old military family. A career officer, he entered the Imperial army as a cadet in 1895 and served in various staff appointments during World War I. A member of the *Freikorps* in 1919, von Leeb made his subsequent career in the Reichswehr and was promoted in 1929 to Major General. From 1930 to 1933 he commanded Military District VII. In 1934 he was promoted to General of Artillery and was assigned as Commander-in-Chief to Army Group II. Dismissed in January 1938, von Leeb was recalled to duty at the time of the Czech crisis, commanding an army into the Sudetenland. Promoted to General in 1939, he was appointed Commander of Army Group C, opposing the French on the Rhine and along the Maginot Line. He privately disapproved of the proposed German army offensive against neutral Belgium, which he believed would turn the world against Germany, and was sceptical of the prospects of victory in the West. Nevertheless, he took an active part in the western campaign and, after the fall of France, was promoted by Hitler to General Field Marshal. On 22 June 1941 von Leeb was appointed Commander-in-Chief of Army Group North based in East Prussia which was to move up through the Baltic States towards Leningrad. Von Leeb's infantry and armoured divisions were initially successful in their drive north, but as the winter approached he advised a retreat from the Leningrad area, which led Hitler to relieve him of his post on 18 January 1942. Field Marshal von Leeb took no further active part in the war. He died in Hohenschwangau, Bavaria, on 29 April 1956.

Leers, Johann von (1902–65) One of the most prolific and vicious literary Jew-baiters in Nazi Germany, Johann

von Leers was born in Vietlubbe, Mecklenburg, on 25 January 1902. In 1929 he joined the NSDAP after studying law at Berlin, Kiel and Rostock and working for a while as an attaché in the Foreign Office. A district speaker and leader of the National Socialist Students' League, von Leers came to the attention of Goebbels (q.v.) and was assigned to write Party propaganda, producing a stream of twenty-seven books between 1933 and 1945 dealing in popularized form with Nazi ideology. An expert on the Jewish question, on theories of 'blood and soil' and the doctrine of the Germanic master-race, von Leers achieved early notoriety with his book *Juden Sehen Dich an* (*Jews Look at You*), published in 1933 and dedicated to the 'gallant' Julius Streicher (q.v.). The book featured photographs of prominent Jews like Albert Einstein (q.v.), Emil Ludwig and Lion Feuchtwanger, under which appeared brief, abusive captions containing the note 'Not Hanged Yet!'. Appointed Professor at the University of Jena, von Leers's other works included *Kurzgefasste Geschichte des Nationalsozialismus* (1933), *Blut und Rasse in der Gesetzgebung* (1936), *Rassen, Völker und Volkstümer* (1939), *Kräfte hinter Roosevelt* (1941), *Juden hinter Stalin* (1943) and the notorious *Die Verbrechernatur der Juden* (1944). In the latter work, von Leers declared that the 'Jews are hereditary criminals' and that Jewry represents 'the principles of anti-God, it is Satanism in action'. He openly called for their extermination as a necessary act. In 1945 von Leers fled to Italy and then to Argentina, where he lived in the colony of German exiles between 1950 and 1955, continuing his neo-Nazi propaganda. Warmly praised by the ex-Mufti of Jerusalem, Haj Amin el Husseini, for having 'always championed the Arabs' righteous cause against the powers of darkness embodied in World Jewry' and for his services to German-Arab friendship, von Leers went to Cairo in the mid-1950s and converted to Islam, calling himself Omar Amin von Leers. His enthusiastic support for rising Arab nationalism and his glorification of Hitler's extermination of the Jews led to his employment in the foreign propaganda service of Colonel Nasser. In Egypt and the Arab world, von Leers found a receptive audience for his call to build an alliance between Germans and Arabs against Zionism, which had allegedly 'stabbed them in the back'. He died in Cairo in early March 1965.

Lenard, Philipp (1862–1947) Nobel Prize winner who held the chair of theoretical physics at the University of Heidelberg and was praised by the Nazis for making science relevant to the political struggle, Philipp Lenard was born in Bratislava (formerly Pressburg in the Austro-Hungarian Empire) on 7 June 1862. The son of a wine merchant, Lenard grew up in an atmosphere of Pan-German nationalism, going to Germany to study physics and completing his doctorate at Heidelberg in 1886. Assistant to the Jewish-born physicist, Heinrich Hertz, Lenard began experimenting with cathode rays in the 1890s, the experimental work for which he was awarded the Nobel Prize for Physics in 1905. Professor of Physics at Kiel from 1898 and later appointed to the chair of theoretical physics at Heidelberg, Lenard was a celebrated lecturer but increasingly out of touch with the modern concepts of physical reality developed by Planck (q.v.), Einstein (q.v.) and Heisenberg (q.v.). Embittered by his belief that the British physicist J. J. Thomson had plagiarized his experimental work, Lenard denounced English 'materialism' and 'egoism' as alien to the spirit of German physics. During World War I he espoused the nationalist theories which perceived the war as a battle between German *Kultur* and western civilization. The defeat of 1918, the Weimar Constitution, the short-lived Munich Soviet and the Versailles Treaty exacerbated his nationalism and drew him to the ideology of *völkisch* racism. He denounced Einstein's theory of relativity on political as well as theoretical grounds. Not only did it abolish the aether (a cherished concept of Lenard) and violate his own intuitive picture of nature, but Lenard deeply resented Einstein's international success, his lionization by the British, his pacifism and left-wing views.

By 1922 Lenard's anti-semitism began to infect his scholarship, alienating him from the mainstream of the German physics community. Following the assassination of the Jewish-born Foreign Minister, Walther Rathenau, in 1922, Lenard refused to observe the day of national mourning which led to threats from Heidelberg union members and a disciplinary hearing against him. Defended by right-wing students, Lenard began to express open support for Hitler and Ludendorff (q.v.) in May 1924 and moved closer to Nazi and *völkisch* circles. In his *Grosse Naturforscher* (1929) Lenard displayed a romantic veneration for the 'Great Investigators of Nature', all of whom he described as of exclusively Aryan-Germanic origin. Lenard's antipathy to the direction of modern physics was based on a belief in an organic universe, a profound dislike of mechanistic materialism and abstract theories, as well as a mandarin love of research for its own sake. Lenard became the leading propagandist of the anti-technology faction in 'Aryan physics', linking his emphasis on the spiritual dimension with the centrality of *Volk* and race and dismissing the supranationalism of science as a 'Jewish fraud'. On good terms with Alfred Rosenberg (q.v.), Rudolf Hess (q.v.) and the *völkisch*-ideological wing of the Nazi Party, Lenard constantly stressed that 'in reality, scholarship – like everything else brought forth by men – is conditioned by race and blood'. Already retired when Hitler came to power, Lenard was too old to play an active role in the Third Reich but his career was held up by the Nazis as a model of true 'German behaviour'.

In 1936 Lenard was the first recipient of the Party's new prize for scholarship, receiving an eulogy from Rosenberg in praise of his long struggle for an 'Aryan' physics. His book *Deutsche Physik* (*German Physics*), published in the same year, was widely disseminated by the Nazis and praised for making science an integral part of the *völkisch*-racist world-view. Lenard was not, however, a very astute politician and like his fellow-Nazi physicist, Johannes Stark (q.v.), failed to perceive the power realities of the Third Reich. As a result, he attached himself to lesser figures like Rosenberg, Hess and Frick (q.v.), failing to gain the support of the top Nazi leaders for his projects. In the last years of the Third Reich he withdrew completely from public life, retiring to a village near Heidelberg. After the war the authorities considered trying him in a de-Nazification court, but the acting Rector of Heidelberg persuaded them that there was no honour in humiliating the aged physicist. Philipp Lenard died at Messelhausen near Bad Mergentheim on 20 May 1947.

Letterhaus, Bernhard (1894–1944) Catholic labour leader and member of the German Resistance, Bernhard Letterhaus was born in Wuppertal-Barmen, Rhineland, on 10 July 1894. After serving in World War I, where he was severely wounded and awarded the Iron Cross (First Class), Letterhaus was involved in working for the Catholic labour unions. In 1928 he became Union Secretary of the West German Catholic Workers' Association and in the same year he was elected as a Centre Party member of the Prussian legislature. After 1933, Letterhaus encouraged underground resistance to the Nazi regime among Catholics. Called up to the army

in 1939 he became a Captain in the *Abwehr* section of the OKW and strengthened his connections with other circles in the Resistance. Arrested in the wake of the abortive July plot, he was sentenced to death by the People's Court on 13 November 1944. The next day Letterhaus was hanged for his part in the anti-Hitler conspiracy.

Leuschner, Wilhelm (1888–1944) Leading trade union member of the Resistance, Wilhelm Leuschner was born in Bayreuth on 15 June 1888. An engraver by profession, Leuschner joined the SPD in his youth and became an active member of the trade union movement. From 1929 to 1933 he was SPD Minister of the Interior in Hesse. In 1932 he was also appointed Deputy Chairman of the German Trade Union Association, a post he held until the Nazi seizure of power. Arrested for the first time on 2 May 1933, Leuschner was sent to a concentration camp where he suffered torture at the hands of his SA guards. Following his release he began to organize clandestine trade union resistance to the Nazi régime. During World War II he worked closely with the circle around General Beck (q.v.) and Carl Goerdeler (q.v.) as the representative of the outlawed trade unions. Politically close to Claus von Stauffenberg (q.v.), he would have been included in a future cabinet had the conspiracy against Hitler succeeded. Arrested for his Resistance activities on 20 July 1944, Leuschner was sentenced to death by the People's Court. He was hanged on 29 September 1944.

Ley, Robert (1890–1945) Leader of the German Labour Front from 1933 to 1945, Robert Ley was born in Niederbreidenbach, Rhineland, on 15 February 1890. After studying chemistry at the Universities of Bonn, Jena and Münster, he participated in World War I as a flier and in 1917 was shot down and taken prisoner by the French. Returning to Münster in 1920, he worked as a chemist with I. G. Farben in Leverkusen until his dismissal for habitual drunkenness. Ley joined the NSDAP in 1924 and a few years later he was appointed *Gauleiter* in the Rhineland. An ardent Nazi and close personal friend of Hitler's, Ley became a member of the Prussian legislature in 1928 and was put in charge of the NSDAP organization in the Cologne-Aachen district. He was elected a member of the Reichstag for the same district in 1930. Implicated in various street and public brawls in the early days of the movement, the coarse, eccentric Dr Ley was a bitter anti-semite who used his Party newspaper, the *Westdeutscher Beobachter*, for conducting a vicious campaign against 'Jewish' department stores and 'Jewish' money power. He specialized in publishing blackmailing articles to extort money, chiefly from Jews. Appointed Reich Organization Leader in November 1932, the pathologically uncouth but enterprising Ley rose in importance after the Nazis came to power, without ever quite reaching the very top rank of the Party leadership.

The prototype of the plebeian, radical Nazi constantly fulminating against bourgeois customs and the 'blue-blooded swine', Ley was an unstable personality and an erratic, inept administrator, whose crackpot theories and sometimes ludicrous public statements did not prevent him from making a personal fortune under the cover of his Party activities nor from enjoying considerable popularity. On 2 May 1933 Ley began a campaign which in a few days successfully 'co-ordinated' the once free and independent trade unions in the Reich into the *Deutsche Arbeitsfront* (German Labour Front). For the next twelve years this monolithic labour organization, which eventually had twenty-five million German workers under its aegis, was controlled by a temperance-preaching alcoholic. The

largest, single mass organization in the Third Reich, the DAF developed into a mammoth empire run by a swollen bureaucracy whose officials came from the NSDAP, the former Nazi unions, the SA and the SS. Its ostensible purpose was to restore 'social peace' in the world of labour by overcoming the class struggle in favour of the unity of the *Volk*. Its paternalistic 'socialism', which legitimized competition in the service of the nation, aimed at winning over the working class to the Nazi way of life by looking after their social welfare and surrounding them with the 'right' cultural atmosphere. Operating with a huge budget, it controlled the hiring and firing of workers, their compensation and insurance, care for the elderly and disabled, while using its funds for workers' education, the construction of buildings and the stabilization of wages. Employers and employees wore the same, simple blue uniform in accordance with the classless Nazi ideology of 'an organization of creative Germans of the brain and fist' which claimed to have made the worker 'an equal and respected member of the nation'. The militant phraseology of the DAF which appealed directly to the mentality of the trenches was designed to stimulate maximum productivity. As Ley put it in a speech in the Siemens electrical works in Berlin in October 1933: 'Every worker must regard himself as a soldier of the economy.'

In compensation for the end of collective bargaining and the outlawing of strikes and all independent trade unions, the DAF sought to divert the working classes by creating an elaborate and sophisticated form of regimented leisure through the *Kraft durch Freude* (Strength through Joy) organization, also headed by Ley. After 1934 this venture in dirt-cheap mass tourism, sport and recreational activities, which involved some nine million German workers in organized leisure, became an important weapon in the modern Nazi version of 'bread and circuses'. Opening up cultural vistas previously available only to the upper classes (theatre, opera, lectures, etc.), it also enabled workers to travel to foreign lands at minimal prices. Apart from the seagoing ships used by *Strength through Joy* travel groups, the DAF owned extensive properties, building societies, banks, insurance companies, publishing outlets and the Volkswagen factory, all of which provided Ley with unlimited possibilities for self-enrichment. The Volkswagen (People's Car) project, which the DAF took in hand in 1938, was a classic example of the fraudulent façade behind which Nazi 'socialism' deceived the working classes. German workers were obliged to pay on an instalment plan before delivery, but not a single car was ever turned out for any customer in the Third Reich, the money was never refunded to the wage-earners and Ley pocketed the profits.

The classless utopia of the *Volksgemeinschaft* which protected the rights of workers was no less illusory, in spite of organizations such as the 'Beauty of Labour' unit set up by Ley to improve working conditions in plants and factories. In reality the principle of *Gefolgschaft* (following the plant leader) was restored in the factories, where employers largely regained their powers while the take-home pay of German workers declined. Tied down by State controls, they found it difficult to move from one job to another, their wages and salaries were frozen and they were obliged to pay increasingly large gifts to a variety of Nazi 'charities'. Thus under Ley's leadership, the DAF served primarily as a vast propaganda organization under the aegis of the Nazi Party, intended to maximize productivity by anaesthetizing the independent political consciousness of the workers. In addition to his role as dictator of the Labour Front, Ley was also made overlord of the Reich housing programme during World War II and

given the task of building and organizing the *Ordensburg* schools – Teutonic order castles where the future Nazi élite was to undergo a combination of Platonic training, the British public school ethos and indoctrination into Nazi racial mythology. Only the toughest and best graduates of the Adolf Hitler *Schulen* were to be admitted to these castles, where the curriculum was defined by Ley as 'four years of the hardest possible physical and mental exertions'. Character training based on sports, tests of courage, education in social poise, etc., was designed to breed a new race of leaders.

Though Ley claimed that the schools opened the door to political leadership for the man in the street, the *Ordensburgen*, with their trappings and mystique of a medieval chivalric order, revealed the quasi-feudal ethos of National Socialist ideas of leadership. Moreover, Ley's deification of Hitler, which took on extreme sycophantic proportions, indicated how deeply his own thinking was impregnated by the *Führerprinzip*. Rabid anti-semitism permeated the anti-capitalist rhetoric of the Nazi labour boss no less intensely. In a speech in Karlsruhe in May 1942 Ley declared: 'It is not enough to isolate the Jewish enemy of mankind, the Jews have got to be exterminated.' Captured by American troops after trying to flee to the mountains near Berchtesgaden, Ley committed suicide on 24 October 1945 in his prison cell while under arrest and awaiting trial at Nuremberg.

Lichtenberg, Bernhard (1875–1943) Catholic martyr of the Nazi régime who died in consequence of his fearless denunciation of the persecution of the Jews, Bernhard Lichtenberg was born in Ohlau, Silesia, on 3 December 1875. Ordained as a Catholic priest in 1899, he served as a military chaplain during World War I. After the war he became a Berlin City Councillor, representing the Catholic Centre Party. In 1932 he was appointed Pastor of St Hedwig's Cathedral in Berlin and six years later he became its Provost. On 28 August 1941 Father Lichtenberg sent a sharp letter of protest to Reich Medical Leader, Leonardo Conti (q.v.), denouncing the euthanasia programme and supporting the position taken by the Cardinal Archbishop of Münster, Clemens von Galen (q.v.). Father Lichtenberg demanded that the Chief Physician of the Reich answer for the crime of killing mentally ill persons, 'which will call forth the vengeance of the Lord on the heads of the German nation'. The euthanasia action was in fact called off, but Lichtenberg was arrested on 23 October 1941 for the much more dangerous offence of having publicly prayed for the Jews and even demanding that he be allowed to join them on their journey to the East. The Berlin Provost was one of the very few German priests to have openly condemned the anti-semitic persecution. For this 'crime' he spent two years in Berlin's Tegel prison. He died on 3 November 1943 while being transferred to Dachau concentration camp.

Liebermann, Max (1847–1935) President of the Berlin Academy of Art until his forced resignation in 1933, Max Liebermann was one of the great innovators in *fin-de-siècle* German art, who ended up as an aesthetic conservative. Born in Berlin on 20 July 1847, the son of a prosperous, respectable Jewish merchant family, Liebermann travelled widely as a young apprentice painter before finally settling in the German capital in 1884, where he remained until his death. In his youth he was strongly influenced by the Barbizon school in France and the Dutch masters. An honest observer whose realism was touched by impressionist light, Liebermann achieved wide popularity with his appealing landscapes, genre scenes and penetrating portraits. Only occasionally

did he turn to explicitly Jewish themes in his work, though he was proud of his ancestry, never denying his origins for all his patriotic German identification. In the stuffy Wilhelminian atmosphere of the 1890s, Liebermann introduced a mini-revolution in German art by pleading for French impressionism at a time when this was still unpalatable to academic taste. In 1898, the same year that he became a member of the Berlin Academy, Liebermann founded the Berlin *Sezession* which helped pave the way from academic to modern art in Germany. A rebel in his time, Liebermann was out of sympathy with the new schools of modernism that subsequently developed, such as expressionism, cubism and fauvism, which were too far removed from nature for his taste. As President of the Berlin Academy in the 1920s he became the target of the younger generation of painters, including such expressionist radicals as Emil Nolde (q.v.). For all his conservative patriotism, the fact of Liebermann's Jewish origin also damned him in the eyes of Nazi philistines. In the Third Reich his work was denounced as an example of 'decadence' and included in displays of so-called 'degenerate art'. Removed by the Nazis from his position as the head of the Berlin Academy, he was forbidden to continue his artistic work. Liebermann died in Berlin on 8 February 1935 at the age of eighty-eight before he could be subjected to the ultimate humiliation of being compelled to leave his homeland. His widow was less fortunate, committing suicide in 1943 to avoid being sent to an extermination camp.

Lischka, Kurt (born 1909) Deputy head of German security and criminal investigations in occupied France and Chief of the German police in Paris, Kurt Lischka was born in Breslau on 16 August 1909, the son of a bank official. After studying law and political science in Breslau and Berlin, Lischka was active in different district courts and worked in the Provincial Court of Appeal in Breslau. He entered the SS on 1 June 1933, reaching the rank of SS Major five years later and being promoted to SS Lieutenant-Colonel on 20 April 1942. On 1 September 1935 Lischka joined the Gestapo and in January 1940 became head of the Gestapo office in Cologne. Transferred to France, he became Knochen's (q.v.) deputy in November 1940 in the security police and SD throughout occupied French territory. He also served from 15 January 1943 as Commander of the security police and SD in Paris, as well as chief of the department which oversaw the internment camps and which executed detainees.

Lischka's forte was 'the Jewish Question', in which he had specialized since 1938 when he took over the *Referat* IVB (Jewish Affairs) in the Gestapo. At the end of 1938 he had been appointed head of the Reich Centre for Jewish Emigration in Berlin and, during the war, had been instrumental in planning and supervising the deportation and subsequent murder of 80,000 Jews in France and of other 'enemies' of the Third Reich. Lischka was arrested on 10 December 1945 after going into hiding in Schleswig-Holstein. He was interned by the British and then by the French, before being handed over to the Czechs on 2 May 1947 for his activities at the end of the war when he was head of the *Referat* for the Bohemian Protectorate in the Reich Main Security Office. Released and returned to West Germany on 22 August 1950, Lischka lived unmolested in the Federal Republic even though a French court sentenced him *in absentia* to hard labour for life on 18 September 1950 for his wartime role in the 'Final Solution' in occupied France. Lischka worked for a time as a commercial employee and even became a judge in the Federal Republic, his French life-sentence notwithstanding.

Thanks to the efforts of the French

Jewish lawyer and Holocaust survivor, Serge Klarsfeld, Lischka was eventually brought to trial in Cologne at the end of the 1970s. He was accused of war crimes together with his former adjunct in Paris, Ernest Heinrichsohn (Mayor of Burgstadt, Bavaria), and Herbert-Martin Hagen, a top SD official in occupied France who had also been sentenced to life imprisonment *in absentia* but nonetheless became a prominent West German industrialist after the war. The Cologne War Criminals Trial against Lischka, Hagen and Heinrichsohn was the most important trial of ex-Nazis since the Eichmann (q.v.) trial in Jerusalem and regarded by many as the 'last major Nazi trial'. On 2 February 1980 the Cologne County Court found Lischka guilty of war crimes and sentenced him to ten years' imprisonment.

List, Wilhelm (1880–1971) General Field Marshal dismissed in September 1942 for failing to break through in the Caucasus, Wilhelm List was born on 14 May 1880 in Oberkirchberg, the son of a doctor. A professional soldier who served as a General Staff officer during World War I, List joined the *Freikorps* in 1919 and from 1923 to 1926 held troop and staff commands in the Reichswehr. In 1927 he was appointed head of the Army Organization Department in the Reichswehr Ministry. Promoted to Major General in 1930, he became Commandant of the infantry school in Dresden, and in 1932 was made a Lieutenant-General. In 1935 he was given command of the Fourth Army Corps in Dresden and then, following the *Anschluss* in 1938, was transferred to Vienna as Commander-in-Chief of a new army group. Promoted to *Generaloberst* in 1939, List commanded the Fourteenth Army in the attack on Poland and the Twelfth Army in the invasion of northern France in 1940, earning promotion to General Field Marshal in July of the same year, after the stunning German victory. In February 1941 List drew up the agreement with Bulgaria enabling the Wehrmacht to attack Greece by passing through Bulgarian territory. From June to October 1941 he was Commander-in-Chief of the German army in the Balkans. During the invasion of the Soviet Union, List commanded Army Group A in the Caucasus, holding this position from 7 July until 10 September 1942 when he was dismissed by Hitler, who blamed him for failing to break through on the Russian front. Tried at Nuremberg, List was sentenced to life imprisonment in 1948 by an American military tribunal. Pardoned and released in 1953, Wilhelm List died in Garmisch on 18 June 1971.

Lohse, Heinrich (1896–1964) Reich Commissioner for the conquered Baltic States and White Russia during World War II, Heinrich Lohse was born on 2 September 1896 in Mühlenbarbek. He was appointed *Gauleiter* of Schleswig-Holstein from 1925 and represented the same electoral district as Nazi member of the Reichstag after 12 November 1933. *Oberpräsident* of Schleswig-Holstein and Prussian State Councillor from 1933, Lohse was made *SA-Gruppenführer* in February 1934. From 1941 to 1944 Lohse was Reich *Kommissar,* Ostland, with his headquarters in Riga during the period when the 'Final Solution' was carried out in the Baltic States and White Russia with the utmost brutality. According to his secret instructions on 27 July 1941, the inmates of the ghettoes under his jurisdiction were to receive 'only the amount of food that the rest of the population could spare and in no case more than was sufficient to sustain life'. His declared object was to safeguard minimal measures 'until such time as the more intensive measures for the "Final Solution" can be put into effect'. Lohse was nonetheless sufficiently disturbed by the mass shootings and sustained pogroms carried out in

the Vilna ghetto and other places to query on 15 November 1941 whether 'all Jews, regardless of age or sex, or their usefulness to the economy [for instance, skilled workers in the Wehrmacht's ordnance factories] were to be liquidated'. The reply which came from the Ministry of Eastern Territories on 18 December 1941 made it clear that 'the demands of the economy be ignored' and referred Lohse to the Higher SS and Police Leaders. For all his concern about irreplaceable Jewish workers, Lohse was not the man openly to challenge the authority of Himmler's (q.v.) police. After the war, Lohse was tried by a British court and sentenced in January 1948 to ten years' penal servitude. He was freed in February 1951 because of ill health and was able to draw a pension from the local authorities in Schleswig-Holstein. Under parliamentary pressure, the Bonn government withdrew the pension, not because of war crimes committed in Russia but because Lohse was adjudged to have been an enemy of democracy during his term as district leader of Schleswig-Holstein. He died in his home town of Mühlenbarbek bei Steinburg in Schleswig-Holstein on 25 February 1964.

Lorenz, Werner (1891–1974) Head of the *Volksdeutsche Mittelstelle* (VOMI), a key division of the SS, Werner Lorenz was born in Grünhof on 2 October 1891. A cadet officer and air corps pilot in the Imperial army, Lorenz joined the *Freikorps* after World War I and was an early adherent of the NSDAP. Independently wealthy with large industrial interests and an estate in Danzig Free State, Lorenz was a traditional nationalist with the reputation of a *bon viveur*. He entered the SS in January 1931 and two years later was elected a member of the Prussian legislature. On 12 November 1933 he became a deputy of the Reichstag for the district of East Prussia. From 1934 to 1937 Lorenz was Commander of *SS-Oberabschnitt* 'North-west' in Hamburg. From 1937 to 1945 he was head of the *Volksdeutsche Mittelstelle*, an office charged with defending the welfare of German nationals living abroad. Completely under the control of the SS, it considered Germans in foreign countries as biologically linked with those in the Third Reich. The office exploited fifth-column techniques, playing an important part in preparations for the *Anschluss*, and aided Konrad Henlein (q.v.) during the Sudeten crisis. During World War II it had a considerable role in the transportation or 'resettlement' of Germans in Poland, the Baltic States and the USSR to the Greater Reich. At the same time it sought to Germanize Poles and other foreign nationals who came under its protection. Many such foreigners found themselves obliged to fight in the ranks of the Waffen-SS for the glory of the Third Reich. The VOMI was eventually merged with the Central Office for Race and Resettlement to form the Reich Office for the Consolidation of German Nationhood. As head of the resettlement staff with the Reich Commissioner for Germanization and in charge of the International Relations Division in the SS Central Department, Lorenz was the chief executive in Himmler's (q.v.) drive to absorb 'racial Germans' into the Reich and extend SS power in the occupied territories. Promoted to *SS-Obergruppenführer* in 1943, Lorenz was a power-seeker, whose record was nonetheless marginally better than some of his contemporaries when it came to the treatment of subject peoples in Nazi-controlled territory. On 10 March 1948 Lorenz was sentenced to twenty years' imprisonment as a war criminal. The sentence was subsequently reduced and, following an amnesty, he was released early in 1955. Werner Lorenz died on 13 May 1974.

Lösener, Bernard (1890–1952)   A 'racial expert' in the Ministry of the Interior, Bernard Lösener was born in 1890, the son of a minor official. After military service in World War I and attendance at Tübingen University, Lösener became a customs official in 1927. He entered the Nazi Party in December 1930 and after the seizure of power he joined the Interior Ministry in April 1933. He had a hand in drafting much of the anti-Jewish legislation of the Nazi régime, especially the Nuremberg race laws of September 1935, and dealt extensively with the complex question of *Mischlinge* (part Jews or offspring of mixed marriages). According to Lösener's own claims, he worked consistently to secure the exemption of quarter- and half-Jews as well as Jews in mixed marriages from Nazi persecution. He calculated that as many as 100,000 *Mischlinge* may have been saved from deportation and death by his determination not to have them equated with full Jews. In 1943 he left the Interior Ministry at his own request and was appointed a judge. In November 1944 he was arrested on suspicion of having helped a couple involved in the July plot against Hitler. Expelled from the Party and imprisoned until the end of the war, he was re-arrested twice after 1945 but eventually released and returned to employment in the civil service until his death in 1952.

Lubbe, Marinus van der (1909–34)   A young unemployed Dutch bricklayer and anarchist, arrested in the burning Reichstag building on the night of the fire (27 February 1933) and subsequently sentenced to death for arson, Marinus van der Lubbe was born in Leyden on 13 January 1909. Van der Lubbe was a homosexual drifter who had frequented the doss houses, shelters and sordid cafés of Berlin before he was discovered by police inside the flaming Reichstag, half-naked, in a hysterical and semi-coherent state. After interrogation at police headquarters, he confessed to being the sole instigator of the fire, though subsequently others were arrested, including Ernst Torgler and Georgi Dimitrov (q.v.), in order to substantiate the spurious Nazi charge that the fire was intended to be a signal for communist revolution in Germany. It was widely believed, however, that van der Lubbe had been manipulated by the Nazis themselves, who used the fire to order the immediate arrest of political adversaries and a day later abrogated all democratic rights and liberties in Germany by emergency decree. Van der Lubbe's mute, bewildered, apathetic behaviour during the Reichstag fire trial, held before the Leipzig Supreme Court at the end of 1933, strengthened suspicions that he had been drugged and manipulated by the Nazis. Although alleged to have made detailed admissions and reconstructions of the facts during his interrogation, van der Lubbe proved unable to explain anything coherently during his trial. It emerged that he had been partially blind for six years, which made the thesis that he had acted alone even more unlikely. Nevertheless, he was found guilty of high treason and insurrectionary arson, being sentenced to death and executed in the courtyard of Leipzig prison on 10 January 1934. The Nazis had previously passed a special retroactive law, the *lex van der Lubbe*, to 'legalize' his execution. They refused to hand over his body to his family for burial in Holland. The controversy over the origins of the Reichstag fire and whether van der Lubbe acted alone or was an unwitting victim of the Nazis have continued to concern historians until the present day.

Ludendorff, Erich (1865–1937) Virtual dictator of Germany during the last two years of World War I during his tenure as Quartermaster-General of the army, and later at the head of the Munich Beer-Hall *putsch*, Erich Ludendorff was born in Kruszewnia, near Posen, on 9

April 1865. Descendant of a Pomeranian merchant family on his father's side, Ludendorff became an army officer in 1881 and was promoted to the General Staff in 1895. In 1908 he was appointed head of the deployment section which helped plan the invasion of Belgium and France during World War I. A strong advocate of universal conscription and increasing the size and armament of the German army, Ludendorff was promoted to Major General and made Brigade Commander in Strasbourg in 1914. Appointed Quartermaster of the Second Army at the outbreak of World War I, he personally led the German troops which rapidly captured the fortress of Liege. In reward for this exploit he was made Chief of Staff of the Eighth Army under General Paul von Hindenburg (q.v.), who had been recalled to restore the front in East Prussia. Working in close unison with his superior, Ludendorff displayed remarkable energy and strategic mastery in bringing about the great German victories over the Russians at the Battles of Tannenberg and the Masurian Lakes in August and September 1914.

In November 1914 Ludendorff and Hindenburg beat back the Russian counter-offensive and continued to maintain German supremacy on the eastern front until the autumn of 1916. On 28 September 1916 Ludendorff became Senior Quartermaster-General following the dismissal of General Erich Falkenhayn with whom he had previously had some sharp clashes. Under von Hindenburg's supreme command Ludendorff helped to relieve the increasingly difficult situation on the western front, and the two men assumed a more overtly political role during the last two years of the war due to the weakness of the civilian leadership. Ludendorff was partly responsible for the decision to send Lenin in a sealed carriage to Russia to promote revolution in the ranks of the Russian army and thus take it out of the war – all the more significant in view of his later obsession with Bolshevism as an instrument of Judeo-Masonic world domination. He was the driving force behind the ruthless terms of the Brest-Listovsk Treaty with the Bolsheviks in March 1918, which revealed the extent of German territorial ambitions during the war. However, following the failure of the German offensive in France at the end of the summer of 1918, Ludendorff began to despair of the military situation and advocated negotiating for peace. Dismissed from his post on 26 October 1918, Ludendorff fled to Sweden where he wrote his war memoirs, *Kriegserinnerungen* (1919). On his return to Munich in February 1919, Ludendorff became closely involved in the rising *völkisch* movement, encouraging counter-revolution in right-wing circles.

In 1920 Ludendorff participated in the Kapp *putsch* in Berlin and, by now convinced that Germany's defeat in World War I had been caused by 'betrayal', did everything in his power to nourish the stab-in-the-back legend. Venerated as a national hero for his victories in World War I, especially in the officer corps and conservative circles, Ludendorff was cultivated by the young Hitler and would have been assigned leadership of the army had the Munich *putsch* of November 1923 succeeded. During the abortive *coup*, he led a column of some 3,000 storm troopers out of the gardens of the Bürgerbräukeller towards the centre of Munich, relying on the magic of his name and renown to win over the armed forces. When the police opened fire on the column, Ludendorff alone did not fling himself to the ground but continued marching calmly on between the muzzles of the police rifles. No one followed this example of heedless heroism and Ludendorff was promptly arrested. Acquitted by the judges of high treason at the subsequent trial in Munich which led to Hitler's imprison-

ment, Ludendorff took over the leadership of the National Socialist Freedom Movement with Gregor Strasser (q.v.) and acted as protector of the banned SA. In the 1924 elections he was elected as a National Socialist deputy to the Reichstag – the Party as a whole won two million votes and thirty-two seats – where he served until 1928. As the imprisoned Hitler's candidate for the presidential elections of 1925, Ludendorff did poorly, winning only 1.1 per cent of the votes, which further exacerbated the growing tensions between the two men.

Influenced by his second wife, Dr Mathilde von Kemnitz (1877–1966), Ludendorff founded the *Tannenbergbund* in 1926, disseminating countless pamphlets and books attacking the 'supranational' powers of Judaism, freemasonry and Jesuitism, and producing a literature so eccentric that even the Nazis disavowed some of his more insane ravings. According to Ludendorff, occult forces 'above the State' had engaged in diabolical intrigues against the German nation which had climaxed in November 1918. The 'supranational powers' had planned the assassination at Sarajevo which sparked off World War I, the Russian Revolution, the entry of America into the war, the Versailles Treaty and other happenings in order to secure Judeo-Masonic world-rule. In his more extravagant fantasies, Ludendorff concluded that Mozart and Schiller had been assassinated by 'the Cheka of the supranational secret society'. Ludendorff's growing persecution-mania led to his discovering 'Jews', 'Freemasons' and 'Romanists' among his own friends and fellowcombatants. Although Ludendorff was a Nazi hero because of his role in the *putsch*, such obsessions provoked top Party leaders like Alfred Rosenberg (q.v.) to ridicule his 'psychosis' and 'perverted political imagination'. For his part, Hitler, at a public meeting in Regensburg in 1927, claimed that Ludendorff was himself a Freemason, a charge which was left unanswered. Relations between Hitler and Ludendorff deteriorated to the point that the latter warned President von Hindenburg in 1933 that 'this sinister individual [Hitler] will lead our country into the abyss and our nation to an unprecedented catastrophe'. Nonetheless, following his death in Tutzing, Bavaria, on 20 December 1937, Ludendorff received a State funeral and was eulogized as a 'great patriot'.

The pseudo-religious movement he had founded, *Deutsche Gotteserkenntnis* (Community of Believers), a new Germanic religion which worshipped the old pagan Norse gods, was officially recognized in 1939 by the Nazi régime. After the war Ludendorff's wife resumed her propaganda against Christianity, freemasonry and Judaism in Bavaria, embracing such outlandish and bizarre theories as the idea that Wall Street bankers had financed Hitler's electoral campaigns. In November 1949 she appeared before a de-Nazification court in Munich and on 5 January 1950 she was found guilty as a 'Major Offender' and sentenced to two years' directed labour. The revived Ludendorff movement was eventually banned by the Federal government in May 1961.

Luther, Martin (1895–1945) Head of the Foreign Office's 'Germany' Department (*Abteilung Deutschland*) and, as Under-Secretary, von Ribbentrop's (q.v.) most powerful subordinate, Martin Luther was born in Berlin on 16 December 1895. He joined the German army in August 1914, serving in railway units throughout the war. A furniture remover by profession, Luther joined the NSDAP and the SA on 1 March 1933, becoming active in Party affairs in the Berlin district of Dahlem. In 1936 he entered the Bureau Ribbentrop, a Nazi Party agency for advising Hitler on foreign policy, in the modest role of forwarding agent in charge of office equip-

ment. The ambitious Luther rose rapidly – in spite of an indictment against him for embezzling Party funds which was eventually dropped – and on 7 May 1940 he was appointed head of the new 'Germany' division (*Abteiling Deutschland*) within the Foreign Office, a position he held until his fall in April 1943. Luther was not only responsible for the entire propaganda of the FO but also for liaison with all Party organizations, the SS and police, becoming one of Himmler's (q.v.) and Heydrich's (q.v.) most powerful agents and gradually undermining the position of his nominal boss, von Ribbentrop.

Luther's talent for organization, his efficiency and skill in bureaucratic infighting, his cold, calculating and unscrupulous methods made him a formidable adversary in the internal power struggles of the Third Reich. Promoted to *Unterstaatssekretär* in July 1941, Luther surrounded himself with young Nazi activists in his department, fighting a determined battle to preserve the traditional prerogatives of the Foreign Office, partly by Nazifying it from within and partly through a policy of bureaucratic imperialism which involved it in new initiatives such as the 'Final Solution of the Jewish Question'. It was Luther, not von Ribbentrop, who participated at the Wannsee Conference of 20 January 1942, working out an understanding with Heydrich for co-operation between the Foreign Office and the RSHA over the murder of European Jewry.

Luther's intimate involvement in the deportation of Jews from western and south-eastern Europe (Russia and Poland were excluded from Foreign Office concern), his remorseless prodding of hesitant governments to undertake more radical measures, reflected his cynical realization that the 'Final Solution' was an opportunity to extend his own power and that of his associates. Luther's dynamic careerism was brought to an end in April 1943 by a premature and unsuccessful coup against von Ribbentrop, which was revealed to the Foreign Minister by the SS itself. Himmler's Adjutant, Karl Wolff (q.v.), sent von Ribbentrop an advance copy of Luther's accusations against him which led to the latter's despatch to the Sachsenhausen concentration camp, just north of Berlin, where he unsuccessfully attempted to commit suicide. Released as the Russians were closing in on Berlin, he died of heart failure in a local hospital in May 1945.

Lutze, Victor (1890–1943) Chief of Staff of the SA in succession to Ernst Röhm (q.v.), Victor Lutze was born on 28 December 1890 in Bevergen. After joining the ranks in 1912, he served as an officer in World War I, entering the NSDAP in 1922 and taking part a year later in the fighting in the Ruhr. An SA leader in 1924 and deputy *Gauleiter* in the Ruhr region, Lutze was subsequently promoted to *SA-Oberführer* in 1928. In 1930 he became a Nazi member of the Reichstag, representing the electoral district of South Hanover-Braunschweig. Appointed Police President of Hanover in March 1933 and *Oberpräsident* (a post he held until 1941), Lutze became a member of the Russian State Council in the same year. Following the Blood Purge directed against Ernst Röhm and other SA leaders, in which *SA-Obergruppenführer* Lutze was closely implicated, he was officially designated by Hitler as Chief of Staff of the SA on 1 July 1934. Lutze held the position until his death in a car crash on 2 May 1943. Under his leadership the SA played an insignificant role in the Nazi State, its influence having declined drastically as a result of the Röhm purge.

M

Mann, Thomas (1875–1955) The outstanding German novelist of the twentieth century, Nobel Prize winner and an unequivocal opponent of National Socialism, Thomas Mann was born on 6 June 1875, the son of a wealthy merchant family in the Hanseatic city of Lübeck. The decline of precisely such a family over three generations was the subject of his first great work, *Buddenbrooks* (1900, Engl. trs. 1924). After the family moved to Munich, Mann worked in an insurance office and studied at university before turning to journalism and freelance writing. Early novels and short stories like *Tonio Kröger* (1903), *Tristan* (1903) and *Der Tod in Venedig* (1913, Engl. trs. *Death in Venice*, 1925) revealed Mann's preoccupation with the relationship between bourgeois life and the modern artistic sensibility, his fascination with death, and the philosophical influence of Wagner and Schopenhauer. During World War I, Mann expressed chauvinistic feelings in a highly sophisticated manner, in his essays on Frederick the Great – admiring the Prussian king's harshness, self-sacrifice and sense of destiny – and in his presentation of the war as a struggle between German *Kultur* and western civilization. Subsequently he was attacked for betraying the cause of German nationalism because of his courageous defence of Weimar democracy in *Von Deutscher Republik* (1923) and other writings and speeches.

A conservative pessimist who nonetheless believed in progress, Mann's second full-length novel, *Der Zauberberg* (1924, Engl. trs. *The Magic Mountain*, 1927), which presented a tremendous panorama of the decay of European civilization, consolidated his reputation as Weimar Germany's leading novelist. In 1929 he received the Nobel Prize for Literature. His anti-fascist convictions found expression in *Mario and the Magician* (Engl. trs. 1930), set in Mussolini's Italy, which demonstrated the dangers of a charismatic conception of political leadership and the powerlessness of the audience in the hands of a hypnotic demagogue. With the advent of the Nazi régime, Thomas Mann, like his novelist brother, Heinrich, and the rest of the family, emigrated to Switzerland, before moving on to the United States in 1938. In 1936 he was officially deprived of his German citizenship and in the same year he was stripped by the Bonn academic senate of his Honorary Doctorate. The Nazis avoided all mention of his name, attempting to expunge his memory from the German consciousness. For his part, Mann took an active part in the anti-Nazi struggle, denouncing the 'terrible complicity of the German universities' in breeding 'those ideas which are ruining Germany morally, culturally, and financially'.

In America, where he taught for a time at Princeton University, Mann composed a number of anti-Nazi essays, including *The Coming Victory of Democracy* (1938). It was in his Swiss and American exile that he completed his monumental four-volume novel, *Joseph und seine Brüder* (*Joseph and His Brothers*), between 1933 and 1944, a moving tribute to the Jews in their darkest hour and to the freedom of the individual against a corrupt tyranny. Mann's final reckoning with Hitler's world, with the mixture of genius and madness in the German 'soul' and the horrors of a collapsing civilization came in his last major novel, *Dr Faustus* (1949, Engl. trs. 1950). Mann died on 12 August 1955 in Zürich, Switzerland, to which he had returned one year before his death.

Manstein, Erich von (1887–1973) General Field Marshal considered by many experts to be the ablest and most talented German Commander during World War II, Erich von Manstein was born Lewinski on 24 November 1887, the son of a General of Artillery. After the death of his parents he was adopted by the wealthy, landowning family whose name he subsequently bore. A professional soldier, von Manstein became an active officer in 1906 and served in World War I on the eastern and western fronts. After holding various troop and staff appointments between 1919 and 1927, he was transferred to the Reichswehr Ministry. By 1933 a Colonel and Department Chief in the General Staff, von Manstein was promoted to Major General three years later and to Lieutenant-General in 1938. From 1935 to 1938 von Manstein was head of the Operations Section in the Army General Staff and for a time he was deputy to Chief of Staff General Beck (q.v.). After Beck's dismissal, von Manstein was sent to command a division in Silesia, but just before the outbreak of World War II he was appointed Chief of Staff to General von Rundstedt (q.v.) during the Polish invasion. It was von Manstein who devised the daring plan for the invasion of France adopted by Hitler – a thrust of concentrated armour through the wooded hills of the Ardennes, seizing the Meuse crossings in the centre of the Allied line. Despatched in January 1940 to command the Thirty-eighth Infantry Corps which

broke through the French lines along the Somme, von Manstein's force was the first to cross the Seine on 10 June 1940. In reward for these achievements he was made General of Infantry in June 1940, received the Knight's Cross and was promoted to General Field Marshal.

After the invasion of Great Britain was called off (von Manstein had been designated to command landing forces in this eventuality), he was placed in command of the Fifty-sixth Panzer Corps in East Prussia and participated with conspicuous success in the operations on the Russian front between June and September 1941. After the invasion of the USSR, von Manstein pushed his forces 200 miles in four days to reach the Dvina and advanced on Leningrad in late July. Held up from taking Leningrad, he mounted a spectacular drive to take Ilmen. On 2 September 1941 von Manstein was promoted to command the Eleventh Army on the south-eastern front and from 1942 to 1944 was Chief of Command throughout this sector. During the first ten months of his command von Manstein defeated the Red Army in the Crimea, in spite of numerically inferior forces, and succeeded in taking 430,000 Russian prisoners. His forces maintained their positions during the severe Crimean winter, storming Perekop, Parpatsch and capturing Sebastopol in July 1942 after a 250-day siege.

Put in command of Army Group Don with the near impossible task of rescuing the beleaguered Sixth Army under General von Paulus (q.v.), von Manstein arrived too late but managed to organize the retreating German forces, preventing the Russians from crossing the Dnieper. The defeat at Stalingrad, in spite of the hopes of the German Resistance and the efforts of General Beck (q.v.) and General von Tresckow (q.v.) in particular, failed to convince von Manstein to abrogate his loyalty to Hitler, despite their differences on matters of strategy.

Though indifferent to National Socialist aims and theories (he had long been Himmler's (q.v.) *bête noire*), von Manstein's professionalism led him to see matters from a narrowly military point of view. Brilliantly successful in throwing back the Russians to the Donetz and capturing Kharkov in February/March 1943, von Manstein was still convinced that the war in the East could be won by avoiding costly, unyielding resistance and allowing deep penetration by the enemy which could be cut off with flank attacks by his Panzer forces. Through a series of personal interviews he was able for a time to persuade Hitler that retreat was necessary to consolidate and fight offensive actions, but the Führer rejected his suggestions for defeating the Russians in the summer of 1943 as too risky. The Russians were given time to reorganize and subsequently inflicted heavy defeats on the German forces.

Although von Manstein conducted a skilful retreat to the Polish frontier, Hitler lost patience with his sophisticated manoeuvring and argumentativeness. When von Manstein again sought permission to retreat on 25 March 1944, he was dismissed from his command of Army Group South and retired to his estate for the rest of the war. Captured by the British, he was brought to trial before a British military court in Hamburg. Cleared of two indictments concerning massacres of Jews, he was found guilty of neglecting to protect civilian life. In his order of the day of 20 November 1941 von Manstein had told the troops of the Eleventh Army that 'the Jews are the mediators between the enemy in our rear and the still fighting remnants of the Red Army and the Red leaders ...' The German soldier in the East, in fighting the Bolsheviks, was 'the bearer of a ruthless national ideology ... therefore the soldier must have understanding of the necessity of a severe but just revenge on sub-human Jewry'. On 19 December 1949 von Manstein was sentenced by the British court to eighteen years' imprisonment, which was later commuted to twelve years. On medical parole from August 1952, he was released in May 1953. He worked for a time as a military adviser to the Federal government and died at the age of eighty-five in Irschenhausen on 12 June 1973.

Mayer, Helene (1910–53) One of the greatest women fencers of all time, Helene Mayer was born in Offenbach, near Frankfurt am Main, on 12 December 1910, the daughter of a Jewish physician and a Christian mother. At the age of only thirteen she won the German foil championship for the Offenbach Fencing Club and in 1928, while still at school, she took the Olympic gold medal in the individual foils for Germany at the Amsterdam Games. In the same year she also won the Italian national championship and by 1930 had been victorious six times in the German championships. World foil champion in 1929, 1931 and 1937, Helene Mayer left Germany in 1932 to study international law in California. She was still studying in the United States when the Nazis came to power in Germany. Initially, the tall, statuesque, green-eyed blonde was portrayed in Nazi propaganda as a national heroine, until her half-Jewish origins were discovered and she was expelled from the Offenbach Fencing Club. Nevertheless, the Nazis were keen to let her compete in the 1936 Berlin Olympic Games because of her outstanding record and to uphold the façade that Jews were not automatically barred from selection for the German national team. Helene Mayer's own reasons for accepting the invitation of the *Reichssportführer* to return to Germany from America were more complex. Firstly, as a German national, there was no other way she could compete in the Games and defend the title she had won in 1928. Secondly, although reared in the

Jewish faith, she felt herself a German and wished to represent her country. Thirdly, she had not seen her mother and two brothers who still lived in Frankfurt (her father had died in 1931) since her departure from Germany. Possibly, pressure was exerted by the Nazi authorities through threats to her family in Germany, though this cannot now be proved. In any event, Helene Mayer competed in Berlin, winning the silver medal in individual foils while the gold was won by the Hungarian Jewess, Ilona Elek-Schacherer, perhaps the outstanding woman fencer in history. On the victors' rostrum, the fair-haired Helene gave the obligatory *Deutsche Gruss*, wearing the white uniform of the German team replete with swastika badge. After the ceremonies were over, she returned to the United States where she became an American citizen and won the US foil championships eight times in all – in 1934–5, 1937–9, 1941–2 and 1946. Helene Mayer returned to Germany for the first time since the Berlin Games shortly before her death on 15 October 1953.

Meinecke, Friedrich (1862–1954) Germany's most eminent twentieth-century historian and editor of the *Historische Zeitschrift* (*Historical Journal*) from 1893 to 1935, Meinecke was born in Salzwedel, Prussia, on 30 October 1862. After studying at the Universities of Bonn and Berlin, he worked for a time in the Prussian Archives and in 1893 was appointed editor of the influential *Historische Zeitschrift*. A leading exponent of the history of ideas, Meinecke was Professor at Strasbourg (1901–6), Freiburg (1906–14) and Berlin (1914–28). A prolific author, his first major work, *Weltbürgertum und Nationalstaat* (1908), attempted to reconcile an optimistic defence of the nation-state with the claims of justice and civilized values. A conservative, nationalist admirer of the authoritarian Prussian tradition –

though he did not play down its excesses – Meinecke nonetheless defended the Weimar Republic after World War I on rational, utilitarian grounds as the least divisive political order. In his influential *Idee der Staatsräson* (1924, Engl. trs. *Machiavellism: the Doctrine of Raison d'État*, 1957) Meinecke explored the tragic antinomy between ethics and power politics, values and causality. Rejecting the view that absolute principles could be found in history, he moved gradually towards the 'objective' relativism and 'historicism' expressed in his *Die Entstehung des Historismus* (1936), a history of the development of historical consciousness which examined the seemingly insoluble relationship between freedom and necessity. In Meinecke's presentation, the German conception of the Individual emerges as the peak of modern western thought.

For all his cultural nationalism, Meinecke was stripped of his editorship of the *Historische Zeitschrift* and his academic position in Hitler's Germany. After the war, Meinecke spoke out against the totalitarian hubris of the National Socialist State, describing the Third Reich (in 1946) as 'not only the greatest disaster the German people have suffered but also their greatest shame'. In his poignant reflections entitled *Die Deutsche Katastrophe* (*The German Catastrophe*), published in 1950, Meinecke re-examined the relation of National Socialism to German history and revised his earlier advocacy of power politics, concluding that Hitler represented 'the breakthrough of a Satanic principle into world-history'. The struggle between the two souls within Prussianism – the civilized and the militarist – had been perverted by the Nazis into a degrading worship of the omnipotent State. Meinecke even revised his earlier admiration for Bismarck and the cult of success, as well as his estimate of the function of the historian, calling for a renewed consciousness of the humanistic currents in German history. On the other hand he glossed over the death factories, the mass murder of the Jews, slave labour and other Nazi crimes against humanity, arguing that Hitler derived his power from his 'demonic personality' and that National Socialism was an aberration in German history. In 1948 Meinecke was appointed Rector of the newly founded Free University in Berlin-Dahlem (West Berlin) by the Allied occupation authorities. He continued to exercise considerable intellectual influence on the historians of post-war Germany after his death on 6 February 1954 in West Berlin.

Meissner, Otto (1880–1953) Head of Hitler's Chancellery from 1934 to 1945, Otto Meissner was born in Bischweiler, Alsace, on 13 March 1880. After attending secondary school in Strasbourg, he studied law and in 1908 joined the civil service with the German State railways. After serving with the infantry in 1915, he was attached to the military administration in the Ukraine under the Skoropadsky régime and briefly served as German chargé d'affaires to the Ukraine. He entered the Foreign Office in 1918 and from 1920 to 1945 served as Chief of the Reich Chancellery under the socialist Ebert, the conservative von Hindenburg (q.v.) and the National Socialist régime of Adolf Hitler. One of President von Hindenburg's most influential advisers and a power behind the scenes, Meissner interceded on Hitler's behalf in his campaign to secure the Chancellorship of Germany. For his services in persuading the ageing von Hindenburg to appoint him, Hitler kept Meissner as his State Secretary at the Presidential Chancellery. In 1937 Meissner was also appointed 'Minister of State'. After the end of the war, three de-Nazification courts failed to establish that Meissner had committed any offences, after he had already been acquitted of war crimes by an American mili-

tary tribunal at Nuremberg on 2 April 1949. All proceedings against him were finally dropped in January 1952. Meissner wrote his memoirs under the title *Staatssekretär unter Ebert, Hindenburg und Hitler* (1950). He died at the age of seventy-four in Munich on 28 April 1953.

Mengele, Josef (1911–1979?) Notorious extermination camp doctor at Auschwitz in charge of selection to the gas chambers and the most horrifying medical experiments, Josef Mengele was born on 16 March 1911 in Günzburg, Bavaria. After studying philosophy in Munich, Mengele took his medical degree at the University of Frankfurt am Main. A convinced Nazi, he became after 1934 a research fellow and staff member of the newly founded *Institut für Erbbiologie und Rassenhygiene* (Institute of Hereditary Biology and Race Research) where he specialized in the study of twins and racial pedigrees. During World War II, Mengele joined the Waffen-SS and served as a medical officer in France and Russia. He was appointed chief doctor in Auschwitz in 1943, where he directed a gas chamber and innumerable selections of victims, proving himself to be a ruthless and pitiless implementer of the 'Final Solution'. In Auschwitz Mengele continued to pursue his pseudo-scientific research into presumed racial differences, anomalies of giants and dwarfs, hunchbacks and other deformities. People afflicted with any sort of physical deformity would be killed for him, on his orders, upon their arrival in the death camp, to provide new material for his studies. There was a special dissection ward where autopsies of murdered camp inmates were performed. Mengele was especially interested in medical experiments on twins, hoping to find a method of creating a race of blue-eyed Aryans that would realize the grotesque dreams of Nazi racial science. After the war, Mengele managed to escape from a British internment hospital and, with the aid of false papers, fled via Rome to Buenos Aires. One of the most wanted Nazi war criminals, Mengele was reported to have been seen by various eye-witnesses in Argentina, Brazil and Paraguay, and substantial rewards were offered for his capture. Naturalized as a Paraguayan citizen in November 1959, Mengele was sought by the Bonn government after 1962 but all efforts to capture or bring him to trial failed. In 1985, after a large reward had been offered in Israel for information leading to his seizure, it was announced that he had most probably died in a swimming accident in Embu, Brazil, on 7 February 1979. In July 1985 a body, presumed to be that of Mengele, was exhumed in Brazil and autopsied by an international panel of forensic pathologists. They concluded that there was a high probability that it was indeed Mengele's last remains, but an element of doubt still persists in some quarters.

Messerschmitt, Wilhelm (1898–1978) One of the great pioneering aircraft designers of the twentieth century, Wilhelm Messerschmitt was born on 26 June 1898 in Frankfurt am Main, the son of a wine wholesaler. A leading aeroplane constructor as well as designer, he founded the Messerschmitt aircraft manufacturing plant in Augsburg in 1923 and three years later produced his first all-metal plane. In 1930 Messerschmitt was appointed Honorary Professor of Aircraft Construction at the Technical College in Munich. During the Third Reich he emerged as one of the foremost figures in the German aircraft industry. At his Messerschmitt Works in Augsburg he produced a series of outstanding fighter planes remarkable for their speed, including the Me-209 and the famous single-seater Me-109 which was first publicly displayed at the 1936 Olympics in Berlin and was subsequently tested and proven during the

Spanish Civil War. During World War II the Me-109 was a highly successful fighter plane utilized extensively in the Polish campaign, in the Low Countries and Scandinavia, not meeting a real challenge until the Battle of Britain. In 1943 Messerschmitt also designed and built the first jet-propelled Me-262 aeroplane. His international reputation and contribution to strengthening the Luftwaffe was rewarded in Nazi Germany by his appointment as Vice-President of the German Academy of Aeronautical Research and *Wehrwirtschaftsführer*. He was also awarded the title of 'Pioneer of Labour'. Interned at the end of the war, Messerschmitt was classified as a 'fellow-traveller' by a de-Nazification court in 1948. Subsequently he was employed in the construction of cabins and prefabricated houses but a decade later was once again a designer of jet aeroplanes for NATO and the West German air force. From 1969 Messerschmitt was a partner in one of West Germany's largest private concerns, the aircraft company Messerschmitt-Bölkow-Blohm (MBB). He died at the age of eighty in a Munich hospital.

Meyerhof, Otto (1884–1951) One of the innovative giants in the field of twentieth-century biology and biochemistry, Otto Meyerhof was born in Hanover on 12 April 1884, the son of Jewish middle-class parents. After attending school in Berlin, Meyerhof studied medicine in Freiburg, Berlin, Strasbourg and Heidelberg, where he received his doctorate in 1909 for a dissertation in the field of psychiatry. A clever, skilful experimenter with broad philosophical interests, Meyerhof qualified as a university lecturer in physiology at Kiel in 1913 and five years later became titular Professor there and Professor Extraordinary in 1921. A year later, while still at Kiel, he received the Nobel Prize (awarded in 1923) and in 1924 he went to the Kaiser Wilhelm Institute of Cytophysiology in

Berlin to work under Otto Warburg. Meyerhof was the first biochemist to recognize the importance of applying thermodynamics and energetics in the analysis of chemical processes taking place in the living cell and to explore the function of a cell in terms of physics *and* chemistry. He was the first to prove how the aerobic and metabolic processes in the body, i.e. those requiring the presence of oxygen and those receiving no oxygen, were linked. The ratio of anaerobic decomposition to aerobic recombination subsequently came to be known as the Meyerhof quotient.

In 1929 Meyerhof became Director of the Kaiser Wilhelm Institute of Medical Research in Heidelberg – which emerged as the international centre of cytology research in the 1930s – and was simultaneously appointed Associate Professor at the medical faculty of the University of Heidelberg, an honour which he lost again as a result of Nazi pressure. Meyerhof initially believed, like many other Germans and Jews, that Hitler would not last long, but by 1936 it was becoming clear that his position in Nazi Germany was untenable. He was allowed to go on working at the Heidelberg Institute until 1938, when the Nazi race fanatics obliged him to emigrate to Paris. Meyerhof left Paris following the Nazi invasion of France in May 1940 and fled south. He reached the United States via Lisbon in October 1940 and subsequently became Professor of Physiology at the University of Pennsylvania in Philadelphia. In 1949 he was once more appointed Associate Professor in Heidelberg as a reparation for the wrong done to him under the Third Reich. He died in Philadelphia on 6 October 1951.

Milch, Erhard (1892–1972) General Field Marshal and Armaments Chief of the Luftwaffe, Erhard Milch was born in Wilhelmshaven on 30 March 1892, the son of a naval apothecary. After serving in World War I in an air force

fighter group, Milch joined the *Freikorps* and in 1920 commanded a Police Air Squadron in East Prussia. From 1920 to 1926 he held various posts with commercial airlines. In 1926 he joined the Lufthansa civil aviation company in Berlin, became a member of its Board of Directors and for the next seven years played a key role in its development. In 1933 Milch entered the NSDAP and the Luftwaffe, and on 22 February was appointed by Hermann Goering (q.v.) as State Secretary in the Reich Air Ministry, a position he held until the fall of the Third Reich. As Armaments Chief of the air force, Milch entrusted eminent technicians from leading industrial firms with managing the separate areas of armaments production and achieved Goering's high regard for his executive ability and efficiency. His half-Jewish origin (his mother was a Jewess) did not prevent his rapid promotion, since Goering arranged for his spurious 'Aryanization' by persuading his mother to sign a legal document that he was not her child. Appointed Major General in 1934, Lieutenant-General in March 1935 and General in November 1938, Milch commanded the Fifth Air Fleet at the outbreak of World War II. On 19 July 1940 he was one of three air force officers to be promoted to General Field Marshal. In the same year he directed air operations against Norway and received the Knight's Cross. Inspector-General of the Luftwaffe from the beginning of the war, Milch took over the Technical Directorate of the Air Ministry in 1942 after the death of Ernst Udet (q.v.). In the same year he was made virtual dictator of transportation in Nazi Germany, along with his close friend and political ally, Albert Speer (q.v.). Both men tried unsuccessfully to alert Goering and Hitler to the need for radically reducing the manufacture of bombers in favour of increasing fighter-plane production, before it was too late. The reports of Milch's experts on enemy armaments and the dramatic rise in American production curves were dismissed by Goering as Allied propaganda. On 17 April 1947 Milch was sentenced by the Military Tribunal at Nuremberg to life imprisonment as a war criminal. On 31 January 1951 the American High Commissioner commuted his sentence to fifteen years' imprisonment. Milch was eventually amnestied and released on 4 June 1954. He continued to work as an industrial consultant in Düsseldorf and died at Wuppertal-Barmen on 25 January 1972.

Model, Walther (1891–1945) General Field Marshal and one of Hitler's favourite commanders, Walther Model was born on 24 January 1891 in Genthin, near Magdeburg, the son of a music master. A professional soldier, Model held various regimental, staff and adjutant appointments during World War I before joining the Reichswehr in 1919. A loyal Nazi, he was made head of the Technical Department in the Army General Staff in 1935 and promoted three years later to Major General. He commanded the Fourth Army Corps during the Polish invasion and was Chief of Staff of the Sixteenth Army in the French campaign. In 1940 he was promoted to Lieutenant-General and in February 1942 to General, receiving the Oak Leaves of the Knight's Cross. Appointed General of Panzer troops in October 1941, Model commanded the Third Panzer Division and then the Ninth Army with great energy and panache during Operation Barbarossa. His ruthless offensive drive carried him to the gates of Moscow. After commanding Army Group North, he was transferred to Army Group South in 1944, and then in June of the same year, having just been promoted to General Field Marshal, he was moved to Army Group Centre to stem the Russian summer offensive. Nicknamed 'the Führer's fireman' for his ability as a troubleshooter,

Model's middle-class background, his energy and lack of conservatism appealed to Hitler, who also appreciated his blunt, direct manner. Model was not only capable of standing up to the Führer and answering back, he also knew how to circumvent his orders when the military situation demanded it. His loyalty to Hitler was, however, never in doubt and, after the failure of the July 1944 plot, he was appointed to replace von Kluge (q.v.) on 17 August as Commander-in-Chief of the Army West. Model held back the Allied armies at Arnhem and commanded the Ardennes offensive, displaying considerable talent in organizing meagre resources. In April 1945 his Army Group Four, consisting of the Fifteenth and Fifth Panzer armies, was encircled in the Ruhr pocket. Nevertheless he held out for eighteen days against superior American forces until forced to surrender over 300,000 German troops. On 21 April 1945 Model shot himself in the ruins of the Ruhr rather than be taken prisoner by the Allies.

Mölders, Werner (1913–41) An outstanding fighter pilot, Mölders was born in Gelsenkirchen on 18 March 1913, the son of a secondary schoolteacher. In 1931 he joined the Reichswehr and then the Luftwaffe four years later. During the Spanish Civil War he was the most successful German pilot of the Condor Legion, downing 13 aircraft in 1938–9. Following the outbreak of World War II, Mölders was promoted to Major and received command of a fighter squadron in June 1940. His fighter group was particularly successful in the Eastern campaign and Mölders himself notched up 115 victories in the air before his early death. On 16 July 1941, following his 101st triumph in aerial combat, he was the first officer to receive the Knight's Cross with Oak leaves and Swords. Mölders died in a plane crash provoked by poor weather conditions on 22 November 1941, on his way back to Berlin from the eastern front to attend the flyer Ernst Udet's funeral. In National Socialist propaganda Mölders served as a hero and role model for German youth. The British Secret Service sought to counter this cult after January 1942, using a forged letter that suggested Mölders might have been killed for opposing the war and National Socialism on the grounds of his strong Catholic faith.

Moltke, Helmut Graf von (1907–45) Legal adviser to the Counter Intelligence Department of the German High Command (OKW) and a leading figure in the Resistance, Helmut von Moltke was born on 2 March 1907 in Kreisau, Silesia. The great-grandnephew of Field Marshal von Moltke who had led the Prussian army to victory over France in 1870, he was the descendant of one of Germany's most distinguished and aristocratic families. Von Moltke's Anglo-Saxon and 'pacifist' inclinations derived from his parental background – his mother was partly English and both his parents were Christian Scientists – and came to the forefront in his later call for the re-Christianization of Germany as the only answer to National Socialist ideology. A farmer on his Silesian estate and a jurist who practised law in Berlin, von Moltke was from the outset opposed to Nazism, which he believed had degraded Germany and would lead it to disaster. In 1933 he founded the Kreisau Circle, which met at his family estate in Silesia. The group, which consisted of professional people, army officers and academics, and espoused a broad spectrum of political views, was full of high-minded, noble idealism. It was von Moltke who was responsible for widening its appeal by bringing trade union and socialist members into the Circle. During the war he advocated a new Christian socialist morality, which would be the prelude to rehumanizing

Germany. His Circle was less concerned with overthrowing Hitler – something he personally shied away from – than with the shape of the New Order that would emerge after Nazism. 'To us,' von Moltke declared, 'Europe after the war is a question of how the image of man can be re-established in the breasts of our fellow-citizens.' An expert on international law and legal adviser to the *Abwehr* from 1939 to 1944, von Moltke used his position to help victims of Nazism, prisoners of war and forced labourers. He also maintained secret contacts with the West, until his internment in January 1944 for tipping off a member of the peace circle of his imminent arrest. After the July plot of 1944, von Moltke was charged with treason, even though he had taken no part in the plans for assassinating Hitler. During his trial before the People's Court, it became apparent that he was being condemned not for any specific actions but for his Christian beliefs. He was hanged in Plötzensee prison in Berlin on 23 January 1945.

Mühsam, Erich (1878–1934) German anarchist and a prominent participant in the Bavarian revolution of 1918–19, Erich Mühsam was born on 6 April 1878 in Berlin, of Jewish middle-class parents. A Bohemian intellectual and a prolific dramatist, Mühsam emerged at the end of World War I as one of the leading agitators for a federated Soviet Republic in Bavaria. The violent tone of his revolutionary speeches and writings provoked an intense backlash among conservative and nationalist circles in Munich. Mühsam was acutely conscious of the danger of Nazism and, after his release from prison in 1924, sought to organize a united front of revolutionary groups to oppose the radical Right. Several of his literary works from the Weimar period satirized the threat posed by Nazism. His story 'Die Affenschande' (1923) mocked their racial doctrines, while his chanson 'Republikanische Nationalhymne' (1924) attacked the judicial system for its harsh punishment of leftists and molly-coddling of right-wing *putschists* and 'Feme' murderers. His last play *Alle Wetter* (1930) envisaged the possibility of a Nazi seizure of power, which in his scenario is happily averted. Mühsam was a *bête noire* of the Nazis long before 1933 and marked down by Goebbels (q.v.) as one of those 'Jewish subversives' who would be liquidated once they were in power. Unfortunately for Mühsam he delayed his departure from Germany too late and was arrested a few hours after the Reichstag fire in February 1933. During the next year, which he spent in captivity in Sonnenburg, Brandenburg and Oranienburg concentration camps, he was subjected to every conceivable torture and indignity. Beaten and taunted by the camp guards, pieces of his beard were ripped out to make him resemble the caricature of an orthodox Jew. His battered corpse was found hanging in a latrine at Oranienburg on 10 July 1934.

Müller, Heinrich (1901–45?) Head of the Gestapo (Section IV of the Reich Security Headquarters) during World War II and Adolf Eichmann's (q.v.) immediate superior, responsible for implementing the 'Final Solution', Heinrich Müller was born in Munich on 28 April 1901, of Catholic parents. During World War I he served as a flight leader on the eastern front and was awarded the Iron Cross (First Class). After the war, the ambitious Müller made his career in the Bavarian police, specializing in the surveillance of Communist Party functionaries and making a special study of Soviet Russian police methods. Partly because of his expertise in this field, he was picked out by Reinhard Heydrich (q.v.) to be his closest associate and second-in-command of the Gestapo. From 1935 the short, stocky Bavarian, with the square head of a peasant and a hard,

dry, expressionless face, was virtual head of the Gestapo, even though he was not a member of the Nazi Party. Müller was politically suspect to influential members of the Party, who resented his past record in the Munich State Police when he had worked against the Nazis. Not until 1939 was he officially admitted to the NSDAP. Yet the stubborn, self-opinionated Müller was highly regarded by both Himmler (q.v.) and Heydrich, who admired his professional competence, blind obedience and willingness to execute 'delicate missions' such as the elimination of leading generals (the Blomberg-Fritsch affair), spying on colleagues and despatching political adversaries without scruple. Müller combined excessive zeal in his duties with docility towards his masters. The model of the cold, dispassionate Police Chief and the bureaucratic fanatic, Müller was rapidly promoted by Heydrich to SS Colonel in 1937, SS Brigadier on 20 April 1939, SS Major General on 14 December 1940, SS Lieutenant-General and Police Chief on 9 November 1941.

As head of *Amt* IV (Gestapo) in the RSHA from 1939 to 1945, Müller was more directly involved in the 'Final Solution of the Jewish Question' than even his superiors, Heydrich, Himmler and Kaltenbrunner (q.v.). He signed the circulating order requiring the immediate delivery to Auschwitz by 31 January 1943 of 45,000 Jews for extermination and countless other documents of the same tenor, which reveal his zeal in carrying out orders. In the summer of 1943 he was sent to Rome to pressurize the Italians, who were proving singularly inefficient and unenthusiastic in arresting Jews. Until the end of the war, Heinrich Müller continued his remorseless prodding of subordinates to greater efforts in sending Jews to Auschwitz. In his hands, mass murder became an automatic administrative procedure. Müller exhibited a similar streak in his treatment of Russian prisoners of war and gave the order to shoot British officers who had escaped from detention, near Breslau, at the end of March 1944. Müller's whereabouts at the end of the war are still shrouded in mystery. He was last seen in the *Führerbunker* on 28 April 1945, after which he disappeared. Though his burial was recorded on 17 May 1945, when the body was later exhumed it could not be identified. There were persistent rumours that he had defected to the East (he had established contact with Soviet agents before the end of the war), either to Moscow, Albania or to East Germany. Other uncorroborated reports placed him in Latin America.

Müller, Ludwig (1883–1946) Head of the so-called German Faith Movement and Reich Bishop, Ludwig Müller was born at Gütersloh on 23 June 1883. Navy chaplain in Flanders and Turkey during World War I and pastor at Wilhelmshaven between 1918 and 1926, Müller was transferred to the Military District of Königsberg, East Prussia, where he became known for his nationalistic sermons and his anti-semitism. Following the Nazi rise to power, in May 1933 Müller became Hitler's plenipotentiary for all problems concerning the Evangelical Church. He established himself as the leading figure in the Association of German Christians, a neo-pagan church which was an offshoot of the Nazi movement seeking to harmonize belief in Christ with the 'blood and soil' doctrines of Nazi ideology. On 23 July 1933 Müller was elected Reich Bishop and in August of the same year Prussian *Landesbischof*, using his authority to mobilize Protestant support for Hitler and the Third Reich against the *Bekenntniskirche* (Confessional Church) organized by Martin Niemöller (q.v.), which considered Christianity incompatible with the Nazi world-view. The new Confessional Church, whose strongholds were in northern and central Germany, opposed Müller's election and the policy of *Gleichschaltung* in the spiritual sphere which he embodied. Despite his total support of the Nazi régime, Müller's influence gradually declined and he became a marginal figure after 1935. Hitler never showed much interest in ecclesiastical questions and did not see in Bishop Müller a man of sufficient stature to carry out any far-reaching transformation of the Protestant church or its reunification with the Catholic church. Bishop Müller committed suicide in Berlin in March 1946.

N

Naujocks, Alfred (1911–60) A leading figure in Reinhard Heydrich's SD (Security Service), the intelligence service of the SS, and a specialist in its dirty tricks department, Alfred Naujocks achieved notoriety as the man who started World War II by leading the fake 'Polish' attack on the German radio station at Gleiwitz, Upper Silesia, on 31 August 1939. Born on 20 September 1911 and briefly an engineering student at Kiel, Naujocks was the type of young ruffian who proved to be so useful in the street-fighting phase of Nazism. A well-known amateur boxer, he was frequently involved in brawls with communists. He joined the SS in 1931 and three years later enrolled in the SD, becoming one of Heydrich's most trusted agents. In 1939 he was made head of the sub-section of Section III of SD *Ausland* and put in charge of such special duties as fabricating false papers, passports, identity cards and forged notes for SD agents operating abroad. He was responsible for devising the scheme to bombard England with forged banknotes (Operation Bernhard) in the early phase of World War II. On Heydrich's instructions, Naujocks had earlier supervised and led the feigned 'Polish' attack on the German radio station at Gleiwitz, near the Polish frontier, which was presented by Nazi propaganda as an act of aggression which justified the German invasion of Poland. Naujocks led a small force of SS commandos, dressed in Polish uniforms, who seized the Gleiwitz transmitter on the evening of 31 August 1939 and announced that 'the time had come for war between Poland and Germany'.

After completing the operation, Naujocks and his men left behind the body of a condemned criminal from one of the concentration camps, as if he had been killed in the attack. The day after this fabricated 'provocation', the German army crossed into Poland.

On 8 November 1939 Naujocks was involved in another escapade, the kidnapping of two British intelligence agents in the little town of Venlo on the German–Dutch border. Naujocks again did the knuckleduster work in this operation, which was designed to give the Germans a pretext for invading Holland on the grounds that the Dutch had violated their neutrality. Naujocks was dismissed from the SD in 1941 for disputing one of Heydrich's orders and transferred to the Waffen-SS. In 1943 he was sent to the eastern front and the following year served as an economic administrator with the occupation troops in Belgium. While in this nominal post, he carried out a number of murders of members of the Danish Resistance movement. Naujocks deserted to the Americans in November 1944, but found himself placed in a war criminals' camp at the end of the war. He escaped from custody before he was due to be tried by an Allied tribunal. It has been alleged that Naujocks was involved after the war in running ODESSA (*Organization der SS Angehörigen* – 'Organization of SS Members'), the Nazi escape organization, together with Otto Skorzeny (q.v.) who handled contracts with the Spanish government, supplying passports and arranging for funds. Naujocks and his associates handled the 'tourists' (i.e. Nazi criminals) going to Latin America, being responsible for their reception and protection there. He was later reported to have settled in Hamburg, where he pursued his business activities until his death on 4 April 1960 without being brought to account for his wartime 'exploits'.

Naumann, Max (1875–1939) Founder and Chairman of the militant, right-wing *Verband nationaldeutscher Juden* (League of National-German Jews), Max Naumann was born in Berlin on 12 January 1875, the son of a merchant. After obtaining a degree in law from the University of Berlin in 1899, he was admitted to the bar. In 1902 he received a Reserve Officer's commission in the Bavarian army – non-baptized Jews were denied such commissions in the Prussian Reserve Officer Corps – and during World War I he distinguished himself as an infantry commander, being awarded the Iron Cross (First and Second Class). Descended from a long-established West Prussian family, Naumann emerged after World War I as the foremost advocate of the total assimilation of Jews into the German national community (*Volksgemeinschaft*). On 20 March 1921 he founded the League of National-German Jews, which called for the conscious self-eradication of Jewish identity, the expulsion of East European Jewish immigrants from Germany and criticized Jewish behaviour in quasi-anti-semitic terms. Author of *Vom Nationaldeutschen Juden* (1920) and *Sozialismus, Nationalsozialismus und Nationaldeutsches Judentum* (1932), Naumann focused his attack on the *Ostjuden* whom he described as 'dangerous guests from the East', noxious bacilli in the German national organism who were racially and spiritually inferior to German Jews. Equally, he denounced Zionists as a foreign body within the German *Volk*, a threat to Jewish integration and purveyors of a 'racist' ideology which served British imperial interests.

His special hatred was reserved for cosmopolitan, rootless, Jewish left-wing intellectuals. Chairman of the League from 1921–6 and its chief ideologue and spokesman throughout the Weimar Republic, Naumann was reinstalled at its head in December 1933 under Nazi pressure. Naumann's organization had originally supported Ludendorff and other right-wing politicians during the early 1920s, though he himself was a member of the right-of-centre German National Party (DVP). After 1929 it was increasingly oriented to the radical Right and was the only Jewish group to support a Nazi-led national revolution. Naumann personally endorsed the NSDAP in 1932 as the only party capable of realizing the 'rebirth of Germandom'. This stance totally isolated him from the overwhelming majority of German Jews. In spite of their ultra-German patriotism, Naumann and his circle were unsuccessful in convincing the National Socialists to accept their goal of mass assimilation or to grant them a special status in the Third Reich. The *Verband nationaldeutscher Juden* was dissolved by the Gestapo in 1935 because of attitudes 'hostile to the State' and its monthly journal was obliged to cease publication. Naumann himself was temporarily incarcerated in *Columbia Haus*, the notorious Gestapo prison in Berlin, but freed after a few weeks. He died of cancer in Berlin in May 1939.

Nebe, Arthur (1894–1945?) SS General and head of the criminal police (KRIPO) from 1933 to 1945, Arthur Nebe was born on 13 November 1894, the son of an elementary school teacher. After volunteering for military service during World War I, Nebe joined the criminal police and reached the rank of Police Commissioner in 1924. A professional policeman and the author of an authoritative treatise on criminology, Nebe entered the NSDAP and the SS in July 1931. A few months later he also joined the SA. Even before the Nazis seized power Nebe was their liaison man in the Berlin criminal police, with close links to the SS group led by Kurt Daluege (q.v.), who in April 1933 recommended him as Chief Executive of the State Police. The former Chief of the Berlin CID under Weimar, Nebe was now given the task of reorganizing the criminal police in the Third Reich. As head of the KRIPO and a top Gestapo official, Nebe played an important part in the establishment of the totalitarian police system. In September 1939 he was put in charge of *Amt* V (the fifth branch) of the Reich Main Security Office, which was responsible for the criminal police. Promoted to the rank of *SS-Gruppenführer*, Nebe was later given command of *Einsatzgruppe* B between June and November 1941, an extermination group whose headquarters were in Minsk (White Russia) and which also covered the area of the Moscow front. During this period of five months, Nebe was credited with the 'modest' number of 46,000 executions. During Himmler's (q.v.) visit to Minsk in July 1941, Nebe was instructed to find new methods of mass killing. (After the war an amateur film showing a gas chamber worked by the exhaust gas of a lorry was found in his former Berlin flat.) It has been suggested, however, that Nebe was not himself personally responsible for the massacres of Jews in his area and that he was already working with the Resistance circle led by Colonel Oster (q.v.). Nebe's alleged disgust at mass murder is somewhat weakened by a letter he wrote on 28 June 1944 recommending the use of so-called 'half-breed asocials' (i.e. gypsies) from Auschwitz for human guinea-pig experiments such as drinking sea water. Despite his very questionable record, Nebe was apparently involved in the July 1944 plot against Hitler. Though not under suspicion, he chose to go into hiding on an island in the Wannsee and was betrayed

by a rejected mistress. According to official records, Nebe was executed in Berlin on 21 March 1945. On the other hand, in September 1956 he was sighted in Turin, Italy, and later reported to be with the SS commando leader Otto Skorzeny (q.v.) in Ireland in the winter of 1960. He was gone by the time members of a Jewish vengeance squad, sent to take him, arrived on the scene.

Neurath, Constantin Freiherr von (1873–1956) German Foreign Minister from 1932 to 1938 and subsequently Reich Protector of Bohemia and Moravia, Constantin von Neurath was born in Klein Glattbach, Württemberg, on 2 February 1873. The son of a court official of the King of Württemberg, von Neurath studied law and then began a diplomatic career, entering the German consular service in 1901. From 1903 to 1908 he was Vice-Consul in London and for the next six years a Councillor in the German Foreign Office. From 1914 to 1916 he was embassy Councillor in Constantinople and the following year he became head of cabinet of the King of Württemberg. In 1919 von Neurath was appointed Ambassador in Copenhagen and from 1921 to 1930 he served as Ambassador in Rome. Transferred to London as Ambassador from 1930 to 1932, von Neurath joined von Papen's (q.v.) cabinet as Foreign Minister on 2 June 1932. The frock-coated, aristocratic diplomat retained his position under von Schleicher (q.v.) and, during the early years of the Third Reich, lent a façade of respectability to Nazi foreign policy with his conservative attitudes. Von Neurath's function was nonetheless largely ornamental and his influence was reduced by the existence of a rival Party Foreign Office under Joachim von Ribbentrop (q.v.) which actually initiated policy.

Following the Hossbach Conference of 5 November 1937, where Hitler revealed his plans for annexing Austria and Czechoslovakia and his readiness for war with the western powers, von Neurath expressed his alarm and on 4 February 1938 found himself out of office as Foreign Minister. To maintain the moderate façade, Hitler appointed him President of a Reich secret cabinet, a phantom organization without any real power. From 1938 to 1945 he was Reich Minister without Portfolio and a member of the Council for Reich Defence, but his influence on foreign policy was minimal. After the German invasion of Czechoslovakia, von Neurath was appointed Reich Protector of Bohemia and Moravia on 18 March 1939, a move designed to make Hitler's annexation look respectable to the Anglo-Saxon world.

In his new post, von Neurath was responsible for dissolving the Czech Parliament and political parties, abolishing freedom of the press, closing down Czech universities, crushing student resistance, persecuting the churches and adopting the Nuremberg racial laws in the Protectorate. Even these draconian measures were not considered strict enough by Hitler, who summoned von Neurath to Berlin on 23 September 1941 for a dressing down. Von Neurath wished to resign but was allowed to go on leave instead, being replaced by Heydrich (q.v.) and officially succeeded by Frick (q.v.) on 25 August 1943. An SS General (from 19 June 1943) and a member of the Nazi Party from 1937, von Neurath joined the clandestine opposition to Hitler in a passive role. At the Nuremberg trials after the war, von Neurath was found guilty of war crimes, crimes against peace and crimes against humanity. On 30 November 1946 he was sentenced to fifteen years' imprisonment. After serving eight years of his term, he was released from Spandau prison in November 1954 for reasons of health. He died in Enzweihingen on 15 August 1956.

Niekisch, Ernst (1889–1967)   A leader of the National Bolsheviks in Weimar Germany who spent eight years in Nazi prisons for his Resistance activities, Ernst Niekisch was born on 23 May 1889 in Trebnitz. A school teacher by training, Niekisch grew up in Bavaria, joining the Bavarian Social Democrats in 1917 and editing their party newspaper. Actively involved in the Bavarian revolution of 1918–19 (he was Chairman of the Workers' and Soldiers' Council in Munich), Niekisch was sentenced in June 1919 to two-and-a-half years' detention in a fortress for his role in the 'Soviet' experiment. Between 1922 and 1926 Niekisch returned to the SPD – he was Secretary of the German Textile Workers' Association in Berlin – but he fundamentally rejected its Marxist internationalism and its weak stand against the Versailles Treaty. In 1926 he became a member of the *Altsozialisten* (Old Socialists) Party and editor-in-chief of its newspaper in Dresden. He was also editor and publisher of the journal *Widerstand* (*Resistance*) which strongly opposed Stresemann's pro-western foreign policy. An anti-western revolutionary nationalist, who believed in German-Russian co-operation and was convinced that the spirit of Potsdam was incarnated in the Soviet Union, Niekisch was the ideological leader of 'National Bolshevism' in the Weimar Republic. His attempted synthesis of extreme nationalism – directed against the Versailles Treaty, French influences and Jewish 'domination' – with revolutionary socialism had some impact on the Nazi Left, including the young Goebbels (q.v.), Gregor Strasser (q.v.), Ernst Röhm (q.v.), and also on non-Nazi nationalists like the writer Ernst Jünger (q.v.). But no rapprochement was possible with the German Communist Party, which was too ideologically rigid and bound by Marxist-Leninist 'internationalism' to attract Niekisch and his followers. The National Bolsheviks remained a small sectarian group which had no further *raison d'être* in Nazi Germany.

A resister all his life, Niekisch soon found himself at odds with the Third Reich and tried to organize oppositional circles in the big cities like Berlin, Munich, Nuremberg and Leipzig, without much success. Arrested by the Gestapo and imprisoned in 1937 for these conspiratorial activities, he was sentenced to life imprisonment by the People's Court on 10 January 1939. Niekisch spent the rest of the war in Nazi prisons and was fortunate to survive the experience, troubled as he was by a severe illness and virtually an invalid. He became a Marxist in the post-war years and in his *Das Reich der Niederen Dämonen* (1953), reflecting on the Third Reich, he emphasized the failure of the German middle classes and their lack of moral resistance. 'Hitler saw that there was simply no crime that could draw upon him the detestation of the German *Bürgertum*. ... The bourgeois had the government which they deserved.' Disillusioned by the crushing of the East Berlin workers' revolt in 1953, Niekisch gave up his membership of the ruling SED Party and settled in West Berlin, where he died on 23 May 1967.

Niemöller, Martin (1892–1984) Protestant pastor who was the guiding spirit of the anti-Nazi Confessional Church, Martin Niemöller was born in Lippstadt, Westphalia, on 14 January 1892. A submarine Commander during World War I, who was awarded the decoration *Pour le Mérite* for his services, Niemöller studied theology after the war and worked for the Inner Mission, Westphalia, between 1924 and 1931. From 1931 until his arrest in 1937, he was pastor of the Berlin-Dahlem church. Like many other German Protestants, Niemöller had originally welcomed the Nazi rise to power as the beginning of a national revival, and his autobiography,

From U-Boat to Pulpit (1933), was widely praised for its patriotism in the Nazi press. Niemöller shared the anti-communism of the National Socialists and their detestation of the Weimar Republic, which he himself had branded as 'fourteen years of darkness'. By the beginning of 1934 Niemöller, however, was disillusioned as Hitler began to 'co-ordinate' the Evangelical Church and subordinate it to State authority with the help of Reich Bishop Ludwig Müller (q.v.). To protect the Lutheran church against these inroads, Niemöller founded the *Pfarrernotbund* (Pastors' Emergency League) in 1934 and took over the leadership of the *Bekenntniskirche* (Confessional Church), becoming the central figure in its resistance to the Nazi-oriented German Christians. At its General Synod in May 1934, the Confessional Church declared itself the legitimate Protestant church of Germany and attracted some 7,000 pastors to its ranks. Enraged by Niemöller's rebellious sermons and his widespread popularity, Hitler ordered his arrest on 1 July 1937. Tried before a special court in March 1938, Niemöller was found guilty of subversive attacks against the State, but was given the relatively mild sentence of seven months in a fortress and a fine of 2,000 marks. Following his release, he was re-arrested on Hitler's express orders and spent the next seven years in concentration camps in 'protective custody', until his liberation by Allied forces in 1945. In 1947 he was elected President of the Protestant church in Hesse and Nassau, a position which be held until 1964. A convinced pacifist, he frequently spoke out against the danger of nuclear weapons and sought contacts with the eastern bloc. He lived in Darmstadt after his retirement in 1965 and was appointed one of the six Presidents of the World Council of Churches between 1961 and 1968. Martin Niemöller died in Wiesbaden on 6 March 1984.

Noether, Emmy (1882–1935) Born on 23 March 1882 in Erlangen, Emmy was the daughter of a famous mathematician, Max Noether (1844–1921), the foremost authority of the algebraic-geometric school in Germany. Being a woman, she was refused habilitation in Göttingen under the Wilhelminian régime and even under the Weimar Republic she was denied a full Professorship, in spite of her outstanding role in the foundation of modern algebra. In 1922, after much opposition, she was made an *ausserordentlicher Professor* (unofficial Extraordinary Professor) at Göttingen, but her income came from a lectureship in algebra. The 'Aryan' clauses of the first Civil Service Act in April 1933 led to her dismissal, though she continued for a time to receive some of her students at her home, one of them regularly showing up in SA uniform. Another of her prize pupils, Teichmüller, a dedicated Nazi, continued to publish mathematical papers during the Third Reich, using her controversial abstract methods without quoting her. Defending her in Nazi Germany was a risky business, not only because of her sex and Jewish origin, but also in view of her well-known socialist and pacifist leanings. Described by Herman Weyl (q.v.) as the greatest woman mathematician in history, Emmy Noether was a pioneer in the field of non-commutative algebra and an inspiring teacher, whose students later developed many of her ideas. Forced to emigrate to the USA, she was appointed Professor and lectured in mathematics at Bryn Mawr College (Pennsylvania) until her death on 14 April 1935.

Nolde, Emil (1867–1956) Eminent German expressionist painter and printmaker who joined the Nazi movement in 1920, Emil Hansen (his original name) was born on 7 August 1867 at his parents' farm near the village of Nolde in Schleswig-Holstein. In the 1890s he taught industrial art in Switzerland and travelled extensively in Europe during the following years. In 1901 he married and adopted the name of his birthplace, Nolde. For a while he belonged to a group of artists called *Die Brücke*, based in Dresden, who used expressionist techniques to criticize society. In 1910 Nolde was one of the young artists rejected by the Berlin *Sezession* and responded by attacking its President, Max Liebermann (q.v.), in a furious open letter. Perhaps the most individualistic and certainly the most 'Nordic' of German painters, Nolde revived the art of religious painting – his most famous work was *The Last Supper* – using glaring colours to express inner feelings with an almost demonic strength. His nine-panel *Life of Christ*, painted before World War I, depicted Christ and his apostles in such a distorted, ugly manner that the church authorities intervened to have it banned.

It was not until the 1920s that Nolde's visionary landscapes, his supernatural, mystic art, became widely recognized (his sixtieth birthday in 1927 was celebrated all over Germany), a delay which grated on the somewhat egomaniac, reclusive painter who could never forgive any criticism of his work. An early member of the Nazi Party, Nolde displayed the exaggerated nationalism, xenophobia and anti-semitism which was widespread in German border regions such as his homeland in Schleswig-Holstein. He had been repelled by his earlier stays in France and Italy, denouncing the 'sweetness' of the impressionists who could not touch his 'tougher Nordic senses'. He was no less scathing about cubism and constructivism, opposing on principle all forms of aesthetic as well as genetic miscegenation.

Nolde's early writings were also full of vituperative statements about Jews to whom he denied 'soul and creative spirit' (*Geist und Schöpfergabe*) and whom he accused of introducing materialistic greed into the art world. He attacked the 'Jewish intellectual spirit' of Herwarth Walden (Director of the avant-garde *Sturm* gallery in Berlin and a pioneer of abstract art) and the art dealer Paul Cassirer for exhibiting only French artists and their German imitators. According to Nolde, Jews were incapable of understanding an art rooted in German soil. When the Nazis came to power, Nolde praised the 'uprising against Jewish power, dominant in all the arts' and expected to be exalted as the most German of all artists.

In the first years of Nazi rule, Nolde was indeed a tolerated, if controversial, figure and he was offered the position of 'President' of all State art schools and a Berlin Academy Professorship, both of which he refused in order to preserve his independence. Initially championed by Goebbels (q.v.), who appreciated his work, Nolde nonetheless became a target of Nazi hostility as artistic life in the Third Reich came under the domination of philistine mediocrities. Following

press attacks on his work as *Entartete Kunst* ('degenerate art'), over forty of his canvasses and about a thousand etchings, woodcuts, lithographs and watercolours were confiscated in 1936. The following year, twenty-six of his oils and works in other media were included in the notorious Munich exhibition of 'degenerate art' and held up to ridicule. The most 'Nordic' of German painters found himself persecuted and out of touch with Nazi aesthetic ideals. Expelled from the *Reichskammer der Bildenen Künste* in August 1941, all of Nolde's humiliating attempts to win Nazi approval proved to be in vain. Officially deprived of the right to exhibit, Nolde continued to paint watercolours in secret in his North Sea cottage in Schleswig-Holstein. He continued to produce works in the style he pioneered fifty years earlier, until his death in Seebüll, North Friesland, on 15 April 1956, at the ripe old age of eighty-eight.

O

Oberg, Karl (1897–1965) Supreme Head of the SS and Police in occupied France from 1942 to 1945, Karl Oberg was born in Hamburg on 27 January 1897, the son of a Professor of Medicine. He enlisted in the army in August 1914, fighting as a Lieutenant on the western front in September 1916 and receiving the Iron Cross (First and Second Classes). After the war he was involved in suppressing a mutiny and participated in the Kapp *putsch* in Berlin. In January 1921 he was business manager of the Escherich Organization in Flensburg and then liaison man between various Reichswehr formations, the government and local patriotic leagues in Schleswig. In 1926 he returned to Hamburg as the representative for a wholesale paper merchant and two years later took a job with a wholesale tropical fruit firm. As a result of the world economic crisis the firm was liquidated within a few months and Oberg remained unemployed until the end of 1930. He then bought a tobacco kiosk in Hamburg with the help of a small family loan. In 1932 Heydrich (q.v.) took him into the SD where he became one of his closest collaborators, following him to Munich and then Berlin, to found the main office of the Security Service. Oberg's promotion was rapid. SS Captain in March 1934, SS Major in July 1934, Oberg was promoted to SS Colonel in 1935 and acted as Heydrich's right-hand man in the SD, respected for his 'decency', his bureaucratic meticulousness and discipline.

Differences between the two men, partly caused by age differences (Oberg was seven years older than his arrogant superior), led Oberg to return to the SS where he took command of the Twenty-second SS Regiment in Mecklenburg and was subsequently head of the SS *Abschnitt* IVA in Hanover until December 1938. In January 1939 Oberg was appointed Police President at Zwickau in Saxony and then in September 1941 became SS and Police Leader in Radom, where he took part in the extermination of Jews and the hunt for Polish workers. Promoted to SS Major General in April 1942, the tall, stockily built, bespectacled North German was sent to Paris on 7 May 1942 as Himmler's (q.v.) personal representative to take command of the SS and SD in occupied France.

Oberg's appointment as Supreme Head of the SS and Police in French territory led to a radical change in the relationship between the military administration and the German police, which henceforth possessed executive powers and were responsible for the security of troops behind the lines. Completely independent of General von Stuelpnagel (q.v.), Oberg proved himself a disciplined Nazi, at the same time ensuring the obedience of French collaborationist and militia groups and making his Gestapo officers thoroughly feared and detested by the local population. Oberg was responsible for publishing the Jewish badge decree for occupied France shortly after his arrival and for various repressive measures undertaken against the French Resistance. After the Allied invasion of Normandy and the liberation of Paris, Oberg and his men retreated and he returned to Germany in December 1944 where he was appointed Commander-in-Chief of the Weichsel Army under direct orders from Himmler. At the end of the war Oberg went into hiding in a Tyrolean village but was arrested by American military police in June 1945. Sentenced to death by a court in Germany, he was extradited to France on 10 October 1946. On 22 February 1954 Oberg and SS Colonel Helmuth Knochen (q.v.) appeared before a Paris military tribunal sitting in the Cherche-Midi prison. Although Oberg had already been interrogated 386 times, his trial was again adjourned. On 9 October 1954 he was once again sentenced to death, but this was commuted to life imprisonment by a presidential pardon ratified on 10 April 1958. A further decree of 31 October 1959 reduced the sentence to twenty years' forced labour from the date of the sentence. Oberg was finally pardoned by President Charles de Gaulle and repatriated to Germany in 1965, where he died on 3 June of the same year.

Ohlendorf, Otto (1908–51) Head of *Amt* III (Security Service) of the Reich Main Security Office during World War II and organizer of mass murders in the southern Ukraine in 1941–2, Otto Ohlendorf was born in Hoheneggelsen on 4 February 1907, the son of a peasant. Educated at a humanistic *Gymnasium* in Hildesheim, he later studied law at the Universities of Leipzig and Göttingen, graduating in July 1933. In October 1933 he became assistant to Professor Jessen at the Institute of World Economy at the University of Kiel. He specialized in the study of National Socialism and Italian fascism – he was subsequently the only top SS leader to be familiar with the syndicalist elements and organizational structure of fascist Italy. In January 1935 Ohlendorf became departmental head at the Institute of Applied Economic Science before entering the SD and working under Professor Reinhard Höhn in the following year.

Parallel to his promising academic career, the intelligent, idealistic Ohlendorf had been active in the National Socialist Students' League in Kiel and Göttingen as well as teaching at the Party school in Berlin in 1935. He had been one of the first members of the newly constituted NSDAP back in 1925 (when he was only eighteen), entering the SS a year later and also fulfilling various SA duties in his home district. The highly educated lawyer and economist was promoted to Major in the SD in 1938 and the following year became head of *Amt* III of the RSHA, a position he retained until the end of World War II.

Ohlendorf's security services provided intelligence information of a unique kind in the Third Reich, prying into the lives and thoughts of ordinary citizens in Nazi Germany and acting as a secret and relatively candid recorder of 'public opinion' for the benefit of the leadership. Although Ohlendorf's research workers were secret police agents, his activities were much disliked by Himmler (q.v.), who characterized the SD chief as 'an unbearable Prussian, without humour, defeatist and anti-militarist and a professional debunker'. When Himmler organized his special extermination units for service in the USSR, Major General Ohlendorf's bureaucratic career was interrupted; from June 1941 to June 1942 he was made Commander of *Einsatzgruppe* D which operated at the extreme southern end of the eastern front. Attached to the Eleventh Army, the academically trained bloodhound and his units in the Ukraine were responsible for the execution of 90,000 men, women and children, mostly Jews. In contrast to some other group commanders, Ohlendorf ordered that several of his men should shoot the victims at the same time 'to avoid direct personal responsibility', since, as he claimed later at Nuremberg, it was 'psychologically, an immense burden to bear' for the executioners. As for the mass murder of Jews in Nikolaiev, Kherson, in Podolia and the Crimea which his units carried out, Ohlendorf later defended it from the dock as a historically necessary task to secure *lebensraum* for the German Reich in the East. Recalling precedents such as the murder of gypsies in the Thirty Years' War and even the Biblical Israelites' extirpation of their enemies(!), Ohlendorf asserted that history would regard his firing squads as no worse than the 'pressbutton killers' who dropped the atom bomb on Japan.

Having completed his stint as an organizer of mass murders, Ohlendorf returned quietly to the Reich Ministry of Economics, where in November 1943 he became the manager of a committee on export trade and a delegate to the Central Planning Board. Promoted to SS Lieutenant-General in November 1944, Ohlendorf still retained his post as head of *Amt* III in the RSHA. He even figured as a 'liberal' member in Himmler's entourage, suggesting at the end of the war that the *Reichsführer-SS* surrender himself to the Allies in order to vindicate the SS against the 'calumnies' of its enemies. Himmler's right-hand man, Walter Schellenberg (q.v.), seriously proposed Ohlendorf as the member of a cabinet list which would be presentable to the Allies. His judges at Nuremberg took a very different view of the attractive, youthful-looking secret service chief, describing him as a Jekyll and Hyde character, some of whose acts defied belief. Sentenced to death in April 1948, he spent three and a half years in detention before being hanged, along with three other *Einsatzgruppe* commanders, in Landsberg prison on 8 June 1951.

Olbricht, Friedrich (1888–1944) Chief of Staff and Deputy Commander of the Reserve Army, one of the leading members of the July 1944 conspiracy to assassinate Hitler, Friedrich Olbricht was born in Leisnig on 4 October 1888. A professional soldier who served in World War I as a regimental Adjutant and General Staff officer, Olbricht was transferred after 1926 to the Foreign Armies Branch of the Reichswehr Ministry. After the Nazis came to power he was appointed Chief of Staff of the Dresdner Division and then in 1935 of the Fourth Army Corps in Dresden. From November 1938 to March 1940 he was Commander of the Twenty-fourth Infantry Division and then promoted to head of the General Wehrmacht Office in the OKW. From 1940 to 1943 Olbricht was Chief of Staff and head of the Supply Section in General Fromm's (q.v.) Reserve Army, exercising direct authority over all troops stationed in the Reich for garrison or replacement purposes. After February 1943 Colonel General Olbricht became involved in building up a military organization in Berlin, Cologne, Munich and Vienna, which could take control after the planned assassination of Hitler. Following the failure of the attempt to blow up Hitler's personal aircraft and the arrest of a number of conspirators, Olbricht, together with Claus von Stauffenberg (q.v.), began planning Operation 'Valkyrie', which involved a move on Berlin by troops mobilized by the Resistance. On 15 July 1944 Olbricht issued orders for 'Valkyrie', but von Stauffenberg's attempt on Hitler's life was postponed at the last moment and the operation had to be explained away to General Fromm as a 'surprise exercise'. On 20 July 1944, when von Stauffenberg's bomb exploded at Hitler's headquarters in Rastenburg, Olbricht was at the War Office in Berlin in charge of organizing the *coup*, but delayed for three crucial hours until von Stauffenberg arrived in the capital. By the time the 'Valkyrie' signal was given and Fromm arrested, it was already known that Hitler had survived the attempt on his life. The conspirators were increasingly confused in their actions and precious time was wasted, enabling the Nazis to restore control of the situation. Fromm was released by loyal officers and promptly had Olbricht, along with von Stauffenberg, arrested and shot by a firing squad on the same day (20 July 1944) in the yard of the War Ministry building on the Bendlerstrasse in Berlin.

Ossietzky, Carl von (1889–1938) Leading German pacifist and anti-Nazi journalist, Carl von Ossietzky was born in Hamburg on 3 October 1889, the son of Germanized descendants of a Polish Catholic family. An office employee in Hamburg, von Ossietzky married an Englishwoman in 1913. Conscripted into the army where he served as an infantryman during World War I, his earlier pacifist convictions hardened into a profound detestation of all forms of militarism. In 1920 he was appointed Secretary of the German Peace Society in Berlin and two years later helped found the pacifist *Nie Wieder Krieg* organization. Nothing was more devastating for the cause of peace and democracy, von Ossietzky declared, 'than the omnipotence of the generals'. Involved in the founding of the Republican Party in 1924, von Ossietzky became associate editor of the daily *Berliner Volkszeitung* and a regular contributor to the left-wing political weekly, *Die Weltbühne (The World Stage)*. In 1927 von Ossietzky assumed the editorship of this periodical, which was the organ of the non-partisan, left-wing intelligentsia and espoused such radical causes as sexual and penal reform, reconciliation with France and working-class unity. Von Ossietzky concentrated his fire in particular against German chauvinism, militarism and attempts to rearm Germany secretly in defiance of the Versailles Treaty.

In a scandalous trial he was accused of treason and sentenced in November 1931 by the Leipzig Supreme Court to eighteen months' imprisonment for providing details about the secret reconstruction of the German air force. In fact this 'secret' information had already been mentioned in a Reichstag debate and observance of the Versailles Treaty stipulations was even written into the German Constitution. Amnestied in December 1932, von Ossietzky continued to fight the bias of the judiciary and attack the abuses of militarism. Embracing the communist thesis that fascism was already in power (under Chancellor Brüning, q.v.), von Ossietzky failed to distinguish clearly between bourgeois democracy and National Socialism, a mistake for which he was to pay with his life. Refusing to flee abroad when the Nazis came to power, von Ossietzky resumed publication of *Die Weltbühne*. He was arrested immediately after the Reichstag fire in February 1933 and sent to Papenburg-Esterwegen concentration camp as an 'enemy of the State'. Suffering from tuberculosis, which he contracted in the camp, he was transferred to a Berlin prison hospital in May 1936. While still an inmate in Esterwegen, von Ossietzky had been awarded the Nobel Peace Prize for 1935, an action which infuriated the Nazis. Hitler responded with a decree of 30 January 1937 forbidding Germans to accept any Nobel Prize in the future. While in custody, von Ossietzky's condition deteriorated still further and he was finally transferred to a public hospital in Berlin, where he died on 4 May 1938.

Oster, Hans (1888–1945) Chief of Staff to Admiral Canaris (q.v.) at the *Abwehr* and a staunch anti-Nazi, Hans Oster was born in Dresden on 9 August 1888. The son of a Protestant churchman, Oster had fought in World War I as a General Staff officer and later joined the Reichswehr. From 1933 Oster served in the War Ministry, becoming head of Department 2 of the *Abwehr* which dealt with financial and administrative questions and kept the central list of agents. A conservative by inclination and an early opponent of Hitler, whom he regarded as the 'destroyer of Germany', Major General Oster was strongly against Nazi war preparations, passing on to the Allies warnings concerning German plans for aggression against Holland, Belgium and Denmark in 1939–40. A central organizer of the German Resistance, Oster also unofficially extended help to Jews through various 'front organizations' under the protection of the *Abwehr* abroad. This was one of the factors which caused his dismissal from the *Abwehr* in April 1943. Under observation by the Gestapo for some time, he was arrested on 21 July 1944 after the abortive plot against Hitler. He was hanged on 9 April 1945 in Flossenbürg concentration camp for his participation in the conspiracy.

P

Papen, Franz von (1879–1969) Reich Chancellor in 1932 and Hitler's Deputy Chancellor during the first two years of National Socialist rule, Franz von Papen was born in Werl, Westphalia, on 29 October 1879, the son of an old Catholic noble family. He began his career as a Lieutenant in a feudal cavalry regiment and in 1913 became a Captain on the General Staff. During World War I he served in Mexico and Washington as military attaché at the German embassy, being expelled from the United States in 1916 for sabotage activities. Briefly a battalion Commander in France, he was made head of the Operations Section of the army in Turkey and sent in 1918 to Palestine as Chief of the General Staff of the Fourth Turkish Army. Entering politics a few years after the war, von Papen became a member of the Catholic Centre Party group in the Prussian legislature from 1920 to 1932. Identified with the anti-republican right wing who sought the restoration of the Hohenzollern monarchy, von Papen became Chairman of the management committee of the Catholic Centre Party newspaper, *Germania*, and his marriage to the daughter of a leading Saar industrialist secured him good connections with big business circles. A member of the aristocratic *Herrenklub* (Gentleman's Club), von Papen's Catholic conservatism, his pseudo-Christian nationalism and links with the Reichwehr made him an ideal front-man for the upper classes in Weimar Germany who dreamed of the restoration of an authoritarian State where their privileges would be secure. Though hitherto a political nonentity who lacked any experience of administration, von Papen became Chancellor of Germany on 1 June 1932 in succession to Heinrich Brüning (q.v.), thanks largely to the support of General von Schleicher (q.v.). His conservative cabinet of 'the barons' enjoyed the support of President von Hindenburg (q.v.), the Reichswehr and big business, but had no solid majority in the Reichstag.

Within two weeks of coming to power, von Papen lifted the ban on the SA and the wearing of the Hitler uniform and began sweeping away the final debris of the Weimar Republic. He dismissed republican high officials and governors of provinces, replacing them with 'nationalists'. On 20 July 1932 he unconstitutionally deposed the Social Democratic government of Prussia under Otto Braun and appointed himself Reich Commissioner of Prussia. This act of appeasement vis-à-vis the Nazis was not met with any determined opposition by the SPD, which failed to call for a general strike or to mobilize the Prussian police. Von Papen's authoritarian experiment had too narrow a class basis to succeed and neither in the Reichstag nor in the nation as a whole could he win a mandate for his reactionary policies. Increasing pressure from General von Schleicher convinced President von Hindenburg that von Papen should be dismissed on 3 December 1932. Determined to gain revenge on his successor, von Papen now began the disastrous intrigues which were to put Hitler in the saddle on 30 January 1933.

At the beginning of January 1933 he met secretly with Hitler at the house of the Cologne banker, Kurt von Schröder (q.v.), to devise ways of bringing down the new Chancellor, von Schleicher. The immediate object of the conspirators – to induce von Hindenburg to sanction a joint Hitler-von Papen government – succeeded, but its premise that the Nazi leader could be 'tamed' and 'restrained' by a team of non-Nazi nationalists proved to be a wild delusion. Von Papen was appointed Vice-Chancellor on 30 January 1933, remaining at his post until 3 July 1934, thereby providing a legalistic façade of middle-class respectability while the Nazis consolidated their control.

Outmanoeuvred by Hitler, the German Nationalists, led by von Papen and Hugenberg (q.v.), epitomized the bankruptcy of the conservative upper classes in their opportunist irresponsibility and their collaboration with National Socialism. On 17 June 1934, in a speech to students at the University of Marburg, von Papen voiced conservative fears by calling for an end to the threatening activities of the extreme Nazis and the SA. 'Have we gone through an anti-Marxist revolution', he asked, 'in order to carry out a Marxist programme?' Calling for greater freedom and a transition to a more democratic State, he alluded favourably to the Hohenzollern monarchy and advocated a renewal of national life in accordance with the principles of Christian conservatism. Hitler was enraged by the speech, contemptuously describing von Papen as a 'worm' and a 'ridiculous pygmy attacking the gigantic renewal of German life', while Goebbels (q.v.), who had suppressed dissemination of von Papen's remarks, returned to his venomous onslaughts on the upper classes as the enemies of National Socialism.

The Röhm purge of 30 June 1934, in which the real author of von Papen's speech, the conservative philosopher, Edgar Jung, was murdered along with other close colleagues, indicated that the

Nazis were now ready to tear off the veil of respectability and dispense with their Nationalist fellow-travellers. Von Papen narrowly escaped with his life – the SS were disposed to finish him off but Goering (q.v.) bailed him out – and he resigned the Vice-Chancellorship shortly afterwards. Nonetheless, by the autumn of 1934 he was once more collaborating with the Nazis, this time as German Minister Extraordinary to Vienna (in 1936 he officially became Ambassador), helping to allay suspicions that Hitler had been involved in the assassination of the Austrian Chancellor, Dollfuss. In his ambassadorial role, von Papen – who claimed in his memoirs that he had stayed on 'only in order to prevent a general European conflict' – played a large part in the arrangements for the Anschluss.

The high-minded aristocrat, for whom discretion was always the better part of valour, fundamentally agreed with Nazi territorial ambitions in central and eastern Europe. He continued loyally to serve Hitler, or as he preferred to put it, the 'German Fatherland', as Ambassador to Ankara between 1939 and 1944. Arrested by American troops at the end of the war, von Papen was tried at Nuremberg and acquitted on all counts on 1 October 1946. A German de-Nazification court reclassified him, however, on 1 February 1947 as a 'Major Offender' and sentenced him to eight years' labour camp and forfeiture of property. Following an appeal, he was released in January 1949. In 1952 von Papen published his memoirs, Der Wahrheit eine Gasse, which appeared in English translation the following year. They were chiefly notable for revealing his insatiable self-importance and astonishing complacency. He died in Obersasbach on 2 May 1969 at the age of eighty-nine.

Paulus, Friedrich von (1890–1957) Commander-in-Chief of the ill-fated

Sixth Army defeated at Stalingrad, Friedrich von Paulus was born in Breitenau on 23 September 1890, the son of a civil servant. A professional soldier, he joined the Imperial army as a cadet in 1910 and during World War I served as an Adjutant and General Staff officer on both the eastern and western fronts. Between 1920 and 1939 von Paulus held various regimental and staff commands, helping to organize the armoured troops. Promoted in January 1939 to Major General, he participated in the victorious drive of the German army under von Reichenau (q.v.) through Poland, France and Belgium. On 3 September 1940 von Paulus was appointed Senior Quarter-master in the OKH (Army High Command) and Deputy Chief of Staff under General Halder (q.v.). Responsible for planning Operation Barbarossa, the invasion of Soviet Russia, von Paulus was awarded the Knight's Cross in May 1942 and on 30 November 1942 he was promoted to General. Several months earlier, von Paulus had been given command of the Sixth Army (his first operational command), which opened its campaign on 28 June with the intention of reaching Stalingrad and occupying the part of it which stretched along the Volga before surrounding the whole city.

By mid-October 1942 von Paulus's forces had reached Stalingrad, but they became bogged down in weeks of exhausting house-to-house fighting, coming under severe Russian pressure. Von Paulus begged for more troops, for arms, fuel, food and winter clothing for his beleaguered army, but received no aid. When the Soviet counter-offensive began on 19 November 1942 and led to the Sixth Army's encirclement in four days, von Paulus asked for permission from Hitler to withdraw rather than stand firm and risk complete annihilation. Hitler, who categorically refused to abandon the Volga, ordered the Sixth Army to hold their position, for 'by

their heroic endurance they will make an unforgettable contribution toward the establishment of a defensive front and the salvation of the western world'. Though von Paulus knew that further defence was senseless and that his 285,000-strong army was rapidly disintegrating, he held on through December 1942. Hitler showered a series of promotions on his doomed officers, even making von Paulus a General Field Marshal in January 1943, in the hope that this would strengthen their resolve to die gloriously at their posts. He was enraged when von Paulus surrendered the dazed, frostbitten, half-starved remnants of his Sixth Army to the Soviet forces on 31 January 1943.

Stalingrad was the decisive turning-point of World War II and the capitulation of some 90,000 surviving German troops symbolized the end of the Wehrmacht's military dominance. Von Paulus was taken into Soviet captivity and eventually agreed to broadcast from Moscow on behalf of his Russian captors. After learning of the conspiracy against Hitler in July 1944 he joined the National Committee for a Free Germany, a Soviet-sponsored organization. After the war von Paulus was called as a witness for the Russian prosecution at the Nuremberg trials in 1946. The Russians kept him in prison until 1953, when he was released and permitted to settle in East Germany, where he died four years later.

Pfitzner, Hans (1869–1949) Leading German composer of strong nationalist leanings who essentially subscribed to the Nazi creed in his old age, Hans Pfitzner was born in Moscow on 5 May 1869, the son of a musician. A pupil of Iwan Knorr at the Academy of Music in Frankfurt am Main, Pfitzner became a music teacher and conductor in various German towns after 1892, including Strasbourg where from 1908 he was Director of the Conservatory and the Municipal Opera between 1910 and 1926. Among his best-known works were *Der Arme Heinrich* (1895), *Die Rose vom Liebesgarten* (1901) and above all the opera *Palestrina* (1917). Appointed a professor in 1913, he became Bavarian *Generalmusikdirektor* (General Music Director) in 1920 and taught the master class at the Bavarian Academy of Arts. A traditionalist composer and champion of romanticism, who devoted much time and energy to combating the 'modernist' danger, Pfitzner was strongly influenced by the nationalist movements in European music after World War I. Constantly stressing the German character of his music – one of his compositions was even entitled *Von Deutscher Seele (On the German Soul]* – Pfitzner was widely admired in right-wing circles as a great patriotic composer, but his fame was restricted to Germany and his music had little impact in other countries. A rancorous, hyper-sensitive artist who was constantly complaining that his genius was not sufficiently recognized, Pfitzner saw himself as continuing Wagner's struggle on behalf of German values and culture even into the Nazi period. He wanted to save the nation through his music and to save music through a revitalized Germany. For all his periodic rancour against Goering (q.v.) and other Nazi leaders, Pfitzner supported their crusade against 'modernism' and the intrusion of 'foreign, subversive' elements, such as jazz, into German music. A recipient of the Goethe Medal in 1934 and other honours, he continued to be productive during the Third Reich. A cello concerto appeared in 1934 and in 1939 Furtwängler (q.v.) conducted the first performance of his *Kleine Symphonie*. Pfitzner participated in Nazi projects for bringing art to the people, conducting a concert of his own symphonies in 1937 in the unconventional setting of a railway repair shop. Pfitzner's works were widely played in Nazi Germany and he received the *Ehrenring* of

the city of Vienna in 1944. He died in Salzburg on 22 May 1949, shortly after his eightieth birthday.

Planck, Max (1858–1947) Internationally known German physicist who introduced the quantum theory and won the Nobel Prize for Physics in 1918, Max Planck was born in Kiel on 23 April 1858. After studying at the Universities of Munich and Berlin, Planck devoted himself for years to clarifying the concept of entropy and demonstrating its importance in thermodynamics. From 1889 until his retirement in 1928 he taught theoretical physics at the University of Berlin. In 1900 he developed the revolutionary idea that the energy emitted by an oscillator could take on only discrete values or quanta. His contributions to quantum theory found confirmation in Niels Bohr's theory of atomic structure (1913) and in the new physics of the 1920s. Appointed President of the Kaiser Wilhelm Society for Scientific Research (later the Max Planck Society) in 1930, he adopted an attitude of prudential acquiescence and delaying tactics when the Nazis came to power in 1933. As Max Born (q.v.) put it: 'The Prussian tradition of service to the State and allegiance to the government was deeply rooted in him. I think he trusted that violence and oppression would subside in time and everything return to normal. He did not see that an irreversible process was going on.' Planck nonetheless openly opposed some of Hitler's policies, especially the persecution of the Jews. A friend and supporter of Einstein's (q.v.), he bravely defended his greatness as a scientist before the Prussian Academy of Sciences and organized the memorial for Fritz Haber (q.v.) in 1934, in spite of warnings from the Ministry of Education. Planck failed in his efforts to delay the dismissal policies of the Nazi régime and his hopes for some kind of accommodation which would preserve the traditions of German scholarship were to be disappointed. His second son, Erwin Planck (1893–1945), a civil servant who became Under-Secretary in the Reich Chancellery under von Papen (q.v.) and then von Schleicher (q.v.), was executed by the Gestapo for his part in the unsuccessful attempt to assassinate Hitler in 1944. In addition to this family tragedy, Max Planck suffered many hardships during the war, including the loss of his home in a bombing raid, before being rescued by American forces in 1945. He died in Göttingen on 3 October 1947.

Pohl, Oswald (1892–1951)   Chief of the SS Economic and Administrative Department during World War II, Oswald Pohl was born in Duisberg on 30 June 1892. After serving in World War I, Pohl entered the NSDAP in 1922 and four years later was made an SA leader. A naval officer by profession, Pohl rose to the position of Senior Paymaster Captain. His organizational talents caught the eye of Heinrich Himmler (q.v.) and, on 1 February 1934, Pohl was made *SS-Standartenführer* and Chief Administrative Officer in the Reich Main Security Office. In June 1939 he was appointed a Ministerial Director in the Reich Ministry of the Interior. In the same year he joined the 'Circle of Friends of Heinrich Himmler' – a group of wealthy patrons drawn from the top echelons of industry, banking and insurance, who played a leading role in supplying Waffen-SS units with arms and uniforms during World War II, in return for certain practical advantages and honorary rank in the SS. Pohl himself reached the rank of *SS-Obergruppenführer* and from 1942 to 1945 was a General of the Waffen-SS. In 1942 he was appointed head of the *SS-Wirtschafts und Verwaltungshauptamt* (or WVHA), which was the Economic and Administrative Main Office of the SS. Its sphere covered all works projects for concentration camp inmates as well as the camps inspector-

ate – altogether a gigantic concern designed to squeeze the maximum use out of captive labour for the profit of the SS. Pohl was thus put in charge of the 'economic' side of the Nazi extermination programme, as part of Himmler's drive for greater efficiency and his desire to secure the financial independence of the SS. Pohl saw to it that all valuables seized from gassed Jewish inmates – including clothing, human hair, tooth fillings, gold spectacles, diamonds, gold watches, silverware, bracelets, wedding rings and foreign currency, etc. – were sent back to Germany. Here the booty was melted down and sent in the form of ingots to a special SS account in the Reichsbank. Pohl went into hiding at the end of the war, disguised as a farmhand. Arrested in May 1946 he initially admitted that the existence of death camps had been no secret in Germany: 'In the case of textile and valuables,' he declared, 'everyone down to the lowest clerk knew what went on in the concentration camps.' Pohl was tried on 3 November 1947 by an American military tribunal and sentenced to death. After spending three and a half years in the Landsberg death cells he was finally hanged as a war criminal on 8 June 1951.

Popitz, Johannes (1884–1945)   Career bureaucrat and Prussian Minister of Finance from 1933 until 1944, Johannes Popitz was born in Leipzig on 2 December 1884. An outstanding scholar who studied law, economics and political science, Popitz was made a Privy Councillor in 1919 and from 1925 to 1929 he was State Secretary in the Ministry of Finance, serving for a time under the socialist Finance Minister, Rudolf Hilferding (q.v.). An Honorary Professor at the University of Berlin, Popitz was not a member of the Nazi Party, but in January 1933 he was named Minister without Portfolio and Reich Commissioner of the Prussian Ministry of

Finance. From 21 April 1933 until 1944 he held the position of Prussian State Minister and Minister of Finance. He was awarded and accepted the highly prized Golden Party Badge of Honour in 1937. A right-wing conservative and monarchist who favoured the Crown Prince Wilhelm, eldest son of the former Emperor Wilhelm II, as successor to Hitler, Popitz became very active in Resistance circles in 1938. A member of the Berlin *Mittwochsgesellschaft* (Wednesday Circle) of academics, civil servants and industrialists, which acted as an intellectual forum of conservative opposition, Popitz gradually moved into the very centre of the conspiracy against Hitler. In the summer of 1943 he engaged in secret negotiations with Himmler (q.v.), trying to win his support for a *coup d'état* and to persuade him to join in attempts to negotiate a satisfactory peace with the Allies. By the autumn of 1943 Popitz was already being watched, but he was not arrested until the failure of the July 1944 plot. Imprisoned on 21 July 1944 and condemned to death by the People's Court on 3 October, his execution was held back by Himmler, who was secretly still seeking to negotiate with the Allies. Popitz was finally hanged at Plötzensee prison on 2 February 1945.

Porsche, Ferdinand (1875–1951) German car designer born in Maffersdorf, Bohemia, on 3 September 1875, the son of a master-plumber, the young Porsche learnt his father's trade and also became a handyman and technician, improving his skills through evening courses. He worked for a Viennese motor firm before World War I and in 1916 was already General Director of the Austro-Daimler company in Wiener-Neustadt. After 1921 he worked for Daimler in Stuttgart, building motors which were the first post-war successes of the German automobile industry. He also designed cars for the Auto Union, including a racing car in 1933 which for many years would be the most successful automobile in international racing competition. In 1934 Porsche (who three years earlier had set up his own independent studio) produced the plans for a revolutionary cheap car with rear engine, to which the Nazis gave the name Volkswagen ('People's Car'). The German Labour Front and its leisure organization, 'Strength through Joy', financially promoted the vehicle and Hitler himself provided the initial sketches. Porsche presented him with a complete design for his 49th birthday on 20 April 1938. In the same year Porsche received the German National Prize for Art and Science from Hitler, who greatly admired his inventive genius. Porsche became manager of Volkswagen (by now the largest German car firm) in 1938 and a year later the car was ready for mass production. However, German workers, despite their instalment contributions, never received a single model as all production was diverted to the war effort. In October 1940 Porsche was appointed Honorary Professor for mechanical engineering, aeronautics and electrical technology at the Technical University of Stuttgart. During the war years Porsche was above all involved in the construction and design of tanks and armoured vehicles. After World War II, his Volkswagen 'Beetle' became a record-breaking German export. Together with his son, he also designed the sports car that bears his name. Porsche died in Stuttgart on 30 January 1951.

Prenn, Daniel (born 1905) The top-ranked tennis player in Germany between 1928 and 1932, driven out of the Third Reich because of his Jewish origins, Daniel Prenn was born in Poland in 1905. An engineer by profession, Dr Prenn first achieved prominence in the German tennis world in 1926, when he was ranked tenth in the national lists. A talented sportsman who as a student at the Technische Hochschule in Charlottenberg had been a member of winning teams in both handball and football, Prenn first won the German tennis championships in 1929 and by 1932 was ranked first in European tennis. Energetic, extremely steady and calm, Prenn was endowed with a stocky but strong physique, and possessed a wide variety of strokes and deadly placements which wore down his opponents. In 1932, his best year, Prenn was ranked sixth in the world and, together with his friend Gottfried von Cramm (q.v.), scored a great victory over the British team of Fred Perry and Bunny Austin to win the European zone of the Davis Cup. Three years earlier he had won both his singles' matches when Germany defeated Britain in the Davis Cup competition.

Following the Nazi rise to power, Prenn, however, was barred from further competition and from the national squad. In April 1933 the German Tennis Federation had passed an official resolution declaring that 'No Jew may be selected for a national team or for the Davis Cup'. The *Reichssportführer* sent Prenn (who was abroad) a telegram asking him not to participate in international tennis competitions but to return to Germany. This he refused to do, but his wife received the *Reichsmedaille* on his behalf from Franz von Papen (q.v.) to mark the German Davis Cup victory in the European zone. Prenn left Germany and moved to England, where he made a new life and became a British subject. He continued to play tennis and in 1934 was ranked seventh in the world in doubles, but he never quite matched the brilliance of his per-

formances in Germany. In 1955 his eldest son Oliver (born 1938) became British junior tennis champion at Wimbledon and his youngest son was one of the world's leading racket players.

Prien, Günther (1908–41) German U-boat Commander who carried out a bold attack on the British fleet anchored at Scapa Flow in October 1939, Günther Prien was born on 16 January 1908 in Osterfeld. After joining the commercial marine at the age of fifteen, he served as an officer on the Hamburg-Amerika line, resigning in 1931 during the Great Depression. In 1933 he was recalled to the navy, and in October 1939 Prien, who was then a Lieutenant-Commander, was ordered by Admiral Doenitz (q.v.) to attack the British fleet at its anchorage in the Orkney Islands. Prien carried out his dangerous mission at nightfall in treacherous tides, skilfully navigating past blockships in one of the narrow entrances, and succeeded in sinking the giant battleship, the *Royal Oak*, before escaping through the same narrow passage and reaching his home base safely. Prien's exploit was a severe shock to British morale – twenty-four officers and 800 men went down with the ship – but in Germany he became a national hero, receiving the Iron Cross (First Class) and a personal audience with Adolf Hitler. Prien subsequently went on to command U-47 in the Battle of the Atlantic and at Narvik. He is believed to have died in the North Atlantic on 7 March 1941. His memoirs as a U-boat Commander sold over 750,000 copies in Germany and the post-war English edition, *I Sank the Royal Oak*, did well in Great Britain.

R

Rademacher, Franz (1906–73) Head of the 'Germany' III Department (*Abteilung Deutschland*) under Martin Luther (q.v.) during World War II and the 'Jewish expert' in the German Foreign Office, Franz Rademacher was born on 20 February 1906 in Neustrelitz, Mecklenburg, the son of a locomotive engineer. After attending a humanistic *Gymnasium* in Rostock, Rademacher studied law at the Universities of Munich and Rostock, passing his second *Staatsprüfung* (State examination) in April 1932 and becoming an assistant judge. A member of the NSDAP from March 1933 (he joined the SA in the summer of 1932 but left two years later), Rademacher entered the Foreign Office as Legation Secretary at the end of 1937. In 1938 he was assigned as chargé d'affaires to the German embassy in Montevideo, Uruguay, a post he held until in May 1940 he returned to Germany, taking over the Jewish *Referat* in *Abteilung Deutschland* under Martin Luther. A career-minded bureaucrat who brandished his pseudo-scientific anti-semitism very conspicuously, Rademacher was closely involved in the planning for the 'Final Solution' during the three years he served under Luther.

In 1940 he drew up the so-called Madagascar Plan, which envisaged a massive expulsion of European Jewry to the French colony, but this project was dropped once the war with the USSR created the possibility of sending Jews to the East and implementing a 'Final Solution' in Europe itself. Rademacher believed in the necessity of such a 'solution', though initially he had not envis-aged systematic extermination. In constant contact with Adolf Eichmann's (q.v.) office, acting sometimes as a messenger boy for his liquidation arrangements and sometimes as an intermediary between him and the Foreign Office, Rademacher's name appears on countless documents concerning the deportation of European Jews to death camps in Poland. He supervised the murder in cold blood of Jews in Belgrade in October 1941 by Nazi occupation forces, for which he was later sentenced after the war. He was also involved in the deportation of Belgian, Dutch and French Jews. After April 1943, following the fall of Luther, Rademacher's own career in the Foreign Office was in a shambles and he enlisted as a naval officer until the end of the war.

Arrested by the Americans in September 1947, then released in the belief that he was small fry, Rademacher was finally brought to trial in February 1952 and sentenced to three years and five months for the Serbian massacres. He broke bail in September 1952 and was smuggled out of Europe via Marseilles by a neo-Nazi network, going to Damascus. He could not be extradited from Syria, whose government thoroughly approved of anyone convicted of crimes against the Jews. In July 1963 Rademacher, however, was imprisoned by the Syrians for allegedly slandering the Syrian State and accused of being a NATO spy, a charge of which he was later acquitted. He suffered two heart attacks and was released from prison in October 1965. He returned penniless to West Germany in September 1966, was re-tried and sentenced to five-and-a-half years' imprisonment, but was set free because he had already served part of his total sentence. In January 1971 the Federal Court in Karlsruhe overruled this verdict and ordered a further trial, but Rademacher died in Bonn on 17 March 1973 before this could take place.

Raeder, Erich (1876–1960) Grand Admiral and Commander-in-Chief of the German Navy until 1943, Erich Raeder was born in Wandsbek, near Hamburg, on 24 April 1876, the son of a middle-class family. He joined the navy in 1894, becoming an officer three years later. During the 1914–18 war, Raeder was on staff and fleet service, taking part in mining operations, hit-and-run raids on the British coast and a number of naval battles. After a period working in the naval archives (he wrote a book on cruiser warfare), he was appointed Vice-Admiral in 1925 and on 1 October 1928 he was promoted to Admiral and Chief of the Naval Command, a position he held until 1935. Promoted again in 1935 to the newly created rank of 'Generaladmiral', he was made Commander-in-Chief of the Navy by Hitler, a post in which he was responsible for rebuilding Germany's naval strength. Raeder initially opposed the march into the Rhineland – as he did the later invasion of Soviet Russia – but subsequently justified Hitler's decision. In 1937 he accepted the award of the Nazi Golden Party Badge, and, in a speech two years later, defended National Socialism as a movement born of the spirit of the front-line soldier and a truly German experience. On 'Heroes' Day' 1939, Raeder declared his full support for 'the clear and relentless fight against Bolshevism and international Jewry whose nation-destroying deeds we have fully experienced'. On 1 April 1939 Raeder accepted the rank of Grand Admiral. He was responsible for the policy of unrestricted U-boat warfare, urging Hitler to concentrate efforts on the disruption of British sea communications and emphasizing the need to defeat England before launching any attack on the Soviet Union. Raeder's desire to avoid a war on two fronts, however, was ignored by Hitler, and the growing differences between them over strategy led to his enforced retirement on 30 January 1943 and replacement by Admiral Doenitz (q.v.) as Commander-in-Chief of the Navy. Raeder was tried and sentenced to life imprisonment as a war criminal by the International Military Tribunal at Nuremberg on 1 October 1946. However, he was released on 26 September 1955. His two-volume memoirs provided a whitewash of Hitler's imperialist policies and his own role in building up and expanding German naval power to serve the ends of the Third Reich. In the second volume, *Mein Leben. Von 1935 bis Spandau 1955* (1957), Raeder described Hitler as 'an extraordinary man worthy of becoming Germany's leader'. He died in Kiel on 6 November 1960.

Rauschning, Hermann (1887–1982) Nazi politician who subsequently exposed the corruption and ruthlessness of Hitlerism and the National Socialist régime, Hermann Rauschning was born in Thorn, West Prussia, on 7 August 1887. The son of an old Junker family, he studied history, music and *Germanistik* at Munich and Berlin. A Lieutenant in the infantry during World War I, Rauschning, who was wounded in action, subsequently became a cultural-political leader, active in ethnic German organizations in Posen. In 1926 he moved to Danzig Free State where, six years later, he became the Chairman of the Agricultural League. A member of the NSDAP and a trusted colleague of Hitler's, Rauschning was appointed President of the Danzig Senate in 1933–4, after the Nazis had won a narrow absolute majority in the elections to the

Danzig Parliament. In August 1933 he signed a treaty with Poland on behalf of Danzig and faithfully represented German interests and the Nazi propaganda line in the Free State. Increasingly, however, Rauschning, who had aroused the antagonism of the Nazi Old Guard as an upstart and opportunist ever since his appointment by Hitler, became disillusioned with National Socialism. In 1935 he fled to Switzerland and eventually settled as a farmer in the United States where he lived after 1948 in Portland, Oregon. Rauschning was the author of two of the most influential early works exposing the nihilistic character and the dangers of Nazism, *Revolution des Nihilismus* (1938, Engl. trs. *The Revolution of Nihilism*, 1939) and *Gespräche mit Hitler* (1939, Engl. trs. *Hitler Speaks*, 1939). Both books were conceived as a warning to the free world that Hitler would stop at nothing to satisfy his lust for power; the Nazis, recognizing its timeliness, went to great lengths to ban Rauschning's *Gespräche* even in neutral Switzerland. After the war, Rauschning's efforts to return to German political life failed though he continued to publish works, dealing mainly with Germany's position between East and West. Rauschning died on 8 February 1982 in Portland. He was almost ninety-five years old.

Reichenau, Walter von (1884–1942) General Field Marshal who was the most political of Hitler's generals, Walter von Reichenau was born in Karlsruhe on 8 October 1884. A professional soldier, he entered the Imperial army in 1903, becoming an officer in the Prussian field artillery and serving on the General Staff during World War 1. Subsequently attached to the Reichswehr, he was promoted to Major General and head of the Army Supply Office. Already head of the Wehrmacht Chancellery under the Weimar Republic, von Reichenau became Chief of Staff and per-

sonal adviser to General von Blomberg (q.v.), the War Minister, in 1933. Cold, purposeful and Machiavellian in outlook, von Reichenau regarded the National Socialists as an indispensable battering-ram against Marxism and planned to harness their revolutionary drive for his own career ends and the interests of the army. A calculating cynic and opportunist, uninterested in moral considerations, von Reichenau was the prototype of the modern, technically trained officer who had thrown off the feudal blinkers of his caste and saw in National Socialism a mass movement which, if tamed at the right moment, would strengthen the hand of the Reichswehr.

A crucial figure in the army's policy-making circle after 1933, von Reichenau had demonstrated his unconditional support for Hitler when, in August of that year, together with von Blomberg, he compelled his fellow officers to take the oath of unconditional obedience to the 'Führer of the German Reich' and 'Supreme Commander of the Wehrmacht'. Determined to eliminate the revolutionary pretensions of the SA as a rival to the Wehrmacht, he negotiated an agreement with Himmler (q.v.) and the SS in February 1933 and again in May 1934 which made the Röhm (q.v.) massacres of June 1934 possible. Von Reichenau and von Blomberg were behind the deliberate political decision to keep the army in barracks and not to intervene in the wave of terror and intimidation which finally destroyed the few remaining remnants of democracy in the Third Reich. The army, von Reichenau declared, would not give succour to those persecuted by the régime or to its political opponents. Promoted to General on 10 January 1935 and chosen to replace General Wilhelm Adam (q.v.) as Commander of the Seventh Army Corps, Munich, it is not surprising that he approved the training of the SS as a military formation. Previously regarded as a desk general without field experience, von Reichenau's political loyalty was rewarded by his appointment in 1938 as Commander of Army Group IV, Leipzig, and at the outbreak of war he was made Commander-in-Chief of the Tenth Army.

Although privately pessimistic about the prospects of victory over the western powers with whom he desired peace, von Reichenau publicly supported Hitler's war plans and was made a Field Marshal after the end of the French campaign in July 1940. Following the invasion of the Soviet Union, von Reichenau commanded the Sixth Army and on 30 November 1941 succeeded von Rundstedt (q.v.) as Commander of Army Group South. After the stupendous SS massacre of Jews in Kiev in September 1941, von Reichenau had been responsible for issuing a notorious order of the day to his troops on 10 October 1941 emphasizing 'the necessity of a severe but just revenge on subhuman Jewry'. The German soldier in the East, according to Field Marshal von Reichenau, was the carrier of an 'inexorable racial idea' which transcended all hitherto accepted codes of military honour. Not surprisingly, he was warmly praised by the murderous *Einsatzgruppen* responsible for the massacres of Jews in occupied Soviet territory, for having secured the co-operation of the Wehrmacht in easing their task. Von Reichenau did not live to see the full fruits of his orders, dying of a stroke on 17 January 1942.

Reichwein, Adolf (1898–1944) Social Democratic politican and pedagogue who became a leading figure in the German Resistance, Adolf Reichwein was born in Bad Ems on 3 October 1898. After serving in World War I where he was severely wounded, Reichwein received his doctorate in 1920. Appointed Professor of History at the Halle Teachers College in 1930, the socialist

philosopher and pedagogue was stripped of his position by the Nazis three years later. From 1933 to 1939 he was obliged to earn his living as a village school teacher before being appointed Director of the Folklore Museum in Berlin. From 1941 Reichwein took part in the deliberations of the Kreisau Circle and was their link man with the Social Democratic wing of the Resistance. Together with Julius Leber (q.v.), Reichwein undertook on 22 June 1944 to make contact with underground communist leaders in East Berlin, on behalf of Claus von Stauffenberg (q.v.). One of the communists turned out to be a Gestapo stool pigeon and this led to Reichwein's arrest on 4 July 1944. Tried before the People's Court and condemned to death on 20 October 1944, Reichwein was hanged on the same day.

Reinhardt, Fritz (1895–1969) Head of the NSDAP School for Orators and from 1933 to 1945 State Secretary in the Reich Ministry of Finance, Fritz Reinhardt was born in Ilmenau, Thuringia, on 3 April 1895. Interned in Russia during World War I, Reinhardt studied economics after the war and founded an international syndicate for taxation in Ilmenau before becoming a tax executive with the Finance Office in Thuringia. After joining the NSDAP he was *Gauleiter* of Upper Bavaria from 1928 to 1930. In 1928 Reinhardt also founded an institute for training local Nazi speakers and, following the Party's success in the elections, the school became a national organization – *Rednerschule der NSDAP* (Party School for Orators) – where the art of public speaking was taught to would-be National Socialist leaders. In 1930 Reinhardt was elected to the Reichstag as the Nazi deputy for Upper Bavaria/Swabia. When the Nazis came to power he was appointed State Secretary in the Reich Ministry of Finance, where he developed a special programme for fighting unemployment by fiscal means and was involved in financing the rearmament of the Wehrmacht. On 1 September 1933 Reinhardt was appointed *SA-Gruppenführer* on the staff of the Supreme SA-Commander and on 9 November 1937 he was promoted to *SA-Obergruppenführer*. Reinhardt was imprisoned in 1945 and released four years later. In 1950 a Munich de-Nazification court reclassified him as a 'Major Offender'.

Reitsch, Hanna (1912–79) Nazi Germany's leading woman stunt pilot and an enthusiastic admirer of Hitler who begged to be allowed to die with him in the *Führerbunker* at the end of World War II, Hanna Reitsch was born in Hirschberg, Silesia, on 29 March 1912, the daughter of an ophthalmologist. The diminutive, slightly built blonde, who was to become a symbol of virile heroism in the 1930s, originally aimed to be a flying missionary doctor in Africa, but turned instead to piloting gliders and powered aircraft with daring and unusual skill. From 1931 when she set the women's world record for non-stop gliding (five and a half hours), extended to eleven and a half in 1933, to her world record in non-stop distance flight for gliders (305 km) in 1936 and her woman's gliding world record for point-to-point flight in 1939, Hanna Reitsch's feats were unrivalled. In 1934 she set the world's altitude record for women (2,800 m), three years later she made the first crossing of the Alps in a glider, and in 1938 the first indoor helicopter flight in the Deutschlandhalle, Berlin. In the same year she also won the German long-distance gliding championships. In 1937 Hanna Reitsch was appointed a flight captain and the first woman test pilot for the new Luftwaffe by General Ernst Udet (q.v.), subsequently performing test flights with all kinds of military planes during World War II. She flew, among others, the little Henschel 293 rocket interceptor and the ponderous

Messerschmitt Gigant transport, and carried out several flights with the V-I in 1944, testing the prototype for the robot bombs that were designed for pilotless flight.

Fräulein Reitsch, who had miraculously survived several crashes, was the first and only woman to be awarded the Iron Cross (First and Second Classes) by Hitler in 1942 for her contribution to civilian flying. A much decorated favourite of the Führer, the brave, patriotic test pilot was politically naïve, refusing to believe that Hitler was implicated in such events as the Crystal Night pogrom and dismissing talk of concentration camps as propaganda. From November 1943 she joined General Robert Ritter von Greim (q.v.), a fanatic flier and like herself an idealistic believer in Nazism, in his air force headquarters on the eastern front line in Russia. She and von Greim were among Hitler's last visitors in the *Führerbunker* in Berlin on 26–29 April 1945, after flying through Russian flak and anti-aircraft shells to reach the Reich Chancellery. On 29 April a physically and morally broken Hitler commanded her and von Greim (the newly appointed Commander-in-Chief of the Luftwaffe) to leave Berlin and rally the remaining Nazi air forces to support a rescue operation. They escaped miraculously through a sea of flames and explosions as Russian troops ringed the city, reaching Admiral Karl Doenitz's (q.v.) headquarters. Hanna Reitsch was later arrested and held in an interrogation centre for fifteen months by the Americans, then released in 1946.

In 1951 she published her autobiography *Fliegen, mein Leben* (Engl. trs. *Flying is my Life,* 1954) and a year later she was the sole female competitor at the International Gliding Championships in Madrid, winning the bronze medal. In 1955 she won the German glider championships (again as the only woman competitor) and in 1957 she took the bronze medal, also setting two

German women's glider altitude records in the same year. Germany's most successful woman flier during three decades, Hanna Reitsch continued to be active as a research pilot after 1954. In 1959 she spent several months in India, becoming friendly with Indira Ghandi and the then-Prime Minister Nehru, whom she took on a glider flight over New Delhi. In 1962 the indefatigable Fräulein Reitsch set up the National School of Gliding in Ghana, where she became a confidante of President Kwame Nkrumah. An exceptional woman, who during her long career set more than forty altitude and endurance records in powered and motorless aircraft, Hanna Reitsch was nonetheless representative in her simple-minded enthusiasm for National Socialism and the personality of Hitler. After the war she appeared to undergo a change of heart, telling an American reporter in 1952 that she was shaken and disgusted by what had happened in the corridors of power during the Third Reich. She died in Frankfurt am Main on 24 August 1979.

Remer, Otto-Ernst (born 1912) Commander of the crack Guard Battalion *Grossdeutschland* stationed near Berlin who was ordered by his superiors to seal off the ministries in the Wilhelmstrasse during the July 1944 plot, the thirty-two-year-old Major Otto Remer's quick turnabout to Hitler's side helped to wreck the conspiracy. Remer, who had been wounded eight times during the war and received the Knight's Cross with Oak Leaves from Hitler himself, had been sent to arrest Joseph Goebbels (q.v.). The Minister of Propaganda reminded him of his oath of loyalty and put him through to Hitler on the telephone to prove that the Führer was not dead as the conspirators had alleged. Remer then withdrew his battalion from the Wilhelmstrasse, occupied the *Kommandantur* in Unter den Linden and

sought to arrest the ringleaders of the plot. For his role in restoring order in Berlin, Remer was promoted to Major General and divisional Commander. After the war Remer founded the neo-Nazi Socialist Reich Party (SRP) in 1950, which polled 360,000 votes in the local elections in Lower Saxony a year later. He heaped abuse on the anti-Nazi Resistance, claiming that they were a 'stain on the shield of honour of the German officers' corps' and had stabbed the German army in the back. He was sentenced in March 1952 to three months' imprisonment – it was never served since he fled into exile – for collective libel of the Resistance circle. A few months later the SRP was dissolved by the Bonn government. Remer resurfaced in Egypt, calling for Germans to help create a strong Arab army to fight their oppression by 'international Jewry', denouncing reparations to Israel as 'brutal robbery' and ranting against 'the inhuman atrocities' supposedly committed by the Jews in Palestine. In more recent years, Remer has become a source of inspiration to the resurgent neo-Nazi movement in Germany while officially denying all connections to it, and has also contributed to the spread of the 'Holocaust denial' mythology. He is one of the symbolically important links between the old- and the new-style Nazism in a reunited Germany.

Renn, Ludwig (1889–1979) Communist anti-Nazi author who came from a Saxon aristocratic background, Ludwig Renn was born in Dresden on 22 April 1889 under his original name of Arnold Vieth von Golsenau. Renn knew the German army and its traditions from the inside, having served during World War I as a company and battalion Commander. During 1919 he was in the *Freikorps*, then after leaving the army in 1920 he studied law, economics and Russian at Göttingen and Munich. After further studies in archaeology and Chinese history, Renn became a freelance writer and joined the KPD (German Communist Party) after publishing his first book, *Der Krieg* (*The War*), in 1928. Written in the impersonal, passionless tone of a field notebook, providing vignettes of an infantry unit's experience in the war, Renn's novel reflected the new realism and sobriety in German literature which coincided with the *Neue Sachlichkeit* (New Objectivity) movement in painting and architecture. In 1928 Renn became Secretary of the Alliance of Proletarian Revolutionary Writers, a position he held for four years, and also edited the communist-oriented journal *Linkskurve* (*Left Trajectory*). His novel *Nachkrieg* (1930) dealt with the security forces of the Weimar Republic, and in 1932 he published *Russlandfahrten* based on his visit to the Soviet Union in 1929. Renn was arrested on the night of the Reichstag fire (27 February 1933) and spent two and a half years in prison. He succeeded in fleeing to Switzerland in 1936 and in the same year became Chief of Staff of the Eleventh International Brigade which participated in the Spanish Civil War. Interned in France in 1939, he was released a year later and settled in Mexico (after brief stays in Britain and America), becoming Professor of European History and Languages at the University of Morelia. From 1941 to 1946 he was a founder and leading figure in *Freies Deutschland* (Free Germany), a movement of exiled anti-Nazi German writers based in Latin America. His communist convictions led him to settle in East Germany after 1947, where he became Professor of Anthropology at Dresden Technical College and a prominent defender of the régime. A member of the communist SED (Socialist Unity Party of Germany), he held several high positions in the cultural life of the GDR and was appointed Honorary President of the East German Academy of Arts in 1969.

Renteln, Theodor Adrian von (1897–1946) Commissioner-General of Lithuania during World War II, Theodor von Renteln was born on 14 September 1897 in Hotsi, Russia. He studied law and economics at Berlin and Rostock between 1920 and 1924. Von Renteln entered the NSDAP in 1928, founding the Berlin branch of the National Socialist High School Students' League and becoming its national leader. In November 1931 the young Baltic émigré was appointed by Hitler to lead both the Hitler Youth and the Nazi Students' League, a victory for the educated, middle-class elements in the Nazi youth movement over the earlier working-class and ideological orientation. Von Renteln resigned from both his positions on 16 June 1932 and was replaced by Baldur von Schirach (q.v.). In the same year he became head of the Nazi *Kampfbund* for small traders and in 1933 founded and led the *Reichsstelle* of German artisans, as well as being elected to the Reichstag as deputy for the electoral district of Potsdam. A defender of *Mittelstand* interests in the Third Reich, von Renteln was head of the Institute for Applied Economics, Chairman of the Disciplinary Court of the German Labour Front and President of the German Co-operative Union in Berlin. Appointed *Generalkommissar* in Lithuania in August 1941, von Renteln was on the Russian list of wanted war criminals. Imprisoned at the end of the war, he was hanged by the Russians in 1946.

Ribbentrop, Joachim von (1893–1946) Minister of Foreign Affairs in the Third Reich from 1938 to 1945, Joachim Ribbentrop was born in Wesel on 30 April 1893, the son of an officer. Educated at Metz and Grenoble, where he studied languages, Ribbentrop then spent four years in Canada as an independent businessman. He returned to Germany in 1914, volunteering for active service and reaching the rank of Lieutenant. At the end of the war he was temporarily military attaché in Istanbul. After the war, Ribbentrop went into business in Berlin as the owner of an export firm for wines and spirits, dealing chiefly with England and France. His marriage to Anneliese Henckel, daughter of the largest German champagne manufacturer, gave him the *entrée* into high society which the snobbish, class-conscious Ribbentrop always craved. Their Dahlem villa on the Lentze Allee was an ideal location for Hitler's secret conferences over the forming of his first cabinet of 30 January 1933. Ribbentrop was a late-comer to the Nazi Party – he joined on 1 May 1932 – but within a year he was a member of the Reichstag representing Potsdam, an SS Colonel and Hitler's adviser on foreign affairs. Accepted by the Führer as a man of the world, von Ribbentrop – the noble prefix was fraudulently acquired – owed everything to Hitler, displaying a degree of sycophantic subservience, Byzantine flattery and desire to please which nauseated even the Nazi Old Guard, who regarded him as a parvenu upstart.

The arrogant, vain, touchy and humourless von Ribbentrop aroused almost universal dislike and contempt for his haughty incompetence. Goering (q.v.) referred to him publicly as that 'dirty little champagne pedlar', while his bitter rival Goebbels (q.v.) remarked: 'He bought his name, he married his money, and he swindled his way into office.' The Italian Foreign Minister, Count Ciano, summed up a widely held view when he observed: 'The Duce says you only have to look at his head to see that he has a small brain.' Hitler, however, would not hear a word against him, once even remarking that von Ribbentrop was 'greater than Bismarck'. Until 1935 von Ribbentrop was primarily concerned with questions of disarmament, but in June of that year he negotiated the Anglo-German Naval Agreement and on 2 August 1936 he

was appointed Ambassador to London. His two-year stay in Britain was disastrous and von Ribbentrop, deeply offended by his social rejection in England, became convinced that Anglo-German antagonism was irreconcilable. Henceforth he portrayed England as 'our most dangerous enemy', while at the same time persuading Hitler that the British would not oppose a policy of violent conquest in Europe by the Third Reich. On 25 November 1936 von Ribbentrop negotiated the anti-Comintern pact with Japan, which was later broadened into the Berlin-Rome-Tokyo Axis.

Appointed Reich Foreign Minister on 4 February 1938, von Ribbentrop reached the peak of his political career between the Munich crisis and the sensational Nazi-Soviet pact which he signed in Moscow on 23 August 1939. The pact paved the way for Hitler's attack on Poland, which von Ribbentrop had convinced him would not be opposed by Britain. The Foreign Minister, who had done everything in his power to frustrate last-minute peace moves, gradually lost influence during the war as diplomatic activity receded in importance. After the invasion of the Soviet Union, most of his time was devoted to futile conflicts with his rivals over his waning area of jurisdiction. The megalomaniac von Ribbentrop tried to compensate by pursuing a more active role in the 'Final Solution of the Jewish Question', ordering his subordinates 'to speed up as much as possible the evacuation of the Jews from the various parts of Europe' and pressurizing the Italian, Bulgarian, Hungarian and Danish governments to this end.

He survived an attempted *putsch* by his own State Secretary, Martin Luther (q.v.), but by 1945 he had lost all influence, even with Hitler, whose political intentions he had in the past always been able to divine and whose favour was the basis of his entire career. Arrested in a Hamburg boarding house by

British soldiers on 14 June 1945, von Ribbentrop was tried by the International Military Tribunal at Nuremberg, where his spineless performance aroused the contempt and scorn of his co-defendants. Von Ribbentrop showed no remorse or understanding of the indictment against him. All that was left of the once haughty Foreign Minister was a hollow, pathetic dependence on the dead Hitler, whose creature he still was, even in the bankruptcy of defeat. Von Ribbentrop was found guilty of war crimes and crimes against humanity and peace. Sentenced to death on 1 October 1946, he was the first of the defendants to be hanged in Nuremberg prison fifteen days later.

Richthofen, Wolfram Freiherr von (1895–1945)   General Field Marshal and Luftwaffe commanding officer during World War II, Wolfram von Richthofen was born in Barzdorf, Silesia, on 10 October 1895. After cadet school at Berlin-Lichterfelde, von Richthofen joined the air force in 1917 and served a year later in the famous Richthofen Air Squadron, whose first Commander had been his cousin Manfred, the legendary flying ace. From 1919 to 1922 Wolfram von Richthofen studied engineering, subsequently joining the Reichswehr and taking part in many air competitions. From 1929 to 1933 he was 'on leave' as a member of the German General Staff in Italy. After a period in the Technical Division of the Reich Air Ministry, von Richthofen was appointed Chief of Staff of the 'Condor Legion' in 1936 during the Spanish Civil War, being promoted in September 1938 to Major General and finally to Commander of the Legion. He returned from Spain in May 1939, commanding an air corps on the western front in September and leading his formations with considerable success during the French campaign. In May 1940 he was awarded the Knight's Cross and promoted in the same year to Gen-

eral of Fliers. A year later he received the Oak Leaves of the Knight's Cross. Involved on the Russian front during 1941–2, von Richthofen was promoted to General Field Marshal in February 1943. Towards the end of the war, he commanded the Fourth Air Fleet in Italy. He died on 12 July 1945.

Riefenstahl, Leni (born 1902)   The most innovative film maker of the Nazi cinema, Leni Riefenstahl was born in Berlin on 22 August 1902 and began her career as a ballet dancer, employed by Max Reinhardt, among others, for dance performances in the early 1920s. In 1925 she made her film début as an actress in *Der Heilige Berg*, the first of a series of well-photographed movies about the Alps made by Arnold Franck, the father of the mountain cult in the Weimar cinema. In the late 1920s, Riefenstahl became the high priestess of this cult, starring in Franck's *Der Grosse Sprung* (1927), *Die Weisse Hölle vom Piz Palü* (1929) made together with G. W. Pabst, *Stürme über dem Mont Blanc* (1930) and *Das Blaue Licht* (1932) which she co-authored, directed, produced and played the leading role in, winning a gold medal at the Venice Biennale. In 1933 she made her last film for Franck, *SOS Eisberg*, before being appointed by Hitler (who greatly admired her work) as the top film executive of the Nazi Party.

The muscular, sportive and beautiful young actress-director now became the ardent cinematic interpreter of such Nazi myths as the 'national renaissance', the cult of virility, health and purity, the romantic worship of nature and the human body. Commissioned to make a full-length movie of a Party Congress, she produced *Reichsparteitag* (1935), a pure apologia for Hitler and his Party, and the powerful Nuremberg Rally film, *Triumph des Willens* (*Triumph of the Will*, 1935) – perhaps the most effective visual propaganda for Nazism ever made. Over a hundred people worked on the film including a staff of sixteen cameramen, each with an assistant, and no fewer than thirty-six cameras were used as well as a huge number of spotlights. Riefenstahl combined melodramatic camera techniques from the silent movies of the 1920s with the dramatic effects of Wagnerian opera to submerge completely the individual in the mass and absorb reality into the artificial structure of the Party convention with its endless parades and show marching. In this work the Germanic imagery of the Nibelungen, extremely magnified and subordinate to an authoritarian human pattern, reappears in the form of a modern Nuremberg pageant. Riefenstahl's film won a gold medal at the Venice Film Festival. It was followed by her classic documentary, *Olympia*, a four-hour epic released in two parts, which was devoted to the Berlin Olympic Games. It received its gala première on 20 April 1938, to mark Adolf Hitler's forty-ninth birthday. Riefenstahl's Olympic films, widely admired for their technical innovation and accomplishment, were awarded first prize at the Venice Biennale and were also honoured by the International Olympic Committee in 1948.

After the fall of the Third Reich, Riefenstahl was one of the few leading figures in the German film industry to suffer for her past glorification of Nazism. She vigorously denied all accusations of romantic involvement or political complicity with Hitler. In recent years, her continuing interest in primitive peoples and their natural environment has found a new outlet in her photographic work during various expeditions to Africa. This has resulted in two remarkable books of photography, *The Last of the Nuba* and *The People of Kau*. In the 1990s there has been a resurgence of interest in Leni Riefenstahl, following the publication of her memoirs and the screening of a documen-

tary film in 1994 about her and her cinematic work, entitled *The Wonderful, Horrible Life of Leni Riefenstahl*.

Rienhardt, Rolf (born 1903)   Rolf Rienhardt, who became Chief of Staff to Max Amann (q.v.) and the most powerful figure in the publishing industry of the Third Reich, was born in Bucha on 2 July 1903, the son of a Lutheran pastor. Having studied law at Berlin and Munich, Rienhardt became legal counsel to the Eher Verlag in 1928, having been drawn into National Socialism through his friendship with Gregor Strasser (q.v.). At the latter's suggestion he was placed on the NSDAP list in the Reichstag elections of July 1932 and re-elected in November. In the same year he became divisional head in the Reich Organization Office under Strasser. Though purged with other Strasser supporters in December 1932, Rienhardt's organizational talents, legal skills and phenomenal capacity for work made him an ideal choice as staff Director in Amann's administrative office for the Party press and as Deputy Director of the Newspaper Publishers' Association. Rienhardt was the real brains and driving-force behind Amann's publishing empire, the man who wrote his speeches and articles, and drafted his most important directives. Rienhardt was a leading personality in the Reich Press Chamber, a member of the German Law Academy, Chairman of the Board of Directors of the *Deutscher Verlag* (formerly Ullstein), Managing Director of *Herold Verlagsanstalt GmbH* (1939) and permanent Deputy Director of the *Reichsverband der Deutschen Zeitungsverleger* (the German Publishers' Association) whose affairs he in effect controlled. The latter position gave him broad powers over the privately owned press, whose gradual liquidation and 'quiet' absorption by the National Socialist press was largely a product of his legal ingenuity and undeviating purpose. By 1939 Rienhardt's position in the publishing field was unchallenged, even though he was only exercising powers delegated by his superior, Max Amann. The latter's inferiority complex vis-à-vis his chief assistant, vastly superior in education and ability, led to increasing tension between the two men. Rienhardt's dilatory handling of Hitler's order to suspend the *Frankfurter Zeitung* finally gave Amann the pretext to dismiss summarily his staff Director in November 1943. Rienhardt left office without severance pay, pension rights or a substantial bank account. He was inducted into the *Leibstandarte-SS* Adolf Hitler Regiment, where he served until the end of the war.

Ritter, Karl (1888–1977) One of the most vaunted film directors during the Nazi period, Karl Ritter was born in Würzberg and distinguished himself as a flier in World War I. An officer until 1919, Ritter then became a designer and painter, first entering films in 1925 as a public relations man for Südfilm and Emelka. In 1932 he was appointed Director and Production Manager for the UFA film company, a post he held until 1945. Ritter was a convinced Nazi who managed to introduce a certain realism and artistry into films that were primarily political and propagandist in orientation. A master of action sequences in the best Hollywood style, Ritter glorified Prussian militarist traditions, the 'heroism' of the Wehrmacht, the spirit of camaraderie and above all the virile bravery of the fighter-pilots of the Luftwaffe – to which he devoted eight films after 1936. Awarded the title of 'Professor' by Goebbels (q.v.), Ritter combined reportage and fiction in his cinematic art, which faithfully reflected Nazi anti-communism in movies like *GPU* (1942) and the militarist ethos of official ideology. His best-known works included *Urlaub auf Ehrenwort* (1937), *Patrioten* (1937) and his homage to the old and

new Luftwaffe, *Pour le Mérite* (1938), which was warmly praised by the leading SS organ for showing the actuality of the Third Reich and 'people as they really are, even with their weaknesses'. Other important films included *Legion Condor* (1939), *Über alles in der Welt* (1941) and *Stukas* (1941), an epic idealization of the Luftwaffe which featured a shell-shocked airman miraculously cured after hearing a performance of Wagner's *Siegfried* at Bayreuth. After the war Ritter emigrated along with many former Nazis to Argentina, where he was head of Eos-Film Mendoza. He returned to Germany in 1954, where he continued to direct films, forming his own company, Karl Ritter-Filmproduktion GmbH. He died on 7 April 1977 in Buenos Aires.

Röhm, Ernst (1887–1934) Chief of Staff of the SA and the only man in Hitler's early career capable of opposing or negotiating with him on equal terms, Ernst Röhm was born in Munich on 28 November 1887, the son of an old Bavarian family of civil servants. Röhm was the prototype of the last generation that sought to eternalize the values of the trenches, the camaraderie of the front-line soldiers in World War I with their restlessness, adventurism and latent criminality masquerading as nationalism. A fat, stocky, red-faced little man who had been wounded three times in the war with half his nose shot away, Röhm became a professional freebooter and swashbuckler after 1918, with boundless contempt for the pharisaism and hypocrisy of normal civilian life. His association with Hitler began in 1919 and they became close comrades – Röhm was one of the few people whom the Führer addressed as *du* in conversation – marching together on the Felderrnhalle in 1923. In these early years of the Nazi movement, the Reichswehr Captain – one of a number of ambitious officers in Munich who had been involved in the plot led by von Epp (q.v.) against the left-wing government in Bavaria – was an indispensable organizer who brought many new recruits into the NSDAP. He had also become the master of a secret cache of weapons in Bavaria, which he hoped to use in a frontal assault on the State. But the failure of the Beer-Hall *putsch* led to his dismissal from the Reichswehr and his temporary withdrawal from political life. Disoriented, he took a number of temporary jobs which frustrated and bored him, before setting off for Bolivia where he spent two years as a military instructor.

Recalled by Hitler after the spectacular Nazi electoral successes of 14 September 1930 to take command of the SA (storm troopers), Röhm rapidly expanded it into a popular army of street fighters, gangsters and toughs. From 70,000 in 1930, the SA increased to 170,000 in 1931, swelled by the growing numbers of unemployed and social déclassés. Röhm regarded this plebeian army of desperadoes as the core of the Nazi movement, the embodiment and guarantee of 'permanent revolution', of the barracks socialism and blind dynamism he had absorbed during the war. The SA fulfilled an indispensable role in Hitler's rise to power between 1930 and 1933, by winning the battle of the streets against the communists and intimidating political opposition. By the end of 1933, however, the SA, which now numbered almost four-and-a-half million men and was seemingly more powerful than the Reichswehr itself, had become disillusioned by the results of the Nazi 'revolution'. It felt cheated of the spoils of office, and the growing bureaucratization of the Nazi movement angered those like Röhm who still dreamed of a *Soldatenstaat* (Soldiers' State) and the primacy of the soldier over the politician. Röhm envisaged a duumvirate with Hitler as political leader and himself as the generalissimo of a vast armed force

to be created by absorbing his SA into the regular army.

As SA Chief of Staff, Reich Minister without Portfolio and Minister of the Bavarian State government, Röhm was still in a strong position at the end of 1933 but fatally misplayed his hand. Failing to understand Hitler's concept of a gradual revolution carried out under the cloak of legality, Röhm united opposition against his plans by his insistence on maintaining momentum in a socialist direction and talking openly about a revolutionary conquest of the State. His populist demagogy alienated the middle classes, the conservative Junkers and the Rhineland industrialists, whose support Hitler still needed. Röhm's demands that the SA become a fully-fledged people's army under his own leadership particularly alarmed the Reichswehr generals, who were no less indispensable to Hitler's long-term plans. Moreover, Röhm had antagonized two dangerous rivals, Goering (q.v.) and Himmler (q.v.), to the point where they considered him Enemy No. 1 and were constantly pressurizing Hitler to cut him down to size, utilizing the SS and the Gestapo to this end. Röhm's own conduct and that of his entourage, given to dissolute homosexual orgies and drinking bouts, loutish behaviour and wildly indiscreet remarks, made the task of his enemies easier. Nevertheless, Hitler hesitated to eliminate his oldest comrade-in-arms, a man to whom he felt a debt of gratitude and a certain warmth, even though he had become a liability and even a danger to his régime.

After warning Röhm not to start a 'second revolution' and after ordering the SA to take a month's leave beginning in July 1934, the decision was taken to liquidate its leader and his closest followers. The guileless Röhm, who suspected nothing, was surprised on 30 June 1934 in a private hotel at Bad Wiessee, a small Bavarian spa south of Munich, where he was taking a holiday with other SA leaders. He was awoken by Hitler and a detachment of SS troops and taken to Stadelheim prison, where he was executed two days later after refusing to take his own life. The Blood Purge, also known as the Night of the Long Knives, led to the deaths of seventy-seven leading Nazis and at least one hundred others, including General von Schleicher (q.v.) and his wife. Röhm was posthumously branded a traitor and accused of having fomented a nationwide plot to overthrow the government. The Nazi régime professed to be scandalized by the homosexual goings-on in his entourage, although this had been well known and tolerated for years. He and his followers were charged with having wanted 'revolution for the sake of revolution', an accusation which came closer to the real reason for his death. By the end of 1934 the SA had lost any political function in the new Nazi State and, with Röhm gone, Hitler no longer had to choose between the nationalist and 'socialist' wings of his movement.

Rommel, Erwin (1891–1944)   Field Marshal and the most popular Commander in the German army, known as the 'Desert Fox' for his mastery of desert warfare, Erwin Rommel was born in Heidenheim, near Ulm, on 15 November 1891, the son of a schoolmaster. He entered the infantry in 1910 as a cadet and distinguished himself in World War I as a platoon, company and battle group Commander. Serving as a Lieutenant in the Alpine battalion in Romania and at Caporetto (Italy), he penetrated deep into enemy territory, taking large numbers of prisoners, as much by surprise and initiative as by military strength. Awarded the Iron Cross (First Class) and the coveted *Pour le Mérite*, Rommel returned to soldiering after World War I, serving mainly as an infantry regimental officer and instructor at the infantry school in Dresden. Never a member of the Nazi Party, he was none-

theless an enthusiastic supporter of Hitler in the early days, acting as a military instructor to the Hitler Youth and then as Commander of the Führer's bodyguard battalion during the Sudeten invasion and the Polish campaign of 1939.

During the invasion of Belgium and France, Rommel was given command of the Seventh Panzer Division which rapidly advanced on the English Channel via the Ardennes in May 1940. In this first campaign Rommel displayed a mastery of tank warfare second only to that of General Guderian (q.v.), using his armour on a narrow front to punch through the opposition and fan out through the breach into the less defended rear areas, causing panic and confusion by the speed of his advance. Characteristically, Rommel always led from the front, in the thick of the fighting, as he was to do later in North Africa. Popular with Hitler as well as with his own men, Rommel was promoted to Lieutenant-General in January 1941 and posted in February to Libya, where as Commander of the German forces his task was to assist the Italians and push the British army back to the Egyptian frontier. As Commander of the Afrika Korps from 9 February 1941 Rommel imposed his personal stamp on the North African campaign, acquiring a legendary reputation for his tactical mastery of mobile desert warfare and ability as a field Commander. Energetic, robust, bold and chivalrous, Rommel was highly publicized and respected by his British opponents whom he defeated at El Agheila on 21 March 1941, pushed out of Cyrenaica in a March–June offensive, defeated again at Sollum and threatened at Tobruk, the only British-held fortress which still endangered his lines of communication.

Rommel's brilliant successes led to his promotion to General on 30 January 1942 and to the sacking of the British Commander, Wavell, who was replaced by General Auchinleck. Rommel, however, was handicapped by logistic and supply problems deriving largely from the fact that the North African campaign was seen as a sideshow in Berlin, where German resources were being concentrated on the Russian front. In November 1941 the British had counter-attacked and forced Rommel back to Benghazi with considerable losses in tanks and men. However, following the delivery of new tanks, the Afrika Korps mounted a powerful renewed offensive which drove the British back to the Egyptian border. On 26 May 1942 Rommel attacked the British defences at Gazala and, though close to being captured, succeeded in taking Tobruk on 21 June 1942, seizing large quantities of British arms and stores. The next day Hitler promoted him to General Field Marshal. The British fell back in confusion to prepared positions at El Alamein, some fifty miles from Alexandria and the Nile delta. Although Rommel's advance was checked by Auchinleck, the latter was soon replaced by General Montgomery as Commander of the British Eighth Army. All Allied efforts were now concentrated on defeating Rommel, and their air supremacy, in addition to supplies of the best material available, decreased the chances of the Afrika Korps in the face of the Allied build-up. Rommel himself was exhausted and suffering increasingly from a stomach ailment which forced him to leave North Africa for Berlin. When the British attacked at El Alamein in October 1942, Rommel had to be recalled from his hospital bed, but only arrived two days after the battle had begun and was too late to influence its outcome. By November 1942 the Afrika Korps was in full retreat along the North African coast and, though they fought a brave delaying action, Rommel's forces were doomed by the Anglo-American landings (Operation Torch) of 8 November 1942.

Rommel was evacuated from Tunisia in March 1943 and given command of Army Group B in northern Italy. At the end of the year he was made Inspector of Coastal Defences in northern France and commanded an army group under von Rundstedt (q.v.), Commander-in-Chief, West. Rommel's strategy for countering the expected Allied invasion focused on preventing any landing and development of an Allied bridgehead rather than relying, as von Rundstedt advocated, on a powerful mobile reserve. Rommel spread out his armour along the coastline, helped site the guns and troop emplacements, ordered four million mines to be laid and devised all kinds of physical obstacles to a landing.

When the Normandy invasion took place he was away in Berlin and, immediately recognizing the significance of Allied air superiority, he twice begged Hitler in June 1944 to draw the proper conclusions and to end the war. Convinced that all was lost, Rommel's loyalty to Hitler had been increasingly strained by the latter's high-handed conduct of the war and he entered into contact with the military conspirators without being a direct party to the plot against the Führer. In view of his popularity, the conspirators hoped to make Rommel the new Chief of State if Hitler was killed. While not opposing their plans, Rommel favoured Hitler's arrest and trial, rather than an assassination attempt. The dispute became academic when he was seriously wounded in an Allied air raid on 17 July 1944 and suffered a fractured skull. Sent home to Ulm to recover, he was convalescing when the 20 July plot failed. Rommel was implicated when one of the conspirators, von Hofacker (q.v.), blurted out his name to the torturers, before dying in agony. On 14 October 1944 two investigating generals came to Rommel's home and offered him the choice of a poison capsule or facing trial by the People's Court for high treason.

Rommel, who feared that he might be murdered on the way to Berlin and that his family would suffer if he opted for the second choice, agreed to swallow the poison. He was given a burial with full military honours and the fiction was maintained that he had died of the wounds he received in France. Thus the reputation of the war hero and loyal Nazi General was preserved by Hitler in the interests of State, in order to maintain German public morale.

Rosenberg, Alfred (1893–1946)   One of Hitler's earliest mentors who became the semi-official 'philosopher' of National Socialism and head of the Nazi Party's Foreign Affairs Department during the Third Reich, Alfred Rosenberg was born in Reval (now Tallinn) in Estonia on 12 January 1893. The son of an Estonian mother and Lithuanian father, both of Baltic German extraction, Rosenberg studied engineering in Riga and architecture at the University of Moscow, fleeing to Paris and then Munich after the Russian Revolution of 1917. Active in White Russian émigré circles and also a member of the ultranationalist, semi-occult Thule Society, which reinforced his obsession with the nefarious role of Jews, Bolsheviks and Freemasons, Rosenberg had the typical 'Germanity' complex of expatriate Germans from the border regions. He joined the NSDAP in 1919 and was introduced to Hitler by Dietrich Eckart (q.v.), whom he eventually succeeded as editor of the Nazi newspaper, the *Völkische Beobachter*, in 1923. An important figure in the early days of the Nazi movement, Rosenberg impressed Hitler by his 'learning', derived largely from the cranky, tract literature of pathological nationalist fanaticism, as well as by his virulent anti-Bolshevism and doctrinaire anti-semitism. In works like *Die Spur der Juden im Wandel der Zeiten* (*The Tracks of the Jew Through the Ages*), *Unmoral im Talmud* (*Immorality in the Talmud*), both published in 1919, and *Das Verbrechen der Freimaurerei* (*The Crime of Freemasonry*, 1921), Rosenberg expressed his crackpot belief in a Judeo-Masonic conspiracy that constantly seeks 'to undermine the foundations of our existence'. According to Rosenberg, Allied Freemasons were responsible for the outbreak of World War I while 'international Jews' had manipulated and controlled the Russian Revolution. Neurotically obsessed with supranational conspiracies and dark, occult powers, he was one of the main disseminators of *The Protocols of the Elders of Zion*, a Tsarist police forgery which exercised a mesmeric influence over some Nazi leaders and millions of their followers.

Hitler's adviser on foreign affairs in the period of the *Kampfzeit*, Rosenberg participated actively in the abortive Beer-Hall *putsch* of November 1923 and was deputy leader of the Party until his resignation in 1924, as a result of feuding with Hermann Esser (q.v.) and Julius Streicher (q.v.). Even in the early years of the movement, Rosenberg was regarded as an outsider and a 'foreigner' because of his Baltic origins, his cramped, pedantic style, introverted temperament and insufferable intellectual arrogance. As editor of the *Völkische Beobachter* he was in constant conflict with Hitler's business manager Max Amann (q.v.) and other Bavarian Nazi leaders who disliked his plodding, earnest, humourless manner. Nevertheless, Rosenberg established himself in the 1920s as the guardian of the National Socialist *Weltanschauung* (world-view), as the leading theoretician of Nazi racism and its chief cultural propagandist. In 1929 he founded the *Kampfbund für deutsche Kultur* (Fighting League for German Culture), which combated so-called 'degenerate art' and advocated the same narrow-minded folk aesthetic which Rosenberg later enforced as President of the Reich Centre for the Advancement of Literature.

In 1930 Rosenberg was elected to the Reichstag as Nazi deputy for Hessen-Darmstadt and published his major work, *Mythus der XX Jahrhunderts* (*The Myth of the Twentieth Century*), which was second only to Hitler's *Mein Kampf* as a 'bible' of the Nazi movement. Though few could understand the author's abstruse style, it had sold over half a million copies by the end of 1936, 680,000 copies by 1938, 850,000 by 1940 and passed the million mark in 1942. The book, which had been many years in preparation (according to Rosenberg it was completed in 1927–8), was deeply influenced by the race theories of the Comte de Gobineau and Houston S. Chamberlain, whose immensely influential *The Foundations of the Nineteenth Century* (Engl. trs. 1910) served as its direct inspiration. The 'myths' which Rosenberg postulated revolved around the mystique of blood purity, which 'under the sign of the swastika' had unleashed a spiritual world revolution, 'the awakening of the soul of the race'. Art, science, law, custom, truth and error, good and evil depended on the racial substance of any given soul, for the whole of world history was presented as nothing but the history of races. For Rosenberg the Teutons were the master-race of 'Aryans', whose values of honour, personality, freedom and nobility reflected the superiority of their 'race-soul'. They were the highest representatives of the Nordic race whose destiny was to rule Europe. All cultural and state-building achievements were attributable to Nordic blood from the 'Aryans' of India and Persia to the ancient Greeks and Romans, and the modern 'Germanic' peoples of the West. By defending 'the myth of the blood' and its superiority over 'the ancient sacraments', Rosenberg claimed to be fighting against the 'psychic bastardization' of the Germans. National Socialism with

its Germanic idea of comradeship was organically opposed to the Christian-Syrian-liberal world idea and to the 'Semitic-Latin' spirit which for Rosenberg was embodied in the Roman Catholic church. Judaism and Christianity were depicted as mortal enemies of the Teutonic soul and its concept of honour. The neo-paganism which Rosenberg preached consciously aimed to extirpate the influence of the Old and New Testaments and eradicate the Christian ideals of love, charity, humility and mercy. The new Germanic faith declared war on Christianity and above all on the internationalism of the Roman church which had sprung from the 'oriental races', in Judea and Syria, which were spiritually alien to the Nordic peoples. In its place Rosenberg affirmed the swastika as the living symbol of blood and race, Wotan-worship, solstice celebration, the old Norse gods and runes. No less vitriolic were his attacks on Jews and Freemasons who, like the Catholics, clung to a supranational religion of humanity which was alien to the German spirit. The Jew in particular was responsible for the ignoble race-destroying doctrines of Christianity.

Rosenberg's muddled hotch-potch of mystical, 'pseudo-scientific', ideological theorizing aroused the Catholic church to an energetic counter-attack in 1934, led by the Munich Cardinal Faulhaber (q.v.), which increased the sales of the book but also undermined its credibility. Although Rosenberg's book was required reading for Party circles and benefited from official sales, it aroused little enthusiasm in the top leadership and was mainly used by Nazi sub-ideologists looking for impressive-sounding slogans. Anti-Nazis seeking some coherence in the eclectic mishmash of official Nazi ideology studied Rosenberg's treatise much more assiduously than Party leaders themselves. The Führer confessed that he found it too obscure to read and besides it contradicted his tactical policy of avoiding a frontal assault on the Christian churches. The Catholic Vice-Chancellor von Papen (q.v.) recalled in his memoirs: 'In our early conversations about Rosenberg and his new "myth" Hitler used such expressions of ridicule that I could not believe these aberrations presented any danger.' Von Schirach (q.v.) observed that Rosenberg had 'sold more copies of a book no one ever read than any other author', while Goering (q.v.) bluntly described the work as 'junk'. Rosenberg's bitterest rival and the man who usurped his position as cultural commissar in the Third Reich, Joseph Goebbels (q.v.), aptly called the *Mythus* 'philosophical belching' while professing to admire Rosenberg's industry. It was Goebbels who coined the sarcastic epithet 'Almost Rosenberg' to describe his rival, the man who 'almost managed to become a scholar, a journalist, a politician, but only almost'. Nevertheless, for all its clumsy, obscurantist mysticism, Rosenberg's *Mythus* did represent the one significant attempt at systematizing the official philosophy of the Third Reich.

In 1934 Rosenberg was appointed 'the Führer's Delegate for the Entire Intellectual and Philosophical Education and Instruction of the National Socialist Party'. Charged with watching over the ideological education and training of Party members, Rosenberg exercised his function with the same narrow-minded, zealous pedantry that he brought to every task. His greatest disappointment was to be passed over for the post of Foreign Minister in 1933 and again in 1938 when he was overlooked in favour of von Ribbentrop (q.v.). As head of the Party Foreign Affairs Department from 1933 to 1945, he was nominally responsible for Nazi Parties in other countries, though in practice this was limited to contacts with fascist organizations in eastern Europe and the Balkans. His visit to Great Britain in May 1933, intended to improve Anglo-German rela-

tions, merely caused increased British hostility to the Third Reich and underlined his practical incompetence. Rosenberg, who had always dreamed of a great Nordic empire under German leadership, brought off one of his few diplomatic successes when bringing the Norwegian fascist, Vidkun Quisling, to Germany in December 1939 to encourage a Nazi invasion of Norway.

In the same year Rosenberg established in Frankfurt his 'Institute for the Investigation of the Jewish Question', declaring in his opening speech that 'Germany will regard the Jewish Question as solved only after the last Jew has left the Greater German living space'. The primary mission of the Institute was the looting of European Jewish library treasures, archives and art collections from their owners to promote Rosenberg's grandiose plans of 'scientific and cultural research'. A special unit called the *Einsatzstab Reichsleiter Rosenberg* (Rosenberg Task Force) had been busy since October 1940 confiscating the great art treasures of France and other occupied countries, with the help of the army, and transporting them to Germany. According to Rosenberg, art objects of all kinds to the value of one billion marks had been sequestered from France alone by January 1941. He had a free hand to sequester all 'ownerless Jewish property' in France, Belgium and Holland, as well as organizing special detachments to confiscate research material and cultural goods belonging to Freemasons. While demonstrating that he was no less ruthless than rival Nazi leaders in such acts of blatant robbery, Rosenberg proved himself a vacillating, incompetent administrator following his appointment by Hitler as Minister for the Occupied Eastern Territories on 17 July 1941.

As far as Jews were concerned, Rosenberg's *Ostministerium* differed only in detail, not in intent, from the draconian policy of ghettoization and then extermination pursued by Himmler (q.v.), Heydrich (q.v.) and the Reich Main Security Office. Similarly, Rosenberg supported the brutal Germanization of the subject peoples, especially in the Baltic lands. But though he had long preached the inferiority of the Slavs, he had evidently never believed that such theories might mean their liquidation. Charged with the administration of the Ukraine, he wrote outraged reports in the autumn of 1942 concerning conditions there and protested at the barbarous treatment of Soviet POWs in Germany, without receiving any response from Hitler. Rosenberg had dreamed of a series of semi-independent satellite régimes in eastern Europe as a security wall against Moscow, without realizing that Nazi policy had decided that the population of these territories would become stateless and an object of extermination. His opposition to the bloody slave-states set up by subordinates like Koch (q.v.) in the Ukraine remained completely ineffective since it was out of touch with the ultimate objectives of Nazi rule in the East. Moreover, Rosenberg's position was far too weak to determine policy in the occupied territories, his authority having been superseded by rivals like Himmler, Goering, Goebbels and Bormann (q.v.), as well as SS and army leaders in the field. The leading ideologue of National Socialism was simply not taken seriously by the technicians of power. At the Nuremberg trial the philosopher of Nazism appeared as a pathetic, broken figure who blamed the degeneration of the National Socialist 'Idea' on his more successful adversaries in the struggle for power. He was found guilty of war crimes and hanged at Nuremberg on 16 October 1946.

Rudel, Hans-Ulrich (1916–82) German fighter ace who flew more sorties than any other pilot during World War II, destroying a massive total of 519 Russian tanks on the eastern front,

Group-Captain Hans-Ulrich Rudel was born in Konradswaldau on 2 July 1916. After attending military school at Wildpark, he was assigned as an engineering officer to a Luftwaffe Stuka formation. Promoted to Lieutenant in 1939, Rudel sank a cruiser and the battleship *Marat* in 1941. In March 1944 he was captured by the Russians after being shot down, but succeeded in escaping. In January 1945 a special decoration – the Golden Oak Leaves of the Knight's Cross – was created for him in acknowledgement of his phenomenal achievements as a fighter pilot. Shot down again in February 1945, Rudel had his right leg amputated.

After the war Rudel fled to Argentina, where he was a prominent member of the German Nazi community. Aided by the Peron government, he acted as a contact man between the Nazi exiles and those in Lower Saxony. On his return to Germany in 1951 he became patron of the ultra-nationalist *Freikorps Deutschland*, and his memoirs, published in Buenos Aires under the title *Trotzdem*, not only glorified war but expressed an unrepentant admiration for Hitler. The idol of the post-war German Right, Rudel became one of the most inflammatory spokesmen and propagandists for the neo-Nazi Socialist Reich Party. In 1956 he returned to South America, living for a time in Brazil and Paraguay and continuing his activity on behalf of the extreme right-wing circles. Rudel remained a controversial personality in West Germany, where two air force generals were dismissed in November 1976 for defending his appearance at an official reunion of former members of the Luftwaffe. Rudel died on 18 December 1982 in Rosenheim. At the funeral jet-fighters of the German air force overflew the graveside in low flying formation – a mark of honour that provoked a further scandal.

Rudin, Ernst (1874–1952) Professor of

Psychiatry at the University of Munich after 1930 and one of the pioneers of Nazi 'racial science', Ernst Rudin was born in St Gallen, Switzerland, on 19 April 1874. He was co-editor of the *Archiv für Rassen-und Gesellschafts-biologie* (Archive for Racial and Social Biology) founded in 1904 and co-founder of the *Gesellschaft für Rassen-hygiene* (Society for Racial Hygiene), established a year later as the brainchild of Rudin's close associate, Dr Alfred Plötz. From 1925 full Professor of Psychology at Basel and Director of the Kaiser Wilhelm Institute for Genealogy and Demography and of the Research Institute for Psychiatry in Munich from 1928, Rudin was one of the leading German representatives at the First International Congress for Mental Hygiene, held in Washington in 1930, where he stressed the importance of eugenics and the systematic study of heredity. When the Nazis came to power, the Minister of the Interior, Wilhelm Frick (q.v.), nominated Rudin as his honorary representative on the Board of Directors of two German racial hygiene unions and appointed him to work together with the Ministry on the reconstruction of the German race.

On 16 July 1933 Rudin took over the leadership of the *Deutscher Verband für Psychische Hygiene und Rassenhygiene* (German Institute for Mental Health and Racial Hygiene) and he was also the chief architect of the 'Law for the Prevention of Heredity Disease in Posterity' which was passed two days earlier and took effect from 5 January 1934. Together with Arthur Gütt (q.v.) and Falk Ruttke, Rudin co-authored one of the first authoritative commentaries on this piece of eugenic legislation, *Gesetz zur Verhütung Erbkranken Nachwuchses vom 14 Juli 1933* (1934), which analysed the purpose and meaning of the new sterilization law. The legislation covered anyone suffering from a hereditary disease who was considered likely to pass it on to his posterity, persons suffering from innate mental deficiencies, schizophrenia, manic-depressive insanity, hereditary blindness or deafness, severe hereditary physical abnormality or even severe alcoholism. The sterilization of such categories, to be determined by specially established eugenic courts, was designed by Rudin to eliminate impure and undesirable elements from the German race.

Reviewing the sterilization laws of the Third Reich in the journal *Deutscher Wissenschaftlicher Dienst* (29 July 1940), Rudin praised Hitler's political leadership for having dared to break 'the terror of the inferior kind of people' by means of 'racial-hygienic measures'. Two years earlier, Rudin had emphasized that 'the importance of eugenics has only become known in Germany to all intelligent Germans through the political work of Adolf Hitler, and it was only through him that our more than thirty-year-old dream has become a reality and racial-hygienic principles have been translated into action'. Among the achievements which Rudin proudly claimed for his eugenics movement was the Nuremberg race law, 'For the Protection of German Blood and German Honour'. On his sixty-fifth birthday in 1939, Rudin was awarded the Goethe Medal for art and science by Hitler and honoured by a telegram from Interior Minister Frick, celebrating him as the 'meritorious pioneer of the racial-hygienic measures of the Third Reich'. In 1944, when he was seventy, Rudin received a bronze medal bearing the Nazi eagle from Adolf Hitler, who lauded him as the 'pathfinder in the field of hereditary hygiene'.

Rundstedt, Gerd von (1875–1953) General Field Marshal and Commander-in-Chief of the western theatre of war between 1942 and 1945, Gerd von Rundstedt was born in Aschersleben on 12 December 1875. An officer in the Prussian infantry from 1893, von Rundstedt served on the General Staff during World War I in Turkey and France. After the war he was promoted rapidly in the Reichswehr, becoming a Major General in 1927 and Lieutenant-General in March 1929. Three years later he was appointed Berlin Military Area Commander and in October 1938 von Rundstedt became a General of Infantry. After heading an army group in the occupation of the Sudetenland, von Rundstedt was retired in October 1938 but was recalled in the summer of 1939, leading army groups in the Polish and French campaigns and receiving the Knight's Cross in September of the same year. As Commander-in-Chief of Army Group South he had outflanked the central Polish forces, preventing them from retreating across the Vistula. In May–June 1940 commanding Army Group A in the invasion of France and the Low Countries, von Rundstedt led the armoured thrust through the Ardennes, outflanking the Allied armies. He was ordered by Hitler to halt in the Dunkirk area, thus enabling the British Expeditionary Force, which was in danger of annihilation, to escape from the beaches and harbour at Dunkirk.

In reward for his services, von Rundstedt was promoted in July 1940 to the rank of General Field Marshal and appointed to command the major part of the forces to invade England, an expedition that never took place. Transferred to the eastern front following the invasion of the Soviet Union, von Rundstedt was appointed Commander of the Southern Army Group (Ukraine) in June 1941 and his armies rapidly overran the Crimea and Donetz basin, advancing as far as Rostov on the Don. Following his tactical retreat from Rostov (in defiance of Hitler's orders), von Rundstedt was relieved of his command in November 1941 and replaced by von Reichenau (q.v.). He was recalled in 1942 as Commander-in-Chief West, responsible for anti-invasion preparations, serving

in this capacity until March 1945, except for two brief intervals when he was recalled. Von Rundstedt's plan of mobile defence was strategically sound, but ultimately failed to prevent the Allied landings in Normandy.

He was temporarily dismissed on 2 July 1944, but nonetheless presided over the court of honour which expelled from the army those generals implicated in the July 1944 plot against Hitler – having refused to commit himself to the conspiracy, though aware of the plans. Von Rundstedt was recalled once again to his command and succeeded in halting the Allied advance by mid-September 1944, stabilizing the defence line and holding it until December. Increasingly paralysed by Hitler's irrational commands, von Rundstedt's Ardennes offensive of December 1944 failed to turn the tide and he ended the war as a British prisoner. The aloof, aristocratic von Rundstedt, an outstanding general and exponent of old-fashioned Prussian military values, was to have been tried by a British court for his illegal order of 21 June 1942 to hand over captured British commandos to the Gestapo, but the trial was dropped because of his ill health. Nor was his possible complicity in the extermination of Jews in July–December 1941, when he commanded the Southern Army Group in Russia, investigated. He died on 24 February 1953 in Hanover.

Rust, Bernhard (1883–1945)   Reich Minister of Science, Education and Popular Culture in Nazi Germany from 1934 to 1945, Bernhard Rust was born in Hanover on 30 September 1883. After studying Germanics, philosophy and classical philology at several universities including Berlin and Munich, Rust became a secondary school *Oberlehrer* (senior master) in Hanover. During World War I he served as a Lieutenant in the infantry, winning the Iron Cross (First Class) and suffering a severe headwound which affected his mental stability. One of the 'Old Fighters', Rust entered the Nazi Party in 1922 and was *Gauleiter* of Hanover-Braunschweig after 1925. In 1930 he was dismissed from his teaching post by the local republican authorities at Hanover – allegedly for interfering with a schoolgirl – but was nonetheless elected to the Reichstag as a Nazi deputy. On 4 February 1933 Rust was appointed Prussian Minister of Science, Art and Education, following the Nazi seizure of power. His steadfast loyalty to Hitler was rewarded by his appointment on 30 April 1934 as Reich Minister of Education, a position which gave him control of German science, public schools, institutions of higher learning and youth organizations. Though more moderate than the rabid ideologues in the Nazi student and teachers' associations, Rust nonetheless presided over the sabotage of Germany's intellectual life in the name of racial purity.

Among the consequences of the Nazi purge of the universities, which he ordered, was the loss of German world leadership in the natural sciences. Over a thousand dons – chiefly Jews, Social Democrats and liberals – were dismissed from the educational institutions of the Third Reich. They included world-famous scientists and Nobel Prize winners such as Albert Einstein (q.v.), James Franck (q.v.), Fritz Haber (q.v.), Otto Warburg and Otto Meyerhof (q.v.), as well as many other distinguished chemists, mathematicians, engineers and jurists. Nazi youth was henceforth to be educated in the spirit of militarism, paganism, anti-semitism and the cult of the perfect Aryan racial type. 'We must have a new Aryan generation at the universities, or else we will lose the future', declared the Reich Minister of Education, echoing his master, Adolf Hitler. In German schools and universities, Jews were presented as the hereditary enemies of Germany, a 'chosen people' of criminals who endangered the

existence of the Third Reich. The mentally disturbed ex-schoolmaster, who presided over the spiritual shipwreck of German science and scholarship, himself committed suicide with the collapse of Nazi Germany in May 1945.

Ryan, Hermine Braunsteiner (born 1919) Former SS guard supervisor in Nazi death camps during World War II, Hermine Braunsteiner was born in Vienna on 16 July 1919. Already a guard supervisor at Ravensbrück concentration camp at the age of twenty, the pale, blonde, blue-eyed Braunsteiner was transferred in October 1942 to the death camp at Majdanek where she remained until March 1944, serving as a supervising warden. She subsequently returned to Ravensbrück after two years and was arrested by the Allied authorities and imprisoned on 6 May 1946. Released on 18 April 1947, she was again imprisoned from 7 April 1948 until 22 November 1949, after an Austrian court of murder had convicted her of charges including assassination, manslaughter and infanticide. Following her second release, she was granted an amnesty by an Austrian civil court from further prosecution in her native country. In 1959 she entered the United States following her marriage to Russell Ryan, an American electrical engineer whom she had met while he was on holiday in Austria. She settled down in the Queens district of New York, receiving American citizenship on 19 January 1963. Five years later the Nazi-hunter Simon Wiesenthal discovered her real identity and the American immigration authorities began procedures in 1971 to revoke her citizenship on the grounds that she had never revealed her Austrian war crimes conviction. Affidavits were submitted by former Majdanek camp inmates alleging that she had taken part in the selection of about two thousand women and children for the gas chambers. She was accused of cruel, brutal and sadistic treatment of defenceless prisoners and of having 'injured and offended the human dignity of inmates' at Ravensbrück. In 1971 a de-naturalization decree deprived her of her American citizenship and on 14 March 1973 an extradition warrant was issued in Düsseldorf demanding that she stand trial in West Germany on charges of killing concentration camp inmates during World War II. She was extradited from the United States and sent back to West Germany after losing her five-year procedural fight to avoid trial. According to one witness at the highly publicized Düsseldorf war crimes trial which began in 1976, she 'seized children by the hair and threw them on to the trucks headed for the gas chambers'. She was known to Majdanek inmates as 'the Stomping Mare' because of the brutal kicks she delivered with her steel-studded jackboots. On 30 May 1981 the sixty-one-year-old former SS guard was sentenced to life imprisonment.

S

Salomon, Ernst von (1902–72) Prussian nationalist author who achieved notoriety for his role in the murder of the German Foreign Minister, Walther Rathenau, Ernst von Salomon was born in Kiel on 25 September 1902, the scion of an old Huguenot family. At the time of the Armistice in 1918, von Salomon was still in the senior class of the Royal Prussian cadet school. Shortly after the war, he joined the *Freikorps*, participating in the fighting in the Baltic and in Upper Silesia. He was also involved in the Kapp *putsch* of 1920 and in nearly all the counter-revolutionary movements which aimed to destroy the hated Weimar Republic, to wipe out the 'shame' of the Versailles Treaty and restore the monarchy. His first novel, *Die Geächteten (The Outlaws)*, which dealt mainly with the *Freikorps* struggle to gain the Baltic States for Germany, depicted the men of 1920 as savage nihilists seeking revenge for their feelings of despair and impotence following the military defeat of World War I. 'We were a band of fighters drunk with all the passion of the world; full of lust, exultant in action. What we wanted, we did not know. And what we knew, we did not want! War and adventure, excitement and destruction...'

Von Salomon's taste for lawlessness and violence, as well as his unregenerate nationalism, led him to participate in the murder of the Jewish-born Foreign Minister, Walther Rathenau, on 24 June 1922, for which he was sentenced to five years' penal servitude. The *völkisch* desperado was released from prison as a result of President von Hindenburg's (q.v.) general amnesty in 1928 and reverted to his favourite pursuit of *putsching*, participating in the bomb-throwing peasants' movement in Schleswig-Holstein. After a few more months in prison where he wrote his first best-selling novel, *Die Geächteten* (1930), von Salomon soon became a favourite of the literary salons, writing *Die Stadt* (The City) in 1932, followed by a characteristic idealization of Prussianism, *Die Kadetten* (1933).

Like other *Edelfaschisten* (noble-minded fascists) such as Jünger (q.v.) and Niekisch (q.v.), von Salomon was a significant forerunner of the Third Reich by virtue of his moral colour-blindness, self-righteous arrogance and irrational nihilism, but was somewhat shocked by the results of the 'National Revolution'. Though he had stirred the hatreds on which National Socialism thrived, he never joined the Nazi Party, despising the 'democracy of the masses' and continuing to prefer his Prussian ideal of a hierarchical, authoritarian State. Von Salomon subsequently claimed that he had been appalled by the brutality of the Röhm Blood Purge of 1934, by the Crystal Night anti-Jewish pogrom and the moral bankruptcy of the Nazi régime. This did not, however, prevent him from being accorded a place in the Nazi Academy of Arts and his books from being recommended by the régime as 'national documents' which portrayed the struggle for the rebirth of a nation. Under the Third Reich, von Salomon's writing was mainly apolitical and he concentrated on a highly successful and well-paid career as a top-level film writer for UFA, the German film company. His best-known screenplays included *Kautschuk, Kongo-Express, Sensationsprozess Casilla* (1939), *Carl Peters* (1941) and *Der Dunkle Tag* (1943). After the war von Salomon was arrested by the American occupation authorities and interned until September 1946, when he was released since nothing incriminating could be found against him.

In 1951 he published a massive 800-page best-seller – it sold more than 250,000 copies in West Germany – entitled *Der Fragebogen* (*The Questionnaire*) – a bitter, cynical, personal testament which exposed his utter indifference to questions of war guilt and repentance. On one level a critique *ad absurdum* of the de-Nazification procedures of the victorious Allies and the 'stupidity' of their good intentions in seeking to re-educate Germans, it was also a cynical apologia for Germany during the Hitler era. The autobiography of a nihilistic, conservative revolutionary who had become a fellow-traveller during the Third Reich, von Salomon's book demonstrated that he had learned little from the experience. Complaining angrily about his 'sadistic' treatment in a post-war American internment camp, he whitewashed the German conscience with his claim that the Americans behaved no less brutally than the Nazis. The moral pretensions of the West were contemptible in the eyes of this unrepentant nationalist for whom the term 'democracy' remained meaningless and hypocritical. With shocking candour, devastating sarcasm and ridicule, von Salomon made the post-war screening of Nazis seem almost as barbaric and inhuman as Dachau and Buchenwald. The success of the book proved that it had evoked a responsive chord in the German national psychology with its amoral indifference to the crimes committed under the Third Reich, its eulogy of Prussian authoritarianism and its contempt for the 'stupid conquerors'. Von

Salomon continued to be a popular and successful author in post-war Germany. He died at his home near Hamburg in August 1972, shortly before his seventieth birthday.

Sauckel, Fritz (1894–1946) Plenipotentiary-General for Labour Mobilization from 1942 to 1945 who conducted slave raids into Soviet Russia and other occupied territories during World War II, Fritz Sauckel was born in Hassfurt am Main on 27 October 1894, the son of a post-office clerk. From 1909 to 1914 Sauckel spent five years as a merchant seaman in the Norwegian and Swedish merchant marine. Interned in a French prisoner-of-war camp during World War I, Sauckel earned his living as a factory worker after the war, before joining the NSDAP in 1923. In 1925 he was made district business manager of the Nazi Party in Thuringia and two years later he was appointed *Gauleiter*. From 1927 to 1933 he was an NSDAP deputy in the Thuringian diet and the leader of its legislative faction after 1930. Appointed Thuringian Minister of the Interior on 26 August 1932 and then Governor on 5 May 1933, Sauckel was elected to represent the district in the Reichstag on 12 November 1933. An Honorary SA General and SS General without function, Sauckel was responsible during the Third Reich for mobilizing German and foreign workers for the Wehrmacht war machine. Promoted to Reich Defence Commissioner for the Military District of Kassel on 1 September 1939, Sauckel was appointed Plenipotentiary-General for Labour Mobilization three years later. He was responsible for deporting five million people from their homes in occupied territories to work as slave labour in Germany, issuing directives that they should be exploited as much as possible for the lowest possible expenditure. His 'protection squads' press-ganged with ruthless efficiency workers who were subsequently imported as slave-labour for the war economy of the German Reich. The slave-labour boss was also responsible for the extermination of tens of thousands of Jewish workers in Poland. At his trial in Nuremberg, Sauckel claimed that he was innocent of any war crimes and had known nothing about the concentration camps, asserting that he had been 'shocked in his inmost soul by the crimes that had been revealed in the course of the trial'. Sauckel's protestations of innocence did not impress the judges. He was sentenced to death by the International Military Tribunal at Nuremberg for war crimes and hanged on 16 October 1946.

Sauerbruch, Ferdinand (1875–1951) A surgeon of international repute and at one time an ardent Nazi, Ferdinand Sauerbruch was born in Barmen on 3 July 1875. After completing his medical studies, he eventually established himself as the chief surgeon of the German army and head of the Charité Hospital in Berlin. His name was one of the most luminous among the 960 professors who in the autumn of 1933 took a public vow to support Hitler and the National Socialist régime. During the Third Reich he was recognized as the leading surgeon in Germany, frequently operating on top Nazi leaders including Hitler and Goebbels (q.v.). It was his medical expertise which restored Claus von Stauffenberg (q.v.) to life in a Munich hospital after he had been gravely wounded in North Africa. In spite of his Nazi inclinations, Sauerbruch was a friend of General Beck (q.v.) and enjoyed the confidence of Resistance circles though only mildly involved in the anti-Hitler plot. After the war Saüerbruch was cleared by a German de-Nazification court. He died in Berlin on 2 July 1951.

Schacht, Hjalmar (1877–1970) Financial wizard of the Third Reich who was President of the Reichsbank until 1939 and Minister without Portfolio until January 1943, Hjalmar Schacht was born to a family of Danish origin in Tingleff, Schleswig-Holstein, on 22 January 1877. Brought up in the United States where his parents had emigrated (his father became an American citizen), he returned to Germany to complete his studies in Kiel, Munich and Berlin, where he received a doctorate in economics. Head of the economic archives of the Dresdner Bank in 1903, he became Deputy Director of the same bank five years later and in 1916 took over the private *Nationalbank für Deutschland* (National Bank for Germany), merging it in 1922 with the Darmstadt Bank. In November 1923 Schacht was made Reich Currency Commissioner with the task of halting the astronomic German inflation and stabilizing the currency, in which he was largely successful, establishing the *Rentenmark* as the basis of a new currency backed by foreign loans. In December 1923 he was appointed head of Germany's leading financial institution, the Reichsbank, remaining at this post until 1930. He participated in the negotiations for the Dawes loan (1924) and had originally agreed to the Young Plan (1929) as head of the German delegation at the reparations conference.

The following year he resigned as President of the Reichsbank in protest at the new reparations regulations embodied in the Young Plan and the increasing foreign debt of the government, steps which drew him closer to Hitler and the National Socialists. Schacht, who in 1918 had been one of the founders of the German Democratic Party but had left in 1926 after turning away from its left-liberal policies, now discovered in Hitler the embodiment of his own ardent nationalism. Impressed by his reading of *Mein Kampf* and by the Nazi success in the 1930 Reichstag elections, Schacht, together with other conservative nationalists, joined the Harzburg Front in October 1931, hoping to use the Nazis in a common alliance to bring down the Weimar Republic. Schacht once declared: 'I desire a great and strong Germany and to achieve it I would enter an alliance with the Devil.' To this end he played a decisive part in bringing Hitler closer to his own banker and industrialist friends. Already in November 1932, he sought to pressurize von Hindenburg (q.v.) to appoint Hitler as Chancellor, and it was on his recommendation that the big guns of German heavy industry – Krupp, United Steel and I. G. Farben – supported the Nazis as well as the German Nationalists in the electoral campaigns of 1932–3. For these crucial services in paving the way for the Third Reich, Hitler reappointed Schacht as Reichsbank President in March 1933 and then as Minister of Economics, a position he held from 1934 to 1937.

As the financial architect of Nazi Germany, Schacht was able to make economic policy without hindrance in the early years of the régime and exploited his intimate contacts with banks, large firms and economic organizations to remarkable effect. A believer in the economies of free marketing, Schacht eased big business out of the clutches of direct Party control, reinforcing the structure of private enterprise and corporate profit margins during his tenure of office. He created the *Reichswirtschaftskammer*, a comprehensive 'Organization of Industry' formed out of former employers' organizations, chambers of commerce and industrial groups. He negotiated highly profitable barter deals with dozens of countries and succeeded in creating credit in a country with little liquid capital and almost no financial reserves. Appointed Plenipotentiary-General for the War Economy on 21 May 1935, it was Schacht who directed the economic preparations for war, making the reconstruction of the Wehrmacht financially possible. For this task he was given almost unlimited powers, and his skill in financing German rearmament made him indispensable to Hitler and the Nazi Party though he never enjoyed their complete confidence. Respected but distrusted, Schacht was the only representative of the old German bourgeoisie still left in the government by 1935.

The first Commissioner of the Four Year Plan, Schacht's policy of financing rearmament and unemployment programmes by greatly expanding public works and stimulating private enterprise, while at the same time seeking to halt devaluation and inflation, soon ran into difficulties with the Nazi Party leadership. In November 1937 he resigned his posts as Minister for Economics and Plenipotentiary-General for the War Economy, being replaced by Funk (q.v.) and Goering (q.v.) as economic overseers. From 1937 until January 1943, he nonetheless remained in the cabinet as Minister without Portfolio, and Hitler reappointed him President of the Reichsbank in March 1938. With the latter's permission, he began to negotiate in London in January 1939 a plan for the emigration of 150,000 German Jews in the next three to five years. The Schacht Plan was linked to the promotion of German exports – 25 per cent of Jewish assets would be put in a cash fund and transferred by increased exports, while 75 per cent would accrue to Germany, in so far as it was not needed for the support of Jews until they emigrated or 'died'. Schacht's dismissal from the Reichsbank Presidency on 20 January 1939, following a new policy disagreement and the outbreak of World War II, put an end to the Plan. Schacht, who did not believe that Germany could economically stand a long war and opposed the escalating arms drive which had subordinated industry to the autarchic needs of the State, renewed his contacts with the restorationist circles of the

Resistance around Goerdeler (q.v.). His private doubts about the Nazi régime which had increased with the years – he had been especially disturbed by the removal of the top generals and the anti-Jewish pogrom of 1938 – did not, however, lead him to a wholehearted commitment to the Resistance.

He was nonetheless arrested on 29 July 1944 after the failure of the anti-Hitler conspiracy and sent to Ravensbrück and then Flossenbürg concentration camps, even though his direct implication in the plot could not be established. He was released from captivity by American troops in April 1945, but appeared before the Nuremberg Tribunal, charged and found guilty of organizing Germany for war. Since the rearmament programme was not considered criminal in itself, Schacht was acquitted in 1946 in spite of the protests of the Soviet judge. A de-Nazification court in Stuttgart subsequently sentenced him, however, to eight years' labour camp as a 'Major Offender'. Shortly afterwards, on 2 September 1948, following an appeal, Schacht was acquitted by a Ludwigsburg court and released. He was definitively cleared in November 1950 of all charges connected with his involvement in the Third Reich. Schacht now began a highly successful second career in the 1950s as a financial adviser to developing countries such as Brazil, Ethiopia, Indonesia, Iran, Egypt, Syria and Libya. He also made a second personal fortune, founding his own foreign trade bank 'Messrs Schacht and Co.' in Düsseldorf in 1953. In the 1960s he continued to be involved in problems of development aid, maintaining close ties with government and business circles in Indonesia and West Africa. Schacht's settling of accounts with his past appeared under the title *Abrechnung mit Hitler* (1949) and his autobiography, *76 Jahre meines Lebens,* was published in 1953. He died in Munich on 3 June 1970.

Schellenberg, Walter (1910–52) Supreme head of the espionage services in the Third Reich and Himmler's (q.v.) right-hand man towards the end of World War II, Walter Schellenberg was born in Saarbrücken on 16 October 1910, the seventh child of a piano manufacturer. After receiving his law degree at Bonn University (where he demonstrated a passionate interest in Renaissance history and its political implications), Schellenberg joined the NSDAP and the SS in May 1933, subsequently entering the Gestapo in the late summer of 1934. The career-minded young adventurer, who spoke English and French fluently, attracted the attention of Heydrich (q.v.) and Himmler, who made him his personal aide. He was entrusted with organizing the *Einsatzgruppen* for the Czech campaign in 1938. Four years later he negotiated on behalf of the Reich Main Security Office (RSHA) with the Wehrmacht over the zones of authority in which these same *Einsatzgruppen* were to enjoy full freedom 'in executing their plans as regards the civil population', in effect, a licence to kill civilians. Schellenberg had earlier been involved in the Venlo incident (November 1939) when he led a detachment of armed Germans across the Dutch border to kidnap two British military intelligence agents. Major Schellenberg, at that time already head of the Gestapo counter-intelligence division, was decorated for his exploit and promoted at the age of only thirty to SS Major General. From 1939 to 1942 Schellenberg was Deputy Chief of *Amt* VI of the RSHA, in charge of the political secret service for foreign countries.

In 1940 Schellenberg was charged with preparing a 'special search list-GB' of 2,700 prominent people in the United Kingdom to be arrested following the projected invasion of Britain. (He also claimed to have written the highly secret handbook, *Informationsheft*, intended to aid the Nazis in looting Britain and stamping out resistance.) Another special mission, this time to Lisbon, Portugal, to kidnap the Duke and Duchess of Windsor – Hitler intended to use them as instruments in his search for a peace agreement with Britain – ended in a complete fiasco. Nevertheless, as Himmler's protégé, Schellenberg was promoted in 1942 to head of *Amt* VI of the RSHA and Chief of Security in the occupied territories. In 1944 he was appointed head of the united SS and Wehrmacht military intelligence, standing second only to Himmler in the Gestapo hierarchy. He used his agents to enter into secret negotiations with the Allies and prodded Himmler to establish contact with the Swedish Red Cross official, Count Folke Bernadotte, about surrendering the German armies in the West. Schellenberg was eventually tried by the American military tribunal at Nuremberg and acquitted of 'genocide' charges, claiming successfully that he had no direct involvement with the 'Final Solution'. He was, however, found guilty of complicity in the murder of Russian prisoners of war and sentenced to six years' imprisonment on 2 April 1949. Released in December 1950, he died in Italy in the summer of 1952, at the age of only forty-two.

Schirach, Baldur von (1907–74) Reich Youth Leader and Governor of Vienna during World War II, Baldur von Schirach was born in Berlin on 9 March 1907, the son of an aristocratic German father and an American mother whose ancestors included two signatories of the Declaration of Independence. On his father's side descended from an officers' family with artistic tendencies and a cosmopolitan background (Carl von Schirach had resigned from the army in 1908 to become a theatre director in Weimar), Baldur grew up in a pampered, well-to-do environment. One of the earliest members of the NSDAP (he entered the Party in 1924 while attending

the University of Munich where he briefly studied Germanic folklore and art history), von Schirach was soon a member of its innermost circle, in spite of his youth. A convinced anti-semite, after reading Henry Ford's *The International Jew* and writings by Houston S. Chamberlain and Adolf Bartels (q.v.), the aristocratic von Schirach was also a militant opponent of Christianity and of his own caste. Throwing himself body and soul into organizing high school and university students for the NSDAP, von Schirach proved himself an outstanding organizer and propagandist of National Socialism. With his infectious enthusiasm and power to inspire youth with the ideals of comradeship, sacrifice, courage and honour, von Schirach was highly regarded by Hitler who also appreciated his blind devotion as expressed in hero-worshipping verses and such sycophantic sayings as 'loyalty is everything and everything is the love of Adolf Hitler'. In 1929 von Schirach was put in charge of the National Socialist German Students' League and two years later he was appointed Reich Youth Leader of the NSDAP, a post which he held until 1940.

In 1933 he organized the gigantic youth march in Potsdam, in which wave upon wave of youngsters greeted Hitler. Already before the Nazi seizure of power, von Schirach's ceaseless propaganda, his idealism and organizational flair for mobilizing youth had succeeded in winning over hundreds of thousands of young Germans to Hitler's cause. In May 1933 he was made Leader of the Youth of the German Reich at the age of twenty-six and in the next few years his cult seemed second only to that of Hitler himself. Placed in control of the Hitler Youth, which by 1936 already comprised six million members, von Schirach used a powerful mixture of pagan romanticism, militarism and naïve patriotism to build up recruits for Hitler's war machine. Young Germans were to be drilled into acceptance of Nazi concepts of character, discipline, obedience and leadership as set out in von Schirach's book, *Die Hitler-Jugend* (1934): they were to be moulded into a new race of 'supermen'. Von Schirach, who fancied himself as a writer and poet, published two books which were best-sellers in 1932, *Hitler, wie ihn Keiner Kennt* (with photographs by his father-in-law, the court photographer, Heinrich Hoffmann, q.v.) and *Triumph des Willens*. The following year, his collection of poems, *Die Fahne der Verfolgten*, and the short biographies of Nazi leaders, *Die Pionere des Dritten Reiches*, were published. Von Schirach taught German youth that their blood was better than that of any nation and devoted his lyricism to hollow worship of the Führer's genius.

Towards the outbreak of World War II, his position, however, was being undermined by the intrigues of Martin Bormann (q.v.) and other enemies. Jokes about his effeminate behaviour and his allegedly white bedroom furnished in a girlish manner, were legion and he was never quite able to live up to his own ideal type of the hard, tough, quick Hitler youth. At the beginning of 1940, von Schirach enlisted as a volunteer in the German army, serving in France for a few months as an infantry officer and receiving the Iron Cross (Second Class). Then, after being relieved of his post as Leader of the Hitler Youth, von Schirach was appointed *Gauleiter* and Governor of Vienna in August 1940. His unorthodox cultural policies in Austria soon aroused Hitler's distrust (fed assiduously by Bormann) and, after a visit to the Berghof in 1943 where he pleaded for a moderate treatment of the eastern European peoples and criticized the conditions in which Jews were being deported, he lost all real influence. Nevertheless, he was on record (in a speech on 15 September 1942) as saying that the

'removal' of Jews to the East would 'contribute to European culture'.

The deportation of 65,000 Jews from Vienna to Poland during his tenure as Governor was a major item in the indictment against von Schirach at the Nuremberg trials. The war crimes tribunal conceded that he did not originate the policy, but had 'participated in this deportation, though he knew that the best they [the Jews] could hope for was a miserable existence in the ghettoes of the East'. Von Schirach admitted that he had approved the 'resettlement' but denied all knowledge of genocide, denouncing Hitler from the dock as 'a millionfold murderer' and calling Auschwitz 'the most devilish mass murder in history'. Sentenced on 1 October 1946 to twenty years' imprisonment for crimes against humanity – which he served out in the company of Rudolf Hess (q.v.) and Albert Speer (q.v.) – the handsome, fair-haired von Schirach appeared to undergo a change of heart, recognizing that he had misled German youth and contributed to poisoning a whole generation which had idolized him. In his memoirs, *Ich Glaubte an Hitler* (1967), issued one year after his release from Spandau prison in Berlin, von Schirach tried to explain the fatal fascination which Hitler had exerted on him and on the younger generation. He now considered it his duty to destroy any belief in the rebirth of Nazism and blamed himself before history for not having done more to prevent the concentration camps. After his release on 30 September 1966, von Schirach lived a secluded life in south-west Germany. He died in his sleep at a small hotel in Kroev on 8 August 1974.

Schleicher, Kurt von (1882–1934) Professional army officer who became the last Chancellor and gravedigger of the Weimar Republic, Kurt von Schleicher was born on 7 April 1882 in Brandenburg. He entered military service at the age of eighteen as a subaltern in the Third Foot Guards, President von Hindenburg's (q.v.) old regiment, and during World War I served as a General Staff officer and Adjutant to General Wilhelm Groener (q.v.) at Supreme Headquarters. After the war von Schleicher helped organize the illegal *Freikorps* and the 'Black Reichswehr' under General von Seeckt (q.v.) and was a key figure in the negotiations with Moscow about training German tank and air officers in Soviet Russia. In 1929 Colonel von Schleicher was made head of the newly created *Ministeramt* (Ministry Bureau) in the Reichswehr Ministry, when his old friend General Groener became Minister of Defence. Von Schleicher was now in charge of the political and press affairs of the army and navy and began to emerge as a talented, unscrupulous intriguer with a nimble mind and a flair for politics. For the next three years von Schleicher was one of the decisive influences behind the scenes who determined the fate of the Weimar Republic. He was largely responsible for the appointment of Brüning (q.v.) as Chancellor on 28 March 1930 and then for his dismissal. Similarly he prevailed on President von Hindenburg to appoint Franz von Papen (q.v.) as Brüning's successor only to bring him down in a web of intrigue.

On 2 December 1932 General von Schleicher became the last Chancellor of the Weimar Republic, lasting for fifty-seven days in office and ruling by presidential decree as had his immediate predecessors before him. He tried unsuccessfully to flirt with the trade unions and create an alliance between the army and the working classes against the propertied classes and the Nazis. The latter he sought to divide by offering Gregor Strasser (q.v.) the Vice-Chancellorship and Premiership of Prussia and by making a deal with Ernst Röhm (q.v.) to bring the SA under the military authority of the Reichswehr. Von Schlei-

cher's 'socialist' policies in military garb and his proposal to break up the bankrupt larger estates in East Prussia infuriated the big landowners and industrialists who feared and distrusted him. The new Chancellor's indifference to traditional class alignments alienated big business. Unable to find a majority in the Reichstag, von Schleicher failed to persuade President von Hindenburg to let him institute a military dictatorship and he was abruptly dismissed on 28 January 1933 after a complicated intrigue in which his old rival, von Papen, played a leading part. Von Schleicher retired from public life though he continued secret contacts with Strasser and Röhm and had not given up all hope of a political comeback. On 30 June 1934 he and his wife were brutally murdered by Nazi assassins in their home in the suburbs of Berlin during the Night of the Long Knives.

Schmeling, Max (born 1905) World heavyweight champion from 1930 to 1932 and the most successful professional boxer in German history, Max Schmeling was born in Klein Luckow, Uckermark, on 28 September 1905. In 1926 Schmeling won the German light-heavyweight title and the following year he became European champion at the same weight. In 1928 he moved up into the heavyweight division, winning the German title. On 12 June 1930 Schmeling defeated the American title-holder, Jack Sharkey, on a foul in the fourth round, in a bout for the world heavyweight championship which was held in New York. In the return fight two years later (on 21 June 1932) held in Long Island City, Schmeling was decidedly unlucky to lose the decision in fifteen rounds and with it the world heavyweight title. The following year he married the film actress, Anny Ondra. The liberal-minded Schmeling who had a Jewish manager, Max Jacobs, found himself unwittingly turned into a symbol of Nordic-Germanic race superiority following his sensational victory on 19 June 1936 over the black American heavyweight fighter, Joe Louis, considered by many the greatest boxer at his weight in ring history. Before a huge crowd in the New York Yankee Stadium, Schmeling caused one of the biggest upsets in boxing history by knocking out the overconfident 'Brown Bomber' in the twelfth round. In Nazi Germany, this triumph – to Schmeling's dismay – was presented in racial terms as a victory that proved Negro inferiority. The return bout at the Yankee Stadium, held before a crowd of over 70,000 spectators on 22 June 1938 which grossed more than a million dollars, was billed as a grudge fight and was more politically and racially charged than any previous encounter in heavyweight boxing history. Joe Louis, who had won the world title in 1937, was determined to vindicate not only himself but also the pride of America and the black people. Within two minutes and four seconds of the first round Schmeling had been knocked out after facing an onslaught of unrelenting savagery from the black American champion.

Following this shattering defeat, Schmeling was never again the same fighter, though he did win the European heavyweight boxing championship in 1939. During World War II Schmeling served in the Wehrmacht as a parachutist and was involved in the spectacular German assault on Crete. After 1945 Schmeling, although over forty, attempted a boxing comeback. He won a few fights but in May 1948 was beaten by another veteran, Walter Neusel, over ten rounds at Hamburg. His boxing career over – Schmeling won fifty-six and drew four of his seventy fights – the former German and world champion remained a popular and much respected figure not only in Germany but also in America. Awarded the Golden Ribbon of the German Sports Press Society and

made an honorary member of the Austrian Association of Professional Boxers, Schmeling became an honorary citizen of Los Angeles and in 1967 received the American Sports Oscar. In the same year he published his autobiography, *Ich boxte mich durchs Leben*. Since 1957 the ex-champion has owned the franchise on a Coca-Cola factory in Hamburg-Wandsbek. Several boxing experts rank him in the top ten of all time among the heavyweight fighters in modern ring history.

Schmitt, Carl (1888–1985) Weimar Germany's most renowned constitutional theorist and the Third Reich's *Kronjurist* (Crown Jurist) until his fall in 1936, Carl Schmitt was born in Plettenberg, Westphalia, on 2 July 1888. Successively Professor of Law at the Universities of Greifswald (1921), Bonn (1922–3), Cologne (1933) and Berlin (1933–45), Schmitt enjoyed a successful career as a teacher and writer on legal and political theory, establishing himself as a formidable conservative critic of the Weimar Constitution which he attacked for having weakened the State and for clinging to a liberalism that was incapable of solving the problems of a modern mass democracy. Schmitt repudiated the liberal antithesis between law and politics, the notion of a government 'by laws and not of men', and the very notion of parliamentary democracy as an antiquated bourgeois method of government. But though a harsh critic of the pluralism of Weimar, Schmitt had opposed the extremists of Right and Left, before the Nazi seizure of power, even supporting General von Schleicher's (q.v.) efforts to block or end the Nazi adventure. With the passage of the Enabling Act of 24 March 1933, there was a decisive change in Schmitt's attitude and later in the same year he described it as the 'provisional constitution of the German revolution', the genesis of a new legal-political order. On 1 May

1933 he joined the NSDAP and rapidly emerged as the leading legal theoretician of the Nazi State. In his *Staat, Bewegung, Volk: Die Dreigliederung der Politischen Einheit* (1933) Schmitt wrote that 'the German revolution was legal – that is, it was formally correct in accordance with the earlier constitution. It stemmed from discipline and the German sense of order.' He emphasized that the central concept of National Socialist State law was 'the concept of leadership' and its indispensable precondition was the 'similarity of racial stock between leader and followers'.

Schmitt, who had not been anti-semitic in his Weimar period (he dedicated his classic work of 1928 on constitutional law, *Verfassungslehre*, to his Jewish friend, Dr Fritz Eisler, and paid homage to the Jew, Hugo Preuss, the creator of the Weimar Constitution), increasingly indulged in racism in order to make his ideological conversion more convincing. Thus he justified the Nuremberg race laws as 'the constitution of freedom' and in October 1936 presided over a conference of university law teachers in Berlin, where he demanded a purging of the 'Jewish spirit' in German law. This opportunism, also visible in other areas, did not prevent the Nazis from regarding him with some suspicion and ultimately as politically unreliable. In the early years of the régime he was protected by his association with conservatives like von Papen (q.v.) and Johannes Popitz (q.v.), and by Goering (q.v.) who made him a Prussian State Councillor and enjoyed patronizing prominent intellectuals and artists. In November 1933 he became Director of the University Teachers' Group of the Nazi League of German Jurists and in June 1934 editor of the leading law journal, *Deutsche Juristen-Zeitung*. But apart from Goering and Hans Frank (q.v.), Schmitt had no connections with the upper Nazi hierarchy, who had their own legal theorists like Werner Best

(q.v.), Reinhard Höhn and Frank himself. Schmitt might protest that the law is 'what the Führer wills', but his status as a late-comer, a traditional conservative and an intellectual made him vulnerable.

Schmitt continued to publish prolifically and to attempt to remove all suspicions concerning his loyalty – he greeted the Röhm Blood Purge as 'the highest form of administrative justice' though he was fortunate enough to escape it – but increasingly he came under attack from Nazi theorists who accused him of neglecting the centrality of race and *Volk*. Nor were his past associations with Jews and liberals forgotten or the fact that he was still a Roman Catholic. In December 1936 the SS organ *Das Schwarze Korps* denounced his anti-semitism as a sham and quoted his earlier opinions, which had been critical of Nazi race theories. Schmitt's Party work came to an end, though thanks to the intervention of Goering and Frank he retained his chair of law at Berlin and his official title of Prussian *Staatsrat*. Eventually he joined the 'inner emigration', but was coolly received, given his earlier willingness to lend intellectual respectability to the Nazi régime. In his memoirs, written in 1950, Schmitt provided a tame and unconvincing apologia for his National Socialist career, claiming that once the Weimar system could no longer protect him, he had no option but to transfer his allegiance to the new régime, as long as it granted him this protection. For all his intellectual brilliance, Schmitt could never transcend the narrow opportunism and fawning subservience which the holders of power inspired in him. Carl Schmitt passed away on 7 April 1985 in his birthplace, but his legacy has continued to provoke intellectual and political controversy in recent years.

Schoerner, Ferdinand (1892–1973) General Field Marshal (appointed in 1945 during Hitler's last days in the *Führerbunker*) and Chief of the National Socialist Leadership Staff of the Army, Ferdinand Schoerner was born in Munich on 12 June 1892, the son of a police official. A commissioned officer during World War I, he was awarded the *Pour le Mérite* for bravery at Caporetto. Entering the Reichswehr in 1919 as a Lieutenant-Colonel, Schoerner did not obtain command of a mountain division until the outbreak of World War II, when he was already over forty years old. A sympathizer with Nazism from his early years, Schoerner was promoted rapidly after 1939 and two years later served as Major General in the Greek campaign – in May 1941 he was awarded the Knight's Cross. In 1942-3 he commanded a mountain regiment in Lapland and a Panzer Army Corps on the eastern front. In February 1944 he received the Oak Leaves of the Knight's Cross and in April he was promoted to General and made Commander-in-Chief of Army Group South in the Ukraine. At the end of July he was transferred to the supreme command of Army Group North on the eastern front. From the beginning of 1944 Schoerner had been Chief of the National Socialist Political Guidance Staff of the Armed Forces and his combination of ideological fanaticism and brutality impressed Hitler, who promoted him at the end of the war to General Field Marshal. 'The Bloodhound', or 'The People's General' as he was sometimes known, was Supreme Commander of the vital Silesian front at the beginning of 1945 and expected by Hitler to perform miracles in relieving Berlin from approaching Russian forces. His drumhead court-martials and ruthless disciplinary measures – he shot privates and colonels with equal zeal for the smallest infractions – were, however, unable to prevent the disintegration of German defences. Schoerner himself fled to the American zone in Austria, was handed over to the Rus-

sians and spent ten years in prison as a war criminal. He returned to West Germany from Soviet Russia at the beginning of 1955, only to be charged with the murder of German soldiers during the last months of the war on the eastern front. He was found guilty of manslaughter by a Munich court in 1957 and sentenced to four-and-a-half years' imprisonment. Schoerner died in Munich on 6 July 1973.

Scholl, Hans (1918–43) and **Scholl, Sophie** (1921–43) Catholic student leaders of an ill-fated but gallant Munich University Resistance circle called 'The White Rose', Hans and Sophie Scholl were born in Forchtenberg, Württemberg, in 1918 and 1921 respectively. Children of the local mayor, they had once been enthusiastic members of the Hitler Youth before going to the University of Munich, a hotbed of student dissatisfaction by 1942, where their mentor was the Professor of Philosophy, Kurt Huber, who opposed and was later executed by the Nazi régime. Hans began his medical studies at the University in 1941, then served as a medical orderly on the Russian front, returning to Munich on study leave the following summer. His younger sister, Sophie, enrolled as a student of biology and philosophy in 1942. At first their activities were clandestine, confined to university circles and the secret printing and distribution of texts such as the courageous sermons of Clemens von Galen (q.v.). They produced leaflets calling for passive resistance and sabotage of armaments factories, and denounced the extermination of the Polish aristocracy and especially the Jews as 'the most terrible crime against human dignity, a crime not to be compared to any similar one in the history of mankind'. On 18 February 1943, the Scholls dropped leaflets from the second floor of the University main building calling for German youth to rise against Nazi 'subhumanity' in

the war of liberation. They also participated in broad daylight in a student
demonstration against the régime on the
streets of Munich, the only occurrence
of its kind in the Third Reich. They
were denounced to the Gestapo by a
Blockleiter, arrested along with four
other students, interrogated and tortured for three days, and sentenced to
death in a summary trial by the People's
Court. On the morning of her execution
(22 February 1943), Sophie Scholl told
her fellow prisoner that she thought
'thousands will be stirred and awakened
by what we have done'. Her leg broken
by the Gestapo interrogators, she hob-
bled on crutches to the scaffold, dying
like her brother with exemplary courage
and dignity. The same evening the students of Munich, instead of revolting as
the Scholls had hoped, ostentatiously
displayed their loyalty to the Nazi
government.

Scholtz-Klink, Gertrud (born 1902)
Nazi Women's League Leader in the
Third Reich, Gertrud Scholtz-Klink was
born in Adelsheim, Baden, on 9 February 1902. A blonde, blue-eyed, slender
little woman with classic features and a
fresh complexion, she had married a
postal clerk at the age of eighteen and
bore him six children (two of whom
died) before she was widowed. An early
member of the NSDAP, she had been
appointed the Party's women's leader in
Baden in 1929. Promoted to the leadership of the NSDAP's Women's Organization in Hessen two years later, she was
active in building up similar groups
throughout South-West Germany and,
when the Nazis came to power, Frau
Scholtz-Klink was made *Reichsfrauen-
führerin* (Reich Women's Leader) of the
Nazi Women's League. She also stood
at the head of the German *Frauenwerk*
(a federal organization of women) and
of the Women's League of the Red
Cross. From July 1934 the German
Labour Front appointed her to lead its

Women's Bureau. As top Nazi women's
leader in an anti-feminist régime,
Scholtz-Klink invariably paid deference
to male supremacy and exercised no real
influence on Party leaders. Her task was
to emphasize the joys of labour and
child-bearing, 'the mission of woman to
minister in the home and in her profession to the needs of life from the first to
last moment of man's existence'. Preaching the cult of motherhood according to
the well-known slogan of 'Children,
Church, Kitchen', Frau Scholtz-Klink
wrapped up in mock-heroic verbiage the
Nazi policy of treating women as breeding machines and beasts of burden for
the greater glory of the Reich. 'The
German woman', she declared,' enthusiastically fights at the Führer's side in his
battle for the universal recognition of
the German race and German culture.'
At a Party rally of 1937 she quaintly
asserted that 'even if our weapon is only
the wooden spoon, its striking power
shall be no less than that of other weapons'. Active in mobilizing women for
labour service, she declared at the 1938
Party rally that 'the German woman
must work and work, physically and
mentally she must renounce luxury and
pleasure'. A good speaker with a rasping
voice who was sent abroad frequently
to propagandize on behalf of the régime,
Frau Scholtz-Klink was the prototype of
the militant Nazi woman. She sought to
teach other German women how to organize their households according to the
policies of the Party and consistently
praised the 'sacred character' of National Socialist conquest and struggle.
After the war she hid for nearly three
years under a false name until she was
arrested and sentenced by a French
military court on 18 November 1948 to
eighteen months' imprisonment. A de-
Nazification court at Tübingen in
November 1949 included her in its list
of 'Major Offenders' as a diehard
advocate of Nazi ideology, but she was
acquitted of guilt for war crimes.

Schröder, Kurt Freiherr von (1889–
c.1965?) Cologne banker who played
a pivotal role in the secret dealings that
brought Hitler to power in January
1933, Kurt von Schröder was born in
Hamburg on 24 November 1889. After
studying at the University of Bonn, he
served during World War I as a Captain
on the General Staff. After the war, von
Schröder became a leading partner in
the firm of J. H. Stein and a wealthy
banker based in Cologne. A founding
member of the Keppler (q.v.) Circle,
von Schröder contributed substantial
funds to the NSDAP, channelling industrialists' money to the Party, and he also
arranged the crucial secret meeting between Hitler and Franz von Papen (q.v.)
which took place at his home in Cologne
on 4 January 1933. At this meeting, the
two men agreed to bring down the government of Kurt von Schleicher (q.v.)
and replace it by an alliance between
themselves. During the Third Reich, von
Schröder held numerous directorships.
He was Chairman of the Board of Directors of the Adlerwerke (Frankfurt am
Main), Felten and Guilleaume
Carlswerk AG, Thyssen Hütte AG,
Braunkohle-Benzin AG (Berlin) and
Boswau & Knauer AG (Berlin), as well
as President of the *Gauwirtschaftskam-
mer* (Regional Economic Chamber),
Cologne-Aachen. Von Schröder was also
appointed President of the Rhineland
Industrial Chamber in Cologne and head
of the Trade Association of Private
Banks. Found disguised as an SS corporal in a POW camp in France, he was
interned by the British after World War
II. Von Schröder was eventually tried by
a German court for crimes against humanity in November 1947, being sentenced to three months' imprisonment
and a derisory fine. On appeal by the
prosecution the fine was substantially
increased in 1948 to 500,000 Reichsmarks; but after the currency reform
and a further appeal by the defence in
June 1950, the final amount to be paid

was insignificant. The former Nazi
banker spent his last years in Hohenstein
bei Eckernförde and is reported to have
died around 1965.

Schultze, Walther (1894–1979) *Reichsdozentenführer* (National Leader of the
Association of University Lecturers)
from 1935 to 1943, Walther Schultze
was born in Hersbruck on 1 January
1894. After serving in World War I in
the air force where he was wounded,
Schultze was demobilized as a First Lieutenant and joined the Epp *Freikorps*.
The leader of a nationalist students' organization, he was a member of the
NSDAP from its inception in 1919,
taking part three years later in the Beer-
Hall *putsch* in Munich. He was at
Hitler's side when the shooting began
and organized the get-away car as well
as the Nazi leader's convalescence in
Uffing am Strafelsee. A physician by
training, Schultze was appointed head
SA doctor in 1923. From 1926 to 1931
he was a Nazi member of the Bavarian
legislature and in 1933 he was made
head of Department VII in the Bavarian
Ministry of Justice. Promoted to Ministerial Director and head of the Public
Health Department in the Bavarian Ministry of the Interior in November 1933,
Schultze was also appointed as Honorary Professor at the University of
Munich a year later. In 1935 Schultze
was nominated as Reich Leader of University Teachers, a position which he
held for the next eight years. He was
responsible for driving Jewish lecturers
out of German universities. In a speech
before the Congress of the Nazi Association of University Lecturers in Munich,
held in June 1939, Schultze emphasized
that the German university stood or fell
'with the type of the combat-ready political, National Socialist fighters who
regard their *Volk* as the supreme good'.
Academic freedom 'must have its limits
in the actual existence of the *Volk*', declared the *Reichsdozentenführer*, who

argued that a 'binding ideology' and not independent scholarship, subject-matter or specialization was the decisive criterion for the university community. The object of his association was to forge a truly National Socialist body of teachers and scholars devoted to the service of the German *Volk*. Schultze was also implicated in the euthanasia programme and the murder of mentally handicapped persons. In May 1960 he was condemned to four years' imprisonment in a de-Nazification trial in Munich for complicity in the 'mercy killings' of at least 380 adults and children. At his trial, Schultze expressed no remorse, declaring that 'never for one moment did I feel that I had committed an injustice or crime'. In August 1979, Walter Schultze died in his villa in Krailing at the age of eighty-five.

Schuschnigg, Kurt von (1897–1977) Austrian Federal Chancellor from 1934 until the *Anschluss* in 1938, Kurt von Schuschnigg was born in Riva, South Tyrol, on 14 December 1897, the son of an Austro-Hungarian army officer. During World War I he served at the front and was taken prisoner by the Italians at the end of the war. After studying law at the Universities of Freiburg and Vienna, he set up as a lawyer in 1924 and became a prominent figure in the clerical-conservative Christian Social Party. Elected in 1927 as the youngest deputy to the Austrian National Council, von Schuschnigg was soon regarded as 'the coming man' in Christian Social circles and in 1932 he was taken into the cabinet as Minister of Justice. From 1933 he also served as Minister of Education under Chancellor Dollfuss. Following the latter's assassination, von Schuschnigg was appointed Federal Chancellor on 25 July 1934 and also held at various times the posts of Defence Minister, Foreign Minister and from 1937 that of Minister for Public Security. A Catholic Pan-German and a rigid advocate of the *Ständestaat* (corpo-

ratist State), Schuschnigg upheld the authoritarian constitution initiated by his predecessor, based on the traditionalist principles of Catholicism, autocracy and legitimacy. Skilfully playing off his rivals against one another, he was able to hold back the fascist Heimwehr and smaller para-military organizations and in 1936 succeeded in ousting the Austro-fascist leader, Prince Starhemberg, from the government and the Fatherland Front. On 11 July 1936 von Schuschnigg concluded the so-called 'July Agreement' by which Austria undertook to preserve a friendly attitude to the Third Reich and to define itself as a *German* State. Though von Schuschnigg rejected National Socialism and *völkisch* ideology, he agreed to release several thousand Nazis from prison, to include several Austrian Nazis in his cabinet and even to allow the penetration of his Fatherland Front by pro-Nazi elements. This was a price he was prepared to pay in the hope of overcoming Austria's diplomatic isolation and obtaining German recognition of her sovereignty and independence. This policy of concessions was severely undermined by the establishment of the Rome–Berlin axis and the withdrawal of Mussolini's support for Austrian independence in 1937.

Having failed to win over moderate nationalists and having alienated the workers by his earlier role in crushing the Social Democrats, von Schuschnigg found himself lacking a mass popular base to rally Austrians against growing German pressure. Summoned to Berchtesgaden on 12 February 1938, the Austrian Chancellor was brutally bludgeoned by Hitler into accepting the appointment of the crypto-Nazi, Arthur Seyss-Inquart (q.v.), as his Minister of the Interior (with control of the police) and into legalizing the Nazi Party in Austria. Hitler lectured his guest on the history of Austria – 'just one uninterrupted act of high treason' – and warned him that 'the German Reich is one of the great powers, and nobody will raise his voice if it settles its border problems'. The threat to Austrian independence drove von Schuschnigg to one last desperate gamble. He announced a plebiscite on 9 March 1938 (to be held four days later) in which the Austrian people were to be asked to vote in favour of an Austria which was 'free and German, independent and social, Christian and united'. Under intense Nazi pressure with the massing of German troops on the Austrian border, the plebiscite was called off and an enraged Hitler insisted on von Schuschnigg's resignation (which took effect on 11 March) and his replacement by Seyss-Inquart. Following the *Anschluss* (during which German troops were enthusiastically welcomed by Austrians as 'liberators') von Schuschnigg was temporarily interned in a Viennese hotel and kept under Gestapo surveillance. Re-arrested in 1941 he was sent to Dachau and spent the rest of the war in various concentration camps. He was liberated by American troops in the South Tyrol in 1945. Two years later he emigrated to the United States where he became a Professor of Government at the University of St Louis and a naturalized American citizen in 1956. His books include *Dreimal Österreich* (1937), his memoirs *Requiem in Rot-Weiss-Rot* (1947, Engl. trs. *Austrian Requiem*, 1947) and *Im Kampf gegen Hitler* (1969, Engl. trs. *The Brutal Takeover*, 1971). Von Schuschnigg returned to Austria in 1967 and settled in the Tyrol.

Schwarz, Franz Xaver (1875–1947) Treasurer of the Nazi Party and a member of Hitler's Old Guard from his early Munich days, Franz Schwarz was born on 27 November 1875 in Günzburg, where he attended high school. After military service Schwarz was employed as a military administrative clerk and then as a municipal official in Munich. Following war service, he

joined the Nazi Party in 1922 and with its refounding in 1925 he became *Reichsschatzmeister* (National Treasurer), a full-time position which he held until the end of the Third Reich, taking over duties previously performed by Max Amann (q.v.). In 1933 he was elected to the Reichstag, representing the electoral district of Franconia. In 1935 he became a Reich Leader and in 1943 he was awarded the title of *SS-Obergruppenführer*. Schwarz died in an internment camp near Regensburg on 2 December 1947. A Munich de-Nazification court posthumously classified him in September 1948 as a 'Major Offender'.

Schwerin von Krosigk, Lutz Graf (1887–1952)   Reich Minister of Finance and a member of Hitler's first cabinet, Schwerin von Krosigk was born on 22 August 1887 at Rathmannsdorff (Anhalt) and educated at Rosslében. He studied law at Oxford and Lausanne, passing his first examination in 1909. In 1910 he entered the civil service in Stettin and passed his final examination in 1914. He served with the Second Pomeranian Uhlans and was awarded the Iron Cross (First Class) for bravery during World War I. In 1920 he was appointed a *Regierungsrat* and in 1929 Ministerial Director in the Reich Ministry of Finance. From 2 June 1932 (when he joined von Papen's cabinet) until 1945, Schwerin von Krosigk remained Minister of Finance and a member of the cabinet. He supervised the financing of Germany's rearmament programme and, unlike the Minister of Economics, Hjalmar Schacht (q.v.), he approved of Hitler's persecution of the Jews and efforts to drive them out of Germany. In May 1945 Admiral Doenitz (q.v.), who had succeeded Hitler, appointed him Reich Minister for Foreign Affairs in place of von Ribbentrop (q.v.), though the post had ceased to have any real meaning. On 2 April 1949 the Nuremberg International Military Tribunal sentenced Schwerin von Krosigk to ten years' imprisonment for war crimes. He was released in January 1951 from Landsberg prison and died the following year.

Seeckt, Hans von (1886–1936) Commander-in-Chief of the Reichswehr in its formative period from 1920 to 1926, Hans von Seeckt was born into a military family in Silesia on 22 April 1886. Appointed to the General Staff of the Prussian army in 1899, von Seeckt distinguished himself during World War I. Promoted to Major General in March 1915, he became Chief of Staff of the Austro-Hungarian Twelfth Army in June 1916 and the following year he was made Chief of Staff of the Turkish army. A member of the German peace delegation at Versailles, von Seeckt was promoted to Lieutenant-General in October 1919 and, from 1920 to October 1926, he was Chief of the Army Command. The monocled, trim, well-dressed Prussian officer, whose political sympathies were monarchist, maintained a cold, impersonal attitude to the republican régime, making no real effort to reconcile himself or the officer corps to the Weimar democracy. Under von Seeckt, the army became 'a State within a State' with its primary loyalty to the military rather than the political leadership, acting as a bridge between the old monarchical system and an as-yet undefined future State. Neutral during the Kapp *putsch* of 1920, von Seeckt used the army to suppress the threat of communist risings in Saxony, Thuringia, Hamburg and the Ruhr, and generally acted behind the scenes in favour of the right wing. Nevertheless, he ordered the armed forces in Bavaria to put down Hitler's attempted *putsch* in November 1923 and took steps to ensure the Republic against the Nazi movement. In the early phase of the movement the Nazis regarded von Seeckt as an enemy and a pawn of 'Judeo-Masonic' influences – his wife was a Jewess – though after 1930 the General allied himself openly with Hitler. Von Seeckt signed the agreement of 1926 permitting Luftwaffe pilots and German tank crews to train on Russian soil and generally favoured a pro-Russian, anti-Polish orientation in the Army High Command. He was dismissed on 8 October 1926 for having offered a military training post to the son of ex-Crown Prince Wilhelm and for having recognized duelling among army officers. After his election to the Reichstag in 1930, von Seeckt drew closer to the Nazis. He was senior military adviser to General Chiang Kai-Shek from May 1934 to March 1935, drafting a full-scale plan to develop a modern Chinese army and a modern arms industry in China. He died in Berlin on 29 December 1936.

Seldte, Franz (1882–1947) Founder of the *Stahlhelm* and Reich Minister of Labour from 1933 to 1945, Franz Seldte was born on 29 June 1882 in Magdeburg, the son of a merchant. After studying chemistry in Braunschweig, he took over his father's chemical factory and became a prosperous manufacturer. He fought at the front in an infantry regiment between 1914 and 1916, losing his left arm in combat and receiving the Iron Cross (First and Second Classes). In December 1918 he founded (together with Theodor Duesterberg, q.v.) the *Stahlhelm*, a nationalist veterans' organization which was to become the largest para-military group in Weimar Germany, along with the National Socialist storm troopers. Seldte called on ex-servicemen to fight against 'the slavery of the Versailles Diktat', demanded 'adequate *lebensraum*' for Germany and decried Marxist internationalism and pacifism as enemies of the nation. Under his leadership, the *Stahlhelm* aided and abetted the Nazi rise to power – in spite of some organizational rivalries – by consistently undermining the stability of the Weimar Republic. Following Hitler's appointment as Chancellor, Seldte became Reich Minister of Labour, a position he held until the collapse of Nazi Germany. Labour Minister for Prussia, a Prussian State Councillor, member of the Reichstag and, from March 1934, leader of the 'co-ordinated' National Socialist German Veterans' Organization, Seldte presided without demur over the dissolution of the *Stahlhelm* and faithfully served the Third Reich. He died in Fürth, Bavaria, on 1 April 1947.

Seydlitz, Walter von (1888–1976) Chief of Staff to Field Marshal von Paulus (q.v.) at Stalingrad where he was taken prisoner by the Red Army and later made President of the German Officers' League in Moscow, Walter von Seydlitz was born on 22 August 1888 in Hamburg, the descendant of a famous military family. After joining the army as a cadet in 1908, von Seydlitz fought in World War I on both the eastern and western fronts. From 1919 to 1930 he held various regimental and adjutant appointments before being transferred to the Reichswehr Ministry. Brigadier from 1934 to 1939, he was promoted to Major General at the outbreak of World War II and held a command in the French campaign. In August 1940 he was awarded the Knight's Cross (and was promoted to Lieutenant-General) for outstanding services during the Russian campaign. General of Infantry from June 1942 and Commander of the Second Army Corps, von Seydlitz was captured by Soviet forces at Stalingrad in February 1943 and in the same year became the first German officer to broadcast from Moscow. One of von Paulus's divisional commanders at Stalingrad and known as a violent opponent of the Nazi conduct of the war, von Seydlitz was appointed by the Russians as President of the 'League of German Officers' in September 1943. Its activities were identical to those of the Free Germany National Committee, formed in Soviet

Russia a year earlier. The aim was to persuade the German army and people to overthrow Hitler, to end the war and establish a 'free' democratic Germany. Many captured German officers and rank-and-file soldiers joined the movement between the autumn of 1943 and the summer of 1944. The failure of the plot of 20 July 1944 convinced the Russians that it had no further value. Von Seydlitz, though having served his purpose, was nevertheless held in prison by the Russians until October 1955. Even after twelve years' captivity he still found himself boycotted by some of the German generals who returned with him from Russia, and he had to wait another nine months until the death sentence passed on him *in absentia* by Hitler was finally annulled in July 1956. He died on 28 April 1976 in Bremen.

Seyss-Inquart, Arthur (1892–1946) Reich Governor of Austria (Ostmark) and then Reich Commissioner of the German-occupied Netherlands from 1940 to 1945, Arthur Seyss-Inquart was born in Stannern, near Iglau, in Moravia, on 22 July 1892, the son of a secondary school teacher. During World War I he served in the Tyrolean *Kaiserjaeger* (Imperial Chasseurs) and was seriously wounded. After 1918 he returned to Vienna, where he became a barrister after studying law at the University and was an enthusiastic advocate of *Anschluss* (Austrian union with Germany). In 1931 the intelligent, pleasant-mannered, ambitious young lawyer secretly joined the Austrian Nazi Party and in May 1937 he was appointed an Austrian State Councillor. During the next year, Seyss-Inquart was Hitler's Trojan Horse in Austria, the pro-Nazi quisling whom he used to pressurize the Chancellor, Schuschnigg (q.v.), and to undermine Austrian independence. Under German pressurize, Seyss-Inquart was appointed Austrian Minister of the Interior on 16 February 1938, with absolute control over the police and internal security. On 2 March 1938 Schuschnigg was forced to resign and though President Miklas at first refused to accept Seyss-Inquart as his Chancellor, he was forced to capitulate. The next day German troops entered Austria and Seyss-Inquart as the new Chancellor also took over presidential powers, forcing a law through Parliament whereby Austria ceased to exist as an independent State and became 'a province of the German Reich'. Promoted to SS Lieutenant-General on 15 March 1938 for his services towards the *Anschluss*, Seyss-Inquart remained Reich Governor of the Ostmark (Austria) until 30 April 1939.

After the setting up of the General Government of Poland on 12 October 1939, Seyss-Inquart was appointed deputy to the Nazi Governor, Hans Frank (q.v.). From May 1940 to 1945 he was Reich Commissioner in the occupied Netherlands where he was responsible for recruiting labour for deportation to Germany and for the rounding up of Dutch Jews. Under his rule the Dutch economy was made completely subservient to the German Reich and living standards declined. Extremely valuable works of art were confiscated and in 1943 textiles and consumer goods seized for the German population. Five million Dutchmen were sent as workers to the Reich and 117,000 out of the 140,000 Dutch Jews were deported to their deaths in Poland. Those Dutch Jews in mixed marriages were given the alternative of deportation to Auschwitz or sterilization, according to regulations approved by Seyss-Inquart on 28 June 1943. Summary justice was also meted out to Resistance elements and collective fines imposed on all Dutch cities where they were suspected to exist. Proposed as Foreign Minister by Hitler during the last days of his life in the *Führerbunker*, Seyss-Inquart was arrested in May 1945 by Canadian troops and tried at Nuremberg. He was found guilty of war crimes,

including direct responsibility for deportations and the shooting of hostages, and was executed in Nuremberg prison on 16 October 1946.

Skorzeny, Otto (1908–1975) Highly publicized commando leader whose daring exploits during World War II raised German morale, Otto Skorzeny was born in Vienna on 12 June 1908. After studying engineering and joining the *Freikorps*, he became a Nazi in 1930. A protégé of his compatriot Ernst Kaltenbrunner (q.v.), whom he had known at the time of the *Anschluss* in Vienna, Skorzeny joined the *SS-Leibstandarte* Adolf Hitler Regiment in Berlin in 1940 after being turned down for the Luftwaffe. After serving in France, the Netherlands and Russia, he was invalided home in December 1942, suffering from gallstones. At first given a desk job, he was transferred in April 1943 to *Amt* VI of the Reich Main Security Office and given charge of a special purposes commando unit, 'Oranienburg'. Skorzeny's task was to develop a school of warfare on 'commando' lines and to this end he studied British methods closely, especially the British attempt to kidnap Rommel (q.v.). His first missions in the Middle East and Russia failed because the General Staff was obstructive with supplies and the political leadership kept changing its mind. At the end of July 1943, Skorzeny was ordered by Hitler to rescue Mussolini, who was then a captive of the new Italian government which sought an armistice with the Allies. The difficult, enterprising raid was carried out on 12 September 1943, when glider-borne troops commanded by Skorzeny were landed on a small plateau in the Abruzzi mountains of Central Italy. The garrison of 250 soldiers guarding Mussolini who was located at the Hotel Camp Imperatore, in an almost inaccessible skiing resort, were taken by surprise and surrendered in a few minutes to Skorzeny's small force of ninety soldiers in gliders. Mussolini was carried off by Skorzeny in a light Storch aircraft after a remarkable take-off and arrived in Vienna the same evening. The cloak and dagger affair was turned into a great success by Goebbels's (q.v.) propaganda machine and Skorzeny was built up as a hero and the 'most dangerous man' in Europe.

Promoted to SS Major General, Skorzeny demonstrated his resourcefulness and quick thinking shortly after the 20 July plot, returning to Berlin to mobilize an SS special duties battalion and giving his support to officers loyal to Hitler. In the autumn of 1944, Skorzeny was called in again to kidnap the Hungarian Regent, Horthy, who was then planning to negotiate an armistice with the Russians. After another spectacular raid, 'Action Horthy' was brought to a successful conclusion and one more deposed Axis ruler was escorted back to Germany by Skorzeny on 17 October 1944. During the Ardennes offensive in December 1944 Skorzeny was given another bold assignment, 'Operation Greif', in which a special brigade consisting of 2,000 English-speaking Germans disguised as American soldiers were ordered to seize the Meuse bridgehead and cause chaos behind the Allied lines. Skorzeny's brigade was unable to hold on long enough to be relieved by the main German force and most of the infiltrators were unable to get back to their own lines, many of them being summarily shot. Nevertheless, the operation caused considerable confusion and a spy fever in the Allied ranks, even leading to the isolation of General Eisenhower for security reasons in case of a kidnap attempt.

At the end of the war Skorzeny served briefly as a divisional Commander in Bach-Zelewski's (q.v.) corps on the Oder front. He was eventually captured by American forces in Styria on 15 May 1945 and tried as a war criminal two years later. An American tribunal at Dachau acquitted him on 9 September 1947 of illegal practices during the Ardennes offensive, after a British officer testified that he had done nothing which his Allied counterparts had not themselves planned or attempted to carry out. After his release, Skorzeny was re-arrested by the German authorities, but escaped from an internment camp in 1948 and then founded a clandestine organisation called ODESSA to help ex-SS members to flee Germany. In 1951 he opened an import-export business agency in Madrid under the protection of the Franco régime and was involved in promoting business between German firms and the Spanish government. He was also a prominent figure in the post-war fascist and neo-Nazi International, trading on his notoriety as a highly publicized war-time adventurer. Skorzeny used his business cover in Spain to reorganize the escape routes for wanted Nazi criminals who had previously fled via Rome to the Catholic countries of Latin America with the help of a Vatican *laissez-passer*. He was able to buy in bulk a steady supply of valid Spanish passports, arrange for funds, set up the travel plans and provide cover stories. Skorzeny purchased a small hotel in Denia on the Spanish Mediterranean coast, from which an escape network to Africa and the Arab countries was established, as well as to South America. He also co-ordinated activities in West Germany with the Waffen-SS veterans' organization HIAG, the *Stahlhelm* and the *Deutscher Soldatenbund* (Federation of German Soldiers) to supply men and money for the escape routes, to press for the release of all war criminals and to orchestrate anti-war-guilt propaganda. At the end of the 1950s he became a landowner in Eire, buying a 170-acre farm where he bred horses and spent the summer months. He died in Madrid on 5 July 1975.

Sorge, Richard (1895–1944) German

journalist and highly effective Red Army spy in Tokyo during World War II, Richard Sorge was born in Baku, Russia, in 1895, the son of a mining engineer. He served in the German army on the western front during World War I and was seriously wounded. After studying at Berlin, Kiel and Hamburg, he became a member of the Communist Party and in 1929 he was made field Commander of Soviet military spies in the Far East, having set up his headquarters in Shanghai while working as the editor of a German news agency. After gaining useful experience in China, Sorge was sent to Japan in 1933 where his cover job was senior German correspondent of the *Frankfurter Zeitung*, the one important newspaper in the Third Reich still relatively independent of the Nazis. Sorge proceeded to establish the first major foreign spy ring in Japan's history, utilizing his excellent grasp of Japanese political affairs and culture to win access to the top diplomatic circles. His hand-picked Japanese collaborators were recipients of highly confidential information from cabinet sources. To strengthen his cover, Sorge posed successfully as a loyal Nazi and also worked as an espionage agent for the German embassy. He had considerable influence with the German Ambassador, Major General Ott, who even allowed him to draft reports to Berlin. Sorge reported to his communist masters in Moscow, by radio or by microfilms passed on through Shanghai or Hong Kong, on the state of preparedness of the Japanese armed forces, their dispositions and political role, on the progress of German-Japanese relations, on Japanese intentions towards China and on her relations with Britain and America. The Russians received advance information from Sorge on the Anti-Comintern pact of 1936 and the German-Japanese military pact four years later. He warned them of Japan's intention to attack the United States and

gave precise information in May 1941 on the German plan to invade the Soviet Union. He even predicted the date of the Nazi invasion to within two days, reporting that it would take place on 20 June 1941, yet the Russians remained in a state of complete military unpreparedness. Subsequently, it became vital for the Russians to know whether Japan's rapid military build-up was directed against themselves – thereby forcing them into a war on two fronts – or against America and Britain. At the end of August 1941 Sorge was able to tell Moscow that there would be no Japanese attack on the Soviet Union that year, a crucial piece of information at a time when the Russians were still close to collapse. Sorge and a Japanese assistant were arrested by police in Tokyo on 18 October 1941 just as the tide of battle in the USSR began to turn in the Russians' favour. He was held in prison for three years and then hanged on 7 November 1944.

Spann, Othmar (1878–1950) Leading ideologist and advocate of the corporate State in post-1918 German-speaking Europe, Othmar Spann was born in Vienna on 1 October 1878. A sociologist who pioneered the philosophy of Universalism (*Ganzheitslehre*), grounded in the 'idealist' tradition of Plato, medieval mysticism and the German romantics, Spann exercised a considerable intellectual influence on *völkisch* circles in Germany and Austria between the wars. A Professor at the University of Brünn between 1909 and 1918 (he was expelled by the Czechs) and in Vienna after World War I, Spann emerged in the 1920s as a semi-official Catholic social philosopher, opposed to the Versailles Treaty, Marxism and democracy and favouring the return to a hierarchically ordered *Ständestaat* (corporatist State). After 1928 he sought to provide the semi-fascist Heimwehr in Austria with a coherent ideology. His efforts were supported by handsome subsidies from the German steel magnate, Fritz Thyssen (q.v.), who approved his corporatist theories, and by Austrian mining interests. In 1929 Spann delivered the inaugural address to the *Kampfbund für Deutsche Kultur* (League of Struggle for German Culture) in the presence of Hitler, Rosenberg (founder of the organization) and other Nazi leaders. He called for a third way beyond democracy and Marxism which would reorganize German society on a corporate basis.

While the Nazis shared Spann's opposition to atomistic individualism, scientific rationalism and the class struggle, they regarded his 'Universalist' ideology as a theocratic, neo-scholastic, conservative doctrine of decay. Spann's hopes for a conservative revolution led by the Catholic camp were seen as an ultramontane attempt to revive the spirit of the medieval Holy Roman Empire, a static form of neo-feudal élitism incompatible with Nazi radicalism. Nevertheless, the National Socialists tolerated the theorizing of such *edelfascist* intellectuals as Spann and his circle, at least until the purge of June 1934 which made them superfluous in the eyes of the régime. Spann and his supporters tried to accommodate to this situation by moving closer to the Nazis after 1930 and acting as the Platonic Guardians of the spirit of a reborn German Reich. But though Spann actually praised the book-burnings of 1933, he nonetheless rejected the crude 'blood and soil' doctrines of nationalism, the biological racialism of the Nazis which he regarded as an offshoot of the age of materialism. Race was much less important than *Geist* (spirit) and, in the eyes of the Spann circle, the nation was essentially a spiritual community. Spann also rejected the biological theorizing of the Nazis on the Jewish question, naïvely believing in a 'clean', decent type of anti-semitism, more in keeping with his idealistic brand of authoritarian

thought. Spann and his followers proposed that German Jewry should be returned to a corporate ghetto of their own within the Third Reich, that they be allowed to live on German soil as wards of society, excluded from active participation in politics, the economy, intellectual and artistic activities. This excessively 'moderate' anti-semitism and Spann's insufferable pretensions to be *the* ideologist of the Third Reich led, after 1935, to open attacks on his theories in Nazi publications. After the annexation of Austria in March 1938, Spann and his son, Raphael, were arrested and sent to Dachau for several months. Maltreated during a Gestapo interrogation, the elder Spann suffered permanent eye damage as a result. He died in Neustift, Burgenland, on 8 July 1950.

Speer, Albert (1905–81)   Reich Minister for Armaments and War Production from 1942 to 1945, Albert Speer virtually controlled all German production during the later stages of the war and became for a while the second most important man in the Third Reich. Born on 19 March 1905 in Mannheim, the son of a prosperous upper-middle-class family of master builders (his father was one of the busiest architects in the city), Speer was educated at the Institute of Technology in Karlsruhe, completing his architectural studies in Munich and Berlin. It was at Berlin University that he first heard Hitler speak in 1930 and came under his hypnotic spell. In January 1931 he became a member of the National Socialist Party, denying, as he subsequently put it in his memoirs, 'my own past, my upper-middle-class origins and my previous environment'. Hitler appeared to the young Speer to offer the complete answer to communism and the political futility of the Weimar system. It was the personality of the Führer, rather than the Party itself (in which he was always something of an outsider), which attracted Speer, who was able through his close personal relationship with Hitler to realize all his youthful architectural ambitions, to design and build for a new order. In 1932 he received his first commissions from the NSDAP and after 1933 he was responsible for the designs and decorations used in the large Party rallies, beginning with the 1 May celebration on the Tempelhofer field. He perfected the Nazi style of public parades, the monumental liturgy of the movement, using inventive lighting effects and rapidly erected flagpoles with great skill to enhance the Reich Party rallies at Nuremberg. His organizing ability impressed Hitler who came to regard him as an 'architect of genius' and gave him a stream of projects to design, including the new Reich Chancellery in Berlin and the Party palace in Nuremberg.

Speer's artistic imagination and technological expertise appealed to the frustrated architect in Hitler, who in 1937 appointed him Inspector-General of the Reich, responsible for rebuilding Berlin and other German cities in the neo-classical, monumental style which he favoured. Speer's task was to convert the visions of a grandiose German Reich into an imposing architectural reality. In 1938, Speer, who already enjoyed the honorary title of Professor, was made a Prussian State Councillor and received the Nazi Golden Party Badge of Honour. A section leader of the German Labour Front, he also headed its 'Beauty of Labour' Department. In 1941 he was elected to represent the electoral district of Berlin West in the Reichstag. The many posts he held during the war included General Inspector of Water and Energy and head of the Party's main office for technology. From 1942 he was also a member of the Central Planning Office. In February 1942 he succeeded Fritz Todt (q.v.) as Minister of Armaments and War Production, demonstrating remarkable gifts as a manager of

industrial enterprises on a gigantic scale. During the next three years Speer was the greatest employer of manpower in Nazi Germany and performed miracles in rapidly expanding war production capacity in spite of massive Allied bombing attacks. Output was increased from 9,540 front-line machines and 2,900 heavy tanks in 1941 to 35,350 machines and 17,300 tanks in 1944 under Speer's relentless prodding and efficiency. In his role as Minister of Armaments, Speer not only kept the German military machine in the field – thereby prolonging the war by at least two years – he also showed no scruples in exploiting all the slave labour he could get his hands on. Nevertheless, in the final stages of the war, Speer became increasingly disillusioned with Hitler's policy of 'victory or annihilation' and tried to protect German industry from the Führer's orders to destroy all areas threatened by the advancing Allied armies.

Though he never sought contact with the conspirators of 20 July 1944, Speer did contemplate killing Hitler, then abandoned the project, attempting till the end to combat with rational argument the illusions of the fantasy world in the *Führerbunker*. Speer's loyalty to Hitler did not lead him to abandon his critical intelligence or independent will, though he continued to shelter behind the fiction of being a strictly 'non-political' specialist. In contrast to other Nazi leaders, Speer, however, did acknowledge the guilt of the régime when brought before the International Military Tribunal at Nuremberg in 1946. He recognized the inadmissibility of obeying orders as an excuse for serving a criminal State and admitted his personal responsibility for the slave labour in the factories under his authority and for his collaboration with the SS when it provided concentration camp prisoners for his production lines.

Speer was found guilty of war crimes against humanity, but it was recognized in mitigation that '... in the closing stages of the war he was one of the few men who had the courage to tell Hitler that the war was lost and to take steps to prevent the senseless destruction of production facilities'. Speer was sentenced to twenty years' imprisonment on 30 September 1946 and the Russians (who had voted to hang him) kept him to the full term. He was released from Spandau prison in 1966. During his imprisonment, Speer wrote the first draft of his best-selling memoirs, *Inside the Third Reich* (published in 1970), which gave a detailed, dispassionate account of his years at Hitler's side and the rivalries within the Nazi hierarchy. One of the most impressive descriptions of the inner workings of the Third Reich, it strengthened the view of many historians that Speer was a man of integrity and honour in comparison with the criminal leaders who were his associates. His personal qualities notwithstanding, Speer was the prototype of the intellectual technocrat without whose efficient and loyal service the modern totalitarian State could never have consummated its lawless acts of violence. He died in a London hospital on 1 September 1981 during a visit to Great Britain.

Speidel, Hans (1897–1984) Wehrmacht General who was Rommel's (q.v.) last Chief of Staff in France, Hans Speidel was born on 28 October 1897 in Matzingen, Württemberg. A professional soldier who served as an active officer from 1914 to 1944, Speidel became involved in the plot against Hitler after being called to France by his old friend, Rommel, to take charge of Army Group B. Appointed on 14 June 1940 Chief of Staff of the Military Governor of Paris, General Heinrich von Stuelpnagel (q.v.), Speidel worked closely with him to draw Rommel into their plans, in the belief that the war was lost and Germany was heading for inevitable catastrophe. Fol-

lowing the failure of the July 1944 plot, Speidel was removed from his post in France and interrogated by the Gestapo, but denied all knowledge of the conspiracy. He was acquitted by a court of honour and thus avoided the fate of other members of the Resistance movement. In 1949 he published *Invasion 1944. Ein Beitrag zu Rommels und des Reiches Schicksal*, a glorification of Field Marshal Rommel, which provided a detailed account of the political conspiracy and an outspoken condemnation of Hitler's lack of moral principles. According to Speidel, the rank-and-file in the army as well as the leaders had full confidence in Rommel's rather than in Hitler's leadership and supported the conspiracy. After the war, General Speidel became Konrad Adenauer's (q.v.) military adviser. He represented the Federal Republic of Germany in NATO and in November 1959 he was appointed head of the Army Department in the Federal Defence Ministry. From April 1957 to September 1963 he was Commander of all NATO forces in central Europe. He retired on 21 March 1964 and henceforth concentrated on his academic work at Tübingen and his writing in the field of military science. Hans Speidel died in Bad Honnef on 28 November 1984.

Spengler, Oswald (1880–1936) Cultural historian and an intellectual forerunner of the Third Reich who ended up as a critic of Nazism, Oswald Spengler was born in Blankenburg, Harz, on 25 September 1880. From 1908 to 1911 he was a senior high school teacher in Hamburg and then a freelance writer in Munich. His most famous work, *Der Untergang des Abendlandes* (*The Decline of the West*), was originally conceived in 1911 as a critique of German foreign policy in the late Wilhelminian era. Spengler expanded the scope of the book to create a new cyclical philosophy of history (*the* 'philosophy of the future' as he claimed), a morphology of culture whose inspiration derived from Goethe and Nietzsche. Combining dazzling erudition in the fields of history, politics, art, mathematics and the physical sciences, Spengler prophesied the drying up of western cultural productivity and the emergence of a new age of Caesarism, dominated by the ruthless competition of power politics, high technology and social organization. The choice for the West, and in particular for Germany, was 'to stand fast or go under – there is no third way'. The decline of the West had begun in the nineteenth century, an age of materialism, formlessness, perpetual warfare and mass democracy, which Spengler hated. The downward curve of a decaying megalopolitan civilization could, however, be arrested by a return to Prussian traditions of leadership and organization.

Spengler's two historical volumes, published between 1918 and 1922, made a tremendous impression, coming as they did in the wake of the German defeat. In subsequent political polemics like *Preussentum und Sozialismus* (1920), which called for an alliance between classical Prussianism and the non-Marxist working-class élite, Spengler tried to persuade public opinion in the direction of the 'conservative revolution'. As a severe critic of the Weimar Republic and liberal parliamentary democracy (which he considered an imported English ideology alien to German tradition), Spengler supplied the radical Right and the Nazis with powerful ammunition and helped create a mood favourable to their ascent to power. In 1933 Spengler published *Jahre der Entscheidung* (*Years of Decision*), which welcomed the national revolution as a liberation of 'the deepest instincts in our blood'. But though, initially, he saw in National Socialism a 'mighty phenomenon', he was quickly disillusioned by Hitler and by the Nazi racial doctrines which he regarded as childish nonsense.

Spengler openly rejected the violent anti-semitism of the Nazis, remaining one of the very few right-wing thinkers who favoured the assimilation of the Jews. The Nazis, in turn, objected to Spengler's pessimistic determinism, to his conservative élitism and his evident disdain for the *Volk*. Increasingly he found himself isolated in the new German Reich which he had prophesied, out of touch and unable to identify with the goals of its political leadership. He died in Munich on 8 May 1936.

Sperrle, Hugo (1885–1953) General Field Marshal and air force commander, Hugo Sperrle was born on 7 February 1885 in Ludwigsburg, Württemberg, the son of a brewer. An officer in the Württemberg infantry, he was promoted to First Lieutenant in 1913 and transferred to a military academy. During World War I he served in the air force and in 1919 commanded the air detachment of a *Freikorps*. In 1925 he was appointed to the Reichswehr Ministry and between 1929 and 1933 held various regimental commands. Transferred back to the air force and appointed Brigadier in 1935 in command of *Luftkreis* V, Munich, Sperrle became one of the leading figures in the Luftwaffe. In 1936–7 he led the Condor Legion (the German interventionist force during the Spanish Civil War), letting loose his bombers on Guernica and other Spanish towns and villages. In November 1937 he was rewarded with promotion to the rank of General of Fliers. The following year he was made Commander of Air Force Group 3, based in Munich. Involved in the air attacks on France, Sperrle was awarded the Knight's Cross in May 1940 and in July of the same year he was appointed General Field Marshal of the air force. In charge of air operations against Great Britain during 1940–1, he emphasized the need to defeat the Royal Air Force if German bombers were to launch successful attacks on British targets. After commanding all the air forces in North Africa, in support of Rommel's (q.v.) Afrika Korps, Sperrle was put in charge of the anti-invasion air forces in western Europe in 1944 which were expecting an Allied landing in Normandy. He set up his headquarters in the Palais du Luxembourg in Paris, a former palace of Marie de Medici. The Armaments Minister, Albert Speer (q.v.), after a visit to his headquarters, commented in retrospect: 'The Field Marshal's craving for luxury and public display ran a close second to that of his superior Goering; he was also his match in corpulence.' Tried at the end of the war, the massively built Sperrle was acquitted of all war crimes by the Allied court at Nuremberg. He died in Munich, where he was buried on 7 April 1953.

Srbik, Heinrich Ritter von (1874–1951) Leading Austrian historian and President of the Academy of Science in Vienna after the *Anschluss*, Heinrich Ritter von Srbik was born in Vienna on 10 November 1874. The son of an Austrian civil servant and a Westphalian mother, von Srbik was raised in a Catholic home and educated at the Theresian Academy. After studying at the University of Vienna, he was assistant at the Institute of Austrian History from 1904 to 1912. From 1907 to 1912 he also lectured at the University of Vienna and was then appointed Professor in Graz. In 1922 he returned to Vienna where he was Professor of History until the fall of the Third Reich. From 1929 to 1930 Heinrich Ritter von Srbik was Minister of Education in the Schober cabinet. He established his reputation as a historian with a two-volume biography, *Metternich, der Staatsman und der Mensch*, published in 1925 (the third volume appeared posthumously in 1954), and edited *Quellen zur Deutschen Politik Oesterreichs 1859–1866*, a five-volume sourcebook, published between 1934 and 1938. In his historical works, von

Srbik was preoccupied with the failure of the Germans to achieve a harmonious unity between the concepts of nation, State, empire and territorial sovereignty. His world-view was too rooted in the universalism of the Habsburg Empire to make him a fully fledged National Socialist, but he nonetheless regarded the *Anschluss* as the fulfilment of all his hopes. Much publicized in the Nazi press, von Srbik proved an eager fellow-traveller, putting himself at the disposal of the Nazi régime as a member of the Reichstag in 1938. In the same year he became President of the German Historical Commission and from 1938 to 1945 he was President of the Academy of Science in Vienna. In 1943 he was rewarded with the Goethe Medal for his services to German historiography and continued to produce historical works until the end of the Third Reich. After 1945 he retired to the Tyrol, where he died at Ehrwald on 16 February 1951.

Stangl, Franz (1908–71) Commander of Treblinka extermination camp in occupied Poland from 1942 to 1943, Franz Stangl was born in Altmünster, Austria, on 26 March 1908, the son of a nightwatchman who had once served in the Habsburg Dragoons. After training as a master-weaver, Stangl joined the Austrian police force in 1931, graduating two years later. In 1935 he was transferred to the political division of the criminal investigation department in the small Austrian town of Wels and a year later he appears to have become a member of the illegal Nazi Party. In November 1940 Stangl became Police Superintendent of the notorious Euthanasia Institute at Schloss Hartheim, where the mentally and physically handicapped and also political prisoners from concentration camps were transferred for liquidation. In March 1942, after being sent to Lublin to report to his fellow-Austrian, Lieutenant-General Odilo Globocnik (q.v.), Stangl was given charge of Sobibor death camp, which became operational in May 1942. During Stangl's period as Commandant, which lasted until September 1942 when he was transferred to Treblinka, approximately 100,000 Jews were killed. Following his arrival at Treblinka, the largest of the five Nazi extermination camps in occupied Poland, Stangl proved himself a highly efficient and dedicated organizer of mass murder, even receiving an official commendation as the 'best camp commander in Poland'. Always impeccably dressed (he attended the unloading of transports at Treblinka dressed in white riding clothes), soft-voiced, polite and friendly, Stangl was no sadist, but took pride and pleasure in his 'work', running the death camp like clockwork. He came to regard his victims as 'cargo' to be despatched, recalling in an interview at the end of his life with the journalist Gitta Sereny that he rarely saw them as individuals – 'it was always a huge mass ... they were naked, packed together, running, being driven with whips. ....' Stangl claimed that his dedication had nothing to do with ideology or hatred of Jews. 'They were so weak; they allowed everything to happen, to be done to them. They were people with whom there was no common ground, no possibility of communication – that is how contempt is born. I could never understand how they could just give in as they did.' Soon after the revolt at Treblinka on 2 August 1943 (which contradicted Stangl's convenient rationalizations), SS Captain Stangl was transferred to Trieste to help organize the campaign against Yugoslav partisans.

His next assignment was in Italy as a special supply officer to the *Einsatz Poll*, a strategic construction project in the Po Valley, involving some half a million Italian workers under German command. In 1945 Stangl was captured by the Americans and interned as a member of the SS who had been involved in anti-partisan activities in Yugoslavia and Italy, his earlier record in Poland not being known at the time. He was handed over to the Austrians and transferred to an open, civilian prison in Linz in late 1947 in connection with his involvement in the euthanasia programme at Schloss Hartheim. Stangl simply walked out of the prison and managed to escape to Italy with his Austrian colleague, Gustav Wagner (q.v.), where he was helped by Bishop Hudal and the Vatican network to escape via Rome on a Red Cross passport, with an entrance visa for Syria. In 1948 he arrived in Damascus where he worked for three years as a mechanical engineer in a textile mill and was joined by his wife and family.

In 1951 the Stangls emigrated to Brazil, where he was given an engineering job and after 1959 he worked at a Volkswagen factory, still using his own name. Only in 1961 did his name appear on the official Austrian list of 'Wanted Criminals', though for years his responsibility in the deaths of nearly a million men, women and children had been known to the Austrian authorities. Tracked down by Nazi-hunter Simon Wiesenthal, Stangl was arrested in Brazil on 28 February 1967. After extradition to West Germany, he was tried for co-responsibility in the mass murder of 900,000 Jews at Treblinka and sentenced to life imprisonment on 22 October 1970. He died of heart failure in Düsseldorf prison on 28 June 1971.

Stark, Johannes (1874–1951) Nobel Prize winner in Physics and head of the *Deutsche Forschungsgemeinschaft* (the State organization supporting scientific research) under the Nazis, Johannes Stark was born on the family estate at Schickenhof, near Weiden in the Upper Palatinate, on 15 April 1874. After receiving his doctorate in physics from the University of Munich in 1897, he went to Göttingen three years later and lectured there until 1906. In 1909 he was appointed full Professor at Aachen.

During this period Stark corresponded freely with Albert Einstein (q.v.) and was one of the earliest proponents of modern physical concepts such as the light quanta hypothesis. In 1913 he discovered what came to be known as the 'Stark effect', the splitting of spectral lines in an electric field, and six years later he was awarded the Nobel Prize for Physics in recognition of his work on electro-magnetism. Professor at the University of Würzberg from 1920 to 1922, Stark had to resign his chair as a result of his angry polemics against Einstein and the theory of relativity. His scathing attack on the physics community, *Die Gegenwärtige Krisis in der Deutschen Physik (The Present Crisis in German Physics*, 1922), which rejected not only the relativity theory but also the Bohr-Sonnenfeld quantum theories as 'dogmatic', increasingly isolated Stark among German physicists and drove him out of academic life for eleven years. Stark's status as an intellectual pariah, his acute sense of victimization and his combative nature drove him into the arms of the *völkisch* movement and as early as 1924 he declared his allegiance to Hitler.

Racism became a weapon against those who had cast him out of academia, and Stark's deep aversion to theory found expression in his attacks on 'Jewish' physics as being unconcerned with the observation of facts, with experiment or scientific objectivity. Stark joined the Nazi Party on 1 April 1930 and, together with Philipp Lenard (q.v.), was the foremost physicist to try to integrate natural science into the Nazi world-view. After Hitler's rise to power, Stark attempted to reorganize German physics under Nazi leadership and to gain control over the direction of scientific research. As President of the Imperial Institute of Physics and Technology from 1933 to 1939 and of the *Deutsche Forschungsgemeinschaft* until 1936, Stark outspokenly denounced theoretical physics, stressing the importance of applied research for technology, industry, economic self-sufficiency and war production. According to Stark in his *Nationalsozialismus und Wissenschaft* (1934), the scientist's first duty was to the nation and leading scientific positions in the Nazi State could only be occupied by nationally conscious, ethnic Germans. Exact, disinterested observation of natural phenomena was, according to Stark, a function of the Nordic racial soul, 'overwhelmingly a creation of the Nordic-Germanic blood components of the Aryan peoples'. Jewish scientists, on the other hand, were depicted as egocentric, born advocates 'unencumbered by regard for truth', mixing facts and imputations, concerned with formal exposition and above all 'interested in self-advertisement and commercial exploitation' of their work. Lacking, according to Stark, the aptitude for true creative activity in the natural sciences, 'the dogmatic zeal and propagandistic drive of the Jewish scientist leads him to report on his achievements not only in scientific journals but also in the daily press and on lecture tours'.

Similarly racist arguments were advanced in Stark's *Jüdische und Deutsche Physik* (1941), but by this time Stark's influence on the German physics community had greatly declined. Not only had he violated the accepted professional values and undermined the scientific standing of German physics, he had also managed to antagonize the Reich Minister for Science, Education and Culture, Bernhard Rust (q.v.), the SS and various Party agencies. Caught up in intra-Party intrigues, Stark made the fatal mistake of choosing Alfred Rosenberg (q.v.) as his patron and suffered the consequences as the latter's influence declined. During his trial in Bavaria after the end of the war, some of the top German physicists, including von Laue (q.v.), Heisenberg (q.v.) and Sommerfeld, testified against

Stark. On 20 July 1947 he was found guilty as a 'Major Offender' and sentenced to four years' hard labour. The classification was later reduced and his sentence suspended. Stark died in Traunstein on 21 June 1951.

Stauffenberg, Claus Schenk Graf von (1907–44) Chief of Staff to the Commander of the Reserve Army and the key figure in the attempted assassination of Hitler on 20 July 1944, Claus von Stauffenberg was born in Greifenstein Castle, Upper Franconia, on 15 November 1907, the descendant of a long line of military aristocrats. On his mother's side he was a great-grandson of the Prussian General von Gneisenau, one of the heroes of the German War of Liberation against Napoleon, and he was also related to another celebrated general of the period, Yorck von Wartenburg. His father was Privy Chamberlain to the last king of Württemberg, and the young von Stauffenberg grew up in a cultivated and devoutly Roman Catholic family atmosphere. Handsome, brilliant, with a passion for the arts and literature as well as horses and sports, von Stauffenberg was strongly influenced in his youth by the poetic mysticism of Stefan George. Nevertheless, he opted for a military career, joining the army as an officer cadet in 1926 in the famous *Bamberger Reiter*, the Seventeenth Bamberg Cavalry Regiment. A monarchist in his early years and a profound believer in the rebirth of Germany's grandeur, von Stauffenberg was not initially anti-Nazi, though doubts in his mind were sown by the Crystal Night anti-Jewish pogrom and later reinforced by his experiences. Von Stauffenberg's devout Catholicism also contributed to his growing conviction that Hitler was the incarnation of evil and that the Nazi régime must be liquidated to preserve Germany's honour and save it from destruction. Posted to the War Academy in Berlin in 1936 and promoted to the

General Staff two years later, von Stauffenberg served with distinction as a staff officer in General Hoepner's (q.v.) Sixteenth Panzer Division during the Polish and French campaigns. Transferred to the Army High Command in June 1940, his disillusionment came during the Russian invasion where he was sickened by the brutality of the SS and the mass slaughter of Jews, Russians and prisoners of war.

His experiences in the Soviet Union, where he was responsible for recruiting Russian prisoners of war, turned him into a socialist and it was under his influence that the German Resistance took on a leftist slant and, for a time, a pro-Russian orientation. After he had made contact in Russia with Henning von Tresckow (q.v.) and Fabian von Schlabrendorff, von Stauffenberg quickly became one of the leading conspirators, concentrating on building up an organization that could take over power once Hitler had been removed. Not satisfied with the conservative, colourless régime envisaged by Beck (q.v.), Goerdeler (q.v.) and Hassell (q.v.), he favoured a new dynamic social democracy and was politically closer to the socialist Julius Leber (q.v.), whom he advocated as the Chancellor of a post-Hitler Germany. Posted in February 1943 to Tunisia as Operations Officer of the Tenth Panzer Division, von Stauffenberg was gravely wounded on 7 April of the same year when he walked into a minefield, losing his left eye, his right hand, half of his left hand and part of his leg. For a time it seemed he might be totally blinded, but he was restored to life at a Munich hospital by the famous physician, Dr Ferdinand Sauerbruch (q.v.). During his recovery, von Stauffenberg resolved to put his qualities of will, energy, military flair and clarity of mind wholly at the disposal of the Resistance and to remove Hitler at all costs. Convinced that the war was lost and determined not to allow Hitler to drag the army and the Fatherland down with him to the tomb, von Stauffenberg devised the 'Valkyrie' plans to assassinate Hitler and set up a military government in Berlin, which would immediately neutralize the most dangerous Nazi organizations: the Gestapo, the SS and SD.

After his recovery, von Stauffenberg was posted back to Berlin and appointed Chief of Staff to General Olbricht (q.v.), Deputy Commander of the Reserve Army. This gave him access to important secret information concerning the military and political operations of the German army, which he utilized in drawing up his plans for seizing power and preparing a necessary network of action. In June 1944 he was promoted to Lieutenant-Colonel and made Chief of Staff to General Fromm (q.v.), the head of the Reserve Army, which gave him an official reason for visiting Hitler's headquarters. He was chosen to carry out the assassination since he was the only conspirator who could attend Hitler's staff conferences without being searched. It was arranged that he would kill Hitler, together with Goering (q.v.) and Himmler (q.v.), at Berchtesgaden on 2 July 1944, but as the Führer was alone the attempt was called off; another plan on 15 July was also postponed. Finally, von Stauffenberg resolved to take the next opportunity even if Himmler and Goering were absent, before the Allies could win a decisive victory in Normandy which would still further weaken the chances for a compromise peace. On 20 July he attended a meeting at Hitler's headquarters in Rastenburg, East Prussia, carrying a bomb in his briefcase. It was detonated to go off ten minutes after he had deposited it unobtrusively against the table support in the map room where Hitler and his chiefs were discussing the military situation. As previously arranged, von Stauffenberg was called away to the telephone, made his way to the exit, passed through two checkpoints after the explosion had taken place and succeeded in reaching Berlin by plane, convinced that Hitler was dead.

Unfortunately, when the bomb exploded, it was farther from the Führer than intended, the briefcase having been moved by one of the officers present after von Stauffenberg's departure. Though four officers were killed and seven seriously wounded, Hitler suffered only minor injuries. The fellow conspirators in Berlin made only half-hearted efforts to execute the *coup d'état*, uncertain whether Hitler was dead or alive. Moreover, von Stauffenberg's associate at Hitler's headquarters failed to sabotage the communications centre, enabling the Führer to learn what was happening in Berlin and a broadcast to be made confirming that he had survived the assassination attempt. Goebbels (q.v.) in Berlin was able to act against the conspirators, who had lost precious time in consolidating their positions, and General Fromm, head of the Reserve Army as well as von Stauffenberg's superior, refused to join the *coup*. After some confusion following his own arrest, Fromm alerted a group of his staff, loyal to the régime, who quickly arrested von Stauffenberg after an exchange of gunfire in which he was wounded. A drumhead court-martial was set up by General Fromm; von Stauffenberg and others, including Olbricht, were taken downstairs into the courtyard of the War Ministry in Berlin, stood up against the wall in the light of a lorry's headlamps and shot. Von Stauffenberg's last words before the bullets hit their mark were: 'Long live our sacred Germany'.

Steinhoff, Hans (1882–1945) Bavarian film director born in Pfafenhoden, Munich, on 10 March 1882, Hans Steinhoff abandoned his medical studies to become a theatre actor and director, before embarking on a new career in the cinema in 1922. A prolific, if frequently mediocre film maker (more than forty productions), whose choice of themes under the Third Reich was often dictated by opportunism, Steinhoff became widely known as the director of the first Nazi film, *Hitlerjunge Quex*, the story of the Hitler Youth martyr Heinz Norkus. Made in 1933 at the dawn of the Third Reich, at a time when the Nazi dictatorship was not yet firmly consolidated, the film is interesting chiefly as a document of the prevailing mood of the times and Nazi readiness to integrate the communists into the national community. Steinhoff's other films tended to be on the heavy side, grandiloquent but lacking in imagination, though his cinematic biographies, *Robert Koch* (1939), *Ohm Krüger* (1941) and *Rembrandt* (1942), were not devoid of merit. The *Krüger* film, which starred Emil Jannings (q.v.) in the title role, denounced English barbarity and the concentration camps in the Transvaal at the end of the nineteenth century, being screened at the very time that Hitler was preparing for his 'Final Solution of the Jewish Question' in Europe. One of the best Nazi films from the technical standpoint, it was highly recommended for its 'political and artistic value' by Goebbels (q.v.) and was awarded the prize as the outstanding foreign film at the Venice Biennale (1941). Steinhoff died in an aeroplane accident at Luckenwalde in 1945.

Stinnes, Hugo (1870–1924) German magnate who emerged after World War I as the country's leading industrialist and was an early financial backer of the Nazis, Hugo Stinnes was born in Mühlheim on 2 February 1870. The prototype of the Ruhr business tycoon who regarded the State as an appendage to his own interests and politics as an extension of economics by other means, Stinnes entered the Reichstag in 1920 as a delegate of the German *Volkspartei*

(People's Party). Stinnes's financial empire included coal mines, coal depots, iron and steel factories, shipping vessels, hotels and newspapers – and he was the leading figure in the *Rheinisch-Westfälische Elektrizitätswerk AG*, which supplied electricity and gas to many towns in Rhineland-Westphalia. After his death in Berlin on 10 April 1924, the business conducted by his sons ran into serious difficulties and had to be liquidated, and a new company was formed in 1925 with the Stinnes family retaining a 40 per cent interest. The eldest son, Hugo Stinnes (born 1897), still controlled vast enterprises including coal mines, Rhine and sea shipping lanes, a glass factory, chemical and hydrogenation plants which produced aviation fuel, and engineering industries employing a large work-force that included foreign workers and prisoners of war. It was alleged that Stinnes was one of the chief beneficiaries of the 'Aryanization' programme introduced by the Nazis after their takeover and there is no doubt that he complied with government directives not to employ Jews in his concerns. Taken into custody by the British occupation authorities in the summer of 1945, Stinnes's links with the Nazi Party could not be clearly established. In June 1948 he was freed under the de-Nazification law.

Strasser, Gregor (1892–1934) Leader of the social-revolutionary North German wing of the Nazi Party and Hitler's most dangerous rival in the early days of the movement, Gregor Strasser was born on 31 May 1892 at Geisenfeld, Lower Bavaria. He was awarded the Iron Cross (First and Second Classes) for his service during World War I as a volunteer in the First Bavarian Field Artillery Regiment. An apothecary by profession, Strasser joined the Epp *Freikorps*, whose aim was to suppress communism in Bavaria, and was active in the Lower Bavarian storm battalion (his adjutant was the young Heinrich Himmler, q.v.), placing it under General Ludendorff's (q.v.) military command. Strasser joined the NSDAP as a storm trooper and commanded an SA detachment during the 1923 Beer-Hall *putsch*, which led to a brief spell of imprisonment. His election in the spring of 1924 to the Bavarian legislature freed him from Landsberg prison and he became co-Chairman of the National Socialist Party together with Ludendorff, excluding 'Old Fighters' like Streicher (q.v.) and Esser (q.v.) and checking the influence of personal enemies like Goering (q.v.) and Röhm (q.v.). During Hitler's imprisonment, Strasser's indefatigable organizational talents enabled the Nazis for the first time to make headway in northern Germany and to found an organization independent from Munich headquarters. Together with his brother, Otto Strasser (q.v.), he founded a weekly newspaper, the *Berliner Arbeiterzeitung* (Berlin Workers' Paper), the fortnightly Nazi newsletter, *NS-Briefe,* for which he hired the young Joseph Goebbels (q.v.) as editor, and his own independent party press, the *Kampfverlag.*

As a member of the NSDAP Reichstag group, which he dominated at this time, Strasser utilized his freedom of action and parliamentary immunity to challenge what he regarded as Hitler's abandonment of the 'socialist' ideals of the movement. In 1926 he opposed Hitler's proposals concerning a plebiscite about grants to deposed princes and, at the Bamberg Party Congress in the same year, the Strasser brothers argued that Nazism must devote itself to the destruction of capitalism, to social justice and the nationalization of the economy. Until his death Gregor Strasser was to insist on the expropriation of the banks and heavy industry and to oppose Hitler's alliance with the Junker nationalists, with the reactionary army leadership and conservative politicians like Hugenberg (q.v.), von Papen

(q.v.) and Schacht (q.v.). Strasser's proletarian anti-capitalism was, however, primarily a means to an end – the establishing of an organic, *völkisch* community and of a new social order which he called 'State feudalism' where the industrial estate would be at the top of the heap. His eclectic socialist programme, which also advocated an alliance with Bolshevik Russia and the anti-imperialist East against the western democracies, essentially aimed at precipitating the downfall of the existing social order.

Gregor Strasser once defined National Socialism as 'the opposite of what exists today'. Between 1926 and 1932 Strasser was Reich Propaganda Leader of the NSDAP and in June 1932 Hitler made him *Reichsorganisationsleiter* of the Party. The rift between them grew, however, when on 7 December 1932 the new Chancellor, General von Schleicher (q.v.), offered Strasser the post of Vice-Chancellor and Prime Minister of Prussia. Strasser, who did not want to split the Party, nonetheless advocated Nazi toleration of von Schleicher's cabinet, which infuriated Hitler who had insisted that he refuse the offer. Strasser gave way and angrily resigned all his Party posts at the end of 1932, a defection which deeply shook Hitler, who feared he was losing his grip on the Party. Strasser left politics, living quietly as the Director of a chemical combine, and was not offered a post in the new Nazi government. On 30 June 1934 he was arrested and murdered on Hitler's orders by the Gestapo, during the Night of the Long Knives. His death and that of the SA leader, Ernst Röhm (q.v.), symbolized the destruction of the Nazi left wing and the vague hopes for a second revolution in the direction of socialism.

Strasser, Otto (1897–1974)   One of the leaders of the revolutionary 'socialist' wing of the NSDAP and younger brother of Gregor Strasser (q.v.), Otto was born in Windsheim on 10 September

1897. After studying law and following a brief period as a Social Democrat, Otto Strasser joined the Nazi Party in 1925 and helped build up a radical, proletarian wing of the movement in North Germany, together with his older brother and the young Goebbels (q.v.). Supporting certain strikes of the Social Democratic trade unions and demanding the nationalization of industry as well as the big banks, Strasser also favoured an alliance with Bolshevik Russia and the revolutionary 'coloured' peoples of the East (China, India, etc.) against the 'declining' West. He stood by the NSDAP's original twenty-five-point programme, emphasizing its socialist content which he took seriously. This brought him on a collision course with Hitler, whom he regarded as having betrayed the original ideals of the National Socialist movement. In 1926 Otto Strasser was made editor of the *Berliner Arbeiterzeitung* and the *National Socialist Letters*, also becoming propaganda chief of the North German wing of the Party. As head of the *Kampfverlag* (Militant Publishers) in Berlin, he controlled an important outlet for disseminating his anti-capitalist ideology, which increasingly embarrassed Hitler in his own efforts to woo and win over the industrialists.

The showdown came on 21–22 May 1930 in a confrontation between the two Nazi leaders over the issue of capitalism and socialism. Otto Strasser refused to submit and was expelled from the Party on 4 July 1930. Six weeks later he formed the break-away Union of Revolutionary National Socialists, known as the Black Front, but it failed to win away Nazi votes from Hitler, even though Otto Strasser claimed a membership of ten thousand. Strasser and some of his followers went into exile in Prague, where they produced a fortnightly paper, *Die Deutsche Revolution*, which attacked Hitler's dictatorship but continued to defend the theory of National Socialism. The Strasser left wing of Nazism was no less racist and antisemitic than its adversaries. In his 'Fourteen Theses of the German Revolution', Otto Strasser proclaimed that it was a German duty to develop 'unique racial individuality' and resist the 'cultural predominance of alien Jewry', which in association with 'the supranational powers of freemasonry and political Catholicism, was either compelled by its racial make-up or driven by its wanton will to destroy the life of the German soul'. Nonetheless, as an articulate opponent of Hitler, Strasser published a stream of books and pamphlets during his exile attacking the political system of the Third Reich and the Führer's betrayal of Nazi ideals. These works included *Die Deutsche Bartholomäusnacht* (1935), which dealt with the Blood Purge that had taken the lives of Röhm (q.v.), the SA leaders and his own brother. Further writings such as *Wohin treibt Hitler?* (1936), *Aufbau des Deutschen Sozialismus* (1936), *Europäische Föderation* (1936), *Kommt es zum Krieg?* (1937), *Europa von Morgen* (1939), *Hitler and I* (1940), *Germany Tomorrow* (1940), *The Gangsters around Hitler* (1942) and *Flight from Terror* (1943) contained a vision of European federation as well as his own reckoning with the past and present. During his exile in Switzerland and Canada, Otto Strasser became an advocate of 'solidarism', a third path between capitalism and communism, which he gave a national-socialist, Christian and decentralized 'Europeanist' colouring. Returning to post-war West Germany, Otto Strasser tried and failed to win public support for these ideas in the 1950s after he had recovered his German citizenship. In other respects he appeared to have learned nothing from the past, still espousing a vicious, demagogic anti-semitism in his journalistic publications. He died in Munich on 27 August 1974.

Strauss, Richard (1864–1949) President of the Reich Chamber of Music from 1933 to 1935 and the most prominent composer to remain in Nazi Germany, Richard Strauss was born in Munich on 2 June 1864, the son of one of the finest French-horn virtuosos of the age. A musical child prodigy, Strauss was engaged in 1885 as assistant to the great conductor, Hans von Bülow, at Meiningen. A year later he was appointed junior conductor at the Munich Opera and within three more years he had already performed at Bayreuth and become a protégé of Cosima Wagner. Before he was thirty, Strauss had won international fame with symphonic poems like the exuberant *Don Juan, Tod und Verklärung* and *Till Eulenspiegel*. In 1898 he was made Royal Prussian Court Conductor in Berlin. By the turn of the century he had not only performed successfully in most West European capitals but was widely recognized as the greatest German composer since Wagner and Brahms. For all his phenomenal success, the young Strauss was a revolutionary innovator and iconoclast who shocked contemporaries with the harsh dissonances of some of his early orchestral works, the deliberate ugliness and macabre eroticism of operas like *Salome* (1905), drawn from the text of Oscar Wilde. With *Elektra* (1909), Strauss began his twenty-year collaboration with the famous Viennese poet and librettist, Hugo von Hofmannsthal. Their greatest success, *Der Rosenkavalier* (1911), a gay, melodious, sensual baroque comedy, brought Strauss to the pinnacle of his fame and popularity. In 1919 Strauss followed in Mahler's wake as Director of the Vienna Opera (a post he held until 1924), but though as productive as ever, his music increasingly lacked the daring, energy and vitality of his youth. Nevertheless, the premières of all his later operas, *Die Frau ohne Schatten* (1919), *Intermezzo* (1924), *Die Ägyptische Helena* (1928) and *Arabella*

(1933), were major events and, under the Weimar Republic, Strauss enjoyed an Olympian status, comparable only to that of Gerhart Hauptmann (q.v.) in the field of drama.

When the Nazis seized power in Germany, Strauss, although no National Socialist, showed little awareness of the implications, lending his name, prestige and fame to the régime and accepting in 1933 the position of head of the Reich Chamber of Music. He agreed to take the place of the exiled Bruno Walter as guest conductor of the Berlin Philharmonic Orchestra and deputized for Toscanini at Bayreuth. He even sent a telegram of support to Goebbels (q.v.) for the measures that the régime was taking against the composer Hindemith (q.v.) and his supporter, Furtwangler (q.v.). Nor did Strauss come out with any public protest against the dismissal of talented Jewish musicians who were often personal friends, though he privately disapproved of Nazi policies in this respect. On the other hand, when Strauss discovered that the name of his Jewish librettist, the renowned writer Stefan Zweig, was to be removed from the opening performance of *Die Schweigsame Frau* (*The Silent Woman*), he threatened to leave Dresden unless it was included. He angrily rejected Zweig's suggestion that a *nom de plume* be used to get round the difficulties with the Nazi régime and wrote an exasperated, teasing letter on 17 June 1935 in answer to his librettist's refusal to write a second libretto for him: 'This Jewish stubbornness is enough to turn one into an anti-semite! This pride of race, this feeling of solidarity – even I note a difference here! ... For me there exist only two categories of people: those who have talent and those who have none.' Strauss claimed to Zweig that he had often told the Nazi leadership 'that I regard the Streicher-Goebbels [q.v.] anti-Jewish campaign as a shame for German honour, as the lowest kind of warfare of talentless, lazy mediocrity against higher genius. I confess openly that I have received from Jews so much help, sacrifice, friendship and inspiration that it would be a crime not to acknowledge this in greatest gratitude.... My worst and most malicious adversaries and foes were "Aryans".' The letter was intercepted by the Gestapo and led to Strauss's dismissal from the Presidency of the *Reichsmusikkammer* and Chairmanship of the Federation of German Composers. Unfortunately, Strauss then wrote a terrified, cringing letter to Hitler, trying to dispel any notions that he did not take his anti-semitism seriously. However craven this behaviour, much of it stemmed from naïvety and the illusion that he was 'above politics', as well as the opportunistic desire to promote his own work through the organizational power of the State.

Strauss's compositions were in fact played, sung and trumpeted through all the opera houses and concert halls of Nazi Germany, inspiring much imitation by younger and lesser colleagues. He continued to compose throughout the years of the Third Reich, working away in his study at Garmisch, cherishing his family – he protected his Jewish daughter-in-law to whom he was strongly attached – and ignoring the cataclysmic political events in the outside world. *Capriccio* (1942), an extensive one-act disquisition on the nature of opera, was his nostalgic and evocative farewell to the medium he had served with such distinction for so long. Only at the end of the war with the destruction of the great theatres in Dresden, Berlin, Vienna and Munich, did he appear to grasp the magnitude of the disaster which had befallen Germany and western civilization. In the autumn of 1945 he took refuge in Switzerland, after writing one impassioned last lament for the Germany that had disappeared forever. On 8 June 1948 Richard Strauss was cleared by a de-Nazification court in Munich of all charges that he had participated in the Nazi movement or benefited from the régime. The eighty-five-year-old composer, one of the giants of German musical history, died in Garmisch-Partenkirchen on 8 September 1949.

Streicher, Julius (1885–1946)   *Gauleiter* of Franconia, founder of the anti-semitic journal, *Der Stürmer*, and Nazi Germany's leading Jew-baiter, Julius Streicher was born on 12 February 1885 in the Upper Bavarian village of Fleinhausen. An elementary school teacher by profession (like his father before him), Streicher served in a Bavarian unit during World War I and, despite a warning for bad behaviour, received the Iron Cross (First Class). In 1919 he co-founded the anti-semitic *Deutsch-Soziale Partei* and two years later joined the NSDAP, taking his own Party membership with him. Streicher was an intimate friend of Hitler and one of the earliest Nazis in northern Bavaria. In 1925 he was appointed *Gauleiter* of the NSDAP for Franconia and his headquarters in Nuremberg became a leading centre for violent anti-semitism in Germany. Streicher's unbecoming conduct and diatribes against the Weimar government led to his dismissal from his teaching post in 1928. A year later he was elected as a Nazi member of the Bavarian legislature. Streicher was a tireless speaker and plebeian rabble-rouser, whose political influence derived largely from the impact of *Der Stürmer*, which he founded in 1923 and continued to edit until 1945. This weekly newspaper became the world's best-known anti-semitic publication with its crude cartoons, repellent photographs of Jews, its stories of ritual murder, pornography and its coarse prose style. Through its columns and through his own endless speaking tours, Streicher reached millions of Germans, imbuing them with his own poisonous brew of hatred, sadism and perversity. The impact of *Der Stürmer* was greatly enhanced by a nationwide system of display cases (*Stürmerkasten*) put up in parks, public squares, factory canteens, at street corners and bus stops, to attract passersby. Their visual impact, their racist slogans and scandalmongering style drew crowds. *Der Stürmer* consistently carried large-print slogans such as 'Avoid Jewish Doctors and Lawyers', and gave listings of Jewish dentists, shopkeepers and professional people whom 'Aryans' were urged to avoid. Those who ignored this advice were in danger of having their own names and addresses listed.

Letters to the editor denouncing Jews – and Germans who patronized them – became a regular feature of *Der Stürmer*, which claimed in 1935 that it was receiving 11,000 letters a week. The 'Pillory' column created a climate of fear and intimidation, not only in Nuremberg – where Streicher dominated all spheres of life – but throughout Germany. Through *Der Stürmer*, Streicher provided a focus for the anti-Jewish measures of Nazi Germany, pressing already in 1933 for the banning of Jews from public baths, places of entertainment, State schools, etc. After Streicher spoke in Magdeburg in 1935, Jews were barred from using public transport. The general campaign which led to the Nuremberg racial laws in 1935 was initiated by his paper. One of Streicher's most enthusiastic readers was Adolf Hitler, who declared that *Der Stürmer* was the only paper which he read avidly from first to last page. Undoubtedly the Führer protected Streicher, raising him to high office and praising him as the 'friend and comrade in arms' who never wavered and would 'unflinchingly stand behind him in every situation'. Although aware of Streicher's widespread unpopularity and unsavoury reputation, Hitler regarded him as a man of spirit, ex-

tremely useful, if not irreplaceable. He considered the Franconian *Gauleiter's* 'primitive methods' to be very effective, especially vis-à-vis the man in the street, and told Rauschning (q.v.) that he gave Streicher a free hand because antisemitism was the most important weapon in the Nazi arsenal.

In spite of repeated requests to suppress *Der Stürmer* as a 'cultural disgrace', Hitler personally ordered that no action be taken and declared that Streicher's material was amusing and very cleverly done. The German public appeared to share this view since *Der Stürmer's* circulation rose from 2–3,000 in 1923 to 65,000 in 1934 and close on 500,000 in 1937. It fluctuated, increased and then during the war dropped to about 200,000. Naturally, the ownership of such a widely read newspaper guaranteed Streicher a considerable income which was the envy of many other *Gauleiters*. Nor were signs of official favour lacking during the Third Reich. In March 1933 Hitler appointed Streicher Director of the 'Central Committee for the Defence against Jewish Atrocity and Boycott Propaganda'. In January 1933 Streicher became a member of the Reichstag for the electoral district of Franconia, and in 1934 he was promoted to *SA-Gruppenführer*. During his time as *Gauleiter*, i.e. until 1939, he enlarged his newspaper business to prodigious proportions, eventually owning about ten newspapers, including the *Fränkische Tageszeitung*. He further extended his personal fortune by expropriating Jewish property in his district and allowing friends to acquire Jewish homes and businesses at a fraction of their real value.

Corrupt, dishonest, sadistic, obscene and brutal in manner, Streicher's sexual peccadilloes and his disreputable transactions eventually became intolerable even to his colleagues and by 1939 Party officials were consistently complaining about his psychopathic behaviour. The fact that he had been charged with rape, admitted horsewhipping political prisoners and derided the virility of other Nazi potentates created a solid front against him that even Hitler could no longer ignore. Streicher's dismissal from his Party posts in 1940 was, however, due less to his venality or pornographic eccentricities than to his specific allegation that Hermann Goering (q.v.) was impotent and that his daughter had been conceived by artificial insemination. It was Goering who despatched a commission to Franconia to examine Streicher's business transactions and personal life, which ultimately led to the latter's downfall. Nevertheless, Streicher was allowed to continue his anti-semitic incitement as editor of *Der Stürmer*, for which he was eventually indicted and hanged at Nuremberg on 16 October 1946. The Nuremberg Tribunal held that 'Streicher's incitement to murder and extermination, at the time when Jews in the East were being killed under the most horrible conditions, constitutes persecution on political and racial grounds ... and a crime against humanity'. Streicher, however, regarded his own trial and death sentence as 'a triumph for world Jewry' and went to the scaffold shouting angrily, '*Purimfest!*' and proclaiming his eternal loyalty to Hitler.

Stroop, Jürgen (1895–1951)   The son of a policeman, Josef Stroop – he changed his first name to Jürgen only in 1941 – was raised in a lower-middle-class, Catholic milieu and volunteered for military service in World War I, from which he returned as a Vice-Sergeant. Appointed SS Sergeant in 1934, Stroop had advanced to the position of *SS-Brigadeführer* and Colonel in the police by 1939. During World War II he proved himself an expert in the 'pacification' of civilian populations in the occupied lands of Czechoslovakia, Soviet Russia, Poland and Greece. A cold, puritanical Nazi who worshipped General Ludendorff

(q.v.) and had absorbed the anti-semitic ideas of his fanatical wife, Stroop idealized authority and power, to which he always displayed servile deference. He savagely put down the Warsaw ghetto rebellion of April–May 1943, which had begun when the Jewish Combat organization, fighting from rooftops and cellars, took on the armoured cars, tanks and trucks of the SS and Wehrmacht. General Stroop had been sent to Warsaw from Lemberg (Galicia) to remove the 56,000 surviving Jews from the ghetto. He moved in to crush the revolt and originally planned to annihilate the ghetto in three days, but the fighting lasted until mid-May with some 300 Germans killed and about 1,000 wounded by the ghetto fighters. Stroop, who treated the liquidation of the Jewish community as a military campaign, had just over 2,000 men at his disposal, including two SS training battalions and some Wehrmacht details. His diaries and despatches, which record the daily killings with cold-blooded brutality, express his surprise that the Warsaw Jews 'despite the danger of being burned alive, preferred to return to the flames, rather than be caught by us'. On 23 April 1943 he complained that his operations were being made more difficult by 'the cunning ways in which the Jews and bandits behave. For example, we discovered that the wagons used to collect the scattered corpses were also carting live Jews to the Jewish cemetery, thus enabling them to escape outside the ghetto.' By 25 April Stroop had combed out much of the ghetto and taken prisoner 25,000 Jews. He noted: 'I am going to obtain a train for T2 [Treblinka] tomorrow, otherwise *liquidation will be carried out* forthwith. Not one of the Jews whom we have caught remains in Warsaw.' On 16 May 1943 Stroop reported that the 'operation' was complete: 14,000 Jews had either been killed in the ghetto or sent to Treblinka death camp and another 42,000 to Lublin labour camps, while unknown numbers had been buried under the débris or burnt alive. Stroop recorded his deeds in a boastful seventy-five-page report bound together in black pebble leather and including copies of all daily communiqués sent to his superior officer as well as photographs with captions in Gothic script like 'Smoking out the Jews and bandits'. The *Stroop-Bericht* was later published in Warsaw in 1960 and a German edition appeared in 1976. General Stroop was awarded the Iron Cross (First Class) in recognition of his services and was then transferred to Greece, where he was appointed a Higher SS and Police Leader. On 22 March 1947 he was sentenced to death by an American military tribunal at Dachau for shooting American pilots and hostages in Greece. He was subsequently extradited to Poland in 1948, retried and executed as a 'fascist hangman' in Warsaw on 8 September 1951.

Stuckart, Wilhelm (1902–53) Nazi politician and jurist who drafted the Nuremberg Laws and their later amendments, Wilhelm Stuckart was born in Wiesbaden on 16 November 1902. After studying law in Munich and Frankfurt, Stuckart fought in the Epp *Freikorps* and was twice imprisoned by the French authorities for opposition activities. An early member of the NSDAP (1922) he became a legal adviser to the Party in Wiesbaden in 1926. Because of his political affiliations he had to resign as a judge in 1932, but within a year he became acting Mayor of Stettin and shortly after was appointed State Secretary in the Prussian Ministry of Education and a member of the Prussian State Council. On 2 March 1935 Stuckart became Secretary of State in the Reich Ministry of the Interior and a few months later co-authored and promoted the Nuremberg anti-Jewish racial laws which placed German Jewry outside the national community. Together with Dr Hans Globke (q.v.) he edited an

authoritative commentary on these laws, *Kommentare zur Deutschen Rassengesetzgebung* (1936), which expounded the *völkisch* concept of the State and developed the theme that the Third Reich 'is the German *Volk* idea become reality'. A leading constitutional expert and loyal SS man – in January 1944 he was promoted to *SS-Obergruppenführer* – Stuckart wrote several works on National Socialist legal theory and tactics. In January 1942 he attended the Wannsee Conference where he responded enthusiastically to the plans for a 'Final Solution of the Jewish Question', proposing the compulsory sterilization of non-Aryans and the dissolution of all 'mixed' marriages. Stuckart, who was also Chairman of the 'Commission for the Protection of German Blood', had a reputation even more severe than that of Heydrich (q.v.) on racial matters. Following his arrest in 1945, the Nuremberg court, lacking relevant documentation, accepted Stuckart's completely false claim that he knew nothing of the extermination programme and sentenced him in 1949 to four years' imprisonment, the term he had already spent in detention since the war. Stuckart was immediately released, living subsequently in West Berlin. He was killed in a car 'accident' near Hanover in December 1953, most probably the victim of a vengeance squad organized after the war to hunt down Nazi criminals.

Stuelpnagel, Karl Heinrich von (1886–1944) Military Governor of France from 1942 to 1944, Karl Heinrich von Stuelpnagel was born in Darmstadt on 2 January 1886. A professional soldier of the old school, who like many of his fellow officers disapproved of the Nazi régime, von Stuelpnagel eventually became the main agent in Paris of the military conspiracy to overthrow Hitler. From November 1938 to June 1940, he served as Quartermaster-General on the Army General Staff and then for the next six months he was Chief of the Franco-German Armistice Commission. Stuelpnagel was then transferred to the eastern front following the invasion of Soviet Russia, commanding the Seventeenth Army until October 1941. On 3 March 1942 he succeeded his cousin, Otto von Stuelpnagel (q.v.), as Military Governor in Paris, a post he held until July 1944. The measures which he took against French Resistance activities, including the execution of relatives and the murder of hostages, were extremely harsh and brutal. Nevertheless, von Stuelpnagel, who had already been active in the Halder-Beck circle and involved in the *putsch* plans of 1939, was in the forefront of the plot to eliminate Hitler and end the war in the West before the anticipated Allied invasion of Europe. His followers succeeded in arresting over a thousand key Gestapo and SS men before news arrived from Germany that the conspiracy had failed. Ordered to return to Berlin, von Stuelpnagel tried to commit suicide near Verdun, but succeeded only in blowing half his face off and blinding himself. The seriously wounded survivor was taken to Berlin, where he was eventually hanged in the courtyard of Plötzensee prison on 30 August 1944. The blinded General had to be led by the hand to the gallows. Like some of the other conspirators, his body was left to hang like an animal carcass on butchers' hooks.

Stuelpnagel, Otto von (1878–1948) Military Governor of France between 1940 and 1942 and a symbol of the most brutal type of Prussian militarism, Otto von Stuelpnagel was born in Berlin on 16 June 1878. From 1898 a Lieutenant in the Second Prussian Infantry Guards Regiment, Otto von Stuelp-

nagel was on active service during World War I. After the armistice his extradition was demanded from Germany for crimes of murder and theft, but he was never brought to book. A member of the so-called 'nobility of the sword', von Stuelpnagel was one of the most influential of the clique of Reichswehr officers who sought to destroy the Weimar Republic from behind the scenes. Already one of Hitler's most devoted followers in the years before 1933, he was called out of retirement for special tasks and reappointed General of infantry in 1940. In October 1940 he was made Military Commander of France, occupying Laval's château at Clermont Ferrand. As Governor of the Greater Paris district, a post he held until February 1942, Otto von Stuelpnagel acquired the reputation of a brutal hangman, responsible for the death of many French patriots and the deportation to Germany of countless others. His proclamations ordering curfews, punishment and execution of hostages were bitterly resented by the local population. After the killing of a German officer in a Paris subway station, he ordered the execution of twenty-two hostages, whose deaths were announced to the French people on red posters. Following French underground activities in Bordeaux and Nantes, another fifty hostages were shot. The terror reached its peak in the autumn and winter of 1941, with mass executions of Jews and communists taken from prison and murdered in a reprisal for actions against the occupying power. Otto von Stuelpnagel was captured in Germany and brought to Paris for trial after the war. He committed suicide by hanging himself in his cell at the Cherche-Midi prison in Paris, while still awaiting trial, on 6 February 1948.

T

Terboven, Josef (1898–1945) Reich Commissar in Norway, Josef Terboven was born in Essen on 23 May 1898, of Roman Catholic parents. After serving as a Lieutenant during World War I, Terboven studied at the Universities of Freiburg and Munich. In 1923 he took part in the Munich *putsch*. A bank clerk by profession, Terboven joined the SA and the NSDAP in Essen during the late 1920s. In 1930 he was elected one of 107 National Socialist deputies to the Reichstag, representing the electoral district of Düsseldorf West. In 1933 he became a Prussian State Councillor and was appointed *Gauleiter* of Essen. On 5 February 1935 Terboven was designated *Oberpräsident* of the Rhine Province and in September 1939 Reich Defence Commissioner for Defence District VI. Following the German invasion of Norway, Terboven was appointed *SA-Obergruppenführer* and Reich Commissioner for the occupied territory on 24 April 1940, a position he held until the end of the war. Terboven's brutal conduct in Norway was warmly praised by Hitler in his 'table talk' (5 May 1942): 'Terboven knew he would have quicksand under his feet', the Führer observed, 'if he did not act ruthlessly.' His cruelty affected all Norwegians, but after the invasion of Russia was especially directed against the tiny Jewish community, many of whom were either executed or deported to Germany. Terboven committed suicide in May 1945 in Norway.

Thaelmann, Ernst (1886–1944) Leader of the German Communist Party shot in Buchenwald concentration camp towards the end of World War II, Ernst Thaelmann was born in Hamburg on 16 April 1886, the son of an innkeeper. Of impeccable proletarian origins, Thaelmann was a transport worker in his early days. He joined the Social Democratic Party (SPD) in 1903 and in the following year became a member of the trade union movement in Hamburg. During World War I Thaelmann veered over towards the Independent Social Democratic Party (USPD) and in 1920 advocated its adhesion to the Communist International (Comintern) at the Halle Congress. Having joined the newly formed Communist Party (KPD) in 1919, Thaelmann was elected to its Central Committee two years later. In October 1923 he supported the abortive communist rising in Hamburg against the opinion of the Party leadership. In 1924 he was elected as a communist deputy to the Reichstag – he served until 1933 – and as Deputy Chairman of the KPD, representing the leftist proletarian wing. From 1925 he was Chairman of the *Rotfrontkämpferbund* (Red Front Fighters' Association), the communist paramilitary organization which in future years was to engage Nazi storm troopers in bloody street battles. In 1926 Thaelmann was responsible for eliminating the ultra-left faction of the KPD led by Ruth Fischer and in 1928 he consolidated his own leadership by driving out the reformist group around Heinrich Brandler. Always loyal to directives from Moscow, Thaelmann was an unconditional supporter of the Leninist-Stalinist course in the Party which refused to tolerate any ideological deviations. From 1924 he had been a member of the executive committee of the Comintern and seven years later he joined its Presidium. Under its directions he adopted the ultra-left turn in 1928 which led the KPD to concentrate its fire on the 'fascist Social Democrats' and the reformist unions. Thus Thaelmann declared in the Reichstag on 2 February 1930 that fascism was already in power in Germany, at a time when the government was headed by a Social Democrat. The massive Nazi gains in the September 1930 elections, however, were dismissed by the communist leadership as 'the beginning of their end'.

In April 1931 Thaelmann confidently announced to the executive committee of the Comintern that the Nazi electoral success (of 1930) 'was in a certain sense Hitler's best day, and that afterwards will not come better days but worse'. In the same spirit, Thaelmann and the communist leaders failed to differentiate between the régimes of von Papen (q.v.) or General von Schleicher (q.v.) and National Socialism, failing to grasp that Hitler would totally eradicate all independent working-class organizations in Germany. Thaelmann's Stalinist strategy against National Socialism, while it embodied violent resistance on the streets, did not shrink from a flirtation with German nationalism. In 1930 the communists adopted the Nazi slogan of a 'people's revolution', calling for 'the national and social liberation of the German nation' and a joint struggle of the masses against the Versailles Treaty, the Young Plan and the 'government of finance capital' allegedly headed by the Social Democrats. Thaelmann's tactics of forging a united revolutionary front of the working class against Nazism was in reality primarily designed to subvert the SPD, the premise being that only the destruction of social democracy could bring victory to the communists. Concentrating his fire against the SPD

rather than the Nazis, Thaelmann even wrote in December 1931: 'By raising the spectre of Hitler's fascism, Social Democracy is attempting to sidetrack the masses from vigorous action against the dictatorship of finance capital.... There are some people who fail to see the Social Democratic forest for the National Socialist trees.'

Thaelmann stood three times as a candidate for the Reich Presidency. In 1925 he had garnered only 1.9 million votes, but in the elections of 13 March 1932 the communist candidate received 4.9 million votes (13.2 per cent) as against 18.6 million (49.6 per cent) for the victorious Paul von Hindenburg (q.v.) and 11.3 million (30.1 per cent) for Adolf Hitler. In the run-off elections of 10 April 1932 Hindenburg won 53 per cent of the votes as against 36.8 per cent for Hitler and 10.2 per cent for Thaelmann. When the Nazis came to power at the end of January 1933 the facile optimism of the KPD leader soon proved to be illusory. He was arrested almost immediately after the Reichstag fire of 27 February 1933 and interned in Berlin's Moabit remand prison as one of Hitler's leading opponents. Thaelmann spent more than a decade in captivity, until he was finally murdered in Buchenwald concentration camp on 28 August 1944.

Thierack, Otto (1889–1946) President of the dreaded People's Court (*Volksgericht*) and later Reich Minister of Justice, Otto Thierack was born in Würzen, Saxony, on 19 April 1889, the son of middle-class parents. He studied law and political science at Marburg and Leipzig, graduating as a Doctor of Law in February 1914. After serving in World War I as a Lieutenant and receiving the Iron Cross (Second Class), Thierack pursued a legal career and was appointed Public Prosecutor in Leipzig and then in Dresden. An early member of the NSDAP and a former leader of the Nazi Lawyers' League, Thierack became

Minister of Justice for Saxony in 1933 and two years later he was appointed Vice-President of the Reich Supreme Court of Justice. From 1936 to 1942 he was President of the People's Court in Berlin, established to provide summary justice *in camera* and without appeal for those accused of crimes against the Third Reich. A Major General in the SS and *SA-Gruppenführer*, Thierack was Reich Minister of Justice from 1942 to 1945. His brief from Hitler of 20 August 1942 empowered him to disregard any existing law in order to establish a 'National Socialist administration of justice'. Thierack worked to make legally practicable the suggestion of Goebbels (q.v.) that various categories of foreigners imprisoned or conscripted by the Third Reich should be press-ganged into concentration camps and 'exterminated by labour'. On 18 September 1942 Thierack came to a monstrous agreement with Himmler (q.v.) for the 'delivery of asocials for the execution of their sentences', drafting the decrees for working to death whole populations who were to be admitted to concentration camps without any charge being offered. Apart from Jews and gypsies the decrees also affected all conscripted eastern workers, especially Russians and Ukrainians. Poles serving more than three years in prison, as well as Czechs and Germans serving more than eight years, were also among the 'anti-social' elements of the prison population to be handed over to the tender care of Himmler's SS.

To make the territories in the East 'fit' for German colonization, Thierack recommended that '... in future, Jews, Poles, gypsies, Russians and Ukrainians convicted of offences should not be sentenced by ordinary courts but should be executed by the *Reichsführer-SS* in view of the leadership's plans for settling the eastern problem'. In a letter to Martin Bormann (q.v.) on 13 October 1942 Thierack revealed, with unusual frankness, the reasons behind this policy: 'The ad-

ministration of justice can make only a small contribution to the extermination of these peoples. No useful purpose is served by keeping such persons for years in German prisons, even if as is done today on a large scale, they are utilized as labour for war purposes.' Thierack explained to Bormann that Himmler's police 'can then carry out their measures untrammelled by the niceties of criminal law'. In spite of such dedication, Thierack was nonetheless criticized by Hitler for not being tough enough and for 'sticking to his legalistic egg-shells'. After the war Thierack was arrested and interned, but hanged himself at Neumünster camp on 26 October 1946 before he could be brought to trial at Nuremberg.

Thorak, Joseph (1889–1952) One of Hitler's favourite sculptors who specialized in technically powerful, brutally muscular male figures, Joseph Thorak was born in Salzburg on 7 February 1889, the son of a potter. Already well known in the 1920s as a freelance sculptor who worked especially in wax, Thorak was influenced by the old Austrian baroque tradition with its strong musical elements and developed an idiosyncratic, sensitive treatment of plastic forms. Trained as a craftsman, the muscle-bound sculptor, whose many portrait busts of politicians included one of Field Marshal von Hindenburg (q.v.), received the State prize of the Prussian Academy of Arts in 1928. During the Third Reich, Thorak became a representative artist of National Socialism with his giant bronze and marble figures of muscular men and heavy-hipped, taut, equally powerful female figures. His marble statue *Two Humans* was singled out for praise by Hitler as an example of 'healthy Nordic eros' in contrast to the 'sensual sex' of the 1920s. From 1937 Professor at the Academy of Visual Arts in Munich, Thorak was commissioned to sculpt busts of Hitler and

Mussolini and some of the monumental figures which flanked the entrances to the new Reich Chancellery. He also worked on such projects as the fashioning of the Berlin Reich sports ground. On Hitler's orders a huge studio was built for him in Upper Bavaria, where he sculpted fifty-four-feet high figures for the Reich *Autobahnen*. After the war Thorak went into retreat but, after he was cleared by a Munich de-Nazification court, began working again on various commissions, including statues for a cloister in Linz. He died on 26 February 1952 at Hartmannsberg in the rural district of Rosenheim, Upper Bavaria.

Thyssen, Fritz (1873–1951) Leading German industrialist who backed Hitler and his movement for fifteen years, contributing over a million marks to the coffers of the Nazi Party, Fritz Thyssen was born in Mülheim on 9 November 1873, the son of a Catholic Rhineland family. His father, August Thyssen, was one of the wealthiest industrialists in Germany and a supporter of the Catholic Centre Party until its participation in the signing of the Versailles Treaty. Fritz Thyssen, heir to the family fortune, became an ardent nationalist who organized passive resistance during the 1923 occupation of the Ruhr, for which he was arrested and condemned by a French court-martial. In the same year he first heard Hitler speak and, impressed by his oratory, his ability to lead the masses and the quasi-military discipline of his followers, gave 100,000 gold marks to the Nazis via General Ludendorff (q.v.). Thyssen was convinced that Hitler could save Germany from Bolshevism and during the next decade was a heavy financial contributor to the Nazi Party, helping them to pay for the Brown House in Munich and to finance their electoral campaigns. The founder and leading shareholder of the United Steel Works (Germany's largest steel trust), he joined the Party in December 1931 after Hugenberg's (q.v.) alliance with the Nazis convinced him that the Young Plan spelled catastrophe for Germany and that only a strong State authority could save the nation. Thyssen brought about the connection between Hitler and the Rhenish-Westphalian industrialists. He invited the Nazi leader to speak before a meeting of industrialists in Düsseldorf on 27 January 1932, where Hitler shrewdly harangued the coal and steel magnates, defending private property and the need for a powerful State and stressing the dangers of Bolshevism. Henceforth, the big industrialists, along with Thyssen, began to increase their contributions to the Nazi cause, smoothing Hitler's road to power.

In September 1933 Thyssen was appointed Prussian State Councillor for life by Goering (q.v.), whom he had specially subsidized as a 'moderate' bulwark against the radicalism of the Nazi Left. On 12 November 1933 he became a member of the Reichstag for Düsseldorf East and in the same year he was chosen to head an institute for research into the corporate state (*Ständische Wirtschaftsordnung*). Thyssen's support for the industrial guild system advocated by the Austrian philosopher-economist, Othmar Spann (q.v.), however, proved irreconcilable with the totalitarian Nazi claim for a leading role in all spheres. By the late 1930s he had become increasingly disillusioned with the régime's rearmament policy (even though it scarcely harmed his business interests), and angered by its anti-Catholicism and persecution of the Jews, which caused him to resign from the Prussian State Council. In a letter to Hitler of 28 December 1939, written after fleeing Germany for Switzerland, Thyssen emphasized that his doubts about the Nazi régime had begun with the dismissal of the conservative von Papen (q.v.) as Vice-Chancellor followed by 'the persecution of Christianity ... the brutalization of its priests ... the desecration of its churches'. Thyssen observed that the Crystal Night pogrom of 9 November 1938 had deeply shocked him – '...the Jews were robbed and tortured in the most cowardly and brutal manner, and their synagogues destroyed all over Germany' – but his protests were to no avail.

The Nazi-Soviet pact of 23 August 1939 and the aggressive war policy of the régime had been the last straw for Thyssen, who wrote to Hitler as 'a free and upright German', claiming to be the 'voice of the tormented German nation' calling for a restoration of 'freedom, right and humanity' in the German Reich. Thyssen's appeal was ignored, he was stripped *in absentia* of his German citizenship and his property was confiscated. In 1941 his memoirs, *I Paid Hitler*, first appeared in English, an anguished settling of accounts with the Nazi régime which 'has ruined Germany', but singularly unreliable in its recounting of his financial relationship with the National Socialists. Thyssen was arrested and turned over to the Nazis by the Vichy police for return to Germany, where he was imprisoned for the rest of the war. He died in Buenos Aires on 8 February 1951.

Todt, Fritz (1891–1942) Famous road-builder and creator of the *Autobahnen* who was also Reich Minister for Armaments and Munitions from 1940 to 1942, Fritz Todt was born in Pforzheim, Baden, on 4 September 1891, the son of a prosperous, upper-middle-class family. After attending high school in his home town, Todt studied at a Munich college of technology before 1914. During World War I he served on the western front and then as a flying observer he was wounded in an air battle. Following the war Todt completed his studies at Karlsruhe and worked as a civil engineer. An early member of the NSDAP – he joined on 5 January 1922 – he was

appointed an SS Colonel on Himmler's (q.v.) staff in 1931 and two years later he was made Inspector-General of the German Road and Highway System. During the next decade the modest, unassuming technologist gathered into his hands responsibility for the entire German construction industry, including military fortifications and the building of the new Reich motorways. By 1938 supreme head of all road-building operations, in charge of all navigational waterways and power plants, Todt was also assigned the task of constructing the Western Wall (known to the Allies as the *Siegfried Line*). He was allowed to dispose of an army of his own workers known as the Todt Organization, in order to complete the Wall in the shortest possible time. As work began to proceed at an accelerated rate in 1939, the Todt Organization combined with various construction firms, army divisions and almost the entire Reich labour service to finish the project before the outbreak of war.

Appointed Reich Minister of Armaments and Munitions in March 1940 (a position he held until his death in 1942), Todt was also responsible for building the Atlantic Wall and a chain of concrete U-boat shelters along the French Atlantic coast. As head of construction within the framework of the Four Year Plan, Todt had frequently clashed with Goering (q.v.), but he enjoyed the high respect of Hitler who made him Inspector-General of roads, water and power in 1941. In reward for building the motorways and the Western Wall, he was the first German to receive the 'German Order' created by Hitler for individuals who had rendered 'special services to the German people'. Entrusted within the Party organization with the Head Office for Technology, all the major technical tasks of the Third Reich concerning Germany's war effort were in his hands. Todt was responsible for building roads in the occupied territories from the northern tip of Norway to the south of France and, during the invasion of Soviet Russia, his organization reconstructed miles of Russian railways, altering them to the standard German gauge as well as establishing depots behind the Moscow front.

In all these massive communications works, SS General Todt had at his disposal a vast army of slave labour as well as several divisions of troops. By the autumn of 1941, however, he was close to despair about the military situation and told his future successor, Albert Speer (q.v.), after returning from a long inspection tour of the eastern front that, given the harsh climate and hardships, 'it is a struggle in which the primitive people [the Russians] will prove superior'. In spite of his pessimism, reinforced by Hitler's refusal to give top priority to increasing equipment for the German army, Todt remained a loyal servant of the régime, while avoiding close personal contacts with Party circles and involvement in power intrigues. He died in an air crash at Rastenburg in East Prussia on 8 February 1942 and his mortal remains were taken to Berlin to be interred there in the military cemetery. Most of his responsibilities, including the Reich Ministry for Armaments and War Production, were taken over by Albert Speer.

Tresckow, Henning von (1901–1944) German General who was one of the leaders of the July 1944 plot against Hitler, Henning von Tresckow was born in Magdeburg on 19 January 1901. An officer during World War I and subsequently a successful stockbroker, von Tresckow rejoined the Reichswehr in 1924. For a time he sympathized with National Socialism, but later opposed the Hitler régime and became the heart and soul of the conspiracy among army officers fighting on the eastern front. At the beginning of World War II, von Tresckow was General Staff officer of an infantry division in East Prussia and distinguished himself in the Polish and French campaigns. Promoted to Major General, he later served as Chief of Staff of the Army Group Centre on the Russian front and tried unsuccessfully to persuade Generals von Kluge (q.v.) and Fedor von Bock (q.v.) to join in a military coup in which Hitler would be arrested and brought to trial. Determined to end the war before the German armies collapsed on the eastern front, von Tresckow began to plan an independent assassination attempt at the end of 1942. On 13 March 1943, assisted by his aide Fabian von Schlabrendorff, he enticed Hitler to Smolensk and smuggled a time bomb into his aircraft which failed to go off on the return flight. Von Tresckow also played a leading role in the plans for several other attempts on Hitler's life during 1943 and in October of the same year joined forces with Claus Schenk Graf von Stauffenberg (q.v.), who now became the central figure in the conspiracy. The Allied invasion of Normandy gave a new urgency to their plans and von Tresckow stressed to those who still hesitated the need to prove to the world and future generations 'that the German Resistance movement dared to take the decisive step and hazard their lives on it'. The failure of von Stauffenberg's attempt on 20 July 1944 convinced von Tresckow to commit suicide rather than endanger other conspirators by revealing information under torture. A Prussian conservative and a man of unusual integrity, von Tresckow took his own life with a hand grenade on 21 July 1944. Before taking final leave of his friend von Schlabrendorff, his last words denounced Hitler as 'the arch-enemy of Germany ... the arch-enemy of the world'. He recalled the Biblical promise to Abraham to spare Sodom if there were ten just men in the city. 'He will, I hope, spare Germany because of what we have done', added von Tresckow, 'and not destroy her. None of us can complain. Whoever joined the Resistance put on the shirt of Nessus. The worth of a man is only certain if he is ready to sacrifice his life for his convictions.'

Troost, Paul Ludwig (1878–1934) Hitler's foremost architect whose neo-classical style became for a time the official architecture of the Third Reich, Paul Ludwig Troost was born on 17 August 1878 in Wuppertal-Elberfeld. An extremely tall, spare-looking, reserved Westphalian with a close-shaven head, Troost belonged to a school of architects (including Peter Behrens and Walter Gropius) who even before 1914 reacted sharply against the highly ornamental *Jugendstil* and advocated a restrained, lean architectural approach, almost devoid of ornament. Troost graduated from designing steamship décor before World War I and the fittings for showy transatlantic liners like the *Europa* to a style that combined Spartan traditionalism with elements of modernity. Although before 1933 he did not belong to the leading group of German architects, Troost's work filled Hitler with enthusiasm and in 1930 he designed the Nazi Party's Brown House in Munich, at the latter's request. In the autumn of 1933 he was commissioned to rebuild and refurnish the Chancellery residence in Berlin. Along with other Nazi architects, he planned and built State and municipal edifices throughout the country, including new administrative offices, social buildings for workers and bridges across the main highways. One of the many structures he planned before his death was the House of German Art in Munich, intended to be a great temple for a 'true, eternal art of the German people'. It was a good example of the imitation of classical forms in monumental public buildings during the Third Reich, though subsequently Hitler moved away from the more restrained style of Troost, reverting to the pomp-

ous imperial grandeur that he had admired in the Vienna Ringstrasse of his youth. Hitler's relationship to Troost was that of a pupil to an admired teacher and he would frequently visit the architect's studio in a battered backyard off the Theresienstrasse in Munich. According to Albert Speer (q.v.), who later became Hitler's favourite architect, the Führer would impatiently greet Troost with the words: 'I can't wait, *Herr Professor.* Is there anything new – let's see it!' The architect would then lay out his latest plans and sketches. Hitler frequently declared, according to Speer, that he 'first learned what architecture is from Troost'. The architect's death on 21 March 1934, after a severe illness, was a painful blow. The Führer revered Troost's work, eulogising him as 'one of the greatest German architects'. He laid a wreath annually on Troost's grave at Munich's North Cemetery. Frau Gerdy Troost, together with the architect Leonhard Gall, completed her husband's project and on 18 July 1937 Hitler himself opened the first official German Art Exhibition at the House of German Art. He praised the building as a 'truly great and artistic structure', uniquely impressive in its beauty and functional in its layout and equipment. He considered this fusion of Hellenism and Germanic tradition in the monumental, neo-classical style as a model for Germany's future public buildings. Hitler remained close to Troost's widow, an interior decorator and fierce defender of her husband's work. She took over Troost's atelier and was rewarded with the title of Frau Professor on Hitler's 48th birthday (20 April 1937). A regular fixture at the Great German Art Exhibitions in Munich, Frau Troost's views on architecture generally coincided with those of Hitler himself. Her two-volume work *Das Bauen im neuen Reich* (1938) was considered an authoritative statement on what was acceptable architecture in Nazi

Germany. In this and other respects, she was in Speer's words, 'an arbiter of artistic taste', especially in Munich. A woman of character, she also fearlessly defended her more liberal modernist taste in painting against Hitler's implacable denunciation of it as 'decadent' and 'degenerate', but to no avail.

Trott zu Solz, Adam von (1909–44) Foreign Office and *Abwehr* official who played an important role in the German Resistance, Adam von Trott zu Solz was born in Potsdam on 9 August 1909, the son of a distinguished, noble family which had produced diplomats and statesmen for several generations. His father had been Prussian Minister of Education from 1909 to 1917, and his half-American mother, of Calvinist-Huguenot stock, was descended from the First Chief Justice of the United States, John Jay. The Protestant piety of his mother and his Anglo-Saxon background were factors in von Trott zu Solz's anti-Nazism, which was strongly tinged by the belief that only the re-Christianization of Germany could preserve it from complete barbarism. A Rhodes Scholar at Balliol College, Oxford, during the early 1930s, von Trott zu Solz established contacts in Great Britain which he was later able to use on behalf of the German Resistance. On his return to Germany in 1934, von Trott zu Solz practised law, published a new edition of Heinrich von Kleist's works with a commentary that celebrated him as a rebel against tyranny, and became active in the Kreisau Circle of opponents of the Hitler régime. By 1939, when he entered the Foreign Office as a protégé of Ernst von Weiszäckers (q.v.), von Trott zu Solz was already one of the leading anti-Nazis of the younger generation, responsible for keeping contacts open with sympathizers of the 'other Germany' abroad. In June 1939 he visited England on what was ostensibly a 'fact-finding mission'

on behalf of the Führer, meeting at Cliveden with the Prime Minister, Neville Chamberlain, the Foreign Secretary, Lord Halifax, and other leading figures in British politics. Introduced as a friend of the Astor family, von Trott zu Solz reported back to the German Foreign Office that Hitler could appease British public opinion, and thereby 'paralyse his enemies', if he withdrew from Bohemia and Moravia. Statements sympathetic to Germany, reported by von Trott zu Solz, however, may have encouraged Hitler to believe that he could invade Poland without fear of British intervention.

Von Trott zu Solz's real purpose was most likely to gain time for the German opposition – as on an earlier visit to Washington in October 1938 – and to avoid a world war, though there are still doubts as to whether he was not a German spy. The British Foreign Office regarded him with distrust, considering that the dossier against him was 'formidable', and did not respond to various peace overtures made by von Trott zu Solz during the war on behalf of the German Resistance. British doubts were reinforced by the fact that von Trott zu Solz and his associates were not in favour of restoring territorial acquisitions gained by Hitler. When, through his *Abwehr* contacts in Switzerland, he met British and American diplomats in 1943–4, he warned that if the West did not offer a decent peace with a non-Nazi Germany, the Resistance would turn to the Soviet Union. In spite of the divided loyalties which afflicted him (he was a strong German patriot), von Trott zu Solz was a convinced anti-Nazi who believed passionately in the ecumenical Christian idea as taught by men like Dietrich Bonhoeffer (q.v.). Tried before the People's Court for his complicity in the von Stauffenberg (q.v.) conspiracy of 20 July 1944, he was sentenced to death and hanged in Berlin's Plötzensee prison on 26 August of the same year.

Tschammer und Osten, Hans von (1887–1943) Secretary of State in the Reich Ministry of Interior and *Reichssportführer* in Nazi Germany, von Tschammer und Osten was born in Dresden on 25 October 1887. He entered the NSDAP in 1929 and in January 1931 became an SA Colonel. In March 1932 he was promoted to *SA-Gruppenführer* and leader of the SA-Group Centre. In March 1933 von Tschammer und Osten was elected a member of the Reichstag for the electoral district of Magdeburg. On 19 July 1933 he was appointed Reich Sport Leader and in January 1934 head of the Sport Section of the *Kraft durch Freude*, the National Socialist recreational organization which was designed to improve the morale of German workers and stimulate their productivity. As Reich Sport Leader, von Tschammer und Osten implemented the Nazi policy of boosting German prestige abroad and maintaining public enthusiasm for the régime at home through the promotion of sports. From 1933 onwards all sports were 'co-ordinated' and great attention was given to physical training, active participation in sports and endurance tests, at the expense of academic education. Sporting prowess was made a criterion for entrance to schools, for school-leaving certificates and even for certain jobs. Nazi sports policy also emphasized the goal of demonstrating 'Aryan' racial superiority in international competition. Under von Tschammer und Osten and his successors, German Jewish athletes were, for example, systematically hindered by being denied adequate facilities and the opportunity to compete, and Jewish sport was first ghettoized and then totally eliminated by the pressure of the police State and its propaganda policies. As head of the Reich Sport Office, von Tschammer und Osten was responsible for the institutionalized system of apartheid which developed, though it was temporarily and hypocritically modified to enable Nazi Germany to stage the Olympic Games in 1936 in Berlin. He died on 25 March 1943.

U

Udet, Ernst (1896–1941) Famous fighter pilot and Director-General of Equipment for the Luftwaffe, Ernst Udet was born in Frankfurt am Main on 26 April 1896. One of Germany's leading aces during World War I, credited with shooting down sixty-two enemy planes, Udet was awarded the *Pour le Mérite* decoration and later achieved further renown as a stunt flier, with flights over Africa, America, Greenland and the Swiss Alps. Appointed Brigadier in 1935, Udet was made Chief of the Technical Office in the Reich Air Ministry a year later. In 1939 he was promoted to Inspector-General of the Luftwaffe and was made responsible for Air Force Procurement. A talented designer, Udet favoured speed and manoeuvrability in aircraft as a result of his own experience as a fighter pilot, but lacked expertise in the field of long-range bombing and transport problems. Udet concentrated on developing single-engined fighters such as the Messerschmitt-109 (which he had personally flown in 1937), the dive-bomber Junkers 87, and light and medium bombers which corresponded to his own inclinations and the concept of the Luftwaffe as primarily a tactical force. The failure of the Luftwaffe during the Battle of Britain to inflict a decisive defeat on the Royal Air Force undermined Udet's standing with Hitler and Goering (q.v.). The flight of Rudolf Hess (q.v.) to Britain in May 1941 – Hess had originally turned to him to get the chance to fly his own plane – and Udet's confident assertion that he would never reach his destination, further lowered the Führer's opinion of his competence. An easy-going cosmopolitan by outlook and taste, uninterested in power intrigues, Udet became increasingly depressed by his capricious treatment at Goering's hands and the latter's blindness to reality. Following the failures of the Luftwaffe on the eastern front and a major quarrel with Goering, Udet committed suicide on 17 November 1941. The Nazi régime covered up the affair, attributing his death to an accident which had occurred while he was testing a new air weapon.

Ulbricht, Walter (1893–1973) Communist Party leader who fled Nazi Germany and subsequently rose to become Head of State and ruler of the German Democratic Republic (East Germany), Walter Ulbricht was born in Leipzig on 30 June 1893, the son of an atheist jobbing-tailor. Ulbricht received only eight years of formal education, leaving school to become a joiner and picking up his Marxism in the pre-1914 working-class youth movement. In 1912 he entered the Social Democratic Party (SPD) in Leipzig. Following military service during World War I, Ulbricht became one of the founders of the new German Communist Party (KPD) in 1919. His rapid rise as a Party functionary coincided with the Bolshevization of the KPD. In 1923 he was already a member of the Party Central Committee. A year later he was sent to Moscow to be trained as a Comintern official, later working as a Party instructor in Prague and Vienna, as well as representing the KPD in the Russian-dominated Third International. From 1928 to 1933 Ulbricht was a communist deputy in the Reichstag for the electoral district of South Westphalia. Appointed district secretary for the Berlin-Brandenburg district in 1929, Ulbricht organized communist resistance to the Nazis in the last years of the Weimar Republic. In October 1933 he succeeded in fleeing Nazi Germany with the help of false papers, establishing a KPD foreign committee in Paris and then participating in the Spanish Civil War (1936–8), where he was given the task of liquidating Party members allegedly disloyal to Moscow.

From 1938 to 1945 Ulbricht remained in the Soviet Union where he survived the great purges and during World War II served in the Political Administration Bureau of the Russian army, working chiefly among German prisoners of war. He was a co-founder of the National Committee for a 'Free Germany', established in Soviet Russia in 1943. In 1945 Ulbricht returned to Germany with the Red Army as the leader of a group organized to establish communist political authority in the Soviet-occupied eastern zone. A driving force behind the elimination of all non-communist political parties in eastern Germany, Ulbricht became Deputy Premier of the newly established German Democratic Republic (GDR) in 1949. In 1950 he was appointed Secretary-General of the Socialist Unity Party (SED), the successor to the decimated pre-war German Communist Party. For the next two decades Ulbricht imposed his personal stamp on East Germany as a loyal ally of the Soviet Union and guardian of Marxist-Leninist ideological orthodoxy. Ulbricht's hard-line communist policies and authoritarian leadership style were combined with the encouragement of scientific and technological efficiency and the repression of working-class and intellectual dissent. First Secretary of the SED from 1953 and Chairman of the Council of State from 1960 (thereby combining State and Party leadership in his own hands), Ulbricht was responsible a year later for the building of the notorious Berlin Wall to stop the daily flight of refugees to the West. The Wall was the physical symbol of Ulbricht's Stalinist siege mentality and his opposition to normalizing relations with West Germany. In spite of the world-wide condemnation it aroused, the Wall doubtless contributed to improving East Germany's economic performance and consolidating Ulbricht's political power. In 1968 Ulbricht sent East German troops into Czechoslovakia, once again proving himself Moscow's most reliable ally in eastern Europe. By the time of his replacement by Erich Honecker as Secretary-General of the SED in May 1971, the unpopular and widely disliked Ulbricht had outlasted all his rivals and enemies and held power for a quarter of a century. He died in Döllnsee, near East Berlin, on 1 August 1973.

V

Veesenmayer, Edmund (born 1904) Reich Plenipotentiary and Hitler's deputy in Hungary towards the end of World War II, SS Major General Edmund Veesenmayer was born in Bad Kissingen on 12 November 1904. After studying economics, he lectured at Munich Technical College and the Berlin School of Economy. An early member of the NSDAP, he subsequently made his career in the SS before being transferred to the German Foreign Office as Wilhelm Keppler's (q.v.) protégé. Veesenmayer frequently travelled to the Balkans and was used on confidential missions by the Foreign Office. He also had considerable business interests in Austria, being a member of the board of Donauchemie AG (Vienna), the Länderbank AG (Vienna) and the Standard Elektrizitäts-Gesellschaft (Berlin). From the spring of 1941 he was attached to the German legation at Zagreb, recommending the deportation of Serbian Jews. This became Veesenmayer's special area and he later wrote long reports to von Ribbentrop (q.v.) complaining about the failure of Hungary and Slovakia to renew deportation of Jews. Promoted on 15 March 1944 to SS *Brigadeführer*, Veesenmayer was sent to Hungary as Reich Plenipotentiary where, from March to October, he engaged in anti-semitic activities and was intimately involved in the 'Final Solution', providing Adolf Eichmann's (q.v.) commando with diplomatic cover. Nominally, Veesenmayer was still responsible to von Ribbentrop and the Foreign Office, but he reported primarily to Ernst Kaltenbrunner (q.v.) at the RSHA on his efforts in securing the co-operation of the Hungarian authorities with the German police in implementing the liquidation of Hungarian Jewry. On 2 April 1949 the International Military Tribunal at Nuremberg sentenced Veesenmayer to twenty years' imprisonment for war crimes. He was released from Landsberg prison in December 1951, thanks to the intervention of the US High Commissioner in Germany.

Voegler, Albert (1877–1945) Leading German industrialist and General Manager of the Vereinigte Stahlwerke (United Steel Works) under the Weimar Republic and the Third Reich, Albert Voegler was born in Borbeck, in the Ruhr, on 8 February 1877. An engineer by training, Voegler was already a prominent figure in the German steel industry before 1914. From 1906 to 1912 he was Director of Union AG for Iron and Steel Industries at Dortmund and a close collaborator of Hugo Stinnes (q.v.). In 1915 he was appointed General Director of German Luxemburg Mining AG, a position he held until 1926. in 1920 he was elected to the National Assembly as a delegate of the German People's Party, serving for four years. (He was elected again as a member for the electoral district of Westphalia South in 1933.) A member of the Dortmund Chamber of Commerce, Voegler succeeded Emil Kirdorf (q.v.) as Chairman of the Rhineland-Westphalian Coal Syndicate in 1925 and a year later he was appointed General Director of the largest German steel works, Vereinigte Stahlwerke AG, Düsseldorf, a post he continued to hold until 1935. From 1930 to 1933 Voegler was one of the prime sources of funds from industrial circles to Hitler's Nazi Party. He was present on 20 February 1933 at a secret meeting held in Goering's (q.v.) Reichstag Presidential Palace, hosted by Dr Schacht (q.v.), where future Nazi policy was explained by Hitler to a group of leading businessmen who responded by contributing three million marks to Party coffers. Hitler promised to eliminate the Marxists, to restore the Wehrmacht, to rearm Germany and to end free elections, a programme that was enthusiastically received by Voegler and his colleagues in big business circles. Under the Third Reich, although never a member of the Nazi Party, Voegler became President of the Kaiser Wilhelm Institute of Science and Research and in 1934 he was appointed Reich Plenipotentiary for the socialization of Rhenish-Westphalian coal pits. He was Chairman and a member of several Boards of Directors in Nazi Germany, including the AG für Energiewirtschaft (Berlin), Deutsche Röhrenwerke AG (Düsseldorf), Elektrizitäts-AG (Nuremberg), Deutsche Edelstahlwerke AG (Krefeld), Ruhrstahl AG (Witten), Ruhrgas AG (Essen), Westfälische Union AG für Eisen und Drahtindustrie, Harpener Bergbau AG (Dortmund) and Rheinisch-Westfälische Elektrizitätswerk AG (Essen). After the 20 July 1944 plot against Hitler's life, Ernst Kaltenbrunner (q.v.), the head of the security services, wanted to indict Voegler and two of his colleagues in heavy industry for 'defeatist' conversations, but the prominent industrialist was protected by the intercession of Albert Speer (q.v.). Voegler committed suicide in Dortmund on 13 April 1945 following his arrest by American troops.

Wagner, Adolf (1890–1944) National Socialist politician and Bavarian Minister of the Interior after the seizure of power in 1933, Adolf Wagner was born on 1 October 1890 in Algringen, Lorraine. An officer during World War I, then Director of a mining company in Bavaria, Wagner joined the NSDAP in 1923. Together with Max Amann (q.v.), Schwarz (q.v.) and Hermann Esser (q.v.), he belonged to the old Munich comrades of Hitler. In 1924 he became a member of the Bavarian diet and on 1 November 1929 he was appointed *Gauleiter* of the NSDAP for Munich-Upper Bavaria. In March 1933 Wagner was made *Staatskommissar* (State Commissioner) for Bavaria and in April of the same year he became Minister of the Interior and Deputy Prime Minister of Bavaria. As a result of his instructions, the numbers of those arrested rose considerably, including non-communist opponents of the Nazi régime. Wagner also served as a Reichstag member for the electoral district of Upper Bavaria-Swabia from 1933. A member of the clique who helped massacre Röhm's (q.v.) followers, he was appointed in 1935 to the personal staff of Hitler at the Brown House in Munich. On 28 November 1936 he was made Bavarian Minister of Education and Culture. Adolf Wagner played an active role in this capacity in securing financial pledges from wealthy industrialists and bankers to finance the building of the House of German Art in Munich. At the opening of the Great German Art Exhibition in July 1937 he was the master of ceremonies and he was always

highly visible at the Day of German Art festivals held in the Bavarian capital. Though notorious for his drunkenness and womanizing, this coarse, despotic Bavarians with his wooden leg and thick duelling scar, liked to make speeches about art and culture. In September 1939 he was appointed Reich Commissioner for Military Districts VII and XIII. However, Wagner's health began to fail soon after the outbreak of war and he was eventually obliged to resign his various posts. He died on 12 April 1944 and was given an impressive funeral, which Hitler personally attended out of respect for one of his closest associates among the Old Guard fighters.

Wagner, Gerhardt (1888–1938) Plenipotentiary for Health in the Party Office and Leader of the National Socialist Chamber of Medicine, Gerhardt Wagner was born on 18 August 1888 in Neu-Heiduk. Co-founder and head of the *Nationalsozialistischer Deutscher Ärzte-Bund* (National Socialist German Doctors' Association) from 1932, he was appointed Reich Medical Leader two years later. A member of the Reichstag (*Wahlkreis* Pfalz) from 12 November 1933 and Nazi Medical Leader for Franconia, Wagner was one of the most rabid Jew-baiters in Hitler's entourage. Already in September 1935 the former *Freikorps* man and archetypal Nazi physician had emerged as a notorious public advocate of the anti-Jewish racial laws, in a speech which he made at the Nuremberg Party rally. The orator, a protégé of Rudolf Hess (q.v.) (who was his patient), advocated sterilization for Jews as well as defectives. In the same speech Dr Wagner emerged as the godfather of the euthanasia programme and an advocate of the survival of the fittest, deploring the millions of marks spent each year on children and adults afflicted with congenital diseases such as blindness, deafness, dumbness and mental illness.

Wagner, Gustav (1911–80) Deputy Commandant of the Sobibor extermination camp in eastern Poland, Gustav Wagner was born in Vienna where he joined the then illegal Nazi Party in 1931, attracted by their programme of unifying all German-speaking people. Arrested for daubing swastikas and putting up posters, he was eventually smuggled over the border into Germany in 1934 in order to avoid further arrest. He reported to a local SA detachment and was employed on guard duty outside a camp. Having joined the SS, he was sent in 1940 to Schloss Hartheim near Linz, a centre for killing off the mentally sick and handicapped. The institution was run from Tiergartenstrasse 4 in Berlin, headquarters of the so-called 'Foundation for Institutional Care'. Handpicked on the basis of his Hartheim record to help build the Sobibor camp (he arrived there in March 1942), he was promoted in September 1943 to *SS-Oberscharführer* and received the Iron Cross from Himmler for his proficiency as a mass murderer. Between May 1942 and its closure in late October 1943, approximately 250,000 Jews were killed in Sobibor. As the senior NCO in the camp and second-in-command at Sobibor – he was also Franz Stangl's (q.v.) deputy at Treblinka – Master-Sergeant Wagner was in charge of 'selection' and ordered the deaths of hundreds of thousands of Jews. Known to his victims as the 'Human Beast', he has been described as an insatiable sadist and 'one of the most brutal thugs' in the camps, who incited others to hang, beat and kill prisoners. According to one survivor, Wagner 'didn't eat his lunch if he didn't kill daily. With an axe, shovel or even his hands. He had to have blood.' Another survivor recalled: 'He was an Angel of Death. For him, torturing and killing was a pleasure. When he killed he smiled.' Not by chance, the revolt at Sobibor in October 1943 took place during Wagner's vacation. On his return he was ordered to close the camp and was subsequently transferred to Italy where he again participated in the 'Final Solution'. He ended the war in an American POW camp, from which he was released on producing false papers. Sentenced to death *in absentia* by the Nuremberg Tribunal, he laid low as a building labourer in Graz, where he met his Austrian compatriot, Franz Stangl, the ex-Commandant of Treblinka. The two men proceeded south to Rome, escaping with the help of the Vatican via Syria to Brazil, where Wagner was admitted as a permanent resident on 12 April 1950. There he lived happily and freely in a Bavarian-style house outside São Paulo until his arrest on 30 May 1978. Wagner had been spotted among the guests at an old comrades' gathering to celebrate Hitler's eighty-ninth birthday by two reporters of a Rio de Janeiro newspaper. Extradition requests from Israel, Austria (where Wagner had been a citizen) and Poland were rejected by Brazil's Attorney-General. On 22 June 1979 the Brazilian Supreme Court also turned down a West German extradition request. Wagner, a dedicated Nazi, showed no remorse for his crimes. In a television interview about the exterminations at Sobibor (BBC, 18 June 1979), he commented: 'I had no feelings... It just became another job. In the evening we never discussed our work, but just drank and played cards.' Gustav Wagner committed suicide in São Paolo on 15 October 1980.

Wagner, Robert (1895–1946) *Gauleiter*

of Alsace-Baden during World War II, Robert Wagner was born on 13 October 1895 in Lindach. He volunteered for military service and served in an infantry regiment during World War I, remaining an active Reichswehr officer until 1924. One of Hitler's earliest followers, Wagner participated in the Beer-Hall *putsch*, standing trial with Hitler in 1924. Imprisoned six times for political rowdyism, Wagner was *Gauleiter* of the NSDAP in Baden from March 1925 and a member of the Baden diet from 1929 to 1933. A member of the Reichstag (*Wahlkreis* Baden) from 1933, Wagner was appointed *Reichsstatthalter* on 5 May of the same year. Responsible for reorganizing the Nazi Party in Baden, he was also Chairman of the local branch of the *Nordische Gesellschaft* (Nordic Society). Between 1940 and 1945, Wagner was Chief of the Civil Administration in Alsace. At Hitler's instigation, he carried out the deportations of October 1940, as a result of which more than 6,500 Jews from the *Gaue* of Baden and Saarpfalz were summarily expropriated and dumped into the unoccupied zone of France, without any previous warning. Wagner was imprisoned in 1945 and sentenced to death by a French military court. He was executed in Strasbourg on 14 August 1946.

Wagner, Winifred (1897–1980) Richard Wagner's English daughter-in-law, mistress of the Bayreuth Festival during the Third Reich, she was born in Hastings as Winifred Williams. Having lost both her parents before the age of two, she was adopted eight years later by a distant German relative of her mother, Karl Klindworth, a musician who had been an early supporter and friend of Richard Wagner. In 1914 he took his seventeen-year-old ward for the first time to the Bayreuth Festival. A year later she was married to Siegfried Wagner, the forty-five-year-old son of the famous composer. Winifred first met

Adolf Hitler (an ardent admirer Wagner's music) in 1923 at a time whe he was still an aspiring political agitatc During his imprisonment after the unsu cessful Munich *putsch*, Winifred se him food parcels and the paper on whic *Mein Kampf* was written. Hencefor her loyalty to Hitler and Nazism nev wavered. In 1930 when both Siegfri(and the aged Cosima (wife of Richa Wagner) died, the thirty-three-year-o Winifred found herself mistress of tł Festspielhaus. During the Third Rei(she turned it into a cultural shrine, oı of the annual highlights of the Na calendar and the glory of the Germ; opera season. By 1933 her relationsh with Hitler had grown so intimate th there were even rumours of a marriag Haus Wahnfried, the Wagner home Bayreuth, became the Chancellor's f vourite retreat from the cares of Stat Hitler, who regarded himself as patrc of the annual festival (it received gene ous government assistance and was cor pletely exempt from taxes), remained close friend of the family and treat(Winifred's children as his own. In Alb(Speer's words, 'he was gay, paternal the children, friendly and solicitous t wards Winifred Wagner'. No doubt tł had a great deal to do with his her, worship of Richard Wagner, who Hitler acknowledged as a major intelle tual influence and whose music reign(supreme during the Third Reich – len ing itself perfectly to Nazi myth-makin Bayreuth and Wagnerian art served an epic ritual or secular cult of Germ; nationalism, of Nordic self-realizatio *völkisch* creation and visions of gra deur. Like Hitler, Winifred Wagner b lieved profoundly in these values and Nazism as the fulfilment of her fathe in-law's aesthetic ideals. After the c(lapse of the Third Reich, she was forbi den, among other things, to run tł Bayreuth Festival, which she made ov to her sons Wieland and Wolfgang. 1975 she broke her long silence in marathon filmed interview with Hans-Jürgen Syberberg, where she appeared utterly unrepentant concerning the past. Her political view remained unbending, but what was more striking was her love for Hitler, the man who had always shown unfailing *Herzenstakt*. 'To have met him', Frau Wagner declared, 'is an experience I would not have missed.'

Waldeck-Pyrmont, Josias Erbprinz von (1896–1967) SS General who was Himmler's (q.v.) first blue-blooded recruit and a nephew of the Dutch Queen, Waldeck-Pyrmont was born in Arolsen/ Waldeck family castle on 13 May 1896. Entering the army as a cadet, he served in World War I and was severely wounded. After the war Waldeck-Pyrmont studied agriculture and joined the NSDAP on 1 November 1929. On 2 March 1930 he entered the SS in Munich as Adjutant to Sepp Dietrich (q.v.) and in September of the same year he became Himmler's Adjutant and staff chief. Promoted to SS Lieutenant-General, Waldeck-Pyrmont was also elected in 1933 as member of the Reichstag for the district of Düsseldorf-West. Himmler's first recruit from the old aristocracy, he rose to become Higher SS and Police Leader for the district of Kassel-Mainfranken in 1939 and during the war was promoted to SS General and General of the Waffen-SS. At his headquarters in Kassel he set up a 'Bureau for the Germanization of the Eastern Peoples'. In 1944 Waldeck-Pyrmont despatched the Crown Princess of Bavaria to the concentration camp of Buchenwald, which was under his jurisdiction. He was also responsible for ordering the execution of Ilse Koch's (q.v.) husband, the Commandant of Buchenwald, who had made himself a millionaire by private exploitation of concentration camp labour. After the war, Waldeck-Pyrmont was arrested and sentenced on 14 August 1947 to life imprisonment by an American court at Dachau. Released for health reasons in December 1950, he died on 30 November 1967 at the age of seventy-one.

Warlimont, Walther (1894–1977) Nazi General who was Jodl's (q.v.) deputy in the Armed Forces Operations Staff during World War II, Walther Warlimont was born in Osnabrück on 3 October 1894. A career officer of middle-class background, Warlimont had entered the army in 1913 as a cadet and served in World War I as a Lieutenant. During the Spanish Civil War he led the German volunteers for General Franco and acted as Plenipotentiary of the Reich War Ministry. In 1937, while still a Colonel in the Reichswehr Office of the Armed Forces, Warlimont prepared a report calling for the reorganization of the Wehrmacht under one staff and one supreme commander. The plan, which clearly aimed at limiting the power of the top officer élite in favour of the Führer, provided the basis for Hitler's establishment of the OKW (High Command of the Armed Forces). Warlimont was given the position of Jodl's deputy and Chief of the National Defence section in the OKW, which he occupied from 1939 to 1944, handling questions of recruiting and manpower. Promoted to Major General on 1 August 1940, Warlimont together with Jodl drew up the preliminary plans for Operation Barbarossa, the code name for the attack on the Soviet Union, in December 1940. A loyal Nazi, Warlimont was promoted to Lieutenant-General on 1 April 1942 and appointed head of the Wehrmacht Leadership Staff. On 1 April 1944 he was made General of Artillery. After the war, Warlimont was arrested and condemned to life imprisonment as a war criminal on 27 October 1948. The sentence was commuted to eighteen years and he was released in 1957 from Landsberg prison.

Weichs,   Maximilian   Freiherr   von

(1881–1954) General Field Marshal who distinguished himself during the Polish and western campaigns at the beginning of World War II, Maximilian von Weichs was born in Dessau on 12 November 1881. He entered the Reichswehr in 1919 with the rank of Captain after serving in World War I as an Adjutant. Promoted to Major General in 1933, he organized and commanded the First Panzer Division in the new German army, three years later. In 1938 he commanded the Thirteenth Army Corps which invaded Austria and the Sudetenland. General of Cavalry from October 1937, von Weichs was awarded the Knight's Cross in July 1940 following his participation in the western campaign. Put in charge of the central sector in the Balkan campaign, he was then transferred to the Russian front, commanding an army group in the southern sector. In February 1943 he was promoted to General Field Marshal. In April 1944 von Weichs was Commander of all German troops stationed in Hungary. In February 1945 he was awarded the Oak Leaves of the Knight's Cross. Von Weichs died in Rösberg-Cologne on 27 September 1954.

Weill, Kurt (1900–50) One of the most celebrated popular composers in Weimar Germany and pioneer of the *Singspiel* (song play), a cross between opera and musical comedy, Kurt Weill was born in Dessau on 2 March 1900, the son of a Jewish reform cantor. Descendant of a long line of rabbis but the 'least pious Jew of the family', Weill matriculated in 1918 from the famous *Hochschule für Musik* in Berlin and was accepted two years later as a student at the Prussian Academy of Arts. Influenced by the Italo-German composer Ferruccio Busoni, by Schönberg and Mahler, he developed a conception of 'gestic' music capable of presenting mass emotions and generalized symbols in an unabashedly popular style. His first

great success was the satirical farce *Die Dreigroschenoper* (*The Threepenny Opera*), based on a theme about proletarian life using modern American jazz rhythms and a text by Bertolt Brecht (q.v.). The combination of Weill's jazzy tunefulness and Brecht's cynicism, together with the performance of Lotte Lenya (Weill's non-Jewish wife and greatest interpreter), helped to make the play a phenomenal success as a ballad opera. The opening 'Ballad of Mack the Knife' became a world-wide hit. Brecht and Weill also collaborated on *Happy End* (1929), *Der Jasager* (*The Yes-Sayer*, 1930), a parable of Leninist virtue, and *Die Sieben Todsünden* (*The Seven Deadly Sins*) – a transition to his later career as a composer of Broadway musicals. Weill's last work in his German period was *Der Silbersee* (*The Silverlake*, 1932), performances of which were disrupted in Magdeburg by the Nazis. Weill's progressivism, his mockery of middle-class conventions and his Jewish origin made him anathema to the Nazi régime, which denounced his work as degenerate intellectualism. He fled to France in 1933 when about to be arrested and then emigrated to America two years later, where he composed popular folk operas such as *Knickerbocker Holiday* (1938), *Street Scene* (1947) and the Broadway musical *Lost in the Stars* (1949). He died in New York on 3 April 1950.

Weiss, Wilhelm (1892–1950) Editor-in-Chief of the *Völkische Beobachter* and President of the Reich Press Association, Wilhelm Weiss was born in Stadtsteinach, Bavaria, on 31 March 1892. In 1911 he joined the German army and served in World War I, where he reached the rank of Captain. Severely wounded (he lost his left leg in air combat), Weiss was posted to the Troop Office of the Bavarian War Ministry, where he wrote military commentaries for the Press Department. Registered for two years at the University of Munich, he did not take a degree but joined the Bayern *Freikorps* and a multitude of other paramilitary and veterans' organizations. In 1922 he was chief editor of the nationalist paper *Heimatland* and a year later took part in the Hitler *putsch*. Between 1924 and 1926 Weiss was chief editor of the *Völkische Kurier* and on 1 January 1927 joined the *Völkische Beobachter* as Alfred Rosenberg's (q.v.) assistant, taking over much of the editorial work and supervising the editorial staff. In 1933 the pliant Weiss became deputy editor and in 1938 he was made Editor-in-Chief, a role he had in fact exercised for some years without the title. As editor of the official Nazi newspaper with the largest circulation in the Third Reich, Weiss became the leading figure in German journalism. Appointed in 1934 by Goebbels to head the Reich Association of the German Press (*Reichsverband der Deutschen Presse*), Weiss had enthusiastically supported the imposition of coercion and control over the press by the political leadership, declaring that: 'Journalism today is no longer a middle-class business, and those who inwardly remain Philistines will certainly not be encouraged by us to clothe their tender souls in National Socialist garments.'

In practice, however, Weiss did not rigorously enforce the Editor's Law which he had supported as head of the Reich Association of Journalists. On the other hand, he never repudiated or distanced himself in any way from the Nazi system. Indeed, he was the recipient of many Party honours including the Golden Party Badge and the Service Cross, being promoted to the rank of *SA-Obergruppenführer* in 1937. A member of the Reichstag from 5 March 1933 (*Wahlkreis* Potsdam), of the People's Court and the *Reichskultursenat*, Weiss rose high in spite of his average intelligence, his reserved nature and the enmity of Reich Press Chief, Otto

Dietrich (q.v.). His efforts to improve the professional standards and the news coverage of the *Völkische Beobachter* were largely undermined by the dictatorial policies pursued by Hitler and Dietrich during the war. By 1945 Weiss had become completely disillusioned with the coercive system he had once supported. On 15 July 1949 a Munich de-Nazification court sentenced him to three years' imprisonment (which he had already served in internment camps), confiscation of one third of his property and suppression of professional rights for ten years. Weiss died on 24 February 1950, while his appeal was still pending.

Weiszäcker, Ernst Freiherr von (1882–1951) Foreign Office diplomat who served the Third Reich as State Secretary and later as Ambassador to the Holy See, Ernst von Weiszäcker was born in Stuttgart on 12 May 1882. After serving as a naval officer during World War I, he entered the Foreign Office in 1920 occupying various consular and diplomatic posts. From Consul in Basel (1922) and embassy Councillor in Copenhagen, he rose to the position of Minister in Oslo (1931–3) and Minister to Switzerland (1933–6). In 1937 he was appointed Ministerial Director and, following von Ribbentrop's (q.v.) nomination as Foreign Secretary, he became Chief State Secretary in the Foreign Office in Berlin, a post he held until 1943. For the last two years of the war, the compliant von Weiszäcker was German Ambassador to the Vatican. Arrested and placed on trial as a war criminal by the Allies, von Weiszäcker was sentenced on 2 April 1949 to five years' imprisonment by an American military tribunal at Nuremberg. Eighteen months after his conviction he was released under a general amnesty. In 1950 von Weiszäcker published his self-justificatory memoirs, *Erinnerungen,* in which he depicted himself as a man of the anti-Nazi Resistance, claiming that he had always opposed

Hitler's foreign policy and that he had accepted honorary rank in the SS for purely decorative reasons. An old guard diplomat, von Weiszäcker doubtless viewed the permeation of the Foreign Office by Nazis with some distaste, but this never prevented him from initialling any of the murderous documents which were submitted for his approval. He died in hospital at Lindau am Bodensee on 4 August 1951 soon after his release.

Wels, Otto (1873–1939) Social Democratic Party leader and Chairman of the SPD between 1931 and 1933, Otto Wels was born in Berlin on 15 September 1873. An upholsterer by profession and a long-time member of the SPD, Wels was elected to the Reichstag in 1912 and served until 1920 in the socialist parliamentary group. Between 1920 and 1933 he was again one of its representatives in the Reichstag and from 1931 a member of the Party Central Committee. As Party leader, it was Wels who on 23 March 1933 rose to oppose Hitler's request for special powers under the Enabling Act, the last genuine public debate to take place in Germany for twelve years. It was a courageous personal intervention in defence of democracy, though the content of Wels's speech revealed not only his limited intellectual scope but also how far removed the Social Democrats had become from the language of political liberty and international proletarian solidarity. Wels claimed that the Social Democratic Party was no less patriotic than the Nazis. He rejected the notion of German war guilt, reparations, and the exaggerations of the foreign press about the internal situation in Germany, and did not oppose Hitler's programme of rearmament and economic autarchy. Shortly after he was to emigrate to Prague and then, in 1938, he went to Paris, where he continued to lead the exiled SPD until his death on 16 September 1939.

Wessel, Horst (1907–30) Young Berlin SA leader who became a venerated martyr of the National Socialist movement, Horst Wessel was born in Bielefeld on 9 September 1907. He joined the NSDAP in 1926 and composed the simple marching song known as the 'Horst Wessel Lied'. After his death this tune was raised to the status of a national anthem, sung at public meetings and used as a musical background to the Nuremberg rallies of the 1930s. The young storm trooper was killed in a brawl in Berlin on 23 February 1930 and the furore over his death was cleverly manipulated by Goebbels (q.v.) to swing public sympathy in favour of the Nazis and against their enemies on the Left. The unsavoury details of his life were suppressed – Wessel was in reality a cheap pimp – and he was transformed into the ascetic hero of innumerable *Kampfzeit* epics, film canonizations and commemorative cantatas by the Nazi propaganda machine.

Weyl, Hermann (1888–1955) Arguably the greatest mathematician of his generation, Hermann Weyl was born in Elmshorn, near Hamburg, on 9 November 1885 and received his doctorate at Göttingen in 1908. Professor at the Technische Hochschule in Zürich (1913), he subsequently became Professor of Mathematics at Göttingen (1930) and for a brief time Director of its famous Mathematical Institute, following the racial purge of April 1933. As a mathematician Weyl made major contributions to quantum mechanics and relativity theory in works like *Raum, Zeit, Materie* (1918). In his *Die Idee der Riemannschen Fläche* (1913, Engl. trs. *The Concept of a Riemann Surface*), Weyl created a new branch of mathematics by uniting function theory and geometry, opening up the modern synoptic view of analysis, geometry and topology. He produced the first unified field theory, in which the Maxwell electromagnetic field, as well as gravitational field, appeared as a geometrical property of space–time. Another major achievement was his creation of a general theory of matrix representation of continuous groups and his discovery that many of the regularities of quantum mechanics could best be understood by means of group theory – an idea which he expounded in his *Gruppentheorie und Quantenmechanik* (1928). Weyl's gift for lucid exposition was also apparent in his influential writings on the philosophy of mathematics. Weyl's efforts to salvage mathematics at Göttingen from the ravages of Nazi officialdom proved unsuccessful and he soon left to join Einstein at the Institute of Advanced Studies, Princeton (USA), where he remained until 1951. Weyl, who died in Zürich on 8 December 1955, wrote in his memoirs: 'I could not bear to live under the rule of that demon [Hitler] who had dishonoured the name of Germany, and although the wrench was hard and the mental agony so cruel that I suffered a severe breakdown, I shook the dust of the fatherland from my feet.'

Wiechert, Ernst (1887–1950) A best-selling author of non-political novels in the Weimar Republic, initially tolerated by the Nazi régime and then persecuted in his own homeland, Ernst Wiechert was born in East Prussia, whose scenery and countryfolk provide the background to several of his novels. Following army service in World War I, Wiechert became a secondary-school teacher in Königsberg, then in a Berlin *Gymnasium* where he observed with growing concern the Nazism already rampant at schools and universities in the last years of the Weimar Republic. When Hitler came to power in 1933, Wiechert was retired from his school duties and left Berlin to live in Bavaria. At first, the Nazis tolerated and tried to exploit his work, claiming him as a poet of 'blood and soil'. The heroes of his quasi-mysti-

cal novels, who found solace in humble, non-urban pursuits, were far removed from what was condemned as 'asphalt literature' in the Third Reich. Nevertheless, novels like *Die Majorin* (1934) were criticized for failing to reflect the 'positive experience of war' and the resurrection of the nation. Wiechert's humane, religious outlook was attacked as an escape into inwardness and sterile traditionalism. Following 'subversive' remarks at a public lecture before students at Munich University in 1935, Wiechert was closely shadowed. A second address at Munich University in 1937, where he declared himself part of the conscience of Germany and warned that the nation 'stands already on the edge of an abyss and is doomed by the eternal law' if it failed to distinguish between right and wrong, made him a marked man. In 1938 he was sent to Buchenwald concentration camp as a 'seducer and corrupter of youth' and an enemy of the Reich. Four months later he was released, more or less a broken man, forbidden to publish anything in the future. Nevertheless, because of his influence, the Nazi managers of literature ordered him to take part in a literary meeting in Weimar where he was used as an advertisement for the 'generosity' of the régime. After the war, Wiechert wrote a stirring book about his experiences in Buchenwald, *Der Totenwald* (*Forest of the Dead*), published in Switzerland in 1946. He moved there, following threats to his life from former Nazis in Bavaria. Wiechert, looking back on the Third Reich, claimed that until 1938 most Germans had only a vague inkling of the terror that was perpetrated in the concentration camps. He defended the record of the working class, in contrast to the aristocracy, the army, the churches and the intellectuals under the Nazi régime: 'Never did the German worker bear a heavier load than during these twelve years, but never more honourable.' Wiechert's best-known novels and novellas include *Der Totenwolf* (1924), *Die kleine Passion* (1929), *Jedermann* (1931), *Die Magd der Jürgen Doskocil* (1932), *Hirtennovelle* (1935), *Der Kinderkreuzzug* (1935) and *Das heilige Jahr* (1936).

Wiedemann, Fritz (1891–1970) Hitler's regimental Adjutant and superior officer in World War I – the future Führer was a despatch bearer on his staff – and subsequently his political adviser on foreign affairs, Wiedemann was born on 15 August 1891 in Augsburg, Upper Bavaria. Pursuing an army career, he was promoted to Lieutenant in 1912 and during World War I he was Battalion Adjutant and Commanding Officer of the Seventeenth Bavarian Infantry Regiment. After the war Wiedemann retired and became a farmer in Lower Bavaria. In 1934 he joined the NSDAP, becoming Hitler's personal Adjutant, and was frequently sent on unofficial diplomatic missions. Active in Austrian affairs in 1936–7, he worked with the German Ambassador, von Papen (q.v.), against the incumbent Chancellor Schuschnigg (q.v.). In July 1938 he went to London for talks with Lord Halifax and in 1939 he was sent to San Francisco as German Consul-General. After his expulsion to Germany in June 1941, he was appointed German Consul-General in Tientsin (China), holding the post from October of the same year until his arrest by the Americans in 1945. Wiedemann, who had held the rank of *SA-Brigadeführer* since 1935, appeared as a witness at the Nuremberg trials where he was sentenced to twenty-eight months' imprisonment. Released in 1948 he subsequently lived as a farmer in southern Germany until his death in 1970.

Wiener, Alfred (1885–1964) The General Secretary of the *Centralverein Deutscher Staatsbürger Jüdischen Glaubens* (Central Organization of German Citizens of the Jewish Faith) in Wiemar

Germany, a refugee from the Third Reich and founder of the Wiener Library, Alfred Wiener was born in Potsdam on 16 March 1885. After attending grammar school in Bentschen, Poznan and then in Potsdam, he studied at the Universities of Berlin and Heidelberg, where he took his doctorate in Arab literature. After World War I, Wiener became the syndic and executive officer of the *Centralverein*, the largest Jewish organization in Germany, which at its peak represented 300,000 people, over half the Jewish population in the country. Its ideology was assimilationist, emphasizing that Jews were national Germans entitled to full equality and differentiated only by religion. It offered legal protection to Jews, fought against the erosion of Jewish identity and the flood of anti-semitic propaganda which was sweeping Germany in the 1920s. Wiener was particularly active in this struggle, regarding anti-semitism as a test case of German democracy and constantly protesting against the indifference of the authorities, the silence of the press and public apathy. His brochure *Vor Pogromen?* (1919) warned of the consequences of the pseudo-scientific hate-mongering which was perverting German nationalism under the eyes of the authorities, and he attacked the leniency of the judiciary in the early days of Nazi subversion. Wiener's appeals to the conservative middle classes fell on deaf ears and he was obliged to leave Germany in 1933, fleeing to Holland where he established the Jewish Central Information Office. This was the nucleus of the massive documentation on the perils of Nazism which he accumulated in the late 1930s and transferred to London in 1939. The renamed Wiener Library played an important role in the British government's propaganda warfare against Nazi Germany and as source material for the British military, officialdom and the press about the Third Reich. After the war, the Library provided crucial information in the prosecution of war criminals and subsequently developed into a major archive for the historical study of Nazism and the Third Reich. Wiener frequently visited Germany in the 1950s and sought to create a spirit of reconciliation between Jews and Germans while warning against any recrudescence of Nazism. He died in London on 4 February 1964.

Winnig, August (1878–1956) Former trade union official who welcomed the Nazis in 1933 as providing the 'salvation of the State' from Marxism, August Winnig was born in Blankenburg, Harz, on 31 March 1878 – the youngest son in a large family – and experienced grinding poverty and disillusionment in his childhood and adolescent years. Organizer of the masons' union, he was editor of its organ *Der Grundstein* from 1905 and elected its Vice-President in 1913. Winnig belonged to the 'social-imperialist' wing of the German Social Democratic Party (SPD). In 1917–18 he was Minister Plenipotentiary to the Baltic Provinces and Reich Commissioner for East and West Prussia. In 1919 *Oberpräsident* of East Prussia, he was removed from office a year later and expelled from the SPD for his participation in the Kapp *putsch*. Winnig's literary works in the last years of the Weimar Republic and under the Third Reich provide an illuminating account of the history of German social democracy between 1878 and 1933, and of his personal odyssey; they also reflect his love of nature, his Christian beliefs and working-class background. He was best known as the author of *Vom Proletariat zum Arbeitertum* (1930), of the autobiographical trilogy, *Frührot* (1924), *Der Weite Weg* (1932) and *Heimkehr* (1935) – and also of the political essays in *Wir hüten das Feuer* (1933). In *Europa: Gedanken eines Deutschen* (1937), Winnig set out his own conservative nationalist credo. His Lutheran convictions

led him to oppose the neo-pagan tendencies in the Third Reich and to withdraw from politics into the 'inner emigration'. Winnig died in Bad Nauheim on 3 November 1956.

Wirmer, Joseph (1901–44) Centre Party politician and lawyer who played an important part in the Resistance movement, Joseph Wirmer was born on 19 March 1901. Wirmer had been expelled from the *NS-Rechtswahrerbund* (National Socialist Lawyers' Association) for defending Jews. A skilful negotiator, he brought together the conservative wing of the Resistance around Carl Goerdeler (q.v.) and Social Democrats like Julius Leber (q.v.), who were politically closer to the young aristocratic leader of the conspiracy, Claus Schenk Graf von Stauffenberg (q.v.). After the failure of the attempt on Hitler's life, Wirmer was arrested and executed by order of the People's Court on 8 September 1944.

Wirsing, Giselher (1907–75) A prominent political journalist and Nazi expert on foreign affairs, Giselher Wirsing was born in Schweinfurt on 15 April 1907. Before the Nazi seizure of power, he was a luminary in the circle of antidemocratic intellectuals around *Die Tat*, whose anticapitalist yearnings were close to the Strasser wing of the NSDAP. In 1933 Wirsing joined the Nazi Party and the SS, working for a time in Alfred Rosenberg's Frankfurt Institute of Research into the Jewish Question. He was considered an expert on the 'Jewish question' in the Middle East, publishing *Engländer, Juden, Araber in Palästina* (1938) which echoed Rosenberg's analysis of Zionism and 'the triumph of the secret leadership of world Jewry'. Wirsing claimed that Great Britain had become a decadent, 'judaized' plutocracy, 'largely ruled by Jewish *Diktat*'. In works like *Hundert Familien beherrschen das Empire* (1940) and *Der*

Masslose Kontinent. Roosevelts Kampf um die Weltherrschaft (1942), Wirsing gave vent to his deep hostility to Britain and the United States. He was for a while an editor of the *Münchner Neueste Nachrichten* and between 1943 and 1945 he edited *Signal* – an illustrated quality magazine aimed at readers outside the Reich. A representative of the higher political journalism in Nazi Germany, he joined the editorial staff of the conservative Stuttgart weekly *Christ und Welt* (*The Christian and the World*), acting as its Editor-in-chief between 1954 and 1970. After the war he travelled widely, wrote books on Third World development and foreign affairs, and advocated stronger German ties with the Arab world. He condemned Adenauer's reparations agreement with Israel and lost no opportunity to denounce 'Israel's aggressions' against the Arabs as well as Anglo-Saxon imperialism in the Middle East. Wirsing died in Stuttgart on 23 September 1975.

Wirth, Christian (1885–1944) SS Major and head of the death camps organization in Poland (1942–3), Christian Wirth was born on 24 November 1885 in Oberbalzheim, Württemberg. As a non-commissioned officer in World War I on the western front, his bravery was rewarded by the golden Military Cross (*Militär-Verdienstkreuz*) – one of Imperial Germany's highest decorations. After several years in quiet obscurity, employed as a builder, Wirth re-emerged as a police officer in Württemberg and in the 1930s became notorious for his special methods of investigation in criminal matters, which eventually resulted in his arraignment before the Württemberg *Landestag*. Nevertheless, by 1939 Wirth had reached the rank of *Kriminalkommissar* in the Stuttgart criminal police (KRIPO), a department of the Gestapo under Arthur Nebe (q.v.). Towards the end of the year, Wirth was sent to Grafeneck psychiatric clinic for 'euthanasia duties', the first of fourteen such institutions in the Reich, where death was eventually to be administered by gassing and lethal injections. Wirth was then transferred to Brandenburg-an-der-Havel, a former prison converted into a euthanasia establishment, where he became the administrative head. At the end of 1939 he carried out the first known gassing experiments on Germans certified as incurably insane; these were watched by Brack (q.v.) and Bouhler (q.v.) of the Führer's Chancellery, from whom he was to receive orders during his later activities as Inspector of the Extermination Squads at Belzec, Sobibor and Treblinka in Poland. It was in Brandenburg that the idea of disguising the gas chambers as a shower-room was first perfected, at Bouhler's suggestion.

Wirth's 'excellent' record in exterminating incurables undoubtedly led to his highly 'confidential mission' in eastern Poland in the summer of 1941. Since mid-1940 he had been a roving inspector of euthanasia establishments throughout Greater Germany – some of them, such as Hadamar and Schloss Hartheim in Austria, which Wirth briefly commanded, were to provide future personnel for the death camps in Poland – and in July 1941, Bouhler and Brack decided to send him to Lublin to set up a new euthanasia establishment, the first outside the Reich. By the end of 1941 Wirth had been assigned to begin the extermination of Jews in Chelmno (Kulmhof), the first of five Nazi death camps in Poland to become operational. During the next eighteen months, he was given responsibility for overseeing the murder of more than two million Jews in the death camps of Belzec, Sobibor and Treblinka, in co-ordination with Odilo Globocnik (q.v.) and the SS police headquarters in Lublin. Wirth, a gross and brutal individual, whose verbal coarseness and cruelty richly earned him the epithet 'the savage Christian', prided himself on the system of terror he evolved in the extermination camps and the efficiency of the methods of gassing which he designed. He also claimed to have pioneered the use of Jewish *Sonderkommandos* – thereby forcing physically stronger Jews to bury their own people, before they, too, were killed. Though his bragging was notorious among his staff, there can be no doubt that as Commandant of Belzec he did have a hand in the evolution of new gassing techniques. A survivor of the Belzec camp, where 600,000 Jews were murdered, recalled Wirth as 'a tall, broad-shouldered man in his middle 40s, with a vulgar face – he was a born criminal. The extreme beast.... Although he seldom appeared, the SS men were terrified of him. He lived alone waited on by his Ukrainian batman, who delivered reports to him from the camp each day.' Following the liquidation of the Belzec camp by the autumn of 1943, Wirth was promoted to *SS-Sturmbannführer* and, together with his commando, was sent by Himmler to Trieste in Yugoslavia to join other German units. According to one account, Wirth was killed in street fighting with Yugoslav partisans on 26 May 1944. He may also have been the victim of a Jewish vengeance squad organized to hunt down Nazi mass murderers.

Wisliceny, Dieter (1911–48) SS Major and Eichmann's (q.v.) deputy, responsible for the mass deportation and murder of Jews from Slovakia, Greece and Hungary, Dieter Wisliceny was born on 13 January 1911 in Regularken, the son of a landowner. A failed theology student who had worked briefly as a clerk in a construction firm, Wisliceny was unemployed when he became a member of the NSDAP in 1931. In 1934 he joined the SS and in June of the same year entered the SD. At one time Eichmann's superior in the SS, he became his deputy during World War II and one of his 'Jewish experts', serving as an official in

the Reich Central Office of Jewish Emigration. From September 1940 he was attached to the German delegation in Bratislava as an adviser on Jewish questions to the Slovak government. Wisliceny, who belonged to the more educated stratum of the SS and was more concerned with money than a career, acquired a reputation in Slovakia for accepting bribes. Less fanatical than Eichmann, he accepted 50,000 dollars from the Jewish relief committee in Bratislava for delaying deportations from Slovakia in 1942. In 1943–4 Wisliceny was sent to Greece, where he headed the *Sonderkommando für Judenangelegenheiten* in Salonika, introducing the yellow badge and preparing deportations. In March 1944 he was called to Budapest to join Eichmann's special operations unit. Wisliceny, who liked to have himself addressed as 'Baron' by the Hungarian Jews, was actively involved in the bargaining for Jewish lives, but the instalments paid to him did not prevent the deportations to Auschwitz. At Nuremberg Wisliceny was a witness for the prosecution and gave shocking details about the 'Final Solution'. It was to him that Eichmann allegedly said that he would 'leap into his grave laughing', because the feeling that he had five million people on his conscience was to him 'a source of extraordinary satisfaction'. Wisliceny was eventually extradited to Czechoslovakia, standing trial in Bratislava where he was executed on 27 February 1948 for complicity in mass murder.

Witzleben, Erwin von (1881–1944) General Field Marshal of the Wehrmacht, Erwin von Witzleben was born in Breslau on 4 December 1881. An active officer from 1901, he served on the western front during World War I and was appointed Berlin Military Area Commander when the Nazis came to power in 1933. Assigned to Defence District III and given command of the Third

Army Corps in 1935, he was promoted to Lieutenant-General. In 1939–40 he commanded the First Army and following the fall of France he was named General Field Marshal on 19 July 1940. Von Witzleben was Commander of Army Group D in France and in overall charge of the Army West when he was retired from active service by Hitler. A veteran conspirator – he had three times failed to make a *putsch* – von Witzleben was chosen to be the military head of the Resistance circle and would have become Commander-in-Chief of the Wehrmacht in a new government had the plot to remove Hitler succeeded. Arrested on 21 July 1944 following the failure of the plot, he was the most broken and pathetic of the conspirators brought before the People's Court. His execution on 8 August 1944 was a particularly grisly affair. The sixty-three-year-old Field Marshal was pushed into a cellar at Berlin's Plötzensee prison, placed under a meathook and, half-naked with a running noose around his head, he was lifted and slowly strangled.

Wolff, Karl (1900–84) Chief SS and Police Commander in Italy and previously Chief of the personal staff of Heinrich Himmler (q.v.), Karl Wolff was born in Darmstadt on 13 May 1900, the son of a wealthy district court magistrate. He was on active service during World War I, rising to the rank of Lieutenant in the Guards and receiving the Iron Cross (First and Second Classes). From December 1918 to May 1920 he was a Lieutenant in the Hessian *Freikorps*. For the next five years he worked as a commercial clerk in various firms and from 1925 to 1933 was the proprietor of an advertising enterprise in Munich. He entered the NSDAP in 1931 and by March 1933 was already an SS leader. From March to June 1933 Wolff served as Adjutant to the right-wing nationalist Governor of Bavaria, General

Ritter von Epp (q.v.), and in July of the same year became Himmler's personal Adjutant. A member of the Reichstag for the district of Hessen from 1936, Wolff rose rapidly in the ranks of the SS. Made an SS Lieutenant-Colonel on 30 January 1934, he was promoted to SS Brigadier on 4 July 1934, to SS Major General on 9 November 1935 and to SS Lieutenant-General on 30 January 1937. He received the Golden Party Badge of the NSDAP on 30 January 1939 and was made Lieutenant-General of the Waffen-SS on 3 May 1940. Virtually Himmler's deputy from the nomination of Heydrich (q.v.) as 'Protector of Bohemia', he was also his chief liaison officer with the Führer. In 1941 he accompanied Himmler to Finland and received the Grand Cross of the Finnish White Rose with Swords in 1942. In the same year Wolff was promoted to *SS-Obergruppenführer* and Colonel General of the Waffen-SS.

In September 1943 Wolff became German Military Governor of northern Italy and Plenipotentiary to Mussolini during the last two years of the war. Convinced by the end of February 1945 that the war was lost, he established contact through Italian and Swiss intermediaries with Allen Dulles, the representative of the US Office of Strategic Services. His negotiations behind Hitler's back in Zürich led to the early surrender of German forces in Italy. For this service the elegant, smooth SS General was not tried at Nuremberg, appearing instead as a willing prosecution witness in full military uniform before the court. Sentenced to four years' hard labour by a German court in 1946, he spent only one week in prison. He subsequently became a highly successful advertising agent in Cologne, later building an elegant lakeside villa on the Starnberger See from his earnings. The exhibitionism of 'the SS General with the clean waistcoat' proved, however, to be his undoing. His memoirs published during the Eichmann (q.v.) trial in 1961 drew the public's attention and that of the Bavarian Justice Ministry to his wartime activities as a key figure in Himmler's immediate entourage and in the building up of the SS State. The amiable, aristocratic-looking Wolff was arrested on 18 January 1962 and charged with complicity in the mass murder of Jews. He was accused of sending at least 300,000 Jews to Treblinka death camp. In a letter of 13 August 1941 Wolff had professed to be 'particularly gratified with the news that each day for the last fortnight a trainload of 5,000 members of the "Chosen People" has been sent to Treblinka' and he was charged with arranging for additional railroad cars to facilitate the deportation of Jews from ghettoes and other areas where they were concentrated. Wolff was also accused of complicity in the shooting of partisans and Jews behind the front near Minsk, where he had been present as Himmler's Chief of Staff, and it was claimed that he was a willing participant in the 'Final Solution' in an advisory and consultative capacity. The assizes of the Munich County Court did not accept Wolff's denials of any knowledge of the death camps and sentenced him on 30 September 1964 to fifteen years' penal servitude and loss of civil rights for ten years. The sentence was softened in view of his 'otherwise blameless life' and contribution to shortening the war, and in 1971 he was released. Karl Wolff died in Rosenheim on 15 July 1984.

Y

Yorck von Wartenburg, Peter Graf (1903–44) A prominent member of the German Resistance and direct descendant of the famous Prussian general of the Napoleonic era who had helped bring down Bonaparte, Peter Yorck von Wartenburg was born in Klein Oels, Silesia, on 17 November 1903. The son of one of Germany's most renowned and aristocratic families, he studied law and politics at Bonn and Breslau, then worked in the civil service, rising to the rank of senior government Councillor. He served as a Lieutenant in the Polish campaign during World War II and from 1942 he was attached to the War Economy Office. One of the founders of the Kreisau Circle and a cousin of Claus Schenk von Stauffenberg (q.v.), he shared the latter's contempt for Hitler and National Socialism. One of the first conspirators to be arrested after the abortive plot of 20 July 1944, Yorck von Wartenburg's conduct in the People's Court was both dignified and brave, in the face of Roland Freisler's (q.v.) insults and provocations. Asked why he had never joined the NSDAP, he answered simply: 'Because I am not and never could be a Nazi.' His Resistance activity, like that of other members of the Kreisau Circle, was based on Christian conviction, the rejection as he explained to Freisler of 'the totalitarian claim of the State on the individual which forces him to renounce his moral and religious obligations to God'. He was hanged on 8 August 1944.

Z

Zangen, Wilhelm (1891–1971) Leading German industrialist and head of the *Reichsgruppe Industrie* (German industry Association) after 1938, Wilhelm Zangen was born in Duisburg on 30 September 1891. An excellent businessman and first-class technician, Zangen had already reached positions of high responsibility in his late thirties. A member of the NSDAP from 1937 and of the SS as well as of the German Law Academy, Zangen held the title of War Economy Leader under the Third Reich and from December 1934 until 1957 he was Chairman of the Board of the Mannesmann tube rolling mills in Düsseldorf. General Director of the Mannesmann concern, which employed slave labour during World War II, he became head of the German Industry Association in 1938 and was also Vice-President of the Chamber of Industry and Commerce in Düsseldorf and deputy head of the Reich Economic Chamber in Berlin. Zangen's directorships included AEG, the Deutsche Bank, Kronprinz AG of the metal industry in Solingen-Ohligs and the machine factory Meer AG in München-Gladbach. From 1957 to 1966 Zangen was Chairman of the *Aufsichtsrat* (Board) at Mannesmann. He died in Düsseldorf on 25 November 1971.

Zeitzler, Kurt (1895–1963) Chief of the General Staff of the German army from 1942 to 1944, Kurt Zeitzler was born in Cossmar-Luckau on 9 June 1895, the son of a parson. After serving in World War I as Commander of an infantry regiment, Zeitzler continued his career in the Reichswehr, establishing himself as an able staff officer and expert in mobile warfare. Under the Third Reich, Zeitzler was promoted to a series of demanding positions while still a relatively young Commander. Attached to the Army Command in 1937–8 as a Lieutenant-Colonel, he served as a corps Chief of Staff during the Polish invasion and then in the 1940 campaign of von Kleist's (q.v.) Panzer army in France. From March 1940 to April 1942 Zeitzler was Chief of Staff of the First Panzer Group and then, as Major General, Chief of Staff of Army Group D under von Rundstedt (q.v.) in the West. A master of improvisation, Zeitzler's string of successes in exacting posts impressed Hitler, who appointed him Chief of the Army General Staff on 22 September 1942 in succession to General Franz Halder (q.v.). Hitler evidently hoped that Zeitzler would conduct the Russian campaign with more vigour than the old military leadership and that he would not question the Führer's methods of command. By the autumn of 1942, however, it was apparent that the German position in Russia was precarious and that a temporary retreat was necessary. Zeitzler urged Hitler to allow the Sixth Army to withdraw from Stalingrad where they were being encircled by Russian forces, or at least to authorize a breakout while it was still possible. Hitler rejected this advice, though after the final surrender of von Paulus's (q.v.) Sixth Army, Zeitzler was able to persuade the Führer to make strategic withdrawals from Moscow and Leningrad. The failure of the planned German offensive at Kursk (July 1943) and then the

Crimean collapse in 1944 disillusioned Zeitzler, who sought to resign on several occasions. He went on sick leave and on 20 July 1944 he retired for reasons of ill health. In January 1945 Hitler had him dismissed from the army and deprived of the customary right to wear uniform. Zeitzler died at Hohenasschau, Upper Bavaria, on 25 September 1963.

Ziegler, Adolf (1892–1959) President of the Reich Chamber of Art and Hitler's favourite painter, Adolf Ziegler was born in Bremen in 1892. An officer during World War I, Ziegler was subsequently trained at the Arts Academy in Weimar and took up painting. From 1925 in personal contact with Hitler, he joined the Nazi Party and later became the expert on the arts in the Reich Leadership of the NSDAP in Munich. A mediocre painter, if technically accomplished, Ziegler was known for his prim, pseudo-classical, waxwork nudes and his depiction of ideal Aryan types. His artistic 'realism' left nothing to the imagination – not for nothing was he known as '*Meister des Deutschen Schamhaares*' – but his work enthused Hitler who commissioned him to paint the portrait of his blonde niece, Geli Raubal,

reputedly the only deep love of his life. Professor at the Munich Academy of Fine Arts from 1933, Ziegler became the foremost official painter of the Third Reich. In 1936 he was appointed President of the Reich Chamber of Visual Arts, a position he held until his dismissal in 1943. In 1937 he was authorized by Hitler to strip all galleries and museums in the Reich of so-called 'degenerate art', including some 16,000 examples of expressionist, abstract, cubist and surrealist works of art. The paintings of such 'degenerate' artists as Max Ernst, Franz Marc, Max Beckmann, Emil Nolde (q.v.), Oskar Kokoschka, George Grosz and Kandinsky were confiscated on Ziegler's orders as head of the purge tribunal. In July 1937 Ziegler organized the Exhibition of Degenerate Art in Munich, which, to the great embarrassment of the Nazis, proved to be the most popular display of painting ever staged in the Third Reich. More than two million visitors came to see the works rejected by Hitler while a concurrent exhibition of 'approved' works of art aroused far less interest. Adolf Ziegler died in September 1959 at the age of sixty-seven in Varnhalt near Baden-Baden.

Glossary

Abteilung: Branch, Section of Main Department or Office.

Abwehr: German Military Counter-Intelligence headed by Admiral Canaris.

Adolf Hitler Schulen: Adolf Hitler Schools.

Adolf Hitler Spende: Adolf Hitler Fund.

Afrika Korps: Special unit formed to aid the Italians in North Africa, which became part of the German Panzer Army under Rommel in January 1942.

Alte Kämpfer: 'Old Fighters' who were early members of the Nazi Party.

Anschluss: Union between Germany and Austria carried out in March 1938.

Auf Gut Deutsch: *In Plain German*, anti-semitic paper edited and published by Dietrich Eckart in post-1918 Munich.

Auslandsdeutsche: Germans living abroad.

Autobahn: Superhighway. Name given to German motorway system.

Bekenntniskirche: Confessional Church in Nazi Germany.

Blitzkrieg: Lightning War, first used by the Germans in their invasion of Poland.

Blood Purge: Night of the Long Knives on 30 June 1934 when the SA leadership was massacred.

Blut und Boden: 'Blood and Soil'. Slogan of Nazi agrarian romanticism.

CDU: Christian Democratic Union.

Deutsche Arbeiterpartei (DAP): German Workers' Party founded in 1919 by Anton Drexler.

Deutsche Arbeitsfront (DAF): German Labour Front founded in 1933 by Robert Ley.

Einsatzgruppen: Task Forces. Special mobile formations which carried out the massacres of Jews, communists and partisans on the eastern front during World War II.

Einsatzkommandos: Special killer units which were individual detachments of the *Einsatzgruppen*.

Endlösung, Die: The 'Final Solution'. Cover name for the plan to exterminate all the Jews of Europe under German control.

Freikorps: Free Corps. Paramilitary units which sprang up all over Germany after the military defeat of 1918.

Freundeskreis Heinrich Himmler: Circle of Friends of Heinrich Himmler from the business world, who financially supported the SS.

Führer, Der: The Leader (Adolf Hitler).

Führerbunker: Leader's Bunker in Berlin where Hitler committed suicide.

Gau: District.

Gauleiter: District Leader of the Nazi Party.

Gestapo (Geheime Staatspolizei): Secret State Police, later incorporated into the Reich Main Security Office and headed by Heinrich Müller.

Generalgouvernment: German-occupied Poland administered by Hans Frank from his headquarters in Cracow.

Gleichschaltung: Co-ordination.

Herrenvolk: Master Race.

Kampfbund für Deutsche Kultur: League of Struggle for German Culture founded in 1929 by Alfred Rosenberg.

Kampfzeit: The Time of Struggle. Term applied to the early days of the Nazi movement.

KPD: Communist Party of Germany led by Ernst Thaelmann.

Kraft durch Freude: Strength through Joy. A National Socialist recreational organization controlled by the German Labour Front.

Kriminalpolizei (**KRIPO**): Criminal Police headed by Arthur Nebe.

KRIPO, see *Kriminalpolizei.*

Lebensborn: Spring of Life. SS stud farm which was the brainchild of Himmler's programme for the creation of a pure Aryan race.

Lebensraum: Living Space. Code word for the desire of Germany to expand into central and eastern Europe.

Leibstandarte-SS **Adolf Hitler**: SS Bodyguard Regiment Adolf Hitler.

Luftwaffe: German Air Force under Hermann Goering.

Mittelstand: Middle Class.

Nationalkommittee Freies Deutschland: National Committee for a Free Germany.

NSDAP (*Nationalsozialistische Deutsche Arbeiterpartei*): The National Socialist German Workers' Party, full title of the Nazi Party.

NS Deutscher Studentenbund: National Socialist German Students' League.

NS Lehrerbund: National Socialist Teachers' League.

OKH (*Oberkommando des Heeres*): The High Command of the Army.

OKW (*Oberkommando der* **Wehrmacht**): The High Command of the entire Armed Forces.

Ordensburgen: Order Castles for training the future Nazi élite.

Ordenspolizei: Order Police. Uniformed police force.

Organization Todt: Semi-military government agency under Fritz Todt concerned with the construction of strategic highways and military installations.

OSS: United States Office of Strategic Services under Allen Dulles which was based in Europe and maintained contacts with the German Resistance.

Ostministerium: Reich Ministry for the Occupied Eastern Territories created in 1941 under Alfred Rosenberg.

Panzer: Armour. Formations of tanks or tanks themselves.

Parteikanzlei: Hitler's Chancery directed by Martin Bormann.

POW: Prisoner of War.

Rasse-und Siedlungshauptamt: SS Central Office for Race and Settlement responsible for the racial purity of the SS and settlement of colonists in conquered eastern territories.

Referat: A 'desk' within the section of a Ministry.

Referent: The official or expert in charge of a *Referat.*

Regierungsrat: Government Councillor.

Reichsführer-SS: Reich Leader of the SS. Position occupied by Heinrich Himmler from 1929 to 1945.

Reichsführung-SS: Reich High Command of the SS.

Reichskanzlei: Chancery of the Reich Chancellor directed by Heinrich Lammers

Reichskanzler: Reich Chancellor, i.e. Adolf Hitler.

Reichskommissar: Reich Commissioner.

Reichskommissar für die Festigung des deutschen Volkstums: Reich Commissioner for the Strengthening of Germandom. Office occupied by Himmler after 1939.

Reichskulturkammer: Reich Chamber of Culture.

Reichsleiter: Reich Leader. Highest ranking Party official.

Reichsschatzmeister: Treasurer of the Nazi Party.

Reichssicherheitshauptamt (**RSHA**): Reich Main Security Office formed in 1939. Its departments included the Intelligence Division, the Gestapo, the Criminal Police and the SD.

Reichssportführer: Reich Sports Leader.

Reichsstatthalter: Reich Governor of a region or district.

Reichstag: Parliament. Stripped of its legislative function during the Third Reich, its role was largely decorative.

Reichsvereinigung der Juden in Deutschland: Reich Association of Jews in Germany. A compulsory organization of all Jews (as defined by the racialist Nuremberg Laws of 1935) in Nazi Germany. It replaced the previous framework called the *Reichsvertretung der Juden in Deutschland*.

Reichsvertretung der Juden in Deutschland: Reich Representative Council of German Jews headed by Rabbi Leo Baeck.

Reichswehr: Defensive Land Forces. Name given to the limited standing army under the Weimar Republic. In 1935 it was renamed the Wehrmacht.

Rotfrontkämpferbund: Red Front Fighters' Association. Paramilitary arm of the German Communist Party during the Weimar Republic.

RSHA, see *Reichssicherheitshauptamt.*

SA (*Sturmabteilungen*): The storm troopers or 'Brownshirts' founded in 1921 as a private army of the Nazi Party under Ernst Röhm. Hitler's first bodyguard, later eclipsed by the SS after the massacre of its leadership in June 1934.

Schwarze Korps, Das: *The Black Corps.* Official weekly newspaper of the SS.

Schutzpolizei: Protection police. Regular, uniformed, municipal and country constabulary.

SD (*Sicherheitsdienst*): Security Service of the SS founded in 1932 and directed by Reinhard Heydrich, which became the sole intelligence service of the Nazi Party.

SPD: Social Democratic Party of Germany, outlawed in 1933.

SRP: Socialist Reich Party.

SS (*Schutzstaffel*): Protection squads formed in 1925, the black-shirted personal bodyguard of Hitler which grew into the most powerful organization within the Nazi Party and the Nazi State under the leadership of Heinrich Himmler.

Stahlhelm: Steel Helmet. Nationalist ex-servicemen's organization founded in 1918 by Franz Seldte.

Standarte: SS regiment.

Totenkopfverbände: Death's Head Formations employed as concentration camp guards under the direction of Theodor Eicke. In 1939 they formed one of the first SS formations of the Waffen-SS.

USCHLA (*Untersuchungs- und Schlichtungs-Ausschüsse*) National Socialist Party courts with the power of life and death over Party members, headed by Major Walter Buch.

Vergeltungswaffen: Reprisal Weapons. The secret weapons, the V-1 and V-2, launched against Britain towards the end of World War II, which Hitler hoped would bring victory to Germany.

Vichy: French government established by Marshal Pétain during the Nazi occupation of France.

Volk: Race.

Völkisch: National, racial, ethnic.

Völkische Beobachter: *Racial Observer.* The official newspaper of the Nazi Party.

Volksdeutsche: Ethnic Germans.

Volksdeutsche Mittelstelle (VOMI): German Racial Assistance Office founded in 1936 and headed by Werner Lorenz.

Volksgemeinschaft: The People's Community. Nazi slogan expressing the allegedly classless form of national solidarity to which the régime aspired.

Volksgenosse: Member of the *Volk.* Racial comrade.

Volksgericht: People's Court presided

over by Roland Freisler from 1942 to 1945.

Volkssturm: People's Army. German Home Guard in World War II.

Volkswagen: People's Car.

VOMI, see ***Volksdeutsche Mittelstelle.***

Waffen-SS: Armed SS élite. Combat formations of the SS which also included non-German SS units after 1940.

Wahlkreis: Electoral Disctrict.

Wehrkreis: Military District.

Wehrmacht: The Armed Forces, i.e. the army, air force and navy.

Wehrwirtschaft: War Economy.

Wehrwirtschaftsführer: War Economy Leader.

WVHA (***Wirtschafts-und Verwaltungshauptamt***): Economic and Administrative Main Office of the SS, formed in 1942 and headed by Oswald Pohl. It administered the concentration camps and controlled the economic enterprises of the SS.

Comparative Ranks

German ARMY	SS	British	American
Generalfeldmarschal	Reichsführer-SS	Field Marshal	General of the Army
Generaloberst	SS-Oberstgruppenführer	General	General
General	SS-Obergruppenführer	Lieutenant-General	Lieutenant-General
Generalleutnant	SS-Gruppenführer	Major General	Major General
Generalmajor	SS-Brigadeführer	Brigadier	Brigadier General
Oberst	SS-Oberführer	Colonel	Colonel
Oberst	SS-Standartenführer	Lieutenant-Colonel	Lieutenant-Colonel
Oberstleutnant	SS-Obersturmbannführer	Major	Major
Major	SS-Sturmbannführer	Captain	Captain
Hauptmann	SS-Hauptsturmführer	Captain	Captain
Oberleutnant	SS-Obersturmführer	Lieutenant	First Lieutenant
Leutnant	SS-Untersturmführer	Second Lieutenant	Second Lieutenant

NAVY		British	American
Grossadmiral		Admiral of the Fleet	Fleet Admiral
Generaladmiral		Admiral	Admiral
Vizeadmiral		Vice Admiral	Vice Admiral
Konteradmiral		Rear Admiral	Rear Admiral
		Commodore	Commodor
Kapitän zur See		Captain	Captain
Fregattenkapitän		Commander	Commander
Korvettenkapitän		Lieutenant-Commander	Lieutenant-Commander
Kapitänleutnant		Lieutenant	Lieutenant
Oberleutnant zur See		Sub-Lieutenant	Lieutenant Junior Grade
Leutnant zur See		Acting Sub-Lieutenant	Ensign

AIR FORCE		British	American
Reichsmarshall		Marshal of the RAF	United States Marine Corps and United States Air Force officer ranks are the same as United States Army ranks
Generaloberst		Air Chief Marshal	
General der ... (unit concerned)		Air Marshal	
Generalleutnant		Air Vice Marshal	
Generalmajor		Air Commodore	
Oberst		Group Captain	
Oberstleutnant		Wing Commander	
Major		Squadron Leader	
Hauptmann		Flight Lieutenant	
Oberleutnant		Flying Officer	
Leutnant		Pilot Officer	

Bibliography

Abshagen, Karl Heinz, *Canaris* (Stuttgart 1949)

Ackermann, Josef, *Heinrich Himmler als Ideologe* (Göttingen 1970)

Adam, Peter, *Art of the Third Reich* (New York 1992)

Adam, Uwe Dietrich, *Judenpolitik im Dritten Reich* (Düsseldorf 1972)

Addington, Larry H., *The Blitzkrieg Era and the German General Staff, 1865–1941* (New Brunswick 1971)

Allen, William Sheridan, *The Nazi Seizure of Power* (London 1966)

Alquen, Gunter d', *Die SS: Geschichte, Aufgabe und Organisation der Schutzstaffel der NSDAP* (Berlin 1939)

Arendt, Hannah, *The Origins of Totalitarianism* (New York 1951)

Arendt, Hannah, *Eichmann in Jerusalem* (London 1963)

Aronson, Shlomo, *Reinhard Heydrich und die Frühgeschichte von Gestapo und SD* (Stuttgart 1971)

Balfour, Michael, and Frisby, Julian, *Helmut von Moltke: A Leader against Hitler* (New York 1972)

Barkai, Avraham, *Das Wirtschaftssystem des Nationalsozialismus. Der Historische und Ideologische Hintergrund 1933–1936* (Cologne 1977)

Barron, Stephanie, *"Degenerate Art". The Fate of the Avant-Garde in Nazi Germany* (Los Angeles and New York 1991)

Bartov, Omer, *The Eastern Front, 1941–45* (London 1985)

Bartz, Karl, *Swastika in the Air* (London 1956)

Baumbach, Werner, *The Life and Death of the Luftwaffe* (New York 1960)

Baynes, Norman (ed.), *The Speeches of Adolf Hitler*, April 1922 to August 1939, 2 vols (London 1943)

Ben Elissar, Eliahu, *La Diplomatie du IIIe Reich et les Juifs (1933–1939)* (Paris 1969)

Berben, Paul, *Dachau: The Official History 1933–1945* (London 1975)

Berghahn, Volker Rolf, *Der Stahlhelm* (Düsseldorf 1966)

Best, Werner, *Die Deutsche Polizei* (Darmstadt 1941)

Bethge, Eberhard, *Dietrich Bonhoeffer* (New York 1970)

Bewley, Charles, *Hermann Goering and the Third Reich* (New York 1962)

Beyerchen, Alan, *Scientists under Hitler: Politics and the Physics Community in the Third Reich* (New Haven 1977)

Binion, Rudolph, *Hitler among the Germans* (New York 1976)

Bleuel, Hans Peter, *Sex and Society in Nazi Germany* (Philadelphia 1973)

Blumentritt, Günther, *Von Rundstedt* (London 1952)

Bollmus, Reinhard, *Das Amt Rosenberg und seine Gegner* (Stuttgart 1970)

Botz, Gerhard, *Wien vom 'Anschluss' zum Krieg* (Vienna 1978)

Bracher, Karl-Dietrich, Sauer, W., and Schulz, G., *Die Nationalsozialistische Machtergreifung* (Cologne 1960)

Bracher, Karl-Dietrich, *The German Dictatorship* (London 1971)

Bramstead, Ernest K., *Goebbels and National Socialist Propaganda 1925–*

45 (London 1965)

Breitman, Richard, *The Architect of Genocide. Himmler and the Final Solution* (London 1991)

Brenner, Hildegard, *Die Kunstpolitik des Nationalsozialismus* (Hamburg 1963)

Broszat, Martin, *German National Socialism 1919–1945* (Santa Barbara 1966)

Broszat, Martin, *Der Staat Hitlers: Grundlegung und Entwicklung seiner inneren Verfassung* (Munich 1969)

Broszat, Martin, and Krausnick, Helmut, *Anatomy of the SS State* (London 1973)

Browning, Christopher, *The Final Solution and the German Foreign Office* (New York 1978)

Buchheim, Hans, *Das dritte Reich: Grundlagen und politische Entwicklung* (Munich 1958)

Buchheim, Hans, *SS and Polizei im NS-Staat* (Bonn 1964)

Bullock, Alan, *Hitler: A Study in Tyranny* (London 1962)

Burden, Hamilton T., *The Nuremberg Party Rallies: 1929–39* (London 1967)

Burleigh, Michael and Wippermann, Wolfgang, *The Racial State. Germany 1933–1945* (Cambridge 1991)

Carr, William, *Hitler: A Study in Personality and Politics* (London 1978)

Carsten, F. L., *Die Reichswehr und Politik, 1918–1933* (Cologne/Berlin 1964)

Cecil, Robert, *The Myth of the Master Race: Alfred Rosenberg and Nazi Ideology* (New York 1972)

Childers, Thomas, *The Nazi Voter. The Social Foundations of Fascism in Germany, 1919–1933* (Chapel Hill 1983)

Cohn, Norman, *Warrant for Genocide* (London 1967)

Collier, Basil, *The Battle of Britain* (London 1962)

Conway, John S., *The Nazi Persecution of the Churches 1933–45* (London 1968)

Courtade, Francis, and Cadars, Pierre,

Histoire du Cinéma Nazi (Paris 1972)

Craig, Gordon, *The Politics of the Prussian Army, 1940–1945* (London 1967)

Crankshaw, Edward, *The Gestapo* (London 1956)

Crew, David (ed.) *Nazism and German Society 1933–1945* (London 1994)

Dallin, Alexander, *German Rule in Russia 1941–45: A Study in Occupation Policies* (London 1957)

Dawidowicz, Lucy, *The War Against the Jews* (New York 1975)

Dawidowicz, Lucy, *The Holocaust and the Historians* (Harvard 1981)

Delarue, Jacques, *The History of the Gestapo* (London 1964)

Deutsch, Harold, *Hitler and his Generals* (Minneapolis 1974)

Dicks, Henry V., *Licensed Mass Murder: A Socio-Psychological Study of Some SS Killers* (London 1972)

Diels, Rudolf, *Lucifer ante portas: Es spricht der erste Chef der Gestapo* (Stuttgart 1950)

Dietrich, Otto, *The Hitler I Knew* (London 1955)

Documents on German Foreign Policy, 1918–1945, Series D, 2 vols

Domarus, Max, *Hitler: Reden und Proklamationen, 1932–1945* (Würzberg 1962)

Douglas-Home, Charles, *Rommel* (London 1973)

Duesterberg, Theodor, *Der Stahlhelm und Hitler* (Wolfenbüttel 1949)

Eckart, Dietrich, *Der Bolschewismus von Moses bis Lenin: Zwiegespräch zwischen Adolf Hitler und mir* (Munich 1924)

Farias, Victor, *Heidegger and Nazism* (Philadelphia 1989)

Farquharson, J. E., *The Plough and the Swastika: The NSDAP and Agriculture in Germany 1928–45* (London 1976)

Ferencz, Benjamin B., *Less than Slaves* (Cambridge, Mass. 1979)

Fest, Joachim, *The Face of the Third Reich* (London 1970)

Fest, Joachim, *Hitler* (London 1974)

Fitzgibbon, Constantin, *20 July* (New York 1956)

Flittner, Andreas (ed.), *Deutsches Geistesleben and Nationalsozialismus* (Tübingen 1965)

Fraenkel, Ernst, *The Dual State* (New York 1941)

Frank, Hans, *Im Angesicht des Galgens* (Munich 1953)

Franz-Willing, Georg, *Die Hitlerbewegung* (Hamburg 1962)

Freisler, Roland, *Nationalsozialistisches Recht und Rechtsdenken* (Berlin 1938)

Friedländer, Saul, *Kurt Gerstein ou l'ambiguité du bien* (Paris 1967)

Friedländer, Saul, *L'Antisémitisme Nazi* (Paris 1971)

Frischauer, Willi, *The Rise and Fall of Hermann Goering* (Boston 1951)

Frischauer, Willi, *Himmler* (London 1953)

Führerlexikon, Das deutsche (Berlin 1934–5)

Funke, Manfred (ed.), *Hitler, Deutschland und die Mächte* (Düsseldorf 1977)

Galland, Adolf, *The Luftwaffe at War, 1939–45* (London 1972)

Gallo, Max, *The Night of the Long Knives* (New York 1972)

Gilbert, G.M., *Nuremberg Diary* (New York 1947)

Gisevius, Hans Bernd, *Adolf Hitler* (Munich 1963)

Gisevius, Hans Bernd, *To the Bitter End* (London 1948)

Goebbels, Joseph, *Vom Kaiserhof zur Reichskanzlei* (Munich 1940)

Goebbels, Joseph, *The Goebbels Diaries* (London 1948)

Goebbels, Joseph, *Tagebücher 1945* (Hamburg 1977)

Gordon, Harold J., *Hitler and the Beer-Hall Putsch* (Princeton 1972)

Graber, G. S. *Stauffenberg: Resistance Movement within the General Staff* (New York 1973)

Graml, Hermann, *Antisemitism in the Third Reich* (Oxford 1992)

Gruchmann, Lothar (ed.), *Autobiographie eines Attentäters: Johann Georg Elser* (Stuttgart 1970)

Grünberger, Richard, *A Social History of the Third Reich* (London 1977)

Guderian, Heinz, *Panzer Leader* (London 1952)

Hagemann, Walter, *Publizistik im Dritten Reich* (Hamburg 1948)

Halder, Franz, *Hitler als Feldherr* (Munich 1949)

Hale, Oron J., *The Captive Press in the Third Reich* (Princeton 1964)

Hallgarten, George W. F., *Hitler, Reichswehr und Industrie* (Frankfurt 1955)

Hanfstaengel, Ernst, *Unheard Witness* (Philadelphia 1957)

Hassell, Ulrich von, *The Von Hassell Diaries* (London 1948)

Heiber, Helmut, *Joseph Goebbels* (Berlin 1962)

Heiber, Helmut, *Walter Frank und sein Reichsinstitut für Geschichte des neuen Deutschland* (Stuttgart 1967)

Heiden, Konrad, *Hitler: A Biography* (London 1936)

Helmreich, E., *The German Churches under Hitler* (Detroit 1979)

Herf, Jeffrey, *Reactionary Modernism. Technology, Culture, and Politics in Weimar and the Third Reich* (Cambridge 1987)

Hilberg, Raul, *The Destruction of the European Jews* (London/Chicago 1961)

Hildebrand, Klaus, *The Foreign Policy of the Third Reich* (London 1973)

Hillgruber, Andreas, *Hitlers Strategie: Politik und Kriegsführung, 1940–1941* (Frankfurt/M 1965)

Himmler, Heinrich, *Die Schutzstaffel als antibolschewistische Kampforganisation* (Munich 1936)

Hinz, Berthold, *Art in the Third Reich* (New York 1979)

Hitler, Adolf, *Mein Kampf*, 2 vols (Munich 1930)

Hoess, Rudolf, *Commandant in Ausch-*

witz (London 1959)

Hofer, Walther (ed.), *Der Nationalsozialismus: Dokumente 1933–1945* (Frankfurt/M 1971)

Hoffmann, Peter, *The History of the German Resistance 1933–1945* (London 1977)

Höhne, Heinz, *The Order of the Death's Head* (London 1969)

Höhne, Heinz, *Canaris* (Munich 1978)

Hull, David St, *Film in the Third Reich* (University of California Press 1969)

Irving, David, *The Rise and Fall of the Luftwaffe* (Boston 1974)

Irving, David, *Hitler's War* (London 1977)

Jäckel, Eberhard, *Hitlers Weltanschauung. Entwurf einer Herrschaft* (Tübingen 1969)

Jacobsen, H. A., *Nationalsozialistische Aussenpolitik 1933–1938* (Frankfurt/M 1968)

Just, Günther, *Alfred Jodl: Soldat ohne Furcht und Tadel* (Hanover 1971)

Kater, Michael H., *Das 'Ahnenerbe' der SS, 1933–45* (1974)

Kater, Michael, *The Nazi Party* (Oxford 1983)

Keegan, John, *Waffen SS: The Asphalt Soldiers* (London 1970)

Kershaw, Ian, *Popular Opinion and Political Dissent in the Third Reich. Bavaria 1933–1945* (New York 1983)

Kershaw, Ian, *The Hitler Myth. Image and Reality in the Third Reich* (Oxford 1989)

Kersten, Felix, *The Kersten Memoirs, 1940–1945* (London 1956)

Kesselring, Albert, *A Soldier's Record* (New York 1954)

Kissenkoetter, Udo, *Gregor Strasser und die NSDAP* (Stuttgart 1978)

Klarsfeld, Serge (ed.), *Die Endlösung der Judenfrage in Frankreich* (1977)

Kochan, Lionel, *Pogrom: 10 November 1938* (London 1957)

Kogon, Eugen, *Der SS-Staat* (Frankfurt/M 1965)

Koon, Claudia, *Mothers in the Fatherland. Women, the Family and Nazi Politics* (London 1987)

Kracauer, Siegfried, *From Caligari to Hitler: A Psychological Study of German Films* (New York 1946)

Krausnick, H. and Wilhelm, H–H., *Die Truppe des Weltanschauungs–Krieges: Die Einsatzgruppen des SD, 1938–1942* (Stuttgart 1981)

Kuhn, Axel, *Das faschistische Herrschaftssystem und die moderne Gesellschaft* (Hamburg 1973)

Kühnl, Reinhard, *Die Nationalsozialistische Linke 1925–1930* (Meisenheim 1966)

Kwiet, Konrad and Eschwege, H., *Selbstbehauptung und Widerstand* (Hamburg 1984)

Laqueur, Walter, *Russia and Germany: A Century of Conflict* (London 1965)

Laqueur, Walter, *Weimar. A Cultural History 1918–1933* (London 1974)

Laqueur, Walter (ed.), *Fascism: A Reader's Guide* (London 1976)

Laqueur, Walter, *The Terrible Secret* (London 1980)

Leber, Annedore (ed.), *Conscience in Revolt: Sixty-four Stories of Resistance in Germany, 1933–45* (London 1957)

Lehmann-Haupt, Helmut, *Art under a Dictatorship* (Oxford 1954)

Lewy, Günther, *The Catholic Church in Nazi Germany* (New York 1964)

Lifton, Robert J., *The Nazi Doctors: Medical Killing and the Psychology of Genocide* (New York 1986)

Lukacs, John, *The Last European War: September 1939/December 1941* (New York 1976)

Macksey, K. J., *Afrika Korps* (London 1972)

Mann, Thomas, *Tagebücher 1933–1934* (Frankfurt/M 1977)

Manstein, Erich von, *Lost Victories* (Chicago 1958)

Manvell, Roger, and Fraenkel, Heinrich, *Doctor Goebbels: His Life and Death* (New York 1960)

Manvell, Roger, and Fraenkel, Heinrich, *Hermann Goering* (London 1962)

Manvell, Roger, and Fraenkel, Heinrich, *Heinrich Himmler* (London 1965)

Manvell, Roger, and Fraenkel, Heinrich, *Gestapo* (London 1972)

Marrus, Michael and Paxton, Robert, *Vichy France and the Jews* (New York 1981)

Maser, Werner, *Die Frühgeschichte der NSDAP. Hitlers Weg bis 1924* (Bonn 1965)

Maser, Werner, *Hitler: Legend, Myth and Reality* (London 1973)

Mason, David, *U-Boat: The Secret Menace* (London 1972)

Mason, David, *Who's Who in World War II* (London 1978)

Mason, Timothy, *Arbeiterklasse und Volksgemeinschaft* (Oplanden 1975)

Meinck, Gerhard, *Hitler und die deutsche Aufrüstung* (Wiesbaden 1959)

Meinecke, Friedrich, *The German Catastrophe* (London 1950)

Miller, Lane, Barbara, *Architecture and Politics in Germany, 1918–1945* (Cambridge, Mass. 1968)

Milward, Allen S., *The German Economy at War* (London 1965)

Mitscherlich, Alexander, and Mielke, Fred, *Doctors of Infamy* (New York 1949)

Mommsen, Hans, *Beamtentum im Dritten Reich* (Stuttgart 1966)

Mosse, George, *The Crisis of German Ideology* (New York 1964)

Mosse, George, *Nazi Culture* (London 1966)

Mosse, George, *Nazism* (New Brunswick 1978)

Müller, Klaus-Jurgen, *Das Heer und Hitler. Armee und nationalsozialistisches Regime, 1933–1940* (Stuttgart 1969)

Müller-Hill, Benno, *Tödliche Wissenschaft. Die Aussonderung von Juden, Zigeunern und Geisteskranken 1933–1945* (Reinbek 1984)

Nachmansohn, David, *German-Jewish Pioneers in Science 1900–1933* (New York 1979)

Nazi Conspiracy and Aggression, 10 vols (Washington 1946)

Neumann, Franz L., *Behemoth: The Structure and Practice of National Socialism 1933–1944* (New York 1963)

Niekisch, Ernst, *Das Reich der niederen Dämone* (Hamburg 1953)

Noakes, Jeremy, *The Nazi Party in Lower Saxony 1921–1933* (Oxford 1971)

Noakes, Jeremy and Pridham, Geoffrey (eds) *Nasism 1919–1945. A Documentary Reader* (Exeter 1984) 2 vols.

Nolte, Ernst, *The Three Faces of Fascism* (London 1965)

Nolte, Ernst (ed.), *Theorien über den Faschismus* (Cologne/Berlin 1967)

Orlow, Dietrich, *The History of the Nazi Party 1919–1933* (Pittsburgh 1969)

Oven, Wilfred von, *Mit Goebbels bis zum Ende* (Buenos Aires 1949)

Overy, Richard J., *The Air War, 1919–1945* (London 1980)

Papen, Franz von, *Der Wahrheit eine Gasse* (Munich 1952)

Peis, Günter, *Naujocks, l'homme qui déclencha la guerre* (Paris 1962)

Peukert, Detlev, *Inside Nazi Germany: Conformity, Opposition and Racism in Everyday Life* (London 1987)

Picker, Henry, *Hitler's Table Talk* (London 1953)

Picker, Henry, and Hoffmann, Heinrich, *The Hitler Phenomenon* (London 1974)

Poliakov, Léon, *La Bréviaire de la haine* (Paris 1951)

Pridham, Geoffrey, *Hitler's Rise to Power, The Nazi Movement in Bavaria* (New York 1974)

Prittie, Terence, *Germans against Hitler* (London 1964)

Procktor, Robert, *Racial Hygiene: Medicine under the Nazis* (Cambridge, Mass. 1988)

Raeder, Erich, *My Life* (Annapolis 1960)

ische Literaturpolitik: Ein Beitrag zur Publizistik im Dritten Reich (Bonn 1960)

Taylor, A. J. P., *The Course of German History* (London 1945)

Taylor, A. J. P., *The Origins of the Second World War* (London 1963)

Tenenbaum, Joseph, *Race and Reich* (New York 1956)

Thies, Jochen, *Architekt der Weltherrschaft* (Düsseldorf 1976)

Thyssen, Fritz, *I Paid Hitler* (London 1941)

Tobias, Fritz, *The Reichstag Fire Trial* (New York 1964)

Toland, John, *Adolf Hitler* (New York 1976)

Trevor-Roper, Hugh, *The Last Days of Hitler* (London 1950)

Trevor-Roper, Hugh (ed.), *Hitler's War Directives 1939–1945* (London 1964)

Trial of the Major War Criminals before the International Military Tribunal Nuremberg, 42 vols (IMT Nuremberg 1947–9)

Turner, Henry A., Jr, *Nazism and the Third Reich* (New York 1972)

Turner, Henry A., Jr, *German Big Business and the Rise of Hitler* (New York 1985)

Tyrell, Albrecht, *Vom Trommler zum Führer* (Munich 1975)

Vogelsang, Thilo, *Reichswehr, Staat und NSDAP* (Stuttgart 1962)

Waite, Robert G., *Vanguard of Nazism. The Freecorps Movement in Post-War Germany, 1918–1923* (Cambridge 1952)

Waite, Robert G., *The Psychopathic God: Adolf Hitler* (New York 1977)

Warlimont, Walter, *Inside Hitler's Headquarters* (London 1964)

Weinberg, Gerhard L., *The Foreign Policy of Hitler's Germany: Diplomatic Revolution in Europe, 1933–1936* (Chicago 1970)

Weinberg, Gerhard (ed.), *Hitlers Zweites Buch. Ein Dokument aus dem Jahre 1928* (Stuttgart 1961)

Weinrich, Max, *Hitler's Professors* (New York 1946)

Weiszäcker, Ernst von, *Erinnerungen* (Munich 1950)

Welch, David, *Propaganda and the German Cinema 1933–1945* (Oxford 1983)

Wheeler-Bennett, John W., *The Nemesis of Power: The German Army in Politics 1918–1945* (London 1964)

Wiedemann, Fritz, *Der Mann der Feldherr Werden Wollte* (Velbert-Kettwig 1964)

Wiener Library Bulletin. O.S. I–XIX no. 3 (1946–65) Kraus Reprint 1978

Wighton, Charles, *Heydrich, Hitler's Most Evil Henchman* (London 1962)

Wilmovsky, Tilo Freiherr von, *Warum wurde Krupp verurteilt?* (Düsseldorf 1962)

Wistrich, Robert S. (ed.), *Theories of Fascism* (London 1976)

Wistrich, Robert, *Hitler's Apocalypse* (London/New York 1985)

Wistrich, Robert, *Antisemitism. The Longest Hatred* (London 1991)

Wistrich, Robert, *Weekend in Munich. Art, Propaganda and Terror in the Third Reich* (London 1995)

Wulf, Josef, *Martin Bormann – Hitlers Schatten* (Gütersloh 1962)

Wulf, Josef, *Musik im Dritten Reich – Eine Dokumentation* (Gütersloh 1963)

Wulf, Josef, *Presse und Funk im Dritten Reich* (Gütersloh 1964)

Wulf, Josef, *Theater und Film im Dritten Reich* (Gütersloh 1964)

Wutte-Groneberg, Walter, *Medizin im Nationalsozialismus. Ein Arbeitsbuch* (Tübingen 1980)

Young, Desmond, *Rommel: The Desert Fox* (New York 1950)

Zbryek, Z., *Selling the War. Art and Propaganda in World War II* (London 1982)

Zeman, Z. A. B., *Nazi Propaganda* (London 1964)

Rauschning, Hermann, *The Revolution of Nihilism* (New York 1939)

Reichel, Peter, *Der schöne Schein des Dritten Reiches. Faszination und Gewalt des Faschismus* (Munich 1991)

Reitlinger, Gerald, *The SS: Alibi of a Nation* (London 1957)

Reitlinger, Gerald, *The Final Solution* (London 1968)

Ribbentrop, Joachim von, *The Ribbentrop Memoirs* (London 1954)

Rich, Norman, *Hitler's War Aims*: The Establishment of the New Order (New York 1974)

Riess, Kurt, *Gustaf Gründgens* (Hamburg 1965)

Ritter, Gerhard, *The German Resistance: Carl Gördeler's Struggle Against Tyranny* (New York 1958)

Roh, Franz, *Entartete Kunst* (Hanover 1962)

Rosenberg, Alfred, *Der Mythus des 20 Jahrhunderts* (Munich 1934)

Rosenberg, Alfred, *Selected Writings* (London 1970)

Rothfels, Hans, *The German Opposition to Hitler* (Chicago 1963)

Salomon, Ernst von, *Der Fragebogen* (Hamburg 1951)

Schacht, Hjalmar, *Account Settled* (London 1949)

Schellenberg, Walter, *The Schellenberg Memoirs* (London 1956)

Schirach, Baldur von, *Ich glaubte an Hitler* (Hamburg 1967)

Schirach, Henriette, *The Price of Glory* (London/Toronto 1960)

Schlabrendorff, Fabian von, *Offiziere gegen Hitler* (Zürich 1946)

Schleunes, Karl E., *The Twisted Road to Auschwitz* (University of Illinois 1970)

Schmidt, Dietmar, *Martin Niemöller* (Hamburg 1959)

Schmidt, M., *Albert Speer: The End of a Myth* (New York 1984)

Schoenbaum, David, *Hitler's Social Revolution* (New York 1967)

Schroeder, Rudolf, *Modern Art Third Reich* (Offenburg 1952)

Schweitzer, Arthur, *Big Business Third Reich* (London 1964)

Seabury, Paul, *The Wilhelmstra: Study of German Diplomats un(Nazi Regime* (Berkeley 1954)

Sereny, Gitta, *Into that Darkne: Examination of Conscience* (L 1977)

Shirer, William L., *The Rise and the Third Reich* (London 1960)

Skorzeny, Otto, *Skorzeny's Speci(sions* (London 1957)

Snyder, Louis L., *Encyclopedia Third Reich* (London 1976)

Smelser, Ronald, *Robert Ley: Labor Front Leader* (Mariett 1988)

Smith, Bradley F., *Heinrich Hi A Nazi in the Making* (S 1971)

Smith, Bradley F., *Reaching Jud at Nuremberg* (New York 1977

Speer, Albert, *Inside the Third* (London 1971)

Speidel, Hans, *Invasion 1944* ((1950)

Spengler, Oswald, *Der Unterg(Abendlandes*, 2 vols (Munich 1

Spengler, Oswald, *Jahre der E(dung* (Munich 1933)

Stachura, Peter (ed.), *The Sha; the Nazi State* (London 1978)

Stephenson, Jill, *Women in Nazi* (London 1975)

Stern, J. P., *Hitler: The Führer People* (London 1975)

Stevenson, William, *The Borman erhood* (New York 1973)

Stockhorst, Erich, *Fünftausen* (Velbert-Kettwig 1967)

Strasser, Gregor, *Kampf um L land* (Munich 1932)

Strasser, Otto, *Hitler and I* (Bostc

Strasser, Otto, *History in M* (London 1941)

Streit, Christian, *Keine Kar* (Stuttgart 1978)

Strothmann, Dietrich, *Nationals*

Clipping Barnet Library
Stapylton Road
Barnet
Herts.
EN5 4QT
Tel: 020 855

KT-430-598

Please return/renew this item by the
last date shown to avoid a charge.
Books may also be renewed by phone
and Internet. May not be renewed if
required by another reader.

www.libraries.barnet.gov.uk

LONDON BOROUGH

By Mary-Rose MacColl

In Falling Snow
Swimming Home

Swimming Home

MARY-ROSE MACCOLL

Allison & Busby Limited
12 Fitzroy Mews
London W1T 6DW
allisonandbusby.com

First published in Great Britain by Allison & Busby in 2016.
First published by Allen & Unwin, Sydney, Australia in 2015.

Copyright © 2015 by MARY-ROSE MACCOLL

The moral right of the author is hereby asserted in accordance with
the Copyright, Designs and Patents Act 1988.

All characters and events in this publication,
other than those clearly in the public domain,
are fictitious and any resemblance to actual persons,
living or dead, is purely coincidental.

All rights reserved. No part of this publication may be reproduced,
stored in a retrieval system, or transmitted, in any form or by
any means without the prior written permission of the publisher,
nor be otherwise circulated in any form of binding or cover
other than that in which it is published and without a similar
condition being imposed on the subsequent buyer.

A CIP catalogue record for this book is available from
the British Library.

10 9 8 7 6 5 4 3 2 1

ISBN 978-0-7490-2054-5

Typeset in 10.5/15.5 pt Sabon by
Allison & Busby Ltd.

The paper used for this Allison & Busby publication
has been produced from trees that have been legally sourced
from well-managed and credibly certified forests.

Printed and bound by
CPI Group (UK) Ltd, Croydon, CR0 4YY

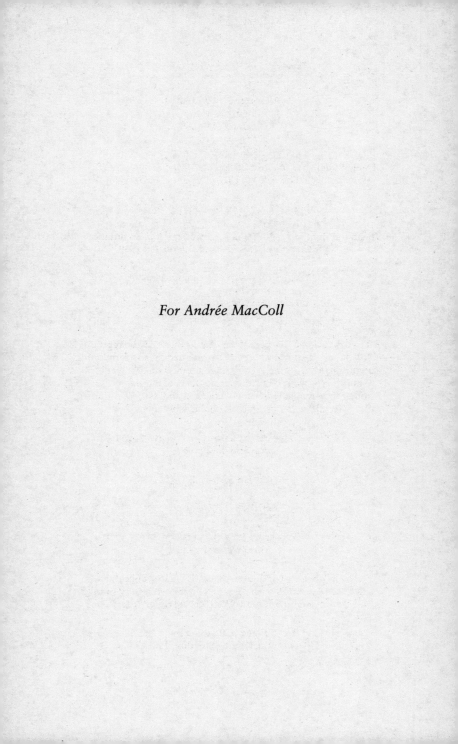

For Andrée MacColl

FAIRER SEX FAILS FATHOMS

American swimmer Miss Gertrude Ederle has been taken unconscious from the icy waters of the English Channel which have proven more than a match for even the strongest female swimmers of the world.

Miss Ederle, eighteen, of Amsterdam Avenue, New York, has been training for the Channel swim since her triumphant return from the Olympic Games of Paris 1924. She set out from France in the early hours of Wednesday and battled rain, fog, shifting tides and freezing temperatures. She was pulled from the water after nine hours by her coach, experienced distance swimmer Mr Jabez Wolffe, just over halfway across from France to the English shore.

Miss Ederle swims with the Women's Swimming Association in New York which produced the swimmers that saw America triumphant in the Olympics, taking more Gold in the water than any other nation, with most medals taken by the women swimmers.

But English swim coach Sir Michael Brossley said he'd seen no evidence in swimmers like Miss Ederle or British swimmer Mercedes Gleitze, also a Channel contender, of the kind of stamina required. 'If women think they can swim the English Channel, then let's find one who can actually do it,' Sir Michael said. 'I think you'll find that these two are the strongest of them and they are not up to the task, nor ever will be.'

Part One

Chapter One

Louisa Quick emerged into a morning as joyous as London offered. Princes Square was wearing summer finally, this late in August, almost as if the strange wintery weather of these last few weeks had never happened. Even Louisa, who rarely noticed anything about her surroundings, noticed the change.

She'd started before dawn at a house in one of the lanes down by the docks; scarlet fever, the rash in full bloom on the chest and arms. Eleven, the lad might have been, twelve at most. He wouldn't last the day, Louisa had thought but hadn't said to the mother. He's terribly unwell was what Louisa *did* say, which the mother already knew. As Louisa had been leaving the house, the sun had illuminated the clouds quite suddenly in a burst of pink. Majestic was the word that came to her mind. From the spectre of death to a majestic dawn.

And now, the sun greeted her again as she came out through the clinic's front door, and oh, the joy of it!

What a gift. For just a moment, here was the world full of possibility. Louisa felt strangely blessed, and although she didn't believe in God, blessed was the word that came to her mind. The still-wet pavement glistened in the sunlight. There were birds – she had no idea where they'd been until today. Louisa's life seemed unimportant suddenly; the waiting room full of patients, the mountain of paperwork in the office, the grumbling nursing staff. All of it gone. Louisa might skip, she thought, or dance a jig, in weather like this. Actually, now that she thought about it, she'd never skip or dance a jig. That was ridiculous. Someone else might skip or dance a jig, Catherine, Nellie even, but not Louisa. Normally, she wouldn't even be outside at this time of morning. She'd be inside, working. Where I would be still, she thought, if it weren't for Helen Anderson.

Louisa had been in the treatment area off the waiting room with a patient when the front desk nurse parted the curtains and told her she was wanted on the telephone. Can I call them back? Louisa had said. The nurse shook her head. They said it was urgent, Doctor. Rooms or here? Louisa had said. The nurse didn't know. It was terrible to admit, but Louisa would hurry more for a patient from her Harley Street rooms. They paid, and expected more. Louisa needed their money for the clinic. She left her patient with the nurse and went to take the call.

Louisa couldn't remember what had been the matter with Helen Anderson when she'd come to the rooms, only that she was one of those patients who knew more than her doctor and wouldn't do as she was told. Louisa saw her

12

again just before Catherine started at the Henley School in the spring. The school's principal, Helen didn't acknowledge their history. Sometimes patients didn't want to see their doctors in other settings, and who could blame them? But when Louisa asked on the telephone if she was all right, Helen sounded exasperated. 'Of course,' she spluttered. 'You must come quickly. Write down the address.' Louisa scribbled down an address as ordered. She was about to ask if anything had happened to Catherine when Helen Anderson rang off. What the devil could be wrong? Louisa thought. It had been a tumour, Louisa recalled now, that she'd excised. Perhaps it had regrown.

Out on Princes Street, Louisa was accosted by a sweet seller and then by Charlie, who roasted chestnuts over an open fire. Louisa gave him a coin, told him she'd be back in half an hour. 'Right you are,' he said. 'I'll save 'em here, Dr Louisa.' He patted his breast pocket – not the cleanest place he could store chestnuts, Louisa thought, but it didn't matter; she didn't eat them anyway.

Louisa hurried through the lane to the Ratcliffe High Way and put her hand out to signal a passing taxicab. As the driver pulled over, she realised she'd forgotten her hat and coat; she must look a fright, her dark brown hair, the armoury of pins it took to secure it – she really needed a cut – adding to the view she was fairly confident others had of her: a woman of difficult-to-determine age a little addled by life. Forty-one, she'd tell anyone who asked. I'm forty-one. At least she'd taken off the stained pinafore she'd been wearing – she'd had to dress a nasty head wound earlier and the apron was still covered in blood.

13

'Why you going down there, Ma'am?' the driver said, tapping the piece of paper she'd handed him.

'I'm a doctor,' she said.

The driver turned around and looked at her with raised eyebrows but said no more.

Louisa rarely took taxicabs, mostly walked where she needed to go, but she didn't have time today. What the devil was the problem with Helen Anderson? she wondered.

Brusque, that was how Louisa's colleague and friend Ruth Luxton had described Louisa. 'Sometimes, Louisa, you are brusque.' Ruth said Louisa was working too hard and she needed a break. Brusque. She and Ruth were both working too hard, truth be told, keeping the clinic running with the money they earned from their Harley Street practices. Louisa had upset one of the nurses, Ruth said. The girl had handed Louisa a swab when she'd asked for something else. She wasn't brusque, she was busy, she told Ruth Luxton. Still, Louisa went and apologised to the girl. She wished they were a bit tougher, these nurses. And, yes, she wished she hadn't been brusque.

The driver turned into John Street. 'Ratcliffe will be faster,' Louisa said, looking at her pocket watch. The line of patients had been out the clinic's front door when she left. It would be all the way down Princes Street by the time she returned, with no other doctor expected in before noon. They were the only medical clinic in the East End, the only care these patients had. You couldn't turn them away.

'No, Ma'am,' the driver said evenly. 'They're digging the sewers, so it's closed further along today.'

'Very well,' she said.

14

The driver stopped in Narrow Street near the Ratcliffe stairs, in front of a group of tired brick buildings. Louisa could see the masts of ships at anchor on the wharf to her left. The driver turned to look at her when he handed her the change. 'You want me to wait?' he said. He smiled, a tooth gone in front, an incisor; he'd miss it when he bit into an apple, she thought.

'Of course not,' Louisa said.

He sighed and shook his head, then drove off.

She looked around. The street was littered with rubbish, including, in the gutter near where she'd stepped out, the remains of what looked like a chicken, feathers and what might have been a claw. She looked up. Most of the buildings had broken windows and looked as if no one lived in them. It was a forsaken place, she thought, such a contrast with the pleasantness of the day, the only relief a group of boys playing football in one of the lanes off to Louisa's left, using what looked like an unravelling cabbage for a ball, a roughly painted line on the end wall to mark one goal, a couple of dustbins to mark the other. They were dwarfed by the buildings on either side of the lane, which were in worse shape than those on the street, windows boarded over or stuffed with newspaper, washing hanging off ledges. But the boys' faces, Louisa saw as she looked over, carried the hope of children the world over, their calls ringing out like an antidote to despair.

'Score!'

'Nah, you was offside.'

'Was not.'

'Was too.'

Louisa thought again of the boy she'd visited early that morning, around the same age as these scallywags. You couldn't always know what would happen, that was the thing. It was what Louisa hated most about her profession. No matter how hard she worked, sometimes it wasn't enough.

'Are you laddies playing the wag?' Louisa called to them.

They scattered quickly then, disappearing like rats into the maze of passageways that ran off every street. Louisa hadn't meant to frighten them. Perhaps they thought she'd come to cart them off to school or, worse, give them a needle.

In among the houses and inns were the large warehouses of the docks. It was to one of these that Helen Anderson had directed Louisa. She stood in front of the dark wooden door, which looked bolted fast. Louisa checked the piece of paper where she'd written the address. She was in the right place, although she couldn't imagine Helen Anderson anywhere here.

Louisa heard cheering down on the bank below. She turned to see that a little crowd had gathered there. She looked out towards the river where someone was pointing. Halfway across was a swimmer, solid, strong, determined, an Oxford or Cambridge freshman no doubt, conquering the Thames on a dare. That must be what they were cheering about. How could you swim in that? Louisa thought. She didn't swim at all and the thought of the filthy river made her sick. But as she watched, the sun shone on the water and it made the swimmer golden. Louisa was mesmerised by his slow, sure stroke. There were two large sailing boats beside the wharf and a steamer coming up the river, half a dozen barges and ferries. What mad boys they were, she thought, a strange feeling building in the pit of her stomach, a nervousness she couldn't account for. Intuition, Ruth Luxton would say. Never underestimate your intuition. Something was very wrong. The taxi driver had gone. She was alone here. Where was Helen?

Just then she saw Helen Anderson herself puffing as she climbed the bank. 'Well, what do you think?' Helen Anderson said. She was flushed, breathless.

'I'm sorry?'

'I'm sorry too, Dr Quick. We've tried to be patient, but this has gone too far.' She had her hands on her hips now, trying to get more air into her lungs.

'What are you talking about?' Louisa said, beginning to wonder if Helen Anderson was in her right mind.

'That.' Helen pointed towards the river, the sun disappearing behind a cloud just at that moment. And then the truth fluttered into Louisa's brain, where it landed lightly and began to work its way into her consciousness. The lone swimmer, turning over now to switch to a perfectly executed back crawl, wasn't Oxford or Cambridge, wasn't a man. It was a woman, a girl. It was Catherine. Of course it was Catherine.

Chapter Two

She'd jumped in feet first from the steps. The water was
deeper than it looked, and she felt as if her body had been
dunked in a bowl of ice and held there. When her feet hit
the bottom, it was soft and squelchy, nothing like the sandy
sea floor at home. She sank down into mud.

No turning back now, she'd thought to herself as she
pushed up. When she reached the surface, she began
to swim, one arm up and over, the other up and over,
kicking with her legs, trying to generate heat. Her head
felt as if it would burst from the cold. She was aware of
the outline of her skull, her jaw. Her lips wouldn't move
properly. They were too cold to blow bubbles. They
were too cold for the laughter that wanted to come,
inexplicably. Was it water that made her want to laugh?
Was it being back in water, even water so different from
home?

She couldn't see her hand in front of her. On the island
you'd never go into such brackish water, where a log might

be a croc. No crocs here, though, no life in the water at all as far as she could tell.

And then she was in the rhythm of the swim, a rhythm she knew so well it was like waking in the morning. It was still cold, but after a few minutes the movement of the swim was creating enough warmth to sustain her. *Keep swimming*. It was her father's voice she heard. Even now, it soothed her. She loved the story, the story of how he'd saved her. *Keep swimming, bonny Cate*, he'd sung that night, and she had kept swimming, or at least she'd held on to him, and by morning, when they reached land, Catherine could swim. That's what her father had said. She doubted it now, having watched other children learn. Swimming didn't come naturally, not even to the Islanders, and Catherine had only been three years old. Her father's story of that night always sounded made up, along with everything he'd told her about her mother, which wasn't much. 'It's because you were so young,' Florence said. 'You don't remember her, so it sounds like a made-up story.'

'What was she like?' Catherine had asked her father. Catherine had no recollection of her, this mother who was the subject of the story – the sailing boat, the storm, her father saving Catherine, losing her mother. Catherine called her Julia. Mother or Mummy would have seemed false. She'd only ever seen one photograph, deep in the bottom drawer of her father's dresser, a photograph Catherine knew she wasn't supposed to see. She'd found her father sitting on the little stool by the bed one day. When he'd looked up, she saw there were tears running down his cheeks, which shocked her. She'd never seen her father cry before. He'd wiped the tears away quickly with one hand, while keeping his other hand, the hand that held the photograph, down by his side. Catherine pretended she didn't notice, but watched from the corner of her eye as he put the photograph in a drawer. Next time he was out at the hospital, she went looking for it.

At first it gave her a fright. Here was a person, a person who had lived. Not the Julia of her imagination but Julia herself, or her likeness at least. This Julia was sitting on the end of a sofa Catherine had never seen in a room Catherine didn't recognise. She had an impression it was somewhere in America, where her mother and father had met, but she couldn't have said why she thought that. Julia was wearing an emerald-green dress with a lace bodice and, high on her head, above her dark red-brown hair, a large bronze-coloured hat with little feathers hanging off the sides.

But it was the face, and especially those eyes looking straight at her, that unnerved Catherine. I know you, those eyes said. I know all about you. It should have reassured Catherine, but if anything the image frightened her. Catherine touched the photograph, touched that face, left her fingerprint on it. She couldn't see herself in this woman the way she saw herself in her father – his laugh, his feet, his way of tilting his head when he was thinking. Still it felt as if the woman in the photograph laid some claim on her. She ran her finger over the image again, wishing, although she wouldn't have been able to say what it was she was wishing for.

'She shone,' her father had told her when she'd asked him what Julia was like.

'Am I like her?'

Her father couldn't speak for a moment. 'Perhaps you are,' he said then. 'Perhaps you are after all, Cate.'

Her father was the only one who called her Cate. She didn't know what her mother had called her. People often said how sad it was, especially other mothers, confirming their own indispensability, but Catherine told them matter-of-factly that you couldn't miss what you'd never had. 'And anyway, I have Florence,' she'd say. 'And Florence is worth ten mothers.' They'd look at her sadly then, as if there were some aspect of their pity she was failing to understand. 'And, also, mothers are quite unimportant really,' she'd say, a grin on her face. They never knew she was teasing. But sometimes when they talked about how sad it was, she'd think back to the photograph and wonder what it might have been like if her mother hadn't died, what it might have been like if her mother was alive.

Florence had been in Catherine's life for as long as she could remember. She *was* like a mother to Catherine. She asked Florence about Julia, not mentioning that she'd seen the photograph. 'Oh, she was a beautiful girl, your mother, a beautiful girl.' Florence shook her head slowly. 'That red hair and those green eyes. But being beautiful can be a curse.'

'She was cursed?' Catherine said.

Florence paused before she answered. 'Being beautiful didn't make her happy. She wasn't happy like you. You're just a bucket of happiness to the brim. It's children that make us women happy.'

'So why wasn't my mother happy?'

21

''Cause children make us sad too.'

'Why?'

'All mothers are sad, because mothering is a giving away, always a giving away.'

A bucket of happiness, Florence called Catherine. Catherine didn't feel that way now; more like a bucket of cold. She lifted her head out of the water and looked towards the far bank. She was veering off course. The point towards which she was swimming – A.J. Smellie Warehouses – was to her left now. It should have been directly in front. She was drifting. That was the thing. You had to account for your drift. Perhaps the tide had turned already. Perhaps she'd miscalculated. Michael could aim for a reef a mile out and use the current to get there by the shortest route. Sometimes he'd swim in the opposite direction of his goal for a while, but always he'd come back to it effortlessly.

She had a sudden memory then. She was standing on the beach with Michael. They were both in shorts without shirts, although Catherine had a singlet on. They might have been seven and nine. The soles of her feet were so hot on the sand she had to hop from one foot to the other to keep them from burning. Oh, to be so warm now, she thought. Michael yelled, 'Go!' She was the faster runner and she beat him into the water, but he dived under and came up thirty yards away from where they went in and won the race, just like he always did.

She swam a few more strokes and looked up again, correcting again slightly, then put her head back under. She should be better at this, she thought. She'd pictured this swim in the weeks since she'd made up her mind to do it, but the reality was so different. *Think about what you're trying to achieve.* Her father's voice. *And don't go to sleep.* The first shock had been replaced now by a deeper feeling, a hankering in her bones to be free of the cold. It was almost comfortable but she suspected being comfortable might be worse. She suspected it might be how she'd give up.

She was drifting again. The tide *had* turned. 'Swim,' she said out loud, which felt good, to have a voice out in this dark old water.

She could see on the bank the girls who'd come down to watch her this morning. They'd be so amazed, she thought, especially Darcy. There were others too, quite a crowd. It would show them she could do something important. What if I don't make it? she wondered. The river had seemed narrow even that morning as she made the crossing in the wherry. But now, in the middle, it seemed so much wider. Her arms were beginning to tire. It was months since she'd swum. If I don't make it, she thought, then stopped herself. *Never plan failure.* Her father again. It was one of the last things he'd said to her. *Never plan failure.* I won't, Daddy.

Chapter Three

Louisa watched her niece swimming, managing to avoid the ferries whose passengers waved and cheered, the boats and barges that looked ready to run the girl down. There was a smell like fresh meat on the turn, sweet, a little rancid. Louisa was afraid. Would Catherine make it across without harm? What if she didn't? What was the girl thinking?

A ferry sounded its horn. Louisa didn't know if it was a warning or greeting but Catherine raised an arm to wave. It seemed a hopeful gesture, Louisa thought. She looked back at the bank where half a dozen girls from the school were waiting, cheering along with the builders from the next-door site. The beauty of the day was with them all, except for Helen Anderson, who was awfully red in the face.

Catherine's arms were bare. They looked so slight as they came up out of the water. But she moved so easily, like a creature born to swim. Even as Louisa knew she shouldn't, she admired her niece's grace.

Catherine had said she wanted to swim, Louisa thought

now, although it was Louisa's housekeeper Nellie who first raised it. She'd cooked pancakes for Catherine's birthday on the third. 'She's fifteen now,' Nellie had said, as if that had anything to do with it, 'and so perhaps she could swim again.'

So was this what Nellie meant? It must have been. And Louisa had ignored her. *You can't ignore children*, Louisa heard her mother say behind her, so clearly she turned and looked, as if her mother was there. 'I wasn't ignoring her,' Louisa said.

Helen Anderson cocked her head. 'I beg your pardon, Doctor?'

'Nothing,' Louisa said. 'I'm sure there's a perfectly rational explanation for this.' Louisa had a hunch there was no rational explanation at all but she desperately wanted Helen Anderson to believe there might be one.

She looked below at the group cheering Catherine on, the girls, the builders and now a few others from neighbouring buildings, Louisa noticed. A motor car pulled up and a man holding a large camera got out, followed by another man in a tan suit. The second man started talking to the girls on the bank.

'I think that might be a journalist,' Louisa said, 'talking to your students.'

'Oh goodness, stop that! Stop that this instant!' Helen Anderson called out, going back down the bank towards the group. 'Just one minute, young man.'

The journalist, a compact lad with blue eyes and a cheeky grin, lifted his hat and said, 'I believe she's one of your students, Miss Anderson. Is this the school's three Rs? Readin', ritin' and the river?'

This was going to be bad, Louisa thought: very, very bad.

They'd tried to be patient, Helen Anderson had said. What did she mean? Had there been trouble for Catherine at the school? Whenever Louisa asked her, Catherine had said it was going well, although in truth Louisa was so busy with work she hadn't really spoken to Catherine lately.

It was Louisa who'd picked Henley, which valued education for women, according to its prospectus, while accepting the importance of manners. Moreover, it was a school that didn't stop for the long summer break all the other local schools had, which meant Louisa wouldn't have to find something to do with Catherine across a summer holiday.

But now, it seemed, either the school had failed or Catherine had, and Louisa had a notion that Helen Anderson, at least, was convinced it was Catherine.

Louisa had a picture in her mind, then, of Catherine on the island at three, running full pelt into the sea behind her father, catching him up, catching him up, Harry pretending to run as fast as he could, letting her grab him around the legs, both of them crashing over into the water, Harry coming up first, shaking the water from his blonde curls. Louisa, waiting on the beach, was afraid, for where was the child? And then, suddenly, there she was, out in the deeper water, calling, 'Daddy! Come on or we'll miss the wave,' just like a little porpoise.

Catherine's mother had drowned, that was the thing. The water was the last place you'd expect to find her, and yet it was like a siren to the girl. Always had been, Louisa thought now.

It was six months after Julia died. Louisa had left London in the January of 1914, in the middle of that cold winter, reaching Sydney nearly two months later in high summer. She'd put off going – selfish, really, but she'd been setting up her practice in Harley Street – and before she knew it, those months had passed. And in truth, she had fears about seeing Harry again, about seeing a child, any child, if she was honest with herself, and especially a child from her own family, the feelings it might arouse in her. Millicent had counselled against her going for this very reason. 'If Harry wants to come home, he will,' their mother said. But Millicent was already a little addled by then, good days and bad, and Louisa didn't put much stock in what she said. Louisa felt it was her duty to go to her brother and do her best to convince him to come home, no matter how she herself might feel. Perhaps, too, she wanted him back in her life. At any rate, she set out, hopeful.

Australia was warm, delightful for the first days, but then, as Louisa moved steadily north – Brisbane, Townsville, Cairns – the weather became hot then unbearable, relieved only by the sea. It was late on a Sunday when the last ferry pulled in beside a long pier that jutted out into a little bay. Louisa stepped down the gangplank and onto the jetty. To one side was a muddy bank and to the other a long, curved beach. Although there was a good breeze, the heat blasted her now that she wasn't on the water.

Harry was waiting at the shore end of the jetty. When he saw his sister, he took off his hat and waved it madly, reminding her of the guileless boy he'd been. 'Louie!' he called. 'My, but it's good to see your face.' He came towards Louisa with his arms outstretched. They embraced warmly. When she pulled away finally, she saw tears pricked his eyes. Poor Harry, she thought then. He'd suffered terribly, she knew. 'Thank you,' he said. 'Thank you for coming.'

He looked so well, it occurred to Louisa, not so much the grieving husband she'd expected. 'Oh goodness, Harry,' she said. 'It's the least I could do. And it's taken long enough.' She smiled, holding on to his hands, which he seemed in no hurry to free from her grasp.

'Yes, it has,' he said, returning the smile with a boyish grin. 'But I'll forgive you as it's an awfully long way.' He let go of her hands and then took her arm to lead her off the pier, taking her portmanteau in his other hand. He was quite cheerful, Louisa thought.

Only a year separated them, Louisa older, and they'd grown up like twins, although Harry always towered over his sister physically and Louisa worked harder at her studies. Left largely to their own devices – their mother had taken up a post at the London School of Medicine for Women before Harry was walking, and their brother Alexander was six years older than Louisa and off at school – they'd always been close. Harry was tall like their father George and had the curliest hair of the three children. When he was a child, it was like wires sticking out of his head, and red like their father's had been, though it was tamer now, Louisa noticed, and more sandy coloured. He'd been the favourite of their grandmother in Edinburgh; she always made Napolean cakes especially for Harry. But after he married, he'd distanced himself from the Quicks and from Louisa in particular. She never understood why, and since he'd moved away, she couldn't easily address it with him.

Besotted was the only word for it, Millicent had said.

'Our Harry is besotted with an American girl.' Their mother had gone over for the wedding. 'Delightful,' she said. 'Absolutely delightful people, even if they are Catholic.'

'Does she want to be a missionary too?' Louisa had asked. Harry had first visited Australia with Alexander, who'd taken over the family shipping company. They'd extended the mail service, which meant their ships passed through the Torres Strait to Australia's north. Harry and Alexander stopped at the port at Thursday Island and then spent a month in Cairns. Alexander wanted Harry to go into the business with him, Louisa realised later, but Harry was set on following his mother and Louisa into medicine. The visit to the island only cemented his plan. When he came home, all he talked about was the hospital they were building on Thursday Island and the marvellous Torres Strait Islanders. He finished his medical studies and then spent six months training at Johns Hopkins in America, where he met Julia Freebody. They married so quickly Louisa wondered if Julia had been pregnant, but Catherine was born eleven months later, after they'd left for Australia and Thursday Island, where Harry had secured the post as hospital doctor. So it had been a love match. And Julia was more than happy to go to a remote place, Millicent told Louisa when she came home from the wedding. 'Aren't they marvellous, Louie? Aren't they just?' That's when Louisa asked, Does she want to be a missionary too?

Louisa wondered at first when Harry stopped writing if Julia was one of those possessive types – some of Louisa's friends had married men like this – but Julia hadn't seemed that way the one time Louisa had met her. She seemed an uncomplicated girl to Louisa; a bit lost, if anything.

They'd come to England on the way through to Australia. Louisa had travelled down from Edinburgh, where she was finishing her surgical training, to the family house at Aldeburgh in Suffolk to see them. Harry was as besotted as Millicent claimed. Julia was polite, smiled a lot, but she wasn't really there. That's what Louisa would have said if asked. 'I didn't get a chance to get to know her because she wasn't really there.' Awfully young, Louisa decided, too young to make up her mind about anything. And, yet, married. Louisa herself was only in her middle twenties, but Julia was nineteen. No interest in the vote, or medicine, or any of the issues of the day, as far as Louisa could tell. Hunting, Millicent had said. The girl goes hunting, shoots with the fellows. But other than that, harmless, if an odd match for Harry, who, like the rest of the Quicks, had an opinion on everything, and, Louisa realised when she thought about it, had never fired a gun in his life.

After they left, Harry rarely wrote home and never came back to visit, even after Catherine was born. Louisa asked her mother was there something she, Louisa, had done to offend him. They'd always been so close and now he hardly even acknowledged his sister. Millicent said he was just getting on with life. 'He's married with a family now.' Louisa had missed her brother, and the opportunity she might have had to be an aunt to the child. She sometimes wondered if Millicent had breached Louisa's confidence and told Harry what had happened. Perhaps he knew and judged Louisa harshly. Alexander had always blamed her, so perhaps Harry would too.

She regarded him now. He didn't look as if he was

judging his sister at all. He looked genuinely relieved to see her. The cream linen suit and broad-brimmed hat looked well on him. It had been four years, Louisa realised.

On the ferry, Louisa had sat outside with the Islanders, hoping to find a breeze. Their skin was beautiful, with such a depth to the colour. She had to stop herself from staring. But it was more than skin colour she was drawn to. Strangely, they reminded Louisa of the women of the East End, who were generous with their time and inexhaustibly, and, given the cruelty of their lives, inexplicably happy. One shy young woman offered Louisa a white fruit with a brown hairy skin. Coconut, Louisa thought. She shook her head no, although it smelt delicious. There was something about these women with their full smiling faces, the easy way they had with one another and with their children, that wasn't there even in the East End women. They looked free, Louisa thought.

Harry held a parasol over his sister's head as they made their way to the buggy. 'Florence said to bring this,' he said, twirling it before handing it to her. 'You'll burn in a minute otherwise.'

Louisa didn't know who Florence was but didn't ask. Had Harry met a woman on the island? she wondered. It would be no bad thing if he were to remarry, Louisa thought then.

They took a dirt road towards the town centre, sitting up front in the open buggy, Harry gently guiding the horse. Oh, the heat of the place. While the horses moved quickly enough, the breeze they created was as hot as the air. It would make anyone want to kill themselves, Louisa thought. She nearly said so, until she realised that, given his loss, talk of death probably wouldn't do Harry any good. But surely he noticed the heat. She looked across, but he appeared oblivious.

Louisa had expected the island to be populated by those natives she'd seen on the ferry. Back in London, she'd gone to the library and located in an atlas the islands to Australia's north. They were home to the Papuans, the atlas said, and the Papuans were cannibals. The people on the ferry didn't look as if they'd eat each other. What's more, when Harry took her through the main street of the town, it was full of Europeans rather than natives, men in suits like Harry's, arm in arm with young women in colourful dresses with parasols against the sun, workers in shirtsleeves and knickerbockers, girls and boys in cotton shorts or skirts.

Harry laughed when she asked him about the cannibals. 'Wrong islands,' he said. 'New Guinea is north of here, and I didn't know the Papuans were cannibals. They come across in canoes sometimes to Saibai or Boigu in the north of the Strait when they're sick. Occasionally the native healers bring them to me. Blood poisoning, a labour that goes on – but I've never heard of them eating each other.' He laughed again, as if Louisa had made some great joke.

Under the trees along the street they did see more Islanders, their skin as dark as coal, the little children running naked and laughing, soft voices drifting over to her on the breeze.

'These people are peaceful, more or less, as far as I know,' Harry said. 'And who wouldn't be, living here?'

She looked out towards the turquoise water. It drew her in.

'There were different groups on the different islands,'

32

Harry said. 'But they were always linked by trade. There's a chap at Cambridge I met after I came here the first time. He's studied all the different cultures. The Islanders are mostly Christian now, but we English haven't always understood their ways of doing things. Those canoes you might have seen down on the beach; they can get anywhere in them. They're beautiful boats.

'Then there was a magistrate back in the nineties, a chap named Douglas, who worked closely with them. He had a lot of respect for the Islanders.' Harry looked at her. 'I do too. The protector system takes away their rights same as for the Aboriginals on the mainland. They can't even travel island to island as easily any more. It's just wrong, Louie.' Louisa agreed it was.

Further along the main street, she noticed a group of young men outside one of the stores. They had sun-browned skin and short black hair and they all wore cotton shirts and trousers. Louisa thought they might be Chinese.

'Japanese, actually,' Harry said when she commented. 'Good lung capacity.'

'Lung.'

'Pearls,' Harry said. 'They're divers.'

'Pearls,' Louisa said.

'Mother-of-pearl,' he said. 'The shell. We supply half the world's buttons.'

They turned out of town and up the only hill on the island, a gentle incline of red dirt from which you'd be able to survey the sea on all sides. Harry pointed. 'That's the house.'

From a distance, it looked like a castle, Louisa thought, built from stone, a belltower on one side, flags flying from the front. 'A stupid thing I did,' he said. 'I think I wanted to impress Julia.' He winced.

'I'm so sorry for your loss, Harry,' Louisa said, patting his knee. 'I should have come sooner. Mama sends her love, dear boy.'

'Well, you've come,' he said. 'And I'm very glad you have.'

'Do you want to tell me about it?' Ruth Luxton had said it would do him good to tell the story.

'About what?' he asked.

'About Julia. What happened to Julia,' Louisa said.

'Yes,' he said. 'When we get to the house. Later.'

As they wound their way up the hill, Louisa thought Harry might come home now after all. He'd been quite adamant about the island, Louisa remembered. He and Julia were going to start a new life there, he'd told Millicent, another hint in hindsight that their old life, the life involving the Quicks, was somehow flawed. It was as if he'd become religious. Perhaps Julia's Catholicism was more strident than Louisa had realised. She did wear a cross on a little chain about her neck, now that Louisa thought about it.

As they drew nearer, the house was no less imposing. The roof was made of slate tiles and they were indeed stone walls, Louisa saw now – they must have carried it block by block in boats and then up the hill from the jetty. The whole lower floor was surrounded by a deep portico. Harry led Louisa up a small set of stairs and through the large front door. He left her bag in the hall and sat her down in the parlour while he went to fetch a cool drink. It took some time for Louisa's eyes to adjust to the dimness. There were double sash windows onto the verandah on two sides, she'd seen from outside as they entered, but they were closed now, and covered with heavy velvet drapes of a deep moss green. There was a sickly smell of flowers past their time. Louisa had an urge to tear back the drapes and open the windows. She felt as if she were suffocating in the humid air. Harry had lost his young wife to the sea outside these windows; perhaps that was why the drapes were closed.

'Lord, Harry, how do you survive the heat?' she said when he came back.

He smiled. 'You get used to it,' he said. 'And there's the monsoon. It's that breeze you could feel from the shore. It brings the rain. Usually by this time of afternoon, we'd have a shower at least. That helps too.'

Louisa's eyes had adjusted now. She could see the room was furnished richly, with two sofas and two big chairs. It was spotlessly clean but looked strangely uninhabited. There were no dead flowers, and yet the smell persisted.

They were sitting sipping their cold water when Louisa heard a voice outside. 'Where is she? Where?' A moment later, the door burst open, and filled the room with light.

She was a beautiful child, with long chestnut hair that fell down her back in a wave, green eyes and dark skin, a handful of freckles thrown across her cheeks, and wit, if the speed at which those eyes surveyed Louisa was anything to go by. She was a Quick, Louisa could see, even in the way she stood, toes out, ankles together, like Millicent and Louisa both. Harry, too, now that she thought about it. Duck-footed Quicks. A dancer, Mrs Quick, one of Louisa's governesses had suggested to Millicent. Young Louisa could be a dancer. Hah! Millicent had crowed. More like a poor skeleton.

Louisa looked at Catherine's face and found herself feeling so tender she couldn't trust herself to speak. She stared.

'You must be Louisa,' the little girl said, sounding grown up.

Louisa smiled. 'And you must be Catherine,' she said finally, tears pricking her eyes. She had an urge to touch the child, to take her in her arms, which she resisted.

Harry cleared his throat and Louisa took her eyes off the child, reluctantly, and looked at him. He looked as proud as punch, and she knew immediately what had helped him through his loss. It was Catherine.

The little girl walked over and stood in front of Louisa and smiled. She took Louisa's hands in her own little hands. She leant in and kissed her aunt on each cheek. Then she pulled away and twirled. She wore a blue-and-white gingham dress with white socks and little black boots, and a blue ribbon in her hair.

'She's so beautiful,' Louisa said to Harry.

'We've done our best with her,' Harry said, his voice gruff with emotion, looking from his sister to his daughter, tears in his eyes.

'I truly am beautiful,' the little girl said, twirling again in the dress. 'Florence made me put on a dress.' She leant in. 'It's awfully uncomfortable, though.' She smiled. 'Florence is bringing the tea,' she said. 'I wasn't allowed to carry the tray. It's too dangerous,' she added, opening her eyes wide.

As if on cue, a native woman came in with the tray. She

wore a blue cotton dress with a white apron tied at the back. So Florence was the help, Louisa thought.

Catherine maintained a steady chatter directed at Florence. 'She's here. It's Aunt Louisa, see? She's very beautiful, isn't she? And she's a proper lady, just like Sister Ignatius said she would be.' The girl ran over to Florence and wrapped her arms around the woman's legs. Florence put her hand to Catherine's head. Louisa noticed the woman's long, delicate fingers.

'I should have introduced you,' Harry said. 'This is Florence, who saved us.' He looked briefly at the native woman and away. 'She looks after Catherine.'

The woman nodded. 'Pleased to meet you, Ma'am,' she said. She smiled gently with her mouth closed.

Louisa noticed a look pass between Harry and Florence then. She had a distinct impression of being shut out, as if there was something between the pair that they weren't saying.

'Catherine's been looking forward to your visit, haven't you?' Harry said, his eyes flicking to Florence again and then back to Louisa.

The little girl smiled and curtsied. 'Where did you learn those lovely manners?' Louisa said. She still felt the urge to reach out, although it was fading now in the face of whatever was going on between Harry and Florence, which she couldn't fathom. The looks between them were full of meaning. She recalled Alexander saying something about Harry and a native woman in Cairns, but Louisa hadn't listened. Alexander had never liked Harry, too many years between them and Harry so adored by their mother.

37

Alexander had been concerned, Louisa remembered now. Could the woman have been Florence? Surely not.

'From Sister Ignatius,' the girl said. 'She said you would be a lady, and I must curtsy to a lady.'

Louisa laughed. 'I'm your aunt, Catherine, your daddy's sister. You don't have to curtsy to me.'

Catherine smiled conspiratorially. 'I know that,' she said in a whisper. 'But it was very important for Sister Ignatius.' Then she ran to Florence. 'Oh, Florence, isn't it wonderful to have Aunt Louisa here with us? Aren't we so lucky? Well, aren't we?'

'Yes, she's your family,' Florence said, stressing each syllable of the word family. Florence flashed Louisa a look. It was as if she were sizing Louisa up.

Catherine was prattling on about the shells she'd found on the beach yesterday. One of them, if you listened carefully, had kept the sea inside, and Catherine would show Louisa, if she liked, once they'd had some tea. But they were most definitely going for a swim that afternoon. Daddy had promised. And scones, there were scones, with real jam they'd made from the mulberries they'd grown in the winter, even though Sister Ignatius said you couldn't grow mulberries on the island. But Florence could grow anything: 'Can't you, Florence,' Catherine said. Florence only smiled.

When Florence left the room, Catherine trailing behind her, Louisa said to Harry, 'Interesting woman.'

'Who?' he said.

'Your housekeeper, Florence. Catherine adores her.'

'Oh,' he said. 'Yes. We'd be lost without Florence. She does so much around the house. And for Catherine.'

'That must be a relief,' Louisa said.

Harry looked at her. 'Florence was the housekeeper in Cairns when Alexander and I were there,' he said, as if reading her thoughts. 'She's Islander. When we had Catherine she came back here and we . . . She helped and now . . . I can't do it all.' So Alexander was jumping to conclusions, as usual, Louisa thought, but, still, there was something.

'Of course you can't,' Louisa said, noting how he skirted over the loss of Julia. Harry would tell her about it when he was ready. 'You're the only doctor here?'

He nodded. 'I have a chap comes up from Cairns once a month, but other than that it's just me,' he said. 'It's not as hard as it sounds. It's more like having a big family. You don't really take time off.' He frowned at Catherine, who had come back into the room quietly. She'd sat on the floor at first but then had moved to Louisa's lap. 'You don't need to be bothering your aunt,' Harry said, more sternly than needed.

'Oh, she's all right,' Louisa said, putting her arms around the little girl. She smelt sweet, Louisa thought. Harry was still frowning at his daughter, preoccupied with his thoughts.

'Well, you're right at home, Catherine,' Harry said. 'Come, let's get down to the beach before dark.' The little girl sprang from Louisa's lap, just like the Scotties when Louisa mentioned a walk.

Louisa had no bathing suit to change into and wouldn't have dared bathe in the sea anyway – she couldn't swim. She remained in her woollen skirt and blouse, leaving the jacket in her room, which was on the upper floor next to Catherine's looking out towards the sea. Although the sun would soon set, the heat was relentless. It would never be cool here, Louisa thought.

Catherine had shed her dress and was wearing shorts with a boy's singlet that was too big for her. Harry was in trunks with an old button-up shirt and a wide-brimmed straw hat. They climbed down a path behind the main house that took them to a cosy beach scalloped by rocks at one end and palms at the other. There was a little boathouse above the beach itself. Catherine had scooted ahead, Harry following her. Louisa, who'd carefully picked her way down the path, took a moment to peer through the briny window of the boathouse. There was a sailing skiff on mounts inside. She wondered if this was the boat Harry had taken out when Julia drowned.

Catherine took to the water as if she lived there, running out alone into the sea and then diving under, terrifying Louisa. In the twilight, she watched her little niece swimming out into the sea and catching the gentle waves back in with her father. Catherine was not like a person, Louisa thought then. She was like a sea creature. That was what she smelt like. It was the sea, clean and pure and alive. Wild, that's what Alexander had said before Louisa left England. That child is growing up wild.

Watching her in the water now at fifteen, Louisa couldn't help thinking that swimming was what Catherine had been born to.

Chapter Four

'We were out sailing,' Harry said suddenly, looking not at Louisa but at Florence. They were in the front parlour. After returning from the beach, they'd eaten dinner – cold chicken and salad followed by jelly and cold custard – in the conservatory that gave onto the back terrace. Catherine had fallen asleep in Florence's lap over on the sofa, and Florence was sitting there quietly stroking the child's hair while Louisa and Harry talked. The drapes and windows were still closed to the sea, although Louisa thought she could hear it in the distance. A breeze blew in through the front door of the house.

Louisa was surprised that Florence had remained with them after dinner. She'd got up to leave and it was Harry who'd asked her to stay. Catherine, for her part, seemed accustomed to Florence being a part of their life together. Florence was just like a mother to the child, Louisa thought.

Harry had been drinking; whisky before dinner and now

a glass or more of port. Was that how he managed after Julia's death? Louisa wondered.

He smiled weakly now. 'We'd taken lunch and headed for Banks Island, which is north of here. Florence's people are from there, aren't they?' he said, and she nodded gently. 'I do a monthly clinic and I used to take them sometimes. Julia liked to get out and about.'

The way he said Julia's name made Louisa look up. There was something in his voice. Was it anger? Louisa thought it might be.

'You have to understand the weather patterns here,' he said, putting his glass down heavily on the table in front of him. 'It can be fine, not a cloud in the sky, and you think you'll head out. It was a blue day, wasn't it, Florence?'

Florence didn't answer him, only sat looking down at Catherine.

Harry turned back to Louisa. 'Actually, Florence said there was a storm coming. Florence, do you recall?'

Florence looked up at him now and nodded slowly.

'You knew. I wish I'd listened. Later, I wished I'd listened. You understand the weather.' He pointed at Florence, took another sip of his drink. Louisa had the urge to put the bottle away from him.

The clinic was soon dispensed with, he said, so they ate their picnic and afterwards Harry and Catherine had a swim. 'She couldn't swim,' he said, referring, Louisa assumed, to Julia – and they made for home in good time. 'Banks Island is a couple of hours away even if the wind is up. And we were lucky, I thought. The breeze was good. But then the sea got rough, the wind whipping up such a

42

swell. Still no storm that I could see, but I know boats. I know what you do. I did it all right. I did everything to stop it.' He looked up at her. 'I did my best, Louie.'

'Of course you did, darling,' she said, noting the awful anguish in his eyes. 'God, it must have been awful, Harry.'

He saw the storm front then, he said, approaching from the south-west, between them and Thursday Island. He pulled into a bay near one of the unpopulated islands, thinking they would be protected there until the storm passed. But even in the shelter of the bay the sea was wild. 'The anchor wouldn't hold and we were soon swept back out.' He shook his head, looking as if he might cry. 'She shouldn't have . . .' He stopped and sighed.

The storm was furious, he said. 'When the mast cracked, I knew we were done for.' He paused. 'You can't do anything without a mast. We just had to wait and hope.' He shook his head. 'You've no idea what it's like.'

He drank again then, pausing so long Louisa thought he might have forgotten he was telling the story. She looked across at Catherine, who twitched in her sleep, as if her father's telling of the story was being lived in her very dreams. Florence was still stroking the girl's hair and Louisa had the strangest urge to tell her to stop. She's not yours, she's ours, Louisa wanted to say.

Later, Louisa told Ruth Luxton how she'd felt about Florence with Catherine. 'Was it because the housekeeper was black?' Ruth had asked.

'Of course not,' Louisa said. 'At least, I don't think it was. I think it was because I realised Catherine was family for the first time, that I owed her something, that she's a Quick.'

Harry followed Louisa's eye to Catherine. 'I couldn't provide comfort. That's the thing. I couldn't help her.' He stared at Florence. 'A boat overturns relatively quietly,' he said. 'It's as if nothing is happening and yet your whole world is falling apart. Catherine screamed when we went in the water.' He swallowed hard. 'She was a wee thing, and it was cold enough at night, in a storm, thunder and lightning all around and the wind and rain. The swell, Louisa, it's likely to tear anything out of your hands. I just held on to Catherine, of course. Through it all.'

'Of course,' Louisa said. 'It's what anyone would do in your situation.'

They only had the one life preserver, he explained. He left Julia the life preserver and swam with little Catherine for an island. The storm passed, he said. He was able to save his daughter but not his wife. The life preserver washed ashore the next morning. Julia was gone. 'Why couldn't she just hold on?' he said, glaring now at Florence.

Florence was a study in repressed emotion, Louisa thought. Her face was set tight, her arms folded around Catherine. Louisa couldn't say what the other woman's feelings were, only that she was having trouble keeping them in check. Later Louisa said to her, 'It was a shame my brother's wife didn't listen to you that day, about the storm.' Louisa saw that tight mouth again before Florence replied, 'Sad day, Miss. Sad, sad day.'

The next morning, they took breakfast in the dining room off the kitchen. Louisa could feel the blast of heat when they opened the French windows to the back terrace. She'd slept fitfully and the woken house felt more oppressive not less, despite the bright sun that came in through the windows when she pulled open the drapes. Downstairs, she noticed that the windows in the back wall of the house, built against the hill, were open. They were the only windows that didn't look at the sea.

Catherine was in the yard with Florence, who was hanging out the washing. The little girl was running between the sheets and Florence was pretending she couldn't find her.

'She's bright, Harry,' Louisa said. They were still sitting at the table. 'What will you do about school?'

'She already goes to school,' Harry said. He didn't look any worse for the night's drinking. Perhaps he hadn't had as much as Louisa thought.

'Here?'

'Yes, here,' he said. There was a touch of argumentativeness in his tone. Louisa didn't know why. 'By rights, she shouldn't start for another year or two, but she was so keen and the nuns all know her from the hospital. So she started early.'

Louisa sat forward in her chair. 'That's all very well for the basics. But what about if she wants to go on, Harry? Surely they don't have the subjects she'll need.'

'The nuns are French, so Catherine's already learning the language. One of them plays piano and Catherine's keen to learn. She'll read with me, write, mathematics, a bit of science. There's nothing wrong with the school here, Louie.' He looked at her. 'And here is where her mother . . . Here is where she started.'

'Of course,' Louisa said. 'I'm just worried about you.

45

If you were at home, I could help with Catherine.'

He sighed. 'Louisa, I'm sorry. But the island is the safest place for Catherine.'

Later, she thought about his use of the word *safest*. It was an odd word, she thought, and how he reckoned his daughter would be safe on an island surrounded by the sea that had taken his wife, Louisa hardly knew.

'And she's happy, aren't you?' Catherine had run up and jumped into her father's lap. He smiled and nuzzled his face in her hair.

'I most certainly am,' Catherine said, in that little adult voice of hers. And then suddenly, as if to confirm she was still a child, she jumped down and dipped her finger into a bowl of cream and put it in her mouth. She watched Louisa as she did this.

Harry looked at his sister. 'I suppose I should tell her she's not to do that,' he said, 'but I don't seem to have the necessary . . . will, I suppose, to correct her. She's so very precious.' He patted his daughter's head. Again, Louisa thought of Julia, of Harry's loss. No wonder he clung to his daughter. Catherine was still focused on that creamy finger, sucking the life out of it. After she removed it from her mouth, she smiled widely.

'Come with me,' she said to Louisa, offering the sticky hand, which Louisa took.

Catherine led her back inside and out onto the front verandah. 'You'll feel better out here, Aunt Louisa. Daddy thinks it keeps the cool air in to have all the windows shut, but Florence says it just makes it hotter.'

'I think I'd have to agree with Florence,' Louisa said,

thankful for the moist breeze that came from the sea, 'although I don't know that anything would make it comfortable.' She regarded the child. 'You like Florence, don't you?'

Catherine nodded. She sat down facing Louisa. 'I don't have a mother.' She sighed, another adult gesture, as if she'd learnt this was how she should act.

'I know. That must be very hard.'

She nodded. 'You could be my mother.'

Louisa smiled. 'No, I can't be your mother.' The breeze was delightful over her face.

'Why not?'

'Well, for a start, I live in England. And second, I'm your aunt.'

'You could come here and be a nurse and be my mother. Also, I know third comes after second.' She smiled as if the matter were now settled. 'And you need to take off some of your undergarments or you'll simply boil to death.'

Louisa laughed. 'How do you know?'

'Sister Ignatius told me. I don't wear any unders but bloomers.' She leant forward. 'It's all right for ladies in the heat.'

'Catherine, about what you said before, I wouldn't be a nurse. I'm a doctor. If I came here, I'd still be a doctor.' It was important, Louisa thought, that girls understood from an early age that women, too, could be doctors.

'Oh very well,' the little girl said. 'But then we'll have two doctors and who will do the nursing?'

She spent the day exploring the island with Catherine and Harry. They took the trap down to the town centre, and from there to a church built in memory of lives lost when a ship struck a reef and sank. They went to the Catholic church, too, next to the school Catherine attended. There was a service being held. The Islanders were singing. Their harmonies were beautiful, Louisa thought, and the church was filled with light.

In the afternoon, they went down to the beach again. Louisa could see what appealed to Harry about his life on the island. Many people stopped to greet them, but it was more than being a big fish in a little pond. He felt at his ease here, Louisa saw. And the island did have a strange charm, she thought.

That night, Louisa had the dream. Someone was chasing her, chasing her, a pursuer whose face she never saw. She couldn't run, and she couldn't scream. And then a child crying – not Catherine, not any child Louisa knew. And then she was awake, and the feeling she had was sadness not fear, tears on her face she couldn't remember shedding. Her body was wet with sweat.

Ruth Luxton had told her to give herself time. How much time, Ruth? she'd wanted to ask but hadn't. Now she could hear water lapping at the beach below. It was the sea at peace, no hint of a pursuer, no crying child, just birds greeting a new day. It was so incongruous with the dream. She lay in bed and waited for the sun and the comfort it would bring.

After she rose and dressed, she went downstairs. Harry was on his way to the hospital. He asked her to walk Catherine down to the school. The day before, she'd taken Catherine's advice, removed her corset and camisole, leaving only her brassiere and linen blouse. Today she took off her heavy wool stockings and petticoat, too, but had to wear the wool skirt as she had nothing cooler.

They walked through town, the heat becoming increasingly oppressive with every minute in the sun. Louisa thought she might die in her skirt and boots, the sun beating through the parasol she carried. She could almost feel the top of her head burning. Catherine was oblivious. She was like a tree, Louise thought, taking her energy from the sun.

As they walked along the waterfront, Catherine pointed out three children about fifty yards from the shore. 'They're the Walton boys,' she said, 'from Hammond Island. I don't like them. They pull my hair.'

Further out in the water from the Walton boys Louisa saw a woman in a dinghy. She was standing up, brandishing a very large rifle. 'What's she got a gun for?' Louisa said, horrified.

'Sharks,' Catherine said matter-of-factly. 'That's their mother.'

The schoolhouse was a single room in a little timber cottage with window openings that had no glass and a doorway with no door. Louisa met the nuns who taught Catherine. The one Catherine had mentioned, Sister Ignatius, was one of those wise old owls, with bright eyes behind wire-rimmed spectacles and a veil crooked on her head. She seemed pleased that Catherine had her aunt visiting. 'We worry about the child too,' she said, as if Louisa had expressed anxiety, which she hadn't. There was another young nun, a Sister Ursula, who'd studied science in Brisbane, Sister Ignatius told Louisa. 'We're very proud she's chosen a vocation.' She was a dear, the younger nun, Louisa thought.

After leaving Catherine, Louisa went on to the hospital, where Harry had agreed to meet her. It was a sprawling building, two rooms in front, a built-in verandah down one side and extensions to the rear, on the edge of the peninsula.

They treated Europeans and natives both, Harry said. 'On the mainland, they split them, the natives in one place and the whites in another. We don't do that – and I'm against it. A patient's a patient, don't you agree?' Louisa smiled. He knew she did.

Louisa met the nurses and then toured the two wards. Harry said the work varied. Pearl divers suffered the bends. Occasionally, there were shark attacks. 'They're usually dead before they're pulled from the water,' Harry said, 'but we've had a couple of bites you wouldn't have thought anyone could survive, but then the natives do. They don't always come to me. They like their own healers. Other than that it's just run-of-the-mill.'

Afterwards, they shared lunch in Harry's office. It was Louisa who brought up the future. She'd decided to be open about her purpose. 'Harry, the truth is I came here to convince you to come home,' she said.

He shook his head. 'I won't come back to England. I'm happy here, Louie. So is Catherine. And it was the last place we . . .' He didn't finish. 'But I did want to talk to you. There's something I really need to tell you.' He breathed in, out, regarding her carefully. 'At the hospital here, we need nurses,' he said finally, 'and I agree Catherine needs her family. She needs a woman in her life, actually. I thought you could . . .'

'You thought I could what?' Louisa said.

'You could come here and take up one of the nursing positions. With your training you'd be ideal.'

'You thought I could just give up medical practice and come here?' She tried to keep her voice level but failed. She expected this kind of attitude from Alexander but never Harry, who'd always respected her vocation. 'You weren't thinking I'd just up and leave my practice?' So this was where Catherine had got the idea.

'Well, I was, actually. She's just a baby.' He swallowed hard and blinked, perhaps to stop the threat of tears, but Louisa found it hard to sympathise. The hide of her brother, thinking she would give up everything. Really! Louisa was a doctor, same as he was. She couldn't just give it away. How dare he expect her to?

Louisa left the island two weeks later. Harry had made it clear he would not come home to England under any circumstances, and Louisa made it clear she had no intention of uprooting and moving to Australia. She'd done the right thing, she told herself. She'd visited her brother. She'd asked him to come home. He hadn't agreed. Still, Louisa had felt awful leaving the little girl. After she departed the island, she could still smell Catherine's hair in her clothes, and it brought tears to her eyes. On the ship home, she often found herself crying. Ruth Luxton would surely have approved. She was always one for expressing strong emotion. But not Louisa. She'd stand out on the deck alone and the tears would come unbidden. This won't do me any good at all, Louisa thought. Still, the tears would come.

And there things had stood. Louisa wrote at Christmas every year, and for Catherine's birthday in August. She had clothes made for her niece. She had to estimate Catherine's size because Harry never responded when she wrote and asked. She had a dressmaker run them up: a blue-and-white gingham dress with a red sash, just like the one Catherine had worn the first time they met, and a pretty hair ribbon to match; another year, a green silk dress, although Louisa had no idea where Catherine would wear it; gloves and shoes, skirts, blouses, socks and stockings. Louisa would keep them for a week or so, looking at them each day, and then send them, always with a little message. She never heard back from Catherine, and from Harry she just had the most general news, nothing about the clothes, and nothing about his daughter.

Louisa thought of Catherine often, it was true. She'd experience that familiar aching in her chest, not really for Catherine, she knew. For another child, a child who never was.

Chapter Five

She could hear their cries now, like gulls in the evening. *Swim-mer, Swim-mer, Swim-mer.* The sun was shining on her face and it made her feel she might be warm again even though it carried so little warmth. The bank didn't seem to come any closer. She wasn't tired. She wasn't even cold now. She was beyond cold. As the cries grew louder in her ears and she started to make out people on the bank, she had an inexplicable desire to turn around and swim back to the other side. She didn't want to return to dry land, to London. She just wanted to swim away.

Always plan success, her father sometimes said. Had he known? she wondered. Had he known his days were numbered? Had he been given some warning, some inkling that this might happen, that he might leave her without a home, without him? It had been Sister Ursula who'd told her. Sister Ursula had come to the house with Roy Macklin, the police officer, that Sunday morning. Her father had left two days before, to travel to Cairns with the harbourmaster's wife, who'd become ill during her confinement. But then Sister Ursula and Sergeant Macklin were at the front door. They were so sorry, they kept saying. Sister Ursula stayed through the morning but Catherine didn't want her there, in the house. She liked Sister Ursula, but she wanted to be small again and climb into Florence's lap and have Florence rub her shoulders and sing a song. She felt very frightened and alone.

She wondered now if she could just keep swimming, head out to the North Sea, down and across the Atlantic to the Indian Ocean, eventually the Arafura Sea, then the green of Saibai or New Guinea and from there to Thursday Island. The Torres Strait could be treacherous, she knew. So many ships had been wrecked and so many lives lost. The Islander families were mostly fishermen or divers, and most had lost someone to the sea. But the sea could be kind too. Catherine and Michael had swum wherever they'd wanted to. The Islanders called Catherine Waapi, fish. Michael was Bid, dolphin. The sea would protect them, Catherine believed.

One day at school in London, one of the other girls, Darcy, had said that Mercedes Gleitze was going to swim across the English Channel. Darcy had read about it in the paper. Catherine had said she, Catherine, might swim the Channel too. She didn't know why she'd said it. She had no idea whether she could actually swim across the Channel but she wanted them to know she could swim. Darcy had told her she was a liar, that she couldn't possibly swim the English Channel. She couldn't even swim the Thames. Of course I could, Catherine had said. She'd seen the Thames.

She'd thought it would be easy. But she soon realised it wouldn't be easy. The Thames was a tidal river. The sea could rush in and out. There were many boats. It might be more treacherous than she'd realised.

If you could swim the English Channel, she thought now, surely you could swim to Australia, for it would only be more distance. You could sleep while swimming on your back, she thought, as she turned over onto her back.

The Arafura Sea was warm year round, so different from this oily, cold river. In the Torres Strait, the islands to the north and west were rock, originally part of the mountain range that divided the east of Australia from the interior, her father had told her, tracing the line in the atlas from the mainland north, north, north and off the tip of Australia's most northern point. He believed the islands had once been a land bridge between Australia and Papua New Guinea. 'Boigu and Saibai – where I go for the clinics – are only a few miles from New Guinea,' he said. His finger ran over the island they'd visited the day her mother drowned, but he didn't say anything about it. 'If you look at the map,' he said, 'you can see where the bridge was. A giant might still use it.' He smiled, stepping from island to island with his fingers.

On the island, she would never have worried about getting cold. They'd dry themselves in the sun after they swam. They'd sit on the sand for a while and then dive back into the sea. It only ever felt soothing. Oh, that feeling of the breeze on your skin giving you just a hint of a chill on those hot, hot days and then, when you'd heated up, the plunge into the cool water. At home, she'd have dived off the end of the jetty. Michael always swam with her, every afternoon after school. When they were older, they'd set out swimming while Harry paddled in a canoe with Florence. They'd meet up on one of the nearby islands and cook fish for lunch. 'You must put those days in the past, darling,' Louisa had said. 'You have to move on.' Catherine had tried. She really had. But it was all so different and new.

And Michael? Catherine thought suddenly. What was Michael doing without her? She imagined his life going on, the life they'd shared, whereas her own life had completely changed. It seemed unfair.

She looked towards the bank. 'I'm swimming,' she said out loud. 'I'm swimming the Thames.'

She was wearing the woollen swimming suit she'd bought at Peter Robinson with Nellie. It had short sleeves that dragged through the water and a skirt over leggings. There were much better suits, sleeveless without a skirt, but Nellie said they were racy. On the island, Catherine had swum in a boy's costume, thin straps on her shoulders and bare legs. But you couldn't do that in London, Nellie said. You have to wear a woman's suit, she said, and at your age it needs to cover you. It took effort to get on and Catherine didn't have an opportunity to swim in it before she took to the river. It weighed her down now, and chafed under her arms and around her neck. She was wearing a rubber cap that made the water roar in her ears. Oh, Daddy, she said to herself now. Why did you have to leave?

Those mothers who felt sorry for Catherine, the ones who said it was so sad to be without a mother, she'd never understood them, not really, not until her father was gone.

And then Catherine knew what they were talking about. 'Learning to swim,' her father had said once, 'is like learning how to breathe again. It's that simple, and that complicated.'

Learning to live without him was like learning how to breathe again too, she realised now.

It had been a day much like any of the others in the months since his death. People had stopped leaving food at the house, although Mrs Watson had asked just a week before what Catherine was going to do now. She'd accosted Catherine in town. While Florence was seeking out green beans, Mrs Watson asked Catherine when the family was coming. At first, Catherine had been confused. As far as she was concerned, the family was Florence and Michael, and Florence was just getting beans. When Florence returned, Mrs Watson smiled and left. Florence asked afterwards what Mrs Watson had wanted, but instead of telling Florence the truth, Catherine said Mrs Watson had wanted to know about her daughter's spelling. 'She can't spell very well at all,' Catherine said, 'but I didn't tell Mrs Watson.' By then, Catherine had figured out what Mrs Watson actually meant. When were her father's family, the Quicks, or her mother's family, the Freebodys, coming? For surely they would come.

Catherine didn't know her mother's relatives, now living in Canada, and she'd only ever met her aunt Louisa once, when she was little. She couldn't even remember her, except that she'd smelt like flowers. There was her father's older brother Alexander, but she didn't know him well either. He'd always seemed stern.

She'd been out swimming with Michael in the morning and then Florence had made breakfast for them, bubble and squeak using last night's vegies. Michael had walked with her to school. In the afternoon, he'd left early to go home and help Florence take some cakes back down to the school for the bake sale the next day. Catherine had stayed back to help Sister Ursula with the younger ones. She'd been helping teach for over a year now. Sister Ursula was trying to convince her to sit the university scholarship exam. She could go to Brisbane, Sister Ursula said, board with Sister Ursula's family there and go to the university to study science. Sister Ursula was trying to get Catherine to think about her future. Catherine hadn't been interested before but now she wondered if that was what she should do after all. Her father had talked about the university too. She didn't want to leave the island, but now she knew she'd have to do something. If she went to Brisbane to study, she thought, she could come back to the island as a teacher.

Catherine had left the school around four and hurried up the hill, intending to have another swim before dinner. She ran up the path, opened the front gate and stopped.

There was a woman seated on the verandah, perched forward in a canvas-backed easy chair, Catherine's father's chair. The woman was dressed in a pale linen blouse and a long dark skirt, and her feet, clad in boots, were crossed at the ankles. They didn't quite reach the floor. She had a hat pulled over her head but you could see wisps of hair sneaking out. When she stood Catherine saw she was tiny. She came forward, said Catherine's name.

Catherine realised she must be the woman from the

government, the one Florence had said would come. 'They won't let you stay with us,' Florence said. It was what Sister Ursula said as well. 'You're a white girl, Catherine, and they won't let you stay with a black family.' It's what Mrs Watson had meant too, Catherine knew. But Michael isn't black, Catherine wanted to say to them all. If skin colour was the determining factor, Catherine was nearly as dark as him.

When Catherine was small, she didn't know Florence had a child of her own. If anything, Catherine assumed she herself was Florence's child. But one day, just after Catherine's fourth birthday, they were at the harbourmaster's office, waiting to meet the ferry to pick up the mail. Someone had left a newspaper on the bench in the waiting area. In the top left-hand corner of the page was a photograph of a group of children, four dressed in frocks, two in pants too big for them, all holding toys. Above was a headline: homes are sought for these children. Half-castes, they called them, and quadroons. Catherine remembered the words because they were words she didn't know.

Catherine was about to ask Florence what a quadroon was but Florence had turned and was rushing outside. Catherine looked at the newspaper again. Underneath the picture was an advertisement for White's Jelly Crystals, which were Catherine's favourite.

She found Florence on the steps but Florence wouldn't speak, and she was shaking as if cold. Catherine went back inside and asked the woman behind the counter for a glass of water for Florence. While she waited, she studied the newspaper. Someone had handwritten a note below the photograph. *I like the little boy in centre of the group but if taken by anyone else, any of the others would do, as long as they are strong.*

The photograph had affected Florence but Catherine didn't know why. Before she went back outside with the water, she tore the photograph from the newspaper and shoved it in her pocket. They walked home together and by the time they'd got to the top of the hill Florence was better. Catherine didn't mention what had happened in the harbourmaster's office for fear of upsetting Florence again.

'They took him away, I think,' Catherine's father told Catherine later that night when she asked him. Florence was downstairs. Catherine was in bed. 'I don't know all the details, but I think they took a baby from her when she was living in Cairns.'

'What do you mean?' Catherine said, not understanding. 'What's this?' She pointed at a word.

'"Quadroon",' he said. 'It means a quarter black and three-quarters white. "Half-caste" is half black and half white.'

'They took Florence's baby?' Catherine said.

Her father nodded. He looked at the clipping again. 'Did Florence say anything about it?'

Catherine shook her head. 'She was crying, Daddy, and Florence never cries.'

'No, she never does,' he said absently, still staring at the picture.

The next morning Catherine's father came to her room and sat on the bed beside her. He'd spoken to Florence. The Protector had taken Florence's child when she was in Cairns, Catherine's father said. 'The baby's daddy was white, so the child wasn't as black as Florence.'

'I thought I was Florence's children,' Catherine said.

Her father smiled. 'No, darling, you're not Florence's.'

'Will they take me away?'

'Of course not.'

'How do you know?'

'It's different for the natives.'

'Why?'

He didn't answer straightaway. 'I think they want the children to grow up with our values, not the native values.'

'Was my mother native?' Catherine said.

'No,' he said emphatically. 'Why do you ask that?'

'You said they took Florence's child because he looks white. They want children who are white.'

'Your mother was American. You know that.' He looked upset suddenly. 'Anyway, I wouldn't let anyone take you away.' But Florence was the most fierce person in Catherine's life. If Florence couldn't stop them, then no one could, Catherine thought.

'They take the children to families who can provide schooling,' Catherine's father said.

'But we have a school.'

'Yes, we do,' he said. 'And they've left the Islanders alone until recently, but Florence was on the mainland. It's different there for the blacks.'

'Why?'

'I don't know,' her father said. 'The government says the blacks are less civilised than white people.'

'Florence?'

'No, not Florence.'

'Then why did they take her baby away?'

'I really don't know,' Catherine's father said. 'But I'm telling you this because I promised you I wouldn't lie, not about important things.' He patted her head and smiled. 'Stop asking questions now,' he said.

Three days later, her father came home early. He found Catherine playing out on the back lawn. He spoke quietly. 'I'm going to tell you something, but you're not to tell Florence. You know my friend, the doctor in Cairns who comes here, Dr Andrews?' Catherine nodded. 'Dr Andrews says there's a new Protector in Cairns. I have an appointment when I go there next week. It may be that Florence can see her child. But you mustn't tell just in case. You must tell Florence I'm going to Cairns for work.' He put his finger to his lips and bent down and kissed her hair. 'I love you so much, wee Cate.'

The next week, he went to Cairns and Catherine knew not to say anything. A month later he went again and she'd all but forgotten their conversation.

Florence and Catherine were on the verandah shelling peas, and they'd been talking about whether or not to go back down to town to meet him on the evening ferry. But then she saw him walking up the path. There was someone with him, Catherine saw, a child. Florence began to moan softly and then cried out. They weren't words Catherine knew. The child – a boy, Catherine thought, judging by the shorts – broke free from Catherine's father and ran towards Florence. They met at the gate and she gathered him up in her arms, his long legs on either side of her hips. He had snot coming out of his nose, Catherine noticed when she caught up, a nasty brown-coloured snot that Catherine knew from her father meant an infection. He was nearly as big as Catherine, with black hair and blue eyes, and he was skinny. His eyes darted around nervously, and he wouldn't let go of Florence.

When Catherine's father reached them, he stood a few feet away from Florence; he was out of breath but staring, a look of concern on his face. The child, still in Florence's arms, was sobbing too.

'Dr Harry, how have you done this?' Florence was saying.

Catherine was confused. Who was this child? And then she remembered. This must be Florence's child, the one her father had mentioned. Her father had found him and brought him back.

'He's back to stay,' Catherine's father said.

The boy, Michael, two years older than Catherine, wouldn't speak. He was sick in his kidneys, Catherine's father told Florence later that night. Florence fussed over him. Catherine watched as his large eyes took in the scene around him. Catherine's father stood in the background, watching the two of them.

The doctor in Cairns knew the Protector, and they convinced him to release the child, Catherine's father told Florence. 'I had to imply that I'm the boy's father, but never mind. He's here to stay, that's the main thing.' Michael had been placed with a family in the last year. Before that, he'd been with another family outside Cairns. Catherine's father didn't know much more than that, and Michael wouldn't talk that first night, nor for many nights that followed.

In all the commotion, Florence hardly noticed Catherine, who had a bath and put herself to bed. That's where she was when Florence came to tuck her in. 'It's my baby back,' Florence said. 'This is the best day of my life.'

'Yes, I suppose it is,' Catherine said, not looking up.

'Are you all right?'

'Of course I am,' Catherine said. She knew she should be happy for Florence, but for some reason she just wanted to cry. She focused on her hands outside the covers, and said nothing.

Florence sat down. 'So many changes,' she said. She stroked Catherine's hair and then took the girl's hands from the covers and held them. She regarded the little fingers. 'You know, don't you, that you're my spirit-child?'

'Am I?' Catherine said. Her mouth turned down, even though she tried to stop it, and tears filled her eyes. She shook her head.

'Oh yes. I knew you first time I saw you. We've been in the world a long time, you and me. I saw you in your daddy's arms and I knew you were my spirit-child. It's good my boy's home. This is where he belongs. But you're still my spirit-child. I couldn't have come through without you. I won't forget that.'

'Will you go away now?' Catherine asked, her bottom lip quivering as she spoke.

'Go away? What for? Who's going to look after you if I go away? Oh no, we're all going to live together. It's going to be fine. There's enough for everybody here. You know that.'

And all at once, it was like the sun coming out. Catherine had thought, without even knowing she was thinking it, that Florence would leave her now, just as her mother had gone. But Florence wasn't going.

It wasn't all smooth sailing. It was a long time before Michael would leave the house. And Catherine, who'd always been the centre of everyone's world, was suddenly on the edge. She was one of those who was trying to help instead of being a child herself. It was Catherine who enticed Michael to school finally. He was up the mango tree in the front yard. 'What you doing up there?' she called one morning, bored with his silence. He didn't answer. She climbed up to a branch below his. 'Come on, I'll take you to school.' He looked down at her, his eyes wild. 'You think they'll take you away?' He nodded slightly. 'Nah, not Sister Ignatius. She won't let anyone take you away. Promise. Come on.'

And to everyone's great surprise, including Catherine's, he climbed down from the tree, took her hand, and went with her. From then on, it was settled: they were a family.

The little woman on the verandah came all the way forward into the sunshine. 'Hullo,' she called. She was English – or Scottish, like Catherine's father.

'Hullo,' Catherine said. She remained at the gate.

The woman came out to the steps. 'Catherine, my dear, it's me. Do you remember me?'

Catherine shook her head. The woman took off her hat. She looked familiar, kind grey-green eyes the colour of the sea on a cloudy day, and little spectacles she peered through. 'I'm your Aunt Louisa, Harry's sister.'

The relief! She wasn't from the government after all.

'Oh,' Catherine said. 'What are you doing here?'

Louisa laughed. 'I'm here to . . . After Harry. Come up out of the sun, my dear. Let me look at you. Goodness, you're a giant.'

Louisa's blouse was light blue, the same colour as Catherine's, and they both wore grey skirts, Catherine saw now. And Louisa must have purchased her hat in the little shop in Samson Street in Cairns. It was the same hat Catherine had chosen, straw, with a wide brim and a wide black band. 'At least we're in uniform,' Catherine said, gesturing to her skirt and top.

Louisa laughed, looking up at Catherine. 'Yes. Do you think they'll mistake us for twins?'

Catherine laughed too then. Louisa had stood back to make room for Catherine to come up the stairs. They stood facing one another. Catherine was a head taller than her aunt. Neither made a move to embrace.

'I've been at school,' Catherine said, and felt a sudden urge to cry. Louisa was so obviously her father's sister, a tiny version of him, like him in the face most of all, especially her eyes. 'I teach the little ones now.'

'Well, isn't that wonderful?' Louisa said.

Catherine looked down at her shoes, not sure what else to say. She'd only started wearing shoes to school this year – Sister Ursula's idea – to set an example for the younger ones. The year before, she'd graduated from dungarees and a shirt to a skirt and blouse. It was Florence who insisted on this. When you didn't have a mother, Catherine had learnt, everyone was your mother.

Later that afternoon, Catherine and Michael went for their swim. They saw the turtles on the far reef, the same two they'd been seeing all year. Will your aunty stay with us? Michael had asked Catherine afterwards. I think so, Catherine had said, at least for a little while.

But after dinner, Catherine realised Louisa may as well have been from the government. Her plan was to take Catherine away. Louisa and Catherine were out on the front verandah. 'This is where you and I sat when I came to visit when you were small,' Louisa said. 'Do you remember?'

'No,' Catherine said.

It was then that Louisa told her. 'You don't need to worry, Catherine. I'm going to take you back to London with me.'

'London?' Catherine said. Louisa nodded. 'I can't leave the island. I'm needed at the school.'

But Louisa had been to the school, she said. She'd spoken to the nuns and they'd agreed – even Sister Ursula. They all agreed, Louisa told her. Catherine needed to leave the island and go to a proper school.

'I'm at a proper school,' she said. But at fourteen, she was subject to the will of others.

'You can't stay here without your parents, Catherine,' Louisa said. 'And that's final.'

'I have Florence.'

'Florence can't look after you properly. She . . .'

'She what?' Catherine said.

Louisa didn't respond. Catherine knew the way the natives were viewed. Florence had talked to her about it. 'They think we're idiots,' she said, 'like monkeys. They speak slowly, as if we might not understand them otherwise. They're the stupid ones, eh?' Catherine laughed. 'They don't know how to catch a fish like Michael does, or make a roast chicken like I do. Oh, actually, I think they do know how to make a roast chicken,' Florence corrected herself. 'I think I learnt that from Julia, now that I come to think of it.' Florence had a habit of shrugging and covering her mouth when she said something incorrect or funny.

But in the end, even Florence took Louisa's side. 'You have to go,' she said when Catherine told her what Louisa intended. 'I don't like it, but Louisa is right. She spoke to me. That's your future, not here. And Louisa, she didn't get to have children. She should have you.'

'No,' Catherine said. 'I'm not going. I'm happy here. I'm going to teach. You don't really want me to go?' She was almost in tears.

Florence was fiddling with her hands in her lap. She looked down at them. 'Louisa is your people,' Florence said firmly. 'It doesn't matter how much we love each other; I'm not yours. And Michael's not either.' She looked hard at Catherine. 'You and my boy – you couldn't have children, Catherine. It would be wrong. You wouldn't be allowed to keep them. The Protector will take them. And there's no Dr Harry to help us. You know as well as I do what that means.'

'You think they'll take Michael again?'

'No, he's too old for the Protector. But if you and Michael . . . you know what I'm talking about.'

Catherine blushed.

Florence looked at her sharply. 'You must go. You have

to trust me. You must go.' She softened then. 'You like your aunt. And she's a doctor, like your daddy. She's giving you an opportunity that you could never get here, Catherine.'

'But, Florence, what will you ever do without me?' The tears came now, falling down her face.

'Oh goodness. You mustn't worry about me.' Florence wiped Catherine's tears away. 'I got the prize, Catherine. I got to raise you. I got to work for Dr Harry. I got given a second chance with my boy. No other mother gets all that without having to pay something back.'

Chapter Six

Louisa watched as Catherine reached the bank. She was shivering visibly as she climbed the stairs. Louisa was about to go down to her when a building worker took off his coat and wrapped it around the girl. One of the others produced a blanket, which they put around her shoulders. They were cheering all the while: 'Swim-mer, Swim-mer, Swim-mer, Cath-rine, Cath-rine, Cath-rine.'

The reporter Louisa had seen earlier had got through the crowd and was talking to Catherine now. Catherine smiled as she spoke. Her eyes, that intense green in the soft light of London, the Quick green, were on fire. She was Harry's daughter right then, Louisa thought. She looked like all those paintings of the saints, as if that baptism in the filthy Thames had beatified her. She still hadn't seen Louisa but her eyes scanned the bank as if looking for someone.

Suddenly, Helen Anderson stepped into Louisa's line of sight. 'Now you see why I didn't want to discuss this on the telephone. We've never had a girl do something like this. There are rules at the school. The girls must not leave during school hours.'

Louisa nodded. 'I really don't know what to say. Catherine asked me about swimming a few weeks ago, but I didn't think she meant . . .' Louisa had a flash of memory then, Catherine with the boy, Michael, the two of them long and lean as they ran together into the sea, his dark skin, hers almost as dark because of the sun. It had unnerved Louisa to watch them, and it had strengthened her resolve to remove Catherine from the island.

'We have a rule,' Helen Anderson was saying. 'If girls leave the school grounds without permission, expulsion is automatic. She took eight girls with her. *Eight*. It was carefully thought out, the whole thing. The girl who came to me, the only one who came to me – one of our prefects, Darcy Williams – said Catherine's been planning it for a month. Catherine told them all to come and watch.'

'Well, the eight on the bank were just following,' Louisa said. 'They shouldn't be expelled.'

'If we bend the rules for one, we're done for, I'm afraid. Dr Quick, I don't like to do this, but I don't want to see Catherine back at Henley.'

'What, you mean from now?'

Helen Anderson nodded.

'What am I supposed to do with her?' Louisa said. She thought of the long line of patients back at the clinic.

'It's not as if this is the only problem,' Helen Anderson said.

'Well, this is the first I've heard of there being any problems at all, Miss Anderson,' Louisa said. 'I wish you'd contacted me before now.' It was no good blaming Helen Anderson,

Louisa knew, but she couldn't help herself. What a mess.

'I suggest you talk to the girl,' was all Helen Anderson said.

Louisa walked towards her niece. Catherine was standing below them on the bank, surrounded by men. She looked up at her aunt, frowned slightly and then burst into a smile. 'I did it, Louisa. I swam.'

Louisa put a hand on her forehead. She was planning to be stern, to tell Catherine that what she'd done was inexcusable, that now she'd be expelled from Henley, and she'd caused trouble for eight other girls. These were the words forming in her head. But when she got close to her tall, lithe niece she found, almost in spite of herself, she was returning Catherine's smile. She couldn't help it. The other girls were still chanting Catherine's name. The reporter was trying to get Catherine's attention again. Catherine was still smiling at her aunt. They were eye to eye for once, Louisa higher on the bank than Catherine was. Louisa felt tears forming in her own eyes. She swallowed hard. 'Yes, you did, Catherine,' she said. 'Yes, you did.'

It was ten months before, in the October, that Louisa had received the wire. HARRY PASSED STOP LOUISA GUARDIAN CATHERINE STOP CONTACT WITHERSPOON CAIRNS ASAP STOP ENDS. When she first read it, she thought Harry must have passed some test. It was the shock, she supposed later. She was in shock. It was only when she reread that she understood. Her brother Harry was dead.

Heart failure, Alexander told her three days later when she visited his office at Southampton. Alexander came out to meet Louisa in the foyer and they embraced briefly and stiffly. He took her back to his office, which looked out over the keel of a ship in dry dock below. The office had always seemed cold to Louisa. Alexander had nothing personal on the desk, and there was no view to speak of. He gestured for Louisa to sit down in the only visitor chair, in front of the desk.

Alexander wasn't as tall as Harry. Like Louisa, he took after their mother's side rather than their father's. He had their father's curly hair, though – blonde rather than red – and George's fine profile and sharp eyes. He'd followed their father into the shipping business. Now it was his whole life. Today he wore an expensive suit, cut perfectly around his muscled frame. He'd taken off the coat and had hung it on the back of his chair, before sitting down and facing his sister. Gold cufflinks and a silk-backed vest completed the picture of a successful man in his prime.

Alexander was named executor in Harry's will, he said. He'd had word from Harry's solicitor too. Harry had been in Cairns, Alexander told her. He'd been at the hospital in the morning, to assist in surgery, and had been about to set out on the return journey back to the island. His heart stopped just like that. One minute he was alive, the next he was dead, according to Alexander. Their father had died of a heart attack. Alexander was older than Harry by seven years. It had shaken him, Louisa could see.

'Harry's named me Catherine's guardian,' Louisa said.

'I know. You'll have to go for her,' Alexander replied.

'Someone will,' she said. 'I've got the clinic.'

'Well, she can't stay on the island, Louisa, and she can hardly travel unaccompanied. We can sort out the house and estate later, but you must go for the child, and soon. She's terribly exposed there.'

'To what?' Louisa said.

Her brother looked at her.

'I know she can't stay there, Alexander,' Louisa said, annoyed at the way he always tried to run everything. 'I'm not totally without wit. But I can't leave the clinic at a moment's notice.'

'Surely the poor can survive a couple of months without you.'

Alexander had always been like this. He saw himself as the one in charge in a way even their father didn't. When Louisa had been arrested during the protests for the vote – she'd marched on Whitehall with the others and then she'd thrown a rock through a window – it was Alexander who'd told her she should be ashamed, Alexander who'd arranged for her to be released from prison early. He said she'd worried their mother unnecessarily: 'And for what, Louisa? Some stupid idea about the vote.'

Louisa regarded her older brother now. He was probably right. She would have to go to Australia. It was a six-week journey at the minimum, which would take her through to the end of the year. She didn't want to feel resentful of Catherine, but she hardly knew the girl. Why should Louisa now drop everything in order to care for Harry's child, the child he'd made it impossible for Louisa to be close to? Harry should have come home. 'I'm not inclined to motherhood, Alexander.'

Alexander only shrugged. 'Well, you're a woman, which puts you in a better position than I am to go.'

Alexander knew what had happened to Louisa. Millicent had confided in him, against Louisa's wishes. He'd blamed his sister. She looked at him now. 'I have my work,' she said, 'just as you do.'

'Yes, I know, your work. But now Catherine Quick is officially part of your work – it says so here.' He'd picked up the telegram and handed it back to Louisa. 'I really must go.' He stood and took the jacket from the back of his chair, put it on in one fluid movement and started towards the door.

'What about the funeral?' Louisa said.

'They're having something on the island, the solicitor said. There's that native family Harry was close to.' Alexander looked hard at Louisa. 'A total Harry mess.' He stood at the door waiting for his sister.

'What do you mean?'

Alexander shrugged.

'The native family – that's the housekeeper, Florence, you're talking about?'

Alexander shrugged again.

'I did notice that Harry seemed very close to Florence,' Louisa said. 'But you don't think . . .'

Alexander held his hand up. 'I'm not saying anything,' he said, 'except that Harry was Harry. Just go and see what you can do. You can have an island Christmas.'

On the train back from Southampton, Louisa sat by herself and looked out the window at the bleak winter landscape. Oh, Harry, I wish it had been different, she thought. I wish . . . Just what did she wish? That he'd come home when she'd asked? That she'd gone to Australia, as he'd asked, to help with Catherine? Perhaps. Louisa's life

75

had been a series of decisions, she thought, that had left her just a little stranded. Sometimes she felt as if the life she might have lived was there, just off to the left somewhere. She might have stayed on the island, mightn't she? She might have cared for the child. It would have helped ease her own pain, surely. But she hadn't.

Louisa had done something useful with her life since then. She and Ruth had run the hospital during the war, and then they'd opened the clinic. And the clinic was marvellous. Everyone said so, even those who hated the poor. Louisa cared for so many families now. But not your own family, she thought, with a bitter taste in her mouth. It was Ruth Luxton she imagined saying that, although Ruth had never said it and never would, Louisa knew. Ruth had been a good friend, Louisa's best friend. But Ruth had her own family, five children, and they'd always come first.

Louisa and Harry had lost one another along the way. 'And now you're gone,' she said out loud to herself. She sat there as the countryside chugged by, the tears rolling down her face matching the tears of rain rolling down the windowpane.

At home that night in London, Louisa looked at the telegram again. Alexander was right. Someone would have to go for Catherine and Louisa was named. And then Catherine would have to live somewhere. She couldn't stay on in Australia alone. She couldn't really go to Alexander, a confirmed bachelor. There was Julia's family but Julia was an only child and her parents, in Canada now, were aged. Julia's father had a sister, Louisa recalled, who had children. They were in New York, or Long Island. Those children must be grown now, must have children of their own. She could go to one of them, it occurred to Louisa, to someone who'd been a mother already. Catherine would surely fare better with an experienced mother.

The next morning, Louisa told Nellie about her visit to Alexander. She said she might contact Julia's family about Catherine going to America to live. Nellie was appalled by the idea. It would be wrong, plain wrong, she said, to send Catherine to Julia's family, whom she hardly knew. Nellie didn't care what sort of family Julia came from. 'She's your blood, Louisa,' Nellie said. 'You can't just refuse her. And it's your side she knows best.' But how could she explain to Nellie that of all the things Louisa felt she could do in life, mothering was not among them?

Louisa asked Ruth Luxton later in the day, but Ruth was surprised too. 'She's your kin,' Ruth said. 'Of course you must take her in. And you'll never regret it if you do.'

There it was. The world would be happier if there were not only more children, but if those women who hadn't had children would just go and have a few. 'You'll never regret it,' was their song. Louisa didn't believe them. Not everything you decide in life comes without regret, she'd found. There were more than enough experiences that led to much regret. And many mothers' lives, as far as Louisa was concerned, were full of regret. But Ruth and Nellie were right, Louisa realised. Whatever else she was, Catherine was her kin. Louisa would have to go and fetch her niece and bring her home. She'd have to do the best she could.

Thursday Island was much the same as it had been eleven years before. She'd left London as soon as she reasonably could, but she'd had to recruit another surgeon for Princes Square and that took a month, and then transfer her surgical patients from the rooms to another surgeon. She didn't get away until December, spending Christmas in her stateroom on the ship. She had to stop in Cairns en route this time, to meet Harry's lawyer, Mr Witherspoon, an older chap, rail-thin, with sharp eyes that regarded Louisa as if she might be plotting to steal her brother's estate on the spot. Not that the estate was worth much, that ridiculous house and whatever Harry had put away of his government salary. Louisa did her best to assure Mr Witherspoon that she had Catherine's best interests at heart.

Witherspoon's concern seemed to be that Harry had left his estate to Louisa rather than in trust. He'd left it to Louisa outright. Louisa did think this was strange but not all that strange. Harry knew he could trust his sister on that score. On the other hand, even her own solicitors had said there would be a trust. It didn't much matter, except that Witherspoon seemed worried on Catherine's behalf.

As he'd been going through the file, Witherspoon had said there was something missing. He located a document number but no corresponding document. He remembered something, he said, and he'd ask his clerk to do a search. He'd find it, he assured Louisa, and if it included instructions to set up a trust for Catherine, Louisa could be very sure that's what he would do. But for now, Louisa just needed to sign papers to make her Catherine's guardian.

Louisa saw a copy of Julia's death certificate on the file. Harry had certified the death, which was most irregular. Her brother would know he shouldn't certify the death of a relative. Mr Witherspoon was unperturbed about it.

78

Drowning was the cause of death, Louisa noted, but she also knew that Julia's body had never been found. It should have been *Missing, Assumed Drowned*, which would have triggered an enquiry. It was odd, she thought, but perhaps Harry wanted as little fuss as possible.

Louisa read the documents she had to sign, feeling for the first time the weight of the responsibility she was taking on. She had to warrant to care for the girl, to be 'totally responsible for the minor's welfare,' the agreement said.

The trip north from Cairns did nothing to ease Louisa's mind and, she realised, it had taken her three months to get here. Harry had died in October and now it was early February. They'd had word through the solicitor that Catherine had stayed on in the house with Florence, the housekeeper, and was still attending school. The police officer on the island, a chap by the name of Macklin, had been appointed guardian *pro tem*, although he hadn't done much as far as Louisa could see. Now Louisa had signed a document that gave her full responsibility for this fourteen-year-old girl of Harry's. How could Louisa possibly manage this additional responsibility? She couldn't manage all the things she had to do as it was.

As the buggy had come through town on Thursday Island, Louisa noticed the native children under the trees in the main street, only now they wore dresses instead of shorts and shirts. There was what looked like a green silk dress in the oriental style Louisa remembered well – how dear it might have been with Catherine's eyes – and a linen blouse and skirt in blue. They were the clothes Louisa had been sending for Catherine over the years, worn by the native children. No wonder Harry had never answered when she'd asked about the clothes. Louisa wondered if he'd even given them to Catherine or had just handed them around. The children did look lovely, she thought, even if that bow around the boy's arm should have been in his sister's hair.

After she'd met with Sister Ursula from the school, who, eleven years on, was now in charge, Louisa went up to the house. Florence answered the door. She looked taken aback by Louisa's arrival, as if she hadn't been expecting Harry's sister, although Louisa had wired ahead. Florence didn't look a day older than the last time Louisa had met her. She was polite but far from friendly. She had a grown boy with her.

'This is my son, Michael,' Florence said. 'We were just on our way to the school.'

Michael was tall and lean, with a body that communicated strength, soft blue eyes and a smile that made you want to smile back. He was carrying a basket. He didn't say much to Louisa but he did take her offered hand. He leant down to her in a kindly way and told her that Catherine was teaching down at school but was sure to be home soon to go for a swim. 'We go every afternoon,' he said, smiling. 'She likes to beat me out to the reef.'

Louisa said she'd wait on the verandah where it was cool and, yes, a glass of cold water would be lovely. What a delightful young man, she thought. She didn't know where he'd been the last time she'd come to the island.

Catherine came bounding in the gate about half an hour later. She was older, of course. She had Harry's eyes and her mother's chestnut hair combined with the Quick red and darkened to auburn, her skin browned by the sun. Across her nose and cheeks was still that band of freckles. She looked straight at Louisa. She was much calmer and more demure than Louisa had expected she'd be. The wild creature Alexander described had grown into a thoughtful young woman, Louisa saw. She was tall, too, like Louisa's father and Harry.

They didn't get to speak until later, after dinner. Catherine had gone swimming with Michael when he and Florence had returned from town. While they were still down at the beach, Florence came out to the front verandah, which overlooked the sea, flecked with gold in the last of the sun. 'Dr Louisa, if I may have a word.' Her tone was polite, but her face was fierce.

'Of course, Florence. Sit down.' Louisa gestured to the chair opposite. Florence remained standing.

'I'm not sure what your plans are, but I do know that Catherine is keen to stay on the island.'

'Catherine doesn't know what she wants right now,' Louisa said, surprised at Florence's frankness. 'Things have been very hard for her, and it's up to us to make them easier.'

Florence narrowed her eyes, setting her jaw tight. 'I've been with Catherine her whole life. I'm the only one now who has. And Dr Harry did something for me I'll never forget. If Catherine wants to stay, it would be fine with me, more than fine. I have some money saved. I just want to make sure you know that.'

'But, Florence, you're not thinking she could spend the rest of her life here, on the island? What about her education?'

'She's at the convent.'

'That's not what I meant. Look, you can help Catherine right now, or hinder her. It's up to you. I know that the best place for her is England, where she can develop to her fullest potential.'

'How do I help the child most?' Florence said. 'The Protector said my son was better off with a white family, and I was so young I believed him.' She paused, looked out at the water. 'Dr Harry couldn't know he was going to die, that's the thing. And I need to have Catherine's best interests in my heart too. That's why I don't know, Louisa. I don't know if there are things I should tell you.' Florence looked as if she might cry.

'What things?' Louisa said sharply, but Florence shook her head and didn't respond. Louisa waited and then said, 'I can assure you there's nothing to worry about. Catherine will be with her family. She'll be happy, I'm very sure. And you have no blood tie to the girl.' Louisa paused but saw no flicker of feeling on Florence's face. She still stood there, saying nothing.

Louisa sighed. 'I'm sorry, Florence, but Catherine must come to England. It will be easier for her if you and your son let her go with your blessing.' She looked at the other woman. Florence's face was hard to read. She watched Louisa for a moment more and then turned and went back inside.

Chapter Seven

'I want to stay here,' Catherine said, almost before Louisa had finished explaining what was to happen. Her mouth was set in a line and she glared at Louisa as she spoke. They were alone, but Louisa had the feeling that Florence and Michael weren't far away. She wondered then if Florence had already spoken to Catherine, had warned her.

Why hadn't Louisa anticipated this? 'Well, that's not possible, dear,' Louisa said. 'I know you've had a difficult time. But you can't stay here. There's no one to look after you.' They were sitting together in the parlour, which was so stuffy the first time Louisa had visited. Now the windows were all open, the curtains pulled back. They looked out into the deep of evening, the sound of the native crickets heavy in their ears and, beyond, the sound of the sea.

'Florence will look after me,' Catherine said. 'She's always looked after me.'

Louisa had watched from the house that afternoon as Catherine and Michael had run down the hill together and dived into the sea. They were like puppies, bumping into one another as they raced, his naked chest, her bare legs. Louisa had never thought of herself as prudish, but in that swimming suit, a man's suit, Catherine's knees and shoulders were exposed. She showed no modesty whatsoever. And with a lad close to her own age. Louisa knew what could happen in these situations, what men were capable of, even seemingly nice young men like Michael. It sent a shiver through her.

'They're natives,' Louisa said to Catherine in the parlour, knowing this wasn't what she meant. The girl only looked confused. 'They're not your people.'

'Yes they are,' Catherine said. 'Of course they are. I've grown up with them.'

Louisa sighed. 'Catherine, I'm your guardian. I'm named in Harry's will. I can't fail in my responsibility here.'

'I have to go?' Catherine said.

Louisa nodded.

Catherine burst into tears then and fled the room. Louisa could hear her sobbing all the way up the stairs. Oh dear, Louisa thought. I'm worse at this business than even I expected I would be.

'We love Catherine,' the woman was saying. She was too close to Louisa's face. 'In fact, if she were to remain on the island, we'd be more than happy to help with her management.' Louisa was racking her brains for a name. She'd met this woman the day before. Catherine didn't like her, Louisa had thought at the time, and then Louisa had forgotten to ask why. Was it Wharton? Or Smithson? It was a name like that, she was sure.

84

Now, the woman had accosted Louisa and Catherine in the main street. Louisa had come to send a wire to Alexander, confirming their departure date, although given Catherine's reluctance, she might need to revise it. Catherine was still insisting she could stay on the island, but Louisa was more certain than ever that the correct course was to have her come to England where they'd find a good school.

Louisa and Catherine had met this woman – Watson, yes, Mrs Watson – who was staring at Louisa now, waiting for a response. Management, she'd said. She'd be happy to involve herself in Catherine's management. The look of hope on the woman's face made Louisa uncomfortable. Why would she want Catherine to stay on the island? What was it to her?

'I've tried my very best to get her to see,' Mrs Watson said. 'But she simply will not, Dr Quick. Can I say what a great honour it is to have you among us? I feel I am in the presence of a giant of the movement.'

She had particularly red cheeks and Louisa was finding it difficult to know if they were rouged. She reminded Louisa of those patients who came to her rooms with no real ailments to speak of other than the experience of an average life. If they paid on the way out, should she care? That's what Ruth Luxton said. But Louisa was a surgeon, unaccustomed to doing nothing. She was happiest in theatre, where patients didn't talk so much, where she could fix their problems without having to spend hours listening to their complaints. So she was disinclined to be tolerant of Mrs Watson.

'I appreciate everything you've done, Mrs Watson,' she

said, swallowing the name in case she still had it wrong.

'The girl is living with natives currently, which we, Jack and I, feel is compromising her reputation.'

Louisa shook her head. 'As I say, I appreciate everything you've done, Mrs Watson, but you will be aware that Florence Cunningham has been in Catherine's life since Catherine was born. Florence is like a member of the family.'

It had crossed Louisa's mind again since she'd arrived on the island that Florence and Harry might have had some sort of tryst. This was what Alexander had implied that day in Southampton, although he'd never made anything explicit and he probably had no evidence. It wouldn't do to dwell on this notion, Louisa knew, but Catherine's skin was as dark as some of the natives', almost as dark as Michael's. Could there have been some relationship that Julia agreed to cover over? Or worse, could Harry and Florence have conspired to harm Julia, poor young thing that she was? Well, that was ridiculous. Harry didn't go to the island in time to impregnate another woman and then bring his American wife into the picture. And even if the timing added up, Harry would never have acted so dishonourably. But he had brought the boy, Florence's son Michael, home to the island. Catherine had told Louisa the story. Why had he done that for a child who wasn't his? At the very least, Harry held Florence in high regard. Was Michael . . . Louisa put any thoughts of Harry's relationship with his housekeeper away, stared at the block of a woman in front of her. 'So I would think you might think twice before you would say something like that,' she said.

Mrs Watson left them soon after, but Louisa could see

there was something changed in her niece. Catherine had looked angry as the woman spoke, and Louisa had realised the girl would have defended Florence. Now she looked at her aunt with a small smile on her face.

'Why did you say that to her about Florence?' Catherine asked.

'Florence *has* been like family to you. I didn't like what the woman was implying, that there was something wrong with that. Did you tell me yesterday you know her daughter?'

'Yes,' Catherine said. 'I teach her reading. She's a sweet little thing. She comes to school looking like a little princess and goes home looking like a street urchin. I'm surprised her mother would trust me with her, frankly. I lead her astray.'

'I think the plan is to bring you back to the straight and narrow, Catherine, and have you caring for her children.'

'Oh,' Catherine said. 'I never thought of that.'

'And if that's the alternative, surely you'd prefer to come back to London,' Louisa said.

'I can't just stay here?'

'I think you know the answer to that in your heart, dear.'

Catherine looked sad then, but also as if, for the first time, she did know the answer.

Louisa was relieved. She'd been worrying about what she'd do if Catherine refused outright to come to London. 'It must be nice to be so wanted, sweet girl,' Louisa said now. 'Florence means well and she's a good woman. She's been wonderful to you. I have no doubt of that. But I visited the school again. They can't do for you what you need. You could be anything, Catherine – a doctor, a lawyer. There are no limits for women, not any more. You must see that.'

'Are you sure, Aunt Louisa?' Catherine said.

'Of course I am,' Louisa said.

On their last full day on the island, Louisa watched Catherine swimming out beyond the break, beyond the jetty, so far out Louisa lost sight of her. There was a reef three miles out, Catherine had told her. It was nothing for the girl to swim that far in a day. Catherine was so at home here, and the beauty of the place, the green of the water, the easy way the natives had with one another, affected Louisa too. She'd ended up staying for a whole month. It was true she had to finalise Harry's estate and clear the house of his personal effects. But the island had a way of slowing a person down. It was quite delightful, even with the heat, Louisa thought. Perhaps Catherine should stay here after all and Louisa should stay with her. Oh good Lord, your brain is melting, Louisa told herself. Of course the girl should come to London. What on earth would she do for the rest of her life otherwise? She shouldn't assume a man would look after her. Louisa knew what folly that was.

Before they boarded the ship in Sydney, Louisa took Catherine to a draper in the city to have dresses made up. Catherine agreed the materials were lovely, ran her fingers over the silks and velvets, but Louisa could see she had no interest in fine dresses. They'd packed what they could of the clothes she wore on the island, but mostly she'd worn Harry's old shorts and a man's shirt with her big straw hat.

Only on school days did she even bother with shoes, so they didn't take much in the end.

Louisa had three plain woollen skirts and three linen blouses made, along with two dresses in the new style, hemmed just below the knee – which Louisa agreed to on the seamstress's advice; she herself was against the shorter skirts, which she felt were unnecessary – and an evening dress in a dark green silk that set off Catherine's hair.

Catherine wanted to go to a beach before they left for London and so Louisa arranged for them to visit the little seaside village of Coogee. The beach had a small headland at one end and a pier at the other. Louisa and Catherine walked out on the pier in the afternoon and bought ices. Catherine wanted to swim, so while she was changing into a bathing suit Louisa rented for her – Louisa had made sure to leave Catherine's men's swimming suit back on the island – Louisa watched two little girls in white frocks, long socks and black leather shoes. They looked so dear, Louisa thought to herself.

'Look at those girls, Catherine,' she said when Catherine returned. 'Aren't they sweet?'

Catherine smiled. 'That's how you'd like me to look,' she said. 'But I look more like him.' With the girls was a boy of around twelve in a button-up cotton shirt and serge shorts, socks falling down around his ankles, scuffed brown leather shoes.

'Yes you do, I'm afraid,' Louisa said. 'Did you not want to get new clothes for England?'

'I don't much care,' Catherine said, and ran off and leapt into the sea.

*   *   *

On the journey back to London, Catherine either sat in their stateroom staring out the porthole, or went up on the main deck to stare at the ocean from there.

'You like the sea,' Louisa said one afternoon when she found Catherine on the deck.

'When I was a little girl,' Catherine said, 'I told my father that I loved swimming so much I wasn't sure if I was a boy or a fish. He said I was neither. I was a girl who loved the water. I said I most certainly wasn't a girl and since he was sure I couldn't be a boy, I might have to be a fish. That was my name on the island, Waapi. It's the word for fish.'

'What was it about the water you loved so much?'

'I still love it,' Catherine said, looking squarely at Louisa. 'I feel as if I could dive in here. I feel sometimes I could swim forever.'

'We used to go to the beach at Aldeburgh, where my mother's family lived,' Louisa said. 'We had our holidays there every summer. I used to go into the water to paddle but I couldn't swim.' Louisa had never learnt. When they went to the seaside her brothers would swim. Louisa wore a swimming skirt and blouse. Even if she'd known how to swim, she couldn't have carried the weight.

When she was very small, Louisa remembered, her father would throw a rope out and she'd hold on while she bathed. Once she'd let go of the rope without thinking and had been swept out with the current. Before she knew it, the water had overwhelmed her. As she bobbed up, she could see her father stepping out of his shoes and throwing off his jacket and hat. It was as if he was moving very slowly, but he must have been going fast for he soon reached her and lifted her up and told her to make herself floppy.

'Can you hear me, Louie?' he said, his arms tight about her.

'Of course I can hear you,' she said. 'Don't be scared, Papa.'

'I'm not,' he said.

'Then why are you hurting me?'

He stopped squeezing so hard.

They came up onto the beach a long way from where they'd left their towels and he carried her all the way. He said they weren't to tell Mama what had happened.

Louisa smiled at Catherine now. 'My mother was a great fan of children being outdoors, but I was never taught to swim. Harry was a fine swimmer.'

'He was very keen for me to be able to swim well,' Catherine said, 'and more proud of my swimming than anything I did at school.'

'Yes, he was,' Louisa said. They were exposed to the oncoming breeze, which was building as the afternoon progressed. 'Come in now, and we'll get ready for dinner.'

'You go in,' Catherine said. 'I'll just stand here a while.'

Catherine had none of the training most young women had for life, Louisa thought. Perhaps that was a good thing, although it would always make her stand out. The fact that she seemed not to care was probably a blessing.

Chapter Eight

When Catherine reached the bank, she looked around for Darcy. She saw Ida and some of the other girls but no Darcy. She climbed the stairs. She was shivering, she realised. One of the workmen had come down and was wrapping his coat around her shoulders. 'Aye, you made it, girl.' She grinned. There was a man taking pictures. She could smell the fire of the flash. It was a warm smell. Someone came with a blanket and wrapped that around the jacket. Catherine would have loved a cup of hot tea, Nellie's cure for everything.

Suddenly she saw Louisa up on the bank with Miss Anderson. They were both frowning, looking at Catherine. How did Louisa get here? Catherine thought.

Ida came down the bank. 'You did it!' she called out, then added, more quietly, 'But you're done for.'

'Why? Where's Darcy?'

'That's just it. She told Miss Anderson. Did you see Miss Anderson's here? She's fuming.'

'Am I in trouble?'

Ida nodded, eyes wide. 'Darcy did you in. She came over last night, said she felt it her duty to warn the authorities of your intended swim. She told me I shouldn't come. What a snake. I'm so sorry.'

Catherine couldn't stop shivering. 'But it was Darcy's idea,' she said, her teeth chattering between the words.

'I'm sorry,' Ida repeated. She was moving away now, as Louisa approached.

Louisa looked angry too. 'What on earth were you thinking, Catherine? Are you all right? You might have been run over.'

'I did it, Louisa. I swam.'

Louisa's face softened into a smile. 'Yes, you did, Catherine,' she said. 'Yes, you did.' She looked back towards the group on the bank. 'But we're in real trouble now.'

She'd farewelled Florence at the ferry, a quick hug in the end for there was no time for more. Florence shook her head. Catherine saw there were tears in Florence's dear eyes.

And then, as the ferry pulled away, Catherine saw Florence's frame slump over on the jetty, as if someone had punched her. She was supporting herself against one of the pylons. Catherine couldn't bear to see her so upset.

'We knew the day would come,' she'd said to Catherine the night before. 'It just came too soon.'

Catherine wished more than anything that Michael had come to say goodbye, that he'd been there to look after his mother now. Catherine couldn't bear it. She looked away from Florence and towards the sea.

One evening, just before she left, Michael had gone swimming alone. A dolphin had swum with him, he said. 'I asked Bid to watch over you. He said you'll come back.' Michael leant in. They hugged one another.

'We could run,' he said. 'Take a boat up to Saibai. They'd never find us.'

But Catherine knew that would be wrong. She felt it was her duty to go with Louisa now. Here was an opportunity to go to a school, a real school where she would learn the ways of the wider world. Louisa was right. Catherine's future for now lay in London. If she was to come back to the island, if she was to have power over her own life, she needed to go with Louisa and learn how.

Michael looked upset then. 'You *do* want to go,' he said. She didn't answer him.

'Fine,' he said. 'Go. But don't expect I'll wait around for you to come back.'

She looked back towards the jetty once more now, and there was Michael. He ran down past Florence towards the end of the jetty. 'Waapi!' he called out. 'Come back to us, you hear? You come back to us, or I'll come get you.' He waved then and grinned. She didn't call out but waved back, tears streaming down her cheeks. He turned and went back to Florence, put his arms around his mother.

After she left the island, after she was all those thousands of miles across the sea, it would be Florence who Catherine would think of at night before she slept: Florence's soft kind voice, her smile, her smell, which Catherine never smelt after she left Thursday Island, of coconut and frangipani, luscious and safe. She'd think of her last swim with Michael, his laugh, and she'd remember that view of the two of them, Michael and Florence, together at the ferry as Catherine sailed away from them.

Chapter Nine

By the time Louisa finished work, it was after nine. She'd seen her list of patients in the rooms, and then visited her post-operative patients at the hospital. On the way home, she'd dropped in to visit the boy with scarlet fever she'd seen early that morning. She'd been relieved beyond measure to discover that he'd turned a corner.

'Oh, Doctor, do you think he's going to be all right?' the mother said.

'He's better,' Louisa replied. 'Much better. The fever's broken. He's not out of the woods but he can see his way from here with a bit of help. Chips of ice, if you can get them; a washer to suck, if not.'

The woman let out a breath and her shoulders relaxed. The frown that had seemed permanently etched on her face was gone suddenly.

'How can we thank you, Doctor?' she said as Louisa was leaving. She went out through the back door and came back in carrying a dead animal of some sort, a bird by the look of it, a chicken. 'Fresh plucked today,' she said kindly. 'Will you not take it, Doctor?'

'That's very thoughtful of you. But can I suggest you make him a broth with that bird? I'll warrant by about lunchtime tomorrow he'll be ravenous and his throat will be sore but he'll take a warm broth.

'And it's you who saved him,' Louisa said. 'Not me.' She was never comfortable with praise and, anyway, it was true. If ever a boy was healed by a mother's love, this one was. 'I just came and watched you do it. It's you who sat up through the nights and hoped. It was your care, your strength, that saved your boy. Now, go sit with him a bit while he's awake and I'll pop in early tomorrow.'

Louisa had always liked coming home to her little house in Wellclose Square. She could walk to and from the clinic with ease, and whatever might be happening in the world outside, she always felt safe here. Even though she knew Catherine and conflict were within on this particular evening, the house was still home.

Louisa unlocked the door and went inside, hung her coat and hat on the stand in the entry and put her bag on the little table. There was a narrow central hallway with rooms on either side. She passed the formal sitting room – or parlour, as Nellie called it – such as it was: a sofa and two large chairs, velvet curtains, a fireplace, flowers on a little table that were looking tired by the end of the week, a rug on the floor, a tiger skin that someone in some branch of the Quick family had shot on safari. Louisa wasn't quite clear how the tiger had come to rest in Wellclose Square, but that was where he lay.

The parlour wasn't a room that welcomed the visitor, Louisa had often thought, although she never understood quite why, the tiger notwithstanding. She herself would become gloomy if she sat too long in the room, although the dogs liked it well enough, or at least Sooty did. He spent his days in front of the grate hoping for a fire, lying on the tiger's backside. Marble was always more particular, preferring the kitchen where Nellie spent much of her day and scraps could be had. Louisa had inherited the dogs from Millicent when she was no longer able to care for them. Sooty did as he pleased but was mostly happy. Marble was more cantankerous, withdrew affection unless treats were forthcoming, barked at flies or the moon or rocks. Louisa had been glad of the dogs after Millicent died. They were a link to her mother, and until Nellie arrived they were the only creatures there to talk to in the evenings; unlike everyone else in her life, they didn't talk back.

On the right, further along the hallway, was the dining room. It was so far from the kitchen Louisa didn't bother eating in there unless there were visitors, and the dining table was spread now with her papers, along with Catherine's school books. She wouldn't be needing those for a while, Louisa thought bitterly.

At the back of the house, Louisa had had a carpenter add a small room with a bath, which was glorious and by far Louisa's favourite room. There was a family story about baths, Millicent's father demanding that when his three daughters went off to boarding school they be allowed to have a weekly bath. It was unheard of, but the school acquiesced. 'So you see, hot baths run in the family,' Louisa

98

had told the carpenter, who was less interested in the story that she thought he ought to be.

Upstairs were two bedrooms. Nellie and Catherine shared. Nellie had offered to move to the back of the kitchen – really a pantry where she'd have been on a mattress on the floor – after Catherine arrived but Catherine insisted she stay in the room. 'So long as you don't mind company,' she told Nellie. 'It will make me less lonely.'

Louisa found Nellie at the back of the house in the kitchen now. Louisa looked a question. 'In bed,' Nellie said quietly. Nellie had come to collect Catherine from the clinic after the swim. 'I think she's sleeping.' There was beef and boiled potatoes, Nellie said, taking down a plate for Louisa.

'I'm not hungry,' Louisa said. 'I'll take it for lunch tomorrow.'

'You must eat,' Nellie said.

'Just not tonight.' She sighed. 'God, Nellie, what are we to do with her?' Louisa took a bottle of scotch from the pantry and sat down at the table against the wall. She poured herself a dram and drank it down. She took a big breath into her lungs and exhaled.

'It's not been easy for her,' Nellie said.

'No, I suppose it hasn't. But if I compare her to you, Nellie – look at what you've done with your life.' Dear Nellie had endured so much more than Catherine had. She'd lost her entire family to the influenza in 1919 and had spent a year or more on the street before she'd come to Princes Square. She'd come through so courageously. 'Catherine's had so many opportunities. Harry just adored her, lavished everything on her. Now she's in a very good school. Or at least she was in a very good school. She's got you looking after her. I do what I can.'

'I think that's the thing, Louisa. You're just so busy, and she's of an age where a girl most needs her mother.'

'Well, she hasn't got a mother.'

'I know, but you're in that role, if you don't mind my saying. You're her guardian.'

'Are you saying I haven't done enough?'

'No, of course not,' Nellie said – carefully, it occurred to Louisa. Nellie was not normally careful with her words. 'But, Louisa, I don't quite understand it. It's like you keep her at a distance.'

'What do you mean, Nellie?'

'You're easier with me than with Catherine. She's your blood, Louisa.'

'But she's just so very different from me, Nellie. How can she be so . . .'

'So what?' Catherine said then. Louisa turned around to find her niece standing in the doorway. She was dressed in a baggy flannel nightdress, but Louisa could make out the powerful frame beneath. And if you didn't notice the outline of muscle and sinew in her frame, the fire in those eyes told a story. The dark skin might have paled to a grey in the London winter, but those blazing green eyes demanded attention.

'Ungrateful,' Louisa said flatly. It wasn't what she meant but it would have to do at short notice. She looked away and then back at the girl. She tried to be more reasonable. 'Catherine, I just can't imagine doing something like that –

swimming the river. Something I'm very sure you knew you shouldn't do.' This wasn't what she meant either.

Catherine didn't respond, just stood with her arms folded, that fierce look in her eyes.

Nellie sat down across from Louisa. 'I do think she's been very unhappy at the school.' She was frowning hard, as if she were trying to make Louisa understand.

Louisa felt a flash of anger. She had so much on her plate already and Catherine had done something entirely stupid. 'Unhappiness doesn't lead the rest of us to jump in the river.' She looked up and saw the girl's face. Catherine looked so young, and the fierceness in her eyes looked more like fear now. 'You knew you shouldn't,' Louisa said more gently.

The girl gave a small nod. 'I wanted . . .' She sobbed suddenly, an awful noise.

'What?' Louisa said, standing up, moving towards Catherine without thinking, putting her hand up near the girl's head, which was bowed now, not quite making contact. 'What did you want, Catherine?'

Catherine looked up, her face distraught, but didn't respond.

'Very well,' Louisa said. 'Back to bed and we'll talk more tomorrow. Perhaps Helen Anderson will have calmed down by then. We can but hope, my dear.' Louisa tried to smile encouragingly, but the look on Catherine's face when she raised her head, the sadness there, just about broke Louisa's heart.

'I don't ever want to go back there,' Catherine said then, her voice shaky. 'I just want to go home, Aunt Louisa. I hate it here. I hate school. I hate everything.'

Nellie had tried to warn Louisa about this, Louisa recalled now, over breakfast in the kitchen a week ago. Louisa was reading a letter from the new health inspector. They were sending an official to inspect the clinic and Louisa had just read their list of requirements. She would have laughed if it hadn't been so serious. Sooty waddled up – they were getting so fat; she wished Catherine would walk them – and she threw him a biscuit. 'Who's a good boy?' she said distractedly and gave him a little pat.

'She's unhappy,' Nellie said.

'What about?' Louisa said, still reading the letter.

'The school.'

'What's wrong with the school?'

'Ask her.'

So when Catherine came downstairs in her uniform a few minutes later, Louisa said, 'School's going well?' without looking up from the notes she was making about the health inspector's letter.

'Oh yes,' Catherine said.

Louisa looked at Nellie, who said to Catherine, 'Go on, ask her.'

Catherine shook her head.

'Ask her what?' Louisa said. She took off her spectacles and looked at Catherine.

'I . . .' Catherine said, then stopped.

'What?'

'Just, I was wondering if I might swim now that it's coming into summer.'

'Swim,' Louisa said, putting down the letter. 'What for?'

'I just . . . I've always been able to swim.'

102

'Oh,' Louisa said. 'I suppose you have. The chaps swim up at Hampstead Ponds, don't they, Nellie?' Nellie had mentioned the ponds the week before on Catherine's birthday. This must have been why.

Nellie nodded enthusiastically.

'I don't see how, dear,' Louisa said. 'Can't you run in the park?'

Louisa regarded her niece now. Catherine looked desperately unhappy. Louisa hadn't listened. Nellie was right. Things had gone very wrong for Catherine, and Louisa hadn't listened.

Louisa was a surgeon. What she loved most about surgery, what she'd loved from the beginning, was its clarity. You cut or you didn't. Staring at Catherine now as she stood unmoving in the kitchen, Louisa felt at a loss.

Nellie broke the silence. 'Come, child, let's go to bed. Your aunt's right. We won't sort this out tonight.' Nellie always knew exactly the tone to take with Catherine. Where did she learn that? It must have come from having younger siblings, although Louisa had Harry. Perhaps Nellie was just better at it. At any rate, it was clear that everything Louisa did when it came to Catherine was wrong.

What *would* they do now? Louisa wondered. Find another school, start again? Louisa had hoped Catherine would settle in, that her memories of the island would fade and she'd come to love London, to love Louisa too. She grimaced. Love was not what her niece felt for her, that was certain. If anything, Catherine had become more unhappy in the months since they'd arrived in London. And rather than forget the island, it was all she thought about.

If she'd known Catherine would be so unhappy, would she have acted differently? Should she have left the girl in Australia? Of course not. Should she have picked a different school? Was the change just too severe?

She poured a second dram of scotch and took herself off to her study to go over the day's reports. Who was it who'd said that scotch was the antidote to all fear? Louisa couldn't remember. Although she hardly knew herself why she felt so angry with Catherine, she couldn't overcome her feelings. Nellie was right. She had pushed the child away. And she'd been unfair. Underneath the anger was a feeling she knew well, even as she tried to push it back down: it was fear; deep gut-wrenching fear that only hard work or strong drink would keep at bay.

What happened to her had not become any more clear in the intervening years. She could not construct a memory that made sense. As time went by, she settled on a story she told herself, the story Jonathan had told her the next day. But now, on nights like this, she wondered whether there was another story, a story she must know in some part of herself. A true story.

He offered to walk Louisa home and she was thrilled. They'd both worked late, an emergency occasioned by a rail accident – a boy who'd gone under a train and had survived, miraculously. The boy had lost a leg but Jonathan had saved his arm. Louisa was so happy to have been the one selected to assist, and then elated by what surgery had achieved for the patient.

Jonathan Pyne was handsome and clever and, of all

the Edinburgh surgeons, he was the only one who was supportive of women. He was training Louisa and three others, two from Scotland, one from France. Ruth Luxton, who had done her general surgical training with him, had urged Louisa to seek him out when she wanted to specialise. 'You were born to surgery, and so was he,' Ruth said. 'You'll hate him, though. I know I did.'

But Louisa had liked him from the start. He was witty and self-deprecating, and everyone except Ruth had a crush on him, Louisa quickly learnt. If he hadn't been married – his theatre nurse; three sons – then any one of the women training with him would have accepted him as a suitor.

At her door, he said, 'I'll see you inside.' Louisa knew he was married, knew he had children. If she'd thought about it at all, she'd have said she knew it made her safe.

It was from here that her memory of the night's events refracted into single sensations, unrelated to one another, that never collected themselves into a whole experience. She might recall a smell of sweet fruit, dark hair on a wrist, or a damp chill in the air, but not put these individual sensations into a context. This was what was most unnerving.

The next morning, Jonathan himself gave her a version, and for many years it was easier to accept his view. It seemed so sure. 'How are you today?' he'd said, just before he was to go into theatre, a sly smile on his face, his hands in the air in front of him, clean. He'd winked. As if they had been lovers. That's what his smile said, the wink. Was that what he believed? she wondered. Was that what he believed they had been to one another?

Now, with the intervening years, she blamed memory

entirely. She told herself of course she wouldn't be able to summon the details. Of course they would be blurred. Still, the incomplete images came to her, harmless ones and some that were not harmless, and she would do her best to remain calm until they passed. They always passed. And for that, she could be thankful.

Part Two

Chapter Ten

Catherine woke to the sound of a bird in the back garden. It was the one she'd heard before, and she'd been meaning to ask Nellie what it was. Its song was so long and sweet, nothing like the parrots back on the island that screeched and squawked the morning awake. This one was a well-mannered bird, the kind of bird her aunt would like Catherine to be. But Catherine was more a screecher and squawker, she thought, however much she wished she could be a quiet little singer.

She got up from her bed and looked out the window for the little bird but all she could see were the motor cars on the street and people hurrying along the footpath on their way to work. A soft rain fell. It would be cold on the way to school, she thought.

This was Catherine's life now: the city, the school, her aunt and Nellie. At first, she'd been able to conjure up the smells of the island – the kelp growing near the rocks or drifting in after a storm, the coconuts the boys threw down from the trees and cracked, the sun itself, which had a smell like hot linen – but all that was gone now. And she couldn't remember the colours, only that they were much brighter.

Catherine opened the window wide and put her head outside. It *was* cold. To her right, the construction noise on Commercial Road had started up. It was later than she'd thought, the morning sun hidden behind clouds. But at least she'd been wrong about the rain. Catherine jumped down the stairs two at a time. Why hadn't Nellie called her?

'Have you made your bed?' Nellie said when Catherine found her in the kitchen.

'Of course,' Catherine said. 'Is Louisa gone?'

'Yes, and you're lucky. She's fit to fry a cat this morning.'

'What does that mean?'

'Furious would be my summary. Now, go back up and make your bed and then we'll have some breakfast. And a talk.'

'Is there any mail for me today?' Catherine said.

'Hasn't been yet.' Nellie was such a sweet person really, Catherine often thought, but she seemed to think she had to be in charge. She was tiny and solidly built with rosy cheeks and black curly hair that bounced around as she spoke – it was hard to take offence at anything someone so sweet-looking said. But, all the same, she was awfully bossy, Catherine thought.

Catherine considered refusing about the bed. What could Nellie do? And how did she know Catherine hadn't made her bed? She was pondering this on the way up the stairs when she stopped suddenly.

She remembered.

Yesterday she'd swum. For the first time since she'd left

Australia, she'd swum. And she'd managed *that* swim, the swim the girls at school said Catherine couldn't possibly do. She'd shown them, she thought. She'd made it across, landing exactly where she'd intended. Miss Anderson, the principal, had seen her. The girls had seen her. Louisa had seen her.

Catherine had tried her hardest to fit in at Henley, the school where, Louisa said, she would be challenged. It was going to be different from the little island school, her aunt said, and Catherine would have to use her brains. Nellie had taken her to buy the uniform: a grey wool pleated skirt, a white linen blouse, a tie, blazer, gloves and hat. They were like restraints, Catherine thought, the skirt so tight around her legs it was difficult to move, the hard shoes that hurt her feet and clacked against the sidewalk. But the worst thing was the stockings. Catherine could not for the life of her see how Nellie gathered them into a little foot that you could poke your own foot into. When she tried to pull them on, she tore them. 'Never mind, I can darn them,' Nellie said, smiling kindly.

It was Nellie who took Catherine on her first day, walking the mile from Wellclose Square to the high gates that fronted Henley. Louisa had been planning to take her but she was called to the hospital. Even Nellie looked unsure, Catherine thought. There were little clumps of girls on the footpath outside the gates. Even though Catherine looked the same in her skirt and blouse, she also knew she was totally different from these girls with their fair skin and English accents. She was one of the tallest too, and many of them stared at her, perhaps because she was new. It made her self-conscious. How strange to come from the island, where she was one of few whites – many of the European children were off at boarding schools on the mainland, so that most of the students at the local school were natives – to a place where everyone was white and yet feel she was the one who was different.

Catherine went first to Miss Anderson's office. She was put in with the juniors for her lessons, since – as the teacher said to her on the first day – she'd have learnt nothing much among the savages. The littler girls were kind but Catherine felt like Gulliver in Lilliput among them. At lunch, she sat with the older girls. Ivy Somerville was nice to her from the start, offering her a place at their table, and Darcy, almost as tall as Catherine, gave a little speech of welcome.

After a week, Catherine moved up to the class with the bigger girls. They were reading *Jane Eyre*, which Catherine had already read, and doing French verbs Catherine already knew. She didn't find the work difficult, although her new teacher, Miss Mason, said her handwriting was atrocious. She had trouble with needlework, and the ball games they played weren't familiar. But school in London wasn't harder than it had been on the island, Catherine quickly realised. It was just different.

It might have been Ida who'd first mentioned swimming, but it was Darcy who'd urged Catherine on. Ida and Darcy couldn't swim at all, Catherine knew. But of all the girls, Darcy had some understanding of what was involved in the Thames swim because Darcy's father was a swimmer. When Catherine had said she was sure she could swim the Thames, Darcy had urged her on.

Darcy had befriended Catherine at the beginning. But

then there was a day when Darcy was sitting in the dining room with the older girls and Catherine came in and they all went quiet. Catherine had a sense they'd been talking about her. Darcy looked at Catherine and said, 'You look like a boy.' A few of the other girls giggled. Catherine didn't know what to say. Darcy said it again. 'Are you a boy? Are you secretly a boy?' More giggles. Catherine shook her head.

'Don't mind her,' Ivy said later. 'She's just jealous. You got a higher score than her on the spelling.' It was true Catherine had done better than Darcy in the spelling. But Darcy was the most popular girl in the class, a prefect. Why would Catherine's doing well in spelling bother her?

The Islanders were not like this. Catherine really *was* different from them, in skin colour if nothing else, but Catherine was accepted as one of them. Catherine's teachers on the island were kind. Her teacher at the new school, Miss Mason, was not. 'Did they not teach you this?' she'd say, even when Catherine knew an answer. Catherine quickly stopped speaking up in class, and became wary around Darcy, who was sometimes friendly and sometimes not.

Miss Mason taught them French. Catherine had taught French to the younger students on the island. But instead of this helping, it only seemed to make matters worse. One day when Ivy was worried because she'd forgotten her French copybook, Catherine had offered to swap. Catherine gave Ivy her own copybook, which she'd already filled in, thinking she could manage getting into trouble better than Ivy since she'd never forgotten her own book before. 'Miss Mason won't know,' Catherine said as she scratched out her name. But Miss Mason did know, and blamed Catherine.

113

'You think you're very clever, young lady,' Miss Mason said. 'But we'll see who feels clever soon.'

No one had ever hit Catherine before. The nuns on the island were gentle, and Catherine's father would never have dreamt of striking her. When Miss Mason brought the cane down on her open palm, the pain was excruciating. But worse than the pain was the look of satisfaction on Miss Mason's face. Why would the teacher enjoy hitting her? Catherine wondered.

As well as the caning, Catherine had to visit the principal's office to tell Miss Anderson what she had done.

'We don't like liars here, Catherine,' the principal had said. 'Did you lie?'

Catherine only nodded, still smarting from the cane on her fingers, unable to trust her voice.

'Would you like me to speak to your aunt about this?' Miss Anderson said. Catherine didn't answer. 'I didn't think so. Well, I'm willing to let this incident go, but you must never be a liar again. Do you understand?'

Catherine only stared at her. She was still upset after being hit but underneath her upset, she was angry. How dare they? she thought. How dare they hit someone for helping a friend? What kind of place was this?

'Very good,' the principal said finally. 'Dismissed.' Catherine stood there for a moment, staring at the principal, and then turned and walked out.

Catherine thought of telling her aunt what was happening at the school. But when Louisa asked how school was going, she found herself saying it was going well. She wanted to please Louisa, who'd made so much of how carefully she'd selected Henley. If Catherine wasn't fitting in, it must be Catherine's fault.

Catherine had thought by swimming across the river she would show them all – those girls, her teachers, even Louisa and Nellie – that she could do something. She hadn't thought through what might happen next, but at least something would be different, she thought. It would say to them, 'This is who I am. This is what I can do.' But it hadn't been like that at all. Louisa had been angry. Miss Anderson had been angry. And as for Darcy, she hadn't even turned up to watch. It was the worst possible thing to have done, Catherine thought now. Darcy had known exactly what would happen. How could a person do that to another person?

Catherine looked in her closet. It wasn't all bad. At least she wouldn't be putting on her white blouse and tie today, or that awful wool skirt that stopped her from running. Not the blazer, nor the gloves, nor those horrid shoes.

She made the bed, after a fashion, pulling the eiderdown over the disorderly sheets, and went back downstairs. 'Nellie, I don't have to go to school.'

'No, you don't,' Nellie said as she put a plate of buttered toast and a glass of milk on the table. 'What a little idiot you are.'

Not Nellie too, Catherine thought then.

'It's a stain on your character. Have you seen this?' It was the morning paper. There was Catherine on the riverbank.

'That's me!' she exclaimed. 'I'm in the news!'

'For goodness' sake, don't let your aunt hear you talking like that. Look at you – you look like a harlot.'

Catherine had no idea what a harlot was, only that it was

something you shouldn't be. It was something to do with Nellie being an East End girl, Catherine was sure, because she'd heard the word once before. It was what one of the nurses at the clinic called Nellie. She and Catherine had gone to Princes Square. Nellie was in seeing Louisa about something. She was an East End girl before she met Doctor Louisa, one nurse said to another. A harlot, the other nurse whispered. I never knew.

Later, Catherine had asked Nellie what they meant.

'East End girl is a working girl,' Nellie said. 'Did they not have them in Australia?'

Catherine shook her head.

'I had to do bad things, Catherine, very bad things.' Nellie's voice, normally loud and clear, sounded small and afraid. She didn't sound like bossy Nellie at all.

'Oh, Nellie, you're a dear,' Catherine had said. 'There might be badness in the world. But not one bit of it was done by you.'

Catherine looked at Nellie now. 'I don't much care what they think of me,' she said, although she did care what Louisa thought. 'If it means I never have to go back to that awful place, I don't much care.'

'Yes, you do, Catherine. I know you do. Now, sit down and tell me why you did it and we'll work out what we can do from here to fix it.'

Chapter Eleven

The headline, the speedy quick, was designed to grab attention, Louisa thought, but they hardly needed it with those legs. Louisa was thankful right then that her own mother was no longer alive. Millicent abhorred attention-seeking stunts, herself having been the focus of so much unwanted newspaper attention. That she managed to break through into medical practice with such quiet determination and decorum underscored her achievement, Louisa knew. It was what Millicent hated about the women who marched for the vote – they became shrill, which Millicent could never abide.

Louisa looked more closely at the photograph of Catherine in her bathing suit. The blanket was still wrapped around her shoulders, but those legs were totally exposed. Catherine was surrounded by men, the builders, all grinning. Her name was in the headline, Louisa's name. The story that followed was more muted than the photograph but no less damning.

At just fifteen years of age, Australian-born Catherine Quick successfully crossed the tidal Thames yesterday.

Miss Quick is the niece of London doctor Louisa Quick, who has been outspoken in these pages about support for women's health in London's East End, where she operates a hospital and clinic for families. Perhaps her niece is showing her aunt's fiery nature, making her plunge in the narrows from the Globe Wharf to Ratcliffe.

According to Stan Grant, a ferryman who watched the swim, most who try have no idea of the pull of the tides. 'That river's a snake, she rises 20 feet every day, a sly mistress. But this were a canny lass, swam at the turn and made it in good time.'

Amateur Swim Club President Colonel Reg Maudsley said it was a reckless swim for a girl. 'Make no mistake. She's just a girl, with none of the strength of lads who've got into trouble. I say she was lucky and she should be charged with recklessness. Imagine if other girls followed her example. Then where would we be?'

Asked if Miss Quick should try out for the Olympic team, Col. Maudsley said, 'Certainly not. We want swimmers, not posers, and if I had my way, those girls would stay covered up in the house where they belong.'

But ferryman Grant, who's been on the Thames since his boyhood, said he'd never seen the likes of Miss Quick. 'She swam a way I'd never seen before,'

he said. 'Using her two arms like windmills and her
feet like paddles. She was fast.'

Louisa left for work soon after, telling Nellie to let Catherine sleep. 'But when she wakes up, get her to write a letter to the principal apologising for what she's done.'

'A letter,' Nellie said, looking at Louisa.

'Yes, a letter,' Louisa said.

'You don't think, Louisa, that you should stop for a minute and consider whether it's the right school?'

Louisa was standing at the front door. She turned back to look at Nellie. 'The school. The school is fine, Nellie. It wasn't the school that swam in the river yesterday.'

'No, I suppose not,' Nellie said. 'But . . .'

'But what?'

'She's a good girl, Louisa.'

'No doubt,' Louisa said, looking at her pocket watch. 'I must run.'

At the gate, she saw the postman coming down the street, so she waited. 'Mornin', Dr Louisa,' he said congenially.

'Good morning, Eric,' Louisa said. 'I'll take the mail.'

'Most people don't like me to give 'em their letters because it's bad news. But this one's come a long way, and it smells good.'

It was postmarked from Cairns in Australia. It was addressed to Catherine. It must be from Florence.

'Thank you, Eric,' Louisa said. She held the envelope to her nose and sniffed it. She couldn't smell anything.

'Had you goin' there, Doc,' Eric said jovially. He laughed all the way to the next house.

119

Very droll, Louisa thought. She put the mail into her satchel and continued on to the clinic.

The reception nurses had seen the article about Catherine, as had the patients Louisa saw in her first session. They all mentioned it.

'Surely women can do anything these days,' Ruth Luxton said when she and Louisa met up mid morning. 'I say good for her.' In Catherine's first month in London, Louisa had brought her into the clinic over a few weekends. She and Ruth had worked together, painting an old lockup in the back garden where they now stored medical supplies. Ruth had told Louisa she thought Catherine had tremendous spirit, 'Just like you,' she'd said. The two of them had got on well, Louisa had noticed, feeling a twinge of something. Was it jealousy? she wondered.

'Don't be ridiculous,' Louisa said to her friend now. 'Women can do anything, but why would they do this?'

'This Grant fellow says he's never seen the likes of her.' Ruth had the paper open on the desk. 'He sounds like he knows his river.'

'The chaps standing on the bank with her were not celebrating Catherine's achievement,' Louisa said.

'How do you know?'

'Oh, you are being naive on purpose, Ruth. Those builders weren't interested in her achievement. They were interested in her legs.'

Ruth smiled. 'You are too disbelieving in goodness, Louisa.'

'And you are far too trusting,' Louisa said. 'Just like bloody Catherine.'

Ruth looked at her. 'Are you all right? You look exhausted.'

'Oh, Ruth, this is so much harder than I thought it would be. Why has she done this?'

Ruth shrugged. 'She's a strong character, Louisa, which you already knew. But I do think perhaps you're underestimating the upheaval she's been through. Coming to live here was an enormous change, and it's not that long since she lost her father.'

'You sound like Nellie. Why can't she just be a good girl like I was at her age?'

Ruth laughed. 'You just rebelled a little bit later, Louisa.' She stared at the photograph. 'Is she happy at the school?'

'I thought so, but now she says not.'

'Do you talk to her?'

'Of course I talk to her.' Louisa thought about it. When was the last time she and Catherine had talked? Had they ever really talked?

'I do wonder why you're finding it so difficult with Catherine,' Ruth said. She paused then. 'Louisa, does it upset you?'

Louisa sighed. 'Perhaps I'm brusque,' she said, too sharply. 'That swim was just unthinkably stupid. The water is jolly cold, and what if she'd been run over by a boat?'

'That is a good point. But she wasn't,' Ruth Luxton said. 'She's just a girl, Louisa, like you were once. Maybe she doesn't conform quite as easily. That's not necessarily a bad thing. And maybe she doesn't fit in at the school. That's where I'd start. At her age, you need to spend time with her. She'll tell you what's going on but you have to give her time. You have to get to know her.'

Louisa looked at her friend blankly. And when am I supposed to do that? she wanted to say, between two and three in the morning?

It was 4 p.m. and Louisa was about to leave the rooms for the day. She'd seen a run of surgical patients – an excised tumour post-op, excellent prognosis, a tiny woman heavily pregnant booking for a caesarean operation to deliver her of the giant she was carrying, and an unmarried woman of breeding with a fiercely unwanted pregnancy. Louisa came out to the waiting area to let the nurse on the desk know she was planning to go home. The nurse pointed towards the office. 'There's a man to see you, Doctor,' the nurse said quietly.

Louisa frowned, whispered, 'I've finished my list.' She wanted to get home early so she could talk with Catherine. Whatever the swim in the Thames meant for the future, Ruth Luxton was right. Louisa had expected too much of Catherine, and hadn't taken the time to help her settle in at the school. Louisa herself remembered starting school. She was only a year younger than Catherine and it *had* been difficult. Why couldn't Louisa have taken this into account? And now she wondered if Henley wasn't quite the school she'd hoped it would be. Perhaps Nellie had a point. Louisa was keen to get home and work out what they could do from here.

The nurse shook her head. 'Not a patient,' she said quietly. 'An American.' Louisa looked at the nurse, who only shrugged.

122

She went into the main office. Sitting in the chair by the large oak desk was a middle-aged man with wavy silver hair combed straight back. He looked vaguely familiar, Louisa thought. 'I'm Dr Quick,' Louisa said. She could smell a fragrance. There were no flowers here. Was he wearing perfume?

The office was still furnished in the dark timbers Louisa had inherited from her predecessor, a dour surgeon who'd finally retired at the age of eighty-six. Louisa and Ruth had taken over his rooms but they hadn't bought new furniture and equipment, as they'd needed everything they earned to establish the clinic. There had never been any spare money since to refurnish.

'Doctor Quick.' He stood and walked towards her. He was a head taller than Louisa and of slim build. He had a kind of pent-up energy to him, as if he might be called upon to sprint at any moment, but at the same time he seemed perfectly at ease. Over one arm he had a dark overcoat and in that hand, his left, a dark grey trilby. He smiled, held out his other hand. It was one of those disarming smiles that expected to be returned.

Louisa smoothed her hands on her skirt. They were still wet from scrubbing after the final patient. He took her hand in his and for a moment she thought he might kiss it. But he shook it instead and stood there. 'I'm Manfred Lear Black.' His voice was soft, his accent stretching and accentuating the 'a' in Black. He smiled again and Louisa saw the flash of white teeth, creases at his dark eyes.

'Mr Black,' Louisa said. She knew the name, Manfred Lear Black. He'd been in the papers. The mad American, they called him. Something about an aeroplane. 'Do sit down.' She flicked her eyes up to the clock on the wall above the desk behind him. He turned.

'I'm sorry,' he said. 'I had intended to make an appointment but when I telephoned I was told you are booked solid for the next month. I took the liberty of popping by.' He said 'popping' as if trying the word out.

His accent was strong on certain words, like the accents of the Americans she'd worked with at Johns Hopkins. 'Well, Mr Black, you're here now. How can I help?' She smiled gently, the way she did for patients who had something difficult to tell her. She assumed he would be coming about a wife or daughter with a medical problem. Sometimes the men came first, especially if it was an unwanted pregnancy.

'Yes, I'll come straight to the point. I've been told you are immune to charm.' Louisa didn't respond to this. 'I have a clinic in Baltimore not unlike your Princes Square, linked to Johns Hopkins. I believe you know Dr Emily Masterton.'

'Emily, of course,' Louisa said. Emily had done her studies at Johns Hopkins University and had stayed on. 'We trained together.' Louisa had gone to Johns Hopkins after she'd finished in Edinburgh, following in her brother Harry's footsteps. Being at a hospital that cared for the poor, with doctors who were committed to helping others, had helped Harry decide on Thursday Island, but it had also helped Louisa decide to start her own clinic after the war. The Johns Hopkins approach, where doctors respected patients and one another, had been healing for Louisa herself, she'd often thought. It was a gentle place, and Emily and Louisa had been friends.

'Emily is now our chief of medicine,' Manfred Lear Black said. 'We're quite similar to your clinic, a kind of social experiment, or so Emily and the other doctors tell our board. The clinic is doing its best to stop people getting sick in the first place: better food, better hygiene, vaccination.'

If only they were doing that at Princes Square, Louisa thought, but they didn't have the time or the resources. 'Yes, Emily was very interested in public health,' she said, glancing up at the clock again. 'And how do you fit into a medical clinic, Mr Black?' she asked.

'My family has an interest in shipping. We've benefited substantially from dockworkers and their families. I have always been of the view that we should give something back. A little like Johns Hopkins himself, although I don't pretend for one minute to fit those shoes. But the clinic.' Black put his hand to his face, wiped it across his mouth. Louisa didn't know where this was leading. 'I have a proposition to put to you, and I thought I ought to come in person so that you'd see I'm sincere.'

'Go on,' she said. There was something in his expression, something she liked.

'I want you to come to Baltimore and spend some time with my doctors. We're planning to offer a major shift to confinement care in hospital. Most women deliver at home, which is not ideal, according to my doctors. We wanted a family specialist to provide us with up-to-date advice on women's health.'

'Me,' Louisa said. 'I'm a surgeon.' Was he being coy about abortion? Louisa was one of the few doctors willing to be outspoken on the issue and on others besides.

Princes Square was shameless, an editorial in *The Times* had claimed recently. Girls the Sally Ann had rejected as amoral had been provided with succour by Louisa Quick and her doctors. Louisa, who tried hard to stay out of the newspapers, couldn't bear this kind of self-righteousness. The Sally Ann refused pregnant women a place to stay if they were unmarried, turned them out on the street. That was what was shameless, as far as Louisa was concerned.

'Your clinic offers family medicine,' Black said.

'But if it's medicine, you'd be better off talking to my colleague, Dr Luxton.'

'Well, I'm talking to you,' he said. He smiled. 'My doctors know you. They know your work. They'll listen to you.'

'But they're in Baltimore,' Louisa said.

'Yes, that's what I'm suggesting. If you could see your way to visiting us later in the year, you could advise us.'

'Visit Baltimore?' Louisa said. 'I can't possibly leave here.' She thought of the clinic, and now Catherine. There was no way she could go abroad in the foreseeable future.

'Of course, we would pay all your expenses, and make a contribution to cover your absence. I know there are moves afoot here in London to require establishments such as yours to meet new health standards. I'd envisage that would involve some additional costs for you. I could be helpful.'

Louisa nodded. How did he know about the new health standards? There had been another letter from the Inspectorate. They were finalising details of a visit. Louisa knew her clinic didn't have a chance of passing the inspection. If they closed the clinic, what would happen to all those families?

'We don't have to decide anything today,' Black said, regarding her carefully. 'But if you want to test my *bona fides*, perhaps you might speak with your brother.'

'You know Alexander?' Louisa said. She sat back in her chair.

'His company has joined with us in the past, and we're about to invest together in a new line. Four more ships, London to New York. Alex is good on the money side.'

'Yes he is,' Louisa said.

Black smiled, tilted his head and regarded her. 'I must say, he's not nearly as charming as his sister.'

'When Alexander told you I was immune to charm, Mr Black, did he also tell you that I once split his lip for calling me a sissy-girl?'

'No, he didn't,' Black said, chuckling. 'As a matter of fact, Dr Quick, we've never discussed you. It was a staff member of mine whose family knows you who gave me that warning, not your brother. I'd hate to be the cause of a second split lip for Alex, although I imagine he could hold his own.' He laughed. 'Come to think of it, he has been a tough negotiator. More than once over the years, I've wished he was on my side of the table not the other. So perhaps another split lip wouldn't worry me unduly. But we must stick to the truth. It wasn't Alex. Now, tell me, am I right in assuming the swimmer I saw on the Thames yesterday is related to you?'

'My niece,' Louisa said, 'Catherine. You saw the newspaper?'

He nodded. 'I saw the swim,' he said. 'Is she Harry's daughter?'

'You knew Harry too?'

'Through Alex. Harry helped me set up the clinic when he was at Johns Hopkins. I should have said at the outset, I'm sorry for your loss.'

Louisa nodded. She'd hardly thought of Harry these last months. 'Catherine lives with me now.'

He nodded. 'Harry's wife, Julia, awful business. I introduced them, you know.'

'Harry and Julia?' Louisa said.

'Yes, she was a Freebody. My mother was a Freebody. Harry came to a little party I had at my house on Long Island. But I lost track after they left Baltimore. I knew they'd had a child, of course. As I say, awful business about poor Julia.' Louisa saw the look of pain on his face, the lines down his cheeks. 'Harry did some wonderful work to set up our clinic. He was one of the most egalitarian fellows I've ever had the privilege to know. A good man.'

'Yes,' Louisa said. 'We were very close growing up, and I'm now Catherine's guardian. You said you saw the swim?'

'I was at a meeting at Globe Wharves to do with this deal we're negotiating. We were called to the window to see this slip of a girl crossing the Thames. Just extraordinary, dodging barges and ferries, swimming against that tide. And then this morning when I saw the name in the newspaper, I put two and two together. My, what spirit she has. She must take after her father,' Black said.

'Perhaps,' Louisa said, feeling the weight of responsibility for Catherine.

'You don't approve, Dr Quick?'

She sighed. Something about his manner encouraged Louisa to open up in a way she wouldn't usually. 'Actually, Mr Black, the swim was not sanctioned by me or by Catherine's school.' She frowned. 'Especially by Catherine's school. As a matter of fact, Catherine is at home right now, waiting for me to get there and tell her what we're going to do. And I have absolutely no idea.' He looked concerned. 'There's no defence I can think of to remedy the situation. She was supposed to be in school. She took eight students with her to watch and now she's been expelled.'

He laughed loudly.

'You think this is funny?' Louisa said.

'Oh, I'm sorry,' he said, becoming serious. But then he started to chuckle again. 'I mean, can't they see the merit in what she did? How does a girl organise a swim like that?'

Louisa hadn't really thought about that. How did she organise it? 'It was a thoroughly irresponsible act.'

'Do you think?' he said. 'Strikes me as a thoroughly courageous act. She swam the Thames, Dr Black. How old is she?'

'Fifteen.'

'Could you have managed something like that at fifteen? I couldn't.'

'I suppose that's one way of looking at it.'

'I have some contacts in swimming, as it happens.' He pulled at one of his earlobes, a gesture Louisa found vaguely attractive. 'Not here but back at home.'

'Swimming,' Louisa said.

'Well, I'm just thinking out loud here but there's a

swimming group in New York – Charlotte Epstein, the Women's Swimming Association. I give them money.'

'Women's swimming.'

'Yes. They teach girls to swim. They trained last year's Olympic team. They won everything.'

'And you give them money?' Louisa couldn't think why.

He put his hand up and flicked the air, dismissing his largesse. 'A little,' he said. 'I lost a sister to drowning.' A look of pain crossed his face then. 'Couldn't swim.'

'I'm sorry,' Louisa said.

He shook his head. 'It was a long time ago. Anyway, it's just an idea. Your niece could come with you – to America, I mean – and swim with the Association while you're in Baltimore. She's at least as strong as Mercedes Gleitze, maybe stronger.'

'Mercedes Gleitze?'

'You don't know who Mercedes Gleitze is?' Louisa shook her head. 'No woman has yet swum across the English Channel. Heck, only five men have succeeded. Mercedes Gleitze is English, from Brighton, and she's come the closest so far. She's trying again this year, and one of our swimmers – that is, the WSA swimmers – Gertrude Ederle, plans to do it first. Matter of fact, she's swimming right now, as we speak. She set out at first light today. Surely you saw that in the paper?' Louisa shook her head. She hadn't seen anything about it. She didn't have time to read the real news, let alone anything about women's swimming. 'It's an exciting battle between England and America, and it may be over tonight. But your young niece would have given both of them a run for their money, I'd warrant.'

130

Louisa stood. 'I'm sorry, Mr Black. This has been very illuminating, but I'm afraid I really must go. Your proposal is . . . totally unexpected. Give me some time to think and perhaps I can write you here in London.' What a ridiculous notion, Louisa thought, running off to Baltimore while Catherine swam. She'd write a polite 'no' after a decent interval.

'Of course.' He stood too. 'Dr Quick, can I say it has been an honour to meet you? Emily speaks so highly of you, and I know my doctors would value your help as we go forward.' He took a breath in and out. 'I had hoped to tempt you with the challenge I presented but I can see you have a full dance card when it comes to challenges with your own clinic and now your young niece. And given that our time is up, I shall have to be the crass American your newspapers love to paint me as.'

He gathered his coat and hat from the chair beside him, put out a hand. She took it. He held it. 'The truth is this. I am a man of considerable means, Dr Quick. I can help you in your work in the East End, if you can help us in Baltimore. We need you. If I may be so bold,' he said. 'Is that how you English put it? If I may be so bold, I will pay whatever it costs. I would envisage your own clinic is going to require substantial work in order to pass the coming inspection. I do want you to know that the money isn't going to be the issue here.' He still had her hand. She was shaking her head, about to let him know she couldn't possibly leave the clinic, when it occurred to her that she could. Of course she could. She could go to Baltimore and visit Mr Black's clinic. She could take Catherine, just as he suggested, and

Catherine could swim with this New York group, which was surely what Catherine would want to do. Louisa could do it, and then Mr Black could give them the money they needed to upgrade the clinic. How marvellous.

'Sit back down, Mr Black,' she said suddenly. 'How would this work? When?'

He smiled but didn't sit, released her hand. 'Ideally, before the end of this year,' he said. 'I go back in November, and any time after that would suit us.'

She regarded him. Gardenias, that was the fragrance. 'For some reason, I find myself liking your idea, Mr Black, and there is nothing crass about money as far as I'm concerned. We run a clinic for the poor. They have no one but us and if we were closed, they'd have no one.'

'You're a lot like your younger brother, Dr Quick. And actually, if you *are* thinking of bringing your niece, I've realised that the winter swim season is much easier in New York than here, as we have so many heated tanks.

'Say, I'm giving a little soirée this Saturday. Perhaps you could attend and bring your niece. I'd like to meet her.' She was about to decline but he held up a hand. 'No need to answer now. There's been a lot to digest. I'll have my man pop by with an invitation tomorrow. May I say again it's been an honour, Dr Quick.'

'Mr Black,' she said, walking him to the office door. She looked behind her at the clock. 5 p.m. Normally to get home from the rooms, Louisa would take the train from Regent's Park to Waterloo and change for Aldgate. She could walk from Aldgate. But she'd still be late.

'Let me drive you home,' he said when she turned back

132

to farewell him. 'I have a car outside.' She started to protest but lamely. He shook his head. 'Truly, it's the least I can do.'

Black's car was a Daimler, parked right outside Louisa's building. When the driver opened the door for her and she stepped in, she felt like the other Harley Street doctors who cared for London's well-to-do. The rich smells of leather and cigars reminded Louisa of her childhood in Edinburgh, at her grandfather's house, when the men would sit around telling stories and smoking cigars. She'd fall asleep in her father George's lap, their voices drifting into her ears.

Black opened the other rear door, got in and sat beside her. She could smell that fragrance again. He was easy company for the journey, making jokes at his own expense about his reputation in the English papers as the mad American, which amused him greatly. He owned a newspaper himself in Baltimore, he said, so he knew the business. But they'd be proven wrong one day, he said. He was sure flight was the way to travel anywhere, he continued, pointing out the traffic they encountered; nothing like New York, he said, but it still takes an age to get anywhere in a motor car. 'And yet, you Londoners don't think we'll take to the sky.' If he'd flown her home, she'd be there now, he said. Louisa should come up some time, he added, and she'd see what he meant.

As they'd pulled up outside her house, Louisa found herself in a happy mood. What a delightful chap, she thought. The driver opened Louisa's door for her. Black got out on his side and came around to her on the footpath.

'I'm sorry that I can't ask you in, Mr Black,' she said.

'I need to talk with my niece about the Thames business and it may be quite delicate.'

He waved her away. 'Wouldn't think of imposing, Dr Quick,' he said. 'My, you have me in good cheer, though. No wonder your patients speak so highly of you.' He leant down and kissed her cheek and while she found herself shocked at the intimacy, he leant back out and smiled and she couldn't help but return his smile. 'Be kind to your niece,' he said. 'She really has done something extraordinary.' Talk about extraordinary, she thought on the way up the front path. She could still feel the warmth of his lips on her cheek.

Chapter Twelve

Louisa found Nellie in the kitchen in a great storm of activity. She was wearing her maid's uniform, a grey skirt, good white apron and bonnet, which she normally only wore when Louisa had visitors. Her face was flushed pink. 'We have the Yardsleys coming,' Nellie said.

'I completely forgot.' Louisa looked at her watch. It was just gone 6 p.m. 'There was a fellow . . . Oh, never mind now. What time are they coming?' Louisa said, all thoughts of her pleasant drive home disappearing into a panic. How could she have forgotten Lord Yardsley?

'Seven,' Nellie said. 'I've done a roast and fought Catherine off the lemon delicious but I wondered what you want to serve for drinks.'

'Something from the cellar. Let me go. Lord Yardsley needs to give me more money, and he won't want to. We'll ply him with drink. You, Nellie, are a gem.'

'He's rich then?'

'Don't you know him?'

Nellie shook her head. 'I don't meet all that many lords, I'm afraid.'

'Oh, well, he is rich, yes. And his wife is so very tiresome. I always have the strangest urge to giggle when she speaks to me. She couldn't be ruder if she tried.'

'And that makes you want to laugh?'

'As a matter of fact it does. Where's Catherine?' she asked just as her niece came in. Louisa found herself smiling. 'Well, Catherine, what are we to do with you?' She tried to say it gently.

Nellie looked at them both. 'Louisa, if I may, and I know we're busy getting ready and we don't have time to talk now, but I did want to make sure you know that there was a girl at the school who's been right nasty to Catherine. I hope Catherine won't mind my saying that this girl was the one who not only urged Catherine to swim the river, but also told the principal. A real piece of work, to my mind.'

'Really,' Louisa said. 'Is that true, Catherine?'

'Yes,' Catherine said. 'And I'm sorry it caused so much trouble, Aunt Louisa. I didn't think about it being wicked. I thought it would show them what I can do. I can't do so many other things at that school, but I can swim.'

'You can swim,' Louisa said. Catherine nodded. It was perfect. Louisa would take Catherine to America. Catherine could visit the women swimmers Black spoke of, and then she and Catherine could go on to Baltimore and spend some time together. It would give Catherine a break after the unpleasantness at Henley, and when they came home they could find a more suitable school. 'Well, Catherine, we don't have to worry about it right now,' Louisa said. 'You weren't happy there anyway, by Nellie's account, and I don't think every school in the world would make you this unhappy.'

'Yes,' Catherine said hopefully. 'I was so happy at school on the island. I loved it more than anything.'

'Yes, well, we'll talk again, my dear. But for now, the Yardsleys are coming.'

'Which means I have work to do,' Nellie said. 'Off now, Catherine, and set the table.'

Millicent would have loved Catherine, Louisa thought. The girl was so untouched by all the things Millicent hated, pretentiousness in all its forms. She was totally without guile. She was also without a number of skills that she might need one day. But really, what did any of it matter?

Louisa followed Catherine into the dining room where the tablecloth had already been laid. 'We haven't shown you how we set table here, have we?' Louisa said. 'It's probably different from what you did on the island.'

Catherine shrugged. 'I don't really remember anyone setting the table.'

'Well,' Louisa said, 'it's useful information. Do you know what goes on the outside?'

Catherine shook her head.

'The first thing you use – which tonight will be the soup spoon – on the side you use it, which is mostly the right. And then you just work your way in. It's very sensible, really.' Louisa opened the drawer on the sideboard and pointed out the silver.

She had intended to set one place and then leave Catherine to do the rest, but she ended up doing them all. 'See, easy?' she said and smiled. Catherine just looked at her.

'I can't thank you enough for getting us ready for tonight,' Louisa said to Nellie when she returned to the kitchen. 'I can't believe I forgot the Yardsleys, but I did. And thank you, Nellie, for letting me know about Catherine. I need to do more. I know that now.' She left Nellie to the rest of the preparations.

Catherine came down soon after, in one of the blue woollen skirts and cream blouses they'd bought in Sydney. She looked presentable enough, except for her hair, which hadn't seen a brush all day. 'Catherine, you could have done more with your hair.'

'If I spent hours,' Catherine said. 'And it would still be hair at the end of it.'

It reminded Louisa of an interaction she'd had with Millicent. Brush your hair, or you'll not come down to meet the visitors, Louisa's mother had said. Louisa had refused, and had stayed in her room through a luncheon. Ruth Luxton was right. Catherine was young and finding her way. And Louisa hadn't always been as compliant as she told herself she had. Millicent met Louisa's attempts at self-assertion firmly. Had it helped? Not really, Louisa thought now. She said, more gently, 'I want us on our best behaviour this evening. I need Lord Yardsley to give me money.'

'Oh, Louisa, is money all you care about?' This was Nellie, who'd come up behind Catherine.

'As a matter of fact, it is,' Louisa said. 'Half of my patients depend on my being able to attract money from the likes of Lord Yardsley.' She thought of Mr Black then, who'd said he'd pay whatever it cost. Imagine having money like that so that you could just do whatever you wanted. Louisa had spent her

138

adult life barely getting by. Although George had done well in shipping, it was Alexander who'd made the most of the family business, and Alexander who'd inherited the wealth. He'd never offered to help Louisa with the clinic and she'd never asked him. Oh, he'd not see his sister destitute, of course, but he didn't see it as his responsibility to provide for what he saw as a pet interest.

Louisa and Ruth Luxton had started their clinic in Princes Square when the Salvation Army vacated their hostel on the site in 1919. They'd worked together in a hospital near Paris during the war. For Louisa, it had been a life-changing experience. No one minded about them being women doctors then; every doctor was needed. When they came back to London, though, things quickly went back to the way they'd been before the war. Louisa and her female colleagues were relegated to women's and children's health. Louisa had loved being able to practise to the full scope of her training as a surgeon, so she came up with the idea to establish her own hospital. They'd started with a day clinic. Other doctors had joined them, all women, and Louisa wanted more than anything to be able to offer surgical services. Eventually they set up a theatre and opened the inpatient service. Now they had the clinic, hospital and a hostel for pregnant women who couldn't afford to go anywhere else.

Some of the women Louisa treated in the rooms in Harley Street were generous enough to donate to the clinic. Others were not. The one thing Louisa had learnt from working between London's well-to-do and London's poor was that poverty was not the characteristic that made people ugly. Poverty did not discriminate between good and bad, clean and dirty, caring and uncaring, or intelligent and stupid. It only changed things like having a roof over your head or not, having enough to eat each day or not. Women in the East End had nothing to fall back on. Many had lost husbands and sons to the war and now wandered the streets all day – they were told to move on if they sat in parks – and then at night went to shelters like the Sally Ann in Hackney or the workhouses closer to Louisa. Even families that were still intact suffered unemployment, which left them destitute. Sometimes it felt to Louisa that the world must change soon, for it was impossible to have so many living so poorly while others lived so well.

Lord and Lady Yardsley were estate owners from Surrey with three grown daughters, all now married with their own families. The Yardsleys had known the Quicks, and Louisa had asked them for money before. Lord Yardsley had always obliged. While the dinner was a thank you, Louisa was also hoping to secure funding for a new X-ray machine; though she needed more than just an X-ray machine now that Princes Square was to be inspected. But Mr Black might provide for this larger cost. She'd push Yardsley to help where he could.

The doorbell rang and Nellie bustled down the passage to answer it. She always greeted guests and took their coats and sat them in the parlour. But when she came back to the hallway on this occasion, she was as white as a sheet, her palms flat against her apron. 'Whatever's the matter, Nellie?'

'Nothing, Miss. The guests have arrived. Actually . . . No, nothing.' Nellie's face was pale.

'Are you quite sure you're well, Nellie?' Louisa asked. 'You look like you've seen a ghost.'

'No, Miss. I . . . The visitors . . .'

'All right,' Louisa said. 'But if you're ill, go to bed. I can look after the Yardsleys.'

But Nellie just shook her head and hurried back into the kitchen.

As Louisa turned to go down the hallway to greet the guests in the parlour she saw Lord Yardsley himself next to the hat stand. He was looking at Louisa wide-eyed, as if he'd had a blow. And then she knew.

Nellie had come to Louisa through the clinic three years before on a bitter February morning. She'd waited on the stoop through the night, the nurse told Louisa quietly. A street girl, the nurse said, sniffing loudly. Louisa came into the waiting room to see a child, no more, with light blue eyes and dark hair, greasy but tied neatly, a skirt caked with mud at the hem, ancient shoes and a dirty blouse. Her fever was high, she had a nasty cough on her chest, and she was in the early stages of pregnancy. She was just turned eighteen, she told Louisa in a tiny voice. By then she'd been living on the street for over a year.

Nellie's family was from Braintree in Colchester, she said, where her father had been a school teacher. Her parents and brother had been taken by the influenza after the war and Nellie alone had survived. She was fifteen. There was nothing put aside, so the family doctor arranged a position for Nellie in a house in London. After two years the young master came home from school. Nellie wouldn't say what had happened but Louisa surmised that the young man had taken advantage of Nellie. She left the house and was living under the Hackney Bridge for a time. She was working the docks area now. She didn't know she was pregnant. Well, Louisa thought. This is what we're here for.

When Nellie had told the story, Louisa was struck by the heart of the girl, which was intact, you could see. She was a good girl, but what chance did she have? Louisa thought to herself that night. The veneer of propriety was so thin. You could tear through it and then have nothing of the civilised world left. The vile creatures who would take advantage of a child like Nellie were there always, ready to rise up from their slime when they saw an opportunity.

The next day, Louisa asked Nellie if she'd be interested in another housekeeping position. There would be a small weekly wage, and room and board. Nellie was hesitant, after her previous experience. 'Where would it be, Miss?'

'It would be at my house,' Louisa said, 'and there are no masters there but me, Nellie – and the two Scotties, of course, the real masters.'

Louisa had thought long and hard about the matter of Nellie's pregnancy. Her responsibility was to tell the girl the truth and give her options but she also knew that Nellie would be faced with a decision she shouldn't have to face at her age.

'She might want the child,' Ruth Luxton said when Louisa consulted her.

'She won't want the child,' Louisa responded, feeling annoyed with Ruth, a rare experience. Louisa and Ruth were generally of one mind on clinical issues.

'She might decide to keep the baby,' Ruth argued. 'Or she might want to give the baby away; these girls often do.'

'Are you against abortion?' Louisa had said, intending to wound.

'It's never a simple decision,' Ruth said. 'And it's hers, not yours.'

'I disagree,' Louisa said, although Ruth's objections rattled her – abortion divided her colleagues, she knew. Some doctors used the law as a way to shirk their responsibilities to their patients, as far as Louisa was concerned. Abortion could be performed if the mother's life was at stake. It often was, as far as Louisa was concerned. Other doctors would fail to act or pass the decision on to a child like Nellie. For goodness' sake, what was the girl supposed to do? She couldn't even look after herself. If she had a baby, it would end any chance she'd have of amounting to anything.

Louisa told Nellie that she had an infection, which was why her period had stopped. Nellie would need to undergo a minor procedure to fix it. The girl readily agreed. When she was well enough to leave the hospital, Nellie moved into Louisa's house at Wellclose Square. She was fine company, with a good brain and a sharp, practical wit that appealed to Louisa. It was soon clear she was not the meek, quiet girl frightened to say her own name who'd come to the clinic that first day. It enlivened Louisa's evenings knowing she was going home not just to the two old dogs and cold meat for dinner but to someone who would challenge her and, more often than not, provide a hot meal. Nellie had a finer moral compass than Louisa, Louisa often thought, a better understanding of right and wrong and of people. Once or twice Louisa wondered if she'd done the right thing in her medical treatment of Nellie. The girl was happy, but Louisa wasn't sure whether she might have wanted to make the decision herself, as Ruth Luxton had suggested.

As for Lord Yardsley, who was standing stupidly in Louisa's hallway now, how could he do that to a child?

Louisa wondered. He must have visited Nellie when she was on the street. 'Oh, Lord Yardsley,' Louisa said in a loud voice, 'clearly you've met our wonderful Nellie.' How could he? she thought again. She turned her face away from him, finding him repugnant. 'And where's dear Lady Yardsley?' she managed to say.

He turned behind him dumbly and there she was, a jewel in emerald green silk. 'Oh, Lady Yardsley, have you met Nellie? She's been with us since . . . We won't speak of that here.' Louisa looked at Yardsley, held his eye until he looked away.

'Dr Quick,' she said. 'So kind of you to invite us. And your little house. It's so . . . quaint.' Lady Yardsley looked up and down the tiny hallway. The paint was peeling from the ceiling, and the rug in the hall looked like a team of hounds had slept on it every night for a decade. At least the lights were dim, so the scene was somewhat softened. The bulbs were blown in the electrical lamps and Louisa hadn't brought the ladder down from the attic to change them, so they had a gas lamp instead. She saw their home as Lady Yardsley might. At least the Scotties were shut up in the upstairs bedroom.

Louisa introduced Catherine, who was standing at the bottom of the stairs. The girl was staring.

'Charmed, I'm sure,' Lady Yardsley said in a way that suggested she wasn't at all charmed. 'You must be the one from the colonies?'

Louisa ushered them into the parlour.

'And you have a tiger,' Lady Yardsley said.

Better than the wolf you have, Louisa might have said but refrained. Instead she smiled at Lady Yardsley. 'We put everything towards the clinic, Lady Yardsley, and there's not much left, I'm afraid. Home is where the heart is. Now if you'll just excuse me a moment . . .'

Louisa went into the kitchen. 'I can serve up if you're not well, Nellie.'

Nellie looked up, her jaw set. 'No,' she said. 'I want to.'

'Do I have to sit through this?' Catherine whispered when Louisa was on her way back to the parlour. She'd come out to the hallway, leaving their guests alone.

'For the clinic, my dear, for the clinic,' Louisa whispered. And then she thought better of it. 'Actually, can you go and talk to Nellie? She's upset. She'll talk to you, I think.'

Lord Yardsley was usually an improvement on his wife but tonight he was without his unusual bonhomie. He was standing in the middle of the parlour still in his gloves and hat. He cleared his throat loudly. 'And so, Louisa, we hear wonderful things about your work.'

'Hat, Yardsley,' his wife said.

'Oh, yes,' he said, removing the hat and gloves and handing them to Louisa, who deposited them in the hall.

'You know,' Louisa said when she returned, 'it's the generosity of folk like yourself and Lady Yardsley that makes the clinic possible.'

'Of course,' he said. 'But we're not doing the work. You are.'

'Oh, you're doing quite a bit,' Louisa said. 'But you're right. We always need more.'

Lady Yardsley spoke then, about someone Louisa didn't know, or perhaps she did, but she lost the beginning and was finding the story difficult to follow now, something

145

about a fish having a spike that someone may have got in their foot. Was it a health story? Perhaps it was.

Catherine came back in. She had a fierce look on her face. 'Catherine, dear,' Louisa said. 'Nellie's made a wonderful dinner. We'll make sure we thank her.'

Catherine nodded tightly. She looked as though she wanted to give Yardsley a piece of her mind. Louisa hoped her niece would be able to hold her tongue.

The dinner was interminable and Louisa felt for Nellie, who came out to serve as usual but looked mortified each time. Lord Yardsley was uncharacteristically quiet throughout the meal, which meant his wife spoke incessantly about nothing. Catherine continued to fume.

Louisa saw her chance. 'Catherine,' she said after the plates were cleared and Lady Yardsley was refreshing herself, 'I worry that Nellie is unwell.' She looked straight at Lord Yardsley as she spoke. 'Go in and help her, my dear. Perhaps you could bring dessert and Nellie could retire early tonight.'

'All right,' Catherine said.

When Catherine left, Louisa turned her eyes to Yardsley but she didn't even need to speak.

'I know your clinic does such excellent work for those less fortunate than the rest of us,' he said. 'And so, with this in mind, I have decided to donate once again.'

'Oh, Lord Yardsley, if only you knew what a difference your support makes.'

He held up a hand to stop Louisa saying any more.

'I haven't yet spoken with Lady Yardsley about a further contribution,' he said. 'So best not mention it. Last year, we were able to give a hundred pounds, I believe. This year, we are able to double that amount because of our good fortune.'

'That will go towards a much-needed X-ray machine. If you were able to see your way clear to another two hundred, making the total four hundred pounds, you've no idea the help we could offer to those less fortunate than yourself.'

He agreed so quickly Louisa wondered if she should have asked for more.

The Yardsleys left soon after dessert, declining port, for which Louisa was thankful. Nellie had retired, as Louisa suggested, and Catherine had done an adequate job of serving the lemon delicious, although the portions might have been more suited to dock workers.

When Louisa returned to the kitchen after seeing the visitors off, Catherine was waiting for her. 'You stay here,' Louisa said. 'I just want to check on Nellie.'

She went upstairs quietly, stood at the door of the room and heard sobbing. She went in. The lamp was out and Nellie was lying on her cot, her face turned to the wall. She must have heard Louisa come in, though, because she said in a voice thick with tears, 'I'm so sorry.'

'Whatever for, Nellie?'

'I brought shame to your house.'

'Oh, goodness me, you never did,' Louisa said. She sat on the bed. 'Turn around now and look at me.'

Nellie half turned and sneaked a glance at Louisa before turning back.

'Oh, Nellie, he's the one who brought shame, not you. You mustn't worry. I don't. Please.'

But the poor girl wouldn't be consoled. Louisa talked

a while more and then offered her a sedative to help her sleep, which she accepted. Once she was settled, Louisa went back downstairs.

Catherine had been tidying in her absence. She was still angry. 'He'd been to visit Nellie,' she said accusingly.

'I know.'

'Why didn't you confront him then?'

'To what end?' Louisa said flatly, looking at her niece.

'Louisa, Nellie's our friend. He'd . . . taken advantage of her.'

'Well, she can go to school next year with his money.' Louisa felt proud of Catherine then, that the girl saw Nellie as someone they should defend. It showed her strength of character.

'I thought you needed the money for the X-ray machine,' Catherine said.

'Well, of course we do. But you judge me harshly, Catherine. Nellie must go to school or she'll be back where she was if anything happens to me.' And he's given us enough to help with both the X-ray machine *and* Nellie's education, Louisa didn't say.

'Is that true for me too?' Catherine said. 'If I don't go to school.'

Louisa nodded. 'Yes,' she said. 'It's crucial to have an education, Catherine. It's the key to the door.'

'The door to where?'

'Freedom,' Louisa said.

Chapter Thirteen

It wasn't until Catherine had gone to bed that Louisa remembered the mail she'd collected in the morning. She was relieved to have some cash for the clinic but she also knew she'd need more money if the inspector required them to meet the new standards. But the extra money Yardsley offered must go to Nellie. Alexander paid Catherine's fees, but he wouldn't pay Nellie's, Louisa knew. He'd see it as a waste. Lord Yardsley, himself the father of daughters, surely wouldn't object to his money being used for this purpose. Louisa only hoped that seeing Nellie in another context might make him realise the harm his sex did. But then again, nothing seemed to stop the demand for women, the younger the better.

Louisa poured herself a scotch and from her satchel took the newspaper she'd bought on her way home. As she did, the letter that the postman had delivered for Catherine came out with it. Louisa had the strangest urge to open it. Perhaps, Louisa thought, there would be information in the letter from Australia that might help her to understand

Catherine. Perhaps if she was careful she could open the envelope and then reseal it so that Catherine would be none the wiser. This was wrong, Louisa knew, but she also knew she was responsible for Catherine and her niece had now been expelled. It would be a small wrong in service of a larger good, Louisa told herself.

When she thought about it, the letters from Australia, one every week, had always unsettled Catherine. Perhaps Florence was putting pressure on the girl to return to the island. Perhaps she was voicing opinions about Catherine's new life. Perhaps there would even be something to shed light on what had gone on in that house on the island, why Harry and Florence had been so strange with one another when Louisa visited. By her second scotch, Louisa had convinced herself that opening the letter was not only an acceptable thing to do, it was imperative.

She set her glass down on the table and focused on the task. The envelope was difficult, glued seemingly by the number of miles it had travelled. She coaxed with her nail. She picked with her thumb. After a few minutes, she tore the envelope open in frustration. She felt the shock of what she'd done then, didn't immediately unfold the page inside. She could remedy this, she thought; she could tell Catherine she'd opened the envelope in error and that she hadn't read the letter. But she *would* read the letter. She knew she would.

It was from the boy, Michael, not his mother, which surprised Louisa. She'd noticed they were close but she hadn't known they were writing to one another; Catherine had certainly never mentioned it. She always took the letters from Australia straight up to her room and read them there. Whenever Louisa asked, she said things were fine. Florence and the family were still in the house, and Florence was housekeeper for the harbourmaster for whom the government had leased the house – Alex had wanted to sell the house when Louisa brought Catherine back to London, but Louisa had said they should leave it for now. They'd leased it. Louisa could dispose of it later.

Catherine had only ever mentioned letters from Florence, never from the boy Michael.

Waapi, he wrote. He had a lovely hand, Louisa thought.

I'm sorry I didn't reply to your last letter. I have not forgotten you and I'm sorry that my last words were angry ones. I see you in every place on the island we've been, which is everywhere. I am hating school and hating home and hating swimming, all because of missing you. I was so glad to have another letter from you, and I won't stop writing again, I promise. Mum says I'm a bad friend and it's a wonder you even bother with me. But you know I will never let you down, Waapi. We are promised, we wrote it together with our bodies.

I worry what will happen. Come home. I love you.
From,
Bid

Louisa looked at the letter again. *We are promised, we wrote it together with our bodies.* If a person had promised with his body, it had to be sexual, surely. What else could it mean? The boy had reached puberty, and Catherine was clearly in the throes of what Dr Hall had called the adolescence. Louisa thought of them running down to the sea together. She'd admonished herself for being concerned about propriety, but perhaps her concern was justified. Had they crossed that line into an adult relationship? Oh, poor dear Catherine.

How dare he? Louisa thought. How dare he take advantage of the girl? And then another thought crossed Louisa's mind. Had Catherine and the boy made life promises to one another? Had the housekeeper, Florence, known? Had she let it happen? Catherine was too young. Oh, what a mess Harry had left. It hadn't been his intention to die, of course, but he'd left Louisa with awful choices.

Louisa felt a shiver, although there was no draught. What was she to do? She must give her niece the letter. That was the correct thing. But was it? Maybe she should hold the letter back. With Nellie's help, she could stop Catherine's letters from going forward, and collect the mail each day to make sure Catherine didn't receive anything. If she took Mr Black's proposal seriously, she could go to America and take Catherine, as he suggested. Perhaps that would help too. More than ever now, Louisa wanted Catherine to forget the island. While she was receiving letters from them, it would pull the girl back to that old life, a life in which she might be imperilled, Louisa thought now.

She took the letter upstairs to her room, opened the drawer where she kept her private papers and slipped it under the pile.

Closing the drawer, she sat down heavily on her bed. She thought of Yardsley and poor Nellie, the boy Michael, who might have taken advantage of Catherine. Were they all like this? Louisa wondered. Surely not. Surely there were good men too in the world.

* * *

She'd said, Yes, I'd love you to walk me home. That was forward of her, she thought later. She shouldn't have used that word, *love*, I'd *love* you to walk me home. She shouldn't have been curious. Alexander had said that. You led him on, Louisa. Did she? Is that what had happened? It was hard now to understand how saying I'd love you to walk me home could lead where it did. But there you are.

When they reached her door and he'd said he would come in, she'd let him. That was her second mistake. None of the other doctors who shared the little flat near the hospital were home. She'd known they weren't. So you *were* curious? Alexander had asked accusingly. Curiosity, too, would hurt you, she learnt that night.

'Where did you study medicine?' Jonathan asked. He was in her sitting room.

She'd started at the University of London, finished at the School of Medicine for Women.

'Did you take lovers in medical school?' he asked.

It was an impertinent question, she knew. She wanted to meet his audacity with her own.

'I would try to impress suitors with my wit,' she said. 'But wit is not such an impressive quality in a woman, as it turns out.'

'It impresses me,' he said.

There was a silence.

'Then you, Jonathan, are easily impressed,' she said, attempting to laugh off his comment.

'On the contrary,' he said, moving towards her.

Later she would tell Ruth Luxton, 'I let him kiss me. I know I did wrong. I let him kiss me but then I told him to go and he would not. And he . . .' She could not bring herself to finish.

He told Louisa he wanted her. She was shocked, said something stupid like, 'I beg your pardon?'

He leant in and kissed her and she could smell rich tobacco and feel the scratch of his beard on her cheeks. She responded without thinking, her arms around him before she knew what was happening. He was not a tall man but he was broadly built and strong. He held her in his arms and for a moment she forgot herself. But then she pulled back from him. 'Dr Pyne,' she said. 'I don't think . . .'

'You must indulge me,' he said, his voice rough. He was pulling at his collar. 'I cannot bear it any longer.' He moved towards her then and Louisa found herself afraid. It was still fun, in a way, a game of cat and mouse, she told herself, but panic was rising like bile in her throat now, and despite her attempts to reassure herself she could feel underneath the fear.

Louisa was twenty-five, a good doctor, but totally inexperienced with men. The truth was she'd taken no lovers in medical school. There had been no one, not ever.

He advanced towards her and she retreated, until suddenly the wall was at her back. Still he kept coming. She was afraid now; a hard, relentless fear that made her breath come in short gasps and her vision blur. It was the expression on his face, the same expression she'd seen just before he began to cut a patient.

Chapter Fourteen

Catherine was sitting at the table in the dining room writing a letter to Miss Anderson – this had been Louisa's suggestion – when she heard the doorbell. She knew not to answer it – Nellie had scolded her before. Catherine was supposed to understand that Nellie was the help, whereas Catherine was the mistress. 'Well, if I'm the mistress, why is it you don't ever do as I say?' Catherine had said to Nellie once.

'That's another matter altogether,' Nellie said. 'But you have to start acting your station, girl, or you'll never be like your aunt.' This was Nellie's trump card. For while she knew that Catherine was unhappy in London, she also knew Catherine admired Louisa. The thing that upset Catherine most about what had happened at the school was that she knew she'd failed Louisa, although her aunt seemed less worried now. That morning, when she'd reminded Catherine to write the letter to Miss Anderson, she also said Catherine mustn't worry herself. We'll find somewhere to go, dear girl, Louisa had said, almost gaily. She'd even sat at breakfast in the kitchen with Nellie and Catherine, sipping coffee and talking about the days ahead. She thought perhaps Catherine could come to visit the clinic while they were sorting out what to do next. Would you like that? she'd said. Catherine said she would, unsure with this new Louisa who seemed more relaxed than the old one but not quite real yet.

I did not mean to cause harm, Catherine had written, which was the truth. She hadn't meant to cause harm. *I only wanted to show that I could achieve the swim which Darcy had told me I could not achieve.* Catherine felt tears threatening. Oh, she longed to be doing something other than this.

Nellie was at the door. 'You've a messenger.'

'What sort of messenger?'

'One that has a message, I'd warrant. Quick sticks. Get your pinnie off and out you go. Plum in his mouth, said he must see Miss Quick and I wouldn't do. Come on now. I haven't got all day.'

Catherine rose, pulled her pinafore over her head and draped it over the chair. As she was walking towards the kitchen, Nellie said quietly, 'Parlour, dear.'

Catherine turned and went to the little sitting room at the front of the house.

On the sofa was a young man dressed in a dark brown suit, his long legs crossed at the ankles. He had a hat in his lap, which he held in his hand as he stood. 'Miss Quick, it's so kind of you . . .' Something went wrong as he moved towards Catherine and he fell forward. Catherine caught him just as he was going over, holding him up under the arms.

'Goodness,' Catherine said.

'I'm so sorry,' the young man said as he righted himself. 'Are you all right?' He had an accent, which was not quite English.

'Of course,' she replied. 'Are you?'

He was at least a head taller than Catherine, willowy with very fair skin and black hair. He smiled. 'Yes. I must have caught my foot in the rug, I think.' He smoothed his jacket and looked behind him at the tiger. He had a high forehead and soft dark eyes. A lick of hair had fallen forward and he pushed it back. He smiled nervously and looked at the rug again. 'That's a tiger,' he said. He seemed a little flustered now. 'I come on behalf of Mr Manfred Lear Black, whom you may have heard of.'

Catherine shook her head. 'I haven't,' she said.

'He's American, staying here for the summer.'

'Oh, the mad American,' Catherine said without thinking.

'Quite. The journalists are fond of calling him that.'

'I'm sorry. I didn't mean to be rude.'

'Don't worry. Mr Black enjoys our English press immensely.'

'Let's sit down,' Catherine said, taking a seat herself on the chair, 'if you feel that might be safe now, Mr . . . ?'

'Oh God, Mackintosh, Andrew Mackintosh. Lovely to meet you, Miss Quick. I'm sorry. The tiger has quite done me in. Mr Black is my employer. That is, I am his confidential secretary. And so.' He returned to the sofa and then, as if suddenly remembering what he was there for, took from inside his suit pocket an envelope and handed it to Catherine. It was addressed to Dr Louisa Quick and Miss Catherine Quick.

'Should I open it?' Catherine said.

'Perhaps wait for your aunt. But I can tell you its contents. Mr Black would be delighted if you could attend a little party on his yacht, the *Aloha*, Saturday coming, to celebrate the marvellous Captain Bone, who brought Mr Black safely to our shores from the great state of Maryland, the United States of America.' This last was said with an accent that perhaps was supposed to be American, Catherine wasn't sure.

'The *Aloha*.'

'Yes, that's Mr Black's yacht. It's moored in the Thames.'

'Captain Bone?'

He nodded.

'Does Mr Black know my aunt?'

'I believe he does, and I understand you are intimately acquainted with the Thames.' He smiled gently, a sparkle in his eyes now.

'Yes.' Catherine found herself blushing.

'Oh, I'm sorry,' he said. 'Is swimming a taboo subject?'

'A little,' she said. 'I got into trouble at school.'

'I bet,' he said. 'But *The Times* says you're a champion.'

'Are you a swimmer?' she said.

He laughed. 'I like the bath,' he said. 'And at Eton, I fell in the pond and a master had to fish me out. No, I'm not fond of water. But I saw you in the newspaper, Miss Quick. Mr Black says it was a fine swim and he *is* a swimmer.'

'Really,' she said. She stood up. 'Well, I'll give the invitation to my aunt.'

'Good then,' he said, standing when Catherine did. 'Delightful. In fact, I'll very much look forward to seeing *you* again, if that's all right.' He put out his hand to

158

shake hers. 'I'm quite safe when standing still,' he said.

'That's a relief,' she said, taking the offered hand. 'And it's been lovely to meet you, Mr Mackintosh.'

Louisa did a run of routine excisions, then saw three patients and caught up on paperwork. She looked at the clock. It had just gone eleven. She went out to the waiting room and said to the nurse on the reception desk, 'Can you ask Dr Luxton to pop into the office as soon as she's free?'

Then she returned to her desk and started writing up case reports on the morning's patients.

Ruth soon came in. 'You look tired,' she said.

'Thank you,' Louisa said. 'Just what I need to hear. Did you know that being told one looks tired does nothing for one's wellbeing?'

'I'm sorry.' Ruth sat in the chair at the side of the desk. 'You do look tired, though – all the time lately.'

'I have a problem.'

'The inspector.'

'Two problems then. Do you know an American businessman, Manfred Lear Black?'

Ruth shook her head.

'He seems to think I should go to Baltimore to visit a clinic he funds. Harry did some work for them, and he knows Alexander. He also saw Catherine's swim. He says it was extraordinary. They swim in America, apparently. Women, I mean. They won at the Olympics.'

'Last year, yes they did,' Ruth said.

'Well, I didn't know that. I don't keep up with women's swimming. Anyway, he seems to know about swimming, and he has a group in New York that Catherine could swim with.'

'And?'

'I can't leave here.'

'Why not?'

'What would happen to the patients?'

'They'd see another doctor? If the clinic's all that's stopping you, Louisa . . .'

'He's offered money.'

'Who?'

'Mr Black. He's rich, and he's virtually told me to name my price. We'd have a chance with the inspector coming.'

'I see. So a wealthy American has offered you an opportunity to help him with a clinic. He also knows a way to help your niece to swim, which, apparently, is what she loves to do. And he's offered to get us out of a real pickle we're about to be in. And you can't see your way clear to going.'

Louisa nodded. 'I see your point.'

'Louisa, darling, this is a marvellous idea. I agree. You haven't had a proper holiday ever. When you went off to get Catherine, you had all those worries about what it would be like. Now, you're finally learning what she needs. Of course you should go. You should go for six months, a sabbatical. There's that young doctor at the London I've been trying to convince to come to us. She wants full-time work. So we'll give her full-time work. Easy. Mr Whatsit can pay her salary.'

'Women's swimming is the next thing, apparently,' Louisa said, not really listening.

'Well, perhaps it is. Wouldn't that be marvellous?'

'Would it?'

'Oh, yes, wouldn't it? Do you remember Lily Smith?'

Louisa shook her head. 'Before your time, the swimming suffragist. Her idea was that she'd swim the Channel to prove women could do whatever men could do and so should have the vote. It's true she put the cause behind by ten years but her failure was an enormous success. It got women swimming. My daughters all swim. I insisted. It's something about our bodies being able to do things. And also, floating. I think floating is marvellous.' She tilted her head and regarded Louisa. 'New York! That young American girl was in shouting distance of Dover when they pulled her out yesterday, apparently, and look at Gleitze. She'll manage it one of these times. She's a typist, you know, who saves up enough money each year to get herself a coach and tugboat . . .'

Louisa hadn't really been listening. She'd been thinking about Mr Black. Earlier that morning, she'd telephoned Alexander, who'd said that yes, he knew Manfred Lear Black. 'Outstanding fellow,' Alexander said. 'Big in the Democratic Party, I believe. They say he might run for office one day. We're about to propose a major partnership with his Baltimore company. It will see us into the US passenger route. But why do you ask?'

'He's interested in our clinic,' she said.

'Oh, yes, he has a similar setup in Baltimore, I think. Harry did some work for them. That's how he met Julia. It would be great for me if you could help him, Louie. He's a tough businessman, ruthless on price. Maybe you can charm him.' Alexander laughed as if the notion that Louisa might charm anyone was a hilarious joke.

She told Alexander that Mr Black wanted her to help

161

with his clinic. 'I'll take Catherine out of school, I think,' she said slyly. Alexander didn't say anything. He'd seen Catherine's picture in the paper, had asked Louisa what the devil she was doing, but hadn't realised Catherine had been expelled. Louisa decided she'd rather keep it that way. The last thing she needed was Alexander on her back.

Louisa had thought the swimming was part of the problem with Catherine. She'd never have dreamt of letting the girl take off her clothes and get in the river like that. She might have sent her up to the ponds in the summer, though, if she'd thought about it more thoroughly. Ruth seemed to think swimming wasn't the problem, that swimming might help. Mr Black had said women's swimming was a field of endeavour now. Louisa wasn't convinced but if it's what the girl wanted to do, then why not let her do it?

When Louisa had gone along to the march with the Pankhurst girls, it had been against her mother's advice. Louisa was all of twenty and it was so exciting to be part of the movement. Her mother said they were shrill, those Pankhurst girls, Millicent's worst criticism of anyone. But exciting was how Louisa described the feeling of freedom she'd had that day. She'd meant to break the window. She wanted to see what would happen. She was arrested with twelve others and thrown in Holloway prison. Six weeks, she served; a surprisingly rewarding experience.

'Violence is never the answer, Louisa,' her mother said. 'You resorted to violence.'

'I broke a window,' Louisa had said, 'in full knowledge, Mother.'

* * *

162

'I had a meeting this week,' she said to Nellie that evening after Catherine had gone to bed. 'A chap named Black, an American businessman. He wants me to go to America. He has a clinic and he needs advice. It would be for a month or two, probably early next year. Catherine's father did some work for them, and this Black fellow knows Alexander. I'd want you to stay here and take care of the house and dogs, just as you did when I went to Australia.'

'Of course,' Nellie said. 'But what about Catherine?'

'That's the thing. Mr Black is interested in women's swimming.'

'Oh, yes,' Nellie said with a look.

'No, not like that. I think he may be quite sincere. He seems very certain Catherine could be a competitive swimmer.'

'Where would she swim?'

'There's a group of women in New York, apparently. It's not what you're thinking, Nellie. I think he may just be a good person.'

'Do you believe in fairy godmothers, Louisa?'

'No, Nellie, I don't.'

'Neither do I,' Nellie said.

Chapter Fifteen

The deck in front of them was lit up with strings of coloured lanterns. They looked beautiful reflected in the water, Catherine thought. The weather had held through the week and tonight it was warm enough to go about in sleeves, Louisa had said before they'd left. Best take a shawl in case, though, she added. It can be chilly down on the river.

Louisa had decided they would go to the party. They were to meet Mr Black, she said, who had asked Louisa to visit his clinic in America. Louisa had said yes. She was going to take some time off from the clinic, she'd told Catherine the night before. Dr Luxton and the other doctors would look after her patients. She would take Catherine with her. 'You'll be able to swim there,' Louisa said. 'If swimming's what you want to do, you'll be able to swim more easily there.'

But all Catherine heard was that they were going to America. America, where her mother's family had come from. Oh, yes, she could swim. But perhaps, too, she could find her people. Mr Black was related to her mother, Louisa said. His mother had been a Freebody, 'or something'.

Louisa had also said that, in the meantime, Catherine wasn't going back to school. She could come to the clinic and help the nurses some days, and once a week, if she wanted, she could go with Nellie up to Hampstead ponds to swim. When they were back from America, they'd work out what to do about school. Catherine wasn't to worry, Louisa had said. She was sure they could get through this difficulty. She'd been very kind.

In front of them now was Mr Black's ship, the *Aloha*, its main deck festooned with those lovely lanterns. Mr Black had sent a car to collect them. The driver had opened the door for Catherine and had called her Miss Quick. It had made Louisa smile. Now they were met by a footman, who led them down a small gangway and along the deck to a set of wooden doors. Catherine could hear a band playing and when the footman opened the doors the music was suddenly louder, like someone's face lighting up when they noticed you. Jazz, Louisa said, that's the new jazz music. You can't help but feel happy when you hear it.

They went inside and found themselves on a landing looking down to an enormous room, the length of the deck. There were more than a hundred people down the stairs, men in tuxedos, women in long gowns, and waiters in white jackets with trays.

Red, white and blue streamers were strung from a central chandelier to each corner. A red carpet led down the stairs. 'It matches your red dress,' Catherine said to Louisa. Her own dress was of a velvet in a deep shade of green.

Catherine had never felt anything so soft that wasn't alive, she'd thought when she first tried it on at the dressmaker in Sydney. She wore ivory slippers and a wrap they'd borrowed from Ruth Luxton's daughter. When she'd come down the stairs before they left home, Louisa had said, 'You look a picture, Catherine.'

Louisa looked so graceful, Catherine had thought, the red silk dress, her hair piled into a chignon, a simple string of pearls around her neck. She looked beautiful. But when Catherine said this aloud, Louisa laughed. And then Louisa had asked was she happy. Catherine had said, 'Yes, I believe I am happy,' because she saw the look on Louisa's face, of expectation, desire to please, and she'd felt sorry for her aunt suddenly. And she *was* happy. She was looking forward to tonight. Andrew Mackintosh would be here, he'd said, and Catherine hoped she'd see him again.

At the top of the stairs was a fellow in tails and white gloves. He had a staff in his hand, and as Catherine and Louisa approached he struck the staff on the floor three times. The crowd hushed. Then he boomed, 'Ladies and gentlemen, I present Dr Louisa Quick and Miss Catherine Quick of London.'

People looked up and smiled, then the party resumed and the footman led Louisa and Catherine down the stairs. 'Oh goodness,' Louisa said. 'It's quite an affair, isn't it? Mr Black said it was a little party. I'm glad now we dressed up.'

Just then Catherine saw Andrew Mackintosh heading towards them from the other side of the ballroom. She waved.

'Who's that?' Louisa said.

166

But before Catherine could respond he was with them. 'Dr Quick, Miss Quick. Mr Black is so terribly sorry he's not here to greet you.' Andrew looked flustered, Catherine thought. 'He's been called away temporarily on an urgent matter, and he's asked me to look after you. Come over and we'll get out of the thoroughfare and find the chap with the drinks.' As he said drinks, his eyes widened and he smiled. He turned to Catherine. 'Did you swim here?'

'Of course,' Catherine said.

Louisa looked at Andrew Mackintosh. 'Have we met?' she said.

'Oh, yes, yes we have,' he said. 'But I was about this tall.' He used his hand to gesture at knee height. 'I'm so sorry. It's been quite a day. You know my mother, Dr Quick. Ada.'

'Ada Mackintosh?' Louisa said.

'The same.'

'Donald.'

'No, Donald's my brother. I'm Andrew, the younger one.'

'Of course. You were the handful.'

'I was the bright spot in my mother's day was the way she mostly put it. But you're quite right. She told me not to touch anything on your desk.'

'And you broke . . .'

He was nodding. 'A vase, yes, expensive. And we bought you a new one and you said it was better than the old one, which was terribly kind of you.'

'It's possible the new vase *was* actually better,' Louisa said.

He laughed. 'Ah yes, entirely, if my mother was involved

167

in its purchase. She has marvellously good taste, unlike her offspring. Come, here's my man to fetch us a drink, which will make everything better.'

He'd led them over to one side of the room, with doors out to the deck. 'Just give me a moment to work out what I do here. I'm not used to all this.' He took from his pocket a wad of bills and peeled off two to give to the drinks waiter, who smiled widely. 'Mr Black insists I take care of "tipping". Do you know what that is?' Catherine shook her head. 'We give money to the staff. I have a hundred pounds, which I'm to ensure everyone gets a little of. I'm not very good at it, I'm afraid. I gave the same chap a pound three times. Thank goodness he's honest. Anyway, it's so lovely you could both attend. I know you're busy, Dr Quick. Mr Black very much wanted to be here to greet you himself.' He turned to Catherine. 'And so, *have* you been back in the drink?' he said.

'You know Catherine too?' Louisa said to him.

'I delivered the invitation for tonight. I work for Mr Black,' he said, gesturing for them to go through a doorway out onto the deck. 'Quieter out here,' he said. There was a gentle breeze now that made the little lanterns swing from side to side. It was all so beautiful, Catherine thought. The white-coated waiter was back and Andrew took a champagne for Louisa, a punch for Catherine, and a champagne for himself. '*Sláinte*, as we say in the old country,' he said, taking a sip. 'I love an employer who appreciates the finer things of life.'

'Catherine mentioned someone had delivered the invitation,' Louisa said, 'but she didn't say the name. I thought you were at Oxford.'

'Past tense, I'm afraid. I just wasn't suited to the life, I suspect,' he said. 'And the week I came down, Mr Black was enquiring about recruiting an Englishman to help him while he's here. One of my father's friends put two and two together. I must say, Dr Quick, Mr Black is awfully glad you could come. And he is amazed by Miss Quick's achievement, that's for sure. He's been following the Channel swimmers these last weeks.'

Black had bought the *Aloha* from the US Navy, Andrew told them. 'But he came across on the *Transylvania* with Captain Bone, which is why we're having this party, to thank the good captain, who's somewhere over there, I think –' gesturing to the left of the ballroom '– and the captain's brother brought the *Aloha*.'

Just then, the crowd parted for a middle-aged man with silver hair slicked back from his forehead. He was frowning slightly, as if concentrating on something down and to his left. He was about Catherine's height, small next to Andrew.

'Now, Mr Mackintosh,' he said, 'are you taking good care of my special guests?' His eyes, a deep brown, sparkled as he smiled. Around them, Catherine saw, conversations had paused as people watched him. It was Manfred Lear Black, she realised.

'I'm doing my very best,' Andrew said. 'Mr Black, Dr Quick, whom you know, and her niece, Miss Quick.'

'Dr Quick,' he said, leaning in to kiss Louisa on the cheek. He turned towards Catherine and looked at her briefly before his eyes slid away. He nodded. 'Miss Quick.'

Catherine didn't know what she'd expected but nothing about the man in front of her was familiar in any way. Had

169

she thought he might remind her of Julia? He didn't, and Catherine felt disappointed suddenly.

'Mr Black, this is quite a party,' Louisa said, looking at Catherine and frowning. 'My mother used to say she didn't often throw parties, but when she did, they were good ones. But this is extraordinary.'

Mr Black surveyed the room. 'Well, thank you, Dr Quick. We're very honoured to have you among us.' His eyes flicked to Catherine again. 'And to have a swimmer of such calibre. You,' he said, smiling. 'What a swim!'

'Mr Black, Aunt Louisa said you're related to my mother,' Catherine said.

'Yes,' he said, 'and therefore to yourself. But I couldn't swim like that, Catherine.' He smiled widely. There was nothing about him that Catherine felt affinity with, she thought again. He could be anyone.

'Mr Black flies, Catherine,' Louisa said, looking at her niece again.

'Well, I do, Dr Quick,' Mr Black said. 'But at functions like this, I keep my wings tucked under.'

Louisa laughed. 'Well, Catherine doesn't show her scales either.'

'Of course not. She'd be smarter than that. That would be showing off. But you have the makings of a champion.' He was still looking towards Catherine, but slightly to her left. 'What do you think of that?' He raised his head slightly, as if peering over spectacles, although he wore none.

Catherine didn't know what to say. She felt a little deflated suddenly. She'd hoped to see Andrew Mackintosh again and he really was very sweet. But she'd also thought that Mr Black would be someone she'd know, and yet, he wasn't at all.

'Catherine is a little embarrassed, Mr Black,' Louisa said. 'We're still discussing with the school what might be done.' This was what Louisa had told her they would say.

'I'd give them a piece of my mind if you were my daughter,' Mr Black said, still looking at Louisa. 'Schools here in London wouldn't know what to do with you, Catherine. And I have some sympathy with that point of view.'

'You didn't enjoy school?' Louisa said.

'I did not,' he said. 'I failed mathematics, as it happens, and yet I'm a banker. I failed English and I'm a newspaper publisher. I think schools are overrated, Catherine. What do you think?' He was still looking at Louisa.

'Well, I didn't much like Henley,' Catherine said. 'I didn't fit in there.' She appreciated his standing up for her. Perhaps the Freebodys would be more accepting of her than the Quicks were.

'We're considering other schools,' Louisa said to Black. 'I do think Henley was less academic than I'd imagined it might be.'

He laughed. 'Good attitude, Dr Quick. The school's the problem, not this one. My daughter's in France. She loves her school because all they do is ride horses and play sport and cook and eat. They even swim, Catherine. But you don't need school when you swim like you do. And the Channel's still there for the taking, girl,' he said. 'Gertrude Ederle gave up this week within sight of Dover. You could give her a run for the Channel next year if you trained. That's what I think. What do you say about that?'

'Can a woman actually swim the English Channel?' Louisa said. 'I mean, physically.'

'Listen to you,' Black said. 'And I heard you were in favour of women's equality.' He pointed his finger at her. ''Course a woman can swim the Channel – and the first one who does will be remembered forever.

'Dr Quick, can I say again what a great honour it is to have you, and your niece, at our little party?' he continued. 'I'm so pleased you could attend. And, Catherine, what you did was an amazing feat and don't let your aunt tell you differently.' He grinned. 'There is nothing finer in the world than a champion. In the newspaper business, we love them. And you, my dear girl, are a champion. I know it. And, as I understand it, we might be going to see more of you?' He gave Louisa a quizzical look.

'Yes,' Louisa said. 'I'm just finalising arrangements for the clinic and then I'll be in a position to talk to you more. But I'm very hopeful we can come to an arrangement.'

'Well, that's fine news,' he said. 'Now, you were asking me about flying, Dr Quick. Catherine, as your aunt already knows, I happen to believe that flying will one day be as normal as taking a train or ferry. It gets your newspapers very excited when I say things like that. Perhaps you've heard of the mad American?' He smiled as he said it. Catherine nodded. 'Have you ever been up?' he said then.

'Up?' Catherine said.

He pointed towards the ceiling. 'In the sky.'

'No,' Catherine said.

'Dr Quick?' Black said.

Louisa shook her head. 'I'm afraid of heights.'

'Hah,' Black said. 'Me too. But when you're up there, you're so high it doesn't seem high at all, if that makes sense. Andrew here will vouch for that.' He smiled slyly.

'Mr Black is referring to the fact that I suffer dreadfully from the air sickness,' Andrew said. 'I'm not at all frightened by how high we are, as I'm too focused on being ill.'

'Oh dear, that sounds like no fun at all,' Catherine said. 'But I think I'd love flying, Mr Black.'

'Say, why don't we take these two gals with us?' Black said to Andrew. 'We're off to Paris first weekend of September.'

'No, I really don't think . . .' Louisa started to protest.

'That's settles it. I'll leave Andrew to tell you where and when. We'll send a car, of course. Pack your glad rags.' He looked at his pocket watch. 'Now, you'll have to excuse me; I must get back to my meeting, unfortunately – an urgent matter. But I did want to make sure I welcomed you personally. It's been a great pleasure to make your acquaintance, Miss Quick, and to see you again, Dr Quick.' He smiled at Louisa, turned on his heel and left them, Andrew following behind him.

'He's quite singular, isn't he?' Louisa said once they were out of earshot.

'Yes,' Catherine said. 'And he's related to me.' Louisa looked perplexed. 'Remember? You said he and my mother are related.'

'Of course,' Louisa said. 'I forgot about that in all the fuffle. You were staring at him, dear, and I couldn't think why.'

'So can we go to Paris?'

'Can we go to Paris?' Louisa said. She was looking after Black, watching the crowd parting again to let him through.

'Yes, can we go to Paris?'

'I don't see why not,' Louisa said. 'It might be fun.'

'And what's a fuffle?' Catherine said.

'I don't really know,' Louisa said absently. 'But I suspect it's the kind of thing that would lead us to Paris.'

It was late, after eleven. Louisa was to one side of the ballroom, watching the dancing. Most of the women wore full-length evening gowns, but there were some in the modern style whose dresses only came to mid calf.

'They do whatever they like,' Ruth Luxton had said to Louisa when women who came to the rooms began dressing in the style, showing their legs, their arms. 'They're just like men.'

'If they wanted to be like men, they'd wear trousers,' Louisa had said.

'Some of them do,' Ruth said.

'But why would they want to look like men?' Louisa said.

'To have the freedom of men. I think they're gorgeous, like flamingos.'

'Flamingos are stupid,' Louisa retorted.

'It was a metaphor, Louisa. No need to be so literal.'

Now it occurred to Louisa that they didn't look like men at all; they were like boys with their flat chests and short hair. And why not? Boys, she thought: that's where freedom is.

174

Andrew and Catherine were among the dancers, laughing and chatting as they tried one of the new dance steps. He was a lovely chap, and Louisa could see that Catherine enjoyed his company. Ada Mackintosh, his mother, had been one of Millicent's patients. Millicent had delivered the two boys, and Louisa had inherited the family after Millicent retired. The other one, Donald, had been lost in France in the war, Louisa remembered now. Poor Ada. She adored her sons. Andrew had grown into a fine young man, Louisa thought, still getting used to his adult limbs by the look of him on the dance floor now. He could do with a bit of fattening up too, Louisa decided.

She was about to go over and tell Catherine it was time they were getting home when she heard a quiet voice behind her. 'Dr Quick?'

She turned around. It was Black.

Louisa had seen him during the evening, standing at the side of the dance floor watching the couples as the band played. On another occasion, he was looking out at the water. She didn't know what he was looking at, but he looked tired, worn down.

'Louisa,' he said in his slow drawl. 'May I call you Louisa?'

'Of course,' she said, 'if I can call you . . .'

'My mother used to call me Lear but everyone else just calls me Black.'

'Lear then,' she said. 'It suits you.' Louisa had had two glasses of champagne and as a waiter approached she began to contemplate a third.

'A mad king?'

'Perhaps. Or perhaps Black, for you strike me as a definite kind of person.' The champagne must have gone to her head, she thought as she turned down the third glass. She should have eaten.

'That I am,' he said. 'I want to talk about Catherine.'

'Catherine?'

He took a long time to respond, so long she thought for a moment he'd forgotten he'd initiated a conversation. Then he looked sharply at Louisa. As he met her eye she felt a shiver. Not drunk then, but hesitant, unsure about something. Those dark eyes – sad eyes, she decided when she thought of him later. There was something compelling about his sadness.

'Catherine,' he said again. He was smoking a fat cigar, drinking what looked like scotch. 'The swimmer.' He smiled but his face looked as if it might at any moment crumple into tears, or laughter. 'The Thames is a terrible river. The tides, Louisa. She may be the best swimmer we've ever seen.'

Louisa put her glass on a nearby table. Why on earth would he care? she wanted to say. 'Mr Black Lear, that swim has created an enormous problem. You probably already know that Catherine grew up on an island very remote from the world. She arrived in London with no idea how to behave, and now she is . . .' Louisa trailed off, looked over towards the dance floor where Catherine and Andrew were still dancing. He had his hand on her back. Louisa wondered should she intervene. 'Please be assured that I will be most happy to come to Baltimore and help you with your clinic in whatever way I can. I would certainly want to bring Catherine as I am very worried about her future, and particularly . . .' Louisa couldn't go on. She thought of the boy Michael, the letter. She must take care of Catherine.

He smiled, took a long sip of his drink. 'Let's take some air,' he suggested, and started towards the doors out onto the deck.

Outside it was chilly and Louisa felt herself shiver in her sleeveless dress. Black took off his jacket and put it over her shoulders. He smiled. Oh, when he smiled. She found herself drawn to him.

'I could tell you things,' he said, 'and I'm sure you could tell me things.' He looked out towards the water, that dark force beneath the ship. 'Ah,' he said. 'Later. We'll talk about all this later.' He went to take her hand. She let him. At first she thought he was about to lead her somewhere but instead he shook her hand, as if they'd made a deal. 'My doctors will be pleased to have you come and visit us, Louisa, and I will wire Charlotte Epstein and make arrangements for Catherine to join the Women's Swimming Association. Meantime,' he smiled again, 'let's pack for Paris.'

Chapter Sixteen

The next morning, Catherine came into the kitchen and asked Nellie for a stamp. Nellie had waited up and they'd told her about the party. The *Aloha* has a croquet court, Catherine had said. Andrew had shown her. Had he gone off alone with her? Louisa wondered. She hadn't even noticed. She must keep a better eye on Catherine. 'And Mr Black is the most marvellous person. He'd taking us up in his aeroplane and even Louisa said we could go.'

'Yes,' Louisa had said, noticing the look of wry surprise on Nellie's face. 'It was a delightful evening. A real gentleman, Nellie.'

'Really,' Nellie had said. 'You're going up in an aeroplane? Well, I never.'

'Catherine, I'll post your letter on my way to the clinic,' Louisa said now.

'Was there any mail for me yesterday?' Catherine said.

'No,' Louisa said before Nellie could answer.

'I haven't heard from Florence,' Catherine said. 'I hope they're all right.'

'We'd know if anything had happened,' Louisa answered.

'Catherine's doing much better,' she said to Nellie after Catherine went back upstairs and out of earshot.

'I think she still misses home. I think that's the source of all this trouble, if you want my opinion.'

'Nellie, listen to me. We must stop describing the island as home. Her home is here, with her family. You left your first home. Many of us do.'

'I left Braintree for London. It hardly compares with what Catherine had to do,' Nellie said. 'But I agree she's doing better. I think she might have a crush on that Mackintosh fellow.'

'Yes, I know.'

'Are her feelings reciprocated?'

'He's terribly sweet with her. But he'd be twenty or more. Catherine's still young. And his mother wouldn't approve. She'd see the Quicks as merchants, I think, and a little beneath her. Still, he's been very kind.' Louisa sat down opposite Nellie. 'I have to tell you something, and I need you to be understanding.' Nellie put down her polishing cloth and looked at Louisa. 'I don't want Catherine sending letters to Australia.'

'What do you mean?'

'I mean, she gives us her letters to post. I want to make sure they don't get posted.'

'But why?' Nellie said.

'It's time for her to move on, Nellie. She's too attached to the past; it's time for her to realise that her future is here.'

'They'll write and say they haven't heard from her.'

Louisa nodded. She would need delicacy here, she knew. 'I will keep their letters,' she said.

'You will what?' Nellie said.

'Nellie, this isn't something I'm going to discuss. I am going to hold letters from Australia, just for a few weeks until we finalise arrangements for this trip to America. And then she can get a stack all at once and we'll send hers. Simple.'

'But you can't do that, Louisa. It's dishonest. She asks about those letters all the time.' Nellie stared at her. 'You've started already. You're already holding letters. She's been asking. Oh, Louisa, you can't be so cruel.'

'I have one,' Louisa said. 'Can't you see the letters are the problem? They keep dragging her back into her old life.'

'No, Louisa, I won't do this,' Nellie said. 'No good will come of it. She's not a child. She's near grown. She has a right.'

'Nellie, I knew you'd be like this. But many things are not black and white in life. There are shades of grey. As a doctor, I deal with them all the time. I don't plan to keep her letters forever, just until we work out what happens next with Catherine, until she has a clear future. Weeks, that's all. Will you help me?'

'Are you sure it's for the best?'

'I am,' Louisa said.

'Well, all right,' Nellie said. 'But only for a few weeks. Then we pass them on.'

'Of course,' Louisa said, believing that this was what they would do, but knowing too that when you begin a deception,

180

it rarely finishes anywhere near where it starts, and it even more rarely has only the consequences you intend.

'You always play that song on the gramophone,' Nellie said that evening. The three were in the parlour, Nellie dusting, Louisa reading case notes. Catherine didn't answer. Louisa looked over at her niece on the lounge. She was sitting there looking into the middle distance, listening to the song. 'It's beautiful,' Louisa said.

Nellie looked at her. 'Not when you've heard it a hundred times today.'

'It's still beautiful. What's it called, Catherine?'

'I don't know,' Catherine said. 'I bought it at the Camden Market.'

'Is he singing "where dreams come true"?' Louisa asked.

'He is,' Catherine said.

'In dreamland,' Louisa said. She smiled. 'I can see why you'd like it.'

Catherine smiled and it filled Louisa with warmth.

'The pair of you are beyond me,' Nellie said. 'I'm going to clean the range. I can't think of anything I'd rather do right now.' She took up her dusting cloths and left them.

Louisa smiled at Catherine. 'I think Nellie grew up in a more industrious household than you or I,' she said.

'Do you think?' Catherine said. 'You seem to be able to manage everything.'

Louisa laughed. 'If only,' she said. 'Why do think Nellie's here?'

'She said it's because you're a Christian woman.'

'Hah. For a start, I am anything but a Christian woman. And second, Nellie's here because if Nellie wasn't here, I wouldn't manage. I don't know the first thing about running a household.'

'But you're a surgeon, Louisa. You don't need to be able to do those things.'

'And what would stop you being a surgeon?'

'I couldn't do that. I can't even get through school.'

'Of course you can,' Louisa said. Catherine's confidence had taken a blow. 'You're a Quick. You can do anything. If you want to succeed in school, you'll be able to. We just have to find the right kind of school.'

'You thought Henley was the right kind of school.'

'Yes, I did,' Louisa said. 'But I was wrong. Or the timing was wrong. Whatever it was, you didn't fit in there. We need to try somewhere else.'

The song had finished and Catherine went over to play it again.

'You like Andrew Mackintosh,' Louisa said.

'He's hilarious,' Catherine said. 'At the party, he was saying that Mr Black loves swimming. Then he started this game where we had to find words for water. He rattled off so many, rain, mist, fog, downpour, sea, ocean, lake, stream, waterfall . . . I can't remember any more. But he had twenty and I'd hardly thought of one.'

'Yes, he's quite charming. His father is a writer.' Louisa had met Ada's husband; he was a difficult man, aloof. That Andrew was so affable was a credit to Ada. 'Florence's son, Michael. Did you like him too?'

'Bid,' Catherine said. She grinned. 'Very much.'

'You were a bit like brother and sister,' Louisa said, trying it out.

'Yes,' Catherine said, 'but more happy. My friends at school liked their brothers and sisters well enough, but they got mad at them sometimes. Michael and I didn't get mad at each other. Sometimes we were almost like one person.'

'I see,' Louisa said. 'Did you like him the same way you like Andrew, then?'

'Oh no,' Catherine said. 'Andrew's funny but Michael was . . .' Her mouth went down at the corners like a child's might. 'I'm sorry, Aunt Louisa, but I just miss home.' She started crying. Louisa felt a stab of remorse now for hiding the letter – Catherine clearly wanted to hear from the boy – although the extent of her upset gave no reassurance at all. Their relationship must be quite developed, Louisa thought, and Catherine was too young.

'I didn't mean to upset you. It has been hard for you, Catherine, but once we set off for America, it will be easier. And you never know. Perhaps you'll go back to the island once you've finished school. But for now, give me a hand with this case, would you?' She wanted to take the girl's mind off that blasted island and wished now she'd never raised it. Louisa went back to her report. 'I'll tell you about it and you tell me what I should do.'

Catherine looked at her aunt, sniffed. 'Are you serious?'

'Of course. Come, sit down with me.'

Louisa explained the details of the case. A young man who'd been superficially injured in the war had ever since experienced a range of odd symptoms: facial tics, involuntary vocal soundings, sometimes foul language. He'd been referred by a physician in Harley Street and Louisa wanted to help if she could. The physician was suggesting there might be a tumour.

Catherine thought for a moment. 'Well, is there a risk that if you operate you'll harm the patient?'

Louisa nodded. 'There most certainly is.'

'And don't you promise not to do harm?'

'Hmmm.'

'So maybe don't operate.'

'That's what I think too. So what if the chap swears too much? I doubt we'll find anything in his skull that causes it. Harry's taught you very well. Most of my work is like this, deciding not to do anything. And when I do do something, it's usually relatively straightforward. See, you could be a surgeon. You could be anything, my dear.'

'Even a swimmer?'

Louisa smiled. 'Yes, even a swimmer.' She looked at her niece. 'But I'm not sure that swimming would be enough for a life. I can't help thinking you'd want more.'

'Aunt Louisa, when you said you weren't a Christian, did you really mean it?'

Louisa nodded. 'I did.'

'Do you believe in God?'

She thought about this question. 'I don't know, Catherine. I really don't.'

'I don't know either,' Catherine said, swallowing hard. 'Florence is Christian. I liked Sister Ursula a lot. I thought at one time I might be a nun.'

Louisa smiled. 'I think every girl thinks that at some

time,' she said. 'I know I did. And I wasn't even raised in a Christian household.'

'Were you and my father close growing up?' Catherine said then.

'Oh my, yes,' Louisa said. 'They called us the twins.'

'What was he like?'

'Harry? Well, he was unexpected. My mother lost a child, a girl before me, and when I came, I think she and my father were overjoyed, a girl to replace Margaret, the baby they lost. But then, just a year later, along came Harry. Our mother was very busy. She was involved in the London School of Medicine for Women and then she found she was pregnant. It wasn't easy for her. She had her work and then these two babies. He was happy, though. Harry was always happy. That's what I remember.'

'So you looked after him?'

'I don't know about that.' Louisa thought back. 'They were different times, Catherine. My mother was trying to do something so important.' She regarded her niece. 'When I was your age, my mother drove me mad. My sister who died, Margaret, had tuberculosis. Mama was convinced it was hereditary and that I would die too. I was sick when I was about ten, which didn't help. Mama was wrong, we now know. It turns out Margaret died because she had cow's milk from one cow only, which was what was recommended at the time. But it gave her tuberculosis over and over. If medical science had inched just a little further along, perhaps Mama would have worried less. But it drove me to distraction the way she ran my life.'

'Did you know my mother?' Catherine said.

'Hardly at all,' Louisa said.

'Do you know if she was happy?'

'I don't,' Louisa said. 'Did she seem unhappy to you?'

'I don't remember her,' Catherine said. 'It was just . . .'

'Yes?'

'Nothing. Just my father never talked about her. And I wondered, you know, if they were happy.'

'Oh, I do know that,' Louisa said. 'Harry adored Julia. In fact, it was quite a joke in our family. Harry was smitten. And he loved you very much, as you know.'

There were tears in Catherine's eyes. 'Aunt Louisa, I'm glad I came here. I mean, I miss the island. I miss Florence. But I'm glad I'm here.'

Louisa swallowed hard. She couldn't trust her voice to answer.

Catherine had gone off to bed and Louisa had sat up to finish her reports. Now her niece was at her bedroom door. 'Louisa, there's someone on the telephone, who says you must come.'

'Yes, yes,' Louisa said, groggy with sleep. She was still in her dream, tired, so tired. She went downstairs, her feet cold on the tiles in the hall. Her eyes wouldn't stay open.

'I've been asked to say sorry for waking you up,' a little voice said when she went to the telephone.

'That's all right,' Louisa said, still half asleep.

'Sally said to tell you it's a beach.' Sally was one of the midwives. 'You need to come, she said. She's worried about the footings.'

'Where is she?'

'Do you know Danby Street?'

'Yes.'

'We're the house at the end of the last row on the left off the road, the river end. We're the one with a light out, Sally said.'

'Tell her I'm on the way.'

Louisa surmised the lad meant a breech, footling, and the midwife needed help with the delivery – quickly.

Nellie was asleep but she found Catherine in the kitchen. 'I have to go out. Do you want to come?'

Catherine nodded quickly.

Louisa went upstairs to dress. When she came down, Catherine was back downstairs, dressed, ready and making tea. 'You won't have time for that,' Louisa said.

'It's for you. I'll put it in a flask,' Catherine said. 'The driver's waiting.'

'Grab the whisky,' Louisa said. Catherine looked at her in horror. 'For the mother, dear.'

They came to the house at the end of the row and the light was indeed shining out into the night. Louisa knocked on the door and they were admitted by a girl who looked like she should be asleep. The house was tiny; it made Louisa's seem palatial. There were two rooms, one a kitchen and eating space, the other a bedroom. The kitchen was filled with small children, none older than six. The boy who'd telephoned, knowable by his face, still flushed with the cold he'd been out in, couldn't have been more than five. Their father was working on the subway, the boy told them.

Louisa could hear moans coming from the bedroom. They went in.

'Nancy, is it?' Louisa said to the woman. 'You remember me from the clinic? I'm Louisa. We're going to help you now.'

Sally, the midwife, stood to go and see to the other children.

'Sally!' Nancy called out in alarm. 'I don't want no doctor.' Many of the East End women were suspicious of doctors, especially women doctors.

Louisa took Nancy's hand. 'I know what you're going through. I've had a child too, you know, Nancy,' she said quietly. 'But the baby's coming out feet first, which we'd rather he didn't. You'll need two of us. Sally won't go anywhere, dear.' She turned to the midwife. 'Stay by her side,' she said. Then she noticed Catherine standing there behind her. 'You go and look after the other children, would you, Catherine?' Louisa said.

Louisa was thankful Sally had been able to keep the mother calm; it was worse when they panicked. As the contractions intensified, they waited, hopeful. If worst came to worst, Louisa could do a caesarean operation, but she'd do everything to avoid it here in the home.

As Sally comforted the mother, Louisa listened to Catherine out in the kitchen. One of the children said, 'We've had no tea, Miss.'

'Are you hungry then?' Catherine replied.

'Oh my, yes.'

'Let's see what we can find.' There was a pause, then Catherine said, 'There's flour and an egg. A treasure trove. What's your name?'

'Alice.'

'Well, Alice, do you know how to make pancakes? I think the two of us might be able to work it out together. What do you say? Do you have a skillet?' Louisa heard the clatter of pans. Then the contractions became more intense and she stopped noticing the sounds outside.

By the time the baby came, another boy, Catherine and the children were clearing up the dishes and tidying the kitchen. When Louisa emerged, one of them said, 'We're cleaning up for Mummy, so she doesn't feel so bad.'

'She's feeling much better,' Louisa said, 'now that baby's here.'

The largest one squealed. 'Is it a girl?'

'Why don't you come in and see for yourselves? Softly now.'

Louisa looked across at Catherine then. She'd put the kitchen in order, wiped all the children's hands and faces, and now she was sweeping the floor. She'd started chopping vegetables for a soup, she said, and would like to get it on before they left.

'I'm just not quite sure what goes in soup,' Catherine said. 'I assumed water because you drink it.'

Louisa laughed. 'Maybe Sally can finish the soup,' she said. 'She'll stay now for the rest of the day.'

There were five of them, Catherine told Louisa on the way home: Alice was six, Tom five, the twins three. 'And there was a one-year-old who sat in my lap while I gave him milk from a cup. But they were lovely children, and Alice so grown up. She told me it was *her* baby coming. The others weren't old enough to look after a baby but she could. How sweet.'

'Did you enjoy going?'

'Oh, yes,' Catherine said. 'It's the first time I've felt . . . useful. I felt useful.'

'Well, you certainly were useful,' Louisa said. 'Normally there's no one there to help with the children. Sally would have gone to them, but it was better to have her with me when we told the mother her baby was breech. She knows Sally.'

'Aunt Louisa, why did you say you'd had a baby?'

'I just wanted to reassure the mother,' Louisa said quickly.

'But you haven't,' Catherine said.

'Of course not,' Louisa said, more sharply than she intended. She felt fear suddenly, as if she were about to be found out doing something she shouldn't. She made herself calm, looked at her niece squarely.

'So that was a lie.'

'Well, strictly speaking, yes. But a white lie.'

'What's a white lie?'

'One you tell to help someone.' Catherine nodded, seemingly satisfied with Louisa's answer. She went on to explain why a breech birth was a concern. 'It's mostly straightforward, like today, but when it's not, it can be awful.'

Catherine seemed hardly to hear Louisa. She was so full of energy. 'And when their mother was crying out, the little ones looked frightened,' she said. 'And I was scared too, because I thought she must have been dying from the sound of it. But Alice, the one I told you about, just said, "Babies hurt coming out." It settled the rest of them down.'

'Those children loved you,' Louisa said. She regarded her niece. 'You were marvellous, Catherine, just marvellous.'

When they arrived home the sun wasn't yet up. Catherine went back to bed. Louisa stayed up, ostensibly to write up the case notes for the birth, but instead found herself sitting in the dining room, staring at the grate.

She told no one, not even Ruth Luxton, not until she was sure. The tender breasts, the missed menses, the nausea. She'd heard enough women report the symptoms.

She debased herself further, went to see him. 'Of course,' he said. 'Of course I'll help. We'll get rid of it.'

'Get rid of it?' she said. 'I don't want to get rid of it. I love you.'

How could she say that after what he did? She felt sick when she thought of this later, telling him she loved him.

'You must understand,' he said. 'I'm married. I have a family. I'm unable to . . . You know that, Louisa.'

That was the moment she realised how very alone she was.

The pregnancy was too far along, she knew, to terminate, and soon it would be obvious to everyone. She went to her mother, who was not unkind. Louisa told Millicent lies, protected him even still. A medical student, she said. The father was a medical student she knew.

'Good God,' her mother said. 'Won't he do the honourable thing? All that study, Louie. How could you?' But her mother soon stopped asking about the medical student, came up with another plan. Perhaps she guessed the truth. Louisa would go through with the pregnancy, her mother said, and they'd find a family through the local doctor at Aldeburgh who could be trusted to act with discretion.

The birth was mercifully quick. She'd hardly felt the first contraction before she was on the floor in the bathroom at Aldeburgh.

She knew her blood pressure was high, had told her mother so. Her mother called the midwife as arranged. 'All these doctors in the family and we're calling the midwife,' was the last thing Louisa said before she lost consciousness. She remembered something; a loud voice. *The baby, we're losing the baby*.

When she recovered, it was Millicent who sat at her bedside, held her hand. 'The child,' she said. 'We lost him. A little boy. A perfect little boy, Louie, stillborn.' Tears in her poor mother's eyes. The cord had been wrapped around his neck. There was nothing to be done.

Afterwards, Louisa would think of the boy as he might have been at various ages; a scallywag, clever, big green eyes, kicking a football in the lane, sick with scarlet fever, roasting chestnuts in Princes Street. Was it wrong that she felt relief more than sadness?

Chapter Seventeen

Catherine rubbed the window and peered out. Mr Black had sent a car for them again, this time to take them to the airfield at Croydon. She wished she'd eaten something as her stomach was beginning to growl. In the predawn light, she could just make out a long, faded track with a light at the far end. In shadow was what she assumed was their aeroplane. It looked like a giant insect from here.

Someone emerged from a squat building to their left. It was Andrew, judging by their height.

'Is it safe today, Andrew?' was the first thing Louisa said when he reached them.

'Hah,' Andrew said. 'It's never safe. I can't stand it. But you'll be able to say you've flown in an aeroplane.'

They made their way across to the little building. 'Our honoured guests,' Mr Black said when they got inside. 'Did you see the aeroplane?'

'No,' Louisa said. 'There was an aeroplane?'

He laughed. 'Well, I'm not going to fly you on my back, Louisa.'

He introduced them to the two pilots when they came in. The senior of the pair was Heindrick, a big man with a barrel chest and booming voice. 'These are the girls then,' was all he said.

The second pilot, younger, blonde hair and blue eyes, was all the way from Canada, Mr Black said. 'His name is Sam. Just don't call him an American. It upsets him.'

Sam came over to Catherine. He wore dark brown wool pants and a leather jacket. He was about Catherine's height. 'Have you ever been up before?'

'No,' she said. 'I can't wait.'

'This is an easy flight,' he said. 'We'll be there in a couple hours – although Mr Black sometimes takes a detour, so you just never know what's going to happen. But make sure you look out the window once we're up.' He had awfully straight white teeth and kindly eyes.

Heindrick went out and came back. The luggage had been loaded, he said. 'We go.'

There were steps up into the aeroplane. The pilots went up first and into the front of the plane, which was separated by glass doors from the half a dozen canvas chairs that had been nailed to the floor for the passengers. Black took the first row, Andrew beside him, Louisa and Catherine behind. Behind them was the spare tank of fuel – the smell was overpowering. Their luggage was piled on the sides of the plane. The bathroom was a bucket in the back.

Catherine could see the backs of the pilots' heads. They wore leather caps now and she watched as Sam put his head out the window, signalling to someone below. After a few minutes, the engine sputtered into life.

'Goodness me, it's loud!' Louisa shouted.

They tracked along at ground level, slowly at first, then turned, picked up speed, the noise of the engines ear-splitting. Catherine could feel the vibrations in every bone of her body. It shook you half apart. They bumped, rose, bumped, rose, bumped and finally rose and were airborne.

The strange feeling in her stomach as they ascended soon passed. The sun was rising and Catherine could see the earth below them recede. She could make out landmarks, now totally transformed. A farm, which from the ground might include a farmer with a wife and children, became squares of crops and a little red roof. It made everything simpler, Catherine thought.

They banked and came back around over the city of London and passed over the Thames. When she saw the Tower Bridge, Catherine thought of the swim she'd done and all the trouble it had caused. She looked over at Louisa. Her aunt looked so fearful, her hands clasped together in her lap, her mouth set, her face pale. Catherine felt a stab of remorse for all the trouble she'd caused, resolved to be better in the future.

She looked out again at the river, which wound its way through the countryside. It was the only detail she could make out now. It was grey, the water here, like the city itself, nothing like the sea at home, whose water was a pure blue-green from a distance and as clear as glass up close. The Islanders believed the sea was alive. But the river, Catherine had found, was a different kind of creature altogether, not wicked, she thought now, but dark and mysterious.

Andrew soon stood, ducking his head because of the low ceiling, and went to the back. Catherine could hear him retching.

She looked out the window again. They were flying over the English Channel. From here it looked so small, as if you could swim it in minutes, she thought. It would be an achievement to be the first woman to swim the Channel, Black had said at his party. Catherine looked down again. It really did look small, for already she could see the green of France.

Before long, they were over what must be Paris, for she saw the Eiffel Tower she'd seen in books.

'Good Lord, we're there already,' Louisa said. Her colour was back, Catherine thought.

'Ain't it great?' Black turned around and said. 'Now, tell me again this will never catch on as a way for getting around the place.'

They passed Paris to their left and flew to Versailles – to visit his daughter's school, Mr Black told them. But it turned out that by 'visiting' he meant flying low over the ground. They could see the roof of the convent, the spires of the church. And sure enough there were the young women of Saint-Marcel's waving to them. Mr Black dropped bunches of flowers that had been packed for the purpose and then they climbed again, at Mr Black's request, to 'go over some alps, please, fellas, to show the girls,' before heading back towards Paris.

When Heindrick came back to talk to Mr Black, he asked Catherine if she'd like to join Sam up the front. She went into the cockpit. You could see the whole world, she thought. The mountains in front of them were covered in snow – she'd never seen it before. 'Oh, it's so very marvellous,' Catherine said.

She took the seat next to Sam and he delighted in her sense of wonder. He said he never got sick of it. He'd learnt to fly in the last months of the war. 'In the end, I didn't get to do much flying,' he said. 'But I haven't been home yet. Plenty of work for pilots now.'

'Do you miss home?' Catherine said.

'Oh, yes,' he said. 'I live in mountains like those ones down there. It's nothing like England. We get so much snow through the winter and even the summers are cold. It's beautiful. But you're not from England either if that accent's anything to go by.'

'I grew up in Australia.'

'Do you miss home?'

Suddenly Catherine thought she might cry. She nodded.

'I'm sorry,' he said. 'I didn't mean to upset you.'

She shook her head. 'I . . . It doesn't usually upset me so much.' She swallowed her tears. 'Tell me more about the mountains,' she said.

In the summers, he said, he and his brother had set a goal to climb every mountain you could see from the town. 'We'd nearly done it too. I'll finish if I ever get back there.'

'I think you will,' Catherine said.

Just then, Andrew poked his head into the cockpit. 'Here you are. I thought you might have jumped in to swim the rest of the way down the Seine.'

Catherine turned to him and smiled. 'You must be feeling better. You're making bad jokes.'

197

'Better enough,' he said. 'You know she's a swimmer?' he told Sam. 'I'm surprised we're not down in the drink.'

'Thank you so much,' Catherine said to Sam before she left the cockpit. She felt strangely light, as if she'd been sitting in the kitchen on the island with Florence rather than up in the sky with a perfect stranger from a country she'd never seen.

Louisa was feeling better too. 'This is not what I expected,' she said.

'I love it,' Catherine said. 'Sam showed me how he flies the aeroplane. He's from the mountains in Canada. It sounds like magic.'

'Aren't there bears in Canada?'

'Louisa, you make everything something to be afraid of.'

'Do I?'

'No, but it was just lovely to . . .'

'To what?'

'Nothing. Anyway, we're landing in fifteen minutes. In Paris, Louisa.'

They came down quickly and landed at the little airstrip with three bumps, a perfect landing, Mr Black said. They caught taxis from the airstrip to the Hôtel de Crillon as the light was fading, passing green fields in late sunshine, cows still out in pasture, little villages. As they approached the city itself, Catherine's eyes couldn't take it in fast enough. Andrew was glib, chattering constantly about what they'd do the next day, pointing casually towards the Arc de Triomphe and the Place de la Concorde as they passed. Andrew had been to Paris, but Catherine was in awe. It was as she'd thought London might be, she realised. It was beautiful.

She and Louisa were sharing an apartment that looked over the Place de la Concorde. They'd giggled when they first saw the bathroom. It had a bidet and Catherine had said there were two lavatories, in case they both needed one, she guessed, not knowing what a bidet was for. Learning its function didn't make it any less funny and the two of them collapsed on the beds laughing at nothing. They unpacked their things, dressed and went down for dinner in the hotel dining room.

The next morning Catherine was in the dining room late for breakfast. She'd been for a walk on her own earlier in the morning and had just kept walking, under a gentle fog. She went down towards the river and through a park where the trees were dropping their leaves. She'd crossed over the river and back, mesmerised at the beauty of the buildings. She'd come upon Notre-Dame Cathedral not knowing what it was at first. She'd gone in and sat for a few minutes. The silence reminded her of nights on the island.

Mr Black came into the dining room now. He saw Catherine and smiled. 'Miss Quick,' he said.

'Hello, Mr Black. I've been out walking.'

'Do you mind if I join you?'

'Of course not. But you're supposed to call me Catherine. I'm just a girl, you know.'

'Catherine, then,' he said and smiled. 'But you're not just a girl. You're a champion. You hear?' He waggled a finger and looked at her mock-sternly. He was very sweet, in his way, she thought. The day before, when they'd dropped the bunches of flowers for his daughter, she'd seen him lean against the window and wave madly. Then he wiped his eye. Catherine had thought it was a tear he wiped away.

He called the waiter over, ordered coffee for himself and a hot chocolate for Catherine, and milk toast and two-minute eggs. Even with Catherine interpreting it took some minutes for the order to be understood, as Catherine herself didn't know what milk toast and two-minute eggs were.

'I used to eat my eggs like that,' she said when the waiter had gone.

'You did?' he said, smiling. 'Well, isn't that something?'

'I wouldn't eat the whites, only the yolk, and then Florence stopped making eggs for me because she said it was too wasteful.'

'I still don't eat the whites,' Mr Black said. 'An indulgence.'

He was in his dark grey suit, his hair neatly combed back from his forehead. It wanted to spring up, by the look of it. His face was pink, like her father's just after he shaved in the morning and Catherine felt a pull of sadness in her heart.

'So, how are you liking Paris?' he asked.

'Oh, it's so beautiful,' she said. 'Thank you so much for inviting us.'

He waved away her thanks. 'Now, Catherine, your aunt does a fine job with her clinic, a fine job that should be recognised. I'm thrilled she's going to come and help us out in Baltimore. Whatever small thing I can do to make her life more pleasant, I'm more than willing. But, my dear, you want to swim.' He raised his eyebrows.

Did she want to swim?

'And I have an interest in swimming.'

200

'Mr Black, swimming got me in an awful lot of trouble.'

'I know that.'

'You don't understand. I was expelled.' Louisa had said they wouldn't tell anyone this but Catherine wanted to tell him. He was a link to her mother, she thought, to the people who might be like her.

'Yes, I know,' he said, as if being expelled was nothing. Louisa must have told him. Catherine was surprised. 'But I also saw you cross that river. And while I am not a betting man, I would bet anything that you are the fastest and strongest woman swimmer on earth. And I'd like to help.'

She didn't respond.

'So what do you think, Catherine?'

'I don't really know,' she said. 'I've never thought about swimming. It just is.'

He laughed. 'That will be great with the reporters. *I've never thought about swimming. It just is.*' He chuckled again.

'Mr Black, you knew my mother.'

He looked at her. 'A little,' he said.

'What was she like?'

'Julia? Oh, they moved away when she was young, so I hardly knew her as a child. I saw her again with your father. She was very pretty, a lot like you.' He smiled. It disappeared quickly.

Catherine nodded. 'I don't remember her and I was thinking that in America, I could meet more people from her family.'

'Her parents are still in Canada,' he said. 'But I'm sure we can get in touch with them. Julia was an only child, wasn't she? There might be others on that side. I should know, I suppose, but I don't.' He eyed her carefully. 'You *do* want to swim as well, don't you, Catherine?' he said.

'I do.' How could she explain to him that his question made no sense? It was like asking if she wanted to breathe.

'Well, let's see if we can work on your aunt so that you can.' He stood then. 'I must go. I'm glad you're enjoying the trip.'

After he left, Catherine noticed that he'd eaten hardly any of his toast and eggs.

Chapter Eighteen

'She could be the one, Louisa.' They were sitting in the little bar across the square from the hotel. Louisa and Catherine had spent the morning with Andrew. In the afternoon Louisa had gone to the Sorbonne, where a doctor she'd served with during the war was now working. They'd spent a couple of hours reminiscing about those days when they thought the sky would be the limit for women doctors from now on. Hah, Louisa could have said now. What young fools they were.

Black had spent the day in the hotel, staving off a bid to buy his newspaper, he said when they met up for a drink. He looked tired around the eyes.

'And she wants to swim,' he said.

'Well, of course she'll want to swim. She also wants to go back to the island.' Louisa thought then of the letters. There had been a second, addressed in a different hand. Perhaps it was from Florence. Louisa hadn't read it – she'd decided that would be unethical – but she hadn't given it to Catherine either. It was September now. Louisa's plan was to take Catherine to America in the New Year – it would take that long to get the clinic sorted out and deal with the inspector. Catherine could meet the swimmers Black had spoken about and then come home and Louisa would find a school. Maybe she could board in Glasgow, Louisa thought, or go to the Spitalfields public school. She needn't go back to Henley. As for the letters, well, Louisa would see.

'I don't think any of us know what we want at fifteen,' Louisa said to Black. She thought of her own girlhood and felt a stab of something. Regret? There was never any question for Louisa. She was going to do medicine. She looked squarely at him. 'I want Catherine to go back to school. It's the only thing that will secure a future for her.'

The waiter came over and Black ordered another martini for himself. Louisa was still going on her first. The hotel's bar was cosy and looked out onto a little square. 'Do you know, I've never really noticed this,' Louisa said, 'but Paris is terribly beautiful.'

'You've never noticed?' Black said. 'How did you miss it?'

'I don't know,' she said. 'I just didn't take it in, I suppose. Always something else to be thinking about.' She took a small sip of her drink. 'Lear, I understand you want advice for your clinic. But why Catherine? Why swimming?' In truth, she was beginning to feel a little uncomfortable. He'd originally come to see her about the clinic, getting her advice, but now he seemed more interested in Catherine and swimming. He'd approached Catherine that morning, Catherine had told Louisa. He'd said something about the English Channel, that she should swim the English Channel.

'Two reasons, both quite selfish,' he said, watching her carefully. 'I mentioned I've had some interest in my newspaper business back in Baltimore. The paper I own, the *Baltimore Sun*, is not the oldest or most distinguished newspaper. I bought into it when it was in trouble ten years ago and found I like being a newspaperman. Our main competition then was the *News*, which was recently bought by Mr Hearst. They have a longer history than us, and they've modernised better. And Mr Hearst is very good at this newspaper business.

'There's a third paper, the *Baltimore Daily Post*. It's a bit like your *Mirror*, lots of pictures, gossip – things, it turns out, readers want. The *Post* is better than us at creating stories people want to read, and the *News* is better at reporting. So we're a bit betwixt and between. All of this is a way of explaining that I do understand why my advisers are urging me to sell. I bought a lemon.' He took a sip of his drink, examined the back of his other hand.

'It's possible I've been a bit slow to realise that the people who want to buy us out are quite serious. I'm under pressure now, you see.'

'I don't see how this is relevant to Catherine.'

'No, I don't imagine you do.' He fiddled with a jar of toothpicks on the table, straightening them. 'It's funny the way things happen. I told you about the Women's Swimming Association. I've been able to support the Association over the years.' He took a cigar from his pocket. 'Do you mind?' She shook her head. He lit up, blew smoke into the air above them. 'And it's become very obvious to me that women's swimming is of interest to readers.'

'Women's swimming,' Louisa said. Pictures of women half naked more like, she didn't say. Is that what had attracted him? 'So your newspaper needs women swimmers?'

'Yes, the blasted *Post* has signed up Lillian Cannon.' Louisa must have looked confused. 'She's a Baltimore native who swam Chesapeake last year. The *Post* is financing her attempt at the English Channel. They got to her before I did. And she has those dogs.'

'Dogs,' Louisa said.

'Yes, Chesapeake Bay Retrievers. Everyone loves them.'

'You think Catherine could beat her?'

'Oh, I know Catherine could beat Lillian Cannon. The Association has another swimmer, a little older than Catherine, Gertrude Ederle. I met Gertrude. She's not what I want.'

'Is she a good swimmer?'

'Yes, but it's more than swimming. Gertrude's New York, which won't go down well in Baltimore. And she's from German stock, which isn't quite what I want either. And I want someone who can communicate.'

'Catherine?'

'Yes. She grew up on an island, learnt to swim from natives, and she's British stock but colonial, which is about perfect. She can talk. If she made good in America, the land where anyone can succeed, wouldn't that be marvellous? She's exactly what I want.'

'Well, you have a whole plan, don't you?' Louisa said, taking another small sip of her martini. It still made her uneasy, she realised. Black had invited them to the party on his yacht. Now he'd paid their way to Paris. He was footing the hotel bill; insisted on it, in fact. Dinner last night and tonight, the accommodation. He was taking them to America, all expenses paid. He was going to contribute to the clinic – they'd come to an agreement. He was going to fund a major upgrade to the Princes Square building. They couldn't do without him now, Louisa realised. If he wanted Catherine to become a competitive swimmer rather than go back to school, would Louisa be in any position to refuse him? Even Catherine was vulnerable to his charm, it seemed. Catherine saw Black as a way to her mother's family. She seemed fascinated by him. He was all she talked about over lunch.

As if he read her thoughts, he said, 'Louisa, I'm not going to push anyone around here. But when I found out who the swimmer I saw was, when I found out that her guardian was you, Dr Louisa Quick, who I'd already intended to visit, I thought something was acting on us here. I am a great believer in serendipity.'

'You said there were two reasons. What's the other one?'

He paused, took a puff of his cigar, blew smoke towards the ceiling. 'I'll tell you another time,' he said. 'You know, when I was Catherine's age, I worked hard. I left school, went into the bank. And then it became a habit, I suppose. I didn't ever get used to not working hard.' Louisa noticed the look on his face, the momentary sadness – it was this she liked in him, this sadness that he wore with such dignity. It was still there when he smiled. It made him more human. Oh, there was the charm, the power of the man, but it was this sadness she could relate to.

She smiled. 'I know what you mean,' she said. 'My

colleagues sometimes ask if I have regrets. They mean not having a husband, not having children. But you see, I don't regret it at all. I have my work. Why would I want children?'

'You have a child now,' he said, narrowing his eyes.

The waiter came with more drinks.

'Yes, I do,' she said after the waiter withdrew. 'And Mrs Black. Is she back in Baltimore?'

He smiled. 'You're thinking of my daughter, of course. Well, there is no Mrs Black. Adeline is the product of an affair I had with a singer here in Paris.' He looked at her squarely. 'Are you shocked?'

Louisa smiled. 'I'm a doctor, Mr Black. It would take more than an unwanted pregnancy to shock me. And Adeline's mother?'

'Died ten years ago,' Black said. 'I sent Adeline to the school. But you are the conundrum, not me. Men don't marry because they don't marry. But women marry. And yet, you never married?'

'No,' she said curtly. 'Do you have siblings other than your sister?'

He shook his head. 'And you, just the two brothers?'

'Yes. My mother lost a child, another girl, after Alexander and before me. She died in my father's arms, apparently.' Inexplicably, Louisa found tears in her eyes, thinking about the sister she never knew taking her last breath, her poor father seeing his child out of life. She breathed in sharply. 'I'm sorry. I don't quite know what's come over me.' His eyes were so soft. 'Anyway, I had two futures to live up to, my sister's and mine. Alexander followed Papa into the business, so he was allowed certain concessions. Harry more or less did as he pleased and nothing he did worried our mother. Were you close to your sister?' He kept switching the conversation back to her, she noticed, and she wanted to know about him, especially as he was now so interested in Catherine.

He nodded but didn't speak, looked out towards the street. 'Do you know, I made a little fun of you before for not noticing the beauty of Paris,' he said finally. 'But when I think about it, I don't believe I've ever noticed it much either.' He smiled. 'I'm not very good at enjoying myself.'

'That's what Nellie, my housekeeper, says about me – that I can't enjoy myself. I enjoy work.'

'Me too,' he said. 'And we could drink to that. But here we are, two lost souls in their sunset years looking for some sort of life.'

Louisa smiled. 'I'm not quite sure I'm ready for sunset yet.' She sipped her drink again. 'And I have a perfectly acceptable life.'

'Well, we could drink to a perfectly acceptable life. You're still worried about Catherine, though.'

Louisa smiled, for this was exactly what she was worried about. Black had a directness she both liked and feared. You never knew where he was going to go next.

'That's good,' he said. 'It's what you should be doing.' He drained his glass and called the waiter to order another. 'You are a good guardian of the child. But I think I understand Catherine better than you realise. I know how it feels to lose your parents at a young age. It knocks you off your feet, the loss of security. I was at school when my father died. They called me back home. I never went back.

209

We didn't have the money.' He frowned. 'I lost my mother not long after, then my sister, and I was on my own.'

'Catherine's not on her own.'

'No,' he said. 'She's not. But it has been difficult for her, and she needs to find her own place. She needs to find her confidence.' He shook his head. 'What do I know? Anyway, Louisa, swimming is what I can help with, and that girl is a swimmer. My friend Eleanor Roosevelt says I'm a suffragist in disguise.' He smiled. 'I'll put you in touch with Charlotte Epstein. You'll like her, and you can be sure that she'll take good care of Catherine. Charlotte's always hosting visiting swimmers. Catherine will be fine.'

Louisa eyed him carefully.

'We're going to have to trust each other if this is going to work, Louisa.'

'I do trust you, Lear,' she said. And she told herself she meant it.

Part Three

Chapter Nineteen

She watched from the upper deck as passengers began to disembark, to be met by family and friends. Many embraced warmly, and tears filled Catherine's eyes. As they'd come into the harbour, she'd looked towards the tall buildings on Manhattan Island like Mr Black had told her to. She'd never seen anything like them, not in London, not in Paris. She saw too the Statue of Liberty, much smaller than she expected, smaller than the buildings, a woman out on her own in the water. It was supposed to represent freedom, but the statue didn't look free to Catherine, anchored there to the rock. The chains at her feet were supposed to be the chains she'd broken. But she looked as if she couldn't get away even if she wanted to. She looked as if she might like to dive in and swim rather than hold a torch for all those Americans but the rock was holding her there.

Catherine wore a long wool coat and a scarf which she pulled up around her neck. She had mitts somewhere but for now just put her hands deep in her coat pockets. It was a different kind of cold from London. A pale sun shone over the water and turned it gold. It was beautiful.

It had taken nearly six months to get here. Ruth Luxton's daughter, May, a violinist in her middle twenties, was coming to New York to attend the Juilliard School. Originally Louisa was to sail with Catherine and May, but then Louisa had decided to defer her own travel for a further month – to make sure the refurbishments at Princes Square were satisfactory – and so Dr Luxton had suggested that Catherine could travel with May, a quietly spoken young woman a lot like Dr Luxton herself. They had a lovely room with a porthole, and for dinner they'd sat most nights at the captain's table because the ship was one of Catherine's uncle's line. Catherine had to wear frocks Louisa had bought for her before she'd left. It was supposed to be an honour, to sit at the captain's table, but Catherine had longed to be free of the confines of the ship and in particular the nightly ritual of dinner. Perhaps that was why she wished Liberty would hoist her skirts and dive in. Perhaps it was Catherine who wanted to be in the water.

May Luxton didn't seem to mind the ship journey. She sat in the cabin and read or went to the engine room where she could practise her violin and no one would be bothered by it. She gave a little performance one night during the trip. Catherine had loved the music. She'd never heard anything like it, she said later. Other than that, May left her alone. For all May knew, Catherine might be off swimming in the ocean every day.

May had disembarked in Newfoundland to visit the Canadian Luxtons before coming down to New York, so Catherine had been alone for the last few days of the journey. She wished she could have stopped in Canada too, to find the Freebodys, her mother's family. She could go across Canada then and see the mountains Sam the pilot had told her about. She wondered would she see Sam in America. Was he still flying Mr Black around?

In the months they'd been organising the trip, Louisa had corresponded with Miss Epstein, the director of the Women's Swimming Association in New York, who would look after Catherine until Louisa arrived. The summer ended and, after an autumn that felt all too brief to Catherine, they were back to winter, London's favourite season. Christmas, New Year, sleet, rain and, finally, Catherine set off in the February. Now it was early March, but spring still seemed a long way off. In all that time, she hadn't heard from anyone in Australia and now, she'd decided, she'd stop writing and pleading with them to reply.

She heard a voice behind her that might have been her mother's but when she looked behind, there was no one there. She always said she never missed her mother, but she missed her suddenly now. When one of the teachers in London had described Catherine as an orphan, she'd been on the verge of correcting the woman. 'That's not true,' she wanted to say. 'I have my father and Florence, and Michael.' But the teacher had been right. Catherine *was* an orphan now, all alone in the world. She had no one. Her father was dead, and Florence and Michael had forgotten her. She had Louisa, but Louisa was hard to fathom, even now.

Catherine had spent her remaining months in London helping out at the clinic. They'd started a little nursery school of sorts in the waiting room. Children accompanying their mothers could stay with Catherine and hear stories or sketch. Ruth Luxton had convinced Louisa to buy some art materials, and they'd designated a corner for them. 'I just love her,' Dr Luxton told Louisa on Catherine's last day. 'But onwards, young woman of the sea,' she said. She hugged Catherine warmly and there were tears in her eyes.

During the summer and autumn, Nellie had gone with Catherine to the Hampstead ladies pond. The English swimmers mostly wore the same kind of suit Catherine had bought, although some wore a more revealing costume, tight to the skin and without a skirt. They swam differently from Catherine too, she noticed, with their heads out of the water, either frog-stroke or a strange sidestroke Catherine had never seen before.

Nellie never took to the water but Catherine became adept as a cold water swimmer. Strangely, now she preferred it; the sting on her skin when she first jumped in, the slow warming up, even the shivering afterwards. And, oddly, the pond reminded her of the island. The water was much colder, of course, but like the island it was an ancient place, a place where many spirits dwelt, as Florence might have said. Catherine wished she could have shown Michael the pond. She wished they could have swum there together.

But now she was travelling to an uncertain future. She was totally unmoored – from her family, her home, from everything familiar. Mr Black was the only person she knew in America. She and Louisa had seen little of him before he'd left London. He and Andrew had gone off flying, to Cairo, then Johannesburg. They'd even attempted Java but they crashed. No one was hurt, but the aeroplane was left behind and then Mr Black had to find another. He called at Wellclose Square, and had Louisa and Catherine to visit at the house he rented in Alderson Street. Catherine liked Mr Black. He was interested in swimming but also in Catherine herself, she thought. She was glad she'd see him again here in America. She'd see Andrew too, she knew, because Mr Black had found a job for him at his newspaper. She was looking forward to that too.

The sun had gone behind a cloud momentarily and the softened light gave the pier before her a gentleness. So here I am, she thought to herself, in America, where my mother's family is from. Perhaps she'd find something of herself here.

Catherine realised she didn't know what she was supposed to do. She hadn't thought of the end of the journey at all. In all the rush to pack and leave, she hadn't asked who would be meeting her. Louisa may have said something, but Catherine had been too excited to take it in properly. Oh, I should have listened, Catherine thought now. I don't even know what to do. She thought then of Louisa saying goodbye at Southampton. Catherine had seen tears in her aunt's eyes, which surprised them both.

'Just remember, dear,' Louisa had said. 'You can do anything.'

'I'm a Quick,' Catherine replied. She found she felt sad too.

'You certainly are,' Louisa said. 'And I'll be right behind you.' Her aunt swallowed then, and tried to smile.

Catherine was just about to go to find a steward to see whether there was any message for her from Mr Black when she saw Andrew, his head well above the crowd, in a navy blue coat with a black hat. She waved madly when she saw him. He held his hat to his chest, waving with his other hand, a grin on his face.

When Mr Black had packed up his London home to return to America, he'd offered Andrew a job. Banking or newspapers? he'd said. Newspapers, for sure, Andrew had replied, he told Catherine afterwards. And so he'd left with Mr Black to start on the *Baltimore Sun* as a reporter.

Catherine was soon down the stairs and along the gangway onto the pier. A minute later, Andrew was with her. 'Mr Black sent me up,' he explained. 'He wanted to come himself but, as usual, he's terribly busy.' She felt a little disappointed. She'd hoped to see Mr Black again. He'd been so very kind to her. But Andrew embraced her warmly. 'You're here. How did we manage this?' He grinned. 'And look at you. You've changed. You're . . . My God, you're beautiful, Catherine.'

He was staring at her. She blushed. 'It's so grand,' she said finally, looking up and along the pier.

'That's the only word for it,' he said, recovering himself. 'New York is the grandest place I've ever been.' He'd changed too, she thought, grown into himself more.

There were windows in the roof of the terminal building and soft light spilt onto their faces. Catherine could still smell the sea but it was mixed now with a smell of fuel and wet wood. She looked around her. Just for a moment, the light above them changed and everything softened. The moment passed, the faces brightened again, and the loud noises resumed. A boat blew its whistle. There were engines and horns sounding constantly from the street outside, and people everywhere shouting to one another. The pier was probably no busier than Southampton, but it seemed busier, more alive. It even smelt busy.

They collected Catherine's suitcase. 'Is this all you've brought?' Andrew said.

Catherine smiled. 'You don't need much for swimming.'

'I brought three trunks,' he said. 'And you need even less for being a reporter; just a pen and notebook, apparently.'

'How is the reporter?' she said.

'Oh, you have no idea what a life I'm leading. I'll tell you about it over lunch.' He looked happy to see her, she thought. But there was something smart looking about him now, a toughness in his manner. Catherine wasn't sure she liked it. It was a little like Mr Black, she thought, but didn't sit well with Andrew. Perhaps it was a way to get by in America.

Catherine soon cleared the Immigration Centre for first-class passengers, and found herself on the street. Andrew took her arm and they walked together happily. The salty smell of the water was soon enhanced by richer smells, a lot like the earth on the island, deep and full of possibility. Andrew hailed a taxi, put a bill into the driver's hand through the window and then opened the door for Catherine. 'I've got better at the tipping business,' he said quietly.

They went to a long narrow cafe that had a row of tables alongside a long counter with stools. 'Baltimore Dairy Lunch.' Andrew pointed to the sign in the window. 'Mr Black's favourite, of course.' He parked her suitcase at the front entrance and took her to a table in the back. He ordered soup and sandwiches for both of them. 'Trust me, it'll be delicious,' he said.

The sandwiches were the most enormous things Catherine had ever seen. The soup was warm and flavoursome, with lots of vegetables. 'I've never had soup for breakfast,' she said.

'Well, where you've come from, it's probably dinnertime, and I'm more in the mood for dinner right at the moment,' he said. 'And anyway, it's eleven-thirty, well and truly lunchtime.'

'There are so many people here,' she said, looking outside at the people hurrying by.

'As it happens, it's all the news at the moment: New York's population is bigger than London's,' he said. 'If you sit here and count, you could probably prove it.'

She laughed. 'Well, they're all out on the streets today,' she said.

'It's like this every time I've been,' he said. 'I have to come up when Mr Black does. I'm still working for him when needed. Last weekend we had another party for Captain Bone, who very kindly brought Mr Black home. Mr Black had a bell made for the *Transylvania*.' Andrew was shaking his head softly. 'I don't know how many nights we sat up working out the most appropriate words to speak at the ceremony to commission the ship's bell. Finally Mr Black just said, "May it ring true," and that was it.' Andrew smiled. 'He's still as ever.'

'So, the reporting?' Catherine said, smiling. 'It makes you smoke those cigarettes?'

Andrew had just lit up. 'It makes you stay up until three in the morning,' he said. 'The demon drink.'

'I thought drink was banned here,' Catherine said. 'That's what Louisa said.'

'Hah. She'd be referring to the Eighteenth Amendment. We call it the Eighteenth Pretendment. Yes, liquor is banned. But there are the speaks, you see, and they are the bane of my existence currently. It's a bar without a front entrance. You have to know the password. But the beer's terrible, and it's laced with ether, which is the real problem. It makes you sick the next morning. And the gin is younger than tomorrow. To be honest, I don't usually surface until eleven or so. I work nights at the *Sun*.'

'Well, you've done well to come for me,' she said. 'And I very much appreciate it.' She smiled. 'But it can't be very good for you if it makes you sick. Don't the police prowl around looking for drink?'

'The police are the first through the door,' Andrew said. 'They're looking for drink, all right – to drink it. Soon as the sarge gets off duty, he's down there with us.'

'And how is your mother coping without you?' Catherine said. Andrew had been worried before he'd left that his mother would miss him.

'There's the problem, of course. Not well at all. She wants me home, keeps sending job notices from *The Times*. Awful, really. I suppose I won't stay here forever.'

Catherine nodded. 'It must be hard to be away from her.'

'Oh, goodness me, no. Not for me. But it's hard on her.' Catherine knew that Andrew's older brother had been killed in the war. 'But you – here you are in New York. And I cannot get over how you've grown up.' The way he said it made her feel heat rising in her throat. 'I'm sorry. I'll stop embarrassing you.' Had she grown up in those months? Perhaps she had. 'At any rate, I've been given strict instructions in relation to you.'

'And what are they?' she said.

'Well, first was your aunt, who told me she was only letting you come to New York unaccompanied because Ada Mackintosh's son would be there to watch over you. And she knew I was a gentleman, she said. Then Mr Black told me that if there are any shenanigans in regard to you, I'm to let him know straightaway. He said I'm to be your big brother and if you get into trouble, it will be on my shoulders.'

'And what exactly are shenanigans?' Catherine said.

'I'm glad you asked, because I asked Mr Black that very question. He said, "Look here, Andy, you know what I'm talking about? You young folk get up to all sorts of caper."' It was a good imitation of Mr Black. 'I told him I'd watch over you.' He became more serious now. 'And I will, Catherine. You can be sure of that.'

She returned his gaze. There was the Andrew she knew, back again for that moment. 'Thank you,' she said.

She looked out to the street again while Andrew went to order more coffee. New York, more than anything, was intense living, she thought. And there were more women, or at least she noticed them more. Their coats were shorter and their heels higher but it was more than that; they were more confident, more alive.

Andrew came back to the table. 'Charlotte Epstein is supposed to come and meet us.' He looked at his watch. 'She must be running late. Well, we'll just have to wait, although I must get the train back to Baltimore by one.'

'I can wait on my own,' she said.

He smiled. 'Having just explained to you the many and varied responsibilities I now have for your general welfare, I'm not going to leave you to your own devices in New York.'

'Andrew!'

Catherine turned to see a tiny bustling woman with dark hair and eyes coming over to their table. She wore a coat to mid calf, tightly belted in the middle. On her feet were bright red boots. She had a toothy grin.

'Here we go,' he said to Catherine as he stood to greet the woman. 'Charlotte, my dear – I have your girl.'

'So you do,' the woman said, holding out her hand to Catherine. 'I'm Charlotte Epstein, hon, but just call me Eppy. Welcome to America!' Her voice was loud but no one seemed to notice.

'Oh, hello,' Catherine said. 'I didn't expect you'd be so . . .' she wanted to say small but thought better of it '. . . young.' She'd assumed that Charlotte would be older, but here she was, a woman in her thirties at most.

'Hah,' Charlotte Epstein said. 'What did you expect, an old troll?' She laughed loudly. 'So, you guys had your lunch?'

'We've just ordered coffee,' Andrew said. 'Sit down, for goodness' sake.' He got up and took a chair from the next table for her. Andrew had written a story about the

Association's swimmers for the newspaper, he said, 'which meant I spent a week in Charlotte's sparkling company.'

She looked at her watch. 'Can't stay. I'm on my own lunch break and I hiked up from the courts.' She sat down anyway and turned to Catherine. 'I work as a court reporter. Okay, I imagine you're keen to get swimming.' She put her hand on Catherine's arm.

'I am,' Catherine said. 'And I saw the harbour coming in.'

'Of course, Catherine nearly dived in to swim to shore,' Andrew said.

Charlotte Epstein laughed again. 'I heard about you.' She waggled a finger at Catherine, but she was smiling. 'The Thames, huh?' She shook her head. 'You don't want to swim in the harbour, my dear. Well, not right at the moment.'

'Why not?'

'Too cold. Now, listen, Andrew is going to take you to my apartment, where you'll be staying. Don't mind the cats. They won't hurt you.'

Catherine nodded.

'And then tomorrow we'll get up together to go to training. How does that sound?' She put a set of keys on the table.

'Wonderful,' Catherine said. 'But where do we swim?'

'Mr Black kindly rents an indoor tank for us. We'll be back in the open water next month, if you're still here.' She smiled warmly. 'I won't confuse you now, but the girls are just dying to meet you, and we'll do a whole lot of lovely things while you're here.'

224

'We must take good care of little Catherine, Charlotte,' Andrew said.

Catherine didn't like him describing her as little Catherine. It made her feel like it was a joke about her. 'I'm hardly little,' she said curtly.

'No, you're not,' Andrew said. 'But we still have to look after you. I've just finished explaining to Catherine that I have instructions from her aunt explaining exactly what my duties are in relation to her care and supervision. Charlotte, be warned. She is quite difficult, apparently.' Catherine didn't like him saying this either. It made her sound badly behaved.

'I'm with Catherine here, Andy,' Charlotte Epstein said. 'She's not little. What a thing to say. And why we're picking on little people is beyond me. Catherine, I must go. And I'm off to New Jersey straight after work for a swim meet. I thought of taking you but decided it would be better to wait for the training session in the morning. I left a snack in the icebox and the guest bed is made up.'

'Thank you so much,' Catherine said.

'Thank *you*, honey. We're all looking forward to having you at training tomorrow. I'll wake you at five.'

'Well, what do you think of your new mistress?' Andrew said after Charlotte left.

'She's lovely,' Catherine said. 'And not grumpy like Louisa.' He laughed but Catherine felt bad immediately she said it. 'I didn't mean that,' she said. 'Louisa isn't grumpy. She's just worried about me. And I've certainly given her plenty to worry about.'

* * *

Charlotte Epstein's apartment was on the third floor of a building on West Fourteenth Street that, from the outside at least, reminded Catherine of the apartment buildings she'd seen in London, plain brick with few adornments and pull-up windows onto the street. From the cafe, Andrew had taken her in a taxi and Catherine couldn't work out the direction with all the high buildings and turns. They were still near the river, she was sure. Andrew said they were at the market end of Chelsea, where he'd been once with Mr Black. He took her suitcase up the three flights of stairs. They left it outside Charlotte's door and Catherine went back down to the street with him. They said goodbye and then he disappeared into a sea of heads, his own poking up every now and then until he disappeared for good. Well, she thought, standing there on the steps, here I am.

Catherine went back upstairs and let herself in. The front door of the apartment led into a small vestibule that opened into the living room. It was cold inside, although not as cold as the street. There was no fireplace, so Catherine kept her coat on. It was getting late now and she could feel the cold descend for the evening.

Though the apartment was smaller than Louisa's house, it was sparsely furnished, so it felt quite spacious. There was a plain rug on the parquet floor in the entry, soft electric lights, a sitting room with a couch and two comfy chairs. The cats were both black, one enormous, one not, and in the kitchen Charlotte had left salted biscuits, bread, something called nut butter and cake. In the icebox was a salad.

The sitting room overlooked a building site and beyond, Catherine was sure, were the docks and the river. She opened the window and smelt the air. It wasn't clean but it was interesting, smoke from engine exhaust, and underneath that the salt and mud of the river. The smell of salt water was so familiar it made Catherine ache for home.

It was a year now since she'd left the island. It seemed so very far away. Michael had been angry about her leaving. He'd told her she should stay, that she owed it to Florence to stay. *You're my sister*, he'd said in the last letter she'd had from him, but then he'd forgotten her altogether. And Mr Black, who'd wanted her to come to America, who was her only link to her real family, hadn't even come to meet her today. Catherine found herself feeling very alone. She took in the smell of the sea, the smell that reminded her of home.

Chapter Twenty

It was still dark when she heard Charlotte Epstein in the kitchen. She got up, dressed quickly and went out, stopping in the bathroom to splash water on her face. The apartment looked different. Catherine wondered if that was because she wasn't as tired. Or perhaps it only came to life when its owner was in residence. Charlotte was small but she took up space. Her face lit up when she saw Catherine. 'Aren't you good to get up without being called? My mother will love you. I've been instructed to bring you over there for dinner tomorrow night. Did you sleep well?'

'Oh, yes,' Catherine said. 'Very soundly.' She felt shy in her pyjamas.

'I came and looked in on you about ten and you were fast off. That's good. But you didn't have your dinner. Have some oatmeal now and then we'll head off to the pool.'

Catherine sat at the little table in the kitchen, adorned with a red-checked cloth and salt and pepper shakers shaped like cats.

'You like it here?'

'Oh, yes,' Catherine said. 'Thank you, it's lovely.'

'My father liked that it's not far from the courts. My mother liked that it was three floors up.' Charlotte smiled. 'But I like that if you look around the corner you can see Lady Liberty. Now, I'll have to go to work after swimming but one of the girls will help you find your way back here. You can stop at the markets if you like. I'll show you where they are on the way. Do you need some money?'

'My aunt went to the bank to get American money for me before I left.'

'Good. We can buy you a subway ticket and you can get anything else you might need at the markets later. Don't worry too much, though. Mr Black has given us more than enough to accommodate you, so don't be at all concerned about any of that. He's very excited about you coming.'

After breakfast, Catherine dressed and packed a bag – the swimming suit she'd bought in London, the cap, and a towel. Charlotte was wearing a long skirt and blouse, with a woollen hat over her hair. She had an enormous satchel over her shoulder. She put on mittens at the door to the apartment building, and made Catherine do the same.

The grass crunched under their feet as they walked across a small park. Catherine was glad then that they wouldn't be swimming in the harbour after all. It should be frozen over, she thought. When she breathed in, the air hurt her lungs. 'Chilly,' was all Charlotte said. She'd pulled her scarf up over her mouth.

Morning seemed forever away but the city was already waking up, cleaners in the shops and factories, cafes preparing the day's meals, bakers about to go home, boys with milk or newspapers to deliver. They went down into the subway, Charlotte navigating the maze of dimly lit corridors and stairs effortlessly.

They caught a train that came out of a tunnel and then crossed a bridge – you could just make out the glint of the water and ferry lights beneath them. 'My grandfather danced across this bridge the day it opened,' Charlotte told her.

They alighted from the train on the far side of the bridge. It was quieter here. Catherine could hear the heels of Charlotte's boots click on the sidewalk. 'Where are we?' Catherine said.

'Brooklyn,' Charlotte said. 'The pool's on the next corner.' They took another right turn down a smaller street.

'You need to understand that Mr Black is our patron,' Charlotte had said on the train, 'and I respect him very much. But we take everyone here, Catherine, good swimmers or poor, so you don't have to worry about being the best.' She nodded as if to herself. 'Frankly, I don't care if you can hardly swim at all. You can come to the WSA. You won't be the first swimmer Mr Black has brought to us. And while we want to encourage the champions, we also want everyone to have an opportunity to swim. Anyway, you swam the Thames. Mr Handley says you must be able to do something in the water.' Catherine had no idea who Mr Handley was.

As they turned the next corner, Catherine saw a dozen young women in long coats with bags slung over their shoulders, waiting outside a three-storey building. They were lit softly by an overhead streetlamp. As she approached, Charlotte called out to them, 'Hey, gals. You are the best girls in the world. What are you?'

'The best girls in the world,' they said in a chorus and then broke into laughter. Catherine smiled along with them, although she wasn't sure why.

When they reached the group, Charlotte said, 'Girls, this is Catherine, the one I told you about. She's come all the way from London to swim with the Women's Swimming Association. Apparently, she's going to be our secret weapon.'

'What about me?' This was from a small, slim girl with square shoulders, in a long pair of pants and jumper, blonde hair cut short, woollen boots.

'Well, you're no secret weapon, Aileen. You're more like the cavalry.'

The girl, who was more than a head shorter than Catherine, laughed. 'You tell my father I'm the cavalry, Eppy. He thinks I'm wasting my time.'

'Your father needs to come and see me, Aileen. I told you that.'

Charlotte Epstein rummaged in her bag for her keys, then opened the front door to the building. It was warmer inside the foyer. There was a sign on the wall that said hotel touraine. There were lounge chairs and lamps on one side and a front desk, unattended now.

'I'm Aileen Ryan,' the small girl said to Catherine, and smiled. 'Swimmer or diver?'

'I beg your pardon?' Catherine said.

'Are you a diver, or just a swimmer?' Aileen said more slowly.

231

'What do you mean, "just a swimmer", Aileen?' Charlotte said. 'Swimming is plenty good.'

'I'm a swimmer, I think,' Catherine said. 'I don't even know what diving is.'

Aileen smiled. 'You know, from a board into a tank.' She gestured with her hand.

'What's a tank?' Catherine said.

'Where do you swim then?' Aileen said.

'The sea,' Catherine said.

'You're from London?'

'Yes, but before that, Australia. I lived on an island. In London, I didn't swim very much.'

They'd gone through the lobby and were walking along a corridor.

'We swim in the sea too,' Aileen said. 'Just not at the moment.'

'On the island, you swim year round,' Catherine said.

'Keep moving, girls,' Charlotte said. 'Mr Handley doesn't like you to run late, and you'll all catch cold and your parents will blame me.'

They followed Charlotte down the narrow corridor to a stairwell. They went down two flights and emerged into a hot, low-ceilinged room with a giant bath along its length.

Catherine stared at it. 'What's that smell?' she asked Aileen. It was something between rotting oranges and kelp.

'Chlorine,' Aileen said. 'It's what they use to keep the tank clean.'

'Is the water warm?' Catherine said.

'Oh, yeah.' Aileen nodded. 'Hey, girls,' she said to the

others. 'Catherine is all the way from Australia and she's never swum in a tank.'

Two girls came over to them. 'I'm Meg Ederle,' one said, 'and this is my sister Trudy.' Trudy nodded. 'She don't hear so good,' Meg said. 'You never swum in a tank?'

Catherine shook her head. She was nervous, she realised. She was thinking of Darcy. But these girls were nothing like Darcy.

'Trudy don't like the tank either,' Meg Ederle said.

Trudy smiled, a lovely, open smile, Catherine thought. This was Gertrude Ederle, Catherine realised, the nineteen-year-old who planned to swim the English Channel.

Their accents were all the same and all different. Meg Ederle sounded almost like an East Ender, but with a twang and something else. German, Catherine learnt later; Meg and Trudy's father, who often came to training, was German. There were five girls in the family, and three of them were swimmers.

Aileen's accent was more subtle, only apparent on certain words. 'Trudy's the second youngest in our team,' Aileen said as she led Catherine to the change room. 'How old are you?'

'Fifteen,' Catherine said. 'Sixteen this year.'

'Well, you're the new youngest then – of the advanced swimmers, I mean. There's lots of younger ones in the junior team. Trudy's nineteen, I'm eighteen.' The girls were all stripping to put their suits on. They wore the new style, woollen bathers cut off at thigh level with straps over their shoulders, rather than sleeves. Catherine's suit was more modest.

'Eppy doesn't swim?' Catherine said, noticing that she hadn't joined them in the change room.

'Not competition. She started the WSA. She's famous.'

'We got to be the best,' another girl said.

'The very best,' still another said.

'My aunt thinks swimming might be a waste of time,' Catherine said. 'I hope she meets Eppy.'

'My father hates swimming too. Don't worry about it,' Aileen said.

'And do you know Mr Black?' Catherine said.

Aileen shook her head. 'Do you live with your aunt?' she asked.

'In London, yes.'

'Where are your parents?'

'My mother died when I was little, and my father last year,' Catherine said.

'You're an orphan, like Anne.'

'Anne?'

'In *Anne of Green Gables*, the book. You haven't read it?'

Catherine shook her head.

'Her parents have died and she's in an orphanage and these people adopt her. They'd meant to adopt a boy so he could help on the farm, but they keep her, even though she's a lot of trouble, and then she goes to school and meets her best friend. She has red hair like yours, only she hates it. Your hair is beautiful.'

Catherine's hair was shoulder-length now. 'Well, like Anne of Green Gables, I don't exactly like it,' she said. 'It makes me stand out in a crowd. And at school . . .' She didn't finish the sentence. She hadn't met a best friend. 'I think I might be about as much trouble for my aunt as Anne was.'

'Nah, you're not trouble,' Aileen Ryan said. 'I have a special sense for such matters.'

When they went back outside, Charlotte Epstein was standing next to a compact man in shirtsleeves and a vest, with thinning silver hair and a neatly trimmed silver moustache.

'Here she is,' Charlotte said, smiling at Catherine. 'Catherine, this is our esteemed coach, Mr Louis de Breda Handley. Mr Handley, may I introduce you to our visiting swimmer, Catherine Quick.'

The man greeted Catherine formally, bowing and taking her hand. 'You will wait here,' he said, 'while I get the other swimmers started on their routines. And then we'll get properly acquainted. Is that all right?' Catherine nodded.

She watched as he went and spoke with each of the swimmers before they started. They swam in four rows, Catherine noticed, different strokes, two on their backs, a few doing frog kicks, four along one wall kicking their legs, and another two, Aileen and Trudy, swimming a crawl.

After a few minutes more, the coach returned.

Standing there in her suit, Catherine felt self-conscious as Mr Handley looked her up and down.

'You need some muscle to swim,' he said. 'May I?' He brought her hands forward. 'Flex.'

She flexed her arms.

'Here,' he said, grabbing her upper arm. 'You need some muscle. But let's get you swimming. The muscle will come.'

He led her over to the tank. They had a section to themselves, roped off from the others.

The coach gestured to the water, and Catherine jumped in. It was like getting into a warm bath. She began swimming. He walked along the pool deck beside her. She could see his pant legs each time she turned to breathe.

She finished a length and stopped.

The coach was frowning. 'Well, you have a style I've never seen,' he said, shaking his head. 'Watch Aileen there.' Catherine looked across towards the other swimmers. 'Do you see that we kick six beats to the stroke and bring our arms up high?'

She nodded, although she didn't know what he meant about the kick. 'You only do two beats to the stroke, or perhaps four. Did you know that?' He used his fingers like kicking legs. 'You'll be faster when you learn to do six, like this –' kicking his fingers faster '– and when you can get your arms higher.' He made windmills with his arms.

For the rest of the session, Catherine had to kick her legs without using her arms. She didn't enjoy it at all, the smelly water, the small space, the other swimmers, and her kicking seemed to get her nowhere. It was nothing like swimming at all. Before she knew it the session was finished, and Charlotte and Mr Handley called her over.

'Well, you've had a great first day,' Charlotte said, looking at the coach. 'But you've learnt some bad habits that you'll have to break, I'm afraid.'

'Will we swim in the sea soon?' Catherine asked.

Charlotte smiled. 'We've entered the Battery to Sandy Hook in May. We train in the harbour beforehand.' She looked at Mr Handley. 'Catherine, for open water we only take the fastest swimmers. And your aunt hasn't said how long you'll be with us yet.'

'Yes, one step at a time,' Mr Handley said. 'Where did you learn your crawl?'

'Pardon?' Catherine said.

'You swim a crawl, same as my girls, but it's different.'

'On the island,' Catherine said.

'Like I said, she's from Australia, Lou,' Charlotte said. 'She swam there, same as Annette Kellerman.'

'Annette never swam the way this one swims,' Mr Handley said. 'It's interesting. You don't get as much chance with your legs when you only kick two beats for each arm stroke, although your legs are strong, and I can see it gives you a very good balance position in the water. You get a lot of mileage from slow kicks. It's those feet.' He looked down and then laughed at his little joke. Catherine had always had big feet.

She went to the change room to get out of her swimming suit.

Aileen Ryan had waited for her. 'Are you staying with Eppy?' she said.

Catherine nodded. 'Just until my aunt arrives,' she said.

Catherine was hoping she'd remember how to get back to Charlotte Epstein's apartment. She had a piece of paper with directions to the train. She took it out now.

'Oh, don't worry,' Aileen said. 'I'll go with you. I don't need to be at school until ten today and Eppy asked if I'd mind. I'd love to take you.'

'Oh, would you?' Catherine said. 'I'm quite bamboozled

here. The buildings make it hard to work out where I am.'
They came back out past the tank. 'It's so small.'

'It's not much fun, is it?' Aileen said. 'Still, when we were
in Paris we swam in the river and it was really disgusting.
And in Antwerp, it was so cold they had to put me in a
warming room every time I dived.'

'Were you at the Olympics?'

'Yep. At Antwerp, I was the youngest. I got silver in
the diving. We nearly weren't allowed to compete because
they didn't want women. And then in Paris, we didn't have
anywhere to train. But don't worry too much about the
tank. Once summer comes, you'll be sick of the water.'

'What's the Battery to Sandy Hook?' Catherine said.

'We swim from Manhattan, near Eppy's place, to Sandy
Hook Beach. The WSA is organising it. We're the favourites,
me and Trudy – if she's in the mood. She did it last year and
beat everyone. I didn't finish because I hurt my shoulder.
And, of course, Helen Wainwright, who is our nemesis,
because sometimes she's faster than me. She's away at the
moment, thankfully. But they're taking three swimmers to
the Channel, so it will be the three of us – me, Trudy and
Helen. Are you swimming Sandy Hook?'

'Apparently not. I don't kick correctly.'

'Ah, don't worry. Mr Handley will get used to you. He
really is a dear – such a gentleman, as my mother would
say. But he never likes to let anyone do anything except
his way. He loves the youngest swimmers best because
they haven't learnt any bad habits, he says. So Trudy is his
total favourite because he had years with her to teach her
his way.'

'I can't swim the way he says, kicking so much. It feels wrong.'

'Don't do it. He'll stop noticing soon. That's what happened with me. He gave up eventually. Then you can do what you like. He played water polo, so he's used to the team all doing the same thing. Swimming isn't really a team thing like water polo. Hey, do you want to come to our beach place at the weekend? We might even be able to dip in the water.'

'Oh, that would be so wonderful,' Catherine said.

'Cold, okay? It's going to be cold.'

'I don't care. I really don't.' It didn't matter if she had to swim through icebergs; anything would be better than that stupid tank.

Chapter Twenty-One

Aileen's mother picked Catherine up from Charlotte's apartment block after Aileen finished school at noon that Friday. Catherine had spent the remaining days of that first week travelling to and from the tank twice each day. She'd gone on the Wednesday to the YMCA pool to swim and watch the divers. She'd met Charlotte's family that night. Charlotte's mother was an older version of Charlotte, and her father kept calling Catherine Katrina. They told her she mustn't ever be lonely in New York. She could always pop in to see any of the Epsteins who seemed to live at regular intervals all over Manhattan. They gave her a map showing where all their homes were. Never too far away, Mrs Epstein said. They were very kind.

Catherine and Aileen sat in the back seat as they drove out of the city to Long Island. Late in the afternoon, they pulled up a long drive lined by pine trees to a white weatherboard house with green shutters and a slate roof.

In the soft light it looked magical, the expanse of the bay behind lit up by the afternoon sun.

'You girls must be positively starving,' Aileen's mother said. 'I meant to pack some snacks but clean forgot. Let's hope there are cookies left over from last weekend!' She laughed. Mrs Ryan had the most marvellous laugh. Mr Ryan, who Catherine met later that first night, was quiet and very serious. He spent most of the weekend behind a newspaper. But Aileen's mother – 'Do call me Dotty, Catherine' – was as much fun as Aileen herself, and Catherine loved her immediately.

'She's a daughter of the American Revolution,' Aileen said at dinner that first night, as if it explained why her mother went into fits of giggles at her own jokes.

Aileen's father looked up over his newspaper. 'She really is,' he said.

On that first afternoon, the two girls helped to unpack the car and went into the large kitchen at the back of the house. It had doors out onto a terrace that overlooked the water. They ate a box of cookies and then Aileen asked if they could go down to the beach.

'Daddy will be up at six for dinner and it's already late,' Mrs Ryan said. 'Why don't you take Catherine for a walk along the point and dip your toes in? And tomorrow you can have the whole day on the beach.'

Aileen's mother had been a runner, Aileen said on their walk, but she'd been stopped by the Amateur Athletics Association. They wouldn't let women run competitively. Or swim, in those days, Aileen added. When Eppy started the WSA, she said, women were not allowed to swim in competitions at all.

Mrs Ryan was all for Aileen's diving, but Aileen's father thought it was nonsense.

'My father is a lawyer, and his father was a lawyer, and so I am to be a lawyer,' Aileen said. 'And if I am to be a lawyer, I must apply myself to my lessons.' She sighed. 'I love diving more than I've ever loved anything. Don't you love swimming that way?'

'I never had to imagine not swimming until I left Australia,' Catherine said. 'It's always been part of my life. I do love it, yes.' For most of the girls she'd met so far at the WSA, Catherine had realised, swimming was a sport, something they'd learnt to do in order to compete. For Catherine, swimming was part of who she was. The only other swimmer who seemed to experience the water this way, she thought, was Trudy, who got into the tank every morning and ploughed up and back, up and back, at speed.

The next morning, Catherine and Aileen ate a hearty breakfast of ham and eggs and fresh bread baked by Mrs Ryan, then set off to explore. They found a cave Aileen had never seen before in the rocks at the point and ate their sandwiches while looking out to the water.

'Eppy says they're putting off deciding about the Channel swim until after Sandy Hook,' Aileen said. 'Trudy might make another try on her own.' Catherine knew the story now. Trudy Ederle had very nearly swum the English Channel the year before, but nine hours into the swim her coach had pulled her from the water. He said she was drowning, and the swimmer who was pacing her agreed. But Trudy herself was furious, the newspaper report said. She told the reporters the coach had fed her something during

242

the swim that had made her groggy. She said there was nothing wrong with her and she could swim the Channel any day of the week. She would be back, she said, her father and sister on either side of her. Trudy's father also came to training, Catherine discovered. He yelled at the girls to swim harder. It made the tank even more unpleasant.

Mrs Ryan said the newspapers had been unthinkably poor in their treatment of Trudy, who was 'just a girl really. Swimming gets people worked up,' she said. 'There were writers even here in America who said it was unwomanly to swim the Channel. They put Trudy in with the flappers. For goodness' sake, she's the butcher on Amsterdam Avenue's daughter. She's no flapper.'

Andrew had been up on the train to see Catherine during the week. They'd gone back to the Baltimore Dairy Lunch for sandwiches. She'd asked him about Trudy Ederle's swim. Trudy's outburst had won her no friends in England, Andrew said, where they called her a sore loser.

Andrew said Catherine should be the one to swim the Channel. 'Yes,' he said. 'Mr Black says you're a champion, and Mr Black knows these things. You could beat the Americans, the Germans and win the Channel for England, our England.'

'It's not my England,' Catherine had said.

'Oh, yes it is,' he said. 'If you win, we'll say you're English. Of course we will.'

Aileen said now that Trudy wasn't aloof. 'She's just in her own world. I don't think she can hear people very well, so she does her own thing.'

A group of dolphins swam past out in the sea.

'Porpoises,' Aileen said, when Catherine pointed them out. They watched them playing in the waves while they shared the last of the soda with cheese crackers.

'Have you ever had a beau?' Aileen asked suddenly.

'What's a beau?' Catherine said.

'A boyfriend, silly.'

'No,' Catherine said. She thought of Michael. 'Well, maybe.'

'Maybe what?' Aileen said.

'Well, not so much a boyfriend, more like a brother.'

'Blech,' Aileen said. 'You can't kiss your brother. Did you kiss?'

Catherine shook her head no. 'There's also another fellow,' she said. 'I knew him in London. He's here now, or in Baltimore. But I'm not sure he's a beau.' Catherine thought about Andrew. She was fond of him, and was glad he was coming to see her. It was someone from home, or from London anyway. When she'd first met him, he'd been so sweet, if a little accident prone. She'd liked him straightaway, and his slight awkwardness had been part of his charm for her. Now, though, he'd changed. He was a reporter for Mr Black's newspaper, smoking those cigarettes and drinking the beer. He'd hardened towards life, she thought, although she wondered if it was just an act. Every now and then his old sweet self would poke through. She wasn't sure of his feelings for her, and she wasn't sure of her own feelings. How would she know? she thought. 'What about you?' she said to Aileen. 'Do you have a beau?'

'Well, there's this boy who lives a few streets away. I'll take you past his house. He's twenty-three and he works at the club at the end of the beach. I don't know if I'll be able to go on without him.' Aileen held her palm to her forehead in mock upset. 'He's *so* handsome,' she said, 'with the blondest hair that flops onto his large forehead – lots of brains, I think – and muscles on his muscles. He swims in the afternoons, so let's hang around all day, just in case.' Her eyes widened. 'Daddy hates him, of course, without even knowing him. I don't dare tell Daddy, actually, for fear he'll go round there with a gun.

'Oh, I'm so glad you're here, Catherine,' she said. 'My best friend, Marlene, left last term, and I've been lonely. But you're just like Marlene – a real friend.'

The next morning, they got up early again and headed for the beach. The day was fine and warm, and they decided to swim out to a shipwreck a mile from shore. The water was freezing, colder than the ponds at Hampstead, but so long as Catherine kept swimming hard, she could manage. The bow of the old ship jutted up out of the water, and the rusted keel was visible, covered now in barnacles. Catherine looked around her. This was what she had missed.

'Oh, Aileen, thank you for bringing me here. What a wonderful place.'

'Holy moley,' Aileen said. 'I couldn't keep up with you. Boy, you can swim!'

They didn't tread water for long, as they started to feel the cold, so they swam back to shore and dressed quickly, and ran along the sand to warm up in the sun.

They never did see Aileen's 'beau' that day, but they had enormous fun looking for him. The rest of the weekend was full of good food and fun, none of the speaking properly and dressing properly and acting appropriately that Catherine had hated at school in London. The time she spent with the Ryans, on that weekend and a number that followed, would remain with her. It wasn't like being with Florence on the island, but it wasn't like being with Louisa and Nellie either. It was just normal, Catherine thought later. She could have settled in and become part of the Ryan family quite easily. It gave her a notion she'd never had before: that she might be able to live somewhere other than the island and it would be all right.

The truth was that Catherine was starting to forget the island. She'd try to remember the smells, but it was difficult. You never smelt coconut in London or New York. It was the strongest memory she had, but she couldn't quite recall it. It was a hot smell, she knew, a wholesome smell that made her think of goodness.

On her last afternoon on Long Island, Catherine watched the sun set with Aileen. They held hands. I could be happy, she thought. I could be happy with these people, with swimming in New York. No one was more surprised to discover she felt this way than Catherine herself.

She fell into an easy routine of swimming morning and evening and spending her days exploring New York. She liked the library on Fifth Avenue, where she could stay all day if she wanted and read newspapers. Outside the library was an ice cream vendor. The worst of the cold weather was over and there were tiny buds on all the trees. Sometimes she'd get one of those ice creams – vanilla or chocolate –

and go and sit in the park and eat it while she watched the people go by. Soon Louisa would come. She'd put off her trip twice now, but she'd wired Catherine that she was finally getting away. When Louisa came, Catherine would leave Charlotte Epstein's apartment and she and her aunt would move into a hotel together. Louisa's last telegram was typical Louisa. MAD HERE STOP SAIL 26TH STOP. That was all. LOVE or even REGARDS probably wouldn't have cost any more, Andrew observed when he saw the telegram. Catherine couldn't imagine Louisa using those words.

All the same, Catherine found that she was looking forward to seeing her aunt again. She was glad to be swimming, she really was, but the tank wasn't what she'd expected. It was so small, like trying to swim in Louisa's bathtub. Catherine would hardly start out before she'd have to turn around. And Mr Handley still said she wasn't swimming properly. The American girls kicked more frequently, while Catherine kicked in rhythm with her arms. She tried hard to do as he said, but it didn't feel normal, and then she would lose speed and he'd tell her to swing her arms higher. She only had one way she could go forward, she told him, and that was the way she was going. He smiled. 'That's good,' he said. 'One way forward.'

Charlotte had been lovely, and Charlotte's and Aileen's families had made sure Catherine felt welcome. She also saw Andrew every week. He came up on the train. Mr Black didn't come, and Catherine found she was disappointed. She told Andrew she'd hoped Mr Black might help her meet her American family but Andrew said he'd hardly seen Mr Black either. There was some trouble with a shipping company he was involved in. Andrew didn't know the details.

Aileen came with Catherine to meet with Andrew one day. After he'd gone back on the train, Aileen said Catherine definitely had herself a beau. As he'd been leaving, he'd shaken hands with Aileen to say goodbye and then he'd leant in to embrace Catherine. But instead of kissing her cheek, his lips brushed hers. He pulled back immediately and apologised, leaving them quickly.

'He's a dish,' Aileen said. 'And he speaks like a prince. Oh, oh, oh,' she said. 'I love him even if you don't.'

Catherine just laughed. 'Oh, Aileen, Andrew's like a big brother. He's not a beau.' But afterwards, she wondered too what his feelings were, what her own feelings were. It was confusing.

Catherine had come to know Charlotte Epstein better. Her experience of court cases trained her well for the many battles she'd fought to get the Women's Swimming Association up and running. Like Louisa, Charlotte was always doing something. She came to swimming training at six o'clock every morning and then left the girls at eight to go to work. She came back in the evenings for training and then went home to work some more.

The girls all wore WSA suits to training. They were more revealing than the suit Catherine wore in England, with straps over the shoulders and cut off higher at the thigh, Catherine told Louisa in a letter. *You will hate them*, she wrote. *They don't even have a skirt!* They were more like the suits the men wore, Catherine thought, more like what she herself had worn at home. Charlotte said if they all wore them to meets, there would be no problem. The girls were used to one another in the new costumes, but some worried they'd be in trouble once they were swimming competitively again on the beaches, which still imposed strict dress codes, policed by beach officers.

'If we get arrested, we'll all get arrested,' Aileen said bravely.

Catherine had laughed. 'They can't arrest me. I'm not even an American.'

'You think that will stop the police?' Aileen said. 'Hah! They arrested Ethelda Bleibtrey on Manhattan Beach, and all she did was take off her stockings. They'll deport you back to Australia, or wherever they like. You might have to become Canadian.' They'd arrested Annette Kellerman too, for wearing a suit just like the WSA suits, but that was before the war, Aileen said.

Charlotte Epstein, who had been listening to them talking, smiled. 'The charge was indecent exposure, if you can believe it. Miss Kellerman gave a great speech in the court about what was needed in order to swim, how you could be pulled under by all those clothes and drown. She said they expected women to go around looking like washing lines.'

Aileen took a bite of the apple she'd brought with her to training, and then offered Catherine some. She shook her head.

'The judge was livid at the beach police,' Charlotte said. 'He threw the case out. They'd never arrest you now, thanks to what Annette Kellerman did.'

* * *

249

One morning in her fourth week, Mr Handley asked Catherine to remain after training. Charlotte hadn't gone to work yet, which was unusual, and the two took her into the small office beside the pool. Mr Handley took the chair beside the desk and Charlotte sat behind it, gesturing for Catherine to take the chair that faced her.

'Catherine, as you know, the WSA has decided to send three swimmers to attempt the Channel this year.'

Catherine nodded.

'And,' Charlotte continued seriously, 'we have to consider a number of factors – not just ability, but also seniority and likelihood of success.'

Mr Handley was silent, though Catherine was aware of him watching her intently.

'We've decided to use the Sandy Hook swim to confirm the decision.'

'Yes,' Catherine said eagerly, thinking they must have decided to let her participate in the first ocean swim.

'But we don't think you should be in the Sandy Hook team.'

Catherine stared at Charlotte. She heard the words, but her brain just wasn't making sense of them. 'I beg your pardon?' she said.

'You're not ready, Catherine,' Mr Handley said. 'You need to improve your style and, so far, you haven't made as much progress as I'd like. In my opinion, as the coach, it would be too risky to allow you to take part in an open-water swim.'

'Risky?' Catherine said. Were they worried about sharks, crocodiles? Where was the risk?

250

'Well, we can only do so much to keep our swimmers safe in the water,' Charlotte said. 'So, after taking advice from Mr Handley, the board has decided that you shouldn't swim with the team.'

Catherine was about to speak, to protest that there would be no risk, when she realised what they meant. They were saying she wasn't a good enough swimmer. 'Oh, of course. Oh. I thought . . . I . . . of course. I'm sorry. That's great news. I mean, that you're sending swimmers to the Channel . . .'

Charlotte's face softened. 'There will be other years, other attempts. And you're still so young.' She put her hand on Catherine's and patted it lightly. 'We had enormous trouble in Paris with Helen and Aileen, and I don't want to go through that ever again.'

Catherine wanted to pull her hand away from Charlotte's and tell them to leave her alone. Instead, she sat there with a stupid grin on her face, trying to pretend that she understood, that none of it mattered.

Mr Handley stood up to leave. He nodded to Catherine then looked at Charlotte, shook his head.

Charlotte sighed. 'Catherine, I have many things to balance, as you can well imagine. You are a promising swimmer, and Coach sees that. And you are willing, if not yet able, to master the stroke . . . But as I say, I have competing priorities. I have to do what's best for the WSA, what gives us the most chance of a win . . .'

But Catherine wasn't listening. All she was aware of was that she'd failed. She'd been expelled from school because of swimming – and now she'd failed at that. Her aunt had only gone along with the whole idea of her swimming because Mr Black said she would be a champion. She wasn't a champion. She wasn't even on the team. She thought she'd found a place here in New York, but it was no place for her.

'It's because you're not American,' Aileen said later when Catherine told her. 'Imagine if we took a Brit over there and they did the Channel first. We have to have an American.'

'I thought they took all swimmers. Anyway, I'm not a Brit.'

'No, you're not. And yes, they do take anyone, but not for this. This is the most important thing ever. This is the English Channel. I don't think they're scared you'll lose. I think they're scared you'll win. I've seen you swim. And I told Eppy; I told her you could beat everyone.'

Catherine didn't believe Aileen. She didn't even think Aileen believed Aileen. But it was awfully sweet of her to say it.

Chapter Twenty-Two

It was late. Louisa was sitting at the table in the dining room. She'd been held up at Harley Street that afternoon, finalising details of the transfer of her patients to the other doctors, and then she'd gone back to the clinic to finish up there. She had papers all over now, things to be handed on or finished before she left the next day. Nellie had gone to bed. The Scotties were on the floor. She should stoke the fire but she'd go to bed herself soon.

On the table in front of her was the pile of letters she'd collected. And today, Nellie had handed her two more, one addressed to Louisa herself. Nellie had asked Louisa was she planning to take Catherine's letters to America and give them to the girl. Was she planning to post Catherine's letters to Australia now?

'Probably,' Louisa had said.

'You have to,' Nellie had said. 'You can't do this, Louisa. You can't keep them from her. You said weeks. It's been months.'

Louisa had let the time slip by. She should have done

something about the letters before Catherine left for America but she hadn't. She'd even taken them out the night before Catherine embarked, but found her courage failed her. How could she give her these letters? How could she say she hadn't sent Catherine's on? Catherine would never forgive her, and the truth was, she'd forgotten Florence and Michael now. She'd been so excited about the trip. She'd been busy at the clinic. She'd been positively bright. It was best now, Louisa thought, to let it go.

Except for Nellie.

'Those people – I met them,' Louisa had said to Nellie. 'They may mean well, Nellie. But they are not Catherine's future. They are her past. Her future is here with us. Surely you, of anyone, can see that.'

'What do you mean me, of anyone?'

'You lost your family, Nellie, and I know you've settled here with me. I know you'll go on to do something great with your life. And while you would never have wanted to lose the baby, your life now is so much more.'

'What baby?' Nellie said.

'Sorry?'

'What baby are you talking about?'

Had Louisa mentioned a baby? Perhaps she had. 'I meant your brother – the baby of the family,' she said.

'I swear to God, Louisa, I do appreciate all you've done for me. I do. I feel blessed that you saw me and decided to help. But I would give it all up to have just one day with my family. I would give it all up in a minute. So, Louisa, you need to think about what you're doing to that girl. And that's all I'll say on the matter.'

'Well, it just upsets her to hear from them,' Louisa said, feeling heat rise in her neck. 'Why do that? She's not going back there. She needs a chance to start a new life.'

Catherine had found a place for herself in the clinic before she'd left for America, and Louisa was sure they could get her back to school after this trip. She could finish her formal schooling and go on to university. She might even become a doctor, Louisa had thought, and wouldn't that be marvellous? Louisa didn't want to tell her the truth now.

The swimming still worried Louisa. Black seemed to think Catherine had the makings of a champion. And Louisa could tell that being in New York with other swimmers was doing Catherine a world of good. She'd made a friend, a young diver whose family had been terribly kind. Charlotte Epstein seemed a very good role model for a female swimmer, and Black had made sure Andrew visited every week to look out for Catherine. Her letters to Louisa were bright and full of interest. Swimming might build Catherine's confidence just as Black had suggested. He hadn't visited her yet, Louisa knew, ameliorating any concern Louisa might have had about his motives in regards to Catherine. But, still, where would it lead?

Louisa found herself thinking about Black, his laugh, low and from his chest, when he saw something that amused him, especially if it was something about the English. Truthfully, she thought of him more often than she'd have liked. She'd see him again soon. And there was probably nothing but childish fancy in her thoughts of him. But still, that smile. He'd been true to his word too. He'd funded an upgrade to the Princes Square facilities – additional bathrooms, an extension of the surgical ward, a new waiting room – to meet all of the requirements the inspector had listed. They'd passed the inspection without qualification.

The two letters joined the other six Louisa had in front of her. She sat there looking at the envelope addressed to herself and then opened the letter.

> *Dear Dr Quick,*
> *We have not heard from Catherine in three months, and the last letter she sent asked why I had not written. I can only assume she is not getting our letters for some reason. You cannot think that we would ever do Catherine harm.*
> *I encouraged her to leave the island, and I trusted you because you are Dr Harry's sister.*
> *My son Michael and Catherine are very close to one another. He is very distressed not to hear from Catherine, and worried. I am worried about both of them.*
> *Please let me know that Catherine is all right.*
> *Sincerely,*
> *Florence Cunningham*

Louisa would have liked to take the moral high ground. How dare Florence suggest that Louisa was doing something untoward? But she *was* doing something untoward, so the moral high ground would remain unoccupied on this occasion. Louisa knew she couldn't easily recover the situation now. At any rate, Catherine *had* moved on. She'd done exactly as Louisa thought she would, and she was much better for it.

Florence wasn't giving up, though.

It was the second letter, which Louisa also opened, that gave her pause.

Dear Catherine,

I hope this letter finds you well. I am writing because I am worried about Michael. He went down to Cairns a few weeks back with a group of boys from here, John and Charlie Mackie, who you know, and some others who've come these last months from Badu. He's been staying with my sister but I got news from her daughter that he's left there and they're not sure where he is.

He has been trying to get work. The thing is, he wants to come to you. He's worried because we haven't heard. I don't like him being in town by himself, and I'm thinking if you just wrote and said you were all right, he might come home. My sister said there's a bad group of boys he's been spending time with. Michael's a good boy, and I don't want any more trouble.

I remain your loving Florence

The notion that Michael would come to London worried Louisa. She would have to tell the truth about the letters. She'd never considered they'd go to such lengths. He must hold Catherine in high regard, Louisa thought. Perhaps it wasn't as she'd assumed. Perhaps he wasn't taking advantage.

Never mind. Once Louisa was there with Catherine in America, she was sure, this would be so much easier. She put the letters back in the drawer, where they belonged. There was nothing for it now; she'd have to go on as she'd started.

Chapter Twenty-Three

On the Friday morning, Catherine was in the change room when she heard voices in the office, Charlotte's and another. Aileen had left to go to school and there was only Catherine and two other girls still getting dressed.

'It appears you may have overestimated your charge,' Eppy was saying, her lovely loud voice clear through the thin wall. 'Coach says she doesn't take instruction.'

She couldn't hear what the other voice, a man's, much quieter, said in reply.

'Swimming is swimming,' Eppy said.

'I want her to stay here,' Catherine heard, the male voice raised now. It was familiar. Oh, my goodness, she thought. It was Mr Black. For no reason she understood, Catherine felt her heart pumping in her chest. She leant towards the wall to listen harder.

'Of course,' Charlotte said. 'I understand.'

'And I think my contributions buy me the right to a view.' It *was* Mr Black, she was sure now, and they were talking about Catherine. Oh, how awful. Eppy had told him Catherine wasn't a good swimmer. He'd spent all that money bringing her here for nothing.

When Catherine came out of the change room, Charlotte came out and beckoned her to come into the office. There was Mr Black sitting on the chair by the desk.

He stood but didn't move to embrace her. 'Catherine,' he said, gruffly, and nodded. 'How are you?'

Catherine found herself pleased to see him and yet embarrassed he'd found out her swimming was not as good as he'd hoped. He looked disappointed, reminding her suddenly of her father when she did something wrong.

'Mr Black.' She was on the verge of tears.

'I hear you're not swimming at your best. You make me look like a liar. Or a fool.'

'I'm sorry, Mr Black,' she said, keeping her tears in check as best she could. She looked at Eppy. 'I'm doing my best, though. Eppy, I'm doing my best, aren't I?'

Eppy nodded. 'Of course you are. Manfred, that's not what . . .'

'You know I brought you here,' he said to Catherine. 'You know I'm counting on you.'

'I do,' she said. 'I'm so sorry.'

'Miss Epstein tells me you've been complaining about the tank.'

'I'm just not used to a small space,' she said.

'Well, maybe that's the problem,' he said. 'What if I found you a bigger space? Would that help?' He came over and stood close to Catherine. Eppy was behind her.

'Yes, I think it would,' she said as confidently as she could muster.

He nodded slowly, looked at his watch. He picked up his hat and coat from Charlotte's desk. 'Let's you and I have a little chat now,' he said to Catherine. 'Charlotte, I'm sure we'll be seeing one another. I go back tomorrow but I'll pop in this evening.' Charlotte stepped out of the way to let him through. Catherine stood there. 'Come on,' he said. 'Charlotte, always a pleasure.'

Charlotte bade Black farewell. Catherine looked behind as she walked along the tank deck with him. Charlotte was standing at the door of the little office, frowning. She looked afraid, Catherine thought.

When they reached the hotel foyer, Mr Black turned to her. 'Catherine, I'm sorry if I was too direct with you.' He looked upset too, Catherine thought. Oh, what a disaster. As if it wasn't bad enough being left off the team. Now she'd disappointed the person she most wanted to please.

'I'm so sorry, Mr Black.' She felt like crying again.

His face softened. 'Please,' he said. 'Don't be upset. Let's go somewhere we can talk. Have you had breakfast?' She shook her head, not trusting her voice right then.

He took her to the diner across the street from the Touraine. He picked a table in the back and pulled out a chair for her, sat facing her. He called the waitress, ordered his usual toast and eggs and she ordered oatmeal with cinnamon and sugar. 'I am sorry,' he said. He looked at her intently. 'But I'm not used to losing, and I'm not very good at it. And I hope you're not either.' He paused, ran his hand over his mouth. 'I didn't like them cutting you from the team without talking to me first. Charlotte shouldn't have done that. I found out quite by accident and I was livid. I'm sorry if I took that out on you. It hadn't been my intention. I was furious, but not with you.'

'Mr Black, I'm really not as good a swimmer as the others. Charlotte was right . . .'

He waved at her to be quiet. 'I don't want to hear that talk, you hear?' he said firmly. 'Look at you,' he went on. 'You have the entire world at your fingertips, girl, and you don't even see it.' He grabbed her hand.

She felt so ashamed. 'Mr Black, I . . .'

'Don't,' he said. 'Don't speak. Let's just let the swimming worry about itself. All right?' He let go of her hand. 'All right?'

She nodded.

'That's my girl,' he said. 'You may not understand this but I lost someone a long time ago, and you very much remind me of her. I want you to be everything you can, Catherine. Do you understand that?' He took a breath in, out. Looking at his face, Catherine thought he might be about to cry.

'I think so,' she said, feeling awfully tender towards Mr Black, who'd been so good to her.

'You're a great girl.' He patted her hand again. 'Now, can you find your way home from here all right?' His voice was tight with emotion. She nodded. 'That's the way.' He stood and looked at his watch. Their food hadn't yet arrived. He threw a bill on to the table.

'Louisa is here next week. I'd very much like to take the two of you to lunch at my club.' He smiled. 'Swim well. I'll see you then.' He stood there a moment more, then he turned and walked away.

* * *

261

They were sitting in the cafe Andrew had taken her to on her first day in New York. Mr Black had sent him up 'to check on our champ', Andrew told Catherine. It was the Monday after Mr Black himself had come to New York. Charlotte had told Catherine she'd be in the Sandy Hook team after all. She was only in the team because of Mr Black, she knew, and Charlotte was angry, Catherine thought. It had been an awful few days.

As she'd walked along Twenty-Third Street with Andrew, she'd seen the buds on the trees, some with leaves unfolding.

'I don't really know why I'm here,' she said.

'Lunch,' he said.

'I meant in a more fundamental way.'

'New York?'

She nodded.

'Well, you don't need a reason. You're in New York because it's New York. And because you swim. Isn't that enough? Louisa will be here soon. She's sure to have you busy rolling bandages in Baltimore or something.'

They'd had their boiled eggs and toast for lunch as the weak sun crept over the top of the building and into the window.

Andrew drank coffee with everything now – a thoroughly Continental sensibility, he called it. He'd lit a cigarette, offering her one and then withdrawing the offer. 'I keep forgetting you're so young,' he said. 'You are growing up before my eyes. Do you want to try one? I'm sure you could now. It'll help you relax.'

Catherine was wearing a light blue sweater and grey

skirt. She needed to gain weight for the Sandy Hook swim. Mr Handley had told them they'd need a good layer of body fat, that the swim would be cold even in May.

She shook her head no about the cigarette. 'I'm not as good as the others,' she said, her mind still on swimming. 'When we race, I come last. I hate that stupid tank.'

Andrew shrugged. 'When I first came to Baltimore, they all hated me because I'm English and I was forced on them by Black. They got over it, and now I'm the star.'

'They don't hate me,' she said, 'although there's a couple who really wonder why I've been picked for the race.'

'Whatever do you mean, darling? You're a marvel. Everyone says. Anyway, who cares about the silly WSA? You could swim for England. You're *our* marvel, not theirs.'

'Am I?' she said. She didn't feel like a marvel. She felt like a freak. She wasn't even that good a swimmer, she thought now. She'd beaten the other children from Thursday Island, but who said they were fast? She was a good swimmer in London because she was the only swimmer. How did she come to think that swimming would help her? 'The only one I can beat is Aileen, and she's a diver not a swimmer.'

'Well, Mr Black must think you're a winner. He told me he's put a thousand dollars on you to win.'

'He's what?' Catherine was shocked.

'He says you're a sure thing. He's wagered a thousand on you for a win. If you lose, he'll give the money to the Association. If you win, well, I don't quite know. But anyway.'

'Oh, goodness,' she said. 'That's just awful. Why did Mr Black do that?'

263

'Faith, he told me. *You gotta have faith, Andy.*'

She shook her head and sighed. This was harder than she'd thought it would be. 'Do you miss home?' she said.

He smiled. 'I miss Mama, and my dog. And I wish I'd brought my ukulele. But I love America. It's so exciting and so real. You can touch it, the mood here. It's not all covered over. When I was at Oxford, it was like I wasn't really alive, or like I was observing everything from a long way away. With Mr Black, everything came to life. I just worry about Mama. She's so lost without me there.'

The waitress came over to the table. 'You folks all done?'

'Yes, the check, please,' Andrew said. After she'd left, he continued, 'You have to be picked for the Channel.'

'Why?'

'Because then Mr Black will find a reporter to go with you. And I hope it will be me. I can visit Mama and Papa, to keep them happy, and then have a month in France.' He smiled again. 'You really are in the doldrums today, aren't you?'

She looked at him.

'You're like the ugly duckling in the fairy tale,' he said.

'How?'

'You're becoming a beautiful swan but you don't know it. You think you want to be a silly old duck.'

Chapter Twenty-Four

New York Harbour smelt of peanuts and dirt. London smelt of the cold, Louisa had often thought, a rather clean smell, one she liked. But peanuts and dirt made her think of childhood, the few times they'd gone to fairs, the smell of the hay for the animals, the roasted peanuts their father would treat them to. That's what America was, she'd thought the last time she'd been here, an almighty fair from which no one seemed to want to go home.

She thought of Harry, who'd come here all those years ago too. He'd gone to Johns Hopkins before Louisa did. And then Alexander had hooked him up with Black and then he'd met Julia.

Louisa looked towards the dock where people waited for their loved ones and felt a pang of loneliness. It was the first time she'd taken a break from work since she'd gone to bring Catherine home, and that was hardly a holiday. She couldn't remember when she'd last taken time for herself. She didn't have much use for holidays, she'd said to

Ruth Luxton when she told her she was going to America. 'I don't know quite what I'll do.'

'You'll find something,' Ruth had said, crisply but kindly. They'd survive, Ruth Luxton said. They really would.

'It was easier when I didn't have time to think,' Louisa said to herself now, causing the young man beside her to look at her askance.

'I beg your pardon?' he said.

'Nothing,' she said. 'Just talking to myself.'

He smiled. 'I usually don't admit it,' he said. 'First time?'

'I beg your pardon?'

'New York. Is it your first time in New York?'

Louisa looked at him. He was young, perhaps middle twenties, with sandy hair and blue eyes. He wore a long coat made of some sort of animal hide and a broad-brimmed hat. 'No,' she said. 'But the first time in a long while.'

'Marvellous,' he said. 'Anything can be possible here.'

Louisa looked at him squarely. 'It's attitudes like that that see people disappointed by life,' she said.

Catherine had wired Louisa that she would come to meet her at the dock and, look, there she was. What a sweet girl, Louisa thought, although Catherine didn't look like a girl any more. She'd grown in just these few weeks. How long had it been? Two months, now that Louisa thought about it. Catherine had come over in March and now it was May. She shouldn't have left it so long, she thought, but there had been so much to do in the end to set up for the trip, and she'd wanted to stay through the health inspector's visit.

Catherine was wearing a pair of long trousers and a

cotton jumper. She was back in those silly trousers, Louisa thought. Her cheeks were ruddy and she grinned as she threw her arms around her aunt.

'Just a minute,' Louisa said, trying to hold Catherine at arm's length then wishing she hadn't.

But Catherine didn't seem to care. She held on to Louisa and hugged her warmly.

Louisa put her arms around the girl and embraced her lightly.

'Oh, I missed you, Louisa.' Catherine laughed and her aunt joined in.

'I missed you too,' Louisa said, finding tears in her eyes. The girl was dear, even if she was so much trouble.

'Mr Black's coming,' Catherine said. 'He's going to take us out to some fancy club. He came to see me, and he shouldn't have done this but he's bet on me to win a race, Louisa.'

'He can afford it,' Louisa said. 'But I didn't realise he'd been to see you. You've been seeing Andrew too, haven't you?'

'Oh, yes, but I do want to do well for Mr Black, Louisa, and I'm very worried that I won't.' Louisa looked at her niece. She did look worried. What did it matter? It was just a swim. Louisa would talk to Black, make sure he wasn't putting pressure on the girl.

Catherine took her aunt to Allerton House on East Fifty-Seventh Street where they'd stay together before Louisa went on to Baltimore. Catherine had already left her suitcase at the front desk, she said. The hotel had been recommended by Charlotte Epstein as one of the new women-only hotels in New York. Catherine talked all the way in the taxi, about the awful tank she had to swim in, the trains that were so much more efficient than in London, the wonderful diners with their sandwiches, and her new friend, Aileen, who had all these made-up words.

The hotel had a simply furnished lobby and a lounge off to one side where guests could entertain. They took an elevator to the twelfth floor. Their room looked over the park across the street. On the top floor was a gorgeous little roof garden, Catherine told Louisa, and a solarium. 'And there's a tank, Louisa. It's small, but bigger than the one we train in, so I'll swim while I'm here.'

That afternoon, Andrew came on the train from Baltimore and took them for tea, on the basis that Louisa wasn't yet ready for an American diner experience. He was affable as ever, if slightly removed from the world. Louisa had gone to see his mother, Ada, after he left for America. She was a strong woman, and she'd loved her two boys so fiercely. And now she'd lost them both, Donald to the war and Andrew to life. There was not much happiness in motherhood, Louisa thought. Ada had told Louisa that Andrew was engaged to be married to an English girl, a girl his older brother had known. Louisa wondered had he told Catherine this. They were close, she could see, and she worried for her niece, who seemed to be keen to find her moorings in New York.

In the evening, while Catherine was at the YMCA pool, Louisa had dinner with Charlotte Epstein in the hotel dining room. Charlotte was exactly as Louisa expected, smart and strong of character. She also had a lovely laugh. She'd been a chaperone for Catherine in New York, although, she said, Catherine was so well behaved she didn't need much in the way of guidance.

Charlotte was clearly less enamoured of Catherine's swimming than Black was, and her view matched Catherine's self-assessment. 'I'll be honest with you, Louisa,' Charlotte said. 'As you'll quickly learn, I don't know how to be any other way. Delightful young woman, but Catherine isn't the swimmer we'd hoped she'd be. She's welcome to stay, of course, but, really, she needs a lot of work before she'll be at competition level.'

They were eating fish in a white sauce; overcooked, Louisa had thought. Nellie was good with fish – good with everything.

'Black's wrong then,' Louisa said. Why the devil bring her all this way? she wondered. 'Frankly, I can't say I'm terribly disappointed.'

Charlotte smiled. 'You're not a fan?'

'Of swimming? I suppose I don't see where it leads. I think you've done a marvellous job to make a place in sport for women. But for Catherine, the water represents something of her past. Don't get me wrong. I'm all for her having this time. But after that, I'd love to see her back in school. She's bright.'

'I know you were very active in the women's suffrage movement,' Charlotte said. 'So were my swimmers.'

'And?'

'Swimming isn't all that different from any number of things women have been shut out of.'

Louisa thought about this. 'We're also shut out of bars.

But I don't intend to campaign any time soon to have us instated there. Some things don't matter.'

'Yes they do, Louisa,' Charlotte said. 'They do matter. Until 1920, there was no Olympic swimming for women. We changed that. Us, the WSA – *we* did that.'

'But that's not why your swimmers get their pictures in the newspaper.'

'I don't care.'

'You don't? It's lascivious.'

'Well, it's lascivious of the fellows who ogle the girls, but it's nothing to do with my swimmers.' Charlotte regarded Louisa.

'Black.'

'What about him?' Charlotte said, a little smile at the corners of her mouth.

'He intrigues me.'

'He intrigues us all, honey.'

'Not like that. I mean his interest. He seems terribly interested in Catherine. He wired me about all this, said he'd had to intervene so she can swim in some race. I *am* sorry he did that.'

Charlotte shrugged. 'Oh, that didn't worry me. He'd probably give us the money anyway if we needed it. You don't have to worry on Black's account. It's the swimming. He's brought us many Catherines over the years.' There was no hint of scandal in Charlotte's voice, Louisa noticed.

'He has? Why?'

Charlotte took a sip of her wine. 'Did he ever tell you about the *Slocum*?'

Louisa shook her head.

'It was a passenger ferry that caught fire in the East River twenty years ago. The *General Slocum*, one of the last big paddle steamers. It was a terrible accident. A thousand died.'

'Oh, how awful.'

'And it was because they couldn't swim. I remember the *Slocum*,' Charlotte said. 'They were pulling bodies out of the water for days. My family were . . . I'll never forget it.'

'And what does that have to do with Black?'

'His mother and sister were on board. They were with him. He was separated from them. He survived. They didn't.'

'Oh,' Louisa said. 'So he supports women's swimming as a way of atoning?'

'Yes. You see, a boy like him would have been taught to swim but not his sister and not his mother.' Like Louisa herself, she thought. 'It's a tragic story. His father had died not long before and so he lost his whole family in the space of a year. Once the association started attracting attention, he came to see me about helping. We couldn't have survived without his support. For him, perhaps it gives him comfort to see that girls swim.

'It was his lawyer who told me about his mother and sister. We were drawing up the contracts. It was a warning, really, that we shouldn't take advantage of Black.'

That night, when Louisa was alone in the hotel suite – Catherine having gone back to the Ryan house from the YMCA – she thought about what Charlotte had told her. Poor Black. To lose your family like that.

She poured herself a scotch. Black had been so young

when it happened; Nellie's age. When Louisa was that age, she'd had everything to look forward to. Oh, later, she'd had her fair share of pain but at twenty-one, she was invincible. Poor Black. The world could be cruel.

So, did he see Catherine as his lost sister? Was he trying to help his sister to swim? Is that why he wanted to believe in Catherine? That was all very well for Black, but it might not be the best for Catherine. Louisa was relieved to hear Charlotte say that Catherine wasn't a strong swimmer. It would make it easier to finish up in America and make their way back home. Catherine would surely be more ready for school now. The girl had forgotten about the island altogether. From here, Louisa was sure that everything would be fine.

Chapter Twenty-Five

It was a cracker of a day according to Aileen Ryan, who thought everything was a cracker: the beach, the sun, the sea, the trolley car they sometimes caught to the place that had the best ice cream. It was her favourite word, Catherine said.

'So?' Aileen said. 'It's better than saying everything's dull.'

'Do I say everything's dull?' Catherine said.

'No,' Aileen replied and laughed. 'I just meant I'd rather be positive than negative.'

'I agree,' Catherine said.

Meg Ederle joined them. 'How's it looking?' she said, a frown on her face.

'It's a cracker,' Catherine said. 'An absolute cracker.'

Meg looked at her. 'What's that supposed to mean?'

Catherine looked at Aileen.

'I give up,' Aileen said. 'Let's get ready.'

The sun was up but the day wasn't yet warm and

Catherine knew the water would be cold. The swim would take them from the Battery at the south end of Manhattan to Sandy Hook at the north end of New Jersey. The tide would be against them for the start of their course, Charlotte had told them, but not to worry; it would soon be in their favour – although, depending on their timing, they might have a struggle at the end.

The dories were lined up along the pier. Each would follow a swimmer. And there they were now, the thirty-four young women, including Catherine Quick, ready to race. There were half a dozen from the WSA. Other swimmers had come from Florida and Texas. Catherine knew she was only swimming because of Mr Black, but Mr Handley had acted as if it had been his decision. He'd said they changed their minds and decided to give her some experience of open-water swimming after all. He looked happy about it, Catherine thought. She and Aileen had been swimming at the beach every weekend, and they'd swum together in the harbour a few times too, but this was Catherine's first race.

Catherine had never grown to like the tank. Every morning there was that foul smell of chlorine. The other swimmers were faster, and Catherine wondered why she was there at all. Charlotte Epstein all but ignored her now, as if she didn't matter. And Mr Black had bet money on her.

A light breeze blew and the tide ran the way of the swimmers, not against them, Catherine thought, watching the water. It would be a day to set a world record, she'd heard someone say in the morning. 'You're our best hope,' Charlotte had said to Meg Ederle. Trudy was the better swimmer, Catherine knew, but Trudy was sick today.

They stood along the pier together in the early morning light. There were newspaper photographers and a small crowd of onlookers. Aileen and Meg Ederle posed for the cameras, giggling in their swimming suits. Then the starter told them to take their marks and they lined up again. He fired his gun. Catherine dived in with the rest, into the blinding cold, emerging to sunlight on the water. Even in this cold, it was beautiful. There was nothing about the water that was not beautiful, Catherine thought.

She knew the race would be long – twenty-two miles on a straight course, and the waters might be kind or otherwise – but she felt more ready to swim than she'd ever felt. Her body opened up to the sea and welcomed it.

As long as she cleared each buoy, she could take whatever course she wanted, Aileen had said. The other swimmers, she knew, were planning to swim through the Buttermilk Channel past Governors Island, but Catherine had decided to swim to the right, towards Liberty, and then come back in towards Sandy Hook. Partly it was because she wanted to go close to Liberty, but it was more than that: the way the sea looked, Catherine thought, it wanted them to go that way. When you swam in the sea, the sea made most of the decisions, Catherine knew.

She settled into an easy pace. Arm up and over, breathe, arm up and over, breathe. After a while, she couldn't see the other swimmers, and she had to look to find the dory that was accompanying her. She became oblivious to time, nothing but swimming now and the occasional correction when she stopped to check the next buoy. The water was cold, the light was soft, but she could be home on the island instead of here in New York Harbour. The sensation of leaving herself behind, of being nothing but her body and the sea, was still the same. 'I swear you came from the sea, Waapi,' Florence always said.

'Do some humans come from the sea?' she asked.

'We all do,' Florence said. 'We're all water babies. But some have a hankering to go back there.'

Charlotte had arranged for a car to take Louisa from Manhattan, where they'd watched the start of the race, down to Sandy Hook in New Jersey, so they could watch the finish on the beach there. You could almost swim it faster than you could drive, Charlotte said.

There had been a small crowd for the early start, including reporters and photographers. The swimmers had looked so vulnerable out there in their costumes, Louisa thought. There was a bigger crowd here at the finish. She couldn't see Andrew. Black was in Baltimore. He'd planned to make the race but couldn't at the last minute. He wired to say he'd see her next week. She'd been disappointed not to see him again.

They were up on the lifeguard stand above the beach.

'Swimming,' Louisa said to Charlotte. 'I'm sorry if I was rude about it.'

'Oh, I don't mind,' Charlotte said. 'You don't swim, so you can't know what it's like to want to and not be able to.'

It was a beautiful day, Louisa thought, warm and sunny, and the water made long, lovely waves on the way into shore. Charlotte pointed to the right of the shoreline, where swimmers were just coming into view.

'Oh, yes, I see,' Louisa said. She felt quite excited now. 'So who's the favourite?' she asked.

'Well, Aileen Ryan is swimming well, and so is Helen Wainwright. They're at loggerheads, those two, always have been. There's another swimmer, Gertrude Ederle, whom you might have heard of, but she's not swimming today. Her sister Meg is in the team, very strong at the moment. They're good in these open-water swims.' She pointed out Aileen and Helen, who were in the lead, along with the British swimmer Hilda James. 'It's going to be very close,' Charlotte said. 'Actually, I hope it's a tie. I couldn't stand to have Aileen and Helen at each other again.'

These three swimmers were ahead of the pack, the rest some way behind. Louisa was looking for Catherine among the swimmers at the back but couldn't see her. She knew Catherine was in a yellow cap – Charlotte had pointed her out at the start. When Louisa couldn't find her niece, she became worried. She started counting heads. 'Where's Catherine?' she said to Charlotte.

'She'll be here,' Charlotte said. They watched a few minutes more, the lead swimmers rounding a buoy and picking up pace now for the final run into shore, all the other swimmers in view. Catherine must be a long way behind, Louisa thought.

Now Charlotte was looking too, scanning the sea.

'I'd better alert the lifeguard captain,' she said. Louisa could hear the fear in her voice.

And then Louisa saw her. 'There she is! By God, she's ahead of them all!'

Catherine wasn't at the back of the pack. She wasn't

with the group to the right of the shore. She'd come from further away, on the left. And she was in the lead – a long way in the lead – on the far side of the group of swimmers. She would beat the others by a mile.

'That's not Catherine?' Charlotte Epstein said.

'I believe it is,' Louisa said. She watched her niece increase her lead with each stroke. She looked so strong, so free, in the water. In that moment, something became abundantly clear.

Louisa understood, as she had not really understood before, that swimming was a part of Catherine, that to take this from her was to take her life from her. Catherine probably had no interest in any of the rights and wrongs of women's swimming, or the suits, or the sport, or the oglers, or even winning and losing. That was all put on swimming by others – by Charlotte, Black and even Louisa. For Catherine, the sea wasn't swimming; it was home.

She surfed in on a wave, which took her almost to shore. She stood and was pushed over by another wave. Oh, the cold. Her hands and feet were totally numb and her lungs hurt. But she was laughing. If this was a calm day, she'd hate to see rough seas. She couldn't believe the race was finished already. The fellow in the boat had kept offering her food, chicken broth, chocolate cake, but she hadn't been hungry.

There was a crowd gathered above the beach, cheering. A dozen ran down the sand to meet her. Mr Handley hurried over with a towel. 'Why didn't you tell me you could swim like that?' he said.

'What?' she said. 'Mr Handley, you were right. The water isn't so cold if you don't think about it. I'm actually sort of warm, to be honest.' She smacked her lips together. 'But my mouth isn't working very well.'

Mr Handley was laughing as he wrapped the towel around her. Everyone was smiling. The photographers were taking pictures. 'I saw fish, a big school of them in front of me. I tried to follow but they were too fast. I've never seen fish like that before, green and black and yellow. They were very beautiful.'

'You know, you won, Catherine,' one of the photographers said. 'The Australian won. What do you think of that?'

She looked at Mr Handley. They were taking pictures of her and she didn't know what to say.

'All right, boys,' the coach said, 'that's enough. You'll terrify the poor girl.'

In the back of the group, she saw Andrew smiling and waving.

'Andrew!' she called. 'Andrew, it's you!'

He came over. 'Well, that was a sight to see, Catherine – you coming in way ahead. There's no one else even finished yet.'

'Really?' She looked around and realised that what the photographer had said was true: there were no other swimmers on the beach. She had won.

'You're going to be famous, girl,' Andrew said. He leant down and kissed her on the mouth. She pulled back, surprised.

'Andrew,' she said.

'I'm so sorry,' he said then. 'I don't know what came over me.'

'No,' she said. 'I really won?' He nodded, smiling.

'Goodness,' she said. 'I didn't think anything like that would happen.'

After the swim, Catherine collected her trophy. A reporter from the New York *Daily News* asked her how she'd won by so much.

'I was lucky,' she said. 'I picked the tides, so that when all the others were swimming against, I was being pulled to the shore and I looked faster. But it's always luck,' she said honestly.

'But you were the fastest swimmer too,' he said.

She thought about this. 'Being fast isn't anything out there,' she said. 'It's the water that gives or not.'

The photographers took pictures of her getting out of the water, getting her award, towelling dry and then once she'd dressed.

Louisa had come down the beach to Catherine after the swim. 'I'm getting sand in my boots,' she'd said first. 'Oh, I'm terrible at this. Well done, Catherine. You've swum amazingly well. You won!'

Catherine smiled.

Her aunt stepped forward to embrace her.

'But I'm all wet, Catherine said.

'Oh, I don't care, darling. You're just a marvel,' Louisa said. She hugged her tightly and didn't let go until Catherine did.

Catherine was exhausted by the end of the post-race

celebrations, happy to get in the motor car that would take them back to the hotel in New York. Andrew and Louisa came with her. When they arrived at the hotel, there were more photographers, sent by the local papers. Catherine could smell the magnesium from their flashbulbs on her clothes for hours after.

Finally they went inside. She'd been seven hours in the water and three hours on the journey back, by which time the evening papers were reporting Catherine's feat. She'd set a new record.

'Is that what reporters do?' she said to Andrew. 'Follow girls like me?'

'It could be worse,' he said. 'Once I had to follow this prize fighter who was a terrible drunk. I think you'd be easier.'

'I didn't mean for them. I meant for me.'

'For you? You're the star, darling. We all adore you!'

The next morning, when Catherine left the hotel to go to the WSA pool, there were half a dozen reporters and twice that many photographers waiting for her. 'Can you tell us what you'll do today, Catherine?' one of them said.

'I'm going to the tank to train,' she said and smiled. 'And maybe I'll swim in the harbour with my friend this afternoon.' When she smiled they took pictures, so she smiled some more. It was strange that they were so interested in her, Catherine thought. All she'd done was swim.

'What's next?' one of them asked.

'I think we swim around Manhattan next Saturday,' she said.

'Are you going to France?'

'No,' Catherine said. 'I haven't been selected.'

'How does that work? Didn't you beat everyone yesterday?'

'Yes, I did,' she said. 'But the WSA will select American swimmers.' She smiled and they took her picture again. They seemed to want to take her picture doing just about anything.

The next day at training, Charlotte Epstein asked Catherine to come into the office. 'What were you thinking?' she said, throwing a newspaper onto the desk.

Catherine looked at her in astonishment. 'I don't know what you mean.'

'You told them you weren't selected for the Channel.'

'Well, I wasn't,' Catherine said. 'I told them the truth.'

'This looks dreadful for us. I've had Black and our chairman on the telephone this morning asking me how we made such a blunder. Black says I promised we'd put you on the team if you won Sandy Hook. He's threatening to withdraw his support. We were going to fix it, Catherine. I would have talked to Mr Handley and . . .'

Catherine shook her head. 'I really don't know what you mean, Charlotte. I just told the truth.'

Chapter Twenty-Six

Louisa had found herself looking forward to seeing Black. They met in the lounge of her hotel.

'I'm so sorry I missed the race,' he said. He embraced her lightly. He smelt fresh.

'Oh, it was something to see,' Louisa said. She sat down and waited as he ordered drinks for them.

'You look wonderful,' he said when the waiter had been dispatched.

'Thank you,' she said. 'It's just lovely to be here. Thank you for suggesting it.'

'I bet Charlotte was surprised,' he said. 'I knew Catherine was the one.' He smiled.

'Yes,' Louisa said. 'We all were pretty surprised, I think.'

'Not me,' he said. 'I know my girl.' The way he said it irked Louisa – *my girl*.

'So now she can come home happy, triumphant and confident,' Louisa said. 'We're very appreciative of what you've done for her.'

He smiled. 'Louisa, she really could be the first woman to swim the Channel, you know.'

'But she's not in the team.'

'She doesn't need to worry about the WSA. Let them take the Ederle girl. We'll take Catherine.'

'We?'

'Me. And you. I'll get her a coach over there. She can go home with you and then train.'

'Lear . . .' Louisa wanted to mention his family but thought better of it. 'I'm not sure any more that this is what she wants, and it's never been what I want for her,' she said firmly.

'Of course it's what she wants,' Black said. 'She was born to it. Anyone can see that.' He thrust his jaw out, a gesture she'd not seen before.

'Born to what, Mr Black?' Catherine had walked in.

'So you did it,' Black said, turning around and standing to greet her. 'I just knew you would. I just knew it. You're my girl.'

He embraced Catherine. Again, Louisa was bothered by the familiarity in his tone, and his embrace was warm. He was staring at Catherine now and the look on his face was hard to read. Pride, Louisa thought. He was proud of her. When he looked at Catherine, was he thinking of the sister he'd lost? That's what you'd have thought watching him now, it occurred to Louisa.

Louisa switched her gaze to Catherine and smiled. 'Catherine, you are in all the papers,' she said. 'And this time, they've actually got pictures of you swimming.' She showed her the pile on the table. 'Mr Black says you could swim the English Channel next.'

Catherine smiled. 'Do you really think so? Do you think I should?'

Black didn't give Louisa a chance to answer. 'Of course you should. You're going to be the greatest swimmer in the world. You'll see.'

The Association made the announcement the morning after the story hit the newspapers. The three swimmers to attempt the English Channel would be Trudy Ederle and Helen Wainwright from the WSA and the Australian Catherine Quick, funded jointly by the Association and Mr Manfred Lear Black.

Catherine had thought Aileen would be selected over Helen Wainwright. She was a better swimmer, and a much better diver. Catherine was going to Aileen's for the weekend but now she worried Aileen wouldn't want her to come. She'd pushed Aileen out of the Channel swim, after all. When she arrived at the house, she hugged Aileen and burst into tears. 'I'm so sorry,' she said.

'Oh, fally-bally! Don't worry, Catherine,' Aileen said. 'I don't mind, really I don't.'

'Oh, Aileen, look at me. I'm the one who's going and you have to stay and I'm crying.'

'Well, that makes perfect sense to me. You're going to leave us, and we don't want you to.' Now Aileen was crying too. 'You've been the best friend. Will you come back?'

'Oh, I do hope so.' They were sitting out on the porch on the swing chair.

'You know, I wasn't going anyway,' Aileen said, smiling through her tears. 'I'm starting Georgetown in the fall.

Daddy wouldn't have let me swim, even if I'd been picked.'

'You mean you're going to university?'

She nodded. 'We visited last week. I'll be in college, with a dorm mate, and the only thing that would make it better would be if it was you. I'm allowed to keep swimming through the rest of the summer, though, and diving. And I'll be watching you. You bet I will.'

When they went inside, Mrs Ryan embraced Catherine warmly. 'You have to come back to us, Catherine. You're our family now. Don't forget that.'

They were such gentle, lovely people, Catherine thought. They had accepted her just as they'd found her, and she would never forget them. Catherine saw, too, that although Aileen was angry at her father for making her give up swimming, she really did want to go to college and study law. She wanted to move on with her life, and she didn't see swimming as the way to do that.

After Louisa left to go to Baltimore, Catherine was frightened to leave Charlotte's apartment because she might see a reporter or photographer. At first she had liked it when they took her picture. It had felt like they were her friends. They called out after her in the street: 'Give us a smile, Catherine.' She quickly got used to the noise of the flash behind her, the smiles on their faces, the big eyes of their flashbulbs staring coldly at her. But they were with her all the time now. She was only to be in New York for another week, and it was as if they couldn't get enough of her.

Catherine had come to hate seeing her image looking back at her from the newspaper page. While others would say, 'Don't you look beautiful?', she felt anything but beautiful. They photographed Trudy, too, and other swimmers. Mr Black's newspaper had a big feature article, written by Andrew, on the Channel contenders of 1926. He put his money behind Catherine Quick, he said, 'the Australian girl who'd made good in America.'

She walked past the newsstand at the station and saw her own face looking out at her, a pasted-on smile, woollen bathers. When she arrived at the tank, Charlotte said, 'You're on page three again.'

'I know,' Catherine said. 'I saw.'

'It's great for us.'

'I hadn't even been swimming,' Catherine said. 'I put my costume on and stood there. I hadn't even been in the water.'

'That doesn't matter,' Charlotte said. 'We need to stay in the papers, Catherine. It's for the sport.'

'Is it?' Catherine said. 'Is it for the sport? Andrew told me it's for the legs.' She thought of Louisa suddenly, what her aunt had said at the beginning about swimming. She'd been right. 'Why do they do that?'

Charlotte shrugged. 'Perhaps it's not ideal, but if it helps us grow our membership and increase donations, then I don't see the harm.'

'It's not your picture.'

In the change room, she asked Aileen, 'Do you think it's right that the papers print pictures of us in our swimsuits even when we're not actually swimming?'

'I've never thought about it,' Aileen said. 'They don't put my picture in the paper very much. They seem to like you the most.' This was said without any ill will, Catherine knew. 'I suppose diving isn't like that swim you did. They're mad keen on the Channel, and it will surely be you or Trudy.' Aileen looked at her more closely. 'But you're crying, Catherine. What's wrong?'

She'd put her suit on and was about to go outside. She sat down heavily on the bench. 'I don't know,' she said. 'I thought it was all good fun at first. But it's all the time, Aileen. I can't go out of the hotel without seeing a photographer. Charlotte said they'd leave me alone after Sandy Hook settled down but they just want to keep at me. Even Andrew.'

'Well, it's his job,' Aileen said. 'He's supposed to do stories for the newspaper. Maybe you need to be more like that Lillian Cannon? She has the dogs.'

'What do you mean?'

'In all the pictures, she has those two big dogs. They swim with her and then they put the dogs in the pictures. It's less about her, I suppose. Or maybe you need to get married and have some children. They're not putting Mille Gade in the paper so much. Or not in her swimming suit, at least. Mostly it's pictures of her hugging her children.' Mille Gade was another New York swimmer who'd announced her intention to attempt the Channel. She had two young children and her husband, a naval officer, was her coach. She said she'd be the first mother across the Channel. It was true they hardly ever pictured her alone in a swimming suit. She always had her children with her.

Catherine laughed. 'You really think it's all right?'

'Of course it's all right. Eppy wouldn't let them do anything wrong.'

Early one morning, just before Louisa was due to return, before any of the photographers were awake, Catherine caught the trolley car down to the pier. She swam out past the first buoy, past the end of the pier, out further towards the ships that were sailing away from New York. Take me home, she wanted to say, but she realised that now she had no home. Even if she could get back to the island, there was no one for her there. They'd forgotten her. She was completely adrift in a sea of her own making.

Chapter Twenty-Seven

Louisa was staying at the Emerson, which had been built by one of Black's friends. The hotel was beautiful, its two-storey foyer lined with white marble and ornate timber carvings. Louisa was in a penthouse suite on the twenty-first floor and she had a view taking in the harbour, city and surrounds. The weather held while she was there, with cold, sunny days and chilly nights. Other than her visits to Black's clinic, she was free to do as she pleased. She wandered Baltimore, a surprisingly pretty city that she'd somehow missed when she'd been there last. Where were you, Louisa? she wanted to ask herself. It was nice to come back now, after so many years had passed, and discover she could enjoy a place so much.

The city was different too. There were motor cars everywhere now, a lot like New York; horses and carts had disappeared. It was cleaner, Louisa noticed, and when she started at the clinic she quickly learnt the diseases that were largely caused by unclean water, which had done such harm when she'd last visited, were unheard of now. Louisa had visited the new School of Public Health, the first of its kind in the world, and Black's clinic had grown from that school's work.

And now the hospital and medical school had blossomed. Black's clinic, in the East Baltimore docks area, had so much more money and equipment than Louisa's Princes Square clinic.

On her last night in the city, before she returned to New York, she and Black had dinner in the hotel restaurant. She was supposed to be giving him advice but, really, they wanted for nothing.

'You seem despondent,' he said. They'd eaten local clams, and now they were eating lobster.

'I suppose I don't know why you brought me here. You have so much more than we do. That X-ray facility is extraordinary. And the theatres! I'd give my eye teeth to have half the set-up you have here.'

He smiled. 'Yes, we've done the great city of Baltimore proud,' he said. 'But there's a network of donors. They've been a great help.'

'From what I hear, no one gives more than you do.' The doctors Louisa met with, including Emily Masterton, couldn't speak highly enough of Black, who gave money and time to the clinic. Their success had largely been dependent on his support.

'Well, Louisa, when I think of giving, I only have to look at Johns Hopkins himself to realise I don't do nearly enough. He had the good fortune to be successful financially, and he gave back. It is incumbent upon those of us who are fortunate to do something for the less fortunate, don't you agree?'

'Of course,' Louisa said. 'And as I say, I really don't know what it is you think I could do for you.'

Black smiled. 'You're too modest, Louisa. We have all the gimmicks, but your quality of care is better. I'm not a fool and neither is my board. That's what our doctors are telling us. They say your care is the best in the world. Your brother was immensely helpful when we were setting up, but I want you to make sure we're on track, especially as we move to confinements.'

'Nurses and midwives,' Louisa said. It was the one thing she'd noticed during the week. His clinic relied heavily on doctors, with less emphasis on nursing care.

'Nurses and midwives?'

'Yes. When my mother did medicine, she had to start in nursing because there was no way for her to work as a trainee doctor. She always said it was her nursing training that made her a good doctor. And she always said if doctors thought more like midwives there would be a whole lot less unhappiness in the world.

'In medicine, we're so busy trying to work out how this bone connects with that bone that we forget sometimes that those bones connect to a patient. Nursing and midwifery start there rather than with the bones.'

'That's just the advice we needed,' he said, lighting up a cigar. He nodded, as if thinking about something.

'But that doesn't mean you just fill the place up with nurses and midwives. At Princes Square we recruited well. We have a physician, Ruth Luxton, excellent with people, who selects the nurses for our wards, our reception, our theatre. And they're very good. Our midwives are just as good.'

'And ours are not?'

She smiled, took a sip of her wine. 'I didn't say that. The Johns Hopkins Nursing School was set up with help from Florence Nightingale. It's a fine school, and if you recruit from the school and make sure you keep standards up, things will stay on track, as you term it.'

He leant back in his chair. He was looking at her intently and seemed about to speak. But he stopped himself, leant back in. 'I want to thank you for trusting me,' he said. 'I'm very glad I was able to assist with your clinic, Louisa. You've had nothing to worry about on that score.'

Whereas previously, Louisa might have been relieved, now his mentioning his help unnerved her a little. She had continued to feel uneasy about Catherine and the swimming. She'd tried to raise the issue with him during the week but he'd always skirted around it, changed the subject. It had even occurred to Louisa that his support for the clinic, even his bringing her to Baltimore to give him advice, was all a ruse to have Catherine swim. That was ridiculous, though, she thought now. He'd been proper in all his dealings with Catherine, hadn't he? Except in relation to the swimming, which he was obsessed with, he'd been kindly.

There was a piano playing somewhere and the music trickled over to them in soft waves.

'I've been wanting to talk to you,' she said.

'About the clinic?'

She shook her head. 'No, about swimming. I don't think Catherine wants it.'

'Wants what?'

293

'The Channel. Charlotte told me you've assigned a journalist now to cover her swim.'

He nodded. 'I've got Andrew on it; Catherine feels comfortable with him. And it will get the others out of her hair if we have exclusive rights. That's all.'

'But your paper stands to benefit.'

He let out a short laugh. 'You think my paper needs to benefit from Catherine? I mean, I should hope we'll benefit. I'm paying for the swim. I have some rights here. And yes, it will help circulation, especially given that the *Post* has Lillian Cannon. But I told you that already.' He waved his hand, dismissing the notion. He looked at her. 'She wants this, Louisa. Ask her yourself. She wants this.'

Louisa saw that he could have anything in the world; that's what his money could do. She nearly told him that she knew about his mother and sister, but she felt he would not take kindly to being confronted with her knowing. It would mean she and Charlotte had spoken of him and Louisa felt sure he wouldn't like that. 'Oh, Lear,' she said, 'I wish the world were a kinder place.'

'What on earth does that mean?'

She looked at him for a long time. 'Life's just not as easy as it could be,' she said finally.

Chapter Twenty-Eight

Catherine hadn't expected anyone to meet them, but there was Nellie, the dear, in a coat and hat, looking like she was dressed for winter although the day was warm.

'It's nearly summer, Nellie. Oh, but it's sweet of you to come.'

'I swear you've grown another foot, Catherine,' Nellie said, hugging her warmly. 'Look at you now, though. You've lost weight. Are you all right?' She looked beyond Catherine, to Louisa, who stood behind her.

'Nellie, dear, it's good to see you,' Louisa said.

'You must come to New York with me next time,' Catherine said. 'Mr Black says I can run the table if I swim the Channel. Do you know what that is? It's a gambling term. It means running the gambling table because you've won so much. Mr Black doesn't gamble, he told me, but he knows all about it. He's been so kind, Nellie. You were wrong to suspect him.'

'Was I now?' Nellie said, looking at Louisa again. 'Let

me look at you properly,' she said, stepping back and returning her gaze to Catherine. 'Yes, you've grown. As for Mr Black, I will reserve judgement, young lady.'

'Listen to you calling me "young lady". You're only a few years older than me.'

'But they're the ones that count. Did you not miss us at all?' Nellie was smiling.

Catherine frowned. 'Of course I did. Especially the food. How I long for one of your beef stews.'

Nellie laughed. 'Oh, that's so kind of you to say, Catherine.' Nellie was proud of the way she looked after them. 'And, Louisa, you're looking marvellous.'

Louisa laughed. 'I feel marvellous. Come, Nellie, let's get Catherine home, so she can show you what she brought you.'

Catherine looked around. 'Louisa, there are no reporters.'

'No what?' Nellie said.

'Doesn't matter,' Catherine said. 'Let's get away.'

They collected the suitcases and took a taxicab back to Wellclose Square.

'So was it very grand?' Nellie asked when she'd made tea. There was fruitcake too.

'Oh, Nellie, New York is so busy,' Catherine said. 'Everyone is going somewhere and has something important to do.'

'And what we do in London isn't important?' Nellie said as she poured.

'It's different. It's just more easy. You know, it reminded me strangely of the island. There are the Negroes, of course. But it's more than the colour of people's skin. It's free, Nellie. It's a place where people are really free.' She thought suddenly of one of the reporters on the day she'd left, asking her to show some leg. That hadn't felt free.

'Are you all right?' Nellie said.

'Oh, yes, fine. I was thinking about something unpleasant.'

'What?'

'Nothing that matters now. And I know how to drink gin.'

'You shouldn't be drinking anything. Is that young Mackintosh fellow corrupting you?'

'Pink gin,' Catherine said. 'It's called a fizz and I'll make us some tonight.'

'We don't have gin,' Nellie said.

'And I didn't know about this,' Louisa said. 'Nellie's quite right. You shouldn't be drinking anything, Catherine.'

'Oh, fally-bally,' Catherine said. 'We'll get some gin. Oh, it's a truly marvellous place, Nellie. You would love it.'

'I'm not sure the Negroes would agree about freedom either,' Louisa said. 'When women fought for the vote they had to take the Negroes out of the equation or it would have failed.'

'The Islanders don't vote in Australia,' Catherine said. 'I hardly think that makes a difference.'

'Of course it does,' Louisa said. 'Voting's the one thing that you can make a difference with. Have I taught you nothing?'

'I couldn't care less for voting,' Catherine said. 'The people in New York are free. I could smell it in the streets.'

'Have it your way,' Nellie said. 'Freedom's a smell then. So what did you bring me?'

Catherine went back out to the front hall and took from her bag the little statuette. She went back to the kitchen. 'You come into New York Harbour and it's the first thing you see. It's freedom and it's a woman.'

Nellie looked at Liberty. 'I do like boiled sweets, you know.'

Catherine laughed. 'Oh, stop it, Nellie. Seriously, it's a symbol of freedom.'

'In your last letter you said you were unhappy.'

Catherine looked at Louisa. 'I was. The swimming wasn't going very well until we could get out of the silly tank we had to swim in. Once I did that, we were fine. Except . . .'

'Except what?'

'Nothing. Oh, I sound ungrateful saying it but they kept putting my picture in the paper, and I didn't much like it. It's not at all private. It's like I'm everyone's.' Catherine walked over to the back door. 'I do like that about London, that no one knows me. And the dogs are glad to have me home.'

'So am I,' Nellie said. 'I just don't run around your feet snorting. Come, sit and have some more tea. I made jam roly-poly, which is what the Scotties are after. No one will put your picture in the paper in this house. And jam roly-poly will put some meat on those bones.'

Oh, but it was good to be home, Louisa thought. Travel was all very well, and she'd had the most marvellous time in

Baltimore, but Nellie gave her a warm hug and the Scotties ran around her feet, crying with delight, as she came in the front door. No, there was nothing like home.

She decided not to go to the clinic on her first morning back, but instead to spend some time in her little house. Catherine had gone in, 'to see what they've done to my schoolroom,' she said. Louisa was in the kitchen with Nellie.

'She has a hunted look,' Nellie said.

'Don't be dramatic, Nellie,' Louisa said, but in truth she was worried about Catherine too. 'They were there all the time in New York. You wonder what they do when there are no swimmers around to photograph. She was in all the papers when she won the race, and then again when they announced the Channel team. It's like a madness over there. But she's back here now and all will be well. You'd have to agree she's in better spirits.

'Yes, she is,' Nellie said. 'She's growing up.' She looked squarely at Louisa. 'And have you given her those letters?'

Louisa shook her head. 'It's been too long now, Nellie. I can't. And anyway, she's stopped asking.'

'I can't help but feel we've done her wrong.'

Louisa wanted to argue with Nellie but found she didn't have it in her to do so. Nellie was right.

'Did she like the swimming?' Nellie said.

'Oh, yes,' Louisa replied, wondering if she should try to explain to Nellie what worried her. She wasn't altogether sure she could articulate it, but it had something to do with Black. 'Anyway, she'll just go over and try the Channel. Mr Black says she has a good chance. And then she'll come home.'

'Won't that just make it harder? Those Channel girls are in all the papers even here. Once they get wind of Catherine . . .'

'Let's worry about one thing at a time,' Louisa said. 'For now, it sounds like she's happy at the clinic. I'm going to do something about a school for her. I think everything is going to be fine.'

Ruth Luxton was waiting for Louisa when she arrived the next morning. 'I'm very happy you went,' Ruth said, embracing her so hard Louisa nearly fell over. 'But, oh, we missed you. Just for your surgeon's hands as much as anything.'

'Not for my surgeon's temperament?' Louisa said.

'Perhaps,' Ruth said. 'I think you get more done in a day than I do.'

'But you do it so much more kindly.'

They sat down in the little office. It was still early and Ruth made tea. 'You're looking better,' she said.

'I am,' Louisa answered. 'I think I've learnt something about myself.'

'And what's that?'

'I think I've spent my whole life since . . . since Edinburgh working too hard.'

'Well, that is good news. How did you come to that realisation?' Ruth smiled. 'Don't get me wrong, Louisa. I've always understood. But it's got to feel good to let that go.'

'Who said anything about letting go? My intention is to hold on as tight as I can.'

They both laughed.

'It was Catherine,' Louisa said.

'Oh, yes,' Ruth said. 'I hear she's been a grand success over there. And the Channel now.'

'It's not so much the success that struck me as the girl herself. You see, Catherine isn't trying to be successful or win races or do anything. She's just happy in herself. Everyone else was so amazed when she won that race, but she didn't even care.'

'I totally agree she's a delightful girl,' Ruth said. 'But what does that mean for you?'

'I think that's how I might have been too, before . . . It's just been a very extraordinary experience to watch her, to spend time with her. Almost an opportunity to travel back in time, to see what might have been.'

'Does that lead to regrets?'

'A little, yes,' Louisa said, tears in her eyes. 'But perhaps also, one day, peace.'

'What a lovely holiday you've had, my dear. We don't get to plan when we're given insight. Now, should we tackle the mountain of paperwork over there?'

'No,' Louisa said. 'Let's not. Let's see some patients and worry about the paperwork later.'

'Well, you really have been transformed. I've never known you to put off paperwork given a chance!'

'There's something else,' Louisa said.

'Yes?'

Louisa hesitated. 'Nothing,' she said finally. She had been going to ask Ruth about the letters, what she should do. Nellie was still insisting that Louisa give them to Catherine, but she didn't want to. It was too late. And what if Catherine didn't forgive her? Maybe after the Channel, when Black was out of their lives, she'd tell her. But maybe she'd just let sleeping dogs lie.

And then, when Louisa collected the post that evening, there it was, a letter, postmarked Cairns, not Thursday Island, addressed to Catherine. It was marked urgent, and so Louisa decided to open it.

Dear Catherine,

I am writing with very bad news. Michael is in trouble. We've been in Cairns for the last month. As I said in my last letter, he went down a couple of months ago to get work with some other boys from here. He was wanting to earn enough money to get over to you and find out what's going on.

But he's been accused of something. Someone held up a store in Samsonvale and they killed the owner. It wasn't Michael. I know it wasn't. But because he'd moved there with a group of boys, they've arrested them all and one of them has confessed.

Michael says none of them did anything and you know he wouldn't do that. But the charge is murder, Waapi. And he's old enough to be hanged.

There's no one I can turn to but you. I don't know any solicitors but Dr Harry's, and he's said he can't help us without money. He says you will help us, being your father's daughter. I've never missed Dr Harry more than in these weeks.

Yours with love,
Florence

Louisa read the letter a second and then a third time. The boy had been charged with a criminal offence. The letter would have taken at least a month to get to London, and Louisa had no idea what might have transpired since Florence wrote. Michael might already have been tried, for all she knew.

He'd been trying to earn the money to come to London, the letter said, to come to London to see Catherine, who hadn't written. Except Catherine had written. She'd written three letters, all of which were in Louisa's possession, along with Michael's and Florence's letters to Catherine. With a sick feeling, Louisa knew that if he had stolen in order to come to Catherine, if he'd killed another human being, she, Louisa, was responsible. She remembered the boy, that lovely smile. She had never meant for something like this to happen. She'd just wanted Catherine to be happy in London.

She went into the kitchen, poured herself a glass of scotch and downed it. She knew if Catherine read the letter she would not only want to help them, she would go to them on the very next ship. Had Louisa misread Michael's first letter, misunderstood the connection between them? Were they indeed siblings, as Alexander had suspected all along? Joined in their bodies? Perhaps the Islanders saw relationships differently.

She wished now she'd just given Catherine the letters and let events take their course. Catherine would probably be forgetting the island in any event. She had a new life. She had the Channel swim coming up and after that, Louisa was sure, she'd return to school.

It had started as a small wrong, hiding one letter. But now it was so much more than that. Louisa put this new letter back in the envelope, went to her room and put the envelope in the drawer with the others.

Part Four

Chapter Twenty-Nine

'Have you two met?'

'No, we haven't,' Harry Quick said. 'And I'd remember.' He grinned at her. God, he must look a fool, he thought. He was trying not to stare. Flowers, she gave off a scent of sweet flowers. The evening had fallen but it was still warm. He pulled at his bow tie, collar, then saw the creeper vine behind her. The smell was the vine, not the girl. Still, he couldn't keep his eyes from her. He felt light-headed.

His hair was in his eyes, he knew, but he couldn't summon his hand to push it back. He stared. Her green eyes seemed more cat-like than human. She wore a red dress. His eyes followed the dress, which fell over her hips like water. Silk, it must be silk. She was watching him. He met her eye.

The other man smiled, taking his arm from around her waist reluctantly. 'Careful, Quick. She's a first-class shot.' He'd invited Harry to a 'little party at the house.' The house was a mansion on Charles Street, high on the hill overlooking the city and the harbour beyond. He was in a tuxedo, his dark hair just starting to grey at the sides, those grey eyes that looked right through a person. Wisdom, Harry had thought when they first met. The man had wisdom.

'I mean it,' he said, trying to get Harry's attention. 'She's in the Maryland Shooters' Association.'

She still hadn't spoken. She regarded Harry and it was the way she held his gaze. She was not to be toyed with, or made a fool. She looked at her companion.

'This is the doctor?' Her voice made her sound younger than he'd thought she was at first; it was a schoolgirl's voice. 'It's so nice you could come tonight. Did you say your name was Harry?'

He nodded. 'And you?'

'Julia,' she said. 'So lovely to meet a friend of Lear's.'

Harry's confusion must have shown on his face.

'Me rather than the king,' Manfred Lear Black said.

'Julia,' Harry said to Black later that night.

'Hmmm?'

'How old is she?'

'Twenty-one.'

'I thought she was younger. Is she at college?'

'Brown.'

He nearly revealed his feelings to Black, but something stopped him.

'So you're cousins?'

Black nodded. 'Her father is my mother's brother.'

'Good.'

* * *

He found her on the terrace on the bottom lawn, which looked out to a lake house. 'What are you doing down here by yourself?' he said, a little drunk on champagne.

'I'm trying to hide,' she said. 'My father wants me to propose a toast.' She wiped her eyes. Harry had the impression she'd been crying.

'A toast to what?'

'To Lear. For his birthday.'

'And you don't want to.'

'No.' She turned to look at him. The moonlight was coming across to them as a thick shimmering line on the lake. 'You're a doctor. You could propose the toast.'

'How would that qualify me?' he said. *'The hip bone's connected to the leg bone . . .'* he sang.

She smiled, gestured with her hand. 'Oh, I don't know. Just . . . let's sit on the grass and we won't be seen from the house and we won't have to do anything they want.'

So they did. Harry was in Baltimore for one more night. She was on her way back to university. If he was going to act, he had to act.

Two hours later, he'd proposed, and she'd said yes.

Chapter Thirty

Cap Gris-Nez, where swimmers were already ensconced for the season, was like a gentle smile. They'd had a rough crossing but as they came down the hill to the sea the Channel was quiet. They'd left England early in the morning of a perfectly calm day too. But about an hour into the journey, a storm had come up, creating a huge swell. The ferry was tossed around. In the worst of the weather, Catherine, who was immune to seasickness, had stood outside watching the water. The rain hit her face and ran down the oilskin coat a crew member had lent her. It was mighty, she thought; a living thing.

'The old girl didn't like us,' Andrew said. He'd been sick for the first half of the journey but was better once the sea calmed. 'You can't be thinking you'll swim it?' he said to her when he came out on deck near Calais.

'Apparently,' she said. 'I think it will be easier on a body than on a boat.' Louisa had wanted to know if Catherine really wanted to attempt the Channel. With all the talk of how challenging it was, how it was a mental as well as physical test, of endurance, of courage, of strength, Catherine had become more nervous. Of course I want to do it, she'd said to her aunt, thinking of Mr Black, who'd been so good to her. She wanted to make him proud. But the journey across was enough to make her pause.

They took the train to Boulogne and taxis from there to Gris-Nez, an unassuming place with two inns, a few houses, not even a store. The beach was defined by the headland at one end and rocks that jutted out at the other. The headland did look a little like a *gris nez*, a grey nose, smelling the sea.

The cape was the closest land point to Dover in England, twenty-one miles away. Some swimmers still tried to go the other way, starting in Dover to finish in France, but the tides were kinder in this direction for the end of the swim. It was less distance for a swimmer than the Battery to Sandy Hook, Catherine knew, except that you could never plot a straight course. The water, now a deep blue, could be treachery or mischief, depending how the seas that ran into the English Channel were feeling on the day. They'd take you north or south at will. Trudy Ederle was within sight of Dover the year before when they pulled her from the water. The Channel had turned sour, and no matter how hard she swam, she could not make headway.

Had it not been for the swimmers who came every summer, the Cape would hardly have a visitor. The day Catherine arrived the sky was a pale blue with a few clouds on the far horizon and she could see the coastline stretch away and disappear into the haze. The water was softly kissing the shoals below and it reminded Catherine of the island suddenly. She felt the pull of home.

Catherine's party was booked at the Hotel du Phare on the hill above the bay, named for the lighthouse that stood at the end of the grey nose. The three-storey hotel was tired, with rickety stairs and creaking windows, no electricity or running water. It was run by a couple who'd made a business of accommodating swimmers and reporters every year. They closed in the winter and opened now when the swimmers intent on conquering the Channel came in. The larger Hotel la Sirène, halfway across the bay and just above the beach, was more popular, but Catherine was glad to be somewhere she might have privacy – the reporters would stay at the other hotel.

The Ederles had gone from Calais to Paris, which left Catherine on her own at the Cape for now. Helen Wainwright, the third WSA swimmer, had pulled out at the last minute with a broken arm. Trudy was doing interviews. The English papers said she was the only one of the swimmers who'd even come close to swimming the Channel before. She was particularly disparaging about Lillian Cannon, for some reason, claiming Lillian wasn't a strong enough swimmer. She didn't mention Catherine at all – perhaps she thought Catherine wasn't even in the running.

Catherine had been secretly overjoyed when Helen Wainwright pulled out, hoping that Aileen might join them in her place. She'd felt a bit lonely on the ferry coming across, even though Andrew was with her. But given the choice, Aileen had opted instead to prepare for university.

Catherine was disappointed her friend wouldn't be with her. It also made her realise that the choice she'd made, to come here to swim, might mean she'd never get back to school, and school was why she'd left the island in the first place.

She'd tried to talk to Andrew about it. 'Louisa's right,' she said. 'I should be at school. That's why I came to London.'

'Oh, I wouldn't think too much about that now,' Andrew replied. 'Mr Black says you can run your own school once you swim the Channel.'

So far, Catherine had been swimming as an amateur, which meant she could not earn any money. After the Channel swim, though, she could turn professional. Andrew said there would be sponsors who'd pay for her name. 'They get you to stand there next to the cars they're selling or wear the clothes.'

'I don't think I'd much like that,' she said.

Andrew had become so much more worldly since going to America. 'What about you?' she asked. 'What will you do next?'

He looked at her. 'Yes. What about me?' he said. 'Mama is very keen on a girl my brother knew. We had a big family discussion about it when I went home.'

'A girl your brother knew?'

'A nice English girl.'

'And you?'

'Ah, Catherine.' He sighed heavily. 'Are we just in the wrong place at the wrong time?' He looked at her. 'You aunt keeps telling me how young you are, and I know that's

313

true. In a couple of years it won't make any difference between us. Would you want to come back to America with me, do you think?'

She had a strange feeling then, the same feeling she'd had when he kissed her in New York. She knew that, if she wanted him to, he'd kiss her again. But she wasn't sure she did want him to. She didn't answer him.

He nodded. 'I see,' he said sadly. 'When Donald . . .' He smiled tightly. 'He was the brave son.'

'So, do you like this girl?' Catherine said.

'I do,' he said. 'I do.' He looked awfully sad, though, Catherine thought.

The wind had freshened again. Andrew said he'd stay in the hotel and read a book, but Catherine walked to the top of the promontory and looked out across the water. Andrew had been like a big brother to Catherine and yet, when he'd kissed her, she'd felt different with him. Aileen had thought Catherine must have a crush on Andrew – who wouldn't? Aileen said – and perhaps she did. But he wasn't the sort of person she felt at home with. The only boy she'd really felt at home with was Michael. Did she feel about Michael the way she felt about Andrew? Did that mean she did have a crush on Andrew? She didn't know. If she could combine how thrilled she'd felt when Andrew kissed her with how safe she felt with Michael, she'd have Aileen's notion of a beau.

She thought of Mr Black suddenly. Of course he wasn't her beau, but there was something about him that felt safe. She wanted to please him, didn't want to disappoint him. He reminded her of her father, she realised, and she felt sad.

She looked out towards England, towards home. Was it home now? On a clear day, you'd see the cliffs of Dover. The smell of the sea filled her with happiness. She was shivering with the cold – the breeze blew straight through her coat – but happy to be back near the water.

The next morning, she woke early, intending to go down to the beach on her own. The weather was settled and the sky was a perfect pale blue. She'd wanted to spend some time by herself, get a feel for the water before Mr Burgess, her coach, arrived.

Catherine and Louisa had met Mr Burgess in London. He was the second person ever to swim the Channel, and Mr Black had engaged him and paid his fee. 'He's the best,' Mr Black had said. 'Can't have my girl with some idiot.'

He was a compact man with steel-grey hair and a grey beard, light blue eyes and dark leathery skin, as if he'd seen too many days at sea. Catherine felt comfortable with him. Very straight, Louisa said. He'll be fine.

'If you know your swimming, Catherine, I know the Channel,' Burgess had said. He'd tried to swim across eleven times before succeeding. 'So I know it better than most men do.' He had a full-throated laugh.

'I know my swimming, Mr Burgess,' Catherine had said, relieved he wouldn't be trying to change her stroke like Mr Handley had. Catherine knew that all five swimmers who'd conquered the Channel to date, including Burgess, had swum the trudgeon, a stroke Mr Handley had shown them that looked odd and was even more odd when you tried to swim it. It was a sort of scissor kick with frog

315

arms. In America, many of the girls had started swimming by learning the trudgeon. It wasn't until Mr Handley took over coaching that they swam a crawl. But Catherine had always swum a crawl, even if it wasn't quite how Mr Handley wanted her to do it. She still kicked two beats for each stroke, or sometimes four, but never six.

Catherine walked down a little path to the sea now. She reached the beach in five minutes but Andrew and the other newspapermen were already down there.

'How you feeling, Catherine?' one of them yelled.

She smiled the way Andrew had said she should. 'I'm feeling like swimming,' she said.

Andrew had said they'd leave her alone now that she was signed to Mr Black's newspaper. Even in London, they'd started pestering her about this swim. The English papers had caught on to the fact that there was a challenger, and they all wanted to know what Catherine thought about what Gertrude Ederle was saying. Catherine replied that it wouldn't be up to Gertrude Ederle, and it wouldn't be up to Catherine Quick. 'The Channel makes its own mind up,' she said. 'There's no telling what will happen.' But then they wrote that she was challenging Gertrude Ederle. Maybe Trudy didn't say the things they attributed to her either. Maybe they just made them up.

When Catherine read the stories about herself in the paper and saw the pictures, it was as if they weren't really writing about her, Catherine. It was as if they meant another person altogether, a person she didn't know, a person she might not like very much.

According to the newspapers, one of them would be

the first woman to swim the Channel. Mercedes Gleitze was planning her attempt from the English side. There were other swimmers too, and the newspapers couldn't get enough of them – or, at least, couldn't get enough of some of them. Another American, Clarabelle Barrett, for instance, was a strong contender, but she was never in the newspaper. Clarabelle came from a wealthy New York family, and had been an early WSA swimmer. When her father died, she'd had to leave the WSA to turn professional and care for her mother. 'One of our great losses,' Charlotte had said. Now she taught swimming in schools. Clarabelle was the only one of them attempting the Channel on her own, with no funding for a trainer or even a pilot boat. She had no newspaper sponsorship, and her friends had lent her money to make the trip to France. The newspapers ignored her. Andrew said she was 'not what we want on page three'.

Aileen had told Catherine that Clarabelle was the swimmer with the most chance of success. She'd swum across Long Island Sound in May, when the water was freezing. She did look like a champion, Catherine thought when they met in France. She was taller than Catherine, over six feet. She had long auburn hair, which she wore tied back. At thirty-four she was older than the other WSA swimmers. She hated the photographers more than Catherine did. And they left her alone mostly, Catherine noticed. 'Because she doesn't look like you,' Andrew said, and smiled. 'She's big and scary.'

Clarabelle wasn't swimming for fame, and there was no one like Mr Black or Gertrude Ederle's father encouraging her either. She wanted money because she wanted to become a professional singer. When her father had been alive, he'd paid for her to learn to sing, but after his death there was no money left for singing lessons. She'd seen the stories on the Channel swimmers and had decided she should at least try. She'd been training all year. She was desperate to succeed, and it made Catherine want success for her.

She looked over at the group of photographers watching her. What she wanted more than anything was to take off her clothes and leave them here on the sand, and dive in and swim. She knew it would be cold, but even the cold wouldn't be enough to deter her. As she waited and watched the sea, photographers snapping their blasted pictures, she realised she would not go in while they were there. She saw Andrew further up the sand, sauntering towards her.

'Good morning,' he said when he reached her. 'Are you swimming or contemplating?'

'Both?' she said.

'Company?' he said.

'I don't want to go swimming with all these fellows here,' she said.

'Why not?'

'I don't know. Can you ask them to leave?'

'Not really. They can snap whatever pictures they like in a public place. You could just strip down to your bathers and let them photograph you getting in the water. They'd love that.'

'But I wouldn't love it,' she said. 'I don't want to, not in front of all of them. I think I'll just go for a walk.'

Andrew looked over to the group of reporters and photographers and sighed. 'Well, they won't be happy until they have something to send back to America. That's how the business is.'

'Why don't you kiss me?' Catherine said.

'Kiss you?' he replied.

'Yes – that would give them something to send back to America.'

'I hadn't thought of that.' He leant in and kissed her on the cheek, his hands still in his pockets. When he pulled back again, his eyes were soft.

He looked over at the reporters. 'It seems that hasn't satisfied them,' he said, and she disliked him then because he was one of them.

'I can't stand this,' she said, and turned and walked through the crowd of reporters and back up the headland towards the hotel.

Chapter Thirty-One

Black must have heard the urgency in her voice on the telephone. He'd only arrived from America the day before. He had a meeting he could cancel, he said, if she could come to the Carlisle at noon. He asked when she was heading over to France. She wasn't sure, she said. He'd be going himself in the next few weeks; by air, he said.

'She's going to do it, Louisa. My girl's going to swim the Channel.' There it was again: 'his' girl. Louisa wondered just how far he'd go to help his girl. She needed him to help her now.

He was in the lobby waiting when she arrived, wearing his lounge jacket and pressed slacks. 'Thank you for agreeing to meet me,' she said. 'Can we walk? I don't think I can sit still for this.'

He offered his arm, smiling hopefully. She didn't take it. 'Are you all right?'

'No, I'm not,' she said abruptly. 'I have done something that I thought was in Catherine's best interests, but it's become complicated and I need you to listen.'

'What is it, Louisa? You look like you've seen a ghost.'

'Yes. Please. Just let me speak. Is there somewhere private we can go? Perhaps I don't want to walk after all.' She had suggested on the telephone that they might walk in the park, but now that she was here, she didn't feel she could go any further. She had a plan, she reminded herself, and she needed Black if she was to execute it.

'Of course.' He gestured to the waiter, stood and spoke quietly to him. He came back to Louisa. 'I'd invite you to my suite, but that might cause a stir, so our man here has arranged for us to use the private lounge.' He helped her up and linked his arm in hers, then placed his other hand on her hand. She calmed a little.

They went into a lounge off the lobby. He closed the door behind him and she sat down at the table by the window. He poured her a drink, a neat scotch, brought it over, then poured one for himself. He looked apprehensive, Louisa thought, as if she might have bad news for him.

'Before you start,' he said, 'it was never my intention to deceive.'

'What are you talking about?' she said. 'Just give me a minute.' She breathed in and out.

'All right,' he said. 'I'm sorry.'

'Deceive?' she said. 'Whatever do you mean?'

'Nothing,' he said. 'Why don't you tell me why you're here?'

'You know Catherine grew up on an island north of Australia?'

He nodded carefully.

'There was a family there, a woman and her child, who were close to my brother Harry.'

'Florence Cunningham.'

She looked at him. How on earth did he know?

'Julia and I wrote one another occasionally. She told me about Florence. I take it that's who you mean? I didn't know she had children.'

'Yes, well, Harry was very close to Florence. My other brother . . . Oh, that doesn't matter now. Anyway, when Catherine came home to London with me after Harry died, she wouldn't settle at school. She just wanted to go back to the island. I began to despair. I mean, she and I didn't know each other terribly well, and I'm not used to children. I know it's no excuse. But it seemed to me that the thing that unsettled her most was news from Australia – from Florence and her son.'

He nodded. 'Of course,' he said. 'You might expect that.'

'Yes. And then one day I collected the post on my way to work. And there was a letter for Catherine. And I read it.' She raised her hand to stop him from talking. 'Yes, I know it was wrong. I know it wasn't mine to read.'

'No, I understand,' he said. 'I would have done exactly as you did.'

The relief! He didn't think she was a terrible person. She continued. 'When I look back now, I . . . I think I misunderstood something in the letter – although perhaps I didn't. But anyway, I made a decision; that is, I kept that one letter to see what happened.

'And then you came along and we were off to New York and swimming, and so I kept the next letter and the next. And I suppose I saw the swimming as a godsend, really, to take her mind off these other things while I sorted something out with a school. I thought she would go over to America and swim a little, and then return to London and go back to school.' She sighed heavily.

'Anyway, I told Nellie to keep Catherine's letters to Australia and not send them, and after a while Catherine stopped writing and talking about the island. And not only that, she was much more happy. She was in New York and all she wanted to do was swim well for you. She admires you, Lear, that's the truth of it.' Louisa was worried it was more than admiration, that Catherine had a crush on Black. She'd lost her parents. She'd lost her home. Oh, Louisa had been so wrong, she saw now.

There was a gardener outside in the drive, pruning something, rosebushes probably – she'd seen rosebushes on the way in. She could hear the regular snip of his shears, the click of the stems breaking.

'Well, that's good news,' he said. 'Well done.'

She smiled weakly and put her fingers to her eyelids, held them there for a moment. 'No, you don't understand. There's been another letter. The boy, the boy Catherine was close to, is in terrible trouble and it's my fault.'

'What boy do you mean, Louisa? Florence's boy?'

'He's Catherine's age or a bit older. His mother says he went to one of the towns on the coast. He wanted to get a job, to earn money. He wanted to come over to see Catherine, to find out why she hadn't replied to his letters. I thought he'd forget. She'd forget. And it was for the best. And now he's in trouble. The boy. He's in trouble, terrible trouble, and it's my fault.' Louisa explained briefly what had happened.

'I don't understand, Louisa. That's not your fault.'

'Well, of course it is. The boy would never have been in Cairns if it weren't for me withholding the letters.

323

And Catherine would never have stopped writing.'

'You can't know that.' He looked at her intently.

'Oh, for God's sake, I'm not seeking your forgiveness here, or some version of Maryland wisdom. Just listen.'

She realised she was close to losing control, and he was doing his best. She needed to calm down. She needed him now like never before. 'I wired Harry's lawyer in Cairns and got him to look into the situation.'

'Witherspoon.'

'You know Witherspoon?'

He hesitated before answering. 'Yes, he's done some work for me on a shipping deal Alex and I were negotiating in Australia.'

'Anyway, at first I was terribly worried, of course, because the letter would have taken some time to arrive and . . . Anyway, Mr Witherspoon's been able to reassure me on that score. The boy's in prison, charged, awaiting trial.

'I thought of going to Alexander, but he and Harry . . . He won't be disposed to help. He'll say I did the right thing.'

'And you think you didn't?'

'Of course not. If he's hanged, it will be because of me.'

'Now, hold your horses there, Louisa. We went from trouble to hanged. Why hanged?'

'I'm sorry. It's just so awful. They robbed a shop. They shot a man. He's dead.'

'This boy did?'

'His mother says no. And Mr Witherspoon says she's right.'

He nodded, breathed in and out slowly. 'All right, Louisa, you need to look at me.' He sat for a few moments, regarded her carefully. She felt like talking but stopped herself. 'So

324

you withheld some letters to help your niece. I don't see a problem with that. It's your job to care for her. And then this boy's done something wrong, or not.' He took a sip of his scotch. 'That's not your fault.' He shook his head. 'Not at all.'

He spoke as if he was used to people agreeing with him, as if he could fix anything, teasing out Louisa's liability as if that would make it all right. And she imagined he mostly could fix anything. But no amount of clever description and running from liability changed what had now happened.

'As far as I'm concerned,' he said, 'you don't have to do anything.'

'Of course I have to do something,' Louisa said. 'I can't keep this from Catherine now.'

'You absolutely must keep it from her now,' Black said, a sense of urgency in his voice. 'She mustn't under any circumstance know this, not now, when she's about to make the attempt on the Channel – not now, when she's left all that island nonsense behind.'

'The bloody Channel is all you think of,' Louisa said.

He looked hurt. 'No it's not. I'm thinking of Catherine, her future. This will give her a confidence nothing else ever could, Louisa, after everything she's been through.' He looked surprised that she thought so poorly of him.

'Well, if the boy Michael is dead, it won't matter. Anyway, Witherspoon can do something, as it happens. He just wants money and so I've told him to go ahead on the basis that I will pay.'

'What for?'

'He says the police aren't really even terribly interested in the case. They want to solve it, and this is an easy way to do so. To take the more difficult way, which means truly solving the crime, they need money.' She felt tears threatening. 'He's a lovely boy, Lear. I met him.'

'How does Witherspoon know this boy didn't do it?'

'Michael was working on a fishing boat. He wasn't even in Cairns when the man was shot. The other boys say they weren't there either. Their alibis would hold in a fair trial, Mr Witherspoon says. It's just an appalling place where some lives are cheaper than others.

'The owner of the boat has signed an affidavit to the effect that Michael was working on the day of the murder, but the police so far have shown little interest. We can take our chances with a trial, Mr Witherspoon said, and he'll represent the boy. But that too is fraught. Witherspoon tells me the quickest way to convince the police to look at the affidavits he's collected is to give them money.'

'A bribe.'

'That's not the word he used.'

'What word did he use?'

'Contribution.'

Black smiled. 'Ah, the world's the world. And I'm guessing that's where I come in – the money.'

She nodded. 'Yes, the money. I told him to go ahead, but I don't have a thousand pounds.'

He took a sharp breath in. 'Oh, that's a lot of money.'

'It's less than you'd spend on one of your parties, I'd warrant, let alone those jaunts up in the aeroplane.'

'Possibly,' he said. 'But those are my parties and my jaunts. This is to help a boy I've never met.'

'It's to help me.'

He took a puff of his cigar. 'If I'm to help, you mustn't tell Catherine.'

'I have to tell Catherine.'

'Ah, we come to an impasse. You now want to unburden yourself of your dishonesty as a way of seeking atonement.'

'No; if I don't tell her, Florence and Michael will.'

'Not if she never sees them again,' he said. 'Which is what you wanted in the first place.'

Louisa stopped then. She wouldn't tell him the whole story. She wouldn't tell him what else she was planning to do. What had happened to Michael – and all because Louisa decided she knew best – made her realise she must now do the right thing.

She'd been wrong taking Catherine from the home she knew and loved. And, she was pretty sure, she'd been wrong about Michael and his relationship to Catherine. He and Florence were more Catherine's family than Louisa was. Catherine was cast adrift not because she was wild and uncivilised as Alexander had claimed but because she'd been taken from the only home she'd known. And, Louisa thought now, it had been a good home.

Louisa was going to do what she could to make up for the harm she'd caused – if only she wasn't too late, she thought now. But she wouldn't tell Black. He would never agree, so bent was he on making Catherine his champion. 'Are you suggesting I go on as if nothing happened? I can't do that, Lear. I just can't. It's wrong.'

'Then you have a problem, Louisa.'

Chapter Thirty-Two

The weather was fine throughout the first week of July and Catherine thought they might try the swim – the sun shone and the water looked like glass day after day – but Mr Burgess was waiting for the right combination of weather and tides.

'The Channel is in charge here, not us,' he said. 'I thought you were the swimmer who already knew that. Anyway, the sooner you learn it, the better you'll be. The Channel tells us when she'll let us swim, and when she won't.'

They needed perfect conditions, but even if the tides were in their favour and the weather looked calm, the North Sea could squall at a moment's notice and ruin a swim.

'The English Channel, my girl, is the most difficult body of water in the world,' Mr Burgess said. 'You're squeezing two grumpy seas into a too-narrow gap, creating a force that has to go somewhere. Often it goes on top of a little swimmer.' It was notorious for claiming ships, and many a fine swimmer had failed, he said, sucking on his pipe thoughtfully.

In the meantime, she spent time in the water every day. She started at twenty minutes. Catherine could have stayed longer. She didn't mind the cold at all, the thrill of the icy water on her skin, even the way it seeped into her bones. She loved the tiredness afterwards, as she drank hot tea in front of the fire. She preferred it to swimming in warm water now, she realised, although Lillian Cannon, who trained with Catherine, told her she'd still rather swim in warmer water. Lillian was sponsored by the *Baltimore Daily Post*, and her dogs were to swim the Channel with her, although Catherine had read a story in *The Times* that said this was cruel to the dogs. The newspapers were just making a story of it, Lillian said. One of the dogs refused to get in the water anyway, Catherine had noticed – he just stood on the beach and howled – so she wasn't sure how they were planning to have them swim the Channel.

Lillian didn't seem to want to win anything. Like Catherine, she just enjoyed swimming. And there was a lightness about her that was lacking in everyone else here, Catherine thought, including Andrew, who was getting very serious about the challenge of the Channel and Catherine's chances. Even Clarabelle Barrett, whom Catherine liked, was serious when it came to swimming. Catherine had asked Mr Burgess if Clarabelle could swim with them but he'd said no. When Miss Ederle arrives, he said, I'll have three swimmers, and that will be enough.

The newspapermen tried to get Catherine and Lillian to be mean about one another, but they had agreed they wouldn't say anything negative about the other. 'Do the newspapers bother you?' Catherine had asked Lillian.

'Oh, no,' Lillian said. 'I don't mind so much. I just cuddle one of the dogs and think nice thoughts and then it's over.'

'I wish they cared more about other things.'

'Yes, it's odd. All we're doing is swimming. Before I left New York, I did a little swim for the newspaper in the river.'

'I remember.'

'And all those sailors from the *Illinois* came out on deck and cheered. You'd think I'd won the war. But do you know, I didn't really even swim. I just dived in with the dogs and then got out. My husband says they like me in my bathing suit.'

The two swimmers often walked along the shore in the afternoons, sometimes followed by the reporters and photographers who Catherine did her best to ignore. If you didn't capitulate, give them a smile and turn their way, they wrote stories with headlines like swimmer sulks or pouting princess. You couldn't win, she knew that well enough.

Lillian had met Andrew over dinner one night. When Catherine said he was a reporter, she noticed that Lillian and her husband Eddie became more careful with him. Lillian wasn't as open. One day on the beach, Catherine asked Lillian about it. 'Oh, I would never talk openly to one of those fellows,' she said. 'The next day, it would all be in the newspaper.'

'He's my friend,' Catherine said.

'Yes, but he's not mine,' Lillian replied.

Andrew did try to help. He told the reporters they weren't allowed to speak to Catherine because they didn't have an exclusive contract. But the photographers were the ones who took everything from you, and Andrew couldn't stop them. At any rate, Andrew himself was sending stories back to America all the while. He was in charge of writing a column in Catherine's name. Initially, she'd told him what things she wanted to write about, but he soon started coming up with his own ideas. Catherine wanted to write about swimming and how it felt, but he said no one would care about that. 'They'll want to know what you're going to wear in the water,' he said. 'The men go naked, you know.' He smiled slyly. Catherine disliked him for it.

The columns were running in the English papers too, and the French. Everyone knew now that Catherine Quick was up against Lillian Cannon and Gertrude Ederle to conquer the Channel. Clarabelle Barrett continued to prepare for her swim but the newspapermen didn't have any interest in her. To Catherine, it was suffocating. It seemed like every day there were more of them ensconced in the other hotel down on the beach, or in the nearby village. What she would remember from those weeks was not the smell of kelp that drifted up from the sea, the smell of salt water on her skin, the smell of the sea air, all of which she loved. What she would remember was their magnesium flashes, which smelt of a match lighting.

The first two weeks of July passed. Louisa still hadn't come over. Catherine was longing to have people she knew other than Andrew around her. Most of all, she wanted to see Mr Black, to show him she was ready for the swim. He'd be so proud. In the hotel she could curl up in a chair and read a book without anyone bothering her. The food was wonderful – chicken in rich sauces, beef steaks with creamy potato, roast lamb – but she wasn't hungry, she found, although she was supposed to be putting on weight for the swim. The problem for the reporters was that there was so little to report, Andrew said. They couldn't leave, in case Burgess suddenly decided it was time to swim, but there was nothing for them to do in the meantime. She knew exactly how they felt, Catherine thought but didn't say.

When the Ederles arrived, Trudy, Meg and their father, things changed. Meg greeted Catherine warmly but Trudy was her usual self, quiet and withdrawn. Her father was furious, Andrew told Catherine, because Mr Burgess was training other swimmers. 'What's the problem with that?' Catherine said, not understanding.

'He's supposed to be Trudy's coach exclusively. Old Papa Ederle is talking to anyone who'll listen. What a bag of wind.' Trudy wanted Mr Burgess to herself, Andrew said.

'But aren't we both swimming with the WSA? I mean, Lillian's swimming with her dogs, and Clarabelle's on her own, but aren't Trudy and I with the WSA, more or less?' The WSA wasn't providing the funding for anyone's swim, as it happened. Mr Black was funding Catherine, and Trudy was funded by the New York *Daily News* syndicate. Mr Burgess had asked Catherine on the first day if he might add Lillian Cannon to his group and she'd said of course. It had been a bright spot since arriving in France, spending time with Lillian and the dogs. Now Trudy wanted Lillian thrown off the team.

Andrew laughed. 'Well, yes, officially you're both representing the WSA. But, you see, Burgess told Trudy he'd coach her and only her. And after last year, Trudy's not willing to share a coach and risk failure again.'

'But swimming together makes it easier, not harder,' Catherine said. 'It's better to have a few of us together.'

'Maybe,' Andrew said. 'But it's not what she wants. I think there's going to be trouble. At least we'll have something to file. Swimmer simmers!'

Catherine turned sixteen, although no one with her knew it and she didn't tell them – not even Andrew. It was odd to be so alone in the world that she had no one left who remembered the day she was born.

It was nearly a year now since she'd been expelled from Henley. She'd had a letter from Aileen, who was getting more excited about starting college. Catherine wondered what on earth she was doing in this little French village not swimming, and Mr Black wasn't even here.

Late in the morning on the day after her birthday, Catherine was down on the beach watching the water. Every day had been the same, relatively calm on the French side, but the tides were wrong or the sea beyond was wild. It was frustrating.

Andrew came down the sand to join her, stopping first to take off his shoes and roll up his long trousers. 'How goes the swimmer?' he asked.

'Oh, you know,' Catherine said. 'Wishing she could swim.'

'Do we know when yet?'

'Mr Burgess says there are three days coming up he likes. It might even be the day after tomorrow, but I think Trudy gets first pick of the day to try.'

'Well, that would at least take her out of contention.'

'You don't think she'll succeed?'

'I think you're the only one who has a chance, Catherine.'

'You know a lot about swimming?'

He smiled. 'You're quite right. I don't. But I know Mr Black. He is rarely wrong and you're his swimmer.'

Catherine nodded but didn't respond.

'Are you all right?'

She looked out towards the water. None of it had been what she'd expected. 'Oh, Andrew, I think of myself here, swimming the Channel, and I don't know if it's what I want.'

'Whatever do you mean?' he said. 'What are you talking about?'

'Nothing,' she said. 'Nothing at all.' He'd never understand, she thought. No one would.

Chapter Thirty-Three

Louisa hadn't seen Catherine when she'd got in late the night before but she left a message suggesting they meet that morning for breakfast. She'd waited in London to make sure everything would go as planned. She hadn't spoken again to Black since they'd met at the Carlisle. She'd agreed reluctantly not to tell Catherine what had happened – and what she, Louisa, had done – but only because it was his money that would get Michael out of trouble. Black wanted Catherine to do the swim. But when the swim was over, however it went, Louisa would have to tell Catherine. It wasn't even a choice now after what Louisa had done. She'd wired Mr Witherspoon. The money was coming, she told him. Do what you can. And then she'd wired Florence.

Catherine came in to the dining room. Oh, the change those few weeks had wrought. Louisa was shocked by the sight of her. Catherine had lost weight when she was supposed to be putting it on. Mr Burgess had told them she'd need to put by some fat for energy and as insulation against the cold. Louisa remembered what Nellie had said when Catherine had returned from New York. Now she could see it herself. The girl was positively haggard, with dark circles under her eyes. It was almost as if Catherine knew without knowing what was happening in Australia. Louisa imagined having to explain to Catherine what she'd done. She should stick to her guns, Black told her. She'd done right, he said. It wasn't wrong to keep the letters from the girl, and it wasn't Louisa's fault if the boy did something stupid. She never had to tell Catherine.

She looked at Catherine walking towards her now. Even her gait was less certain. When Louisa thought back to the girl who'd come out of the Thames, the girl who'd left Australia, even the girl who'd been the first to the beach at Sandy Hook, she could see how this girl was different.

They hugged, Catherine holding on longer than usual, then they both sat. Louisa didn't say anything but the look of concern on her face must have told a story.

'Nothing's wrong,' Catherine said. She smiled, but even her smile was less than it had been.

'Have you been swimming this morning already?' Louisa was upset to see Catherine like this but she was trying not to show it.

'No, just walking with Lillian Cannon. I'll introduce you after.'

'I saw Mr Black in London. He's very pleased that you're here.'

Catherine nodded. 'Mr Black,' she said, her face brightening a little. 'Did you tell him I'm training?'

'Oh, yes, he's very proud,' Louisa said, seeing how pleased it made Catherine. 'Are you sure you're all right, dear?'

'I just . . . I don't even have a minute when they're not there.'

She was close to tears, Louisa saw.

'The newspaper men?'

'They follow my every move. I hate it. Mr Burgess said yesterday that they come in the boat, that they take the whole trip with us. How am I supposed to swim with all that?'

'Poor girl, you never have a minute's peace, do you? They think it's the news.'

'Why aren't they interested in swimming then? Why don't they talk about swimming? They talk about who my boyfriend is, and what I'll wear. But they never talk about kicking or which crawl I'll do.'

'Oh, dear girl. I never would have wished this on you . . . I . . .'

'I suppose you'll say you told me so.' She looked at Louisa.

'Did I tell you so? I don't think I quite thought it through as well as all that. But I do understand. When my mother was doing medicine, all the newspapers wanted to know was whether she blushed when she saw a man naked. She'd done anatomy in her nursing training, so she was well past the blushing stage when they were asking. But they persisted. She was like you in that way, Catherine. She didn't like the limelight. She didn't want to be any different from the others.'

'What did she do about it?' Catherine said.

'Oh, she put up with it until they stopped. Eventually they did. But she never had to endure anything like what you're facing. It wasn't her body they focused on. Do you still want to do this?'

'The swim isn't what's bothering me. Ever since New York, they've been following everything I do. I can't even eat breakfast without someone writing about it. I have to do the swim. For Mr Black.'

'No, you don't, Catherine,' Louisa said. 'If you don't want to swim, you shouldn't swim.'

Catherine didn't respond.

In the afternoon, Louisa watched the training session with Burgess. The newspapermen were down on the beach. They were taking pictures and calling out their questions. Burgess did nothing to stop them and Louisa approached him afterwards and told him that it was bothering Catherine. Now that Trudy Ederle had arrived, the newspapers were making much of the tensions among the swimmers, Louisa noticed. Burgess nodded, said he'd see what he could do.

Louisa had met all the other swimmers during the day. She liked Lillian Cannon, a little blonde girl who meant well. But Trudy Ederle was the one who had what it took, Louisa thought. Like Catherine, she was a good swimmer who loved the water. But unlike Catherine, she saw this as a race, and she wanted more than anything to win.

The next day, Mr Black arrived. He came along the promontory where Louisa and Catherine had been walking. He kissed Louisa on the lips, Catherine noticed, and Louisa didn't turn and give him her cheek like Catherine might have expected. He embraced Catherine briefly, kissing her on each cheek. She found herself so happy to see him. It had been the same when Louisa arrived. She'd been missing them, she realised, wanting familiar faces.

'Let's go back to the hotel,' Mr Black said. 'What a wild place we've brought you to, Catherine.'

'Catherine's still worried about the reporters,' Louisa said when they were back at the hotel lounge. 'They follow everything she does.' She turned to Catherine. 'Mr Black and I spoke of this in London. He can help.'

'Maybe,' he said. 'The thing is, it will only get worse once you swim the Channel.' He was looking at Catherine and his eyes were kind. 'But to be the first woman to do that, Catherine – what an achievement.'

'I know, Mr Black,' Catherine said, 'but at the moment I don't even want to go swimming because the reporters are watching and taking their pictures.'

'Just ignore them,' Black said.

'How do I do that?'

'By taking no notice. That's what I do. In England, they call me the mad American. That's what you first heard about me, am I right? In Baltimore, I own the newspaper, so they tend to write what I want. But in New York, I'm a big bully with shady leanings, according to the *Post*. I'm a friend of Franklin and Eleanor, which makes me corrupt. That's just how they work, Catherine. They need sensation. Truth is, swimming isn't interesting. But swimmers are. That's why they want you. I'll see what I can do.'

It's different for you, Catherine wanted to say. They

don't take a picture of you with hardly any clothes on and have the world look at it. She would never have understood how this might feel until it happened to her.

Catherine had a flash of memory then. She was on the island, running down to the sea with Michael. They would have been nine and eleven, she guessed. They got to the beach, hot from the run, and decided on the spur of the moment to swim. They stripped off and ran into the sea.

It was Florence who took Catherine aside afterwards. 'Where were your bathers?' she wanted to know.

'I left them at the house,' Catherine said. 'We weren't planning to swim.'

She still remembered the feel of the water on her body, the freedom it gave her. But she also knew, from Florence's face, that something was wrong.

'You mustn't do that, Catherine,' Florence said.

'Why not?'

'You just mustn't. There are bad men . . . You must wear your bathers.'

Catherine wanted to ignore Florence. It felt so marvellous to have the water flowing over her skin. She tried several times to get Michael to go along with her after that, but he wouldn't. The memory came back now. It was innocent, she knew, but Florence had made her feel guilty. It was the same feeling she had when the reporters followed her around, as if she, and not they, were at fault.

The next day there were squally showers, and it felt as if the weather matched Catherine's mood, changing constantly, restless. She wanted to be doing more than swimming out

340

to the rocks and back. Mr Burgess sensed her restlessness. Now he was training Catherine separately from Trudy Ederle, so there wouldn't be further trouble. Sometimes Lillian Cannon still swam with Catherine, which Catherine didn't mind, but Trudy wanted to work on her own with her coach.

Catherine was down on the beach waiting for Mr Burgess when she saw up on the sand a tall blonde man in swimming trunks with a sweater over them, a towel around his neck. She thought he must be another Channel likely. But then he waved and called out her name. The accent. She looked again.

'Sam?' she called back. It was Mr Black's pilot. 'What on earth are you doing here?' She ran towards him.

When they met, he embraced her warmly.

'I flew Mr Black over to come see you and Dr Quick. I brought trunks; I thought maybe we could swim together.'

'You swim?'

'I'm the Lake Louise champion.'

'What does that mean?'

'It means this water will be warm as far as I'm concerned.'

She laughed. 'Oh, goodness but it's wonderful to see your face.'

'Yeah,' he said, grinning. 'You look like a real swimmer.'

'I'm just waiting for my coach,' she said. 'We swim to the point and back a few times. It's all about acclimatising and the right tides. We're lucky this morning. No reporters.' She grinned, so happy to see him.

'I read your column in the paper,' Sam said.

'I don't write any of it. Andrew writes it for me.'

'I wondered. It doesn't really sound like you.'

'That's because it's not me. Oh, it's good to see you. So you're still working for Mr Black?'

'This is my last run with him.'

'Why?'

'I'm going home.'

'Are you Sam, to Canada?'

He looked at her. 'I just can't stay any more,' he said. 'I thought I'd go on and be a pilot, you know, like that fellow Lindbergh. Mr Black even offered to fund a flight. But I need to be back in the mountains. I'm just not happy anywhere else.' He looked sad for a moment, then brightened. 'But you – it turns out Mr Black was right. You're a champion.'

'I suppose I am. I think it's grand you're going home.' Catherine felt tears in her eyes. 'Look, now, here's the coach. I'll introduce you and we can swim together.'

Catherine realised she'd lost touch with everything that mattered to her. Andrew was writing her column. She didn't even look at the words he wrote now. He was just like the other reporters. All he cared about was getting a story. Seeing Sam made her remember what it had been like, nearly a year ago now, when she'd been happy. And it was very different from how she felt now.

Chapter Thirty-Four

'Now it's my turn for confessions,' Black said. He grimaced. They were at the bar in the hotel down on the beach, the day after he'd flown in. Louisa had told him that she'd wired the money to Witherspoon and all had gone as planned. She nearly told him the rest then – that she'd borrowed from Nellie's education fund and had sent that money directly to Florence, and wired her to come with Michael once Mr Witherspoon had secured his release; that Nellie was right now taking them to Wellclose Square, that they'd be there when Catherine came home. She knew she'd have to tell Catherine the truth about the letters, even if meant she lost her niece. Nothing that she'd seen so far in France did anything but confirm that this was the right course of action.

There were other diners, mostly locals, a few reporters. Louisa had seen Andrew and a young woman huddled in a corner but hadn't spoken to them.

'I think I already know,' she said.

'You do?'

'Your mother and sister. Charlotte told me.' She reached across to take his hand. The night before, he'd kissed her. They were out on the front porch of the hotel. The rich smell of a cigar lingered in the air. Louisa felt the sea air and thought of Aldeburgh and her childhood. She could hear the water against the rocks below them. Was there ever a chance to start again in life? It felt right then as if there was. Just at that moment, Black had leant in and kissed her on the lips, gently, almost chastely. She closed her eyes. 'Oh,' he'd said softly then.

But now he was shaking his head. 'No,' he said, withdrawing his hand. 'It's not that, although that's part of all this.' He sighed heavily.

'I can't imagine what it must have been like.'

'No you can't,' he said curtly. 'But, Louisa, there's more I have to tell you. Please, just let me speak. After last night, I can't go on with a lie.' He looked at her then, and she saw the despair on his face.

He was married, she thought suddenly. Of course. He was married and he'd never told her. She stared at him. He shifted uncomfortably in his seat.

'I had planned to tell you the first time we met. That was my intention. I told you I knew Harry . . .'

She nodded.

'Well, I also knew Julia.'

It was the way he said her name. Louisa stared at him.

'There's no easy way to say this,' he said. 'I'm Catherine's father.'

'You're what?' Louisa said.

'I'm Catherine's father,' he said again.

'What are you talking about?'

344

'Julia, my cousin – we were lovers.'

She heard a clock somewhere tick a minute by. Louisa looked at him. 'Harry's wife, Julia.' She couldn't put this together. 'But you said . . .'

'Julia was my cousin, my *first* cousin.' He'd said Julia was a Freebody. Someone in his family, his mother, was a Freebody. He'd never even hinted they were closely related, or knew each other well.

He paused, took a long pull on his drink. 'After the *Slocum* . . . I'd lost my mother, my sister. I'd lost them. And Julia . . . We didn't know one another well when she was growing up. They were in the Midwest for a time. But then they came back. She and my aunt stayed a summer at my house on Long Island.'

He put his drink down. 'The thing is, I knew. I knew we could never . . . I was older than Julia by ten years. She was my first cousin. I knew it would never . . . So I introduced her to Harry. Harry, the poor sap. I introduced her to Harry, and she said yes to spite me.'

'Oh,' Louisa said, feeling sick inside.

The week before the wedding, Black said, Julia's mother had asked him to accompany her to New York so she could make the final preparations. Harry was still at Johns Hopkins. 'I said yes, of course. I shouldn't have. I knew I shouldn't have. And then . . .' It was their last night together; he was aware that they would probably never be alone again. 'The thing is, I'd always been chaste. We both knew, though. You do . . . Have you ever loved anyone, Louisa?'

She shook her head.

'Well, you don't know what I'm talking about. I let my

guard down. That final night, Harry was supposed to meet us. He telephoned the hotel to say he was in surgery and for us to go on to dinner. He wouldn't make the last train, he said, so would I take Julia back to the hotel and he'd wait until morning?

'So I did.' He looked ashamed. 'For Julia, I think it was the last moment before she signed up for life with Harry. I believe she loved him, Louisa. I have to believe that.'

'God,' Louisa said flatly. 'She married him because you're her cousin? How could she marry someone out of spite?'

Louisa thought of Catherine then, who'd been let down by them all. Poor dear Catherine.

'I should have told him,' Black was saying. 'But I thought . . . After that there was the wedding. I met your mother. Alex came over. I tried to talk to Julia. I felt awful for what I'd done. And I saw Harry, so happy.'

'But Catherine wasn't born until eleven months later,' Louisa said. 'You can't be her father.'

He was quiet for a few moments, staring at the table. Then he looked up. 'It didn't end there,' he said. 'I saw her again, after the wedding. We met at a cafe. I went there to tell her that we mustn't see one another again, to apologise.

'But I'm sitting there in the cafe, Louisa, and it's all I can do not to reach across and touch her. I'm not proud of those feelings. I'm not proud of many things I've done. We were together again that day. In a hotel.'

'And Julia?'

He didn't answer.

'Poor Harry,' Louisa said. 'But why are you so sure Catherine is your child?'

'She is.' He said it with considerable force. 'Julia wrote me from Australia and told me.'

Louisa realised suddenly why Harry had been so hard to read about Julia's death. 'So did she die in a sailing accident with Harry?'

Black shook his head slowly.

'What happened?'

'I went to the island after she wrote and told me about Catherine. She was desperate. She wanted me to come. I couldn't just abandon her, not once she'd had my child. I was fully prepared to take responsibility for what I'd done. You see, Louisa, I'd done so much wrong already.' He took a long pull on his drink.

Poor Black, Louisa found herself thinking, no matter what he'd done. 'So I went to the island. I told Harry the truth. I told him I was sorry and that the best course would be for him to seek a divorce on the grounds of unfaithfulness. And I would marry Julia and take Catherine. When I think back to how stupid I was, assuming he would just capitulate, I can hardly believe myself. I was wanting to make this one thing right. I wanted to make sure I didn't let her down.' There were tears in his eyes.

'And Harry wouldn't,' Louisa said.

'He said Julia could leave him, but she couldn't take Catherine – and if she tried, he'd follow her and he'd find her.'

'So what did you do?' Louisa was still in shock, she realised. Black believed he was Catherine's father, and if he was right, Harry and Catherine were not related at all. And Louisa. Louisa was not related to Catherine either. This couldn't be, she thought. It just couldn't be. Would she lose

347

her niece now? She couldn't bear that thought. She focused on what Black was saying.

'This is the thing, Louisa. What I should have done was walk away. But I couldn't then. You see my dilemma. I'd told the truth, however much I regretted doing so. Julia said she'd come with me and leave Catherine with him. But I knew she'd blame me one day if she lost her child. And to be honest, if it hadn't been for Catherine, I wouldn't have been there in the first place. I'd already decided to let Julia go. I wouldn't have interfered in their marriage except that the child was mine. Whatever wrong I'd done, I wanted her to be happy. I didn't want to harm anyone.'

'So what happened?'

'We were at an impasse. I wouldn't leave without the child. She became more desperate. At one stage, she even told me Catherine wasn't mine anyway. She only said it out of desperation, she said later. "You wouldn't have come, though, would you, if it weren't for the child?" she said. "You wouldn't have come just for me?" And it was true: I wouldn't have. I wish I'd lied to her about that. She might not have . . .

'I went back to Cairns to talk to the lawyers. She was just desperate for us to be together, not in her right mind. My lawyer was working with Witherspoon on what could be done. But Julia must have lost hope. She could see what would happen. She knew you Quicks would never give up, that Harry had his family behind him. The courts would favour him, she was sure.'

'How?'

He looked up at her, and the pain on his face was hard to bear. 'How what?'

'How did she die?'

'She shot herself.'

'There was no sailing trip, no storm?'

He shook his head.

'And that's how you know Witherspoon,' Louisa said, 'and Florence Cunningham.'

'I left the island and I gave Harry my word I wouldn't go back, that I would do no further harm to the child I'd harmed so much already.'

'But you did come back into Catherine's life.' That was why he'd come to them, pursued Catherine, the swimming. It was nothing to do with Louisa and his Baltimore clinic.

'Witherspoon wrote me when Harry died. He's probably just looking to make a dollar from me but his client is Catherine, and he said he was concerned that her estate was at risk.'

'Because of me,' Louisa said. He nodded. She looked at him. She thought about what he was saying, that Julia had told him the baby was his. Women knew these things usually, Louisa had found. But Catherine was a Quick, surely. Louisa had always said so. Had she just seen what she wanted to see? 'So you think you're Catherine's father?' Louisa said.

'I know it, Louisa.'

'No,' Louisa said. 'You're not. Oh God, Black, what a mess you've had to live with.' She put her hand out. He took it. 'I'm sorry, but Catherine is a Quick. I can show you pictures of my mother if you want, and of me. Catherine was the spitting image of me as a child. She's definitely Harry's.'

'You can't be sure of that,' he said, withdrawing his hand.

'Yes I can,' Louisa said. 'I'm really sorry that you've been through all this. Harry didn't believe Julia. He knew Catherine was his.'

'He never said a word about any of it. I think now he held on in a desperate bid to make Julia stay. '

Yes, Louisa thought, Harry was besotted with Julia. It was believable he'd have been desperate to make her stay. Did he use Catherine in this way? Surely not.

'So when I came to you about the letters, why didn't you tell me then?' She felt angry now.

'I nearly did. It made me realise that whatever I do now, I've been wrong to come back into Catherine's life like this. You've been a good guardian, Louisa.' His voice broke on these last words.

'What was your plan exactly – to take Catherine back to America and tell her the truth?'

'When I saw her swim across the Thames that day, I was proud, I think. And yes, my family. I lost my family for want of swimming. I lost my family because I took them on a ferry trip. I thought I could hook Catherine up with the WSA and it would be good for everyone. It would give her confidence. I didn't think of any future, not then. I came to London just to see, to see that she was all right with you, to keep an eye on her. I didn't know what you were like. I'm so sorry. She's my kin.'

Louisa wished he'd stop saying that. It wasn't true. Louisa was sure it wasn't. Although, was she sure? Perhaps he was right. Perhaps he was Catherine's father and Louisa saw the Quicks in Catherine just because she expected to. Surely not. Still, it was enough to shake her.

'So you saw her swim in the Thames because you were watching her,' Louisa said.

He nodded.

'And Alexander? Did you go into business with my brother because of this?'

'No,' Black said. 'Alex was how I met Harry in the first place. I didn't even start the negotiations.'

'And now you want to tell her?'

'I do not,' he said. He shook his head. 'When you came to me, when the boy was in trouble, I saw how much you care for her, how hard you're working to help her. It was like having a bucket of water thrown in my face. I saw suddenly and so clearly what I've done. It's hard to describe what it's like to fail so spectacularly, Louisa.' He looked at her helplessly. 'What should we do?'

'Was Julia the only one for you?' Louisa said.

'Louisa, I never gave you any kind of understanding.'

'I wasn't planning to make a claim on your heart, Black. I was just curious,' she said, keeping her voice even.

He nodded. 'No, if I'm honest. No. We didn't know one another well enough, and she was so young. Later I wished I'd been stronger.'

'And Catherine,' Louisa said, thinking of her niece suddenly, her niece who might not be her niece. 'Catherine will be upset to learn any of this.'

'Of course she will. Telling her that the man she thinks is her father lied to her for her whole life. I can't imagine what that would do to her.'

* * *

351

Louise and Catherine had a morning to themselves; the reporters and photographers were gathered down at the other hotel where Trudy Ederle was staying. The reporters were camped down at her hotel, hoping to fuel the feud so they'd have some news to tell.

'I have to talk to you about something,' Louisa said.

'What?' Catherine said. 'What's so serious?'

'Sit down,' Louisa said. They were in the little lounge at the hotel that overlooked the terrace and the sea. Louisa had slept poorly the night before, dreamt again of being chased, a monster catching up, catching up. When she woke, her head was clearer. She couldn't do anything about Black. Perhaps he was indeed Catherine's father – he seemed very sure – but Catherine had spent her whole life with Harry, and Harry had named Louisa Catherine's guardian. As far as Louisa was concerned, she was responsible for her niece, and she would continue to be responsible whatever happened. If Black tried to interfere, she'd deal with it as best she could. For now, though, she had to go on as she'd intended.

As she'd been getting ready this morning, she'd thought how oddly things had turned out. She hadn't wanted responsibility for Catherine. It had been Nellie and Ruth Luxton who'd pushed her. She's your blood, they'd said. You can't refuse her. And now, it seemed, perhaps she wasn't blood-related at all, and yet Louisa had never been more committed to anything in her life than she was to Catherine's welfare.

She knew she still had to tell Catherine the truth about what she'd done. More than ever, Catherine had a right to know that there was an alternative life for her, the life she'd chosen in the first place, even if it meant Louisa would lose her.

'Catherine, I did something I shouldn't have done,' Louisa said.

Catherine had picked up the newspaper from the table between them. 'It says here I'm a greater swimmer than . . . someone, I can't find them now, an Italian chap. I'm so glad Mr Black is here, Louisa. Have you noticed the reporters are leaving me alone now? I'm sure he's done something. He's been so good to me . . .' Catherine looked up at her aunt. 'What's wrong? You look like you've seen a ghost.'

Catherine looked serious suddenly and Louisa felt a pull of emotion. She smiled hopefully.

'Did you know Andrew's getting married?' Catherine said.

'Is he? Yes, I think I did know that, dear.'

'Yes, to some girl his brother was engaged to. I think he's getting married to make his mother happy. Can you believe that?'

'Oh, I see,' Louisa said. 'Poor boy. Catherine, you need to listen to me, darling. I've done something I shouldn't have and I have to tell you.'

'I mean, I'm not upset about it, Louisa, if that's what's worrying you. I don't even like Andrew any more. He's become one of those awful reporters. We're very different.'

Louisa nodded. 'Yes, you are,' she said. 'But we need to talk.'

'Shoot,' Catherine said. It was a term the Americans used. Andrew had started her on it.

'Do you remember when you swam the river?'

'The terrible Thames,' Catherine said.

'The terrible Thames. Well, afterwards, do you remember you kept wondering why you weren't getting any letters from the island? You waited every day for news and they didn't write. And you wrote to Michael and he still didn't write.'

'No, he didn't,' Catherine said.

'The thing is, I shouldn't have done this, and it was with good intentions, but I think I didn't see quite how much . . . What I mean to say is, I didn't want to do the wrong thing.'

'Louisa, what are you talking about?' Catherine said.

'He did write.'

'Who?'

'Michael. He wrote. A few times. And I didn't pass on the letters.'

'What do you mean? You hid them?'

'I hid them.'

'Why are you telling me now?'

'I couldn't go on in a lie.'

'You took my letters, Louisa? You hid them and lied to me?' Catherine's voice was failing her. 'Why would a person do that?'

'I thought he'd taken advantage of you.'

'What do you mean?'

'I thought he'd . . . I thought he was your lover.'

'He's my brother, Louisa. He's been in my life since we were little. How could you think that?'

Louisa was embarrassed. 'I read one of his letters to you.

He said you were joined in body. I assumed.' She looked at Catherine flatly.

Catherine stared at her. 'We were joined in body. Swimming. It's when you swim the three islands together. You're joined in body. The islands are the body. But, Louisa, how could you do that? How could you stay friends with me?'

It was this question that broke Louisa's heart, for it showed not only how young Catherine was but the extent of the breach of trust. Louisa could tell herself she had Catherine's best interests at heart, but it was simply wrong, what she'd done.

'And Nellie? Did she go along with this?'

Louisa looked at her. 'No. Nellie said it was wrong. And Nellie was right. I'm sorry, Catherine.'

'Where are the letters?'

'At home, in London,' Louisa said. 'As soon as we get back, I'll give them to you. I did the wrong thing. But I really did believe it was for the best. I know I haven't been very good at this, but I was worried. I thought if I brought you to London, and sent you to a good school, it would open up the world to you; you'd find you could do and be anything as a woman.'

'And now look at me,' Catherine said. 'I'm not anyone.'

She rushed from the room, leaving Louisa sitting alone, looking out towards the sea.

The next day, the third of August, was Catherine's birthday. Louisa had wanted to make sure she told the girl the truth before that, whatever the consequences. Black was back in

Paris. They hadn't spoken of Catherine again before he'd left.

Louisa had brought from England a little gold chain with a heart-shaped locket. Catherine came into the dining room, which Louisa and the hotel owners had decorated for lunch. Andrew was there, Lillian Cannon and her husband, the coach Burgess, the young pilot, Sam. Louisa had made Andrew promise that there would be no reporters or reporting, that this would truly be a private party.

Catherine hadn't spoken to her aunt since Louisa had told her about the letters, and Louisa didn't know what the girl was thinking. She still hadn't told her about the trouble Michael was in, but there would be time for that later. She was losing Catherine now one way or another, and it was what she deserved.

After lunch, Louisa gave Catherine her gift. 'I had it made,' she said. 'I am sorry, Catherine. I truly am.'

Catherine looked at her. 'What you did, I just can't believe it. But, Aunt Louisa, you really have no idea who I am. It's not even my birthday today.'

'Yes it is,' Louisa said. 'It's the third of August.'

'No, my birthday is the twenty-seventh of July – it was a week ago.'

'Your birthday is *when*?' Louisa said.

'I told you – the twenty-seventh of July.'

'But last year . . .'

'Last year, you weren't even home on the twenty-seventh. I was too scared to tell you because you'd gone to all the trouble of planning a celebration for the third of August. So I just let it go.'

Louisa looked at her niece. 'How do you know?'

'How do I know what?'

'How do you know you were born on the twenty-seventh of July?' The twenty-seventh of July, a date etched in Louisa's consciousness.

'I've always known,' Catherine said. 'What's the matter, Louisa? You've gone awfully pale.'

There was a knock on Catherine's door just after midnight. 'Come on, out of bed. It's time.' It was Mr Burgess. Trudy Ederle was sick. Mr Burgess had been down to her hotel in the afternoon and ruled her unfit. Without telling the Ederles, he'd made other plans.

Catherine dressed quickly and came down the stairs. Mr Burgess had got the cook out of bed. There was a plate of stew and potatoes on the table.

'I'm not hungry,' she said.

'It's not food, it's fuel, girl,' Mr Burgess said. For the first time since she'd met him, he seemed excited.

Clarabelle Barrett had failed. She set out on the first of August and swam bravely, Mr Burgess told Catherine, but a fog 'so thick she couldn't see her hands' made her give up after twenty-two hours in the water. The Channel had thrown its worst her way and the fog just did her in. Mr Burgess said the Channel decided who would succeed and who would fail and the swimmer had nothing to do with it. Miss Barrett was within shouting distance of the coast. 'A sight I know well,' Mr Burgess said.

'Was she all right?' Catherine wanted to know. 'Afterwards, was she all right?'

'Aye,' said the coach. 'She knew it beat her, and she won't be back. But that's not your concern. Your concern is getting yourself across.'

Lillian Cannon and her dogs were returning to America the next week too. She'd made two attempts herself, Catherine knew, the second shorter than the first. It was just too difficult, she'd said, which had given Catherine pause. If Lillian had found the swim too difficult, if Trudy had failed the year before, and if Clarabelle now hadn't managed it, how would Catherine succeed?

As if he guessed her thoughts, Mr Burgess said she had to think of one thing and one thing only out in the Channel tonight.

'What's that?' she said.

'The swim. Just think of the swim. No one ever swam a long way by thinking of the opposite shore. You let me worry about Dover, and we'll be fine.' He would be in the pilot boat. They both knew the rules. She could take sustenance, bottles of broth, cake, crackers, tied to a pole extended from the rowboat, so long as her hands never touched the boat or a person.

The newspapermen would follow them in a second boat, Catherine knew, but, Mr Burgess said with a twinkle in his eye, he'd forgotten to alert the boatman. 'Let's have the water to ourselves for a while,' he said. 'You don't like all that other stuff.'

'Thank you,' she said.

'You're going to do this swim, girl. You really are,' he said. 'Now, is there anyone else you want to wake up, that tall young fella that hangs off you like a puppy?' At first she thought he meant Sam but he was talking about Andrew.

She shook her head, then reconsidered. 'Yes, there is,' she said.

'Hurry up then,' he said.

She took the steps two at a time and knocked softly at the door.

Louisa must have been up because she came to the door quickly, in her nightdress and socks, her hair a mess. 'Catherine,' she said. 'Are you all right?' She looked so tiny standing there.

'I'm going. I'm swimming,' Catherine said. 'And I wanted to tell you, just in case anything happens. It's all right, Louisa. Really it is. Not what you did. That was terrible. But you've been a good aunt, such a good aunt. I'll just send the letters and explain what happened as soon as we get home. All right?'

'Of course,' Louisa managed to say. 'Can I come in the boat? I'd like to be there.'

'Can you dress quickly?'

'Yes.'

'We'll meet you down there.'

They made their way by lamplight down to the little beach. Sam was there and Catherine was relieved. He'd said he'd swim with her when she was feeling tired and she was glad that Mr Burgess had remembered to wake him. Sam would go on the pilot boat with Mr Burgess. And coming towards them now was Louisa, tiny in her cardigan and woollen skirt.

'Come on, girl,' Mr Burgess said to Catherine. 'Let's get you ready.'

He and Louisa helped Catherine to slather grease and lanolin over herself. 'Stinks,' Catherine said. She was wearing her woollen suit. She knew it would chafe on such a long swim and she'd already decided what to do about that. Through the night, she was going to take off the suit and leave it in the dory until first light and then do her best to put it back on. She hadn't told Burgess but knew he'd agree.

'You'll be glad of the grease when you're out there,' was all Mr Burgess said, his eyes bright in the midnight. Then he looked up toward the inn. There were lights bobbing down the hill. 'Quick, here come the newspapermen. Pity their boat's not here. Let's row out quiet now. I'm not letting them on with us. Just you and me and the Channel, eh?' They'd moored the pilot boat out in the bay. The boatman had been the one to see Mr Burgess himself safely across all those years ago.

There was no time for goodbyes. Catherine dived into the waves while Mr Burgess rowed out with Louisa and Sam. They cheered her on quietly, although she'd hardly swum fifty yards. There was a moon rising over the water. Catherine was swimming the Channel, she thought, and it had happened just like that.

Chapter Thirty-Five

The water hadn't felt cold when she'd set out. That was the strange thing. Perhaps it was the excitement. But now all she was aware of was the cold. The muscles of her arms had cramped an hour ago but now they were past cramping. The weather had been kind so far, although Mr Burgess said they were far from out of the woods. It had been a bad season, he'd said the week before, too few days that were on a swimmer's side.

Mr Burgess had rowed with her for a while to keep her spirits up, and he'd given her some broth and chocolate cake. Her hands were numb now when they brushed against the woollen suit at her hips. She knew she had to keep moving or her body would begin the process of shutting down. Her body was begging to shut down, in fact. It would be the easiest thing in the world, to curl up here, to sleep.

She suspected this was what had happened to Trudy Ederle the year before. She'd gone to sleep in the water and another swimmer had pulled her out. Later Trudy said she'd been fine but the other swimmer saw her go under and come up, water flowing out of her mouth, he said. She also said she was sure her coach – the Scot Jabez Wolffe who'd attempted the Channel twenty-two times and failed – had fed her whisky with the beef broth. Mr Burgess would not be feeding Catherine whisky, he'd assured her. 'But, I won't think twice about pulling you out, girl,' he'd said. Catherine knew that Trudy's father had told Burgess he wasn't to take Trudy out of the water without her permission. Mr Burgess had made Mr Ederle and Trudy sign a waiver to release him from any legal responsibility. If Catherine was unconscious, she thought, of course she'd want him to pull her out of the water. It was only a swim, for goodness' sake.

Trudy's father wanted his daughter to win. Catherine's father had never been like that. He'd only ever encouraged her. Now she had Louisa, and she'd disappointed her at the start, she knew. She hadn't been the girl Louisa had wanted her to be. They'd both learnt along the way, Catherine thought now. But in telling Catherine what she'd done, hiding the letters from Australia, Catherine had felt, strangely, that while Louisa went the wrong way about showing it, her aunt truly cared about her. She cared enough to intervene to protect Catherine's interests. Louisa was on her side in a way her father had been on her side, she realised; in a way she imagined her mother might have been on her side.

She'd so much wanted to please Mr Black. She couldn't remember when she'd decided she wanted to swim the Channel, to become the first woman to do that. Mr Black had told her the newspapermen would only become more interested in her once she succeeded. He was ambitious on her behalf, not like Trudy Ederle's father but not that different either, when Catherine thought about it. She didn't think she wanted that for herself. In truth, she'd have liked Clarabelle Barrett to be the first woman. She was the one of them who most needed money.

Mr Black had come to see Catherine the evening before, after he'd returned from Paris. He'd wished her a happy birthday. She didn't bother explaining that it wasn't her birthday. 'I have to talk to you, Catherine,' he'd said, looking very serious.

'We might be making the attempt tomorrow,' she said. 'Mr Burgess says the tides look good.'

'Well, that's the best news.'

'What did you want to talk about, Mr Black?'

'Nothing, honey. Nothing that can't wait until we get to Dover. If you go in the morning, I'll fly overhead. I'll come down low and wave. Will you wave back?'

'Of course,' she said.

'I'm glad you're a swimmer,' he said. 'I lost my sister and mother to drowning.'

'I know, Mr Black. Louisa told me.'

'And I don't have anyone left but you.' It was so odd, the way he'd looked at her as he said it. It gave her a thrill but something about it frightened her too.

She was cold now in her bones, nothing left inside to keep them warm. They'd hit a squall and Mr Burgess had recalculated their route, which would see her swim an extra two miles. She was more than halfway there, he said, but she wasn't, if she knew what he meant, which she didn't, because nothing made much sense to her right then.

She made herself think of the island, the warm sand under her feet, so hot in the middle of the day you could burn your feet on it, Michael's long brown body, his smile. If she wrote to him, would he be the same? Would he understand that it hadn't been her fault, that Louisa had stopped the letters? Would anything be the same? She thought of Florence, dear Florence, and wept.

The grease and lanolin, designed to stop the worst of the cold and chafing, had worn off now. She wondered why they bothered with it. She never did get her swimsuit off. She'd worried she wouldn't be able to put it back on and the photographers, who surely would catch them up soon, would snap the picture of a lifetime. Her suit was hurting at her shoulders and underarms. But pain was a better sensation than the cold, which frightened her.

Louisa had asked her once whether when she was swimming, she thought of her mother. Louisa meant her mother drowning. She'd said no but it was a lie. On a long swim, she always thought of her mother. She thought of the way Julia had given up. Sometimes, like now, she would talk to her. You didn't hold on, she'd say. You had a life preserver and you didn't hold on. Why not? I would have held on, she'd say to her mother. I would have stayed with you, no matter what.

The twenty-seventh of July. The twenty-seventh of July was Catherine's birthday. And all these years, Louisa had thought her birthday was the third of August. Not because she'd got the date wrong, as Catherine had assumed, as

364

Louisa had pretended after lunch that day, not because her brain was so addled she couldn't keep a date in her head, not because she didn't care enough, but because she had been told Catherine was born on the third of August. By her mother Millicent. By her brother Harry. Because if they'd told her the truth, that Catherine was born on the twenty-seventh of July, she'd have known what they were hiding from her.

On the twenty-seventh of July that year, Louisa's own child was born: the child her mother had told her was a boy, a boy who'd died.

She could remain here in the water forever, she thought suddenly, swim on and on. *Until what?* said a voice she didn't recognise. Until she ran out of energy and life ended, she thought. She looked across at the pilot boat. For hours now it had been nothing but a haze of lights. She'd swum through the night, Sam diving in to swim alongside her when she needed company, and she'd lasted through the morning, the afternoon, and now it was another night. She would finish alone, she knew. It was the end or not, she knew.

The newspapermen were on the boat behind them, the photographers wanting their pictures, reporters wanting their stories. They'd caught up now. They wanted a dream, she thought, a winner with long legs and a lovely smile. Catherine could be that person. She was sure she could. That way led to fame and to fortune. And everyone wants that, Mr Black had said. Everyone wants that. 'You're a model of what it means to be a modern woman,' he said. 'What do you think of that?'

Mr Black said he wanted to talk to her when she made land. She already knew what he was going to say. He'd sponsor the next swim and the next. He'd been so good to her, and she felt she owed him something. He wanted her to become an American citizen, to swim for the US in the Olympics in 1928.

Her father had told her the story of the selkie, half woman, half seal, who came to live among men and dried out for want of the sea. Someone had stolen the selkie's skin so she couldn't go back. In one version of the story, the selkie left a child, like Catherine's mother left her. In the water the world was quiet but the sound of her breath was loud. What a lovely thought, the quiet of the sea floor and no one to worry about.

She could hear the shouts. It was Burgess. 'Catherine, are you all right?'

She waved. Had she dozed off? Perhaps she had. One arm up and over, the other, and this way you go forward.

She could see the shore, barely, the lights of Dover, hear Mr Burgess yelling from the boat. 'That's the Forty Lights,' he said. 'You're there, girl! You're nearly there! Just keep swimming.'

She didn't know that it had been less than thirteen hours since she'd left France. She didn't know that once she completed this last mile, she would not only be the youngest person to swim the English Channel. She would not only be the first woman, she would set a record, beating the last swimmer by over three hours. The tides had been kind, the Channel had admitted her, and Catherine had kept swimming.

The journalists called to her. 'How are you feeling, Catherine?' 'Are you tired?' 'Are you nearly there?'

They were like ants, she thought, like nothing. She knew other swimmers had faltered in the last mile, and she understood why. It wasn't fear of failure, it was fear of success. She was beyond any particular emotion, joy or sorrow or pain. That's what swimming was for her, she realised, a way to come to this place in herself. She felt not tired, but beyond tired, beyond cold. And, yet, fully alive.

Mr Burgess was telling her to turn to the right. She saw she'd come too far over. They were supposed to come in at Deal but he'd decided to make instead for Kingsdown. She could see little lights on the beach, thousands of them. The word had got out while she'd been swimming, Mr Burgess said. They'd transmitted their stories to their newspapers and had made the late morning editions. Crowds on the beach were there to welcome her, Catherine Quick, the first woman to swim the English Channel.

She couldn't see anyone on the boat now. She was almost past them, she thought. For a few moments, she became disoriented, couldn't see the boat itself, couldn't see the lights on the shore either now. Had she lost consciousness? She rolled over and thought she could float here forever. She heard, in the distance, a voice. It was a voice she knew; not Mr Burgess, although it must have been him. Again, someone was calling her name. She looked to where she thought the boat was but still couldn't see it. She stopped a moment, rubbed her goggles. It was infuriating trying to keep up in the darkness. The voice again. It was calling her name. Not Catherine – her other name. 'Waapi, I can see you in the light! I'm coming. I'll swim you in.'

And then, Mr Burgess was there in the dory. 'Who *is* that?' he said.

'Catherine,' Louisa said. 'It's all right.'

There were lights everywhere around her now, from the pilot boat, and from the shore, even a beam from the lighthouse trained towards her. She could make out his funny little head bobbing up and down in the water in silhouette.

'Michael!' she yelled. 'Over here, you idiot. I'm over here.'

'Just tell him not to touch her,' Mr Burgess said. 'It will disqualify her.'

She heard Louisa cheering. Catherine looked up to Burgess.

Michael came closer. 'Waapi,' he said. 'It's really you.'

'It is,' she said, swimming to him and throwing her arms around his neck. 'It's me. You smell like coconut.'

Chapter Thirty-Six

'Well, that's good you told her the truth, Louisa. I don't know what possessed you to lie.'

'I thought it was best for her,' Louisa said. She'd told Nellie everything – well, almost everything.

'But it wasn't best for her,' Nellie said.

'Yes, I know that now, but I didn't know it then.' She looked at Nellie's dear face. Catherine had disqualified herself from the race. Mr Burgess was devastated. He thought she was fine but she must have had a madness come upon her, he said. 'A madness,' Louisa had said. 'A bit of sense, more like.'

Andrew had returned to America with his bride, after covering Trudy Ederle's successful swim of the Channel. The girl he'd married was from a nice London family. They might even make a go of it, Louisa thought, although Andrew had liked Catherine more, she was sure. Catherine, for her part, had had enough of reporters to last a lifetime, although she and Andrew had parted friends.

Catherine was packing to go home to the island. Sister Mary Ursula was moving to another school in two years, and a government school would take over. Catherine would do her training in Brisbane, staying with Sister Mary Ursula's family, so she could be the teacher at the school. Louisa would go with her. Nellie was going to Louisa's old school in Glasgow.

Sam the pilot was already home in Canada. He'd sent them a telegram promising to visit the island, so long as Catherine came to visit his mountains.

Louisa kept the truth about her own past to herself for now. She knew she'd have to tell Catherine – she was entirely cured of managing other people's lives for them – but not yet. For now, the girl had enough to contend with. For Louisa, Catherine was the good that had grown from something awful. Here was the child born from that violence. Here was the fact that made it bearable. Here was Catherine. Louisa would leave the clinic, of course she would. She would take up the still-vacant post as the doctor on Thursday Island, and remain with Catherine, her daughter.

Florence had been waiting with Nellie on the beach. She looked at Louisa, and Louisa saw only kindness in those eyes. 'I know,' Louisa said quietly. 'Catherine's birthday.'

Florence nodded. 'I'm sorry. There's a letter. Mr Witherspoon found a letter in his files. I'm glad you know. I wondered whether to tell you.'

Louisa took the letter from Florence and put it in her bag, watched her brave niece on the shore hugging Michael while the onlookers stared. They thought she must be mad, like Burgess did, devastated to have failed. But Catherine hadn't failed. She had swum the Channel. She just wouldn't have to deal with being a Channel swimmer.

How had Louisa ever assumed Michael and Catherine had been lovers? The girl was perfectly innocent, Louisa should have realised. He was a brother to her. It was Louisa's own experience, she realised. She'd seen everything through a particular lens, of her own experience. Michael was not like Jonathan. Hardly any men were like Jonathan.

'And it's not the only lie I told,' Louisa said to Nellie now.

'There are more?' Nellie said.

'Yes, Nellie. I lied to you.'

'When?'

'Do you remember when you first came to the clinic, and you were very sick, and your period had stopped?'

Nellie nodded. 'And you told me some story about a little procedure, when in fact I was pregnant.'

Louisa stared at her. 'How did you know?'

'I guessed, but also, Dr Luxton talked to me. She said I had choices. I wanted to stop the pregnancy. I didn't have any way of caring for a child when I was so sick, and I knew that.'

'So why did you never tell me?'

'Dr Luxton said you'd tell me I was sick and needed a little procedure and that it would help her immensely if I didn't tell you about our little chat. So I didn't. But I knew.'

Thank goodness for Ruth Luxton, who had been so happy to learn Louisa's news. Ruth was recruiting new

371

doctors for the clinic. 'I'd pack your bags for you if I could, Louisa. You must go with her now.'

'So would you rather have known, or not known?' Louisa asked Nellie.

'I'd rather not have had to make that decision. But if the decision had to be made I knew it was me who had to make it.'

Nellie was right. One day, Louisa would tell Catherine the truth, she thought. One day she would let her know who she was and where she'd come from. For now, though, what was important was that Catherine knew she was going home.

Dearest Louie,

If you are reading this letter, then I am gone and Catherine is your ward.

Firstly, I want you to know that I am sorry to be the bearer of this news. You have been a good sister, and I have wished many times I'd told you the truth when you came to Australia. My reasons for not telling you have been entirely selfish. At first I didn't want to make you angry with our mother, who did her best. But then I didn't want to lose what I had.

I had hoped you would never need to know, to be honest, for I was so sure that knowing would be more difficult than not.

Louisa, I did not set out to deceive you, and you must believe me that Mama did only what she thought was best.

When Julia and I came through England, Julia was

372

expecting a child, the child you have always believed was Catherine. But Julia lost the baby on the ship. I wrote and told Mama that Julia was expecting. She told you, I think. I also wrote when we lost the baby and my letter must have arrived when you were at Aldeburgh awaiting the birth of your own child. Mama chose not to tell you. Perhaps in her mind she already had plans. Whatever her reasons, it made the next steps easier.

Your blood pressure was high in the labour and you fell into unconsciousness soon after the birth. All of this you know. But Mama made a decision about the child. She decided that if you knew the child lived, you would spend your days worrying about what you'd done. You might even decide to keep the child, which Mama thought would be wrong for both of you. She told you it was a boy. But the child was Catherine.

The midwife, Mary Breen, had a baby herself, you might recall, a boy of nearly two. She breastfed your baby on the ship to Australia. Mama was particular about that. No cow's milk after Margaret. Mama paid Mary's fare to Australia and back, since Julia couldn't feed a baby. In Cairns we found Florence, who'd lost her own child and could feed ours.

When Julia died, I wondered if I should tell you the truth. I hope I did the right thing. You were so busy with your work, and I thought to know you had a child would be the last thing you'd want. And in truth, I loved Catherine so dearly I couldn't stand the idea that she might be taken from me.

So Catherine is your child, Louisa. I hope you will love her as much as I do.

Your loving brother,
Harry

Harry. All those years, he had kept the truth from Louisa. Florence too. How could they? How could they not tell her? She supposed he thought Louisa might make some claim on the child, might want to take her. He was right. Louisa would surely have taken Catherine back to England at three, once she knew. She wouldn't have left the child motherless on the island. How could Harry have been so selfish?

'We all do our best,' Ruth Luxton said. 'You did your best, Louisa. He did his best. And look what you got. You got a daughter.' The word still didn't make sense to Louisa, who felt anything but a mother.

Black had come to see Louisa in London before he left for America and she'd told him everything; she saw no reason not to.

'What a fool I must look,' he said.

'Both of us,' she said. 'I'd started to think you might be right about Catherine, to be honest, that she was your child. Julia must have known, of course. She must have loved you very much.'

'Yes, she did,' he said. He paused, regarded Louisa carefully. 'We won't see each other again then?' he said.

'Probably not,' she said.

'I'll be sad about that.'

'I will too,' she said. She took the hands he offered her and held them. His were warm and soft. She could see the loss in his eyes. He'd lost so much. What would happen to him now? she wondered.

'Will you go to the island?' he said.

'I will. That's where Catherine wants to be for now. And they haven't replaced Harry.'

'So you'll be the doctor.'

'I'm guessing I will.'

He smiled. 'Well, you know me, Louisa. Don't be surprised if I fly over your way to visit some time soon.' He became serious then. 'Did you expect it to end like this?'

'I'm not quite sure this is the end,' she said. 'It feels much more like the beginning.'

Chapter Thirty-Seven

'You don't trust yourself,' Catherine said. 'That's the biggest problem.' They'd been in the water since three that afternoon, or Catherine had. Louisa had mostly the skirted the shallows.

Catherine still took the children swimming every afternoon after school and she'd told Louisa that they were easier to teach, 'even though they haven't had much of an education yet. That's what you always told me was the key to something. Not to swimming, it seems.'

Catherine saw the look of disappointment on Louisa's face and softened. 'But I know it's not easy learning something new.'

Louisa was wearing the bathing costume they'd bought in Cairns four weeks before, when Catherine came home from university for the July holiday. It was in the new style, with short legs and shoulder straps. Louisa had told Catherine she felt terribly daring. But to Catherine, Louisa looked so small and delicate, and she was so fair compared with everyone else on the island. Like a tiny flightless bird, Catherine had thought, tears in her eyes for no reason she could articulate.

'I'll teach you to swim,' Catherine had said. Louisa loved her work at the hospital, Catherine knew. Already she'd raised money for a hostel for women. They were training Islander midwives and nurses, and one day, she said, Islander doctors. But she'd resisted getting in the water. 'You can't live on an island and not swim,' Florence had said. Louisa had just smiled.

It had taken the entire first lesson to convince Louisa to go in at knee level. She hadn't enjoyed the water, not even the delightful chill on her skin, and now, after four lessons, Catherine was wondering if they should give up. At the very least, you had to be able to float on your back; you could save yourself if you could do that. But every time Louisa tried, she'd panic, fold at her hips and go under the water. She needed to find her buoyancy but couldn't seem to do it.

In the third week, Catherine had tied a rope around her wrist and looped the other end around Louisa's waist. 'I can reel you in if you get into trouble,' she'd said. But it didn't make any difference. Louisa couldn't trust herself or Catherine.

Today Louisa had managed a full five seconds on her back before she panicked and went under, coming up spluttering as Catherine got there to pull her up out of the water. There was a hint of a smile as she'd started to float and Catherine had been hopeful, but the next try was the worst yet.

'What are we going to do with you?' Catherine said now, and laughed. 'I think you hate the water.'

'I think the water hates me,' Louisa said.

Catherine shook her head. 'No, you're a Quick, born to the sea.'

We're both Quicks, Catherine thought, still defining what that means.

It was a year ago, when they first came back to the island, that Louisa had sat down with Catherine on the front verandah and told her the story. September, already warm, the weather glorious, the island just as it had always been. Louisa's story reminded Catherine of Harry's story about Julia, although, Louisa assured her, this one was a true story too. Louisa was Catherine's mother. 'You're the baby I carried, the baby I truly believed I'd lost,' she said at the end, her voice tight with emotion. 'I didn't know whether to tell you, but I decided there should be no secrets.' She smiled weakly then, and looked across at Catherine. She looked afraid.

Catherine had sat for some minutes without speaking. It was an odd sensation, hearing something so surprising, and yet, unsurprising. Finally, she said, 'Is it all right if I keep calling you Louisa?'

'Of course. What else would you call me?' Louisa said. 'The thing I want impress on you, and the reason it's taken me this long to tell you, is that I want you to always know that Harry loved you. Of that I am very sure. I wanted to wait until we were here, until you were back in your home so you could take it all in.'

Catherine nodded, looked out to the sea which was her home. 'I mean, if I don't call you Mother or Mama. Is it all right if you don't feel like my mother? Florence feels more like my mother, and even Florence . . . I've never really had a mother.' Catherine didn't feel emotional at the time, although later when she was on her own, she cried, even though she couldn't say quite why she was crying. And they weren't unhappy tears, just tears.

'That's probably a good way of looking at it.' Louisa had said. 'We shouldn't worry too much about it, I shouldn't think.' Catherine couldn't see her aunt's face but she could hear that her voice was still tight.

'The Islanders often give babies to others,' Catherine said.

'Yes, I know,' Louisa said. 'When they come in to the hospital, it's not always easy to know who's who. The important thing is that you know the truth. It's just what it is, Catherine, nothing more.' She turned to her and smiled again.

'What I'm trying to say is that it doesn't really matter,' Catherine said. 'The Islander babies belong to everyone. It's not that different from what happened with us, is it?'

Later that week, Catherine told Florence what Louisa had told her. 'You said once that mothers are always sad,' Catherine said to Florence. 'Is that what you meant?'

'Oh, it's more sad for Louisa. She's your mama, like I'm Michael's mama. But she didn't get to raise you and that's always hard for a mama. That's always sad.'

'But the Islander babies go to other mothers.'

'That doesn't mean it's easy for the mothers,' Florence said now. 'Even the ones who give their babies willingly feel that sadness. A mother might know that someone else won't have children unless she gives them a child, so she does it for them, for all of us, but it's not ever an easy thing.' Florence looked at Catherine.

'But that's not what happened to you and Louisa,' she

said. 'Louisa's mother didn't tell her. That wasn't right.'

Catherine looked at her aunt in the water now. Her curly hair, cut short, flopped on to her face. The late afternoon light softened her features. 'Am I very exasperating?' Louisa said.

'You really are,' Catherine said. They both laughed. 'We'll go home after one more try.'

'We couldn't just give up now?' Louisa said. She'd managed to work her way back to the shallows where she could stand up easily.

'You can't live on the island and not be able to swim,' Catherine said. She untied the rope from Louisa's waist and took Louisa's arm and led her back out to the deep. The day was ending, the water burnished bronze suddenly in front of them as the sun emerged from under a cloud. They could hear seagulls overhead and the voices of the fishermen who were cleaning their catch on the beach. She looked across at Louisa, her eyes ablaze with life. 'You are my mother,' she said. 'Just do it.'

And Louisa did. 'I'm floating!' she cried out. 'Oh my, I'm floating. Catherine, I'm in heaven.'

Just then they heard the sputtering buzz of an engine, so unlikely here on the island. Catherine looked up just as Louisa pointed. It was a little airplane, two wings, an engine like an annoying insect now, and although they couldn't see, Catherine was sure that she knew the identity of the pilot and his passenger.

Writer's Note

I was inspired by the lives of Dr Louisa Garrett Anderson and Van Lear Black, who never met in real life, as far as I know, and who have only scant biographical details in common with the fictional Dr Louisa Quick and Manfred Lear Black. In his early twenties, my great uncle René MacColl was Van Lear Black's confidential secretary, but that, and a subsequent distinguished career in journalism, are all he had in common with the fictional Andrew Mackintosh. René MacColl's memoir *A Flying Start* was also an inspiration. He writes with style and wit.

Gertrude Ederle was the first woman to swim the English Channel. Other swimmers who existed outside these pages include Mercedes Gleitze, who made the crossing on her eighth attempt in 1927 and went on to a career as a distance swimmer. Lillian Cannon and Clarabelle Barrett never attempted the Channel again after 1926. The fictional Aileen Ryan shares an outstanding diving career and small stature with Aileen Riggin. Many great women swimmers have been lost in the wash of history.

I'm indebted to John Zarrillo, archivist at the Brooklyn Historical Society, who found the Hotel Touraine for me, and to the Women's Swimming Association, New York, without which this book would never have had a reason to be.

Writing a novel is a swim of sorts. Thanks to those beside me, or in the pilot boat, readers, writers and dear friends, and some who are all three, in Brisbane and Banff. Thanks Brisbane neighbourhoods, Bar Merlo Paddington, Canberra. Thanks the Banff Centre and Wild Flour, East Hotel and Silo. Thanks Gurrumul. Thanks *Qweekend*.

Thanks all those inspiring readers I met through *In Falling Snow* and especially the book clubs that are keeping reading alive. Thanks Lisa Mayocchi who gave me notebooks. I've been sustained by the Ryans, the Pooles, the Cravens, the Wilkins-Ruckels, and Bardon 7/6.

Cathy Sinclair tells me the truth when no one else will. Lenore Cooper, Suzi Jefferies, Louise Ryan and Theanne Walters are on the swimming advisory committee in my mind. As for companions in the water, Kim Wilkins and Kris Olsson are right beside me, and Louise Limerick and Kate Morton know that swimming has been everything.

I set out with my agent Fiona Inglis in the pilot boat. There's an outstanding team at Allen & Unwin, Christa Munns who corrects the course repeatedly, Ali Lavau who sang me out of a murky draft, and Sarina Rowell who saved me from prohibition. Nada Backovic surrounded our swim in something beautiful.

Thanks also to Susie Dunlop and the team at Allison and Busby, especially Lesley Crooks and Sophie Robinson who took exquisite care to bring this story to new readers.

Occasionally, you are carried by strong tides to the right place. Annette Barlow had to carry me an unreasonably long way this time.

David has always been on my team, and Otis gives me a reason to swim at all.

Mary-Rose MacColl
Brisbane, July 2016